The Middle East
and the United States

FOURTH EDITION

The Middle East and the United States

A Historical and Political Reassessment

EDITED BY

David W. Lesch
Trinity University

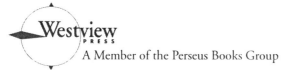

Westview
PRESS
A Member of the Perseus Books Group

Copyright © 2007 by Westview Press, a Member of the Perseus Books Group.

Published in the United States of America by Westview Press, A Member of the Perseus Books Group, 5500 Central Avenue, Boulder, Colorado 80301-2877, and in the United Kingdom by Westview Press, 12 Hid's Copse Road, Cumnor Hill, Oxford OX2 9JJ.

Find us on the world wide web at www.westviewpress.com

Westview Press books are available at special discounts for bulk purchases in the United States by corporations, institutions, and other organizations. For more information, please contact the Special Markets Department at the Perseus Books Group, 11 Cambridge Center, Cambridge, MA 02142, or call (617) 252-5298, (800) 255-1514 or email special.markets@perseusbooks.com.

Library of Congress Cataloging-in-Publication Data
    The Middle East and the United States : a historical and political reassessment / edited by David W. Lesch. — 4th ed.
        p. cm.
    Includes bibliographic references and index.
    ISBN–13: 978-0-8133-4349-5 (pbk. : alk. paper)
    ISBN–10: 0-8133-4349-6 (pbk. : alk. paper)
    1. Middle East—Foreign relations—United States. 2. United States—Foreign relations—Middle East. I. Lesch, David W.

DS63.2.U5M43 2006
327.56073—dc22

2006022860

The paper used in this publication meets the requirements of the American National Standard for Permanence of Paper for Printed Library Materials Z39.48–1984.

10   9   8   7   6   5   4   3   2   1

To those who made a difference,
Louis Cantori, Robert O. Freedman, and Nadav Safran

Contents

Part Two

Arab-Israeli War and Peace

Part Three

Gulf Wars

Part Four

Retrospective and Reassessment

Preface to the Fourth Edition

The third edition (3e) of *The Middle East and the United States* was published in January 2003, but the final manuscript was delivered to Westview Press by mid-2002; therefore, the contributors who were writing on topics that delved into current events had limited information on the full effects of the tragedy of the terrorist attacks of September 11, 2001. The immediate repercussions of 9/11 included the US-led invasion of Afghanistan in October 2001 to evict the Taliban ruling regime and the rising chorus in the administration of George W. Bush in early 2002 of going to war to topple the Iraqi regime of Saddam Hussein. These were early indications of the foreign policy shifts being implemented by the Bush administration, so 3e in retrospect really was only able to scratch the surface in examining and assessing them.

Since mid-2002 we have witnessed at least as much change as that which had accrued between the publications of the second and third editions. In September 2002 the Bush administration unveiled its national security strategy, more commonly referred to as the Bush doctrine, which, among other things, advocated the application of preventive war through preemptive action in order to deal with rising threats, particularly within so-called "failed states," before they became an imminent danger to the United States—in other words, before another 9/11 occurred.

Of course, the most spectacular application of the Bush doctrine was the US-led invasion of Iraq in March 2003 that removed the regime of Saddam Hussein. The global war on terror launched by the Bush administration in the wake of 9/11 continued unabated, however, focusing on rooting out al-Qaida elements in Afghanistan and Pakistan, centering on the search for al-Qaida leaders Osama bin Laden and Ayman al-Zawahiri, but it also extended to other parts of central and south Asia, the Middle East and North Africa, and even into Southeast Asia in search of and to help governments counter and eradicate threatening Islamic extremist groups.

The United States and its allies, however, would soon become bogged down in Iraq by a lethal insurgency led by a combination of Iraqi elements and a small number of foreign so-called Jihadists. For the Bush administration it has become something of a race against time, attempting to facilitate the formation of a viable and representative Iraqi government so that the United States could begin drawing down upon its troop presence in Iraq. This is a tall task to say the least, especially amid declining poll numbers for President Bush as the casualties in Iraq mount and the strategic and intelligence rationale for going to war come under increasing scrutiny with the mistakes in each category having been revealed. All the while the unpopular war in Iraq as perceived in the region itself has contributed to unprecedented anti-Americanism. The complexities of the Middle East have also complicated the Bush administration's attempts to promote democracy in the region, in what became a central tenet of administration policy, in the face of rampant authoritarianism (among friends and foes alike) and the rising political power of organized Islamist movements.

In the meantime, the Arab-Israeli front, and more specifically the Israeli-Palestinian dynamic, has ground to a virtual halt in comparison to the spate of peace negotiations in the 1990s. The Oslo and Madrid peace processes were declared dead and buried in the wake of the failure of Camp David in July 2000 and the subsequent al-Aqsa *intifada* that erupted in September 2000. With the victory of Likud hardliner Ariel Sharon as Israeli prime minister in early 2001, combined with a weakened and discredited Palestinian Authority President Yasser Arafat (at least in the eyes of Tel Aviv and Washington), no so-called "road maps" to peace could revive the process. Instead, Israel began to act unilaterally, first with its withdrawal from the Gaza Strip in summer 2005 followed by the stated intentions of the governing coalition to do the same in the West Bank minus the largest Jewish settlement blocs and East Jerusalem. Meanwhile, the two venerable icons—and implacable foes of each other—have effectively passed from the scene: Yasser Arafat died in November 2004 and Ariel Sharon suffered a debilitating stroke in January 2006 and as of this writing is still in a coma. The new party the latter founded in late 2005, Kadima, won the most seats in the March 2006 elections, with Sharon acolyte Ehud Olmert becoming prime minister and vowing to continue with the plan of unilateral withdrawal. The political situation in Israel and within the Palestinian territories is anything but defined, however, especially with the victory of Hamas in the January 2006 legislative elections that resulted in its unexpected and unprecedented assumption of power. A wait and see attitude seems to be the order of the day as the repercussions of the political changes, if not upheavals, of early 2006 shake themselves out. As is usually the case, there seem to be more questions than answers regarding the ever-elusive prospects of a comprehensive Arab-Israeli peace.

In addition to being updated and revised, the new edition has also been reorganized in a way that, in my opinion, better reflects the melding of history and current events regarding US involvement in the Middle East. Essentially, I have condensed Parts One and Two (that focus mostly on the effects of the superpower cold war in the Middle East) from the first three editions into one part; therefore, this edition has four parts compared to five in the first three. This is the result of history accumulating before our very eyes over the past five years that requires coverage and examination. Because page counts and book prices are an important part of the process of putting together a volume such as this, by necessity some previous excellent contributions to the first three editions needed to be excised in order to keep the page count, and therefore the price of the book, at a reasonable level—to say this was difficult is an understatement, but hard choices needed to be made. As a historian, it was against my very nature to sacrifice some history in order to more adequately cover recent events, but what has transpired in the Middle East has been transformational, so it needed to be done.

Again, I have asked some friends and accomplished colleagues to make contributions to this volume; indeed, five of the twenty-five chapters are new. Now that there has been sufficient distance to attempt a reassessment, Jeremy Pressman engages in a critical examination of the Madrid and Oslo peace processes up to and through the failure of Camp David in 2000. Robert O. Freedman, who graciously volunteered to remove his excellent chapter on Russia's role in the Middle East surrounding the 1991 Gulf war that was a pillar in the first three editions, contributes a salient new chapter on the Bush administration's first term in office (and a little bit thereafter) vis-à-vis the Arab-Israeli arena. Obviously the US-led war in Iraq is the single most important event in US–Middle East relations since 3e; as such, two chapters are devoted to this that build upon other updated ones in the Persian Gulf section of the book. Steve Yetiv writes on the rationale of the Bush administration for going to war against Iraq in the first place, while Ali Abootalebi critically analyzes "what went wrong" in Iraq that led to the quagmire the United States found itself in soon after the initial military phase. Finally, Jon Alterman examines the Bush administration's attempts to promote democracy in the region, its prospects for success, and its intended and unintended consequences.

There are a number of people who have helped to bring this volume together. First and foremost, as always, I wish to thank the contributors themselves, many of whom revised and updated their chapters (and some for the third—and probably last—time), especially those who comment on recent and/or current events; they are dependable and committed scholars one and all. Ms. Eunice Herrington in the Department of History at Trinity University has once again been of inestimable assistance, as she has been ever since the first edition—she probably deserves to be listed as co-editor by this time! I have worked with Karl Yambert, senior editor at Westview Press, on several projects—it is always a pleasure to do so. I wish all authors could have an editor as supportive and competent as Karl. Lastly, of course, I want to thank my wife, Suzanne, and my son, Michael, who continuously lift my life and spirits, which more than compensates for the rather dreary task of updating, revising, and compiling this volume!

I am also dedicating this volume to three colleagues, scholars, mentors, and friends: Louis Cantori, Robert O. Freedman, and the late Nadav Safran. I have now been teaching full-time for over fifteen years. It is long enough to observe how my own students have grown and prospered and to realize that with some of them I made a difference, sometimes a life-altering one. It often compels me to again appreciate those who made an important difference in my professional life—and beyond. If it were not for Lou Cantori and Bob Freedman at the University of Maryland-Baltimore County where I was an undergraduate, I would never have entered this field. Taking their classes and becoming their advisee generated my passion for the Middle East, which at first was simply a reflection of their own. Both continue to be dear friends and important guides in my career. Next to peace in the Middle East, I think what all three of us want the most in this world is another World Series victory for the Baltimore Orioles (and it is a close second!!). Nadav Safran was my advisor when I first entered Harvard University's Center for Middle Eastern Studies. It was he who encouraged me to go on and obtain a Ph.D. rather than enter the workforce immediately after my master's degree—one of those life-altering decisions for which I am forever grateful. He was a friend, mentor, and enthusiastic "president" of the CMES Shaykhs intramural basketball team—he is missed.

As I have mentioned in each of the first three editions, there are always going to be some topics that I wish were covered. A lot of this depends on the seemingly infinite vagaries of circumstances, challenges, and personalities that an editor has to deal with; a good part of this is determined by size and cost because we do not want students to have to pay an exorbitant price for this book. I have long come to the conclusion that before anyone has the right to critically review an edited volume, they must have first done one him/herself!

Note on the Text

One of the challenges of compiling an edited volume written by different individuals is ensuring stylistic consistency among chapters. In particular, many authors have used their own system of transliteration. I generally retained each author's style except for names and terms that appear throughout the text. In these cases, I selected one variation of spelling, which is often the more recognizable version rather than a strict transliteration: for example, "Hussein" rather than "Husayn" or "Hussain"; "Faisal" rather than "Faysal" or "Feisal"; "Nasser" rather than "Nasir"; and "Mussadiq" rather than "Mossadeq," "Mossadegh," or "Musaddiq." Many of the chapters include a diacritic mark (') for the important Arabic consonant 'ayn; however, I have eliminated the diacritic mark for the Arabic hamza ('). One hopes few exceptions have slipped through.

In addition, the body of water bounded by Iran, Iraq, and the Arab Gulf states is known either as the Arabian or Persian Gulf; this book has no particular preference and allows the individual authors to choose for themselves which appellation to utilize. The war in the Middle East in 1990–1991 is generally known in the United States as the Persian Gulf crisis and Persian Gulf war, a conflict that was precipitated by the surprise Iraqi invasion of Kuwait. In the Gulf itself, this event is generally referred to as the Second Gulf war (the first being the Iran-Iraq war of 1980–1988), the Kuwaiti crisis, the War to Liberate Kuwait, the Iraqi crisis, or simply the Gulf crisis and war, the latter being employed by most contributors in this book. Some references to other conflicts have also been standardized. For instance, two major conflicts involving Israel are generally referred to as the 1967 Arab-Israeli war and the 1973 Arab-Israeli war; however, the first is also known as the June War or Six Day War, the second as the October War, the Yom Kippur War, or the Ramadan War. In certain instances, individual contributors employ these terms.

Since the international community, including the United States, still recognizes Tel Aviv as the official capital of Israel, some of the contributors use Tel Aviv rather than Jerusalem in some references to Israeli policy even though the seat of government in Israel is clearly located in Jerusalem. Generally, I let the authors decide.

D. W. L.
Jerusalem, Tel Aviv

The Map Project by Justin McCarthy, Middle East Studies Association of North America, Inc. 2003

Introduction

David W. Lesch

US involvement in the Middle East has spanned the breadth of this country's existence, beginning most dramatically with the administration of President Thomas Jefferson, which tried to stop pirating by the North African or "Barbary" provinces of the Ottoman Empire in the early 1800s. This was a war to ensure freedom of navigation on the high seas, which was essential for US trade, as the new republic no longer enjoyed the benefits of British naval protection. Aside from this early encounter, US interaction with and interest in the Middle East during the nineteenth century was limited to the private activities of missionaries and merchants. In the following century, however, World War I propelled the United States onto the world stage—and into European politics—in a role it had neither sought nor experienced before. As the war was winding down, the United States quickly developed an interest in the disposition of the Middle East provinces of the defeated Ottoman Empire. The result was the first significant official foray by Washington into the region in the twentieth century: the King-Crane Commission was sent to Syria, Palestine, Lebanon, and Anatolia to inform American policy on the future of the region. Nonetheless, no US administration gave the region a high priority during the interwar years (1918–1939), although there was some interest in the growing involvement of multinational oil companies in the Middle East.

The strategic value of the region became clear in World War II, when, in 1942 and 1943, Anglo-American forces attacked and defeated German-Italian forces in the North African campaign. Soon, the realization that the reconstruction of Europe and Japan—as well as the postwar economic boom in the United States—would become more and more dependent upon Middle East oil (which makes up more than two-thirds of the world's known reserves) boosted the policy significance of the region in the eyes of Washington's policymakers. Moreover, the strategic value of the Middle East became linked to the emerging cold war between the United States and the Soviet Union. Washington dutifully grasped a global foreign policy and came to believe that it was the only nation that could successfully prevent Moscow from extending its influence in the region in the wake of the weakened British and French imperial positions. As a result, the Middle East became a policy priority for post–World War II administrations. The emergence of the state of Israel in 1948 reinforced US interest in the Middle East, but this event also complicated

Washington's relations with and objectives toward the Arab world, as Arabs increasingly perceived US and Israeli interests as being one and the same. Complication and complexity came to define the US–Middle East relationship during the forty or so years of the cold war, intertwined as it was with the decolonization process, Arab nationalism and state building, the Arab-Israeli conflict, the "Arab cold war," the growing strength of OPEC (the Organization of Petroleum Exporting Countries), and Islamist movements. The end of the US–Soviet cold war in 1989 resolved some tensions and mitigated others in the Middle East. However, the regional environment produced by the termination of the cold war was soon altered by the 1990–1991 Gulf war, which created new tensions and problems.

The Madrid peace process, which was launched after the Gulf war in 1991, and the Israeli-Palestinian Oslo accords, which followed in 1993, engendered a great deal of hope that a comprehensive Arab-Israeli peace could be achieved. The process proceeded in fits and starts but made significant progress; the 1994 Israeli-Jordanian peace treaty, the Israeli-Syrian negotiations, and the regional multilateral talks that for a time paralleled the Madrid process nurtured hopes for peace. Unfortunately, the overall goals set forth in the 1990s were not achieved, and the Oslo and Madrid peace processes came to an end with the eruption of the al-Aqsa *intifada* in 2000 that followed the failed last-gasp attempt by the Clinton administration to settle the Israeli-Palestinian final status issues.

In the wake of the failure to conclude the Madrid and Oslo processes, combined with continued economic problems in the Muslim world amid the general prosperity of Americanized globalization, a virulently anti-American form of Islamism arose that increasingly found violent expression through such groups as Osama bin Laden's al-Qa'ida, the culmination of which led to the tragedy of September 11, 2001. The United States, under the leadership of President George W. Bush, reacted to 9/11 in a dramatic manner. The distance traveled from the secure, if not invincible, feeling Americans enjoyed prior to 9/11 to the sense of vulnerability in the aftermath of the attacks was enormous. It was this feeling that in large measure produced a consensus in the United States in support of President Bush's more assertive foreign policy. This became manifest in the US-led invasion of Afghanistan in October 2001 that successfully evicted the ruling Taliban regime by the end of the year. It became even more apparent in the enunciation of the administration's national security strategy in September 2002, otherwise known as the Bush doctrine, which, among other things, advocated the application of preventive war through pre-emptive action in order to deal with rising threats before they could injure the United States and its interests. In March 2003, the Bush doctrine became the rationale for the US-led invasion of Iraq, which toppled the regime of Saddam Hussein. Amid the global war on terror spearheaded by the Bush administration after 9/11, the United States has become ensconced in a quagmire in Iraq generated by a lethal insurgency composed of Iraqi elements and a small number of foreign Jihadists. As many questions surround US foreign policy in the Middle East now as in the immediate aftermath of 9/11. Has the Bush doctrine failed? Will Iraq turn out to be its one-time application? How can the United States repair its sullied image in the region? How can it improve its relations with countries whose authoritarian nature runs counter to the administration's stated commitment to the promotion of democracy in the region? Can Arab/Palestinian–Israeli negotiations be reactivated in the wake of all of these changes, or will unilateralism and an ever-fragile non-belligerency come to characterize this arena over the long term? It is within this atmosphere that old and new problems meet, where history and politics meld together, and where conflict and hope for peace exist side by side.

This volume endeavors to cover these issues. Part 1, titled "From Idealism to Realism: Wilsonian Intent to Cold War Practice," begins with an examination of the King-Crane Commission, which emanated from the idealistic intentions of President Woodrow Wilson's Fourteen Points enunciated near the end of World War I—particularly that of self-determination for subject peoples—and which was ostensibly created to assess the wishes of the native population in Syria regarding postwar independence. The commission did not quite fit the reality of European politics or, for that matter, American politics, and as James Gelvin points out in Chapter 1, it was not as idealistic as it seemed, as it simply reflected and transferred democratic elitism. Indeed, by examining the King-Crane Commission from the Syrian perspective, Gelvin concludes that the commission actually established a pattern for subsequent US encounters with nationalism and state building in the Middle East that had unforeseen and often deleterious results for both the United States and the region.

The incipient nature of US policy in the Middle East evident in the immediate post–World War I period became more pronounced following what has been called the great divide of World War II, which awakened policymakers to the necessity of a more active and goal-oriented foreign policy commensurate with the onset of the cold war and related regional issues.[1] Yet, there was still the strong desire rooted in the American heritage to portray the United States as anything but a second-generation imperialist merely trading places with the Europeans. This schizophrenia made itself apparent in US development diplomacy toward the Third World in the immediate post–World War II period and was evident in President Harry S Truman's Point Four program, which was intended to be something like a Marshall Plan for the Third World. The inherent difficulties of this policy framework in light of the new global and regional realities in the Middle East were exemplified by the short but dramatic mission of Truman's special assistant to the Middle East, Edwin Locke Jr., whose story is examined by Paul Kingston in Chapter 2.

The manifest great divide in the Middle East, where a cold war–based, realpolitik foreign policy supplanted any pretense of a developmentally based one, can arguably be seen in the Muhammad Mussadiq crisis of 1953, when covert efforts primarily engineered by the United States succeeded in overthrowing the popularly elected Iranian prime minister. At the time, Washington and London thought Mussadiq would tilt Iran toward the Soviet Union, which was viewed as an unacceptable strategic setback that could also have led to a potentially disastrous superpower confrontation. The Mussadiq crisis reveals how the United States began almost instinctively to follow in the footsteps of British imperialism, demonstrating a preference for the status quo rather than the forces of change. This episode and surrounding events are examined by Mark Gasiorowski, who details—and is critical of—US policy in the matter (Chapter 3) and by Sir Sam Falle, who provides the on-the-ground viewpoint (Chapter 4). Falle was a high-level official in the British embassy in Tehran at the time of the crisis and maintains that US and British actions were correct—not only then but also in retrospect.

The perceived success of the Iranian coup reinforced the Dwight D. Eisenhower administration's emphasis on a more interventionist policy, which was characterized by covert activities designed to fight the Soviets in the cold war in the Third World through tactics short of nuclear confrontation. The Mussadiq crisis seemed to be repeated in various ways in the Middle East throughout the remainder of the decade, some with perceived equally positive results, some with more negative results.

Peter Hahn (Chapter 5) offers a description of this transitional stage in US diplomacy toward the Middle East as strategic necessities of the cold war became the paramount consideration by studying Washington's relationship with Egypt from the last stage of the King Farouk regime to the early Nasserist period ending with the Suez crisis in 1956. Elie Podeh (Chapter 6) further covers US strategic policy in the Middle East by focusing on the creation of a regional pro-West defense pact, specifically the seminal 1955 Baghdad Pact, the role of the United States in its formation, and the repercussions of its consummation. David Lesch and Erika Alin (Chapters 7 and 8 respectively) examine the Syrian and Lebanese crises of 1957–1958 and the associated complex political environment of the Middle East in the 1950s, when the international cold war in the region was at its height and was superimposed on the Arab-Israeli conflict, Arab state building, and the emerging Arab cold war. This section ends with a discussion by Malik Mufti (Chapter 9) on the relationship of the United States with pan-Arabism, specifically that proffered by Egyptian President Gamal 'Abd al-Nasser versus that espoused by the Ba'thists in Iraq and Syria following the 1956 Suez crisis and bridging the Arab cold war to the seminal 1967 Arab-Israeli war. Mufti concludes that US policies under Eisenhower and his secretary of state, John Foster Dulles, as well as those under the John F. Kennedy and Lyndon B. Johnson administrations, which have been "roundly criticized" in the past (as in this volume), have been to a large extent misinterpreted and were actually much more prescient and successful than is popularly perceived, especially as the United States began to see Arab nationalism as an antidote to communism. As others have observed, however, the objectives may have been achieved despite US policy, especially as the dynamics of Malcolm Kerr's "Arab cold war" tended to define the political and diplomatic parameters in the Middle East during this period.[2]

Since the emergence of the state of Israel in 1948 and the subsequent Arab-Israeli conflict, there seems to have been a recurrent cycle of conflict followed by missed opportunities for peace or the establishment of something less than a comprehensive peace, which in turn has created an environment in which tensions continue and issues remain unresolved, which then leads to the resumption of some form of conflict—and so forth and so on. The role of the United States in this process has varied considerably, from pacifier to antagonist, from mediator to peacemaker, from belligerent to bystander. Part 2, titled "Arab-Israeli War and Peace," examines the role the United States has played in this seemingly never-ending cycle. At the close of the cold war, there was a widely held perception that this cycle could be terminated with a sustainable comprehensive peace in the Arab-Israeli arena, and a number of important steps were made to facilitate the achievement of this. However, as the breakdown of the Oslo and Madrid peace processes and the current situation in the region demonstrate, there remain significant obstacles to a complete resolution of the Arab-Israeli dispute.

Fawaz Gerges begins this section (Chapter 10) with a discussion of the 1967 Arab-Israeli war, which initiated the peace process as we know it today and effectively brought the superpower cold war together with the Arab-Israeli issue. In the 1969–1970 War of Attrition and the 1973 Arab-Israeli war, the Soviets became intimately involved, the result being a near superpower confrontation during the latter stages of the 1973 hostilities. In examining the impact of the 1967 war on Arab nationalist perceptions of the United States, Gerges argues that the war had a "devastating negative impact" on Arab views of the US role in the peace process. Nevertheless, the "indispensable and preponderant" role of Washington in this process was made abundantly clear: the United States "held most of the cards."

Janice Stein (Chapter 11) discusses the intricate, tension-filled, and dramatic superpower negotiations during the latter stages of the 1973 Arab-Israeli war, the results of which altered the international and regional configuration in the Middle East and contributed to a "second cold war" between the Soviet Union and the United States that lasted until the early 1980s. Bernard Reich (Chapter 12) then analyzes the "special relationship" that developed between Israel and the United States during the "peace process" of the 1970s and 1980s leading up to the Israeli-PLO Declaration of Principles through to its apparent unraveling with the al-Aqsa *intifada* that began in September 2000. JoAnn DiGeorgio-Lutz (Chapter 13) discusses the "precarious nature" of the US-PLO relationship during this same period from the Palestinian perspective.

Jeremy Pressman contributes a new chapter (Chapter 14) that outlines the Oslo and Madrid peace processes through the failed Camp David meeting in July 2000 and critically examines the roles played by each of the principal players, including the United States. In the process, Pressman offers some cogent reasons why both the Oslo and Madrid accords broke down. In another new contribution, Robert O. Freedman (Chapter 15) covers in intricate detail the policies of the George W. Bush administration toward the Arab-Israeli arena during its first and early second terms in office. In doing so, Freedman reveals the complexities of the Arab/Israeli dynamic and the challenges facing any resumption of serious negotiation.

Part 3, "Gulf Wars," focuses on the series of events leading up to and following the Iraqi invasion and occupation of Kuwait in August 1990, the subsequent liberation of Kuwait by the US-led international coalition in February 1991, and the US-led invasion of Iraq in 2003 and its aftermath. This period marks the most intimate involvement of the United States in the Middle East. The Gulf wars have climaxed more than a half-century of US vital interest in the Persian Gulf area. US policy has been based primarily on maintaining stability in the area to ensure easy access to and the safe transport of oil—and during the cold war, to keep the Soviets from fishing in troubled waters.

Balance-of-power politics played an important part in US calculations toward achieving these objectives. First, the United States initiated a relationship with Iran through the Mussadiq coup, and then it enhanced this relationship by supporting the shah of Iran as the US "policeman" of the Gulf as part of the Vietnam-induced 1969 Nixon doctrine, which sought to secure US surrogates for its global strategic interests. (The United States envisioned Israel playing a similar role in the heartland of the Middle East.) With the fall of the shah in the 1979 Iranian revolution and with the ensuing Iran-Iraq war, Washington began to see Iraq's Saddam Hussein as its new gendarme in the region, keeping Khomeinism at bay, restoring Gulf stability, and even possibly playing the role that Egyptian President Anwar Sadat never filled—that of leading a moderate Arab consensus toward peace with Israel. US and British support backfired, however, a turn of events that became readily apparent when Iraq invaded Kuwait in 1990, eliciting the decision by the administration of George H. W. Bush to intervene militarily. The 1991 Gulf war, along with the end of the cold war, contributed to a new regional configuration full of prospects for peace and stability as well as conflict and instability. Importantly, this resulted in an enhanced role for the United States in a part of the Middle East that had traditionally been wary of US influence.

US involvement reached a pinnacle with the US-led invasion of Iraq in 2003, fueled by accusations from the Bush administration that the regime of Saddam Hussein was manufacturing and stockpiling weapons of mass destruction (WMD) and had links with al-Qaʻida. According to the prescription of the Bush doctrine, the supposed threat from Iraq needed to be dealt with before it developed into a direct threat to the United States—no one wanted to see another 9/11. Bush administration officials, while assiduously maintaining a commitment to a satisfactory resolution of the Iraqi situation, have admitted that things did not go entirely according to plan. There were no WMD found in Iraq, and no serious Iraqi links to al-Qaʻida were proven. Moreover, a growing insurgency against what is perceived to be an American occupation and a dysfunctional Iraqi government have led to tremendous instability in the country. Neither US forces nor Iraqi forces were prepared to deal with an insurgency, and reconstruction of the country's basic infrastructure has been impeded by constant violence. Officials from both countries are attempting to find the correct formula for an effective government in Iraq so that the United States and its allies can withdraw their troops.

Gary Sick, who served on the National Security Council staff during the Carter administration, begins this section (Chapter 16) with an examination of US policy in the Gulf in the post–World War II era through the period of "dual containment" in the 1990s, particularly focusing on the enhanced role of the United States in the region following the 1979 Iranian revolution. In addition to providing context for this section, Sick also critically analyzes the changing role of the United States in the area, as the interests defined and the subsequent policies enacted by Washington have been adjusted and readjusted in reaction to the frequent shifts in the regional balance of power in the Gulf.

Shafeeq Ghabra (Chapter 17) follows with a discussion, from the Kuwaiti point of view, of the development of the relationship between the United States and Kuwait. Stating that Kuwait, with divergent interests, was something of a reluctant ally of the United States during the Iran-Iraq war, Ghabra concludes that although much work is still needed to solidify relations between the two nations in order to preserve mutual interests and present a unified and stable presence in an unstable area, the relationship is solid due to a deep level of cooperation in the Gulf wars of 1991 and 2003.

In Chapter 18, Amatzia Baram examines the US-Iraqi relationship that developed out of the Iran-Iraq war and analyzes Saddam Hussein's decision to invade Kuwait. Baram contends that whereas the George H. W. Bush administration perceived the relationship to be a positive development worth nurturing in the aftermath of the Iran-Iraq war, the measures it took in an attempt to curb Saddam Hussein's excesses only compelled Baghdad to conclude early on that the United States and Iraq were on a "collision course"; the Iraqis understood that the achievement of their national goals would have to come at the expense of their relationship with the United States.

Examining the Saudi view of its relationship with the United States before and throughout the period of the Gulf wars, F. Gregory Gause (Chapter 19) concludes that although the dilemma that has traditionally faced Saudi rulers (keeping the United States as its "over-the-horizon" defense while maintaining its distance from Washington for domestic and regional purposes) was smashed with the open reception of US troops during the 1991 Gulf war, a quandary still exists because of domestic public opinion weighted against too close an attachment. Of course, the tensions between the two countries have only been exacerbated in the aftermath of 9/11, as the majority of the terrorists who carried out the attacks, as well as Osama bin Laden himself, were Saudi.

Steve Yetiv and Ali Abootalebi contribute two new chapters (Chapters 20 and 21, respectively) examining the US-led invasion of Iraq in 2003 and its aftermath. Yetiv first outlines the rationale of the Bush administration in making the decision to go to war in Iraq. In doing so, he analyzes the popular perceptions—and misperceptions—of why the Bush administration went against the wishes of most of the international community and invaded Iraq. In the process of his examination, he outlines what appear to be the real reasons. Abootalebi offers a stinging critique of the Bush administration's decision to go to war and the series of missteps it made during and after the initial military phase that led to the seemingly intractable position for going to war in which the United States now finds itself. While outlining this predicament in Iraq, he also examines the important and related US-Iranian dynamic.

Part 4 is titled "Retrospective and Reassessment," and it contains chapters on a variety of historical and current issues of interest. Even though the cold war has ended, its legacy and its aftermath are subjects of intense discussion. Indeed, the theme that links all of the chapters in this section is change—from the cold war to the end of the cold war (and its regional effects upon the Arab-Israeli, Persian Gulf, and Central Asian arenas) to the changing role of Russia (from superpower to supplicant) to the dramatic effects of 9/11 on the region. Many Middle East states are experiencing various levels of severe socioeconomic distress, a situation that has led to a concomitant rise in oppositional Islamist movements, something that is portrayed by many as the new implacable foe of the United States and the West, particularly in the wake of 9/11. There is change in the Arab world as it comes to grips with the roots of this discontent. Many nations in the Middle East are grappling with the problem of regime legitimacy amid rampant authoritarianism and corruption and US attempts to promote democracy in the region. All of this is exacerbated by generational change in leadership positions and the need to define a role in the international community. And finally, amid all of the change in the Middle East and in the international arena, there is the question of what role the United States should play.

From the vantage point of Moscow, Georgiy Mirsky, in an essay derived from scholarly examination and personal experience (Chapter 22), discusses the motivations, ideological commitment, and interests of Soviet policy toward the Middle East during the cold war era and the transformation of this policy in the post–cold war world. Noting that the Kremlin historically preferred to undermine the West through support of national liberation movements (many of which were thoroughly un-Marxist/Leninist), Mirsky observes that the ideological baggage associated with substantiating such policies quickly disappeared following Gorbachev's glasnost (or what Mirsky calls the "de-ideologization" of Soviet foreign policy), clearing the way for a more cooperative relationship with the United States in the Middle East, the one area of foreign policy where the Kremlin still can play an influential role.

Henri Barkey (Chapter 23) examines the increasingly important relationship between the United States and Turkey, one that is composed of strategic as well as economic elements—and the very interesting, close military relationship Turkey has established with Israel. After surveying the post–World War II history of the relationship that reveals the waxing and waning of relations between the two countries based on a variety of circumstances, Barkey describes the close strategic cooperation that developed between Washington and Ankara by necessity as a result of the Gulf war and the sanctions regime implemented thereafter against Iraq. This strategic cooperation was strengthened after the events of 9/11, when Turkey became vitally important to US strategic interests in Central Asia and the Middle East, but then suffered a setback in 2003 when Istanbul, fearing domestic backlash, would not allow the United States to use its territory to launch the invasion of Iraq.

Marvin Weinbaum (Chapter 24) examines the US-Afghani dynamic. After detailing the development of the Soviet-Afghani and US-Afghani relationships in the post–World War II era, he then comments on the seminal period surrounding the Soviet invasion of Afghanistan in 1979 and the changes that it wrought in and outside of the region itself. Weinbaum goes on to analyze the breakdown of the Afghani state following the Soviet withdrawal in 1989, which led to the Taliban takeover by

1996 and the establishment of the al-Qaʿida terrorist infrastructure shortly thereafter. He closes with a discussion of how Afghanistan again arose from "marginality" and acquired a prominent foreign policy position in Washington following the September 2001 attacks, the US-led invasion of Afghanistan, and the attempt to construct a functioning democratic society following the ousting of the Taliban.

Jon Alterman (Chapter 25) offers the final new contribution to this compendium, one that critically examines the Bush administration's attempts to promote democracy in the region, the object of which is to help drain the facilitating swamp of Islamic extremism created by the lack of political space imposed by authoritarian regimes and associated corruption and socioeconomic deprivation. While applauding the promotion of democracy in the region, Alterman criticizes the methodology employed by the United States over the years, which tended to focus on the so-called Arab liberals to the exclusion of other important elements of Arab societies. The efforts at democratization have therefore produced decidedly mixed results and contributed to the rising influence and power of Islamist groups that Washington has been trying to marginalize. While pointing out the mistakes of US policy in this area—and their consequences—Alterman concludes by offering some ideas for American administrations to consider that might produce a more desirable outcome for US and indigenous interests alike.

William Quandt (Chapter 26) offers a retrospective examination of US foreign policy toward the Middle East and a look at what opportunities and problems in the region lie ahead for policymakers. Although acknowledging that many people, particularly those in the region itself, have had good reason to be highly critical of US actions in the Middle East, he asserts that the objectives as traditionally defined by US policymakers have been for the most part achieved, and at least until 9/11, with relatively little cost in human and economic terms, especially when compared to US policy in Southeast Asia. While this relative success may be on the wane in recent years nonetheless, US administrations must begin to define objectives commensurate with the changes that have occurred in the international and regional environment while remaining sensitive to the fact that many of the problems in the region are intrinsic to the area and cannot be solved in Washington.

The rise of Islamist movements in the Middle East has obviously created a good deal of consternation among policymakers in Washington, and the foreign policy and security establishments have been mobilized in a heretofore unparalleled way in an attempt to deal with this issue following the events of 9/11 and the 2003 war in Iraq. Many see this phenomenon as inherently inimical and dangerous to US and Western interests in the region. In an attempt to understand the Islamist perspective toward US foreign policy in the Middle East, Yvonne Haddad (Chapter 27) examines the root causes of Islamism in general as well as its specific views toward the role that the United States and the West have played in the area. She does not paint a very optimistic picture. Haddad offers a glimpse at the potential of continuing conflict in the Middle East unless certain long-standing grievances held by many groups in the region are addressed in what they perceive to be a satisfactory manner.

Even though they are chronological opposites, the first and last chapters address—by design—the World War I period, where much of the Middle East map was artificially drawn by the victorious entente powers. The divisions and issues that resulted from this period are still very much alive today, and in many ways they are still creating challenges and obstacles for US foreign policy toward the Middle East. Indeed, the perception of the United States held by many in the Middle East has changed dramatically over the course of the twentieth century and into the twenty-first century. This is clearly indicated by the positive view toward the United States observed by a US visitor to the region in 1922 (revealed in the epigraph to Chapter 1), in contrast with the antagonistic, paranoid, cynical, and hateful comments typically made by Islamists today, as evidenced in the numerous quotes cited by Haddad in Chapter 27. And as Robert Allison shows in his postscript on the development of the distorted image of the Middle East and Islam held by Americans during the formative period of the United States, climaxing with the Tripolitan war, these types of negative comments flowing back and forth are anything but a recent phenomenon. As will become apparent throughout this book, involvement in the Middle East has been an adventurous and, at times, tumultuous experience for the United States, one that has not been without its successes. But it is also one that has had numerous failures; even what the United States typically considers successes, however, are not always viewed as such by those in the region itself. The United States is certainly by far the most influential outside power in the Middle East, but it is also far from the most popular; the two do not always, and sometimes should not, go together. Is this the dilemma of a superpower with global interests working through a regional environment, or could US policy have been much more discerning and prescient? The answer probably lies somewhere in between.

Notes

1. Raymond Hare, "The Great Divide: World War II," *Annals* 401 (May 1972), pp. 23–30.

2. See Malcolm H. Kerr, *The Arab Cold War: Gamal 'Abd al-Nasir and His Rivals, 1958–1970* (New York: Oxford University Press, 1971).

Part One

From Idealism to Realism

Wilsonian Intent to Cold War Practice

1

The Ironic Legacy of the King-Crane Commission

James Gelvin

In the immediate aftermath of World War I, a US observer in Syria wrote:

> Without visiting the Near East, it is not possible for an American to realize even faintly, the respect, faith and affection with which our Country is regarded throughout that region. Whether it is the world-wide reputation which we enjoy for fair dealing, a tribute perhaps to the crusading spirit which carried us into the Great War, not untinged with the hope that the same spirit may urge us into the solution of great problems growing out of that conflict, or whether due to unselfish or impartial missionary and educational influence exerted for a century, it is the one faith which is held alike by Christian and Moslem, by Jew and Gentile, by prince and peasant in the Near East.[1]

If, during the three-quarters of a century that have passed since these words were written, those who have chronicled the relations between the United States and the nations of the Middle East have had few, if any, opportunities to repeat our observer's findings, they can at least take solace from the fact that the goodwill that may have existed seventy-five years ago has been dissipated precisely because of US intervention in the "great problems" engendered by the destruction of the Ottoman Empire.

The first official US foray into the politics of the post-Ottoman Middle East came about as the result of a suggestion made by President Woodrow Wilson to the Council of Four entente powers (France, Great Britain, the United States, and Italy) assembled in Paris to determine the terms of peace. In an attempt to resolve an acrimonious dispute between Britain and France over the future disposition of the Arab provinces of the Ottoman Empire, Wilson suggested the formation of an interallied commission on Syria. The commission would travel to the Middle East "to elucidate the state of opinion and the soil to be worked on by any mandatory. They should be asked to come back and tell the Conference what they found with regard to these matters. . . . If we were to send a Commission of men with no previous contact with Syria, it would, at any rate, convince the world that the Conference had tried to do all it could to find the most scientific basis possible for a settlement."[2] Although both France and Britain acquiesced to the idea of the commission, neither power appointed delegates to participate in its activities. As a result, the commission became a US commission and thus has been commonly referred to by the names of its two commissioners, Henry Churchill King, president of Oberlin College in Ohio, and Chicago businessman and Democratic Party activist Charles R. Crane. King and Crane traveled to Palestine, Syria, Lebanon, and Anatolia in the summer of 1919 to meet with local representatives. Their findings, filed with the US delegation at Paris, were subsequently ignored by the peace negotiators.

Diplomatic historians have usually cited the King-Crane Commission as either an example of US naïveté in the face of European realpolitik or as a representation of the principles that differentiate the "new diplomacy" from the old. In reality, the legacy of the commission is far more complex. Although the commission's impact on entente policy was doomed from the beginning by a variety of factors—a confusion of secret agreements, historic claims, and postwar realities; the Parti Colonial in France and the Republican Party in the United States; and the British realization that "the friendship of France is worth ten Syrias"[3]—contemporary students of US foreign policy can draw two lessons from the story of the commission. The first lesson is that in diplomacy, as in physics, neutral observers do not exist; rather a world power necessarily influences the object of its interest simply by turning its attention to it, by defining it as a problem to be solved and then framing the possible terms for its solution. Second, a review of the effects of the visit of the King-Crane Commission on the Syrian population[4] underscores the need for US policymakers to reassess the preconceptions and misapprehensions that have guided them, often with disastrous results, when formulating policies that deal with "nation building" and nationalism.

The Doctrine of Self-Determination and Its Application in the Middle East

During World War I and the subsequent peace negotiations, the French, British, and US governments all made declarations that indicated support for self-determination for the peoples of the Ottoman Empire. At the same time, however, all three governments committed themselves to policies that made true self-determination impossible.

For Woodrow Wilson, the liberation of peoples and postwar self-determination were sine qua nons for US participation in the war. From December 1917 through September 1918, Wilson delivered a series of addresses, enunciating US principles in Fourteen Points (8 January 1918), Four Supplementary Points (11 February 1918), Four Additional Points (4 July 1918), and Five Additional Points (27 September 1918). "Self-determination," Wilson warned, "is not a mere phrase. It is an imperative principle of action which statesmen will henceforth ignore at their peril."[5] In Point Twelve of the original Fourteen Points, Wilson directly addressed the status of Turks and non-Turks in the Ottoman Empire, promising the latter "an absolutely unmolested opportunity of autonomous development."[6]

Stung by the revelation of secret agreements reached during the war for a colonial-style division of the Ottoman Empire, and wishing to allay the doubts of Arab nationalists who suspected entente perfidy, France and Britain adopted Wilson's call for self-determination for the inhabitants of the Middle East. On November 9, 1918, they issued the following joint declaration, which they distributed throughout liberated Syria: "The object aimed at by France and Great Britain in prosecuting in the East the War let loose by the ambition of Germany is the complete and definite emancipation of the peoples so long oppressed by the Turks and the establishment of national governments and administrations deriving their authority from the initiative and free choice of the indigenous populations."[7]

In the same statement, however, the two powers displayed their ambivalence to the principle of self-determination by making their support for the doctrine conditional on the acceptance by the indigenes of guidance from "advanced nations":

> In order to carry out these intentions France and Great Britain are at one in encouraging and assisting the establishment of indigenous Governments and administrations in Syria and Mesopotamia, now liberated by the Allies, and in the territories the liberation of which they are engaged in securing and recognising these as soon as they are actually established.
>
> Far from wishing to impose on the populations of these regions any particular institutions they are only concerned to ensure by their support and by adequate assistance the regular working of Governments and administrations freely chosen by the populations themselves. To secure impartial and equal justice for all, to facilitate the economic development of the country by inspiring and encouraging local initiative, to favour the diffusion of education, to put an end to dissensions that have too long been taken advantage of by Turkish policy, such is the policy which the two Allied Governments uphold in the liberated territories.

For many Arab nationalists, particularly those who had preferred sitting out the war in Egypt to joining the British-inspired Arab Revolt of Sharif Hussein and his sons, the Anglo-French statement appeared to be little more than a rationalization for a thinly veiled colonialism.[8] As if to confirm their suspicions, French President Georges Clemenceau visited London in December 1918, where, in the words of British Prime Minister Lloyd George, it was "agreed that Syria should go to France [as a mandate] and Mesopotamia to Great Britain."[9] To mollify the French further, the British (as well as the United States) disavowed any interest in Syria in a meeting of the Council of Four held three days before the peace conference authorized the assignment of mandates in the region.

Whereas the French and British attitude toward both self-determination for the inhabitants of the region and the King-Crane Commission was thus clear, US support for both was surprisingly ambiguous. Its European allies might easily have argued that the United States had, on several occasions, already placed its imprimatur on their wartime and postwar arrangements for the region. After all, not only had Woodrow Wilson issued a statement of support for the Balfour Declaration[10] in September 1918 without bothering to ascertain the attitude of the inhabitants of Palestine toward the establishment of a Jewish homeland in their midst, but one month later he approved the official US Department of State commentary on the Fourteen Points, which recognized the preeminent position of France in Syria and affirmed that Britain was "clearly the best mandatory for Palestine, Mesopotamia, and Arabia."[11] Little wonder, then, that Henry King and Charles Crane, in a memorandum written to the US president before their tour of the Middle East, argued that the mandate for Syria should go to France "frankly based, not on the primary desires of the people, but on the international need of preserving friendly relations between France and Great Britain,"[12] or that, within a week of proposing the commission, Wilson had, according to Ray Stannard Baker, a close associate and head of the US press bureau in Paris, "clean forgotten" about it.[13]

Support among the entente powers for the activities of the commission thus ranged from lackluster to dismissive. The commission's recommendations were nonbinding, and even if the commission were to find, as it did, that Syrian public opinion supported a united Syria and (in ranked order) no mandate, a US mandate, and a British mandate,[14] all three options had already been foreclosed. It was in this context that Lloyd George, like the proverbial Western sheriff who remarked, "First we give him a fair trial, then we hang him," urged his French colleague to support the activities of the commission, but "first let us agree [about the disposition of territory] between ourselves."[15]

The US Perspective on Self-Determination and Public Opinion

Not only did decisions made in Paris preclude the possibility that the King-Crane Commission would influence entente policy, but preconceptions held by both the commissioners and their president—preconceptions about democracy, progress, public opinion, and nationalism that both underlay the commission's flawed procedure and circumscribed the range of its possible findings—impeded the commission's ability truly to "elucidate the state of opinion and the soil to be worked on by any mandatory" in Syria.

The extent to which his father's Calvinism shaped Woodrow Wilson's worldview and principles of his foreign policy is a well-worn cliché.[16] But because Wilson was a historian as well as the son of a Presbyterian minister, he tempered his belief in a mankind tainted by original sin with the optimism implicit in the Whiggism common to the academic milieu from which he emerged. History, for Wilson, was the chronicle of liberty—"the enlargement of the sphere of independent action at the expense of dictatorial authority."[17] From the Greek polis and the confrontation at Runnymede through the ratification of the US Constitution, human progress could thus be measured in two ways: by the multiplication of the personal freedoms available to the (Anglo-Saxon) heirs of this tradition, and by the spread of democracy—the political correlate to this tradition—throughout the world.

In his writings, Wilson argued that the expansion of international trade, print media, and, most important, public education during the previous century had created an autonomous realm of public opinion in most nations that facilitated the global diffusion of democratic ideals and structures.[18] Wilson's definition of public opinion thus differed dramatically from the definition used by his German idealist contemporaries: Rather than being the repository of common sense ("all-pervasive fundamental ethical principles disguised as prejudices"),[19] Wilson's public opinion was an *informed* public opinion shaped by the most enlightened strata of society.[20] This was the public opinion upon which the doctrine of self-determination rested, the public opinion that Wilson charged the King-Crane Commission to elucidate.

The members of the King-Crane Commission shared Wilson's understanding about the nature of public opinion. Their fact-finding consisted of holding audiences with, and receiving petitions drafted by, those whom they considered to be the most important and most representative Middle East opinion makers: thirty-four mayors and municipal councils, fifteen administrative councils, sixty-five councils of village chiefs, thirty Arab shaykhs, seventeen professional and trade organizations, and so on. It should not be surprising, therefore, that in its final report the commission advocated strengthening Syrian nationalism through an expansion of education "in clear recognition of the imperative necessity of education for the citizens of a democratic state and the development of a sound national spirit."[21]

Although members of the King-Crane Commission disagreed about the extent to which the Syrian population was prepared for self-determination and how long "the systematic cultivation of national spirit" in Syria would take, all agreed on the liberal and secular foundations on which Syrians had to base their nationalism. In the conclusion to its final report, the commission recommended imposing a mandate on Syria but optimistically predicted that the period during which a mandatory power would have to oversee Syrian affairs might be brief. According to the report, mandatory control could be relinquished as soon as the leaders of the Syrian nationalist movement demonstrated their sincerity in midwifing a modern democratic nation-state that protected the rights of minorities:

> The western world is already committed to the attempt to live in peace and friendship with the Moslem peoples, and to manage governments in such a way as to separate politics from religion. Syria offers an excellent opportunity to establish a state where members of the three great monotheistic religions can live together in harmony; because it is a country of one language, which has long had freedom of movement and of business relations through being unified under the Turkish rule. Since now the majority declare for nationalism, independent of religion, it is necessary only to hold them to this view through mandatory control until they shall have established the method and practice of it. Dangers may readily arise from unwise and unfaithful dealings with this people, but there is great hope of peace and progress if they be handled frankly and loyally.[22]

In contrast to the findings of the commissioners, the reports filed by William
Yale, one of two technical advisers attached to the King-Crane Commission, cast
doubt on the short-term "possibility of developing among the people of Syria a national spirit upon the community of language which exists, the similarity of race,
the sense of economic dependence, and the germ of nationalism." Yale predicted
disaster without a long-term and energetic mandatory presence in Syria:

> There is a liberal movement among the Syrian Moslems, a movement which under
> proper guidance and with proper assistance may be able to awaken a new spirit in the
> younger generation, might have been able to lessen the fanaticism not only of the ef-
> fendi class but of the lower classes. At the present time this liberal movement was too
> feeble, too weak in numbers and conviction . . . to rally to their support the ignorant
> fanatical masses which are swayed by the Ulemas and the Young Arab Party.[23]

Ironically, the very search by members of the King-Crane Commission for their
counterparts in Syrian society directly (and adversely) affected the latter's ability to
shape Syrian public opinion. Those whom Yale entrusted to nurture "liberal nationalism" naturally believed, like the commissioners, that educational achievement or
professional status entitled them to play a special role in nation building. While actively courting the commissioners, this grouping simultaneously sought to convince
the Syrian population that, having achieved the approbation of the commission, it
would secure Syrian independence through negotiation and compromise—if not
absolute independence, then at least independence under the benevolent guidance
of the Americans or British. The refusal by the entente powers to accept the recommendations of the King-Crane Commission destroyed the credibility of this sodality
within the nationalist movement and thus assured the emergence a new and very
different kind of nationalist leadership.

The "Liberal Movement"

The thin strata of society behind what William Yale (ingenuously) identified as the
"liberal movement" had emerged in Syria as the result of two processes that had,
over the course of the half-century that preceded the dissolution of the Ottoman
Empire, increasingly determined institutions and social relationships in the Arab
Middle East. Both the accelerating rate of integration of the region into the world
economy and attempts made by the Ottoman government to rationalize and
strengthen central control increased the salience of capitalist relations and encouraged their diffusion (albeit unevenly) throughout the empire. These effects, in turn,
not only induced the reconstruction and/or enlargement of certain previously existing social classes, but they prompted the emergence of new social classes as well.
Members of two of these classes, often intertwined through reciprocal ties of interest
and/or consanguinity, formed the core of Yale's "liberal movement": the so-called
middle strata, comprising intellectuals, trained military officers, professionals, and so
on, who were necessary to implement Ottoman "modernization" and state-building

policies, and a reconstituted urban notability whose economic and political status was increasingly based on a combination of land ownership and good relations with Istanbul.[24]

Two types of bonds united these groups with their counterparts in the West. Because both the formation of the middle strata and the post-1860 transformation of the urban notability depended upon the spread of peripheral capitalism and modern institutions of governance in the Middle East, the categories used by these groups to organize the world and their society were coherent with the categories used by analogous groups—both in the metropole and in other peripheral areas—who benefited from, or whose origins can be traced to, the worldwide expansion of capitalism. In addition, elective ties of affinity, nurtured, for example, through education, religious affiliation, and/or wartime experiences, often linked members of these groups to their European counterparts. These natural and emulative bonds not only account for the strategies used by these newly empowered groups to craft state institutions in post-Ottoman Syria, but also explain why, during the same period, an influential bloc readily worked within the parameters set by the Paris Peace Conference in an attempt to win Syrian independence.

The Arab government that was established in Damascus at the close of World War I depended upon individuals from these groups to administer the territory of inland Syria and to mobilize the support of the indigenous population. Working both within the government and through allied political and cultural organizations (the most important of which were al-Fatat, the Arab Club *[al-nadi al-'arabi]*, and the Literary Society *[al-muntada al-adabi]*),[25] the self-proclaimed elite within the nationalist movement (labeled in their own writings the *mutanawwirun, mustanirun,* or *mufakkirun*) designed governmental and extragovernmental institutions to expand the authority of the state, reorganize traditional structures within civil society, introduce mores and values compatible with or derived from those of Europe, and inculcate new national myths and symbols among the population. In a report written in November 1919, for example, British traveler Gertrude Bell described her visit to one such institution, the "School for the Daughters of Martyrs" *(madrasat banat al-shuhada),* which was established in Damascus to educate orphans whose fathers had died during the Arab Revolt. The school, according to Bell,

> is run on private subscriptions by a committee of ladies presided over by Naziq bint al 'Abid, a girl of 21 belonging to one of the best families of Damascus. She is a niece of 'Izzat Pasha, who was the all-powerful Secretary of Abdul Hamid for a period of years, during which he earned great wealth and the bitter recriminations of the C.U.P. [Committee of Union and Progress] when it came into the saddle. In spite of their threats Izzat managed to escape to Europe, where he had already lodged a respectable part of his fortune. Sitt Naziq was educated in a mission school at Beyrut, speaks English, and is the most advanced lady in Damascus. She and her mother sat unveiled among a company of men, a select company, but none of them related to the 'Abid family. Another Mohammadan lady of the committee was present, and she also was unveiled. . . . The mistresses were mostly Christians educated in Beyrut and speaking

fairly good English. Besides the orphans there were an equal number of girls of good
Damascene families who pay for the education they receive. These girls 16 to 18 years
old, were not seen by the men of the party. Girls and children were brought out into
the large garden which surrounds the house to sing patriotic songs. In one of them a
chorus of the elder girls addressed the orphans, reminding each one that her father
died in the cause of liberty and bidding her never to forget that she was "bint ul
'Arabi," while the children replied that they would never forget their birth, nor King
Husain who fought for their race, nor finally (this stanza was specially prepared for the
US Commission) President Wilson who laid down—save the mark—the principles of
freedom.[26]

A more comprehensive picture of the attitudes and activities of like-minded *mu
tanawwirun* during the period preceding the visit of the King-Crane Commission
to Damascus is displayed in an unusual parable, entitled "The True Vision," that
was published on the front page of the official gazette of the Arab government in
May 1919.[27] The fantasy begins with a description of the author at his desk, contemplating the news of demonstrations held in Egypt to show popular support for
Egyptian independence: "We hardly see such good order in the demonstrations of
the most advanced Western nations. I said to myself, 'By God! They unjustly accuse
the East and its people of savagery, immaturity, and an inability to imitate the civilization of the West. What is more indicative of their readiness [for independence]
than this admirably ordered and perfect demonstration?'" Troubled by his medita-
tions and by concerns about the upcoming visit of the King-Crane Commission to
Damascus, the author falls asleep. His dreams transport him to an unfamiliar Middle East location where the inhabitants speak classical Arabic and dress in traditional
attire. In the tent of their chieftain lies a strange mechanism and two mirrors: one
mirror reflects the past, the other forecasts the future. The author, having begged
the apparition for a glimpse of the future, spends the remainder of the dream watching upcoming events unfold, "like in a movie."

The author's first vision is of the near future. On the eve of the arrival of the
King-Crane Commission, "the people of distinction and their intellectuals" *('ilyat
al-qawm wa mufakkiruhum)*, assembled in a general congress, make preparations to
convince the commission that the Syrian population is mature (the words
"*madani*," "*umrani*," and "*adabi*" are used throughout the article) and therefore
merits independence. To accomplish this, as the parable continues, the delegates
plan to use locally based artisan guilds and patriotic clubs to organize demonstrations similar to those of Egypt and to distribute placards among the population calling for complete independence:

In conformity with this plan each citizen placed a sign on his forearm and on his
breast on which was printed "We demand complete independence." Shop owners
placed signs with this slogan written in English and Arabic on their shops. Hardly had
these plans been made when all inhabitants—regardless of religion, sect, and national-
ity—showed these placards . . . and one could not walk down the street without seeing

the signs on every building and wall. As the size of demonstrations swelled, the people daubed this slogan on the tarbooshes of small boys and embroidered it on the frontlets of small girls. I laughed when I saw a bald man with the slogan written on his head. I saw the owners of carriages and horses who placed this slogan on the faces of their horses and the sweets-sellers put the slogan on the lids of containers of sweets and milk. I was truly amazed when I saw the work of the residents of Salhiyye—they spelled out this slogan with lanterns on Mt. Qasiun by night in letters that could be read for seven miles. The people kept up this sort of activity until the delegation left Damascus.

Impressed by the "intelligence, advancement, and worthiness for independence" of Syrians, the King-Crane Commission returns to Paris and convinces the peace conference to offer the Syrians independence. Under the benevolent leadership of Faisal, now king of Syria, and guided by a new congress, presumably composed of the same notables and intellectuals who had convened in the previous congress, the nation can now enjoy the fruits of its independence:

> I saw . . . the people now turning their attention to the founding of schools and colleges until no village remained without an excellent primary school. I saw prosperity spreading throughout the country and railroads connecting populous villages and farms. I saw farmers using the most modern agricultural techniques, extensive trade, and flourishing industry. Damascus appeared to me to be the most advanced of cities in terms of its construction. Its streets and lanes were paved with asphalt and the Barada River was like the Seine, traversing the city from east to west. On its banks was a corniche on which towering buildings stood. I saw Aleppo: its water, brought by canals from the Euphrates, sustained its gardens and parks and anointed its waterless desert. . . . Factories were founded throughout the kingdom so that the country had no need for manufactured goods from the West, but instead exported its products to China, India, and Africa. Its people grew rich, its power increased, and it moved to the forefront of advanced nations.

As is common with prophetic narratives, the accuracy of the dreamer's vision increasingly fades the further it advances into the future. Much of what the author wrote about imminent events did transpire as foretold. The Syrian General Congress, composed primarily of representatives whose backgrounds placed them among the "people of distinction," met in early June 1919 to formulate a consentient list of demands to be presented to the US commission.[28] The Arab government distributed *khutab* (sermons) to be read at Friday prayers and, in conjunction with political and cultural associations and government-sanctioned guilds, sponsored petition campaigns and mobilized demonstrations in support of the "Damascus Program" promulgated by the congress.[29] Local political activists and *makhatir* (government officials assigned to quarters within cities) ensured that shopkeepers throughout Syria placarded their storefronts with the slogan, "We demand complete independence."[30] However, the long-term vision for Syria espoused by the author—

a vision suffused with Eurogenic ideals and expressed through an alien discourse—not only failed to materialize but proved to be far removed from the concerns of the vast majority of the Syrian population.

With adequate resources, it might have been possible for the Arab government and its allies gradually to enlist the support of the Syrian population for its "true vision": The *mutanawwirun* not only enjoyed the requisite social prestige to attract the spontaneous consent of nonelites but, because of their access to institutions of governance, they possessed potentially formidable coercive powers as well. However, on September 13, 1919, the British government decided to reduce its substantial subsidy to the Arab government by half and to withdraw its forces from Syria. This decision undercut both the economic and the political positions of the Arab government and its allies and generated a crisis from which they never recovered.[31] Widely interpreted as portending French rule in Syria ("protection and mandate are synonyms, and are the precursors to annexation"),[32] the action seemed to confirm the bankruptcy of the plan to achieve the complete independence of Syria through negotiation. Almost overnight, the slogan "Complete independence for Syria within its natural boundaries, no protection, tutelage, or mandate *(la himaya, la wisaya, wa la intidab)*" replaced its shorter but obviously inadequate predecessor on placards posted throughout Syria.[33]

The Response of Nonelites to the Failure of the Commission

> The enemy have cloaked themselves in hypocrisy, and
>   enfolded it in rancor and hatred.
> They took an oath of loyalty and they were disloyal,
>   and from among them you have trusted some as
>   allies who were treacherous. . . .
> What is amiss with those who have carried the scales of
>   guidance on their arms, that they have failed to
>   discern the truth?
> If they do not help those who need help and bring
>   success to those who deserve it, then let the
>   scales be broken.
>
>   —Khayr al-Din al-Zirikli[34]

For many in the Arab Middle East, the expansion of capitalist relations and the reorganization of imperial institutions that had taken place during the seventy years preceding the dissolution of the Ottoman Empire induced social changes that ranged from disorienting to calamitous. Not only did the status of those local elites who lacked landed wealth and/or bureaucratic connections decline but rivalry intensified among established and emergent elites for highly coveted posts in the reinvigorated state bureaucracy. The spread of capitalism frequently transformed peasant life: Peasants often found themselves at the mercy of usurers, planted cash crops for export, and supplemented family incomes by participating, sometimes seasonally, sometimes permanently, in the urban labor force. Coastal cities and extra-mural urban areas expanded, and newcomers to cities frequently settled in neigh-borhoods (such as the Maydan in Damascus and al-Kallasa in Aleppo) that lacked homogeneity and established social structures. New demands made by the state (such as the universally loathed conscription), agricultural crises, alterations in pat-terns of land tenure, conflicts on the periphery of the empire and World War I, and postwar inflation and rural insecurity further disrupted the lives of nonelites.

The social and economic shocks experienced by both nonelites and former elites had two relevant effects. First, because the expansion of market relations and the in-trusion of a uniform apparatus of power into previously unregulated or underregu-lated domains increasingly determined the nature and extended the scope of ties among Syrians, the significance of horizontal, associational, and national linkages among the population grew at the expense of vertical, communal, and parochial bonds—a necessary precondition for "proactive" collective activity and what histo-rian George Mosse calls the "nationalization of the masses."[35] Second, the social and economic shocks engendered an ideological backlash among the self-described "ag-grieved" *(mankubun),*[36] who frequently expressed their disaffection through a pop-ulist discourse that extolled the historic ties and common interests that united Syrians into an egalitarian national community, celebrated the central role played by nonelites in preserving "traditional" values, and affirmed the integrity of commu-nity boundaries.

Starting in September 1919, populist activists—disempowered notables, mer-chants, *qabadayat* (local toughs), *ulama,* petit-bourgeois merchant/*ulama,* and so on[37]—took advantage of the opportunities for mobilization that both the pro-longed social transformations and the immediate economic and political crises pro-vided to create the structures necessary for a sustainable populist movement. Over the course of the next nine months, these activists founded an array of intercon-nected organizations (the most important of which were the Higher National Com-mittee *[al-lajna al-wataniyya al-'ulya],* based in Damascus, and local committees of national defense *[lijan al-difa' al-watani])* that challenged the authority of the crip-pled Arab government, the discredited *mutanawwirun,* and the representatives of the entente powers meeting in Paris.

The populist organizations attracted widespread support, particularly among the Sunni Muslim population of inland Syria, for several reasons. As described earlier, in anticipation of the arrival of the King-Crane Commission in Syria, the Arab govern-ment and its extragovernmental allies applied modern techniques for mass mobiliza-tion that had, even before the founding of the populist organizations, acclimated much of the population to participation in national politics. But where the Arab government attempted to reach a settlement with the entente powers through nego-tiation and compromise, the populist organizations preached the more popular doc-trine of militant anti-imperialism and marshaled and/or supplied local volunteer militias and guerrilla bands to resist mandatory authority. The organizations con-nected individuals to a national political machine through neighborhood and village branch organizations and supervisory committees *(al-lijan al-far'iyya, al-lijan al-taftishiyya*) and promoted participation by sponsoring electoral campaigns, demonstrations, military exercises, and charitable activities. Finally, the populist organizations assumed responsibility for services—protecting and provisioning urban quarters, assessing taxes, licensing monopolies, ensuring a "fair price" for grain, providing relief for the indigent and families of soldiers—which the local notability and the Arab government could no longer provide.

In contrast to the anonymous dreamer and his colleagues—who were willing to accept a temporary mandate in exchange for technological assistance and the accouterments of civilization—populist spokesmen articulated a vision for Syria that met the concerns of "the great mass of the nation [that] is not confined to the educated, the notables, and the merchants of the cities who read the daily newspapers, follow international and domestic politics, and are concerned with scientific discoveries and technological innovation."[38] Scornful of the aspirations of the Westernized elites ("[The French] only want to possess the sources of wealth and turn the free population into slaves in the name of progress, and only the Syrians [will] feel the effects"),[39] populist spokesmen eschewed the dichotomization of Syrian society inherent in "A True Vision"—a dichotomization that stigmatized and alienated a vast majority of the population by pitting the cultured and educated formulators of public opinion against the passive nonelites—and expounded a vision of Syria that was both comprehensive and inclusive. Populist organizers thus counterpoised their own definition of public opinion to the definition used by Woodrow Wilson and his epigones in Syria:

> The people possess a spirit which transcends the inclinations of individuals . . . and the nation possesses an independent personality stronger than the personalities of its members. . . . Those who would penetrate the heart of the Syrian people . . . know that public opinion is made from two sources: the first is its historical traditions in which there is strong faith and fidelity. This is fixed and immutable at its core, and even though it changes form it is imperishable and indestructible. The old illiterate, the religious 'alim, the cultured youth all equally respect historical traditions and aspire to the general goal. . . . [T]he people compel outside influences to be compatible with their traditions, and they desire to harmonize the elements of public opinion by making the second element compatible with the first, that is, with historic tradition.[40]

The aggressive posture assumed by the leaders of the populist movement and the potential empowerment of their constituents alarmed both foreign observers and the *mutanawwirun*. Populist rhetoric, suffused with Islamic and apocalyptic images and embellished with anecdotes that described the treachery of "those who would sell the nation like merchandise," foreign conspiracies, French and Zionist atrocities, the defilement of Muslim innocents, and exculpatory vengeance, aroused their apprehensions as well. "Over 90% of the Moslems of Syria are ignorant and fanatical, and can be swayed by their religious leaders," reported William Yale. "They are profoundly anti-Christian and anti-foreign and can be easily led to excesses by the recognized leaders, the clergy, land owners, and tribal chiefs."[41] Similarly, in a letter addressed to a former finance minister, a physician working in the foreign ministry of the Arab government depicted the populist movement as a form of mass pathology: "Individual dementia is among the greatest afflictions I know, but worse still is the complete dementia of a nation. . . . I am not a prophet, yet I see the end result very clearly if the transgressors do not return to their senses."[42]

The transgressors did not, of course, "come to their senses." To the contrary, worsening economic conditions, widening border warfare, the demands made by an apparently incompetent yet increasingly rapacious Arab government, and the announcement of the decision made by the entente powers at San Remo in April 1920 (to divide Syria and impose mandates) boosted support for the populist movement and the organizations it spawned while further undermining the authority of the Arab government and the counsel of the *mutanawwirun*. When the Arab government finally acquiesced to a French ultimatum that threatened unspecified "acts" unless the government accepted a French mandate, antigovernment rioting—which left scores dead in Damascus and hundreds dead in Aleppo—erupted throughout Syria. In the aftermath of this final display of the "state of opinion and the soil to be worked on by any mandatory," the French army marched on Damascus and France began its quarter-century occupation of inland Syria—one year to the day after the departure of the King-Crane Commission from the Middle East.

The King-Crane Commission and the Construction of Syrian Nationalism

> In truth, the politics which followed in Syria were very strange, inasmuch as the intellectuals—the men of public opinion—and the men of the government themselves stirred up, by all means possible, the excitement of the people and pushed it to the extreme. Then, all of a sudden, they retreated before the slightest obstacle which blocked their way, and they abandoned the people who were perplexed, not knowing how to explain their position. . . . This created a situation of enormous emotional turmoil and squandered the trust which the people had placed in their leaders. They openly accused their leaders of treachery to the point that, gradually, that trust was dissolved, and the leaders to whom the people had entrusted the reins of government were not able to lead and they were scoffed at.
>
> —As'ad Daghir[43]

Following World War I, revolutionary violence convulsed much of the non-Western world, from Turkey through India to China and Korea. The situation in the Arab Middle East was no different, with conflagrations erupting in Egypt (1919), Syria (1919–1920), and Iraq (1920). Despite the fact all the affected areas could sustain complex, programmatic political movements (as opposed to movements that might be characterized as temporary, defensive, and prepolitical)[44] because all had been subjected to analogous processes—the uneven and asymmetric spread of dependent capitalism and the introduction of modern institutions of governance—a unique interplay of local, regional, and international determinants ignited and shaped each uprising.

Although Woodrow Wilson had originally proposed an interallied commission merely to ascertain and convey the wishes of the Syrian population, the King-Crane Commission had the unintended effect of catalyzing and, in many ways, defining the political movement that arose to resist the imposition of a mandate on Syria. Gulled by the promise implicit in the commission's tour of Syria, the *mutanawwirun* constructed structures that expedited the mobilization of the population. Because these elites were oriented toward Europe and the peace conference, however, they designed institutions, demonstrations, and propaganda campaigns for the purpose of presenting to an outside audience an image of a sophisticated nation eager and prepared for independence. They thus deferred the task of integrating the majority of the population into their framework of legitimacy. As a result, during the period that preceded the French mandate, the *mutanawwirun* never truly involved nonelites in their nationalist project: They never dickered with the population over questions of ideology and program, they never synthesized a political discourse that was compelling to nonelites, and they never established connections with the population comparable to those that the Wafdist leadership had established with the population of Egypt, for example. In short, the announcement of the formation of the King-Crane Commission and its subsequent visit to Syria initiated an unintended chain of events that culminated in the strengthening of a populist nationalism dissociated from the guidance of the more Westernized nationalist elites.

Notes

1. *Editor and Publisher*, 2 December 1922, iii.

2. Notes by Sir Maurice Pascal Alers from the 20 March 1919 meeting of the Council of Four, in Arthur S. Link, ed., *The Papers of Woodrow Wilson*, vol. 56 (Princeton, 1987), p. 116.

3. British Prime Minister David Lloyd George to French President Georges Clemenceau, 25 April 1919, in ibid., 58:134.

4. Unless otherwise indicated, the term "Syria" is meant to designate the territory of the Middle East that comprises present-day Syria, Lebanon, Jordan, Israel and the Occupied Territories, and western Iraq.

5. Ray Stannard Baker and William E. Dodd, eds., *Public Papers of Woodrow Wilson*, vols. 5–6: *War and Peace: Presidential Messages, Addresses, and Public Papers (1917–1925)* (New York: Harper & Brothers, 1927), 5:180.

6. Ibid., 5:160–161.

7. J. C. Hurewitz, ed., *The Middle East and North Africa in World Politics: A Documentary Record*, vol. 2: *British-French Supremacy, 1914–1945* (New Haven, 1979), 112.

8. For the position of the Syrian nationalists in the Egyptian exile community, see James L. Gelvin, "Popular Mobilization and the Origins of Mass Politics in Syria, 1918–1920," Ph.D. diss., Harvard University, 1992, 209–211. See also Muhibb al-Din al-Khatib, autobiographical manuscript stored in the Dar al-Watha'iq al-Tarikhiyya, Damascus.

9. Link, *The Papers of Woodrow Wilson*, 58:328.

10. The Balfour Declaration (named after British Foreign Secretary Arthur Balfour and issued on November 2, 1917) was in the form of a letter from Balfour to a leading British Zionist, Lord Walter Rothschild; it promised British support for the creation of "a national

home for the Jewish people" in Palestine. The declaration provided a much-needed boost to the Zionist movement by providing the legal framework for continued Jewish immigration and land purchases in Palestine, the twin pillar of the Zionists' policy to make Palestine their national home. The British issued the declaration for a number of reasons: to preempt what was expected to be a similar announcement by Germany; to win the support of worldwide Jewry, especially in the United States and USSR, that would aid the war effort; and to have a group beholden to British interests in Palestine in order to protect the right flank of the Suez Canal, act as a buffer between the anticipated French position in Syria and the British position in Egypt, and provide a land bridge from the Mediterranean Sea to the Persian Gulf (from Palestine across Transjordan and Iraq to the Gulf).

11. Charles Seymour, ed., *The Intimate Papers of Colonel House: The Ending of the War* (Boston, 1928), 153, 199.

12. Link, *The Papers of Woodrow Wilson,* 58:322–326.

13. Ray Stannard Baker in ibid., 56:442. Baker also wrote the following entry in his diary (21 May 1919; see ibid., 58:368) about the circumstances that led to the commission's departure: "[Wilson] told me with a kind of amused satisfaction—he gets very little fun out of his conferences, but he had it today—of the discussion this morning of the Syrian question and of a red-hot conflict of view between Lloyd George and Clemenceau. It seems that Lloyd George calmly proposed to give to Italy (to induce a settlement of the Fiume question) a slice of Syria which Clemenceau had already decided to gobble down. This perfectly frank scramble for territory, which in a moment of anger was fought with all guards down, seemed to amuse the President very much. It also had the effect of once more reviving the plan for the Syrian Commission (King and Crane). The President told the Four, positively, that our commissioners were leaving for Syria on Monday! It has given him his chance."

14. According to the report of the King-Crane Commission, "It is certain from the oral statements that accompanied the petitions that the term, 'Absolute independence,' was seldom used in the sense of an entire freedom from only foreign guidance such as that of a mandatory under the League of Nations, inasmuch as the request was frequently combined with a choice of mandate or a request for foreign 'assistance.' While a few of the Young Arab clubs certainly desired freedom from all foreign control, the great majority asked for independence and defined a mandate to mean only economic and technical assistance." "Report of the American Section of the International Commission on Mandates in Turkey (28 August 1919)," in U.S. Department of State, *Papers Relating to the Foreign Relations of the United States,* vol. 12: *The Paris Peace Conference: 1919* (Washington, D.C., 1947), 767.

15. Link, *The Papers of Woodrow Wilson,* 58:133–134.

16. See Arthur S. Link, *Wilson the Diplomatist: A Look at His Major Foreign Policies* (Baltimore, 1957), 12.

17. Woodrow Wilson, "Political Sovereignty," in *Selected Literary and Political Papers and Addresses of Woodrow Wilson* (New York, n.d.), 91–92.

18. See, for example, Woodrow Wilson, "The Character of Democracy in the United States," in ibid., 89–93.

19. G. W. F. Hegel, *Philosophy of Right,* trans. T. M. Knox (New York, 1952), 204.

20. In an interview with Ida M. Tarbell, Wilson quoted the following lines from "The Princess," by Alfred Lord Tennyson: "A nation yet, the rulers and the ruled— / Some sense of duty, something of a faith, / Some reverence for the laws ourselves have made, / Some patient force to change them when we will, / Some civic manhood firm against the crowd." Collier's, 28 October 1916, 37.

21. For the strategy of the King-Crane Commission, a complete listing of the groups it received, and its conclusions, see "Report of the American Section of the International Commission," cited in note 13 above.

22. Ibid., 863.

23. William Yale, "A Report on Syria, Palestine, and Mount Lebanon for the American Commissioners," Yale Papers, Boston University, Box X/Folder 8/22–23.

24. For details about the "middle strata" and its role in nationalist movements, see E. J. Hobsbawm, *Nations and Nationalism Since 1780: Programme, Myth, Reality* (Cambridge, 1990), 90–94, 117–122; Miroslav Hroch, *Social Preconditions of National Revival in Europe: A Comparative Analysis of the Social Composition of Patriotic Groups Among the Smaller European Nations,* trans. Ben Fowkes (Cambridge, 1985), particularly 129–155. For a discussion of the changing nature of the urban notability during the nineteenth century, see Philip Khoury, *Urban Notables and Arab Nationalism: The Politics of Damascus, 1860–1920* (Cambridge, 1983).

25. It is important to note that, contrary to the assumptions of William Yale and other Western observers, neither the Arab government nor any of the allied organizations were monolithic; moreover, the government and the political and cultural clubs included members who espoused a variety of ideologies and practices. For example, as late as the autumn of 1919, al-Fatat included three factions: the "dissenters" (*rafidun*) who refused to support any mandate; a "pro-British/anti-French" faction allied with Emir Faisal; and a faction that still held out hope for a U.S. mandate. See 'Izzat Darwaza, *Mudhakkirat wa Tasjilat* (Damascus, 1984), 2:76–77, 81–82; Gelvin, "Popular Mobilization," 55–63, 74–85. In this essay, the term "Arab government" refers to the faction of the government that included Emir Faisal, his entourage, and his allies.

26. India Office, London: L/PS/10/802. Gertrude Bell, "Syria in October 1919," 15 November 1919, 11.

27. *al-'Asima,* 7 May 1919, 1–2.

28. See Khoury, *Urban Notables,* 86–88; Yusuf al-Hakim, *Dhikrayat,* vol. 3: *Suriya wa al-'ahd al-Faysali* (Beirut, 1966), 90–97; Safiuddin Joarder, *Syria Under the French Mandate: The Early Phase, 1920–1927* (Dacca, 1977), 209–211.

29. Archives Diplomatiques, Nantes (hereinafter AD): 2430/no no. Cousse to Dame, 18 April 1919; Ministère des Affaires Etrangères, Paris (hereinafter MAE): L:AH vol. 4/237–238; Picot to Pichon, 22 May 1919; MAE L:SL vol. 14/#897; Picot to MAE, 17 June 1919; MAE L:SL vol. 44/3D; Minault (Latakia) to Administrateur du Vilayet de Beyrouth, 18 July 1919; Ministère de la Defense, Vincennes (hereafter MD) 7N4182/Dossier 4/340; Picot to MAE 21 July 1919; MAE L:SL vol. 43/39–41. "Renseignements d'Agent," 10–20 July 1919; AD 2430 Dossier Confidential-Départ/#240, 11 August 1919. For texts of sermons distributed 11 and 18 April 1919, see AD 2343/286, Cousse to Haut Commissionaire, 24 April 1919.

30. MD L:SL vol. 12/32–38. Cousse to Haut Commissionaire, 6 April 1919; Gelvin, "Popular Mobilization," 321–322.

31. See Malcolm Russell, *The First Modern Arab State: Syria Under Faysal, 1918–1920* (Minneapolis, 1985), 93–131.

32. See leaflet entitled, "Independence or Death!" in MAE L:SL vol. 43/72–73, 21 July 1919 (in Arabic with French translation).

33. See Gelvin, "Popular Mobilization," 240.

34. Khayr al-Din al-Zirikli, *Diwan Zirikli: al-a'mal al-shi'riyya al-kamila* (Amman[?], n.d.), 24–25 (translation by author).

35. See Charles Tilly, Louise Tilly, and Richard Tilly, *The Rebellious Century, 1830–1930* (Cambridge, Mass., 1975), 51–53; George L. Mosse, *The Nationalization of the Masses: Political Symbolism and Mass Movements in Germany from the Napoleanic Wars Through the Third Reich* (New York, 1977).

36. For copies of leaflets signed "mankub," see: MAE L:SL vol. 43/62, 64. n.d.; MD 7N4182/Dossier 4/340. Picot to MAE, 21 July 1920.

37. For a listing of the backgrounds of the primary and secondary leadership of the Higher National Committee of Damascus, see Gelvin, "Popular Mobilization," 125–130, 457–458.

38. Muhibb al-Din al-Khatib, "The Job of Guidance," *al-'Asima,* 16 October 1919, 1–2.

39. Foreign Office, London: FO371/5188/E7808/#42. "Arabic Press Abstracts for Week ending June 14, 1920," 26 May 1920.

40. *al-'Asima,* 23 October 1919, 1–2. It is interesting to contrast this statement with one made by Woodrow Wilson: "When I try to disentangle the ideas of the people and endeavor to express them if at first there is disaccord I am not astonished. I have firm confidence that their ideas will rally to mine." Quoted by Daniel Halevy, *President Wilson,* trans. Hugh Stokes (New York, 1919), 244.

41. Yale, "A Report on Syria," 24.

42. Sudan Archives, University of Durham: SA/493/6/51. Amin M'aluf to Ahmad Shuqayr, 1 June 1920.

43. As'ad Daghir, *Mudhakirrati 'ala hamish al-qadiya al-'arabiyya* (Cairo, 1956), 122.

44. See Tilly, Tilly, and Tilly, *The Rebellious Century,* 50–54; E. J. Hobsbawm, *Primitive Rebels: Studies in Archaic Forms of Social Movement in the 19th and 20th Centuries* (New York, 1959), 1–2, 110.

2

The "Ambassador for the Arabs"

The Locke Mission and the Unmaking of US Development Diplomacy in the Near East, 1952–1953

Paul W. T. Kingston

This chapter examines President Harry S Truman's policy toward the Near East[1] during the last years of his administration.[2] It focuses on the creation, in late 1951, of a regional office based in Beirut. Its mandate was to coordinate US economic policy in the region including capital assistance from the Mutual Security Program (MSP), refugee assistance channeled through the United Nations Relief and Works Administration (UNRWA; the United Nations alone will be referred to as the UN), and technical assistance from the Technical Cooperation Administration (TCA), commonly known as Point Four. Truman appointed Edwin Locke Jr., a young banker, to head the office. His official title was special assistant to the secretary of state, and he was given the rank of ambassador with direct lines of communication to the president.[3]

The "Locke mission" is interesting from several perspectives. First, it has become a forgotten episode in the history of US policy in the Near East that reflects a more general scholarly neglect of US policy in the region in the last years of the Truman administration. The prevailing perception is one of drift and frustration caused both by the failure to reach any political settlement to the Arab-Israeli conflict and by the parallel difficulties in pursuing an economic approach to peacemaking, symbolized by the cautious recommendations of the Economic Survey Mission (ESM) in 1949. This chapter suggests, however, that the Truman administration attempted to reinvigorate the economic approach to peacemaking in the early 1950s. As such, the Locke mission emerges as a link between the initial launching of the ESM in 1949 and the later attempts by Eric Johnston under the Eisenhower administration to resurrect the same kind of approach. Finally, the dispatching of the Locke mission also represents a concerted, if failed, attempt to promote a more regional US approach to the Near East, a break from past US emphases on bilateralism.

The main issue at stake here is whether an economic approach to pursuing US objectives in the region was realistic. Certainly, the creation of the regional economic office and the appointment of Locke was greeted in many circles with much fanfare. The *New York Times* carried the story on its front pages;[4] the British, in part influenced by Locke's appointment, transferred their own regional economic office, the Development Division of the British Middle East Office (BMEO), to Beirut;[5] the Arab states were clearly buoyed by the prospects of a stronger US economic presence in the region; and, as we shall see, the announcement won praise—and indeed had been the result of pressure—from those within the US State Department who had persistently called for the application of a Marshall Plan–type policy to the region.

However, despite the promising beginning, the Locke mission ended in ignominy and, ultimately, oblivion: Locke resigned within a year of his appointment without having effected any appreciable shift in US economic policy in the region, and the Beirut-based regional economic office was disbanded. After briefly examining the origins of US economic diplomacy in the Near East, I set out to examine why Truman's economic approach to the Near East faltered so badly. This entails examining the relationship of the Locke mission to the three pillars of US development policy in the region: technical assistance under the Point Four program, capital assistance under the Mutual Security Program, and refugee assistance channeled through UNRWA. Part of the explanation revolves around the person of Locke himself who, in persistently advocating a more pro-Arab line, emerged as an early if unlikely example of that much maligned group of State Department officials known as the "Arabists."[6] Equally important are the vague terms of reference given to Locke that merely masked fundamental conflicts in objectives among the various bureaucratic parties concerned and that served to sap the "collective will" of the Truman administration. Ultimately, however, the question must be examined not at the level of personalities nor of policy implementation but at the level of philosophical approach. Locke represents that generation of Americans who believed that the injection of US finance and expertise into troubled parts of the underdeveloped world could help to create a more empathetic political environment in the short run while laying the foundations for self-sustained growth and, thus, political stability in the long run. The assumptions behind this optimistic approach have now been openly questioned. Capital and technology by themselves rarely promote development; development does not necessarily promote political stability. Nevertheless, these were the assumptions that governed policy in the early cold war and it is worth reminding ourselves how strong their hold was on policymakers and development planners.

The Origins of Truman's Economic Approach to the Near East

The roots of postwar US economic diplomacy in the Near East are found in the wartime participation of the United States in the Middle East Supply Centre

(MESC). Originally created to regulate the flow of imports and exports in and out of the region so as to conserve shipping space for military purposes, the MESC ultimately became involved in promoting regional economic production. It did such a good job at this latter task that some began to consider the idea of continuing the development functions of the MESC after the war. Despite some initial and favorable consideration, the idea was ultimately rejected by the US government and, at the close of the war, the MESC was immediately disbanded. The reasons were three-fold. First, there was a strong desire not to continue to underwrite the British Empire in the region (which, it was felt, a regional economic approach would do). Second, there was an equally strong sense that a bilateral approach to the Near East would better serve US commercial interests by allowing for the unfettered expansion of private trade and investment in the region. Finally, economic orthodoxy in the United States dictated that private investment would best promote economic development in the "undeveloped" parts of the world. Hence, initial US economic policy in the Near East would be based on bilateralism with an emphasis on the private sector.

Three factors forced US Near East policymakers to change these calculations: the Arab-Israeli conflict, the emerging cold war, and the rise of anti-Western Arab nationalism. The Palestine War of 1948 and the subsequent upheavals in the Arab world as a whole, for example, forced US Near East policymakers to think more in regional terms. This led to the initiation of a series of Chief of Mission meetings, the first being held in Istanbul in November 1949. It also resulted in the emergence of a more favorable attitude toward Britain's regional presence, particularly the string of British military bases across the region symbolized by that at Suez and, as W. R. Louis has noted, led US Near East policymakers to defer to, if not underwrite, Britain's regional security system.[7] This ultimately led to the (stillborn) joint Anglo-American proposal to create a Middle East Command (MEC) in October 1951. Finally, this new interest in regionalism was extended to the economic realm, symbolized by the dispatching of the ESM under the auspices of the UN and headed by Gordon Clapp, the former director of the Tennessee Valley Authority (TVA).

Clapp assumed his task enthusiastically and initially considered creating two organizations—one to deal exclusively with refugee relief and the other to deal more directly with economic development. The latter was, in effect, the reemergence of an earlier British proposal to create a Middle East Development Board. He was strongly supported in these views by George C. McGhee, assistant secretary of state for Near Eastern affairs; both believed in the potential of economic development to erase intractable political problems. However, the initial foray into regionalism produced few dividends. The Chief of Mission conferences did not produce a coherent regional approach but merely acted as forums for exchanging information. Moreover, Clapp dramatically scaled down his originally ambitious ideas. Instead of two organizations, the UN amalgamated relief and resettlement functions into one organization, the UNRWA. Such cautiousness was dictated by a number of factors. Clapp himself concluded in his final report that "the region is not ready, the projects are not ready [and] the people and the governments are not ready for large scale development."[8] Moreover, the British changed their tune and raised strong objections to the idea of creating a regional development organization for fear of arousing the indignation of Arab nationalists. Instead, they advocated the creation of a development board in each country.[9] Thus, we witness an interesting shift with Britain, the dying imperial power moving away from a regional policy, and the United States, an emerging imperial power looking at the potential of a regional policy in a more favorable light. The launching of the Point Four program in 1950, however, seemed to offer some consolation and, in its initial years, it became active in the independent states of the Middle East, notably Iran, Lebanon, and Jordan, where the first general agreement under Point Four was signed.

However, in 1951, there was a significant polarization of both the global and regional climate. Driven by the outbreak of the Korean War and sparked by the nationalization of the Anglo-Iranian Oil Company by Iranian Prime Minister Muhammad Mussadiq in March, the assassination of King Abdullah of Jordan in July, and the unilateral abrogation of the 1936 Anglo-Egyptian treaty by the Wafdist government in October, there was a revival of discussions about the utility of economic approaches to diplomacy. Globally, this culminated in the establishment of the MSP, the main task of which was to coordinate all overseas economic, technical, and military assistance programs. Regionally, this led first to an allocation of $160 million for the Near East from the MSP. It then resulted in a US-backed decision by the UN General Assembly to strengthen the ability of UNRWA to promote refugee resettlement as well as relief by giving it an expanded budget of $250 million over three years. Finally, on the strong recommendation of McGhee, President Truman created the regional economic office in Beirut as a mechanism for coordinating all regional economic activity. With the appointment of Locke to head the office on November 13, 1951, it seemed that the regional economic approach to securing peace and stability in the Near East would finally be given a chance to work.[10]

Locke, Point Four, and Lebanon

A youthful forty-one years, Locke seemed an inspired choice to head the new regional economic office, combining both a successful career in the private and public sectors with an interest in the Middle East. His public-sector experience, acquired during and immediately after World War II, was impressive and included such positions as executive assistant to Donald Nelson, head of the War Productions Board (1943–1944), Truman's personal representative to Chiang Kai-Shek in China (1945), and Truman's special assistant in the White House (1946). Locke's natural environment, however, was the private sector, where his demonstrated instinct and friendly charm eventually led to his appointment in 1946 as vice president of Chase Manhattan Bank. He used his position to generate various business opportunities in the Middle East, principally Saudi Arabia, where he entered into negotiations to build both a cement plant and, later, a Coca-Cola plant. His growing involvement in the region eventually earned him a seat on the board of governors of the American University of Beirut. Locke, therefore, was seen as exactly the kind of person who could activate an economic approach to achieving peace and security in the Near East.[11]

Locke arrived in Beirut in early December 1951. It seemed an opportune moment. After protracted negotiations over the terms of US involvement in development activities,[12] the Lebanese government agreed to ratify the Point Four General Agreement in November 1951 and, with the subsequent announcement of Locke's appointment, was looking forward to a significant infusion of US aid into the country. Therefore, Locke, upon his arrival, was given a very friendly and high-profile welcome, the kind befitting a potential new patron. Harold Minor, the US minister in Lebanon, was clearly surprised at the receptivity of the Lebanese to the arrival of Locke—or "Saint Locke," as one leftist Lebanese paper sarcastically noted. In reaction to one of the many receptions in Locke's honor, Minor reported, "I have never in my many years in the Foreign Service attended a function more jovial and friendly. The Lebanese were simply bubbling over with enthusiasm. . . . It was something like a football rally." He went on to suggest that the Lebanese government seemed willing to cooperate with Locke to a degree that "we had hardly dared hope for."[13] Certainly, Locke would turn out to be a darling of Beirut society, hosting numerous dinner parties and, on several occasions, being the personal guest of President Faris al-Khuri at his mountain home. This was the kind of access to the top echelons of power in Lebanon that US representatives had hitherto not known.

From the outset, Locke seemed determined to take advantage of this favorable atmosphere. Having arrived in Beirut only the day before, Locke immediately wrote to his contact in the State Department, Arthur Gardiner, suggesting that a significant expansion of the development program for the Arab states would be needed if his mission was to be a success.[14] Within a week, Locke was also transmitting these ideas directly to Truman, bypassing the State Department and TCA. This was to become a feature of the Locke mission and it revealed the degree to which he perceived (and, as it turned out, misperceived) that he could count on Truman's personal support. Nevertheless, this letter is important, for it sets the tone for his entire mission. The main thing, wrote Locke, is that "a lot more life needs to be put into our aid programs here and in the other Middle Eastern countries." Not only were there "too many plans and too little action" (a complaint heard universally among the recipient governments in the region), but those plans that were being made operational under the Point Four program were making no significant impact economically or psychologically. This, above all, was Locke's self-appointed agenda, "to get these people [the Arabs] thinking in positives rather than negatives." In a classic espousal of the economic approach to peacemaking, Locke emphasized that "if we can get them started in an important way on developing the very attractive natural resources that they have, I believe that the political problems will suddenly become much less difficult to solve."[15]

Locke was looking for impact projects to fulfill his Near East mandate and, in Lebanon, there seemed one ready at hand: the Litani River project. Lebanon had been one of the first countries to receive assistance from Point Four even before a general agreement had been signed. It was in the form of a survey mission for the

Litani River basin and was initiated by the first director of Point Four, Dr. Henry Bennett, upon his inaugural tour of the Middle East as a way of getting activity off the ground for the newly established TCA. Six months later, however, rumblings were surfacing in the Lebanese press about the lack of immediate, concrete results, and there was further fear that the project would be geared to the interests of private Lebanese citizens and, perhaps, Israel. The result was what one report referred to as "a vigorous campaign" in the Lebanese press against Point Four's association with the Litani River project.[16] Although one of Locke's first public actions was to issue a statement deflecting such criticisms, in fact he looked upon them as valid.[17] According to Locke, US involvement in the Litani River project, based as it was on technical assistance, was ill-designed to obtain quick results. Nor was it likely to solicit anything more than "polite unenthusiastic foot-dragging cooperation from [the] Lebanese."[18] Needed was a more significant infusion of development capital, and this was precisely what Lebanon could not provide. Its public finances were insufficient to keep up with the demands for development projects and, even where capital was available, it was tremendously difficult to achieve any kind of political consensus over its use. Nor did the kind of private investment needed for large projects seem to be forthcoming, as demonstrated by the failure of the Syrian government to raise capital for the development of the port at Latakia through the sale of public bonds. In Locke's opinion, an infusion of US development capital would solve both of these problems; it would provide a "take-off" point for sustained economic growth and improve the climate for private investment. All of this would, in turn, lay the psychological foundations for a more solid political alliance.

However, not all US representatives in Lebanon were delighted with the rather spectacular arrival of Locke in Beirut and his promise of a dramatic expansion of US aid to the Middle East. The bulk of this opposition emanated from Lebanon's Point Four team, whose program Locke was pledging to aggrandize. Part of the problem stemmed from confusion over the exact nature of Locke's mandate. When the regional economic office was first created, the local field offices of Point Four were assured that Locke's mandate would not allow him to interfere in the specific work of country programs or to supersede the authority of local country directors. Whether such a distinction could work in practice was problematic; the British certainly had had their share of administrative problems in launching the regionally based BMEO in 1945.[19] By choosing Beirut as Locke's headquarters and by sending him out at a time when the local Point Four office was without Country Director Hollis Peter, Washington seemed to be asking for problems.[20]

They did not take long to appear. Less than a month after Locke's arrival, one member of Lebanon's Point Four staff, Richard Farnsworth, complained in a personal letter to Peter that their operations in Lebanon had been taken over "Locke, stock, and barrel," so much so that the Lebanese government was beginning to submit project requests to Locke's office directly.[21] Well over a month later, Point Four's staff in Lebanon continued to complain about "the Locke concept": "[He] is still 'Mr. TCA' in Lebanon," wrote US official William Crockett, "and I am afraid will remain so as long as he stays in Lebanon."[22] When Peter finally arrived in Beirut at the end of March, he was forced to spend much of his time clarifying the actual extent of Locke's authority to the rather confused Lebanese—and to Locke himself.[23]

Had the confusion been merely administrative, little harm would have been done to basic US policy in the country. However, the real conflict in Beirut revolved around fundamental policy issues—issues that had never been satisfactorily resolved as a result of the amalgamation of Point Four with the MSP in May 1951. Point Four's approach, epitomized by the views of its founding administrator, Dr. Bennett, and shared by most in the field, was based on the idea that development would only come by building up human capital at the grass-roots level. This required a long range development policy based on the provision of technical assistance in such areas as education, health, and agriculture. Moreover, those results had to be part of a cooperative effort, one in which the local government made significant contributions of both finance and manpower. The concern here, of course, was with the long-term sustainability of projects. Those more politically minded in the State Department, however, had little time for an approach to development policy that ignored short-term political imperatives. George McGhee, who in many ways had masterminded the economic approach to peacemaking between the Arabs and the Israelis by first suggesting the formation of the ESM, was clearly unimpressed with the scope and philosophy of the Point Four program as it emerged in its severely reduced form in 1950;[24] Dean Acheson, secretary of state at the time, referred to Point Four in retrospect as "the Cinderella of the foreign aid family."[25]

The emergence of Locke, ostensibly an ambassador for the Point Four program yet an emissary whose ideas turned out to be much at odds with its philosophy, brought this latent conflict over US development policy to the surface. At a meeting in Washington, D.C., between representatives of Point Four and those from the Near East Division of the State Department to discuss Locke's request for an infusion of financial aid into the Litani River project, the two parties found themselves unable to reach any consensus. Whereas the latter argued strongly for Locke's proposal on the basis that the overriding need was to get some large and visible project under way in one of the Arab states, Point Four staff continued to object on the basis that "the principle of picking up the check on partially completed projects was a basic departure from TCA philosophy and policy."[26] After several conversations with Locke upon his return to Beirut, Peter revealed much the same story: "It is quite clear that Ed Locke and I do not see eye to eye on the points of major importance in the Aid Program to Lebanon. I believe he listened politely at my expounding the Point Four philosophy which we feel must be an integral part of each project . . .while he believes there is a real distinction to be made between pure technical assistance on the one hand and economic or financial grant aid on the other."[27]

Peter was further concerned by Locke's propensity to project his ideas about US development policy in the region in an official manner in meetings with Lebanese officials. Fouad Ammoun, Lebanese director-general of foreign affairs, even suggested that Locke had virtually promised them increased amounts of aid, $5 million in fiscal year 1952 and $10 million in fiscal year 1953.[28] This was not only a break in diplomatic protocol, not to speak of constitutional procedure, but it also threatened the viability of the existing Point Four program in the country. The basic dilemma, of course, was that if the Lebanese were led to believe that a large infusion of US capital was imminent, they would be less interested in making the kind of small-scale commitments of local finance that were so important to all Point Four projects. Indeed, this seemed to be the case: At one point in the protracted negotiations over the terms of a Point Four agreement for the almost completed fiscal year 1952, Fouad Ammoun admitted that the Lebanese had not acted more quickly because they were waiting to see what Locke could produce.[29] This also explained, in Peter's opinion, the rather cavalier attitude taken by the Lebanese toward the visit of the World Bank's regional representative, Dorsey Stephens.[30] The dilemma, as US official Victor Skiles stated, was that "[if] U.S. aid is to be accepted not as a cooperative endeavor but as a substitute for local financing . . . we will have failed miserably in the total effort."[31]

Not all disagreed with Locke's ideas, notably Afif Tannous, an agriculturalist of Lebanese origin based with the Point Four team in Beirut. He was understandably delighted to be part of an expanded development assistance program for his mother country. This, however, made the matter potentially more dangerous by creating divisions within the US diplomatic community in the country. For the time being, Minor and Peter worked to maintain a facade of diplomatic unity in order to avoid unduly embarrassing Locke or damaging the prestige of his newly established position. Peter stressed, however, that this was being done at the cost of giving the impression of Point Four staff support for Locke's ideas, which was not always the case.[32] Peter, therefore, warned Washington that Locke's presence in Beirut could jeopardize his own ability to fulfill Point Four's mandate in the country. He wrote: "I do not believe it is too late to obtain the cooperation and enthusiastic support of the Lebanese Government officials for a real Point Four program, but it is hard for them to concentrate on this aspect which requires considerable understanding and foresightedness with the promise of large sums dangling in front of their noses."[33]

Locke and Regional Development in the Near East

Locke's actions in Lebanon during the early stages of his mission cannot be understood without placing them in the broader context of the Near East as a whole. Locke's mandate, after all, was a regional one and would require a regional solution. Here, Locke's diagnosis was similar to that made in Lebanon. What he found was an economic assistance program badly structured to meet the needs of the Near East. US assistance under the Point Four program was judged to be slow and insufficient by Arab governments—a "broken reed" as one Jordanian official remarked. This was particularly so in contrast to the large sums of capital assistance being provided by the United States to Israel, a point that Locke was constantly reminded of during travels to various Arab capitals. Moreover, though the United States was providing capital assistance to UNRWA, the funds were going largely unused due to the reluctance of Arab states to accept anything that smacked of the principle of reintegration. Acceptance of UNRWA assistance for refugee resettlement was looked upon as tantamount to abandoning the rights of the refugees to return to their homes. The result was an aid program ill-equipped to solve the kind of political problems in the region for which it was ultimately designed. It was these political problems that underlay all of Locke's thinking on the matter. As he wrote in a memorandum to Truman: "I feel that I must say frankly to you that our entire economic effort to help the Near East achieve a more secure freedom, a lasting peace and a rising standard of living is in danger of being overwhelmed by political turmoil."[34]

Locke's sense of urgency was further accentuated by the tight legislative schedule in Washington. Before Locke scarcely had his feet on the ground in Beirut, the State Department was already drawing up its proposed budget for the MSP for fiscal year 1953. By mid-February, it had released its initial estimates, which showed little change in the size or distribution of aid to the Near East. Having staked the success of his mission on the need for an increased allocation to the region, Locke once again bypassed the State Department and cabled directly to Truman, expressing his utmost concern at what he saw as the continued drift of US policy in the region. "If we do not (rpt [repeat] not) now (rpt now) make it clear to the Arab states that we mean what we have been saying these past three years about wanting to help them develop their countries, I am mortally afraid we will have lost our last chance and that the reaction to this . . . program will be bitter and sharp, and the inclination to look for other friends greatly increased."[35]

Locke's recommendation to Truman was the establishment of a $100 million Arab development fund designed to provide capital assistance to the Arab states, especially the non-oil states of Lebanon, Syria, Jordan, and Egypt. This would, in effect, add a fourth stream to US development policy in the region, separate and distinct from already existing programs to Israel, UNRWA, and Point Four. The purpose of the fund was to finance the completion of several impact projects in the fields of transportation and/or river development, placing special emphasis on the former as a result of Locke's experiences in China.[36] In all, he presented nine possible projects.[37] In an attempt to make his proposal more palatable to Congress, Locke presented it up as a "one-shot" deal that would pave the way for the greater involvement of the World Bank and private capital.

There had been numerous criticisms made of US development policy in the region, but never had a call for change come so explicitly and forcefully and never from such high levels of government. In effect, Locke was calling for not only a break with the traditional approach to development as advocated by Point Four, but also a significant shift in US policy toward the Arab world. Aid was to be raised to a level on par with that given to Israel, and it was to be given on an unconditional basis, free from linkages with the Arab refugee issue. On this last point, Locke was especially insistent: "If we try bargain for pol[itical] and military advantages as direct quid pro quo, believe results w[ou]ld be nil and our whole position considerably weakened. . . . Realize this entails certain risks but consider it infinitely less than contains as at present."[38] In short, Locke's proposal was a genuine attempt at instituting an economic approach to peacemaking in the Arab world. It advocated a separation of the economic from the political in a way that US contributions to UN-RWA could not.

Locke faced serious obstacles in effecting such a significant shift in US policy in the region. The dissenting views of many Point Four officials have already been mentioned; no doubt, these were joined by opposition from those wary of undermining US support for Israel. However, the most immediate obstacle was time—a problem not helped by Locke's sudden illness in Beirut in mid-February, which forced him to delay a trip to Washington designed to allow him to make his case before the State Department and, if necessary, Congress. By the time Locke returned to Washington at the end of March, the bill to extend the MSP, which made no provision for the kind of program advocated by Locke, had reached an advanced stage in its presentation to Congress.[39]

To compensate for his absence, Locke tried several methods to build support for his proposal. In mid-March, Donald Bergus, then second secretary in the Lebanese legation, was sent to Washington to lobby the State Department. This was accompanied by a flurry of supportive telegrams from US officials in Lebanon and Syria, the latter seeing in Locke's plan an opportunity to break the impasse over the introduction of Point Four into the country.[40] As was mentioned earlier, Locke also took the unorthodox step of building up an Arab constituency for his ideas by officially informing the president and prime minister of Lebanon of his proposal to increase US assistance to the Arab world, much to the horror of Peter.[41] It seems apparent, however, that Locke was really counting on the personal support of Truman. "I beg of you," wrote Locke after falling ill in Beirut, "to give this every consideration. I stake on this proposal such reputation as I may have and feel that it is the only way to get the results I know you want me to get out here."[42]

Truman did not provide the kind of hands-on support Locke was looking for. Although he expressed appreciation for Locke's imaginative approach, Truman passed the buck, so to speak, by referring Locke's request back to the State Department, where it ran aground over conflicting policy interests.[43] In Bergus's initial meeting with officials from the MSP, for example, objections were raised on the grounds that unconditional aid would set dangerous precedents and would probably militate against promoting the kinds of reforms that the United States felt were needed.[44] Averell Harriman, the director for mutual security under the auspices of the MSP, later raised these same issues in a memo to Secretary of State Acheson.[45] In short, the kinds of objections raised by the Point Four team in Beirut seem to have carried much weight in Washington.

Neither did there seem to be a great deal of respect for Locke's political analysis. Crucial to Locke's argument was his oft-repeated view that the political situation in the Near East was "precarious" and "threatening," requiring immediate action. But, to paraphrase Harriman's query, was it so serious as to require amendments to the mutual security bill in such a way that might jeopardize the entire program put forward?[46] There were similar questions raised about whether increased aid to the Arab states would, in fact, improve matters. One memo described Locke's aim of winning the friendship of the Arab world as "an endless task" that did not provide a basis for formulating programs of an extraordinary character.[47] There was particularly strong objection to his idea of divorcing development from the Palestinian refugee issue. In response to one compromise suggestion that Locke's program of capital assistance be confined to Syria as a way of breaking the impasse in relations with that country, Reeseman Fryer, a Point Four official, responded that: "To offer Syria an unconditional development program much greater in magnitude, different in organizational structure and purpose from the programs now getting underway in Lebanon, Jordan, Egypt and Iraq would tend to undermine Point 4 programs in the latter countries by appearing to pay a premium for non-cooperation—'It pays to hold out.'"[48] The only way a program of expanded assistance could be justified, wrote Fryer, was if it was paralleled by an appropriate concession on the part of the Syrian government—one that would have to revolve around the issue of refugee settlement.[49] In short, unconditional economic assistance to the Arab world was out of the question.

Thus, Locke's proposal never did see the light of day. Ostensibly it was rejected on the grounds that its passage through Congress would prove an impossibility;[50] in reality, the Truman administration was not inclined to consider any dramatic changes in its policy toward the Near East. Truman may have wanted "action" in the Near East, but he was not willing to become actively involved himself in promoting such changes. With Locke's proposal also threatening the viability of Point Four's operations in the Near East—it had already shown signs of doing just that in Lebanon—without offering any immediate solution to the Palestinian refugee issue, he was also unable to muster much support within the appropriate bureaucratic circles in Washington. Locke, in short, must have been a rather isolated figure upon his return to Washington, a far cry from his more heady days as Truman's special representative to China and, subsequently, the White House itself. It is this sense of isolation and inertia in Washington policy circles that would eventually lead to Locke's unmaking as a representative of US policy in the Near East.

Locke, the Arab Refugees, and UNRWA

After the proposal to create an Arab Development Fund was shelved, Locke was kept in Washington for an additional month. Part of the reason for Locke's delayed return was to ensure that he did not go back to Beirut completely empty-handed. Due to his own indiscretions, there was a high sense of expectation in such Arab states as Syria and Lebanon of a possible shift in US development policy. This led to the creation of a smaller $25 million fund aimed at financing more moderately demanding projects, which Locke was to draw up in cooperation with the local Point Four country directors. However, the principle reason for delaying Locke in Washington was to brief him more thoroughly on the goals and procedures of both the State Department and his mission. This meant clarifying Locke's role within the Point Four program, a task that met with some success, if Peter's subsequent comments are any guide.[51] Even more fundamental to US interests in the region, however, was the need to make UNRWA more effective. Locke had been appointed as the US representative on the Advisory Commission of UNRWA in late February but had been unable to take up his duties with any seriousness due to his illness and subsequent return to Washington. Since State Department policy now held that a capital aid program for the Arab states only be considered if and when the considerable resources of UNRWA, of which 70 percent came from the United States, were fully utilized, Locke was now instructed to help make that US contribution an effective one.[52] Thus, upon returning to Beirut, Locke's mandate had been clarified: much reduced involvement in the Point Four program and much enhanced involvement in UNRWA.

Locke's appointment to the Advisory Commission of UNRWA came at a propitious moment in its history. In January, the UN General Assembly, including its Arab members, had approved a three-year, $250 million reintegration program designed to remove the refugees from their dependence on international relief. The agreement of the Arab states to this program had been obtained on the theory that settlement and integration would not interfere with the legal rights of the refugees to repatriation and compensation. In the Arab world, it became known as the "Blandford Plan," after John Blandford, the US director of UNRWA, who was a former manager of the TVA. Following the vote, Blandford became involved in a series of bilateral negotiations on specific refugee settlement projects with the Arab states.

Despite Locke's fundamental objection to using UNRWA as a channel for US development (as opposed to relief assistance to the Arab world), he did take an active part in its affairs. Upon his return from Washington, Locke began a series of visits to refugee camps in order to get a firsthand view of actual camp conditions. He would often visit the camps unannounced, meet with refugee leaders, listen to their grievances, and receive their petitions. What he found appalled him: inadequate health and educational facilities, a lack of employment opportunities, complaints about reductions in rations, and particularly vitriolic rhetoric reserved for the West in general and for the "dictator" of UNRWA, Blandford.[53] What was interesting about these trips was Locke's tendency to distance himself from past US policy in the region and to set himself up more as a spokesman for the refugees. After a meeting with refugee leaders in Beirut during early autumn, for example, Locke held a news conference and declared the refugee situation "more serious now than it has ever been" and intimated that he would push for a change in US policy toward these "forgotten people."[54] So delighted were the refugees with this newfound and high-level US advocate that one refugee leader described him as the "Ambassador for the Arabs."[55] It was this image—the public champion of the refugees—that Locke brought to the meetings of the Advisory Commission of UNRWA.

One of the most immediate and acute problems facing UNRWA upon Locke's return was the widening disparity between the growing number of refugees, on the one hand, and the shrinking resources available for relief on the other. Although the Blandford Plan had pledged $50 million for relief, much of that had been earmarked for the first year of the program with the hope that the reintegration program, for which there was $200 million, would increasingly be able to pay the bills in subsequent years. In the absence of any concrete agreements on reintegration projects, however, UNRWA very quickly began to face a financial crisis. Less than eight months after the passage of the program, the estimates for the relief budget for fiscal year 1953 had already been raised from $18 million to $23 million, a figure even Locke felt was optimistic.[56]

In Locke's opinion, one of the reasons for this budgetary crisis was the undisciplined and profligate manner in which UNRWA spent money. To correct the situation, Locke launched within the Advisory Commission a campaign for greater fiscal austerity. Initially, Locke raised the idea of cutting refugee rations, though he avoided making any personal or governmental commitments and eventually backed away from the suggestion for political reasons.[57] A more concerted effort was made to improve the administrative efficiency of the agency. Locke was astounded, for example, that at a time when UNRWA was trying to reduce the financial allocations for relief, the number of staff on its payroll was increasing out of all proportions.[58] There were similar problems with the procurement operations, which Locke described as amateurish and amazingly soft, particularly when it came to the negotiation of prices for wheat purchases from local governments.[59] There was also talk of corruption within UNRWA itself—of supplies like wheat and medicine being sold privately on the open market.[60] To investigate these problems, Locke successfully put pressure on Blandford to hire an outside auditing firm to examine UNRWA's supply division. Although no corruption was actually uncovered, the report revealed, in Locke's words, a situation "even less satisfactory than I had imagined."[61]

The real issue facing UNRWA, however, was how to push forward with the reintegration program, so crucial in solving UNRWA's budgetary problems let alone in improving the plight of the growing number of refugees. Here, the signals were mixed. Jordan had proved reasonably cooperative over plans to finance dam construction and irrigation development on the Yarmuk River. Originally drawn up by a Point Four engineer, Miles Bunger, the Yarmuk–Jordan River scheme was subsequently adopted by UNRWA, which allocated an initial $10 million from the reintegration fund. Negotiations with the Syrian government were slower, but, in the beginning of October they, too, had resulted in a $30 million reintegration agreement.

However, the difficulty of implementing these agreements was quickly apparent, the Syrian agreement being a case in point. Despite his numerous trips to Damascus to meet with Syrian President Adib al-Shishakli—a "stalky little guy" with whom he professed to get on "beautifully"[62]—Locke was never very optimistic about the prospect of significant progress in refugee settlement there. Even after the initial talks between the Syrian chief of state, Colonel Fawzi Selu, and Blandford in February 1952—which some thought was an encouraging start—Locke's summary of the discussions led him to a much different conclusion: "1. [Selu] didn't think the amount of aid in Blandford's Plan was sufficient and moreover felt the Agency should pay for any land it wanted; 2. He was more interested in industrial than agricultural development—he feels the West is turning the Middle East into a great farm; 3. He is worried about competition for jobs between Syrian nationals and

Palestinian refugees . . . If that's progress, I'm the son of a donkey."[63] The substance of the $30 million agreement with Syria in October bore out this initial skepticism. By the end of November, only one project was actually underway—the conversion of a rundown army barracks southwest of Homs into an orphanage; it was expected, at a cost of $100,000, to remove, at most, 200 refugees from the relief rolls. All of the additional agricultural projects under consideration were hampered by the marginality of the land being offered.[64] Debates over the technical and political feasibility of the proposed Yarmuk scheme were causing similar delays in Jordan.

The frustrations over this halting progress spilled over into meetings of the Advisory Commission and were symbolized by the deteriorating relations between Locke and Blandford, the two most prominent Americans involved in UNRWA. There were a variety of issues over which the two locked horns. The conflict over budgetary practices within UNRWA has already been mentioned. This was accompanied by a series of backstabbing exchanges over Blandford's decision to replace UNRWA's US representative in Amman with a former British military officer. Locke, who was somewhat suspicious of British policy in the region, wanted to see Americans in key positions in UNRWA, both to improve its efficiency and to take advantage of any good press, particularly in Jordan, where the most promising program existed.[65] Locke and Blandford also squared off over whether Arab members should be accepted on the Advisory Commission; Blandford eventually succumbed to Locke's strong advocacy of this issue when it received the support of the State Department.[66]

The most substantial dispute between the two concerned UNRWA's approach to the resettlement issue. Locke was critical of Blandford's desire for political agreement before planning the specifics of any resettlement program, an approach that had led to delays in building up the technical arm of UNRWA. In Locke's opinion, this had left UNRWA an "empty shell" and unable to draw up, let alone execute, the kind of reintegration projects that would ultimately attract the cooperation of Arab governments. The result was "a lot of talk and a lot of running around," but no action.[67] Locke felt that by strengthening UNRWA's technical side Blandford would be able to negotiate on a much more compelling, project-by-project basis. It was a position often forwarded by Syrian officials in their negotiations with UNRWA.[68] Thus, he pushed Blandford repeatedly in meetings of the Advisory Commission to hire more technicians who could proceed with the immediate job at hand. Faced with Blandford's persistent opposition, however, Locke reverted to his initial lack of optimism about the prospects for UNRWA's success. The extent of his disillusionment was revealed by comments made in a letter to Truman at the end of September:

> UNRWA . . . is doing a pretty awful job and getting practically nowhere. What meat it would be for a new Truman committee—inefficiency on a broad scale, overstaffing and complete lack of results. The frame of mind of the refugees, now in their fifth year of homelessness, is becoming increasingly desperate. I have come to the firm conclusion that UNRWA is not the answer. No one believes in it anymore, especially in the Near East and least of all the refugees themselves.[69]

"Locke Hits Out at US Aid Policy"

Where was Locke to go from here? (The headline that serves as the title for this section portends his fate.) Although he had been sent to the Near East to activate policy, he had no confidence in the tools at his disposal. He had discarded UNRWA as a viable mechanism for US development policy in the Near East. Neither was he impressed with the potential of the Point Four program to make a noticeable political impact. It was true that the State Department had agreed to the establishment of a $25 million capital investment program for the Near East. However, when Locke convened a meeting of regional TCA country directors in late August to draw up a plan of action, he was extremely unimpressed with the nature and quality of the project proposals, especially those from the Lebanese group, whom Locke described as less than cooperative.[70] Moreover, as the following remarks to Truman indicate, Locke had become increasingly impatient with the "indecisive" State Department: "That organization, as I found out by personal experience last spring, has fallen into the way of doing things by committee and by unanimous vote which means that new ideas are under severe and sometimes almost insuperable handicap."[71] No doubt, this growing antagonism was fueled by rumors that the State Department's recall of Locke was imminent.[72]

These growing frustrations coincided with the marked deterioration of the Near East political climate in the autumn of 1952. Revolution in Egypt, a change of government in Lebanon, continued drift in Jordan, and the uncertainty of the political situation in Syria: All were factors pushing local Arab leaders into championing a more radical anti-Western stance, particularly in regard to the Arab-Israeli conflict and the refugee problem. The opening of the UN General Assembly in the autumn of 1952 provided the Arab states with a diplomatic forum where they could voice their criticisms. The net result was, in Locke's words, an "explosive situation," with the Arab states "feeling their oats," the Israelis becoming more "restive," and the Russians making continuous and discreet advances.[73]

Locke's response to this growing sense of crisis was to revive his old proposal for the creation of an Arab development fund. It was his hope that the deteriorating political situation might now induce Truman to give it personal endorsement.[74] However, with Eisenhower's victory in November and the emergence of a new sense of expectancy in the Arab world about an impending realignment of US policy in the region, Locke changed his tactics. Eisenhower was looked upon as having fewer ties with Israel and as being more conscious of the benefits of closer ties to the Arab states. In order to create some bureaucratic momentum for a policy shift, some diplomats began to advocate a formal reevaluation of US policy in the region.[75] Locke approved of this campaign but saw little hope of its success using normal diplomatic channels. Having first come out to the Near East with the hope of making a psychological impact on Arab public opinion, Locke now reversed his target and sought to make an impact on US public opinion. At the beginning of December, he gave three interviews with a US reporter, all of which appeared in the Beirut newspaper, the *Daily Star,* the second under the byline, "Locke Hits Out at U.S. Aid

Policy."[76] He then gave a talk at the influential Lebanese policy institute, le Cenacle Libanais, on December 6, calling for the formulation of a "new and hard-hitting policy" in the Near East based on the creation of a US-financed Arab development fund that could push ahead with such vital projects as the development of the Euphrates River and the Yarmuk Plan. In effect, it was a rehashed version of the proposal that he had presented to Truman six months earlier.[77]

The reactions to Locke's outbursts were swift and predictable. In Amman, Green, who on the whole was supportive of the kind of approach being suggested by Locke, was taken aback by his public attacks on US policy;[78] in Beirut, Minor was equally shocked at Locke's public policymaking and warned that "I can only see harm in this";[79] and in Washington, those who had become increasingly concerned about the adverse effects that Locke's appointment was having on US policy in the region finally had their excuse for action. One day after his talk at le Cenacle Libanais, Locke was called back, "for consultations" in Washington; one week later he resigned. Thus, less than one year after his high-profile return to public service, Locke was on his way back to the private sector.

What is interesting about "the Locke affair," as it was called for a short time in Beirut, was the reaction it received in parts of the Arab world. When Locke took his criticisms of US development policy public, the Lebanese press responded with support and praise: "The Arab world can only be grateful for such men as Locke who have . . . seen the flow of American policy and have spoken out," read one editorial in the *Daily Star*;[80] "wise and righteous," read another, containing an added hope that Locke would now be free to continue his campaign unshackled by diplomatic protocol.[81] Moreover, when Locke returned to Beirut at the end of December to finalize his affairs, he was given a hero's welcome. The Syrian government hosted a dinner in his honor in Damascus, and the Lebanese government awarded him the Order of the Cedars, the highest honor of state. Clearly, by publicly championing the Arab cause within the Truman administration, Locke had won himself a secure if fleeting spot in Arab history texts. As Peter summed it up, "There can be no question now . . . that he is the man of the hour—the white hope of the Arabs who is assumed to have spoken out on the basis of his convictions."[82]

The affair has since become a forgotten episode in the history of US policy in the region. This may seem somewhat surprising, given Locke's penchant for publicity even after his return to the United States.[83] Moreover, Locke's recommendations were not without support in US policy circles; their roots went back to George McGhee, Gordon Clapp, and the ESM. Nevertheless, history has probably been an accurate judge of the significance of the Locke mission. To start with, even if Locke's ideas did strike a sensitive vein within the State Department, his tactics left much to be desired and lost him the respect of all those who might have lent him support. Moreover, his call for unconditional aid to the Arab states, friend or foe, would never have carried much weight, especially in the context of an intensifying cold war that stressed the importance of helping one's allies. Perhaps the most important reason for the disappearance of the Locke mission from history was its complete overshadowing by the incoming Eisenhower administration, rumored to be interested in pursuing a more evenhanded regional policy. In that sense, Locke found himself all of a sudden swimming with the tide rather than against it.

However, though the Eisenhower administration did make efforts to improve relations between the United States and the Arab world, it never considered the kind of changes to US development policy in the Near East that Locke had hoped to see. The United States did continue to channel its assistance through UNRWA, though with the resignation of Blandford in early 1953 the grandiose settlement plans gradually gave way to the reality of day-to-day relief operations. Moreover, though Point Four did begin to consolidate its presence in the region, it never did receive the kind of capital resources that Locke felt were needed. Finally, by insisting on regional linkages and prior political agreements, the Eisenhower administration, despite the diplomatic efforts of Eric Johnston, was never able to activate the kind of "impact project" approach to development advocated by Locke. In short, what was labeled as "an economic approach" to peacemaking in the Near East has always been burdened with explicit political baggage.

This raises a more general question, one that is ultimately relevant to an evaluation of the Locke mission. Would the kind of more strictly economic approach advocated by Locke have been any more effective? Certainly, the Arab states were calling for it and, in that sense, Locke was really acting as a conduit for Arab views. However, whereas what was called the "TCA approach" may have worked in the context of the developed states of Europe (a debatable point at best), its application in the developing world has proven more problematic. It has taken theorists and practitioners of development many years to realize that modernization was not simply a linear process dependent on the infusion of technology and capital. The development process has been complicated by a whole series of structural and cultural factors, ones that are consistently ignored in the context of aid policies such as those suggested by Locke. These complicating factors have been particularly salient in the Middle East, plagued as it has been by the Arab-Israeli conflict, the extraordinarily high degree of regional interaction, and the superimposition upon them of the cold war. Locke, by so exclusively placing his hopes for an improved relationship between the Arab world and the United States on the provision of more US finance and technology, essentially ignored all of these factors. Thus, although more pro-Arab on the surface, his proposal can in fact be criticized for its insensitivity to the details of Arab politics—a common criticism of US policy in general in the Middle East in the 1950s. Whether linked or unconditional, greater amounts of capital assistance would not have been the decisive factor in winning Arab friendship, nor would they have effected any dramatic and broad-based economic take-off. It might have improved the lives of a few peasants, provided work for a few Arab bureaucrats and technicians, and even settled a few Palestinian refugees—all very laudable on human grounds. However, it could not have effected the kind of broad structural changes in the region that were at the root of its instability. These were simply beyond the scope of US power.

Notes

I would like to thank Myriam Noisette and David Wesl for commenting on earlier drafts of this chapter. Needless to say, all errors of judgment and interpretation are my responsibility. I would also like to thank the Connaught Fund at the University of Toronto for generously funding this research and the National Archives in Washington, D.C., and the Truman Library in Independence, Missouri, for facilitating it.

1. For definition's sake, the term "Near East" is used to refer to the Levant states of Syria, Lebanon, Jordan, Israel, and also Egypt.

2. Truman succeeded the presidency upon Franklin D. Roosevelt's death in April 1945. Elected outright in 1948, Truman served out one full one term; Republican Dwight D. Eisenhower took office in 1953 by defeating Adlai Stevenson in the 1952 presidential election.

3. For background on Truman's policy toward the Middle East in the last years of his administration, see H. Fields, "Pawns of Empire: A Study of United States Middle East Policy, 1945–53," Ph.D. diss., Rutgers University, 1975; J. Hurewitz, *Middle East Dilemmas* (New York: 1953); M. Kolinsky, "The Efforts of the Truman Administration to Resolve the Arab-Israeli Conflict," *Middle East Studies* 20(1) (January 1984); and I. Pappe, *Britain and the Arab-Israeli Conflict, 1948–51* (Basingstoke: 1988).

4. *New York Times,* 14 November 1951.

5. Cf. Parker to Hare, "Transfer of the British Middle East Office from Cairo," 29 December 1951, Lot 57D/298, Near East (hereinafter NE) Files, National Archives (hereinafter NA). In fact, Bill Crawford, the head of the Development Division, responded enthusiastically to Locke's appointment, describing him as "one of the brightest guys to hit this part of the world." Crawford to Evans, 23 January, 1952, Foreign Office (hereinafter FO) 371/98276/E11345/5.

6. Cf. R. Kaplan, *The Arabists: The Romance of an American Elite* (New York: 1993), for a recent journalistic account.

7. Cf. W. R. L. Louis, *The British Empire in the Middle East: Arab Nationalism, the United States, and Postwar Imperialism* (Oxford: 1984).

8. Cf. United Nations Conciliation Commission for Palestine, *Final Report of the United Nations Economic Survey Mission for the Middle East* (Lake Success, N.Y.: 1949).

9. Cf. Laborne to Clapp, 6 October 1949, Morton to Clapp, 8 November 1949, Clapp to Morton, 11 November 1949, Morton to Clapp, 2 December 1949, and Keeley to Clapp, 17 March 1950, all contained in Papers of Gordon Clapp, Box 3, United Nations Economic Survey Mission (hereinafter UNESM), Harry S Truman Library (hereinafter HSTL).

10. For details on the events leading up to Locke's appointment, see "Oral History Interview with Edwin Locke Jr." and "Oral History Interview with George McGhee," HSTL.

11. Edwin Locke Jr., interview by author, 7 February 1994.

12. In 1951, Syria and Yemen had still not signed Point Four agreements. Cf. Pinkerton to US Department of State, "Point IV Agreement with Lebanon," 883A.00-TA/2–2851, and Geren to US Department of State, "Why a Point IV Agreement has not been concluded with Syria," NA 883.00TA/5/28/51.

13. Minor memo, 9 January 1952, Papers of Edwin Locke Jr., Box 4, HSTL.

14. Locke to Gardiner, 21 December 1951, ibid.

15. Locke to Truman, 26 December 1951, ibid.

16. Cf. "Campaign Against Point IV Litani River Project," Beirut to US Department of State, 883A.00-TA/1–752.

17. Cf. "Statement by Ambassador Edwin Locke Jr.," 23 December 1951, Papers of Edwin Locke Jr., Box 4, HSTL.

18. Locke to US Secretary of State, 883A.00-TA/1–3152.

19. Cf. P. Kingston, "Pioneers in Development: The British Middle East Development Division and the Politics of Technical Assistance, 1945–1960," D.Phil. diss., Oxford University, 1991.

20. Cf. Staff Memorandum, US Department of State, "Responsibilities of Ambassador Locke in the Near East," 12 May 1952, Lot 57D/298, NE Files, for details on the policy discussions surrounding the creation of the regional office.

21. Farnsworth to Peter, 16 January 1952, Record Group (hereinafter RG) 84, Lebanon, Classified General Records, Box 28, NA Records Administration (NARA).

22. Crockett to Skiles, 29 February 1952, RG 84, Lebanon, Classified General Records, Box 28, NARA.

23. Peter to Reeseman Fryer, 1 April 1952, RG 84, Lebanon, Classified General Records, Box 28, NARA.

24. Cf. Oral History Interview with George McGhee, p. 44, HSTL.

25. Cf. D. Acheson, *Present at the Creation: My Years in the State Department* (New York: 1969).

26. Cf. Memo of Conversation, "Telegrams from Amb. Locke Proposing the U.S. Complete the Markabi, Kasmie, and Taibe Projects for Lebanon," 883A.00-TA/2–1352.

27. Peter to Reeseman Fryer, 1 April 1952, RG 84 Lebanon, Classified General Records, Box 28, NARA.

28. Cf. "Negotiation of Point 4 Program Agreement in Lebanon," 883A.00-TA/4–2452.

29. Cf. ibid.

30. Peter to Reeseman Fryer, 7 June 1952, RG 84 Lebanon, Classified General Records, Box 28, NARA.

31. Skiles to Tannous, 28 February 1952, ibid.

32. Peter to Reeseman Fryer, 1 April 1952, ibid.

33. Ibid.

34. Locke to Tannous, "Action Program for the Near East," 25 April 1952, Presidential Secretary's Files, Papers of Harry S. Truman, HSTL.

35. Locke to Truman, 19 February 1952, Papers of Edwin Locke Jr., Box 5, HSTL.

36. Locke, for example, justified these priorities by citing the "remarkable success" of the Japanese in developing Manchuria during World War II based on the modernization of infrastructure in the areas of transportation, fuel, and power. Cf. Locke to US Secretary of State, 880.00-TA/3/24/52.

37. These were: improvement to the port of Beirut, improvement to the port of Tripoli, the construction of a port at Latakia, the construction of a natural gas pipeline from Kirkuk to the Levant region, the development of the Litani River, the development of the Tigris and Euphrates Rivers in Syria, the development of the Orontes River, the development of the Yarmouk-Jordan area, and the implementation of the equatorial Nile plan.

38. Locke to US Secretary of State, 880.00-TA/3/24/52.

39. Cf. Harriman to Acheson, 880.00-TA/4/9/52 for background on the legislative obstacles concerning Locke's proposal.

40. Cf. Cannon to US Secretary of State, 880.00-TA/3/15/52, Tannous to US Secretary of State, 883A.00-TA/3/5/52, and Tannous to US Secretary of State, 883A.00-TA/3/17/52.

41. Peter to Reeseman Fryer, 1 April 1952, RG 84, Lebanon, Classified General Records, Box 28, NARA.

42. Locke to Truman, 19 February 1952, Presidential Secretary's Files, HSTL.

43. Cf. Berry memo, "Grant Aid for Arab States for Fiscal Year 1953," 880.00-TA/2/29/52.

44. Cf. Memo of Conversation, "Arab States Development Programs" 880.00-TA/3/17/52.

45. Harriman to Acheson, 880.00-TA/4/9/52.

46. Ibid.

47. Cf. Thorp to Acheson, "Near East Aid Program," 880.00-TA/2/25/52.

48. Reesemen Fryer to Andrews, 9 May 1952, Lot 57D/298, NA.

49. Ibid.

50. Memorandum of Conversation with the President, "The Locke Proposal," 1 May 1952, Dean Acheson Papers, Box 67, HSTL.

51. Cf. US Department of State, Staff Memorandum, "Responsibilities of Ambassador Locke in the Near East," 12 May 1952, and Gardiner to Locke, 15 May 1952, Lot 57D/298, NE Files, NA. See also Peter to Reeseman Fryer, 7 June 1952, RG 84, Lebanon, Classified General Records, Box 28, NARA; and Gardiner to Locke, 15 May 1952, Lot 57 D/298, Records of the Office of Near Eastern Affairs, NA.

52. Cf. Thorp to Secretary of State, "Near East Aid Program," 880.00-TA/5/2/52.

53. Cf. Locke to Gardiner, 4 September 1952, Papers of Edwin Locke Jr., Box 5, HSTL, and Fidler to Locke, "Discussion with Palestine Arab Refugee Leaders," 15 September 1952, Papers of Edwin Locke Jr., Box 5, HSTL.

54. Cf. *Le Soir* (Beirut), 15 September 1952.

55. Cf. "Notes on Locke's Visits to Refugee Camps," Notebooks 1 and 2, Papers of Edwin Locke Jr., Box 4, HSTL.

56. Locke to Gardiner, 4 September 1952, Papers of Edwin Locke Jr., Box 5, HSTL.

57. Ibid.

58. Ibid.

59. Ibid.

60. Cf. Amawi to Locke, 3 October 1952, Papers of Edwin Locke Jr., Box 5, HSTL, for a discussion of possible corruption within the United Nations Relief and Works Administration.

61. Locke to Gardiner, 30 July 1952, and Locke to Gardiner, 24 September 1952, Papers of Edwin Locke Jr., Box 5, HSTL.

62. Edwin Locke Jr., interview by author, 7 February 1994.

63. Locke to Gardiner, 23 February 1952, Papers of Edwin Locke Jr., Box 5, HSTL.

64. Cf. Locke to Gardiner, 29 November 1952, ibid.

65. Cf. Green to US Secretary of State, 320.2AA/9–2752, and Lobenstine to Byroade, 320.2AA/10/4/52.

66. Cf. Funkhouser to Hart, "Arab Membership on ADCOM," 320.2AA/9/12/52, Memorandum of Conversation, "UNRWA Relief Budget and Syrian Membership on the Advisory Commission," 320.2AA/9/17/52, and Lobenstine to Byroade, 320.2AA/10/4/52.

67. Locke to Gardiner, 23 February 1952. Papers of Edwin Locke Jr., Box 5, HSTL.

68. Cf. Geren to US Department of State, "Selo Gives Opinion on U.S. Aid," 883.00/10/16/52.

69. Locke to Truman, 24 September 1952, Papers of Edwin Locke Jr., Box 5, HSTL.

70. Cf. Locke and Peter to TCA Country Directors, Near East, 880.00-TA/8/4/52, and Locke to Gardiner, 6 September 1952, Papers of Edwin Locke Jr., Box 5, HSTL.

71. Locke to Truman, 24 September 1952, Papers of Edwin Locke Jr., Box 5, HSTL.

72. Fidler memo, 9 October 1952, ibid.

73. Locke to Truman, 24 September 1952, ibid.

74. Ibid.

75. Minor to US Secretary of State, 880.00-TA/11/24/52.

76. Cf. *Daily Star* (Beirut), 28 November, 30 November, and 2 December 1952, all found in the papers of Edwin Locke Jr., Box 4, HSTL.

77. Edwin Locke, "The Arab Economy: The Truth and the Challenge," 5 December 1952, Papers of Edwin Locke Jr., Box 4, HSTL.

78. Green to Minor, 3 December 1952, RG 84, Lebanon, Box 28, NARA.

79. Minor to Green, 9 December, 1952, ibid.

80. Cf. *Daily Star* (Beirut), 13 December 1952.

81. *Daily Star* (Beirut), 27 December 1952.

82. Peter to Young, 19 December 1952, RG 84 Lebanon, Classified General Records, Box 28, NARA.

83. At the end of January, Locke spoke at a meeting of the American Friends of the Middle East in which he repeated his criticisms of US development policy in the Near East, this time directing some added invective at officials of the State Department, whom he described as "scrubs." Cf. Daily Star (Beirut), 10 February and 21 March 1953. For a rather unabashedly vicious response from one of the "scrubs," see Bruins to Hart, 320.2-AA/3/23/53.

3

US Foreign Policy Toward Iran During the Mussadiq Era

Mark Gasiorowski

Muhammad Mussadiq, who served as the Iranian prime minister from April 1951 until August 1953, is revered by almost all secular democratic Iranians and admired even by many supporters of the regimes of the shah and Ayatollah Khomeini. He ended a long period of British hegemony in Iran by nationalizing the British-controlled oil industry, instilling a strong sense of national pride in most Iranians, and setting the stage for several decades of rapid economic growth fueled by oil revenues. He also tried to democratize Iran's political system by reducing the powers of the shah and the traditional upper class and by mobilizing the urban middle and lower classes. Although he ultimately failed in this latter endeavor, his efforts made him a hero in the eyes of those Iranians who have dreamed of establishing a democratic regime in their country.

At the start of the Mussadiq era the United States had a very positive image in Iran, created by the small group of US teachers, missionaries, archaeologists, and administrators who had ventured there and by the commitment to freedom, democracy, and independence espoused by the US government and most Americans. The United States initially supported Mussadiq, upholding Iran's right to nationalize the oil industry, trying to mediate an agreement with the British, giving Iran a small amount of economic aid, and generally praising Mussadiq and his democratic aspirations. However, US support for Mussadiq gradually declined, and under the administration of President Dwight D. Eisenhower the United States engineered a coup d'état that drove Mussadiq from office and ended the movement toward democracy he had been leading. The United States thereafter strongly backed the shah, greatly facilitating his efforts to create an authoritarian regime in the decade after the coup. Consequently, the Mussadiq era also marked a period in which the popular image of the United States in Iran began to change from that of benevolent outsider to malevolent supporter of the shah's despotic regime.

This chapter examines US policy toward Iran during the Mussadiq era. It focuses particularly on the strategic considerations that led US officials to change from a policy of supporting Mussadiq to one of opposing and eventually overthrowing him, thus engendering the malevolent image many Iranians still have of the United States. The chapter does not provide a detailed account of the August 1953 coup or the events leading up to it, which are examined at length elsewhere.

Prologue: US Policy Toward Iran Before the Mussadiq Era

Before World War II the United States had little strategic or economic interest in Iran, and relations between the two countries were cordial but distant. The United States had established diplomatic relations with Iran in 1856 but did not send a diplomat of ambassadorial rank there until 1944. During the late 1800s and early 1900s contact between the two countries was very limited, consisting mainly of missionary activity with a handful of US missionaries, teachers, and archaeologists, these Americans created a very positive image of the United States in Iran. Nevertheless, relations between the two countries were evidently of such little importance by the late 1930s that Iran's monarch, Reza Shah Pahlavi, recalled his ambassador to Washington for several years after derogatory comments about him appeared in the US press.[1]

With World War II raging in Europe, Britain and the Soviet Union jointly invaded Iran in September 1941 to establish a supply route to the Soviet army. The invading forces quickly overpowered the hapless Iranian army and forced Reza Shah, who was seen as a German sympathizer, to abdicate in favor of his twenty-one-year-old son, Muhammad Reza Pahlavi, the late shah. Following US entry into the war the United States sent troops to Iran in conjunction with the supply operation, initiating a period in which US-Iranian relations grew rapidly. By early 1944 some 30,000 US soldiers were stationed in Iran, guarding the supply route against bandits and German agents, expanding and improving Iran's transportation system and oil production facilities, and building plants to assemble aircraft, trucks, and oil drums. The United States sent military missions to Iran to reorganize and train the Iranian army and gendarmerie and gave Iran some $8.5 million in lend-lease aid during the war. Unlike Britain and the Soviet Union, the United States did not meddle in Iran's domestic affairs during the war, reinforcing its image as a champion of freedom and independence.[2]

As the German threat eased in 1944, the Soviet Union began to expand its influence and demand oil concessions in the northwestern Iranian provinces of Azerbaijan and Kurdistan, which it had been occupying since 1941. Constrained by its need to maintain the wartime alliance, the United States initially made no effort to block these activities. However, as World War II drew to a close in 1945, the Soviet posture toward Iran grew more menacing and was paralleled by similar activities elsewhere in the world. As US officials grew increasingly concerned about Soviet expansionism, and after Harry S Truman replaced the more diplomatic Franklin D. Roosevelt as president, the United States began to pressure the Soviet Union to withdraw its forces from Iran. Soviet officials demurred, and in December 1945 and January 1946 Soviet-backed rebels established the Autonomous Republic of Azerbaijan and the Kurdish People's Republic in northwestern Iran. Powerless to stop these activities, the Iranian government sought backing from the United States and Britain and petitioned the United Nations (UN) to demand a Soviet withdrawal. US officials issued protests to the Soviet government and strongly supported Iran's position at the UN. Backed by the United States, Iranian prime minister Ahmad Qavam traveled to Moscow in March 1946 and negotiated an agreement under which Soviet troops would be withdrawn from Iran. The Iranian army reoccupied Azerbaijan and Kurdistan in December 1946, crushing the autonomy movements and ending one of the first chapters in the cold war.[3]

As the crisis in Azerbaijan and Kurdistan was drawing to a close, the US Department of State and other US government agencies conducted a thorough review of US interests in Iran. Reflecting the considerable effort US officials had made earlier to eject Soviet forces from northwestern Iran, US officials concluded that Iran was "of vital strategic interest" because Persian Gulf oil would be critical in the event of a war with the Soviet Union.[4] However, despite this finding, no major changes occurred in US policy toward Iran during the late 1940s. US policymakers at this time were pursuing a strategy of "strongpoint defense" in their efforts to contain Soviet expansionism. This strategy called for a concentration of US defense efforts in Western Europe and Japan—on the western and eastern borders of the Soviet Union—and accorded a much lower priority to other regions, including the area south of the Soviet Union where Iran lay. Consequently, though the shah and the various Iranian prime ministers of this period made repeated requests for US military and economic aid, Iran was not given a large aid package under the Truman Doctrine, as were Greece and Turkey, and it received less US aid in the late 1940s than countries like Ireland, Portugal, and Sweden, despite its larger size and poorer economic conditions.[5]

The United States did slowly increase its involvement in Iran in other ways during this period, however. The military training missions begun during World War II were renegotiated and extended in 1947 and 1948. The US embassy staff grew considerably in size, enhancing diplomatic, commercial, and cultural interactions between the two countries. More important, the Office of Strategic Services, the predecessor to the Central Intelligence Agency (CIA) established a station in the Tehran embassy in early 1947 to take over covert operations then being conducted by US military attachés and embassy political officers. These covert operations included intelligence-gathering and propaganda operations aimed at the Soviet Union and its allies in Iran, cross-border espionage and subversion raids into Soviet territory, and efforts to map out escape and evasion routes and organize "stay-behind" guerrilla networks for use in the event of a Soviet invasion. Although these operations were all aimed ultimately at the Soviet Union, they did have the effect of strengthening or weakening various Iranian political actors in minor ways during this period.[6]

In the late 1940s unrest grew steadily among politically active Iranians, due mainly to the absence of meaningful opportunities for political participation and to growing resentment toward the Anglo-Iranian Oil Company (AIOC), a British-owned firm that was earning large profits from its monopoly over Iran's oil industry. Much of this unrest was mobilized and articulated by the Tudeh (Masses) Party, a pro-Soviet Communist Party established in 1941 that had become Iran's largest political party before falling into disfavor after the Azerbaijani crisis. In October 1949 a group of prominent political figures established an organization known as the National Front to press for political reforms and nationalization of the AIOC's assets in Iran. The National Front quickly became extremely popular and managed to elect eight of its members to the Majlis (the Iranian parliament) in late 1949. It was led by Muhammad Mussadiq, a charismatic Majlis deputy from a wealthy landowning family who had established a reputation as an ardent nationalist and democrat and one of Iran's few honest politicians.[7]

By early 1950 US officials had become alarmed about political conditions in Iran, with one describing Iran as "dangerous and explosive" and another warning that it might become a "second China."[8] Simultaneously, the National Security Council was undertaking a major reevaluation of US global strategy, which was codified in the April 1950 document known as NSC–68. The new strategy called for a "renewed initiative in the cold war" involving large increases in military and economic aid to countries located all along the Sino-Soviet periphery—not just those on the western and eastern borders of the Soviet Union.[9] The growing unrest in Iran and this new global strategy together led US officials to undertake a thorough review of US policy toward Iran, which concluded that a major effort had to be made to prevent the Tudeh Party from coming to power and delivering Iran into Soviet hands. As a result, during the following year US officials agreed to provide Iran with $23 million per year in military aid and a modest amount of economic aid; they approved a $25 million Export-Import Bank loan to Iran (which was never actually provided); and they supported Iran's request for a $10 million World Bank loan. They also sharply increased the number of US Foreign Service and CIA officers working in the Tehran embassy and named Henry Grady, a highly respected diplomat, to be the new US ambassador.[10] By early 1951 the United States had positioned itself to play a major role in Iranian politics.

The Truman Administration and the First Mussadiq Government

Throughout 1950 unrest continued to grow in Iran, with political reform and oil nationalization remaining the most contentious issues. Prime Minister Ali Razmara initiated a program of political and socioeconomic reforms but also attempted to implement an agreement with the AIOC negotiated under his predecessors that fell far short of popular demands. In response, Mussadiq and the National Front began to call for outright nationalization of the oil industry, and a member of the Islamist group Fedayan-e Islam (Devotees of Islam) assassinated Razmara in March 1951. The shah then appointed Hussein Ala, a loyal ally, to replace Razmara. The country was swept with a new wave of unrest, leading the Majlis to nominate Mussadiq for the premiership and pass a bill nationalizing the oil industry. Bowing to popular sentiment, the shah appointed Mussadiq prime minister on April 29 and signed the oil nationalization bill into law on May 2.[11]

Nationalization of the AIOC posed a serious threat to Britain's weak economy and dwindling prestige, so the nationalization decree initiated a period of growing confrontation between Britain and Iran. In the following months British officials adopted a three-track strategy aimed at reestablishing Britain's control over Iran's oil industry either by pressuring Mussadiq into a favorable settlement or removing him from office. The first track was a halfhearted effort to negotiate a new oil agreement that would recognize the principle of nationalization but retain de facto British control over Iran's oil. This effort collapsed in August 1951, and the British thereafter refused to negotiate directly with Mussadiq. The second track consisted of a series of hostile measures aimed at undermining popular support for Mussadiq. The most important of these was a successful effort to persuade the major world oil companies to boycott Iranian oil exports. The British also imposed a series of bilateral economic sanctions on Iran and began an ominous military buildup in the region. The third element of the British strategy was a series of covert efforts to overthrow Mussadiq. These efforts continued throughout Mussadiq's tenure as prime minister and were carried out primarily through a network of politicians, businessmen, military officers, and clerical leaders that had been cultivated by British intelligence officers during their long years of intrigue in Iran.[12]

After Mussadiq assumed office the Truman administration publicly expressed strong support for him, recognizing that he was very popular and therefore could serve as an effective alternative to the Tudeh Party. Officials in Washington again undertook a review of US policy toward Iran, concluding that Iran must be kept in the Western camp at all costs because of its strategic location and that a protracted oil crisis might weaken the US economy and threaten US and Western security. Accordingly, for the remainder of Truman's term in office the administration pursued a policy of supporting Mussadiq, opposing British efforts to overthrow him, and attempting to mediate an agreement that would satisfy both parties to the oil dispute and minimize disruption of the world oil market.[13]

Soon after the oil nationalization law was enacted, US officials began to implement a plan to ease the effect of the British oil blockade on the world oil market. Under this plan US oil companies were asked to provide oil to US allies that had been adversely affected by the blockade. Some 46 million barrels of oil were delivered under this plan in the first year of the blockade, amounting to roughly 20 percent of Iran's 1950 production. Although this effort was intended to help stabilize the world oil market, it also reinforced the oil blockade and therefore inadvertently helped to weaken the Iranian economy and undermine Mussadiq's popular support.[14]

At the same time, US officials began a concerted effort to facilitate a negotiated settlement of the oil dispute. They privately advised the British to accept nationalization of the AIOC and agree to a 50–50 division of profits with Iran—an arrangement that had become common throughout the industry by that time. In July 1951

Secretary of State Dean Acheson asked special envoy Averell Harriman to lead a mission to Tehran and London to mediate the dispute. Harriman worked assiduously to bring the British and Iranian positions closer together, inducing the British to send a negotiating team to Iran under the leadership of Sir Richard Stokes. The Stokes mission made little headway, and negotiations between Britain and Iran collapsed in August.[15]

Throughout this period the British had been working strenuously to replace Mussadiq with their close ally, Sayyid Zia al-Din Tabatabai. This had involved direct pressures on the shah to dismiss Mussadiq and appoint Sayyid Zia as prime minister as well as efforts to build support in the Majlis through the British intelligence network for Sayyid Zia's candidacy. British officials even went so far as to work out a set of guidelines for settling the oil dispute with Sayyid Zia. US officials were generally aware of these activities and neither supported nor opposed them. The British effort to install Sayyid Zia had not made much headway by the time the Stokes mission collapsed. Accordingly, in September 1951 British officials began to implement a plan to invade southwestern Iran and seize the oil fields. When US officials were told about this plan, President Truman notified British Prime Minister Clement Attlee that the United States would not support an invasion and urged him to resume negotiations. As a result, Attlee was forced to abandon the invasion plan, telling his cabinet that "in view of the attitude of the United States Government, [he did not] think it would be expedient to use force" in Iran.[16]

Mussadiq traveled to New York in October to address the UN Security Council about the oil dispute. US officials invited him to Washington, hosting him warmly and making another concerted effort to mediate the dispute. These efforts again failed to bring about a settlement. During the following year US officials made a series of additional proposals that called for Iranian oil to be marketed by a consortium of US and other oil companies. When antitrust concerns led the major US oil companies to reject this plan, US officials first tried to persuade US independents to accept it and then, in the fall of 1952, decided to waive antitrust laws to persuade the majors to participate. Despite these efforts, US officials were unable to settle the oil dispute.[17]

Having failed to reverse the nationalization law, to install Sayyid Zia as prime minister, or to seize the oil fields forcibly, the British began to search for other options in their efforts to regain control over Iran's oil. Another option soon materialized. Ahmad Qavam, who had been prime minister during the 1945–1946 Azerbaijani crisis, approached the British seeking support in his bid to replace Mussadiq as prime minister. British officials sent an emissary to meet with Qavam in Paris in March 1952. Qavam told the emissary that he would settle the oil dispute on terms acceptable to the British, and he produced a list of potential cabinet ministers for their approval. The British supported Qavam by accepting his plan to end the oil dispute and having their network of Iranian allies help him. Qavam spent the next several months trying to build support in Iran for his candidacy.[18]

Mussadiq evidently learned about Qavam's activities and suddenly resigned on July 16. The shah then appointed Qavam prime minister. During the next several days the National Front organized a series of massive demonstrations calling for Mussadiq's return to office. Army and police units attacked the demonstrators, killing at least sixty-nine and injuring over 750. Since Qavam had no popular backing, Mussadiq's supporters dominated the streets of Tehran. On July 21 the shah bowed to the popular will and appointed Mussadiq to a second term as prime minister. Qavam slipped quietly into exile.[19]

The Truman Administration and the Second Mussadiq Government

The Qavam episode initiated a period of growing political instability in Iran. Morale in the armed forces dropped sharply. The Tudeh Party became much more active. Mussadiq filled his new cabinet with close supporters and persuaded the Majlis to grant him emergency powers, angering National Front leaders such as Ayatollah Abul Qassem Kashani, Hussein Makki, and Muzaffar Baqai. More ominously, a group of military officers led by General Fazlollah Zahedi began to plot against Mussadiq with the Rashidian brothers, who were the central figures in the British intelligence network. Zahedi had briefly served as interior minister in Mussadiq's first government and had supported the National Front until the July 1952 uprisings, when the resurgence of Tudeh activity and plummeting morale in the armed forces apparently drove him into the opposition.[20]

Kashani, Makki, and Baqai soon approached Zahedi, expressing their dissatisfaction with Mussadiq and thereafter collaborating loosely with him in his plot. Zahedi also obtained the support of Abul Qassem Bakhtiari, a leader of the Bakhtiari tribe who had worked with him in collaboration with German agents during World War II. He then met with the British chargé d'affaires, asking for assurance that the British would not oppose him, would agree to a settlement of the oil dispute on terms similar to those worked out with Qavam, and would obtain US acquiescence in his activities. The chargé reported this to London and was told to help Zahedi. British intelligence officers then provided arms to the Bakhtiari. The chargé described Zahedi's activities to US Ambassador Loy Henderson. Either Zahedi or a close lieutenant also met with Henderson in early September, telling him that a government would soon come to power that would halt the growth of Tudeh influence. Henderson reported these conversations back to Washington but remained noncommittal.[21]

US policy toward Iran during this period was ambiguous. Ambassador Henderson was alarmed about the resurgence of the Tudeh Party and the generally chaotic situation in Iran in the aftermath of the Qavam episode, and he recommended that Washington prop up the Mussadiq government with a large aid package. Although this did not occur, US officials renewed their efforts to resolve the oil dispute and continued to support Mussadiq, both publicly and in private conversations with the British. However, at the same time, CIA officers in Tehran began to turn some of their anti-Soviet covert operations in directions that undermined Mussadiq's base of support. Under a propaganda operation code-named BEDAMN, they distributed newspaper articles and cartoons that depicted Mussadiq as corrupt and immoral and portrayed him as exploiting Kashani. They provided financial assistance to certain clergymen to drive them away from Mussadiq and create a clerical alternative to Kashani. CIA officers with long-standing ties to the Pan-Iranist Party and the Toilers' Party—both had strongly supported Mussadiq—made efforts to turn these organizations against Mussadiq. In a particularly noteworthy case, two CIA officers in the fall of 1952 approached Baqai, who had headed the Toilers' Party, encouraging him to break with Mussadiq and giving him money. Similar approaches may have been made to Kashani, Makki, and other prominent figures.[22]

By November 1952 both the Pan-Iranists and the Toilers' Party had split into pro- and anti-Mussadiq factions; Kashani, Makki, Baqai, and other National Front leaders had openly turned against Mussadiq, seriously weakening him. These three men, like most other Iranian politicians at the time, were extremely opportunistic and may well have had other reasons for breaking with Mussadiq. Moreover, the British were carrying out very similar—and probably much more extensive—covert activities against Mussadiq at this time. Therefore, although these CIA activities may well have helped to undermine Mussadiq's base of support, they were not the only forces operating against him in this period, and it is impossible to say with any certainty how much of a role they actually played in weakening him.

Mussadiq evidently learned about Zahedi's plot and moved to stop him before it could be implemented. As a member of the Iranian senate, Zahedi enjoyed parliamentary immunity and therefore could not be arrested. However, Mussadiq issued arrest warrants on October 13 for the Rashidians and for General Abdul Hussein Hejazi, a close ally of Zahedi. A General Aryana was dismissed from the army in connection with the plot. More important, on October 16 Mussadiq broke diplomatic relations with Britain, claiming British officials had supported Zahedi. This act alarmed US officials and persuaded some of them that the situation in Iran had gotten out of hand.[23]

No longer able to operate from the safety of their Tehran embassy, the British decided to seek US help in their efforts to oust Mussadiq. Christopher Montague Woodhouse, who had been heading British intelligence operations in Iran, was sent to Washington in November to present US officials with a plan to oust Mussadiq. The plan called for a coordinated uprising to be engineered by the Rashidians and certain Bakhtiari tribal elements, with or without the shah's approval. Although the British believed Zahedi was well suited to lead the coup, they proposed several possible coup leaders. Woodhouse met with CIA and State Department officials. Most high-ranking CIA officials favored a coup by this time, although some lower-ranking Iran specialists and the CIA station chief in Tehran were opposed to the idea. State Department officials told Woodhouse that Truman would not support a coup but that president-elect Dwight Eisenhower and his foreign policy advisers probably would.[24]

The Eisenhower Administration and Mussadiq

Dwight Eisenhower entered office in January 1953, and the administration harbored bold plans to restructure US foreign policy in ways that would more effectively contain the Soviet Union. Its new global strategy, which was eventually set out in the October 1953 National Security Council study NSC–162, called for a broad effort to enhance containment while reducing US defense expenditures. An important element of this effort was a decision to strengthen pro-Western countries located along the Sino-Soviet periphery—a project that the Truman administration had begun but set aside as the Korean War and European reconstruction distracted its attention. These countries were to be strengthened with large military and economic aid programs, defense alliances, and, where necessary, covert political operations conducted by the CIA.[25] As a result of this new global strategy, the Eisenhower administration redirected the US military and economic aid programs away from Europe toward the Third World; it constructed a ring of defense alliances around the Soviet Union and China; and it greatly increased the CIA's use of covert operations. With its proximity to the Soviet Union, and Mussadiq's failure to resolve the oil crisis, Iran was a crucial pawn in this new strategy and quickly became a major preoccupation for the Eisenhower administration.

Secretary of State designate John Foster Dulles and his brother, Allen Dulles, who was deputy head of the CIA's covert operations division under Truman and was to become CIA director under Eisenhower, had been following the situation in Iran with growing alarm. Although they did not regard Mussadiq as a Communist, they believed conditions in Iran would probably continue to deteriorate as long as he remained in office, strengthening the Tudeh Party and perhaps enabling it to seize power. In light of Iran's crucial role in the US strategy for containing the Soviet Union, they viewed this possibility with grave concern. The Dulles brothers therefore concluded that Mussadiq had to be removed from office—a conclusion that was not shared at this time by Assistant Secretary of State for Near Eastern and South Asian Affairs Henry Byroade, Ambassador Henderson, the CIA station chief in Tehran, or several lower-ranking State Department and CIA officials. Allen Dulles had met with Woodhouse in November 1952 and expressed his support for a coup to overthrow Mussadiq. The Dulles brothers were ready to begin preparations for a coup by the time Eisenhower was inaugurated.[26]

On February 3, 1953, two weeks after the inauguration, top US and British officials met in Washington to discuss the situation in Iran. At this meeting a decision was made to develop and carry out a plan to overthrow Mussadiq and install Zahedi as prime minister. The operation was to be led by Kermit Roosevelt, who headed the CIA's Middle East operations division. Roosevelt traveled to Iran several times during the following months to prepare for the coup, meeting with Zahedi, the Rashidians, members of the Tehran CIA station, and two Iranians code-named Nerren and Cilley, who were the main operatives in the BEDAMN propaganda operation. A US specialist on Iran working under contract for the CIA was assigned to develop an operation plan for the coup with a British intelligence officer. Roosevelt presented the coup plan to the Dulles brothers and other top US officials in a June 25 State Department meeting. He was directed to implement it immediately.[27]

Zahedi had continued to intrigue against Mussadiq after the exposure of his plot in October 1952. He remained in contact with Bakhtiari tribal leaders, who were given arms and money by the British during this period. His allies in the Majlis undertook a series of parliamentary maneuvers to try to oust Mussadiq. In February 1953 a group of retired military officers loyal to Zahedi and Bakhtiari tribesmen led by Abul Qassem attacked an army column, apparently trying to spark a coup. Mussadiq responded by issuing an arrest warrant for Zahedi, who had lost his parliamentary immunity. Zahedi's allies then organized a series of violent disturbances in Tehran that nearly toppled the Mussadiq government. A similar incident occurred in late April, when several Zahedi associates apparently kidnapped and murdered the commander of the national police, a staunch Mussadiq supporter. Rumors of coup plots circulated throughout the winter and spring of 1953.[28]

Following the June 25 State Department meeting, Roosevelt and his CIA team began to work in loose coordination with Zahedi. They used the BEDAMN network to launch an extensive propaganda barrage against Mussadiq and organize antigovernment and anti-Tudeh demonstrations, adding considerably to the turmoil that was engulfing Tehran. They sought the support of top military officers, arranging to have certain army units participate in the coup. In late July and early August they sent two emissaries to see the shah and obtain his support. When these approaches proved unsuccessful, Roosevelt arranged through the Rashidians to meet personally with the shah. After direct US and British involvement were confirmed through special radio broadcasts, the shah agreed to support the plot.[29]

Having obtained the shah's backing, Roosevelt was ready to proceed with the coup. The shah signed decrees dismissing Mussadiq and appointing Zahedi prime minister. The commander of the shah's Imperial Guard delivered the first of these decrees to Mussadiq on the night of August 15 and was promptly arrested. Army and police units loyal to Mussadiq then set up roadblocks throughout the city, began a massive search for Zahedi, and arrested several of his associates. An armored column that had been assigned to move into Tehran in conjunction with Mussadiq's dismissal failed to arrive. As the coup plot unraveled the shah fled the country in panic, first to Baghdad and then to Rome. Zahedi was brought to a CIA safe house, where he remained for the next several days. Roosevelt made contingency plans to evacuate himself, Zahedi, and a few other participants.[30]

Despite these setbacks, Roosevelt and his colleagues began to improvise a new plan. They distributed copies of the decrees dismissing Mussadiq and appointing Zahedi throughout Tehran in order to publicize the shah's actions. They brought two US newspaper reporters to meet with Ardeshir Zahedi, who told them about the shah's decrees and characterized Mussadiq's rejection of them as a coup, since the decrees were in accord with the constitution. This information was quickly published in *The New York Times*. Ardeshir Zahedi and one of the CIA officers were sent to Kermanshah and Isfahan to persuade the garrison commanders in those cities to send troops to Tehran. The US military advisory group distributed military supplies to pro-Zahedi forces to encourage them to support the plot.[31]

On August 17 Nerren and Cilley used $50,000 given to them by Roosevelt's team to hire a large crowd that marched into central Tehran shouting Tudeh slogans, carrying signs denouncing the shah, tearing down statues of the shah and his father, and attacking Reza Shah's mausoleum. This crowd played the role of an agent provocateur: It generated fear of a Tudeh takeover among Tehran residents and was even joined by many real Tudeh members, who assumed it had been organized by the party's leadership. These disturbances continued on the following day. Mussadiq therefore ordered the police to disperse the crowds, even though the Tudeh was tacitly supporting him against Zahedi and the shah. The Tudeh responded by ordering its members off the streets, removing an important obstacle to Mussadiq's opponents.[32]

By the evening of August 18 the police were closing in on the CIA safe house where Zahedi was hiding. Roosevelt therefore began to look for a new way to spark a coup. Knowing that Ayatollah Kashani was strongly opposed to Mussadiq and had considerable influence over lower- and middle-class Iranians, he decided to seek Kashani's help in organizing another crowd to agitate against Mussadiq. Following the Rashidians' advice, he had two CIA officers meet with Ahmad Aramesh, an influence peddler who apparently had connections with Kashani. They asked Aramesh to ask Kashani to organize an anti-Mussadiq crowd and gave him $10,000 to finance the effort. At the same time, the Rashidians and Nerren and Cilley probably made independent efforts to organize such a crowd.[33]

Although it is not clear whether Kashani or these figures were involved, a large crowd suddenly emerged near the Tehran bazaar in the late morning of August 19. The crowd attacked government office buildings and the offices of newspapers and political parties that supported Mussadiq. It was joined by army and police units and by onlookers who had become alarmed by the "Tudeh" demonstrations of the previous days. Realizing that events had turned decisively against him, Mussadiq refused to order his security forces to disperse the crowd. At the same time, an army unit seized the Tehran radio station and began to broadcast bulletins condemning Mussadiq and supporting Zahedi. An air force general led a column of tanks to the safe house where Zahedi was hiding and rescued him from the police units closing in around him. Military units and large groups of demonstrators then seized the army headquarters and marched on Mussadiq's home, where a nine-hour tank battle ensued. The walls around Mussadiq's house were destroyed and the house itself was stormed; some 300 people were killed. Mussadiq escaped into a neighbor's yard but surrendered to Zahedi's forces the next day. Several days later the shah returned to Iran and personally thanked Roosevelt, telling him, "I owe my throne to God, my people, my army—and to you."[34]

The shah's comment to Roosevelt seems to have been appropriate, for the United States did indeed play a key role in overthrowing Mussadiq and ending the threat he had posed to Iran's autocratic monarchical system. Roosevelt and his colleagues had planned, financed, and led the coup, taking decisive action after the attempt to arrest Mussadiq had failed that later made the coup successful. Zahedi, its nominal leader, hid in a CIA safe house almost until the coup had been completed. The shah was not consulted about the decision to undertake the coup, the manner of its execution, or the candidate chosen to replace Mussadiq, and he had been reluctant to support the coup and had fled the country at the first sign of failure. The British had played only a minor role in the coup, helping develop the initial plan for it—which failed—and directing the Rashidians to work with Roosevelt. Although the AIOC's oil boycott had weakened Iran's economy and thus helped undermine popular support for Mussadiq, many other outcomes could have resulted from Mussadiq's declining popularity. Zahedi and his allies had failed repeatedly to overthrow Mussadiq during the previous year. Although they might possibly have engineered a coup without US help, outstanding arrest warrants greatly hindered Zahedi's activities, and he had no real popular support. No other Iranian appears to have had the popularity of military connections necessary to carry out a coup without external backing. It therefore seems safe to conclude that the United States played a decisive role in overthrowing Mussadiq and severely weakening the political movement he led.

Conclusion

This chapter has emphasized that US security interests—as conceived by the Truman and Eisenhower administrations—required that Iran be kept in the Western camp during the cold war, and therefore it has implied that domestic political conditions in Iran could not be permitted to move beyond certain boundaries in the eyes of US policymakers. Under the Truman administration these boundaries initially were drawn rather broadly: Mussadiq did not seem to pose a threat to US interests, and US policymakers believed he could serve as an effective counterbalance to the Tudeh Party. However, these perceptions slowly changed as Mussadiq remained in power and unrest grew in Iran. When Eisenhower entered office, the more stridently anti-Communist views of his foreign policy advisers and the changing perceptions of Mussadiq among some holdovers from the Truman administration together led the United States to drop its support for Mussadiq and take steps to overthrow him. Consequently, US security interests associated with the cold war and changing views in Washington about how Mussadiq's regime affected these interests were responsible for the fateful US decision to undertake the August 1953 coup.

During the following decade these same considerations led US policymakers to provide extensive support to the shah, building up his autocratic regime as a bulwark against Soviet expansionism. Immediately after the coup they provided him with $68 million in emergency aid, amounting to roughly one third of the total revenue Iran had lost as a result of the British oil embargo. Over $300 million in additional US economic aid was given to Iran during the next ten years. After the coup US officials renewed their efforts to settle the oil dispute, fostering an agreement that permitted Iran to begin exporting oil again in late 1954. Iran's oil income grew quickly as a result of this agreement, exceeding total US aid receipts by 1958 and thereafter serving as the shah's main source of revenue. The United States also began a major effort to strengthen the shah's security forces soon after the coup, reorganizing and training his domestic intelligence apparatus and giving him almost $600 million in military assistance during the next decade.[35]

With the threat from Mussadiq and the National Front effectively contained, the economy growing rapidly, and an increasingly effective security apparatus in place, the shah consolidated his grip on power in the late 1950s and early 1960s. By late 1963 this process had been completed: The shah presided over an authoritarian regime under which organized opposition to his authority was not tolerated, and there seemed little chance that he would fall from power. However, many politicians were aware that Iranians deeply resented the shah's regime; they increasingly blamed the United States for restoring him to power in 1953 and then helping him to consolidate the new regime. This resentment generated a new challenge to the shah in the 1970s that differs from the one posed by Mussadiq: nondemocratic, violent, and deeply anti-American. This new challenge brought the shah's regime crashing down in the late 1970s and created a series of crises for the United States during the following decade that only recently have begun to subside.

The strategic considerations that led US policymakers to undertake the 1953 coup and then build up the shah's regime therefore helped set in motion a chain of events that later destroyed his regime and created severe problems for US interests. One can only hope that the end of the cold war will make it possible for the United States and other major powers to think more clearly about domestic political effects of their actions and thus avoid the kind of outcome that resulted from US policy toward Iran during this era.

Notes

1. Abraham Yeselson, *United States–Persian Diplomatic Relations, 1883–1921* (New Brunswick, N.J.: Rutgers University Press, 1956); John A. Denovo, *American Interests and Policies in the Middle East, 1900–1939* (Minneapolis: University of Minnesota Press, 1963), ch. 9.

2. T. Vail Motter, *United States Army in World War II: The Middle East Theater, the Persian Corridor, and Aid to Russia* (Washington, D.C.: Department of the Army, Office of the Chief of Military History, 1952); Mark Hamilton Lytle, *The Origins of the Iranian-American Alliance, 1941–1953* (New York: Holmes and Meier, 1987), chs. 2–4.

3. Bruce Robellet Kuniholm, *The Origins of the Cold War in the Near East* (Princeton: Princeton University Press, 1980), chs. 5–6.

4. US Joint Chiefs of Staff (hereinafter JCS), *United States Strategic Interests in Iran* (Washington, D.C.), JCS 1714/1, October 4, 1946, p. 6.

5. John Lewis Gaddis, *Strategies of Containment* (New York: Oxford University Press, 1982), chs. 2–3; US Department of State, *Foreign Relations of the United States, 1947*, vol. 5 (Washington, D.C.: US Government Printing Office, 1970), pp. 905ff.; ibid., 1948, vol. 5, pp. 170ff.; ibid., 1949, vol. 6, pp. 528ff.; US Agency for International Development, *U.S. Overseas Loans and Grants: Series of Yearly Data*, vols. 1–5 (Washington, D.C.: US Agency for International Development, 1984).

6. Rouhollah K. Ramazani, *Iran's Foreign Policy, 1941–1973: A Study of Foreign Policy in Modernizing Nations* (Charlottesville: University Press of Virginia, 1975), pp. 159–162; confidential interviews conducted by the author with several CIA officers stationed in Iran during this period.

7. Ervand Abrahamian, *Iran Between Two Revolutions* (Princeton: Princeton University Press, 1982), ch. 5. On Mussadiq's background and beliefs, see Farhad Diba, *Mohammad Mossadegh: A Political Biography* (London: Croom Helm, 1986); James A. Bill and Wm. Roger Louis, eds., *Mussadiq, Iranian Nationalism, and Oil* (Austin: University of Texas Press, 1988); and Homa Katouzian, ed., *Musaddiq's Memoirs* (London: JEBHE, National Movement of Iran, 1988).

8. US Department of State, *Foreign Relations of the United States, 1950,* vol. 5 (Washington, D.C.: US Government Printing Office, 1976), pp. 510, 523.

9. US National Security Council (hereinafter NSC), *United States Objectives and Programs for National Security,* NSC–68, April, 14 1950, reprinted in Thomas H. Etzold and John Lewis Gaddis, eds., *Containment: Documents on American Policy and Strategy* (New York: Columbia University Press, 1980), p. 434; Gaddis, *Strategies of Containment,* ch. 4.

10. US Department of State, *Foreign Relations of the United States, 1950,* vol. 5, pp. 509–529, 551, 604; confidential interviews conducted by the author with several retired CIA officers.

11. Mostafa Elm, *Oil, Power, and Principle: Iran's Oil Nationalization and Its Aftermath* (Syracuse, N.Y.: Syracuse University Press, 1992), chs. 4–5.

12. For a fuller examination of these activities, see Mark J. Gasiorowski, *U.S. Foreign Policy and the Shah: Building a Client State in Iran* (Ithaca: Cornell University Press, 1991), pp. 62–67.

13. NSC, *The Position of the United States with Respect to Iran,* NSC 107/2, June 27, 1951.

14. NSC, *National Security Problems Concerning Free World Petroleum Demand and Potential Supplies,* NSC 138, December 8, 1952, pp. 9–10.

15. Elm, *Oil, Power, and Principle,* ch. 8.

16. Henry Byroade, interview by author, Potomac, Maryland, August 7, 1984; "Record of Interdepartmental Meeting," March 20, 1951, Foreign Office (hereinafter FO) 371/91525; "View that HMG Should Refrain from Any Statement," August 26, 1951, FO/371/91582; "Approach to a New Persian Government," September 8, 1951, FO/371/91590; "Text of Reply from President Truman," September 26, 1951, FO/371/91591; CAB 128/20, pp. 231–234. All of these documents are from the British Public Records Office, London (hereinafter cited as PRO).

17. Elm, *Oil, Power, and Principle,* chs. 11–12, "American Proposal that the Royal Dutch/Shell Group Should Take Over and Operate the Abadan Refinery Considered Impractical," November 6, 1951, FO/371/91610 (PRO); Paul Nitze, interview by author, Washington, D.C., July 5, 1984.

18. "Qavam's Proposals," January 7, 1952, FO/371/98683 (PRO); "Intervention of Mr. Julian Amery," February 7, 1952, FO/371/98683 (PRO); "Qavam's Proposals," March 25, 1952, FO/371/98683 (PRO); "Internal Situation," n.d., FO/248/1531 (PRO); Sir George Middleton, interview by author, London, January 16, 1985.

19. Elm, *Oil, Power, and Principle,* ch. 16.

20. "Annual Report on Persian Army for 1952," September 12, 1952, FO/371/98638 (PRO); "Internal Situation," cited in note 18; *New York Times,* August 15, 1952, p. 2, and August 20, 1952, p. 1; Fitzroy Maclean, *Eastern Approaches* (London: Cape, 1950), p. 266; Henderson to Acheson, July 7 and 21, August 3, 4, and 15, and October 17, 1952, Record Group 84, Box 29. The latter documents are from the US National Archives, Washington (hereinafter cited as USNA).

21. "Internal Situation," cited in note 18; "Tribal Affairs and Tribal Policy," n.d., FO/248/1521 (PRO); "Intrigues Among the Bakhtiari Tribes," November 28, 1952, Record

Group 84, Box 28 (USNA); Middleton interview by author; Henderson to Acheson, September 9, 1952, Record Group 84, Box 29 (USNA).

22. Elm, *Oil, Power, and Principle,* pp. 244–246; confidential interviews conducted by the author with several retired CIA officers.

23. *New York Times,* October 13, 1952, p. 4, and October 16, 1952, p. 6; "Annual Report on Persian Army for 1952," December 9, 1952, FO/371/98638 (PRO).

24. Christopher Montague Woodhouse, *Something Ventured* (London: Granada, 1982), pp. 116–119; Kermit Roosevelt, interview by author, Washington, D.C., June 5, 1985, Henry Byroade, interview by author, Potomac, Md., August 7, 1984, and CIA officer who was working in Iran at the time, interview by author.

25. Gaddis, *Strategies of Containment,* ch. 5.

26. Interviews conducted by author with Henry Byroade and Gordon Mattison, Bethesda, Md., June 30, 1984, Roy Melbourne, Chapel Hill, N.C., February 1, 1984, and several CIA officers who worked in Iran at this time.

27. Kermit Roosevelt, *Countercoup: The Struggle for the Control of Iran* (New York: Mc-Graw-Hill, 1979), pp. 120–124; Roosevelt interview; confidential interview with the Iran specialist, August 5, 1984.

28. Henderson to Acheson, January 19, 1953, Record Group 59, Box 4117; "Internal Affairs," February 18, 1953, FO/371/104562 (PRO); "Internal Affairs," February 24, 1953, FO/371/104562 (PRO); "Internal Affairs," February 28, 1953, FO/371/104563 (PRO); "Dr. Musaddiq's Quarrel with the Shah," February 23, 1953, FO/371/104563 (PRO); "The Murder of Chief of Police Afshartus," May 8, 1953, FO/371/104566 (PRO); "Internal Situation," n.d., FO/371/104563 (PRO).

29. Confidential interviews with several retired CIA officers; Princess Ashraf Pahlavi, *Faces in a Mirror* (Englewood Cliffs, N.J.: Prentice Hall, 1980), pp. 134–140; Roosevelt, *Countercoup,* pp. 147–157.

30. Confidential interviews with several retired CIA officers.

31. Confidential interviews with several retired CIA officers. See also articles published in *The New York Times* during this period.

32. Ibid.

33. Ibid.

34. *New York Times,* August 20, 1953, p. 1, and August 21, 1953, p. 1; Roosevelt, *Countercoup,* p. 199.

35. Gasiorowski, *U.S. Foreign Policy and the Shah,* ch. 4.

4

The Mussadiq Era in Iran, 1951–1953
A Contemporary Diplomat's View

Sir Sam Falle

In the 1950s, I served Great Britain in Iran, Lebanon, and Iraq and at the Foreign Office in London on the Middle East oil desk. These postings gave me a worm's-eye view of a period of unprecedented change in the Middle East. There were revolutions in three countries: Iran, Iraq, and Egypt; I was present at the first two. The causes were intrinsically the same: resurgent nationalism against the British, who were, in any event, beginning to dismantle their empire and to dissociate themselves from their so-called stooges or puppets. In the midst of this change, the British and Americans shared the fundamental policy of denying the region to the Soviet Union while preserving oil supplies for the West, though sometimes they differed on the details. Both countries eventually came to agree on policy and methodology during the Muhammad Mussadiq crisis in Iran, a seminal event not only in Iran but also in the entire Middle East, especially in terms of the development of US foreign policy. In now turning to this episode, I take a different perspective from most who have commented on and written about the Mussadiq period.

When I arrived in Iran in 1949, the cold war was gathering impetus. The British had left India, and Prime Minister Clement Attlee's Labour government hoped for a steady and orderly transfer of power throughout the old empire. The United States had already become, by far, the most powerful country in the free world. The Middle East was disproportionately important, considering its relatively small population, because of its vast oil reserves and strategic position between the cold war adversaries. Arab nationalism, suppressed for many centuries by the Ottoman Empire and briefly by the British and French, was awakening. The Arabs, angry, wounded, and humiliated by the creation of Israel, still felt that they were not yet free from "imperialism." Iran had just emerged from World War II, during which it had in practice been partitioned between Britain and the Soviet Union. The British oil company, then known as the Anglo-Persian Oil Company (later Anglo-Iranian

Oil Company, or AIOC, and then British Petroleum), continued to take the major share of the profits of Iran's oil for itself and the British government.

Thus, the Iran to which I came in 1949 was uneasy. The Soviet threat remained in the north, and the British and their oil company in the south were regarded as imperialist oppressors, even though Anglo-Iranian official relations were correct. The British and also the Russians had deposed Iran's ruthless modernizing ruler, Reza Shah Pahlavi in 1941 for his pro-Nazi sympathies. His thirty-year-old son, Muhammad Reza Pahlavi, sat uneasily on the peacock throne. He had little of his father's courage or ruthlessness, and I suspect he was a reluctant tyrant in his later years. In 1952 he was summed up by one of my Iranian acquaintances: "His Majesty is very, very, weak."[1] At that time he was certainly vacillating and indecisive. Furthermore, he disliked the British for deposing his father; I wrote in an official minute, "The Shah hates our guts." However, on the positive side, it is worth noting that he reacted courageously and not vindictively to an attempt on his life by the Tudeh Party in February 1949. He neither lost his nerve nor ordered reprisals.

The AIOC had been exploiting Iranian oil since the beginning of the century. This cheap oil was of immense importance to the Royal Navy, which had converted from coal just before World War I. "Anglo-Persian" built a great refinery at Abadan on the Gulf and dominated the economic life of Iran. To be fair, it was a remarkable commercial enterprise, providing a living as well as tolerable working conditions for its Iranian employees and investing huge sums of money in Iran. Sadly, however, the leadership of the AIOC failed to understand the nationalist spirit of postwar Iran. More foresight on their part could have saved the United States, Britain, and Iran from a sea of troubles, certainly from Mussadiq and perhaps even from Ayatollah Khomeini. Here I pay tribute to the United States for the famous "golden gimmick," the ARAMCO (Arab-American Oil Company) 50–50 profit-sharing agreement with Saudi Arabia in December 1950, which recognized the fact that the host country would want at least an equal share of the profits; in Iran, the AIOC had actually been paying more taxes to the British government off its profits than it did royalties to the Iranian government. If only AIOC had been equally wise. In international terms it might have made sense for ARAMCO and the US government to have warned the AIOC and the British government in advance of the imminent deal with the Saudis, but this does not excuse us. It should have been obvious which way the wind was blowing. The AIOC had already signed the "supplemental agreement" with the Iranian government in July 1949 (supplemental because it affirmed and augmented the concession of 1933). Although this was an improvement over previous terms, it lacked the apparent clear-cut simplicity and fairness of 50–50 profit-sharing. The fact that the US tax system ensured that ARAMCO did better than AIOC would have under a similar agreement does not affect the main issue. Sir William Fraser, AIOC's boss, saw the danger and tried to dress up the supplemental agreement, but it was too late.

Ali Razmara, chief of staff of the army, was appointed prime minister by the shah in June 1950. He tried to get the supplemental agreement through the Majlis, the

Iranian parliament, but the Majlis forced its withdrawal in December 1950. Nationalism and strong feelings against the company were too strong, even for Razmara to combat, and in any event the ARAMCO 50–50 agreement finally scuppered the supplemental agreement. Razmara had been the best hope, indeed the last hope, for a settlement of the oil crisis anywhere near the AIOC's terms—or perhaps for any settlement at all. He was strong and capable, fully supported by the shah. He was a practical liberal nationalist, to use the jargon of the time. He was prepared to work with the British toward a solution, for which he has, of course, been condemned as an imperialist stooge. On the surface this was a time of relative calm in which a reasonably competent cabinet tried to move forward with a seven-year development plan. The cabinet ministers raised expectations of far-reaching reforms at all levels of Iranian society, and this was, of course, the moment for the AIOC to make an unequivocal 50–50 offer, although Razmara seemed to accept the supplemental agreement.

Razmara was assassinated in March 1951, presumably because of his efforts on behalf of the supplemental agreement. Dr. Muhammad Mussadiq became prime minister in April 1951 with tremendous popular support. His appeal was simple and straightforward: unequivocal nationalism, the nationalization of the oil industry, and the elimination of the AIOC's influence, indeed of all British influence, from Iran. His first act was oil nationalization, on May 2, 1951. This was a heady moment for Iran, and the rejoicing crowds cried, "Oil has been nationalized: Long Live Dr. Muhammad Mussadiq, Iran's beloved prime minister!" And they really meant it, because, at last, they could walk tall, the imperialists had been defeated, and the streets of Tehran would soon be paved with the gold that the AIOC had been stealing from them.

The AIOC was badly shaken but still hoped that the crisis could be solved by negotiation. They sent a representative, Basil Jackson, with a 50–50 offer, which was not accepted, perhaps partly because of its presentation but more so because of Mussadiq's aversion to the British and the company. His position, power, and popularity were based on his nationalization of the AIOC, and it was probably politically impossible for him to allow them to return, certainly not openly, perhaps not even in disguise. This is one of the most important factors in this story.

The United States viewed the crisis with alarm, not out of sympathy for the AIOC but out of fear that chaos and economic collapse in Iran could lead to a Tudeh takeover. This was a dominant theme. In July President Harry S Truman sent a most distinguished and able diplomat, Averell Harriman, as his special envoy to mediate. Mussadiq was better disposed toward the Americans than the British, and Harriman persuaded him to accept a British ministerial mission led by Cabinet Minister Sir Richard Stokes. This again failed; not so much because of its substance but partly on account of its presentation, and mostly because it was British. Indeed, the distinguished historian, Professor Wm. Roger Louis, writes: "It is debatable whether any Englishman, even of the stature of Mountbatten, could have successfully negotiated with Mussadiq."[2] Yet it was not as straightforward as that; the next offer after Stokes was from the World Bank, and it was also turned down on the grounds that it would infringe upon Iranian sovereignty. If we assume that Mussadiq, in his own very theatrical way, had the interests of Iran at heart, this was his first serious mistake. He had been entirely consistent in his opposition to the British for reasons that are easy to understand. But it was foolish to antagonize the Americans, who were fundamentally most sympathetic to him personally and to his ideas. But his rejection of the World Bank offer gave the Americans food for thought and made them understand how intensely different (and difficult) it was to negotiate with him.

On September 25, 1951, the British staff in Abadan were given notice to quit the country. The British government had considered the use of force to protect their great asset, but Prime Minister Attlee was opposed to this. The arguments against intervention were powerful and, if there were any doubt, certainly clinched by US opposition. The next occurrence was an international boycott of Iranian oil, which caused a shutdown of the Abadan refinery and the cessation of the flow of oil. I visited the refinery while it was shut down; nobody bothered me but it was an uncanny experience, seeing that vast complex, all silent and dead.

Early in 1952 I left Shiraz, from where I had followed the above events with increasing disquiet, to take up the post of Oriental Secretary in the British Embassy in Tehran. Things looked bleak but not completely hopeless. We were fortunate in having a brilliant chargé d'affaires, George Middleton, and a first-class, very wise, and experienced US ambassador, Loy Henderson. They worked well together. My job was political adviser and, when necessary, interpreter for Middleton. We were all three in sympathy with Iranian nationalism and recognized that, at that period in time, its personification was Mussadiq, although more and more rational and responsible Iranians were increasingly beginning to doubt his competence and to fear that he was leading the country to economic ruin. Middleton, like Mussadiq, was bilingual in French, and the personal relations between the two were excellent. They had many meetings, often exasperating for Middleton but personally agreeable. Middleton really liked "Mossy" and tried with immense perseverance to reach a settlement with him. I vividly recall one occasion when he returned from a marathon session almost elated: "I think we have done it at last, Sam." He sent his telegram to London describing the proposed settlement. I expressed some skepticism, to his annoyance, but two days later Mussadiq turned the whole idea on its head. This was typical and happened time and time again, but Middleton persisted until even he realized that Mussadiq was not prepared to make any deal. Even though Middleton was British, Mossy liked him back, for he was modern-minded and saw the Iranian point of view. Mussadiq would have been wise to use this able and sympathetic interlocutor in order to move toward agreement, but he always balked at the last moment.

The next significant episode during this period was the Ahmad Qavam interlude in July 1952, when this elder statesman briefly took Mussadiq's place as prime minister. This tends to be represented as a last, desperate attempt by the British to replace Mussadiq with their own man. I was in the thick of all this and can attest that the facts were very different. We were in no position either to depose Mussadiq or impose Qavam, although it was clearly in our interest that he should take over. He was as much of a nationalist as Mussadiq but more restrained, and he regarded the Soviet Union rather than Britain as the principal threat to Iran. Mussadiq's resignation on July 16 was precipitated by the shah's refusal to agree to his prime minister's request for control of the armed forces, which constituted the shah's principal source of influence. Qavam's five-day stay as prime minister is a story in itself. Briefly, however, he fell because the shah lost his nerve, failed to support him, and succumbed to a Tudeh-controlled mob. Both Henderson and Middleton believed Qavam could have held if the shah had backed him. He had considerable support among thinking Iranians. Middleton wrote: "The Shah was in the grip of fear: fear of taking a decision that might expose him to the fury of the populace, should Qavam not, in the event, remain in control. This attitude of the Shah is one of the central features of this crisis; we had long known that he was indecisive and timid, but we had not thought that his fear would so overcome his reason as to make him blind to the consequences of *not* supporting Qavam" (emphasis added). There is more in the same vein and I do not want to belabor the point, but it is important because popular mythology holds that Qavam was doomed from the beginning and his prime ministership was one more example of British stupidity and failure to move with the times. Middleton also wrote:

> The Shah defended his prerogatives against Mussadiq to the point of the latter's resignation and then he began to get cold feet at once and very nearly discouraged the Opposition from voting for Qavam. When the Opposition [in the Majlis] proved encouragingly firm and voted for Qavam, he refused him the support he required to stabilize the situation. When, despite his hesitancy, his troops remained loyal and effective, in the face of physical attacks and powerful propaganda, [contrary to the mythology] he withdrew his backing from them and exposed their commanders to the risks of savage reprisals. He hates taking decisions and cannot be relied upon to stick to them when taken; he has no moral courage and easily succumbs to fear; he is preoccupied with his personal position on the Throne and thinks to retain it by a policy of appeasement; and, I am now convinced, we must see in him a deep-rooted dislike and distrust of the British. He has constantly ignored all sound advice given to him by responsible Persian statesmen and by the United States Ambassador and myself, and is swayed by the advice of his Minister of Court who, I suspect, echoes His Majesty's doubts and fears.

Even Middleton, who had been prepared to give Mussadiq the benefit of every possible doubt, had reached the end of the road, although he was always prepared to go on talking. He wrote:

> If we look beyond this crisis and take a wider view it is clear that the responsibility for Persia's present ills lies principally with Mussadiq and his entourage. His strength lies in his power of demagogy, and he has so flattered the mob as the source of his power that he has, [I fear,] made it impossible for a successor to oust him by normal constitu-

tional methods. His followers, and principally Ayatollah Kashani, have probably gone further than he intended on enlisting the support of the Tudeh for Monday's trial of strength. The chief question now facing us is whether Mussadiq's government or any other (short of a military dictatorship) can avoid the "kiss of death" which is the well-known consequence of flirting with communists.

So Mussadiq returned in triumph on the shoulders of the mob and with the backing of the Tudeh Party. The shah acceded to all of Mussadiq's demands, which he had previously refused, and he became steadily more helpless and terrified. Although Middleton had more or less given up hope for Mussadiq, this was not yet the US position, although Loy Henderson and George Middleton were generally pretty close in their assessments.

When I came to Tehran at the beginning of that year (1952), support for Mussadiq was by no means monolithic. He had, of course, touched the nationalist chord, which was full of resentment against imperialism and the desire of a once great nation to be respected again. But he had delivered nothing positive; he had destroyed but he had not built up, and he had cut off almost all of Iran's revenues. He had not known when to close a deal and had constantly asked for more. He must have understood that, although the US government was sympathetic to him personally and to his nationalist aspirations, there were limits to even its generosity. It could not afford to conclude an agreement that would start a vast series of renegotiations with the world's oil producers. At the same time, he was well aware of US concern that Iran might turn to communism. So he decided to go on bargaining and came with an unacceptable counterbid to the Truman-Churchill proposal of September 1952. This proposal stated that the amount of compensation should be subject to arbitration, that the Iranian government and the AIOC should negotiate on the resumption of oil production, and that the United States would grant $10 million in budgetary aid. Mussadiq demanded £50 million as an advance against oil. The proposal ultimately failed and certainly reinforced a negative view of Mussadiq.

Another major player in all this was General Fazlollah Zahedi. He seemed like a possible focus of opposition to Mussadiq and possibly even a successor. He had been imprisoned by the British during World War II for pro-Nazi activities, a strong point in his favor, from the point of view of most Iranians, for having been on record as opposing the British. Both Middleton and I met him and were favorably impressed. He was tough, clearheaded, and rational. October 1952 was a tense time and ended in the severance of diplomatic relations between Iran and Britain. (It is worth mentioning that, throughout this difficult time for Anglo-Iranian relations, we were never personally harassed and I did not feel any danger or threat.)

I next went to Washington, D.C., as a member of a small delegation to discuss Iran. Many in Washington still thought that Mussadiq was the last, best hope; we disagreed, believing that his remaining in power would lead to a Communist takeover.

What happened in 1953 is now well known: the overthrow of Mussadiq; the restoration of the shah, who had fled for a brief period; and the establishment of a pro-Western government in Tehran under General Zahedi. This was followed by the remarkable consortium oil agreement, which reflects the greatest credit on all concerned and even enabled AIOC to obtain 40 percent of the consortium with handsome compensation.

It is a widely held view among those interested in the history of the Middle East that it was a grave mistake to depose Mussadiq. It is interesting to speculate what would have happened if the Democrats had won in the United States in 1952. Democrat Adlai Stevenson, as president, would presumably have retained Dean Acheson as secretary of state and George C. McGhee as assistant secretary of state for Near East and South Asian affairs and continued to negotiate with Mussadiq. It is impossible to predict whether they would have succeeded, bearing in mind that there were limits to what the United States could concede. Mussadiq did indeed reject the "final offer" by the Republicans on March 10, 1953. With hindsight it could conceivably have been better to continue until some sort of agreement was reached with Mussadiq, but we shall never know. I very much doubt it, even today.

Let us go back forty years. The Korean War had just ended; World War III had been avoided. It was thought at the time that a Communist takeover of Iran would have been a disaster of appalling magnitude and might indeed have led to global conflict. It is questionable whether the United States could have tolerated the Soviet Union on the Gulf. One cannot in any way compare this scenario with what actually happened: a pro-Western government until 1979 and, thereafter, the irritant of Khomeini, who was impartial in his hatred of the superpowers. It was impossible to predict in 1953 that the shah, who was in a relatively strong position at the time of his restoration, could have developed into such a disagreeable tyrant, nor could we have foreseen Khomeini. We saw the immediate danger, and I remain completely convinced that it was right and, indeed, vital, *given the circumstances of the time,* to topple Mussadiq.

While we are considering "what ifs," there is another, intriguing possibility. Let us imagine that the AIOC and the British government had listened to their wisest advisers. A 50–50 oil agreement would have been concluded between the AIOC and the Iranian government no later than 1950. It seems highly probable that Mussadiq would never have come to power. Iran would have become prosperous some five years earlier, and the poverty, misery, and political instability of the Mussadiq years would have been avoided. The shah's throne would not have been threatened, and there would have been far less reason for a passionate, xenophobic nationalist movement. In spite of Iran's endemic corruption, some of the oil wealth would have gone toward development and even filtered down to the people years earlier. It is possible that the weak shah, not having been threatened and terrified to the extent he was during the Mussadiq period, might have developed into a capable and benevolent ruler. He seemed genuinely to want to help his people, and his tyranny was probably motivated by fear as much as anything. So perhaps there would have been less opposition to him, and perhaps he would have survived. Nevertheless, he would still have tried to Westernize too fast, angering the *mullahs,* and his family would have been no less corrupt. Then we can ask whether tough US support could have saved him at the end of the 1970s.

Many scholars have criticized US and British policy vis-à-vis Mussadiq. Their arguments, in summary, are as follows: Mussadiq was a rare phenomenon in Iran in that he was both honest and a democrat. He represented resurgent Iranian nationalism and was both beloved and respected by the Iranian people. He was not a Communist—far from it—and he came from the landed ruling class, although he differed in his humanity and caring approach. Consequently, he was exactly the sort of leader whom the West should have supported, since he stood for nonviolent, progressive change. This was precisely what was needed to combat communism and lead Iran to true freedom and prosperity. Such an Iran would have been friendly to the United States. For the wrong reasons, however, the US government deposed Mussadiq, supported the increasingly tyrannical shah, and thereby helped to bring about the Khomeini revolution, with all its unfortunate consequences for US-Iranian relations. The corollary to this argument is that an oil deal should have been made with Mussadiq, whatever the cost; or, even if this had proved impossible in the medium term, he should have been supported as our last, best hope in Iran and a bulwark against communism.

This chapter spells out the case that favored the deposing of Mussadiq. Clearly it would have been more desirable and in the interests of the United States, Iran, and, indeed, Britain if we could have made a reasonably satisfactory deal with Mussadiq. It might even, with the benefit of hindsight, have been better to make a poor deal than no deal at all. There were, however, limits beyond which it would have been impossible to go without upsetting the global oil business. Maybe it would have been worth it, and the cost to the United States might have been less than that of the Khomeini revolution. It is difficult to say, but, in my opinion, Mussadiq turned down some good offers that might have prevented the crisis.

In 1952 we were very worried about the Soviet, Chinese, and world Communist threats, with extremely good reason: Tensions were high and real. There was the Korean War and Stalin was still alive in all his psychopathic and dangerous malevolence. At the time, the prospect of a communist Iran was alarming and, we thought, could have led to World War III.

The US government was anxious to see, at least up to our visit to Washington in November 1952, that Mussadiq remain in office. It was with reluctance, and after the rejection of its final offer in March 1953, that it decided to support the coup. As for Mussadiq himself, he was probably an honest, sincere Iranian nationalist. He was certainly a brilliant demagogue. It is questionable, to say the least, whether he was capable of running Iran. Many Iranians—by no means all "lackeys of the imperialists"—to whom we spoke at the time were convinced of the contrary. There was a sort of mob rule. To this day, I remain utterly convinced that the Communist danger was too great to ignore and would have produced knee-jerk reactions that could have led to global catastrophe. Not only our intelligence services but an enlightened liberal of the caliber of George Middleton, who tried desperately to reach agreement with Mussadiq, were in no doubt that the lovable old man had to go.

To conclude on a personal note: In the British Foreign Service I was known as "Red Sam." This was because I believed in liberal causes, resurgent nationalism, and the like. Later I was a fervent supporter of both Egyptian President Gamal 'Abd al-Nasser and the Iraqi nationalists. Thus, Dr. Mussadiq was initially a man after my own heart, and I am on record as a remorseless critic of the AIOC. The fact that even I eventually became convinced that he had to be replaced says something; all my beliefs, or, if you like, prejudices, were in the other direction—on his side. Sadly, he could not control the Communists, and they would have removed him from power and replaced him with one of their own.

The Mussadiq crisis of 1951–1953, and, as I see it, the first Iranian revolution, led to two contradictory and consequently misleading conclusions. First, the strength of nationalism and the need for foreign governments and commercial enterprises to come to terms with it were clearly demonstrated. The second point, however, is that foreign powers were nevertheless able to depose at will uncooperative governments in Third World countries. The latter was highly dangerous and led to grievous miscalculation in the 1956 Suez crisis when, as in Iraq in 1958, the former was ignored.

Notes

1. These and other quotes contained in this chapter are gleaned from the personal records of the author.

2. Wm. Roger Louis, *The British Empire in the Middle East, 1945–1951 (Oxford: Clarendon, 1984), p. 652.*

5

National Security Concerns in US Policy Toward Egypt, 1949–1956

Peter Hahn

From the late 1940s through the Suez crisis of 1956, US officials faced a bewildering variety of security problems with regard to Egypt. In the late 1940s, a bitter dispute raged between Great Britain, a cold war partner that wished to remain in possession of its military base facilities in the Suez Canal Zone, and Egypt, a nationalistic state that sought to escape British military occupation. Each side sought US endorsement of its position in this dispute, which remained unsolved into the early 1950s. After the Egyptian revolution of 1952, President Gamal 'Abd al-Nasser negotiated the departure of British forces from his country and challenged the remnants of Western imperialism elsewhere in the region. US officials found it impossible to reconcile Nasser's nationalism to their security interests in the Middle East and therefore sought to undermine his prestige and influence in the region. When Britain decided to wage war on Egypt in late 1956, however, US officials took steps to halt the attack on the grounds of US national security. From the late 1940s to 1956, Washington consistently made policy toward Egypt on the basis of its security interests.

During the decades preceding World War II, Egypt emerged as a region of strategic importance to the British Empire. Britain militarily occupied Egypt in 1882 in order to protect the Suez Canal and lines of communication to India, and it gained enormous advantages during World War I by closing the canal to the Central Powers and by staging troops in Egypt for the Gallipoli and Jerusalem campaigns. Having legally secured the right to occupy Egypt through the 1936 Anglo-Egyptian treaty, the British used the Suez Canal Zone during World War II to deny Axis forces in North Africa easy access to oil fields in the Middle East, to ensure vital communications and transit between the Indian Ocean and the Mediterranean, and to develop a major base that boasted airfields, supply dumps, repair shops, and personnel facilities. At war's end, nearly 200,000 British troops were stationed in the Canal Zone base.[1]

US officials who examined the security situation in the Middle East during the early years of the cold war recognized the immense potential strategic importance of Egypt. As international tensions escalated during 1945 and 1946, defense officials identified the British base in the Suez Canal Zone as a facility of vital importance. In the event of war against the Soviet Union, they reasoned, Western access to the base would prove essential to victory. To promote national security, in other words, US officials would support London's quest to maintain its base in Egypt.

The US-Soviet confrontation over Turkey in 1946 first attracted the attention of Pentagon officials to Egypt. "Any action which threatens Britain's control of the Suez Canal and deprives her of a sizable portion of the Middle East oil fields," the Joint War Plans Committee (JWPC) observed, "threatens her position as a world power." Soviet conquest of the Suez Canal "would have serious adverse effects upon British capabilities in a major war."[2]

Contingency war plans devised in the Pentagon in 1946 also stressed the importance of maintaining access to British air bases in Egypt. In the event of hostilities, according to a war plan code-named PINCHER, US bombers would attack the Soviet Union's oil industry in order to cripple its war-making capability. Bombers would need air bases in Egypt in order to reach a sufficient number of vulnerable targets in the southern Soviet Union. Bombers dispatched from England, Pakistan, or Japan would lack the range to strike such targets. From airfields in the Suez Canal Zone, Western bombers could reach Moscow, the "nerve center" of Soviet power, and a host of other valuable targets. "Early availability of secure V[ery] H[eavy] B[omber] operating bases in the Cairo area," the war plan MAKEFAST added in late 1946, "is essential to the attainment of the strategic air offensive objectives."[3]

Military bases in Egypt also possessed other attractive features. Pentagon planners were confident that bases in the Canal Zone could be defended against the southward Soviet thrust anticipated in the opening stages of war. Egypt's proximity to the Soviet Union qualified it as a staging area for offensive operations into south-central Russia. The Suez Canal corridor enabled provision of the country from the Indian Ocean should the enemy close the Mediterranean. Egypt would likely emerge as a base for psychological warfare measures targeted especially at secessionists in southern Russia. As the JWPC stressed, the importance of possessing bases in Egypt "can hardly be over-emphasized."[4]

Pentagon planners confirmed the importance of British bases in Egypt as the cold war escalated in 1948 and 1949. In June 1948, during the Berlin crisis, the Joint Strategic Planning Group (JSPG) observed that facilities in Egypt needed to defeat the Soviet Union in war "far exceed[ed] those envisaged" in earlier plans. In July, the Joint Chiefs of Staff (JCS) stressed that Egypt remained essential "as a base from which to initiate an air offensive against vital elements of the Soviet warmaking capacity." In December, army officers recognized Egypt's "important role" in any military engagement in the Middle East. In March 1949, US Secretary of Defense James Forrestal confirmed Egypt's abiding importance to US national security. "In the event of global war," the National Security Council (NSC) resolved in late 1949, after the Chinese Communist revolution and the Soviet detonation of an atomic bomb, "the United States would probably wish to use facilities in the Cairo-Suez area in conjunction with the British." Indeed, army planners presumed, "should emergency dictate, the U.S. will avail itself of any facilities held by the British."[5]

From 1950 to 1953, the strategic value of British facilities in Egypt diminished slightly but remained significant. The development of long-range aircraft reduced the importance of Egypt as a launching point for any strategic air offensive against Soviet targets, but the country remained vital as a poststrike landing-and-refueling point for heavy bombers launched from Britain and as a defensive barrier, supply depot, and staging area. Renovations at Abu Sueir, Canal Zone (started in 1949 and completed in 1952) made it the only air base in the Middle East capable of handling heavy bombers. US military officials secretly stockpiled supplies at Abu Sueir and Cairo International Airport. In the eyes of US strategists, national security dictated that British military facilities in Egypt remain accessible to Western powers in the event of war.[6]

US interest in maintaining British military facilities in Egypt for national security reasons conflicted with US interest in mollifying Egyptian nationalism for political reasons. In the late 1940s, Egyptian nationalists began to challenge Britain's presence in their country. Specifically, they demanded revision or abrogation of the 1936 Anglo-Egyptian treaty that authorized the British base in the Canal Zone. Extensive Anglo-Egyptian negotiations in the late 1940s failed to reach a settlement, and nationalists turned to other tactics, including work stoppages, boycotts, and terrorist attacks, to compel the British to leave. Until the early 1950s, Britain resisted the Egyptian demands, and a deadlock ensued.[7]

The Anglo-Egyptian conflict confronted the United States with a thorny dilemma. Some officials of the US Department of State wanted to recognize Egyptian national aspirations in order to ensure the loyalty of the Egyptian people and other Third World nations in the cold war as well as to honor the US ideal of self-determination. To Pentagon officials, however, a British departure from Egypt, in the absence of satisfactory promises by Egypt to allow access to its bases, would imperil national security.[8]

US officials considered access to military bases in Egypt so vital that they repeatedly subsumed their conflicting political interests in Egypt. In May 1946, for example, US officials interceded on London's behalf in Anglo-Egyptian negotiations that had stalemated over the question of Britain's right to return to bases in Egypt after it departed the country. US Secretary of State James Byrnes told King Farouk that he hoped Egypt would avoid "running the risk of undermining the security of the Middle East" in its quest for "full sovereignty." Egypt's hostile reaction to that message made US officials reluctant to intercede again, but they quietly encouraged the British to remain firm in negotiations with Cairo.[9]

In preparation for the Anglo-American "Pentagon talks" of October 1947, US Department of Defense officials insisted that the United States endorse Britain's position in Egypt for reasons of national security. Despite their fears that angering Egyptian nationalists might undermine the very Western interests that the Pentagon wished to preserve, officials at Foggy Bottom agreed. At the talks, State Department officials suggested that Britain appease Egyptian nationalism by agreeing in principle to withdraw eventually from Egypt, but they relented easily when British officials protested that this step would signal weakness. US and British officials agreed that "the British should have the right to maintain [in Egypt] . . . certain strategic facilities . . . during peacetime in such a condition that they could be effectively and speedily used in case of an immediate threat to the security of the Middle East." It would be "dangerous in the present world situation for the British Government to abandon such strategic facilities to which it is entitled by treaty in Egypt." In these Anglo-American talks—conducted as the cold war was intensifying—US officials sacrificed their interest in appeasing nationalism to national security considerations.[10]

US officials showed slightly more concern for Egyptian nationalism in 1949. Because Egypt blamed the United States for the creation of Israel, the war in Palestine had embittered Cairo against Washington. To avoid further alienation, US officials refused a British request to participate in talks between British and Egyptian military officers about the future of the British bases in the Canal Zone. By early 1950, however, State Department officials again interceded in Anglo-Egyptian negotiations to urge the government of Egyptian Prime Minister Mustapha Nahas to recognize that Western defense rights in Egypt were consonant with Egyptian sovereignty. "If Egypt insists that Britain withdraw her troops from the Suez zone," Assistant Secretary of State George C. McGhee told the Egyptian ambassador, "it would result in a weakening of Egypt's military strength at precisely a time when Egypt desires to increase her powers of resistance." In July, following the eruption of the Korean War, McGhee refused an Egyptian appeal for support in negotiations with London, instead warning that "Russian aggression in the Near Eastern area" loomed possible, in which case "it would be essential to our common strategic plans to have the British on the spot."[11]

In late 1950 and early 1951, however, US officials came to fear that unmollified Egyptian nationalism might abet the rise of neutralism in that state and throughout the Middle East. "The Near Eastern nations are at a point of decision," Samuel K.C. Kopper, deputy director of the Division of Near Eastern Affairs, noted in December 1950, "as to whether to cast their lot irrevocably with the West, to remain neutral, or to drift into the Soviet orbit." Pressuring Egyptian leaders to align with the West, McGhee concluded in early 1951, was bound to fail. A compromise solution to the base dispute, McGhee realized, "would outweigh the present advantages of the British position."[12]

In 1951, therefore, US officials devised the Middle East Command (MEC) concept to bridge the gap between strategic and political interests in Egypt. The MEC idea envisioned a multilateral, anti-Soviet defense arrangement that would include Egyptian military officers with headquarters in Cairo. Unfortunately, the chance that Egypt would approve MEC diminished in the summer of 1951, when the United Nations (UN) Security Council, at the behest of Britain and France, passed a resolution censuring Egyptian restrictions on canal shipping destined for Israel.

Before Western powers found the time to propose MEC to the government in Cairo, Prime Minister Nahas had commenced parliamentary procedures to nullify the 1936 Anglo-Egyptian treaty. Egypt summarily rejected MEC.[13]

State Department officials were deeply troubled by Egypt's rejection of MEC, by its abrogation of the treaty, and by a wave of violence between British troops and Egyptian guerrillas in late 1951 and early 1952. The turmoil helped trigger the revolution of July 1952, in which a clique of military officers led by Gamal 'Abd al-Nasser ousted King Farouk. Alarmed by the parallel rise of revolutionary nationalism in Egypt and Iran, Secretary of State Dean G. Acheson feared that the entire Middle East might turn hostile to the West unless Britain made concessions to end its impasse with Egypt. Pentagon officials, on the other hand, favored fully endorsing Britain's stubborn position. The NSC reconciled these positions by resolving in April 1952 "to induce the U.K. to modify its position in ways which, while maintaining basic Western interests, might make possible an early negotiated settlement." But Britain would not be induced to make any concessions, and the Anglo-Egyptian impasse persisted into 1953. In light of national security requirements, US officials refrained from strongly pressuring the British to make those concessions that might have served the US political interest of mollifying Egyptian nationalism.[14]

In 1952 and 1953, changing circumstances in the Middle East and elsewhere rendered the Canal Zone military base less essential to US and British security. British officials concluded in late 1952 that Soviet development of atomic weapons made it dangerous to concentrate 80,000 soldiers in a single base site within Soviet bomber range. Attacks by Egyptian guerrilla fighters, moreover, inflicted severe human, psychological, and financial costs. The Canal Zone base, though still important, seemed to the British no longer indispensable. They decided to move their headquarters to Cyprus, relocate troops to the home isles, and rely on rapid air transit in the event of an emergency.[15]

Similar ideas developed on the western shore of the Atlantic. When Turkey joined the North Atlantic Treaty Organization (NATO) in 1952, the Pentagon began thinking about shifting its Middle East security focus from Egypt to the northern tier of the region. After Pakistan joined the Southeast Asia Treaty Organization (SEATO) in 1954, a northern tier pact offered to complete a chain of anti-Soviet pacts from East Asia to northern Europe. The governments of the northern tier seemed more ready than Arab states such as Egypt to cooperate with Western defense plans. More secure than the lone, gigantic base at Suez, a series of smaller facilities scattered along the Soviet perimeter also provided advantages in intelligence collection and offensive capabilities. For example, Thor and Jupiter missiles, developed in the mid-1950s, could carry nuclear payloads but for only short distances.[16]

In 1953, President Dwight D. Eisenhower and Secretary of State John Foster Dulles approved a shift in US strategic focus from Egypt to the northern tier. Conversations during a tour of the Middle East in the spring of 1953 convinced Dulles that Egypt, beset by rampant forces of nationalism, would not serve as a reliable security partner but that northern tier states would. Turkey and Pakistan, he observed, would serve as cornerstones of a defense pact of states that "are most conscious of the Soviet threat and most disposed to cooperate with western powers." Dulles declared the original MEC idea to be "on the shelf." In 1954, US Air Force officials canceled planned improvements at the Abu Sueir airfield. The northern tier idea came to fruition with the signing of a Turkish-Iraqi pact in Baghdad on February 24, 1955. Britain joined the Baghdad Pact in April 1955; Pakistan joined in September and Iran in October.[17]

In light of Egypt's diminished strategic importance, US officials pressed the British to make concessions needed to break their deadlock with Egypt. With strong US urging, a reluctant Churchill government approved a base treaty in July 1954 (signed in October 1954). The accord terminated the 1936 treaty, provided for withdrawal of British forces over twenty months, permitted British civilian technicians to maintain the base, and authorized the British military to return in the event of Soviet attack on Turkey or any Arab state. British forces completed their departure in June 1956.[18]

US officials hoped that Nasser, with his independence secured, would cooperate with Western security plans, endorse the northern tier pact, and eventually join it. "We are counting on Egypt," Deputy Assistant Secretary of State John D. Jernegan noted on August 16, 1954, "to play an important leadership role . . . in the achievement of United States policy objectives in the Middle East." Nasser talked about forming an Arab League collective security pact and Dulles suggested linking this pact to the northern tier arrangement via an Egyptian-Turkish mutual defense treaty. Nasser's initial reaction and his acceptance of $40 million in US economic aid in late 1954 encouraged US hopes that Nasser would become a security partner.[19]

By early 1955, however, such US optimism seemed unfounded. Nasser refused to accept US military aid because of the standard condition that a US military mission would administer it, a condition that to him smacked of colonialism. He also rejected a secret US plan, which would have violated congressional rules for administering aid, to divert $5 million of the $40 million in economic aid to military hardware purchases.[20]

As negotiations on military aid stalemated, Nasser emerged as a thorn in America's side in the Middle East. He reversed himself on the northern tier idea and became a chief critic of the Baghdad Pact. He claimed as Egypt's mission the riddance of Western imperialism from the Middle East. He reacted strongly to Israeli provocations and responded coolly to the Anglo-American "Alpha" peace plan. In the absence of US military aid grants, Nasser purchased a massive quantity of arms from the Soviet Union in September 1955.[21]

Eisenhower and Dulles at first tried to appeal to Nasser by offering to finance construction of the Aswan dam, and they tried to pacify the Egyptian-Israeli situation by sending special emissary Robert Anderson to broker a deal in early 1956. But Nasser would neither accept the conditions of the dam aid offer nor cooperate fully with the Anderson mission. Worse, in early 1956, he encouraged anti-British rioters in Jordan and Bahrain, continued to criticize the Baghdad Pact, bought weapons from Poland, and recognized the People's Republic of China. NSC officials concluded that Nasser's "positive neutralism actually works in favor of the Soviet bloc since it is directed against established western positions."[22]

US officials had concluded by March 1956 that, despite their efforts to woo Nasser, he had emerged as a threat to their national security interests in the Middle East. With the British, therefore, they concocted the Omega policy, a series of steps designed to undercut Nasser's prestige among Arab peoples and possibly to remove him from power. Omega would "let Colonel Nasser realize," Dulles noted, "that he cannot cooperate as he is doing with the Soviet Union and at the same time enjoy most-favored-nation treatment from the United States." Omega planned for the gradual withdrawal of the Aswan aid offer, but in July, under strong congressional pressure, Dulles canceled the deal abruptly. Nasser retaliated against the Aswan renege by nationalizing the Suez Canal Company and announcing that its revenues would finance the dam.[23]

Nasser's seizure of the canal company provoked the Suez Crisis of late 1956. The British at once resolved to use force to recover control of the waterway and knock Nasser from power, and they eventually conspired with the French and the Israelis to launch a tripartite attack against Egypt that began October 29. President Eisenhower, by contrast, decided early in the crisis that force would threaten US national security interests. A British attack on Egypt would foment Anglophobia around the world, inflame Arab nationalism (and thus imperil oil supplies to the West), and result in a long and costly British occupation of the Suez Canal Zone. For the United States to allow London to wage war on Egypt, Eisenhower told the NSC on July 31, "might well array the world from Dakar to the Philippine Islands against us." A breach with London would "be extremely serious, but not as serious as letting a war start and not trying to stop it."[24]

Accordingly, Eisenhower sought to use diplomacy to delay a British attack, on the calculation that time would cool British tempers and avert war. In late July he dispatched Deputy Under Secretary of State for Political Affairs Robert Murphy and Dulles to London to soothe British anger. In August, Eisenhower and Dulles arranged the London Conference to devise a diplomatic solution to the question of control of the canal, in September they proposed establishment of a Suez Canal Users Association to govern the waterway, and in October they encouraged Britain and Egypt to resolve their differences through negotiations sponsored by the United Nations. Eisenhower also publicly and privately appealed to British Prime Minister Anthony Eden to practice restraint. "The use of force," he cabled Eden on September 3, "would . . . vastly increase the area of jeopardy." The developing world "would be consolidated against the West to a degree which, I fear, could not be overcome in a generation and, perhaps, not even in a century."[25]

Once hostilities began on October 29, Eisenhower moved to end the fighting promptly for three national security reasons. First, he regretted that the attack on Egypt diverted global attention from Moscow's brutal crushing of the rebellion in

Hungary. Second, he feared that the Soviets would politically support Egypt and thereby win favor among developing nations. Unless the United States ended the fighting, Dulles observed, "all of these newly independent countries will turn from us to the USSR. We will be looked upon as forever tied to British and French colonialist policies." "How can we possibly support Britain and France," Eisenhower added, "if in so doing we lose the entire Arab world." US inaction would enable the Soviet Union to seize "a mantle of world leadership through a false but convincing exhibition of concern for smaller nations."[26]

Third, Eisenhower gravely worried about Soviet threats to intervene militarily to defend Egypt. On November 5, one day after crushing the rebellion in Budapest, Moscow threatened to send troops to Egypt and to fire rockets on London and Paris. The JCS interpreted this statement as "serious intent on the part of the Soviets." Eisenhower observed that Soviet leaders were "scared and furious" over Hungary, "and there is nothing more dangerous than a dictatorship in this frame of mind." The president warned Moscow that the United States would defend its allies, but he also tightened his diplomatic and financial squeezes to convince Britain and France to halt the fighting. Both powers accepted a UN cease-fire on November 6.[27]

From the mid-1940s to the mid-1950s, US officials consistently made policy toward Egypt on grounds of national security. From 1946 to 1953, the overriding strategic importance of British military facilities in Egypt compelled them actively and passively to endorse Britain's determination to remain in the Suez Canal Zone over Egypt's strong opposition. Such security concerns, in light of the cold war and the Korean War, convinced officials in Washington to subsume their conflicting political interest in befriending Egyptian nationalism. Only when the move to the northern tier diminished the strategic importance of Egypt did US officials find it safe to pressure Britain to reach a settlement providing for withdrawal of British forces from the Suez Canal Zone.

After the 1954 Anglo-Egyptian treaty, US officials hoped to win Nasser's cooperation with their plans for securing the Middle East against Soviet expansion. But Nasser refused US overtures and emerged as a leading critic of Western influence in the region. Therefore, again for reasons of national security, US officials together with the British initiated the Omega policy to undermine Nasser's prestige in the Middle East and, perhaps, even his power in Cairo.

National security concerns also determined US behavior during the Suez crisis of late 1956. Fear that the Soviet Union would gain politically or intervene militarily compelled Eisenhower to oppose British plans for war against Nasser and then to use his power to halt the attack once it began. Contrary to its political concerns, the United States censured its British ally and rescued Nasser from aggression during the Suez conflict. Such actions were entirely consistent with Washington's national security imperatives, which prevailed, as before, over its competing political interests.

Notes

1. D. A. Farnie, *East and West of Suez: The Suez Canal in History* (Oxford: Clarendon, 1969), pp. 32–93; and Peter Mansfield, *The British in Egypt* (London: Weidenfeld and Nicolson, 1971), pp. 201–219, 265–275.

2. JWPC 450/3, 10 March 1946, Record Group (RG) 218, Records of the Joint Chiefs of Staff, CCS 092 USSR (3–27–45), section 6 (hereinafter RG 218 with appropriate filing designations), National Archives, Washington, D.C. (hereinafter National Archives).

3. "PINCHER," JPS 789, 2 March 1946, US Department of Defense, Joint Chiefs of Staff, Records of the Joint Chiefs of Staff: Soviet Union (Washington, D.C.: University Publications Microfilm, 1978), reel 1; and "Air Plan for MAKEFAST," n.d. [autumn 1946], RG 165, Records of the Army Staff, ABC 381 USSR (2 March 1946), section 3, National Archives.

4. JWPC 450/3, 10 March 1946, RG 218, CCS 092 USSR (3–27–45), section 7. See also JIS 226/3, 4 March 1946, RG 218, CCS 092 USSR (3–27–45), section 5.

5. JSPC 684/40, 2 June 1948, RG 319, Records of the Army Staff, P&O 686 TS, case 1, National Archives (hereafter RG 319 with appropriate filing designations); JCS 1887/1, 28 July 1948, RG 218, CCS 381 EMMEA (11–19–47); unsigned report on Egyptian airfields, 1 December 1948, RG 319, P&O 686, case 273; NSC 47/2, 17 October 1949, Harry S Truman Papers, President's Secretary's Files, Subject File: NSC Series, box 193, Harry S Truman Library, Independence, Missouri (hereinafter Truman Library); and memorandum by Maddocks, 4 February 1949, RG 319, P&O 686 TS, case 9. See also NSC 45, 17 March 1949, RG 273, Records of the National Security Council, National Archives (hereafter RG 273 with appropriate filing designations).

6. NSC 68, 14 April 1950, US Department of State, Foreign Relations of the United States, 1950 (Washington, D.C.: US Government Printing Office, 1959–1990), 1:261–262 (hereinafter FRUS with volume and page citations); Walter S. Poole, The History of the Joint Chiefs of Staff, vol. 4: The Joint Chiefs of Staff and National Policy, 1950–1952 (Wilmington, Del.: Glazier, 1980), pp. 161–172; Bradley to Lovett, 25 June 1952, RG 330, Records of the Office of the Secretary of Defense, CD 092 (Egypt) 1952, National Archives (hereafter RG 330 with appropriate filing designations); NSC 129/1, 24 April 1952, RG 273; and JSPC 684/130, 1 November 1952, US Department of Defense, Joint Chiefs of Staff, Records of the Joint Chiefs of Staff: The Middle East (Washington, D.C.: University Publications Microfilm, 1978), reel 1.

7. Peter L. Hahn, *The United States, Great Britain, and Egypt, 1945–1956: Strategy and Diplomacy in the Early Cold War* (Chapel Hill: University of North Carolina Press, 1991), pp. 94–109, 132–139.

8. See, for example, memorandum of conversation by Battle, 27 January 1952, RG 59, General Records of the US Department of State, 774.00, National Archives (hereafter RG 59 with appropriate filing designations); report by Hendershot, 4 April 1952, RG 59, 611.80; Summary of Discussion, 23 April 1952, and NSC 129/1, 24 April 1952, RG 273; and Bradley to Lovett, 25 June 1952, RG 330, CD 092 (Egypt) 1952.

9. Byrnes to Tuck, 24 May 1946, RG 59, 741.83. See also Tuck to Byrnes, 27 May and 11 June 1946, and Clark to Byrnes, 27 June 1946, ibid.

10. US-U.K. Agreed Minute, n.d. [16 October 1947], Foreign Office (hereinafter FO) 800/476, Records of the Foreign Secretary's Office, ME/47/17, Public Record Office

(hereinafter PRO), Kew Gardens, London. See also Memorandum of Conversation by Hare, 9 October 1947, FRUS 5 (1947):561–562; State Department Policy Memoranda, n.d. [c. early October 1947], ibid., pp. 521–522, 543–544; and Royall to Marshall, 29 September 1947, and Unsigned Memorandum for the Record, 23 September 1947, RG 319, P&O 091.7 (section 2), case 50.

11. Memorandum of Conversation by Acheson, 13 April 1950, Dean G. Acheson Papers, US Secretary of State Series, box 64, Truman Library; and Memorandum of Conversation by Stabler, 17 July 1950, RG 59, 641.74. See also Acheson to Holmes, 17 February 1949, FRUS 6 (1949):194–195.

12. Paper by Kopper, 27 December 1950, FRUS 5 (1950):11–14; and Minutes of Meeting, 2 May 1951, FRUS 5 (1951):113–120.

13. Peter L. Hahn, "Containment and Egyptian Nationalism: The Unsuccessful Effort to Establish the Middle East Command, 1950–1953," *Diplomatic History* 11(1) (Winter 1987):23–40.

14. NSC 129/1, 24 April 1952, RG 273.

15. Memorandum by Eden, 27 October 1952, Records of the Cabinet Office, CAB 129/56, C(52)369, PRO; Minutes of Meeting, 29 October 1952, Cabinet Meetings Minutes, CAB 128/25, CC 91(52)7, PRO; and Minutes of Meeting, 11 December 1952, Records of the British Defence Committee, CAB 131/12, D(52)12/4, PRO.

16. JCS to Lovett, 17 October 1952, RG 330, CD 092 (Middle East 1952); NSC 155/1, 14 July 1953, NSC 5428, 23 July 1954, and progress report on NSC 5428, 7 April 1955, RG 273; and unsigned Memorandum by State Department, 17 May 1954, RG 59, 611.41.

17. Circular Telegram by Dulles, 30 July 1953, RG 59, 780.5. See also Washbourne to Division of Operations, 28 September 1954, and Memorandum for the Record by Logan, 8 December 1954, RG 341, Records of the Headquarters of the US Air Force, National Archives.

18. Shuckburgh diary, 27 July 1954, Evelyn Shuckburgh, *Descent to Suez: Diaries, 1951–1956* (New York: Norton, 1987), p. 233; and Murray to Eden, 3 November 1954, PREM 11/702, Records of the Prime Minister's Office, PRO (hereinafter PREM with appropriate filing designations).

19. Jernegan to Murphy, 16 August 1954, RG 59, 774.13. See also Hart to Byroade, 26 October 1954, and Caffery to Dulles, 6 November 1954, RG 59, 774.5MSP.

20. Caffery to Dulles, 16 September and 27 November 1954, RG 59, 774.5MSP; Memorandum by Operations Coordinating Board (hereinafter OCB) working group, 21 December 1954, OCB.091, Egypt folder, OCB Central File Series, NSC Staff Papers, Dwight D. Eisenhower Library, Abilene, Kansas (hereinafter Eisenhower Library); and Stevenson to Eden, 17 January 1955, Political Correspondence of the Foreign Office, FO 371/113608, JE1057/1, PRO.

21. Byroade to Dulles, 20 May and 9 June 1955, FRUS 14 (1955–1957):192, 234; Powers to Radford, 18 August 1955, RG 218, CJCS (Radford) 091 Egypt; State Department Report, 12 September 1955, IR 7042, Records of the Research and Analysis Branch, RG 59; and progress report on NSC 5428, 2 November 1955, RG 273.

22. Progress Report on NSC 5428, 17 May 1956, RG 273. See also Progress Report on NSC 5428, 2 November 1955, RG 273; Dulles to Macmillan, 5 December 1955, FRUS 14 (1955):820–821; Memorandum of Conversation, [30 January 1956], Dwight D. Eisenhower Papers (Ann Whitman File): International Series, box 20, Eisenhower Library (hereafter Whitman File with appropriate filing designations); Hoover to Dulles, 16 March 1956, John Foster Dulles Papers, White House Memoranda Series, box 4, Princeton University, Prince-

ton, N.J. (hereinafter Dulles Papers with appropriate filing designations); and Eisenhower diary entry, 8 March 1956, Whitman File: Diary Series, box 9.

23. Dulles to Eisenhower, 28 March 1956, Whitman File: Diary Series, box 13. See also memorandum of conversation, 19 July 1956, and Byroade to Dulles, 26 July 1956, FRUS 15 (1955–1957):867–873, 906–908.

24. Memorandum of Conversation by Goodpaster, 31 July 1956, Whitman File: Diary Series, box 16. See also Eden to Eisenhower, 27 July 1956, PREM 11/1098; Minutes of Meeting, 27 July 1956, Whitman File: Cabinet Series, box 7; Memorandum of Conversation by Goodpaster, 28 July 1956, Whitman File: Diary Series, box 16; and Memorandum of Conversation by Dulles, 30 July 1956, Dulles Papers, Telephone Conversation Series, box 5.

25. Eisenhower to Eden, 3 September 1956, PREM 11/1100. See also Dulles to Murphy, 30 July 1956, and Dulles to Eisenhower, 2 August 1956, Whitman File: Dulles-Herter Series, box 5; Minutes of Meeting with Dulles, 1 August 1956, PREM 11/1098; Memorandum for the Record, 12 August 1956, Whitman File: Diary Series, box 17; Position Paper, 11 September 1956, Dulles Papers, Subject Series, box 7; and Lloyd to Eden, 8–12 October 1956, PREM 11/1102.

26. Summary of Discussion, 1 November 1956, Whitman File: NSC Series, box 8; and Eisenhower to Dulles, 1 November 1956, Whitman File: International Series, box 19.

27. Circular Telegrams by JCS, 6 November 1956, RG 218, CCS 381 EMMEA (11–19–47), section 47; Memorandum of Conversation by Goodpaster, 6 November 1956, FRUS 16 (1955–1957):1014; and Memorandum of Conversation by Goodpaster, 7 November 1956, Dulles Papers, White House Memoranda Series, box 4.

6

The Perils of Ambiguity
The United States and the Baghdad Pact

Elie Podeh

On February 24, 1955, Iraq and Turkey signed a military pact, which would later develop into a wider organization, encompassing Britain, Pakistan, and Iran. The Baghdad Pact (BP), as it came to be known, was devised to interlock with a chain of alliances already surrounding the Soviet Union, such as NATO, SEATO, and ANZUS. From a Western perspective, the role of the BP was to defend the Middle East from the Soviet "menace." In many respects, the formation of the BP was a consummation of Secretary of State John Foster Dulles' Northern Tier concept, devised following his Middle East tour as US secretary of state in May 1953. Though supporting it behind the scenes and joining some of its committees, the United States never formally joined the BP. Instead, in early 1957 it launched the Eisenhower Doctrine, which largely superseded the pact.

The BP episode had been considered marginal in American historiography.[1] Recent studies, however, based on declassified archival material, have somewhat corrected this perception. Largely focusing on the role played by the United States and Britain in establishing the pact, these studies offer three interpretations: The first sees it as a US initiative;[2] the second views it as a US initiative "hijacked" by Britain;[3] and the third sees it as a British initiative.[4] These studies, as shown elsewhere, underestimate the role of the regional powers—particularly Iraq and Turkey—in the formation of the pact.[5] Moreover, in analyzing the BP within the framework of US-British relations, most studies do not delve into global and internal constraints that hampered US accession.[6] More specifically, they largely neglect several important questions that would be the focus of this chapter: Why did the United States allow the initiative to be taken over by the British? What was the purpose of US ambiguous policy toward the pact, and how successful was it? How did interdepartmental controversies shape US policy toward the pact? And, finally, what does this episode tell us about the nature of Eisenhower-Dulles relations?

Early Middle Eastern Defense Plans

Until the advent of the Republican administration headed by President Dwight D. Eisenhower and Dulles in January 1953, US interest in the Middle East was limited. This partial aloofness was caused by US extensive involvement in cold war crises and its efforts to contain Soviet expansion in Western Europe, leading to the launching of the Truman Doctrine (1947) and the formation of NATO (1949). But US interest in the Middle East was far from negligible. Strategically, the region was seen as a source of oil; a center of communications; a shield to Africa and the Indian Ocean; and no less important, an irreplaceable offensive base against the Soviet Union. Yet the Middle East was considered a British and Commonwealth responsibility due to Britain's historical role and its control of military bases there.

With the formation of NATO, the United States considered establishing a regional defense organization in the Middle East, but all the available options seemed premature or irrelevant. In the meantime, the bilateral treaties between Britain and several Arab countries remained the basis of Western security.[7] The outbreak of the Korean War in 1950, followed by the Iranian oil crisis in March 1951, led to a change in American thinking. The United States became convinced that the cold war was not confined to the European theater and that remote areas such as the Far East, and by implication the Middle East, were exposed to Soviet penetration. In the long run, the cold war led to the adoption of a new policy called the "New Look." In the short run, both the United States and Britain thought that a more aggressive policy for the defense of the Middle East was required. In September 1951, they launched the Middle East Command (MEC), an allied anti-Soviet pact comprising the United States, Great Britain, France, Turkey, Australia, New Zealand, and South Africa. Egypt was the only regional state to be offered the status of a founding member—a decision determined by the strategic value of the Suez area as well as British desire to overcome the deadlock in the negotiations over the Anglo-Egyptian treaty. Unable to join what was regarded as "perpetuation of British occupation" and suffering from a variety of domestic problems, the Egyptian government rejected the offer and simultaneously abrogated the 1936 treaty. Without Egypt, the MEC idea simply withered away.[8]

The revision of MEC, which took place during the first half of 1952, resulted in a joint US-British project to establish a planning organization located in Cyprus, called the Middle East Defense Organization (MEDO).[9] The July 1952 military coup in Egypt suspended its execution, although it rekindled Western hopes that the new Egyptian regime would be willing to discuss the original MEC plan, especially in light of the contacts held between the CIA and the rebelling officers prior to the takeover. However, Muhammad Naguib and Gamal 'Abd al- Nasser, the two leading officers, refused to commit themselves to any Western defense plans subjecting Egypt to foreign control.[10] It was thus evident that Egypt—the cornerstone of Western strategic planning—had become a stumbling block in the way of establishing a Middle Eastern defense organization. A new line of thinking was needed, and that is exactly what Dulles offered with his Northern Tier concept.

In 1953, Eisenhower's administration devised the "New Look." It derived mainly from the need to reduce military spending. The new strategy came also as a response to the Berlin crisis and the Korean War, which—according to the critical view—left the enemy the freedom to choose the time, place, and conditions of any confrontation. Thus, the policy was designed to protect America's global interests without risking new "Koreas." In addition, it constituted a kind of response to the successful hydrogen bomb tests by the Soviet Union in August 1953, which ended the Western monopoly on this kind of weaponry. The New Look meant that the United States would meet any Communist aggression "with massive retaliation by means and at places of its own choosing."[11] This resulted in a drastic cut of the army and navy budgets; in contrast, the budget of the air force, which was trained to carry out atomic strikes, was substantially increased. The credibility of America's second-strike capacity, however, depended on encircling the Soviet Union with airbases from which US bombers could attack. This necessitated bases in Europe, South Asia, and the Middle East.[12] Because NATO had already been established in Europe and some form of organization in Asia was beginning to take shape (the Southeast Asia Treaty Organization, SEATO, would be formed in September 1954), the Middle East was seen as the remaining vacuum in the strategic belt being constructed around the two communist "behemoths"—the Soviet Union and the People's Republic of China.

Dulles' tour in the Middle East and Southeast Asia in May 1953 proved to be a turning point in the formulation of US Middle East policy. Following his mission, Dulles realized that the Anglo-Egyptian dispute, the Arab-Israeli conflict, and the question of local legitimacy were of more concern to the revolutionary Egyptian regime than were the Soviets. In contrast, the Northern Tier countries—Turkey, Pakistan, Iran, Iraq, and possibly Syria—were thought to be more concerned with this menace and thus constituted a more realistic basis for the creation of a regional organization.[13] In July 1953, Dulles' conclusions were drawn into a National Security Council (NSC) memorandum, which set out the objectives and policies of US policy in the Middle East. In general, the paper urged the development of secret plans for the defense of the area with Britain, Turkey, and other "northern" countries.[14]

The US Joint Chiefs of Staff kept up the momentum by advising the US Department of Defense in November 1953 to encourage Turkey, Pakistan, Iran, and possibly Iraq to create a regional defense organization, thus skirting the thorny issues of the Anglo-Egyptian dispute and the Arab-Israeli conflict.[15] Indeed, the United States was instrumental in bringing about a treaty of friendship and collective security between Turkey and Pakistan, the two most ardent supporters of collaboration with the West, in April 1954. Despite US attempts to portray the agreement as a "local" initiative, it was clear that the United States orchestrated it. The treaty was intended to serve as a nucleus of a wider defense organization subsequently including other Muslim-Arab members, with the formal or tacit endorsement of Washington. When Iraq agreed to sign a military agreement with the United States in April, it seemed that it was to become the first Arab state joining the Turco-Pakistani pact.[16] At that point, Dulles' Northern Tier concept seemed not only innovative but also successful.

The centrality of the Turco-Pakistani agreement in US thinking was reflected in a NSC policy statement in July 1954. After reiterating US interests in the Middle East, and acknowledging receding British influence, it noted that this pact was the first step in the direction of creating an indigenous regional defense arrangement including also Iran and Iraq. It was acknowledged that as long as the Anglo-Egyptian dispute and the Arab-Israeli conflict remained unresolved, the chances for enlisting other Arab states to the organization were slim. Still, the document advised to "associate Egypt with the defense arrangements should she so request, and make clear to her that the 'northern tier' concept does not derogate from the importance the US attaches to strengthening Egypt." The paper also attached importance to the British position in determining the success of the Northern Tier concept, advising the policy makers to invest efforts to "overcome the doubts now held by the UK."[17]

While the Arab world began feeling the first reverberations of the Turco-Pakistani agreement, Dulles was preoccupied with interlocking the chain of pacts surrounding the Soviet Union in Southeast Asia. Following the Korean War, the region remained highly unstable, culminating in the French loss of Dien Bien Phu to the Vietminh forces on May 7, 1954. This was followed by the Geneva conference in July, where it was decided to grant independence to Cambodia and Laos, while Vietnam was temporarily divided into two entities. Western desire to bring stability to the region, as well as to check the spread of communism, led to the establishment of SEATO, comprising the United States, France, Britain, Australia, New Zealand, Pakistan, and the Philippines. The signatories pledged to consult in the event of common danger. A separate protocol extended the protection of SEATO to the territory of Laos, Cambodia, and South Vietnam.[18]

The signing of SEATO enabled Dulles to concentrate on the last vacuum in the chain of pacts—the Middle East. The signing of the Anglo-Egyptian agreement in October 1954 raised US hopes that both Great Britain and Egypt would be more forthcoming in their attitude toward the Turco-Pakistani pact. Soon, however, it became evident that the pact would not serve as a basis for a wider defense organization. Apparently, the United States had misjudged the behavior of three key players: Britain, Iraq, and Egypt. Although the British were considered—and rightly so—a cold war partner, they were keen to maintain an effective political and military presence in the Middle East. The Northern Tier concept, however, threatened to shift the focus of regional defense from Egypt to the countries located on the southern border of the Soviet Union, thus further eroding Britain's influence. The Hashemites in Iraq, for their part, hoped to use the idea of regional defense as a mechanism that enabled them to revise the Anglo-Iraqi treaty and to pose a credible claim for Arab hegemony. Evidently, they realized that even if they joined a US-sponsored pact, it would not constitute a vehicle to revise the Anglo-Iraqi treaty, and by joining an existing non-Arab pact, Iraq had negligible chances for leading this enterprise. The third key player—Egypt—was determined to defend its perceived leading role in the Arab world, which seemed to be challenged by Iraq's moves. As a result of these conflicting interests, the Turco-Pakistani pact was rejected as a basis for regional defense; instead, Iraq and Turkey—with the active support of British and US knowledge—devised a somewhat different formula, which culminated in the establishment of the Baghdad Pact.

The Formation of the Turco-Iraqi Pact

Western defense plans coincided with the aspirations of Nuri al-Sa'id, the Iraqi prime minister, who faithfully served the Hashemite monarchy. Since the early 1950s, Nuri attempted to find a defense mechanism enabling Iraq to improve its standing in the Arab world and to modify the Anglo-Iraqi treaty, which was to expire in 1957 under heavy domestic criticism. Nuri was disappointed that initial Western plans treated Iraq as a minor player. Yet, Egypt's rejection of these plans and the consequent shift in the strategic thinking toward the Northern Tier concept improved Iraq's bargaining position. Nuri was intent on exploiting this opportunity to elevate Iraq to its "deserved" position in the Arab world. It would make up for what Iraq viewed as the regrettable British decision to place the Arab League in Cairo in 1945.

Since Iraq's adherence to the Turco-Pakistani pact did not meet its interests, and as a result of Egyptian-led Arab opposition to the pact, Nuri began searching for another mechanism. His search commenced in London in September 1954, where he raised several ingenious ideas about regional defense, envisaging a central role for Iraq. Although Nuri was convinced that a regional pact without Western participation would be worthless, he came to the conclusion that the first step should be a pact between Iraq and a Muslim-Asian country—a step that the Iraqi parliament would unconditionally approve. An agreement between two equal "oriental" countries would, he thought, help camouflage the subsequent adherence of Great Britain and perhaps the United States as well. Although the visit did not produce any tangible results, it became the starting point for the new defense project. Interestingly, however, Nuri did not disclose all the details of the London visit to the US ambassador in Baghdad, in spite of Iraq's good relations with the United States.[19]

In October, while the British were reviewing their defense plans in light of Nuri's ideas, the latter went to Ankara to promote the possibility of an Iraqi-Turkish pact. Although the talks were tough and inconclusive, Turkish Prime Minister 'Adnan Menderes assured Washington that within six months a "pattern of Middle East defense in [a] manner particularly satisfactory to [the] US and UK" would be established.[20] At that point, it seems that Great Britain and the United States began moving in opposite directions. While the Foreign Office realized that an Iraqi-Turkish pact allowing for subsequent British adherence was a desirable solution, the State Department still thought that the Turco-Pakistani pact was the most appropriate basis from which a "full-fledged defense organization could grow."[21] Moreover, it complained that British thinking on the Northern Tier concept "is not so positive as it was last autumn."[22]

The Iraqi-Turkish initiative gained further momentum during Menderes' visit to Baghdad in early January 1955. On January 13, the two prime ministers published a joint communiqué, pledging to sign a pact aimed at cooperation in the event of external or internal aggression, open to other states "eligible by virtue of their geographical location or their potential contributions."[23] The terms of the statement surprised both Great Britain and the United States, but they were quick to respond favorably.[24] On January 18, Dulles publicly endorsed the Iraqi-Turkish statement, describing it a "very constructive development" in the direction of "building up the so-called 'Northern Tier' of which Turkey and Pakistan are already pioneers," adding that every step closing the gap between Turkey and Pakistan improved the security of the area.[25]

Two possible explanations may be offered for the quick US endorsement of the statement. First, Dulles realized that Nuri and the British Foreign Office would not be induced to join the Turco-Pakistani pact, which did not serve their interests. On the other hand, he could not oppose an anti-Soviet regional defense pact, which served overall US global interests. By encouraging Iraq, the United States was at risk of alienating Egypt. Yet it seems that the force of circumstances made any debate in the State Department or the White House between "Egypt-firsters" and "Iraq-firsters" superfluous. Unaware of the deep Egyptian-Iraqi animosity, Dulles still entertained the notion of holding the rope on both ends.[26] He hoped that the fact that the United States was not directly involved in planning the new venture would enable it to maintain friendly relations with Nasser's Egypt at the same time.[27]

The second reason for the quick endorsement was connected with US world affairs. In mid-January 1955, the United States was deeply embroiled in an East Asian crisis, which threatened to deteriorate into World War III. The previous September, a military and political crisis had ensued between Communist China and the Nationalist Chinese led by Chiang Kai Chek in Taiwan, when the former made a move that was interpreted as an attempt to capture the islands of Quemoy and Matsu, near the Chinese shore. Although the military significance of the islands was doubtful, their conquest by Chou En-Lai's forces was perceived as the beginning of Taiwan's fall. The United States was resolved to face this challenge, even if it meant the use of force. Subsequently, a security treaty was signed with Taiwan in December 1954. In mid-January, however, communist forces made some military moves that propelled the United States to make a stronger commitment. On January 24, Congress approved the Formosa Resolution, which authorized "to use force if, in Eisenhower's sole judgment, an attack on the offshore islands was a part of, or a definite preliminary to, an attack against Taiwan and the Pescadores."[28] Seemingly no direct connection existed between the crisis and the question of Middle East defense, but it is probable that Dulles' preoccupation with the Chinese affair (which would end only in April), prevented him from delving too deeply into the relatively tranquil Middle East situation.

Following the Turco-Iraqi statement, the United States attempted to advance a two-pronged policy: supporting the build-up of a realistic defense organization, including Turkey, Pakistan, Iraq, and Iran and advancing an Arab-Israeli settlement through Operation Alpha.[29] This was a code name for a secret US-British project to bring about an Egyptian-Israeli settlement. Early versions of the plan were drafted already in the second half of 1954, but the actual details were worked out in Washington in January–February 1955. After being endorsed by Dulles and Anthony Eden, the plan was waiting to be presented to Nasser and Ben-Gurion at the earliest possible opportunity.[30] Because Nasser's consent for the project seemed crucial, the United States made efforts not to alienate him over the issue of regional defense. Pursuing these two goals successfully, therefore, necessitated limiting the pact to the Northern Tier countries and preventing Arab states other than Iraq from joining it. In retrospect, these two aims seem irreconcilable, but at that time the State Department thought otherwise.[31]

Egypt, for its part, exerted considerable efforts to frustrate the Iraqi-Turkish move. On January 22, Nasser convened a conference of Arab prime ministers aiming to elicit a resolution forbidding Iraq to sign a military pact outside the framework of the Arab League. After debilitating discussions, the conferees were unable to reach an acceptable formula.[32] Perceiving this outcome a triumph, Nuri continued his negotiations with the Turks. Both the United States and Great Britain closely followed the contacts and, in certain cases, even Dulles and Eden were personally involved. While the Foreign Office's main concern was the appearance of the "umbrella" clause, enabling Great Britain to join the pact at a later stage, the State Department's main concern was the formulation of a document that would not antagonize either Egypt or Israel. The US involvement during the consultations assumed particular importance whenever Nuri showed signs of crumbling under Turkish pressure.[33]

When the nucleus of the future Middle East regional defense organization—the Turco-Iraqi pact—was finally concluded on February 24, both Dulles and Eden were attending the first annual meeting of SEATO in Bangkok. Publicly, they expressed satisfaction, but in private they were concerned that Nasser's anti-pact policy would jeopardize it. Having met Nasser on his way to Bangkok, Eden was convinced that his objection stemmed from jealousy and a frustrated desire to lead the Arab world. Concurring with Eden's assessment, Dulles expressed willingness to support Nasser's claim for Arab leadership once the Arab-Israeli problem was settled.[34] For Dulles, therefore, there existed an inevitable linkage between the future success of the pact and the progress of Alpha. Undoubtedly, Dulles viewed US formal abstention from the pact as an advantage. Moreover, because the United States had special ties with Turkey (through NATO), Pakistan and Iraq (through military agreements), as well as ongoing secret military talks with the British, Dulles did not feel any urgent need to formally commit the United States to this new project.

The US Position: To Join or Not to Join? Stage I

Following the conclusion of the pact, US policy toward Middle East regional defense straddled a thin line: Although it refused to join the pact, it was encouraging—but not pressing—Pakistan and Iran to join. On the other hand, the United

States maintained a posture of neither encouraging nor discouraging the adherence of other Arab states, fearing that such a move would jeopardize Nasser's cooperation with Washington on Alpha. This was a continuation of US policy as outlined in NSC-5428 of July 1954 with one difference: relying on the Turco-Iraqi pact rather than the Turco-Pakistani pact as a major instrument of policy. This change stemmed from the corrected assessment that the provisions of the former provided a better foundation for regional defense than the latter.[35] Unaware of all these complex US interests, its allies considered this policy to be ambiguous.

In early April, when Great Britain was about to join the pact, Dulles was considering a conciliatory approach to Nasser. It aimed at enhancing his prestige and confidence, following his loss of face over the pact and his humiliating defeat to Israel in Gaza on February 28, 1955.[36] Dulles was prepared to grant Egypt political, economic, or military support if it contributed to the consolidation of the Northern Tier or to the progress of Alpha. Dulles thought that the United States would commit itself not to seek new Arab members whereas Egypt would participate in the defense of the Middle East—possibly through the Turco-Pakistani pact, which was less binding than the Turco-Iraqi pact. It is unclear why Dulles thought Nasser would suddenly be willing to participate in any Western-led organization. Perhaps, as indicated above, he did not attach enough importance to the Nasser-Nuri (or the Egyptian-Iraqi) rivalry, hoping that some mechanism appeasing them both would eventually be found. The idea withered away quickly, and the American ambassador in Cairo assured Nasser that the United States had no intention of joining the pact nor pressing other Arab states to do so.[37]

Internally, frustration at US policy toward regional defense came from the State Department. On April 22, Deputy Under-Secretary of State for Political Affairs Robert Murphy submitted a memorandum to Dulles, in which he criticized US policy with regard to regional defense:

> We are not reaping the full benefit of these developments because we lack a comprehensive political-military strategy for the defense of the Middle East. On the one hand, the 'Northern Tier' countries do not know what is required of them; on the other, we are undecided as to our own role and have inadequate criteria against which to measure the effectiveness of our country programs of military aid in terms of regional defense.[38]

Murphy recommended adopting the proposal of the Joint Chiefs of Staff (JCS) for a review of US military-political policy by the National Security Council and to set up a State-Defense working group to formulate policy recommendations. Dulles reacted promptly, and the subject was raised at the NSC meeting on May 5. Although the president was unwilling to revise present policy on the Middle East, it was decided to set up a joint State-Defense committee at the assistant secretary level to study defense problems.[39] These discussions were intended also to prepare for British-US military talks that were scheduled for June–August 1955. A month later, the joint working group submitted clear-cut recommendations:[40]

It will be politically necessary for the US to adhere, probably within a year at most, to a Middle East defense organization. It will be also militarily necessary, so that we may be in a position to influence defense planning and preparations. The best procedure is to adhere to the existing Turk-Iraqi Pact. The timing of US adherence depends upon political developments, primarily in connection with the Arab-Israeli dispute. It should, in any case, follow that of Pakistan and Iran. If there were prospects of a real relaxation of Arab-Israel tensions, our adherence should be delayed until that had been achieved. . . . If there were no such prospects, we should adhere without too much delay, in order to maintain momentum in the regional defense build-up.

A convincing argument on why the United States should join this pact was raised:

Politically, it would be most damaging to our position in the area and our hopes for regional defense if we declined to associate ourselves with these arrangements. At the least, it would dampen the enthusiasm of the countries concerned for a further development of their own defensive arrangements and would greatly reduce the influence we could bring to bear on the direction those arrangements might take. At the worst, it could be interpreted as a reversal of policy and decision that the Middle East could not or would not be defended, thus precipitating a move by the area toward a neutral or pro-Soviet position. In view of our strong advocacy of the principle of collective security in Europe, the Far East and Latin America, it is hard to see how we could justify a refusal to join a collective security organization in the Middle East, the only area directly exposed to communist aggression where we do not now participate in an organization of that kind.

The working group also presented the question of military expenditure ingeniously. It was assessed that $4 billion was the probable cost over a five-year period, which meant that the gross annual amount for all forms of US aid would be $800 million. But since $500 million would be required even if no regional defense plan were undertaken, the net cost of the plan would be only about $300 million annually.

These recommendations were somewhat mollified by a JCS report. But the JCS, too, thought that "the US should decide now, in principle, to adhere to the Northern Tier pact after such a pact is consummated [that is, the accession of Pakistan and Iran]." The timing of US adherence, the JCS concluded, "should not be too dependent upon developments in the Arab-Israeli controversy."[41] The notion that it would be necessary for the United States to adhere, within a year, to a regional organization was also supported by the CIA.[42] These positions gave Dulles the "green light" to defer the decision at least until the "consummation" of the pact. When the British inquired whether the United States would become a full-fledged member or at least associated with military planning, Dulles explained that until the relaxation of the Arab-Israeli conflict, the United States would not accede.[43] A State Department paper confirmed that "the position of close collaboration but non-adherence can in all probability be sustained for 6 to 12 months."[44] Still, to substantiate US commitment, Dulles was willing to establish an informal liaison with the pact organization once it was formed.[45]

The final composition of the pact was sealed with the adherence of Pakistan in September and Iran in the following month. With this, it became a five-member pact, known as the Baghdad Pact, as the organization headquarters were located at the Iraqi capital. With the formation of the BP, the United States established a liaison aimed at coordinating plans and channeling aid. The US ambassador in Baghdad was assigned as a permanent political liaison and the army attaché as a military liaison. The two participated as observers at the opening session of the BP Council, held in Baghdad, on November 21.[46] In this way, the United States thought it was enjoying the benefits of a member without being exposed to the criticism of anti-pact states.

Following the Baghdad meeting, British Foreign Minister Harold Macmillan urged Dulles to reconsider US adherence to the pact. He also attempted to receive US blessing for Arab adherence, but Dulles remained opposed: "An immediate move to expand the BP," he said, "would deny us Nasser's cooperation. If we failed with Egypt, we should then secure the immediate adherence of both Jordan and Lebanon." Once again Dulles rejected US adherence because such a move "would probably have to be coupled with a security guarantee to Israel."[47] In contrast to Dulles' advice, however, Britain and Iraq exerted pressure on Jordan to join the BP in December 1955. This move unleashed a vehement Egyptian-Saudi response that almost toppled King Hussein.[48] Both Eisenhower and Dulles saw the episode as a confirmation that no Arab state having common borders with Israel should join the BP.[49]

The dissatisfaction from what was considered ambiguous US policy toward the BP came from different angles. The first kind of criticism came from members of the pact, pressing for US adherence or for another US commitment. This pressure would intensify whenever a crisis engulfed the region. A typical approach was a letter from Eden to Eisenhower, on March 4, 1956, in which he urged the United States to take "urgent and effective measures to shore up the BP and Iraq in particular." In his opinion, US accession would impress Nasser "more than our attempts to cajole him have yet done." Evoking historical analogies, Eden concluded: "a policy of appeasement will bring us nothing in Egypt. Our best chance is to show it pays to be our friends."[50] Eden's immediate reason for sending this alarming letter was the dismissal of Glubb Pasha, commander of the Arab Legion in Jordan. The urgency was also dictated by British desire to augment the BP before the pact's annual meeting in Tehran. Apparently, the British and Pakistani pressure on Dulles was heavy because it was the first—and only—time he tentatively entertained the notion of joining the BP.[51]

The second kind of criticism came from the US embassy in Baghdad. Acquainted with Iraq's domestic difficulties, Ambassador Gallman thought US refusal to join the BP jeopardized the cooperation of regional states and consequently the general security of the Middle East. In a typical letter to Dulles sent in early January

1956, Gallman wrote that because the United States did not adhere to the BP, "we get all the blame from critic-countries for supporting it, and none of the credit which our friends in the Pact accord only to fellow members."[52] Certain officials at the State Department occasionally shared this kind of criticism.

The third kind of criticism, and perhaps the most important, came from the Department of Defense and the JCS. On February 10, 1956, Admiral Arthur Radford, chairman of the JCS, claimed that the United States was pursuing a confusing policy with regard to regional defense. In order to become more involved in military planning, he recommended joining the pact. Otherwise, he concluded, the BP "will fall apart."[53] Following the Tehran meeting, where all members once more urged the United States to adhere, Secretary of Defense Wilson notified Dulles that early adherence, or an indication of intent, would be necessary in order to avoid the disintegration of the pact.[54] In light of Dulles' continued refusal to join the BP, Wilson asked to place this question on the NSC agenda to determine the desirability of announcing this step during the 1957 BP meeting in Karachi, Pakistan.[55]

Clearly, an interdepartmental controversy emerged concerning the policy the United States should adopt regarding the BP. The military establishment thought US adherence would augment the pact, enhance the US position in the Middle East, and strengthen its security. In contrast, the State Department, and particularly Dulles, objected for a variety of political reasons. It seems that during April 1956, following his return from the SEATO conference in Karachi, he made up his mind against the BP. He particularly resented the British role; they "have taken it over," he told Eisenhower, "and run it as their instrument."[56] Dulles also disliked the fact that the pact had become "a forum for Arab politics and intrigue."[57] Since he assessed that the Senate would not sanction adherence to the pact, the effect of such a failure on the pact, he reasoned, would be far more serious than non-adherence. Such a defeat could also adversely affect an incumbent president in an election year. Finally, he assessed that such a move would elicit pressures to give Israel a security guarantee, resulting in the alienation of the Arab states and perhaps even pushing them in the Soviet direction.[58] In the ensuing controversy between the military and political wings, Eisenhower sided with Dulles.

As a sop to pact members, Dulles informed them that the United States would join the BP Economic Committee, retain an observer status in both the military and countersubversive committees, and request an increase in military assistance to all members in fiscal year 1957.[59] These measures, of course, did not satisfy the members or the US military establishment. Yet the Suez war gave them another opportunity to raise their case, and this time with more vigor.

The US Position: To Join or Not to Join? Stage II

Great Britain's participation in the war had a devastating effect on the BP. In their despair, the Muslim members decided to temporarily suspend Britain from the pact's activities, thus turning it into an Islamic pact. Because there was a fear that the war's reverberations would lead to the fall of the Hashemite regime, it was no surprise that a meeting of the four Islamic members called for the United States to join the BP, especially considering Washington's opposition to and actions taken toward stopping the British-French-Israeli tripartite invasion of Egypt.[60]

At the same time, the severe repercussions of the war brought the Department of Defense and the JCS to raise again—this time more forcefully—their demand for US adherence to the BP. The military establishment presented four arguments in support of this demand. First, the events created a convenient atmosphere for passing such a resolution in Congress. Second, Israel would be now more inclined to accept this development without the United States having to pay the price of a security guarantee. Third, it was the only effective way to counter Nasser's growing popularity in the Arab world on the one hand and to bolster Iraq's shaky situation on the other. Fourth, it would enable more US involvement in military planning, give more control of pact activities, and lead to the establishment of US bases in member states. A strong sense of urgency accompanied the presentation of these arguments; Admiral Radford estimated that if the United States would not act by December 1, the chances would be lost.[61] In the same vein, Ambassador Gallman sent a lengthy report to Dulles, persuasively arguing that should the United States stay out of the BP, it "will slowly die."[62]

All these arguments, however, did not impress Dulles, who was convinced that the war did not change his arguments against accession. A State Department paper enumerated all the pros and cons of such a step but its conclusions were clear: "The disadvantages of US adherence to the Pact are of such a nature that it is concluded that our joining now would not serve the US national interest." The paper listed twelve arguments against and only five in favor of adherence to the BP. Some of the arguments could not be easily dismissed: the possibility that the Soviets would exploit the opportunity and react; the doubt about the effectiveness of the BP in preventing Soviet penetration; the greater involvement in Arab conflicts; and the idea of being associated with Great Britain in local public opinion.[63] It seems, however, that the main goal of the paper was to convince the president not to succumb to the military pressure.

The contrasting views of the military establishment and the State Department were presented to the president on November 21, 1956. Eisenhower was most impressed by the argument that if the British got the United States into the pact—as the matter would certainly appear to the Arabs—Washington would lose its influence with the latter. He also entertained the idea of "building" the leadership of the Saudi monarch as a substitute to Nasser and, with Saudi support, declaring US support of the pact.[64] Eventually, this interdepartmental "battle" resulted in a tepid statement, issued on November 29, to the effect that the United States reaffirms its support for the BP and for the "collective efforts of these nations to maintain their independence."[65] Although important, this declaration was a far cry from the wishes of the BP members.

The inconclusive nature of the discussions with the president led the military establishment to initiate another round in the struggle over the BP. In late November, the JCS prepared a paper listing all the reasons compelling the United States to join the BP.[66] Secretary Wilson incorporated these ideas in a letter to the president on December 4. In this unusual communication, which exposed some of the passions behind its formulation, Wilson indicated that because "we feel so strongly about the need to join the BP," he allowed himself to attach some supporting data. In contrast to Dulles' twelve-point letter, Wilson listed ten advantages gained by adhering to the BP, first and foremost allowing the United States "to fill the political and military vacuum created by the decline of British position." Failure to take this step, the letter concluded, would result in general lack of confidence in US resolve, greater Soviet penetration, and the collapse of the pact.[67] Clearly, in his determination to persuade the president to join the BP, Wilson highlighted not only military but purely political interests as well.

In early December 1956, it became evident that a new—or at least clear—policy for the United States in the Middle East was needed in order to pacify US allies and to resolve the simmering interdepartmental controversy. The important decisions in this respect were taken following several phone consultations between Eisenhower and Dulles. On December 6, Dulles told the president that the Defense Department and the JCS were anxious to join the BP but that he had "considerable reservations" about such a move, which should be a political decision.[68] In their second talk, Dulles listed three possible alternatives open for the United States: adhering to the BP; organizing a new Middle East grouping; or devising a Congressional resolution authorizing the president to use the armed forces and to spend certain sums to bolster military cooperation with US allies. Dulles favored the last option, which would give the United States "maneuverability in the area, which would not exist through the BP or a new Pact."[69] As Eisenhower immediately concurred, it was clear that the die had been cast. On the same day, Dulles discussed the idea with William Knowland, an influential senator and an enthusiastic supporter of the administration. In the following days, the details of what would become known as "the Eisenhower Doctrine" were worked out. Interestingly, Dulles' idea was not novel; Congress had already authorized a similar plea—the Formosa Resolution—during the 1955 crisis over the islands of Quemoy and Matsu.

To ensure the safe inauguration of the resolution, Dulles prepared the ground with the British.[70] His most important task, however, was to convince the military establishment that the resolution indeed offered a better framework for US policy than the BP. On December 20, both the secretary of defense and the JCS chairman expressed satisfaction with the new plan. Admiral Radford stated somewhat apologetically that the JCS supported adherence to the BP "simply to take some major action quickly."[71] After overcoming this major hurdle, the president met a bipartisan congressional leadership on January 1, 1957, which paved the way for the approval of the Eisenhower Doctrine by Congress a few days later.[72]

The Eisenhower Doctrine sealed the fate of the BP. If there had been a chance that the United States would join it, the doctrine made this step superfluous. In late January, Dulles briefed all diplomatic missions to the effect that US adherence was unlikely because joining a pact in which Britain was a member might prove "embarrassing." Moreover, the BP had become a liability because nonmembers perceived it as a Western organization, thus rendering the US concept of an indigenous organization meaningless. As a result, Dulles concluded, the United States would strengthen its allies through bilateral channels and through the Eisenhower Doctrine.[73] The BP Islamic members soon realized that despite the advantages that might accrue from the Eisenhower Doctrine, it adversely affected the fate of their pact. Consequently, they kept pressing the United States, claiming that "we are four zeros and those only add up to zero."[74]

Once more, the United States adopted an ambiguous position: Eisenhower's envoy to the area, James Richards, was instructed to tell member states that the doctrine "in no way supplant[s] the BP."[75] In fact, until the very last moment, Washington kept insisting that "there has been no final decision taken not to join the BP."[76] In addition, on March 22 the United States decided to join the BP Military Committee during the Karachi Council meeting in June. Thus, an anomalous situation emerged: The United States was a full member in several important committees of the BP, yet it was not a member of the pact itself. Another sign of US commitment to the pact was shown when Dulles, for the first time, attended the Ankara annual council meeting in January 1958. But when the members asked the United States to head the command of the BP military forces, the JCS politely declined.[77] All these mixed signals created the impression that Washington did not consider the BP as a major instrument of policy.

On July 14, 1958, a group of army officers headed by Colonel 'Abd al-Karim Qasim overthrew the Hashemite regime in Iraq, leading to its suspension from the BP. Great Britain and the United States discussed the possibility of changing its name, reorganizing it, or even setting up an alternative organization, yet Britain resisted any change because so long as Iraq remained a member, the "umbrella" clause concerning the use of Iraqi installations in wartime was legally binding.[78] This situation had changed, however, when Qasim announced Iraq's formal withdrawal from the BP on March 24, 1959. The remaining members renamed the pact "Central Treaty Organization" (CENTO), with Ankara replacing Baghdad as its headquarters. Iran's withdrawal in February 1979, following the Ayatollah Khomeini's revolution, signaled CENTO's death knell.

Conclusion

US policy toward the BP demonstrated the perils of ambiguity. In terms of success, it was not one of America's finest hours. Ambiguity could well serve US policy, which attempted to satisfy its allies while simultaneously not alienating other potential partners. It ended up, however, disappointing all. In theory, some of Dulles' moves were logical, even ingenious, particularly the Northern Tier concept, which skirted the Anglo-Egyptian impasse over Suez, and the Eisenhower Doctrine, which thwarted the military intention of joining the BP following the Suez debacle. In reality, however, the results amounted to a blunder: First, this policy alienated US allies, as well as potential allies. The main lesson to be drawn from the Baghdad Pact episode from a US point of view is that an ambiguous policy does not necessarily pay off; perhaps it is better to satisfy a limited group of allies than to forge a broad, yet inconclusive, front. Eventually, when the United States came up with a more definite policy—the Eisenhower Doctrine—it was viewed with disdain in the Arab world: Indeed, what goodwill the administration received following its positive stance in the Suez war was lost with the enunciation of the doctrine. Second, the Baghdad Pact episode accelerated the penetration of the Soviet Union, which leapfrogged into the heart of the Arab Middle East with the September 1955 arms deal with Egypt, exactly the opposite of what the BP was intended to accomplish. Even though recent studies show that the entrance of the USSR to the region, particularly in Egypt, preceded the pact, undoubtedly the formation of an anti-Soviet pact in the Middle East deepened Soviet involvement.[79]

The British did not "hijack" the Northern Tier concept from Dulles. Although he somewhat resented their "bossy" attitude regarding the BP, it seems clear that this perceived behavior of the British cannot solely explain US refusal to join the pact. Moreover, because he believed that US accession would antagonize both Egypt and Israel, Dulles preferred adopting an ambiguous position. Such a policy was meant to allow the United States to enjoy the fruits of association without being subjected to the constraints of a formal member.

The greatest mistake of the United States was its failure to comprehend Arab psychology in the postcolonial era and the depth of Arab rivalries. The belief that Nasser could be enticed to join a Western-led pact if only the price was right or that it would be possible to "build" King Sa'ud as an alternative Arab leader to Nasser attested to the shortsightedness of US thinking. Unwittingly, the Eisenhower administration was caught up in a dual Arab struggle: that between Egypt and Iraq for Arab hegemony, and that between Nasser and the Iraqi Hashemites (represented by Nuri al-Sa'id) for Arab leadership. The United States should have reasoned that between these two contenders there was no middle path. Since decolonization in the Third World constituted one of the hallmarks of the 1950s, Nasser-type leaders could promise a better reward for the United States than the Nuri-type, which was largely detested as a result of its long collaboration with the West. Although a policy oriented solely toward Nasser would have not necessarily paid off (as was the case during the Kennedy administration), it could still offer more dividends for the United States than an ambiguous policy alienating all.

Dulles, however, was more successful in his struggle with the military establishment as the political interests eventually prevailed over the military-strategic considerations. It was a classic example of the interplay between domestic and foreign policies, in which the former did *not* affect the latter because of Dulles' central position in the foreign decision making.

Finally, what does the Baghdad Pact tell us about the US decisionmaking process? Was Dulles a "foreign policy czar," as some scholars have claimed?[80] A close scrutiny of US conduct in this episode substantiates Richard Immerman's thesis that in spite of Dulles' impressive hold over foreign affairs, Eisenhower also played an important role in the decisionmaking process.[81] Indeed, Dulles enjoyed a large amount of respect and confidence from Eisenhower. For example, in the controversy between the State and Defense Departments, he supported Dulles even though his personal background made him prone to accept the military view. True, Dulles "invented" the Northern Tier concept and the Eisenhower Doctrine, but the president was intimate with the details and active in the decisionmaking process. Thus, it seems that Chester Pach and Elmo Richardson rightly concluded that the two "forged an extraordinary partnership in the making of foreign affairs."[82] Moreover, the BP episode demonstrates that the analogy of Dulles as an international lawyer who advises and counsels his client-president is not far-fetched. Steven Spiegel claimed that Dulles "always understood that he was the president's lawyer in foreign affairs and that he must maintain his client's confidence in order to retain his portfolio."[83] After all, whereas the lawyer has to show ingenuity, it is left to the client to make the final decision after carefully evaluating the alternatives presented by the lawyer. The fact that the lawyer lost the BP case does not exempt the client from responsibility—at least in this case. Hence, one must conclude that it is the lawyer-client pattern of behavior that typified the Eisenhower-Dulles relations in this episode.

Notes

1. A recent dictionary by David Shavit, *The United States in the Middle East: A Historical Dictionary* (Westport, Conn.: Greenwood, 1996), did not mention the Baghdad Pact at all. Many books dealing with the Eisenhower administration, cited below, hardly discussed this episode. Only one single Ph.D. dissertation has been written on the subject, but it is not based on archival material: Donald James Decker, "The U.S. Policy Regarding the Baghdad Pact" (The American University, Washington, D.C., 1975).

2. Ayesha Jalal, "Towards the Baghdad Pact: South Asia and Middle East Defence in the Cold War, 1945–1957," *International History Review* 11 (1989), pp. 409–433.

3. Nigel Ashton, "The Hijacking of a Pact: The Baghdad Pact and Anglo-American Tensions in the Middle East, 1955–1958," *Review of International Studies* 19 (1993), pp. 123–137.

4. Brian Ried, "The 'Northern Tier' and the Baghdad Pact," in John W. Young (ed.), *The Foreign Policy of Churchill's Peacetime Administration, 1951–1955* (Worchester: Leicester University Press, 1988), pp. 159–181; Richard L. Jasse, "The Baghdad Pact: Cold War or Colonialism?" *Middle Eastern Studies* 27 (1991), pp. 140–156. For an older version of this attitude, see Elie Kedourie, "Britain, France and the Last Phase of the Eastern Question," in J. C. Hurewitz (ed.), *Soviet-American Rivalry in the Middle East* (New York: Praeger, 1969), pp. 189–197.

5. For an analysis of Iraq's role in the formation of the Baghdad Pact, see Elie Podeh, *The Quest for Hegemony in the Arab World: The Struggle over the Baghdad Pact* (Leiden: E. J. Brill, 1995). For an emphasis on the Turkish role, see Ismail Sosyal, "The 1955 Baghdad Pact," *Studies on Turkish-Arab Relations* 5 (1991), pp. 43–116; Ara Sanjian, "The Formulation of the Baghdad Pact," *Middle Eastern Studies* 33 (1997), pp. 226–266.

6. For a study that referred to domestic interdepartmental controversies, although still within the framework of U.S.-British relations, see Magnus Persson, *Great Britain, the United States, and the Security of the Middle East: The Formation of the Baghdad Pact* (Lund: Lund University Press, 1998).

7. Elie Podeh, "The Cold War in the Middle East: The Western Quest for a Regional Defense Organization, 1945–1953," *Orient* 33 (1992), pp. 265–268. On early western Middle Eastern plans, see Persson, *Great Britain*, pp. 66–80.

8. On the consultations leading to the formulation of the MEC, see *Foreign Relations of the United States,* 1951 (Washington: 1977), Vol. V, pp. 144–267. For the Egyptian response, see ibid., pp. 209–210. See also Peter L. Hahn, *The United States, Great Britain, and Egypt, 1945–1956: Strategy and Diplomacy in the Early Cold War* (Chapel Hill, N.C.: University of North Carolina Press, 1991), pp. 109–116: Persson, *Great Britain*, pp. 80–85.

9. On MEDO, see FRUS, 1952–1954, Vol. IX (Washington: 1986), pp. 178–183, 188–191, 198–199, 213–218, 226–234, 249–252, 271–274, 301–305; Hahn, "National Security Concerns," p. 95; Podeh, "The Cold War in the Middle East," pp. 273–274; Hahn, *The United States*, pp. 144–145, 149–154, 156–159, 162; Persson, *Great Britain*, pp. 90–98, 114–116, 119–124.

10. Geoffrey Aronson, *From Sideline to Center Stage: U.S. Policy Towards Egypt, 1946–1956* (Boulder: Westview, 1986), p. 51; Podeh, "The Cold War in the Middle East," p. 274.

11. Nadav Safran, *From War to War: The Arab-Israeli Confrontation, 1948–1967* (New York: Pegasus, 1969), p. 104.

12. For more on the New Look, see Townsend Hoopes, *The Devil and John Foster Dulles* (Boston: Little, Brown, 1973), pp. 191–201; Richard A. Melanson, "The Foundations of Eisenhower's Foreign Policy: Continuity, Community, and Consensus," in R. A. Melanson and D. Mayers, *Reevaluating Eisenhower: American Foreign Policy in the 1950s* (Urbana, Ill.: University of Illinois Press, 1987), pp. 54–55; Dwight D. Eisenhower, *Mandate for Change, 1953–1956* (New York: Doubleday, 1963), pp. 446–447, 451–454; Chester J. Pach Jr. and Elmo Richardson, *The Presidency of Dwight D. Eisenhower*, rev. ed. (Lawrence, Kans.: University Press of Kansas, 1991), pp. 81–82.

13. FRUS, 1952–1954, Vol. IX, pp. 379–386; Podeh, "The Cold War in the Middle East," p. 275; Persson, *Great Britain*, pp. 113–158.

14. Steven Z. Freiberger, *Dawn over Suez: The Rise of American Power in the Middle East, 1953–1957* (Chicago: Ivan R. Dee, 1992), pp. 53–54.

15. Aronson, *From Sideline to Center Stage*, p. 80.

16. Meyer, *Egypt and the United States*, pp. 89–90; Aronson, *From Sideline to Center Stage*, pp. 84–87; Podeh, *The Quest for Hegemony*, pp. 64–76.

17. FRUS, 1952–1954, Vol. IX, pp. 525–531.

18. On SEATO, see Pach and Richardson, *The Presidency of Eisenhower*, pp. 95–96; Hoopes, *The Devil and John Foster Dulles*, pp. 202–261.

19. For further details, see Podeh, *The Quest for Hegemony*, pp. 91–92.

20. FRUS, 1952–1954, Vol. IX, pp. 554–555. On Nuri's discussions in Turkey, see Podeh, *The Quest for Hegemony,* pp. 93–95.

21. FRUS, 1952–1954, Vol. IX, pp. 2402–2404.

22. FO-371, Shuckburgh's Minute, 11 January 1955, V1073/26, 115484; USNA, RG-59, London to Secretary of State, Dispatch 1945, 10 January 1955, 780.5/1–1055. On 10 January 1955, Dulles again expressed concern over the British coolness toward the Northern Tier concept. See USNA, RG-59, Dulles to London, Tel. 3574, 780.5/1 755. Evelyn Shuckburgh, Under-Secretary in the Foreign Office in charge of Middle East policy, admitted that "there does appear to be a difference of emphasis between US and UK." See RG-59, Butterworth to Secretary of State, Tel. 3053, 11 January 1955, 780.5/1–1155.

23. FO 371, Hooper to FO, Tel. 31, 13 January 1955, V1073/12, 115484; USNA, RG-59, Baghdad to Department of State, Dispatch 319, 13 January 1955, 682.87/1–1355.

24. USNA, RG-59, Dulles to Baghdad, Tel. 406, 14 January 1955, 682.87/1–1455. A similar note was sent to Ankara. After hurried consultations with the State Department, the British Foreign Office also gave its blessing to the statement; see FO 371, FO to Baghdad, Tel. 45, 14 January 1955, V1073/33, 115484.

25. Podeh, *The Quest for Hegemony*, p. 103. See also Dulles's congratulatory messages to both Nuri and Menderes, USNA, RG-59, Tel. 406, 14 January 1955, 682.87/1–1455. For more on US reaction, see Persson, *Great Britain* pp. 202–3.

26. See, for example, USNA, RG-59, Dulles to Ankara, Tel. 853, 28 January 1955, 780.5/1–2255.

27. On the development of US-Egyptian relations during that period, there is ample material. See, for example, Hahn, *The United States*; Muhammad Abd el-Wahab Sayed-Ahmed, *Nasser and American Foreign Policy 1952–1956* (London: LAAM, 1989); Meyer, *Egypt and the U.S.*; Aronson, *From Sideline to Center Stage*; Matthew F. Holland, *America and Egypt: From Roosevelt to Eisenhower* (Westport, Conn.: Praeger, 1996).

28. Hoopes, *The Devil and John Foster Dulles*, p. 274. On the whole crisis, see pp. 264–283; Pach and Richardson, *The Presidency of Eisenhower*, pp. 98–102.

29. USNA, RG-59, Memo from Burdett to Hart, 3 February 1955, 682.87/2–355; FRUS, 1955–1957, Vol. XII (Washington: 1991), p. 14.

30. On the Alpha plan, see Shimon Shamir, "The Collapse of Project Alpha," in Roger R. Louis and Roger Owen (eds.), *The Suez 1956: The Crisis and Its Consequences* (Oxford: Oxford University Press, 1989), pp. 81–100.

31. See, in particular, USNA, RG-59, memo from Burdett to Hart, 3 February 1955, 682.87/2–355. On the Alpha project and the Baghdad Pact, see Persson, *Great Britain*, pp. 186–224.

32. On the Cairo conference, see Podeh, *The Quest for Hegemony*, pp. 107–112.

33. For the last round of negotiations in February, see ibid., pp. 118–125.

34. For a report on Dulles-Eden meeting, see USNA, RG-59, Dulles to Washington, DULTE 4, 24 February 1955, 684A.86/2–2455; FRUS, 1955–1957, Vol. XIV (Washington: 1989), pp. 71–72. On Eden's meeting with Nasser, see FO-371, Stevenson to FO, Tel. 269, 21 February 1955, V1073/289, 115492; Enclosure to Dispatch 31, 21 February 1955, V1073/323, 115493.

35. See George Allen's memo, 1 April, in FRUS, 1955–1957, Vol. XII, p. 49. Generally on US policy, see the memo by Allen approved by Hoover, USNA, RG-59, 11 March 1955, 780.5/3–1155. On the attitude toward Pakistan, see Hoover to Karachi, Tel. 1368, 18 March 1955, 780.5/3–755. On the attitude toward Iran, see Dulles to Ankara, Tel. 1206, 25 March 1955, 780.5/ 3–2155. On the attitude toward Arab states, see Dulles to Damascus, Tel. 515, 26 March 1955, 682.87/ 3–2455. The US policy toward the Arab states was cabled to London, see Tel. 5107, 6 April, 780.5/ 4–455.

36. Israel launched the attack—the biggest since the 1948 war—as a response to Egyptian *fidayeen* infiltration. The attack, which resulted in heavy Egyptian losses, had far-reaching consequences for Egyptian-Israeli relations (and by implication Egyptian-Western relations).

37. USNA, RG-59, Dulles to Damascus, Tel. 515, 26 March 1955, 682.87/3–2455; FRUS, 1955–1957, Vol. XII, pp. 45–47, 50–51.

38. FRUS, 1955–1957, Vol. XII, p. 51.

39. Ibid., p. 55; Persson, *Great Britain*, pp. 246–247.

40. For a short summary, see FRUS, 1955–1957, Vol. XII, pp. 63–70. For the full report, see USNA, attachment from Jernegen to Cyr, Baxter, and Jones, 6 June 1955, 780.5/6–655. It was a top secret report with limited distribution. All the quotations cited below were taken from this report.

41. Memo from the JCS to Secretary of Defense Wilson, 16 June 1955, FRUS, 1955–1957, Vol. XII, pp. 70–74. For a comparison between the report of the working group and the JCS report, see ibid., pp. 98–102. For more on the position of the military, see USNA, Scott's memo, 22 June 1955, 780.5/6–2255.

42. USNA, RG-59, Allen Dulles to Jernegen, undated, 780.5/7–2755.

43. The issue came up during US-British military talks held in June 1955; see memo of conversation, 11 August 1955, 780.5/8–1155.

44. The paper was presented to the president on July 11; see FRUS, 1955–1957, Vol. XII, pp. 129–132. For a summary of the US position as approved by the president, see USNA, RG-59, Dulles' memo entitled "US Views on Middle East Defense," 17 September 1955, 780.5/9–1755.

45. FRUS, 1955–1957, Vol. XII, p. 141.

46. The US mission to the council included also Admiral Cassady, the Commander-in-Chief of US Naval Forces, Eastern Atlantic and Mediterranean. See USNA, RG-59, Memo by Russell to Dulles, 18 October 1955, 780.5/10–1855; Gray to Secretary of State, 30 January 1956, 780.5/1–3056; FRUS, 1955–1957, Vol. XII, p. 198.

47. For the exchange of letters, see ibid., pp. 206–207; USNA, RG-59, Dulles to London, Tel. 3132, 5 December 1955, 780.5/11–2555.

48. The Jordanian episode was highly critical from an Arab point of view because it made it clear that if Jordan, a Hashemite ally of both Great Britain and Iraq could not join the BP, then the chances that other Arab states would take this step were slim. For details, see Podeh, *The Quest for Hegemony*, chap. 8; Persson, *Great Britain*, pp. 274–280.

49. See the discussion at the NSC, 22 December 1955, FRUS, 1955–1957, Vol. XII, p. 214.

50. Ibid., p. 249. For Eisenhower's reply, see PRO, FO-371, 10 March 1955, V1075/71, 121272. The same argument was posed by Lloyd to Dulles at the Karachi SEATO conference on 6 March, FRUS, 1955–1957, Vol. XII, p. 250.

51. USNA, RG-59, Dulles (from Karachi) to Hoover, DULTE 14, 780.5/3–856. Dulles sent a four-point program for the U.S. adherence. It was written that the tel. was a "speculative exercise" transmitted without any recommendation because there was no time to seriously discuss it. Concomitantly, Dulles entertained the idea of reaching some truce with Nasser, including a promise not to recruit Arab members to the BP for certain Egyptian undertakings. See Podeh, *The Quest for Hegemony*, p. 198.

52. Ibid., p. 215; Persson, *Great Britain*, p. 246.

53. FRUS, 1955–1957, Vol. XII, p. 248.

54. Letter from Wilson to Dulles, 5 April 1956, ibid., p. 267.

55. Memo from Wilson to the executive secretary of the NSC, 15 May 1956, ibid., p. 298. The issue also came up during a State-JCS meeting on 23 May 1956, see ibid., pp. 299–302.

56. Ibid., p. 270.

57. See Dulles' conversation with the JCS, 9 April 1956, ibid., p. 275.

58. Ibid.; Dulles' letter to Wilson, 23 April 1956, ibid., p. 294.

59. On these measures, see ibid., pp. 269, 282, 285; USNA, RG-59, Hoover to Baghdad, Tel. 908, 4 May 1956, 780.5/5–456.

60. FRUS, 1955–1957, Vol. XII, pp. 319–321.

61. For papers and statements of the military establishment, see ibid., pp. 325, 327–329; USNA, RG-59, Wilson to Dulles, 14 November 1956, 780.5/11–1456.

62. USNA, RG-59, Gallman to Department of State, Dispatch 307, 15 November 1955, 780.5/11–1556.

63. FRUS, 1955–1957, Vol. XII, pp. 331–337. See also Dulles' memo sent to Radford, USNA, RG-59, 17 November 1956, 780.5/11–1756.

64. FRUS, 1955–1957, Vol. XII, p. 341.

65. Ibid., p. 360.

66. Memo by the JCS to Wilson, 30 November 1956, ibid., pp. 361–363.

67. Ibid., pp. 373–376; USNA, RG-59, Wilson to Dulles, 4 December 1956, 780.5/12–456.

68. FRUS, 1955–1957, Vol. XII, p. 390.

69. Ibid., pp. 395–396. In fact, the new grouping was also a new idea. It envisaged incorporating the BP into a new and larger grouping to be called the Middle East Charter, which would also include Saudi Arabia and Lebanon. The idea was soon dropped. See Podeh, *The Quest for Hegemony*, p. 224.

70. FRUS, 1955–1957, Vol. XII, pp. 399–400.

71. Ibid., p. 416.

72. On the meeting, see ibid., pp. 432–437. On the congressional approval and the doctrine, see ibid., pp. 437–439; Spiegel, *The Other Arab-Israeli Conflict* (Chicago: University of Chicago Press, 1985), pp. 83–91.

73. USNA, RG-59, Dulles to all diplomatic missions, 28 January 1957, 780.5/1–2857.

74. See a memo of a conversation between Dulles and Prince 'Abd al-Ilah, the Iraqi Crown Prince, USNA, RG-59, 5 February 1957, 780.5/2–557; 787.11/2–557.

75. FRUS, 1955–1957, Vol. XII, p. 451.

76. See ibid., memo from Rountree to Dulles, 20 June 1957, 780.5/6–2057.

77. USNA, RG-59, the JCS to Murphy, 27 May 1957, 780.5/5–2757. This was a main issue on the agenda of the Karachi council meeting, Henderson to Dulles, Tel. 3331, 6 June 1957, 780.5/6–657; Dulles to Henderson, Tel. 3201, 5 June 1957, 780.5/6–557.

78. PRO, FO-371, FO to Washington, Tel. 236, 13 January 1959, EB10345/54, 132921.

79. That was also the U.S. view at the time. See David Lesch, *Syria and the United States: Eisenhower's Cold War in the Middle East* (Boulder: Westview, 1992), p. 85. It should be noted that the Czech arms deal of September 1955 is often mentioned as a direct consequence of the pact. Recent studies, however, show that the origins of the deal lay in the years before the conclusion of the pact. See Rami Ginat, "Origins of the Czech-Egyptian Arms Deal: A Reappraisal," in David Tal (ed.), *The 1956 War: Collusion and Rivalry in the Middle East* (London: Frank Cass, 2001), pp. 145–168.

80. The term "czar" is taken from Spiegel, *The Other Arab-Israeli Conflict*, p. 59. In connection with the Eisenhower-Dulles controversy, see Pach and Richardson, *The Presidency of Dwight D. Eisenhower*, p. 84.

81. Richard H. Immerman, "Eisenhower and Dulles: Who Made the Decisions?" *Political Psychology* 1 (1979), pp. 21–38.

82. Pach and Richardson, *The Presidency of Dwight D. Eisenhower*, p. 85.

83. Spiegel, *The Other Arab-Israeli Conflict*, p. 59. See also Pach and Richardson, *The Presidency of Dwight D. Eisenhower*.

7

The 1957 American–Syrian Crisis
Globalist Policy in a Regional Reality

David W. Lesch

The Syrian crisis of 1957 (I will refer to it as the American-Syrian crisis) is one of those occasions where the flaws of applying a globalist analytical methodology to the Middle East—in lieu of a serious appreciation of the regional dynamics in the area—are, in retrospect, dramatically revealed. Indeed, the parameters of the crisis itself were determined as much by regional forces as they were by international actors. It was a telling irony, an indication of the policy misconceptions and misapplications surrounding the approach to the Middle East taken by the administration of President Dwight D. Eisenhower in 1957. What started out as a policy designed to isolate and reduce the power of Egyptian President Gamal 'Abd al-Nasser, that is, the Eisenhower Doctrine, was effectively abandoned during the US-Syrian crisis; thus, a modus vivendi was reached with Egypt, whose help Washington sought during the latter stages of the crisis in order to salvage the situation in Syria. Because of this rather embarrassing experience, the Eisenhower administration began to thoroughly realize that the Middle East was much more complex, not simply an area of East-West ingress.

The New US Ally in the Middle East

The American-Syrian crisis officially began on August 12, 1957, when the Syrian government announced the discovery of a US-engineered attempt to overthrow the regime, which the Eisenhower administration believed was close to becoming a Soviet "outpost" in the region.[1] The next day the Syrian government expelled three US diplomats; the United States responded in kind on August 14, declaring the Syrian ambassador to Washington and his second secretary personas non gratas.

The Eisenhower administration, during the height of the cold war, steadfastly held this incident out as a sign of unacceptable growth in Soviet influence in Syria (especially since the leadership in Syria was generally pro-Ba'thist, the new army chief of staff, 'Afif al-Bizri, was thought to be a Communist, and Syria and the Soviet Union had agreed to sign a wide-ranging economic accord a week earlier), with possible calamitous repercussions for the US position in the entire Middle East. With the Suez debacle so fresh in their minds, Eisenhower and his secretary of state, John Foster Dulles, were careful not to appear to be second-generation imperialists and therefore preferred an Arab-led response to "correct" the situation in Syria, either through diplomatic or military pressure. None would be forthcoming.

The administration was confident that it could count on the support of Saudi Arabia to arrange the Arab response, since King Sa'ud, upon his visit to Washington earlier in the year, had been officially touted as an ally of the United States in the Middle East as a counterpoise to Nasser. Winning over Sa'ud had been an unofficial corollary to the Eisenhower Doctrine (announced in January 1957 and passed in March), a rather hastily formulated policy intended to fill the perceived vacuum of power in the Middle East following British and French humiliations at Suez.[2] One of the objectives of the Eisenhower Doctrine was to subvert the alliance Nasser had built to isolate Iraq, then the only pro-Western and Arab Baghdad Pact member. To do this, Washington sought to isolate Nasser—then at his zenith of popularity in the Arab world due to his successes in the Suez crisis—and to halt any further increase in Soviet influence in the Middle East. Thus, Washington had to find an Arab leader who could rival Nasser in prestige and convince other Arab states to turn pro-Western, if not join the Baghdad Pact outright. Because of Saudi Arabia's growing oil wealth and its central position in the Islamic world, Eisenhower and Dulles chose Sa'ud, despite his putative limitations, to rival Nasser and they systematically set about augmenting his stature in the region.

Sa'ud, however, had his own set of objectives that he wanted to achieve through this anointment.[3] The Saudi monarch (or those within the Saudi ruling circles who were guiding him) saw US support as his stepladder to a leadership position in the Arab world. But by choosing this route, he (or they) also invited an inherent contradiction, one that left the king vulnerable and ultimately led to his failure: In order to challenge and possibly assume Nasser's mantle, Sa'ud had to distance himself from Washington's policies. However, this was a given, for Nasser had long set the standard for Arab nationalist leadership, and any pretender to this position had to sufficiently detach himself from the West. Thus, there ensued a schizophrenic Saudi foreign policy, supporting Washington's interests vis-à-vis a four-power conference meeting (between Saudi Arabia, Egypt, Syria, and Iraq) in Cairo in February 1957 and the Jordanian crisis in April 1957 (among other things), yet opposing the Eisenhower administration's policies related to the right of Israeli shipping through the Gulf of Aqaba (Sa'ud was against it, Washington for it) and the Buraimi Oasis dispute (which actually caught the United States between two allies since the dispute pitted Great Britain against Saudi Arabia).

King Sa'ud became the Arab spokesman for the Israeli shipping question following Nasser's convenient abdication of that role in the wake of the Suez crisis and the establishment of United Nations (UN) emergency forces in the Sinai Peninsula. That was a brilliant move by Nasser because he took advantage of

Sa'ud's strong desire to build up his own Arab nationalist credentials and simultaneously hid his own inability to prevent Israeli ships from passing through the gulf by shifting the blame onto Sa'ud, thereby promoting a rift in US-Saudi relations in the process.

There were those, however, who had serious doubts about Sa'ud's usefulness to the United States in the inter-Arab arena. In Cairo, following the four-power conference, a US diplomat remarked, "If after this meeting [the] United States doesn't fulfill what Saud thinks are its promises, the King could react very dangerously. He has staked his reputation and honor on [the] United States and could switch completely if he feels betrayed."[4] The king, as stated earlier, had his own reasons for cooperating with Washington: He wanted US pressure on Israel to withdraw from the Sinai Peninsula (portions of which it occupied during the Suez crisis), as well as solutions to the Suez Canal sovereignty question, the shipping dispute, and the Palestinian refugee problem. Success on any one of these issues would have significantly heightened Sa'ud's standing in the Arab world. Although the United States managed to arrange an Israeli withdrawal from the Sinai (and only after Eisenhower personally intervened with a nationally televised speech designed to pressure Israel), it came through on little else.

Events at the conference also demonstrated that Sa'ud remained ultimately subordinate to Nasser or, more to the point, to Nasser's popular slogans of Arab nationalism and his ability to cause problems for the king within Saudi Arabia. The communiqué emerging from the four-power meeting, despite Sa'ud's attempts to revise it, said nothing about the threat of communism in the Middle East but instead reflected Nasser's stand on foreign policy and inter-Arab issues. This fact was not lost upon US embassy officials in Jeddah, who began to see the chinks in the armor of the US-Saudi partnership and warned the US Department of State in April 1957 that "it was clear [that the] Palestine question, Aqaba, Buraimi and in general, old issues of Zionism and imperialism loom large in Saudi thinking and could easily affect our relations quite seriously."[5] The British, for their part, had been very skeptical of the US plan to build up Sa'ud as a rival to Nasser. As one British official noted, "The Americans may have been deceived both about the area of real agreement between Saudi and American policy and the degree of influence which Saud exercises over his Arab colleagues. Saud must know that Egypt is able to make serious trouble for him in his own country."[6] In retrospect, this observation seems to have been correct on all counts. As a result, by the time the American-Syrian crisis developed, Saudi Arabia and the United States were essentially on different wavelengths regarding Middle East policy. Saudi Arabia as well as other presumed pro-West Arab states, particularly Iraq, were unwilling to take the leadership role in response to the situation in Syria in August–September 1957. This compelled the Eisenhower administration to adopt an alternative and, as it turned out, much more dangerous path toward "correcting" the situation in Syria.

Washington's Response to the Crisis

Both Eisenhower and Dulles felt that the course of events in Syria in August 1957 was "unacceptable." Both believed the United States "could not afford to have exist a Soviet satellite not contiguous to the Soviet border and in the midst of the already delicate Middle East situation."[7] And both were also anxious to take advantage of the initial trepidation expressed by Syria's neighbors, which would subside, it was thought, if the United States did nothing. The administration also knew their friends in the Middle East were looking to it to lead the way, but Eisenhower and Dulles were looking in the opposite direction for a regional response to the crisis, hamstrung as they were by the specter of Suez and Soviet actions in Hungary.

It is clear that the United States was seriously contemplating direct military action against Syria. In a telephone conversation with Chief of Staff General Nathan Twining on August 21, Dulles stated that "we are thinking of the possibility of fairly drastic action."[8] Also on August 21, Dulles wrote to British Foreign Minister Selwyn Lloyd that "it seems to us that there is now little hope of correction from within and that we must think in terms of the external assets reflected by the deep concern of the Moslem states. . . . We must perhaps be prepared to take some serious risks to avoid even greater risks and dangers later on."[9] British Prime Minister Harold Macmillan commented on August 27 that "this question is going to be of tremendous importance. The Americans are taking it very seriously, and talking about the most drastic measures—Suez in reverse. If it were not serious . . . it would be rather comic."[10]

The desire for a regional response supported by Saudi Arabia, however, was most clearly demonstrated in a letter from Eisenhower to Sa'ud dated August 21, 1957: "We believe that it is highly preferable that Syria's neighbors should be able to deal with this problem without the necessity for any outside intervention. In view of the special position of Your Majesty as Keeper of the Holy Places of Islam, I trust that you will exert your great influence to the end that the atheistic creed of Communism will not become entrenched at a key position in the Moslem world."[11]

The constraints upon the willingness and ability of Sa'ud to play this role and the misperception by the administration that the king had significant influence in the Middle East eliminated any hope for a regional response. Macmillan wrote Dulles on August 23 that the "essential point is that the other Arabs should expose the pretensions of the present Syrian regime to be good Arab nationalists and should denounce them for what they are, namely Communists and Communist stooges."[12] The problem was that Syria's neighbors did not agree with Macmillan's assessment. Instead, the White House received two notes from Sa'ud on August 25, one that dealt with the shipping question and the other with Syria. Although their contents are unknown, they were described as being "couched in extremely tough language," suggesting that Sa'ud was placing the blame for the events in Syria squarely on the United States and/or was presenting the administration with a quid pro quo of his own connected with the shipping dispute.[13] In response, the State Department wrote to its embassy in Jeddah: "We find it very disappointing indications you have received of King's attitude toward developments in Syria. . . . In interests [of] Saudi Arabia and in those of all NE [Near East] states we are anxious that [the] King use his political and moral authority to rally opposition in area to present Syrian regime and to facilitate generating of pressures designed to isolate Syria and to work toward an improvement of situation in that country."[14] The US ambassador in Jeddah also emphasized to the king the danger of communism and Soviet influence in the Middle East while trying to play down the relationship with Israel. He was unable to persuade Sa'ud.

Policy Transformation in Washington

Eisenhower faced two major problems with military intervention in Syria. First, during the Suez crisis and the Soviet invasion of Hungary, he had supported the principle that "military force was not a justifiable means for settling disputes."[15] But he was also convinced that Syria was on the road to becoming a Soviet satellite, and he was determined not to let this happen; he was not going to be accused of "losing" any country to communism, much as the Republicans had rhetorically bashed the Truman administration for "losing" China. Thus, the president had to find a way to rationalize this dilemma, first to himself, then to the outside world. He did this by viewing the Syrian situation as inherently different from the Suez crisis. The Arabs, he postulated, were "convinced" that Syria had been clandestinely invaded through infiltration and subversion, whereas during Suez they believed Nasser had acted well within his rights in nationalizing the Suez Canal Company. Eisenhower decided that Arab action against Syria "would be *basically* defensive in nature, particularly because they intended to react to *anticipated aggression,* rather than to commit a naked aggression" (emphasis added).[16] The sticky question of how to deal with subversion, one that critics of the Eisenhower Doctrine had asked when it was announced, had again come to the forefront; the administration was forced to answer it. Now, however, instead of the pretext being an open attack of one country against another, the administration was preparing the way for possible military intervention on the grounds of *anticipated aggression.* All the United States needed was an arbitrary finding that Syria was controlled by international communism.

The second problem facing Eisenhower revolved around the fact that no Arab state was willing to assume a leadership role in response to the crisis. This was apparent when the White House sent an experienced and respected diplomat, Loy Henderson, who was then deputy undersecretary for administration, to the Middle East to sound out Washington's allies in the region regarding the Syrian situation. Unexpectedly, he did not have a solid proposal to put forth to the conferees when he arrived in Istanbul on August 24. In fact, the British ambassador to Turkey described Henderson as having been "inadequately briefed and rather devoid of ideas."[17] The conferees had obviously expected Henderson to arrive with a proposal, but none was forthcoming, and all they could agree upon was that something had to be done soon. Crown Prince 'Abd al-Ilah of Iraq admitted there was no trust between Jordan's King Hussein and himself; the United States had counted on Iraqi-Jordanian cooperation against Syria.[18] The Jordanians insisted that Saudi support was the key to the whole situation; without it Hussein could only leave Turkey to vacation in Italy and Spain, a move that led Eisenhower to conclude that "contrary to what we had been led to believe . . . [Jordan] did not want to join in any move against Syria."[19]

Within the ruling circles in the Arab world, differences of opinion could also be found as to the seriousness of the Syrian situation. They had to be wary of the sentiments of the populace, who were largely sympathetic with the Syrian regime. Henderson was reported to have been "shocked" by the negative reaction of the Lebanese press to his visit to Beirut, a reaction that was typical below the government level in most Arab states at the time. Nowhere was this more evident than in Iraq; the Iraqi government's refusal to lead an all-Arab response against Syria was as important to the disruption of the Eisenhower administration's plans vis-à-vis Syria as Saudi Arabia's decision not to follow the US lead, for if the administration was depending on Saudi political and economic support, it was also depending on Iraq to provide the muscle needed to intimidate or take direct action against Syria.

Henderson's findings left the White House confused. Referring to Henderson's trip to the Middle East, the president would write in his memoirs that "whereas early information had indicated the possibility of prompt Iraqi military action with the Turks abstaining, there were now hints of a reversal of this arrangement."[20] The United States at first wanted Turkey to play a secondary role, conscious of the fact that many Arabs still had a strong distaste for the Turks rooted in the days of Ottoman rule in addition to the fact that action by a North Atlantic Treaty Organization member might enlarge the dispute to the international level with possible Soviet involvement. However, the Turkish government, already bordering the Soviet Union to the north, was very concerned about a possible Soviet satellite coming into being to the south.

With the failure of the Henderson mission, the administration, especially John Foster Dulles, reverted to standard cold war thinking. From this point on, it viewed the US-Syrian crisis as it related to the Soviet Union, with all the trappings befitting the "Munich mentality," something that would have a particularly telling impact on the Turks. In a letter to Harold Macmillan discussing Henderson's findings, Dulles wrote the following:

> There is nothing that looks particularly attractive and the choice of policy will be hard. We are not completely satisfied with any of the alternatives which have thus far been suggested. There are risks involved in and objection found to all of them. We are continuing to explore other possibilities. . . . I do not suggest that we have reached any conclusion in favor of encouraging positive action. However, Loy Henderson has the impression that the Turks are desperately serious about this situation, and I do not think either of our governments wants to try to impose what could be another Munich.[21]

How Dulles concluded that the Turks should be given the green light to proceed militarily against Syria if they chose to do so, thereby contradicting the rationale of an all-Arab response, is not the question that should be addressed at this time.[22] Suffice it to say that, having failed to acquire the support of Saudi Arabia and Iraq, the administration looked elsewhere to "correct" the situation in Syria. However, this move transformed the crisis, already elevated from the bilateral level to the regional level, then from the regional level to the international level, as the Soviet Union felt compelled to intervene in order to protect its potential client state and enhance its standing in the Third World. The Kremlin directly warned Turkey, and by implication the United States, to stay out of Syria. And, contrary to many previous studies of this incident that conclude the Soviet Union purposefully exaggerated the crisis after the climax had already passed in order to gain propaganda points, Moscow quite probably saved Syria from external intervention. Outside Turkey, the players in the region itself were more than ready to end the crisis, but Dulles insisted on some kind of "victory" over Syria, and thus the Soviet Union, and this raised the level of international tension.

Sa'ud Takes the Initiative

As the United States and the Soviet Union were indulging in their superpower standoff, diplomacy shifted back to the regional level as Saudi Arabia entered the scene. Sa'ud saw the incident as an opportune moment to assert himself in the inter-Arab arena by mediating a percolating crisis. On the more practical side, he also wanted to salvage his assets in Syria and pull it again toward the Saudi orbit and away from Nasser's influence. Iraq was unable to do this because its government was unredeemably regarded as a lackey of imperialism—in addition to the fact that it had lost most of its "assets" in Syria as a result of the exiles and trial verdicts following the exposure of the failed British-Iraqi plot (Operation Straggle) to overthrow the Syrian regime in late 1956; but Sa'ud had distanced himself from Washington sufficiently to act the part of an Arab nationalist leader, and he was totally at odds with the British.[23] It was important that he also maintained valuable leverage over other Arab states, namely the knowledge that Saudi Arabia was one of the linchpins to the Arab coalition the Eisenhower administration had hoped to form (i.e., if Syria and Egypt did not support his mediatory efforts he would throw his weight behind the US initiative). As expected, the Syrian regime, which had repeatedly branded Sa'ud an imperialist tool and a US lackey earlier in the year, started praising the Saudi monarch for his farsightedness, compassion, and commitment to Arab causes. The government began to vociferously support Saudi Arabia's position on the shipping and Buraimi questions and initiated a back-and-forth stream of diplomatic visits between Damascus and Riyadh.

En route to receive "medical treatment" in West Germany, Sa'ud made a twenty-four-hour stopover in Beirut on September 7 to consult with various Lebanese officials and, almost assuredly, with Syrian officials as well (an especially likely event in light of the somewhat coordinated sequence of events that transpired soon thereafter). The Syrians, who earlier in the year would have viewed Sa'ud's mediatory efforts as unwarranted interference in Syrian affairs, now publicly welcomed this visit. Almost overnight, the Lebanese, Jordanian, and Iraqi governments started to back away from their earlier condemnation of Syria and began to make noises in support of the Syrian regime. The Saudi ambassador to Syria stated on September 10 that his country would "spare no effort to support, back, and aid" Syria should it be the object of outside aggression.[24] On September 12, a Saudi official was quoted as saying that "Saudi Arabia will not stand with hands folded in the event of any aggression against Syria."[25] Also on September 12, Sa'ud reportedly sent a note to Eisenhower urging patience and forbearance in dealing with the Syrian situation, and he claimed that reports of the Syrian threat had been exaggerated.[26] As the climax to his diplomatic efforts, Sa'ud appeared at the airport in Damascus on September 25, 1957, to "consult" with Syrian officials. (Iraqi Premier 'Ali Jawdat arrived the following day.) Arab newspapers across the Middle East, including Egyptian ones, hailed Sa'ud's efforts.

Nasser's Riposte

This course of events was something Nasser was unwilling to accept, for he had worked extremely hard to keep Syria out of the West's sphere of influence (as well as that of Iraq) and to place pro-Nasserist Ba'thist and army elements in the Syrian hierarchy. Now he was in danger of "losing" Syria to Saudi Arabia or even the Soviet Union.[27] As early as September 11, 1957, Nasser was scheming with Syrian officials to counter Sa'ud. Nasser, along with his commander in chief, 'Abd al-Hakim 'Amr, and the chief of staff of the joint Egyptian-Syrian command, Hafiz Isma'il, met in Cairo with the Syrian chief of staff, 'Afif al-Bizri, and Colonel 'Abd al-Hamid Sarraj, who was the head of Syrian intelligence and the real power in Syria. In retrospect it is clear that at this meeting plans were drawn up for a dramatic move to reestablish Nasser's preeminence in the Arab world. He also intended to build up the pro-Nasser army/Ba'thist faction in Syria (through Bizri and Sarraj) in order to check Saudi advances through President Shukri al-Quwatli and Prime Minister Sabri al-'Asali, as well as Soviet influence through Khalid al-'Azm and Communist Deputy Khalid Baqdash. Nasser thus began a diplomatic offensive that was at first subtle so as not to appear to be in conflict with Sa'ud's popular mediation efforts. In addition, Nasser was well aware of the Saudi monarch's relationship with the Americans and probably realized that he too would benefit from Sa'ud's mediation, for the Egyptian president did not want to be in a position where he would be forced to come to Syria's aid against fellow Arab states, least of all Turkey or the United States, or play second fiddle to the only country really capable of protecting Syria—the Soviet Union. Nasser would cleverly allow Sa'ud to commit himself to a peaceful resolution before he made his move.

That move was to send troops to the Syrian coastal city of Latakia on October 13, ostensibly to defend Syria against Turkish "aggression" (the Turks, with encouragement from Washington, had been steadily massing forces along the border). This was done while Sa'ud was in Beirut attending a soccer match. The contrast of Sa'ud at a sports event and Nasser sending Egyptian troops to the aid of a sister state threatened by outside forces did not go unnoticed, as was, most certainly, Nasser's intent. Helped by a massive propaganda campaign, Egypt became the Arab state that matched words with deeds and honored its defense commitments. *Al-Ahram* (Egypt's government-controlled newspaper) printed on October 14 that the action showed that the defense agreement between Egypt and Syria (entered November 1955) was not "merely ink on paper . . . it is a reality." The Syrian press hailed the arrival of Egyptian troops, and Damascus Radio simultaneously intensified its charges against Turkey for its "provocations" and "aggressions" on the border. On October 17, Syria placed the army on alert and arms were distributed to civilian groups (the Popular Resistance Organization), it would have seemed even more awkward than it already was to have Syrian troops in a state of unreadiness at the exact moment that Egyptian troops were supposedly helping Syria face the imminent threat from Turkey. Had the threat been real, of course, Nasser would not have sent his troops. The Soviet Union had already explicitly warned Turkey and the United States against any action vis-à-vis Syria, so in a sense Nasser was operating under a Soviet defense umbrella. That it was more of a political than a military move is borne out by the fact that only about 2,000 Egyptian troops landed at Latakia, which was a woefully inadequate number for the supposed task. Nasser had effectively turned the tables on Sa'ud and won a tremendous propaganda victory.

In addition to upstaging Sa'ud and regaining the diplomatic initiative in the Arab world, Nasser had other reasons for sending Egyptian troops to Syria at this particular moment. With Egyptian troops on the ground in Syria, Nasser was in a position to regain his influence in the country, manipulate the political process, and protect his Ba'thist/army assets. It also prevented Bizri's advancement in the Syrian power structure through the vehicle of the joint command (Nasser reportedly did not trust Bizri and shared the US view that he was a Communist).[28] The move was also designed to solidify support for Akram al-Hawrani, who was up for election on October 14, 1957, as speaker of the Chamber of Deputies against incumbent Nazim al-Qudsi, a leading member of the traditionally pro-Iraqi Populist Party. Nasser preferred to see Hawrani win election, and the timing of the Egyptian troop landing was intended to help his chances. In view of the fact that Hawrani won by only a slim margin, Nasser's timely assistance could have been a decisive factor in the outcome. It was important to Nasser to have Hawrani in the position of the speaker of the chamber, for it was, ex officio, the vice presidency of the Syrian Republic, and if the president became ill or was away, the speaker would undertake his functions.[29] With Quwatli in his seventies and often ill (in a real or diplomatic sense), this position assumed added significance. Hawrani, as a leader of the Ba'th Party and the key to its link with the military, had essentially become the number-two figure in Syria, and he was therefore in the catbird seat for the next presidential election. In this way, Nasser and his Syrian supporters could continue to keep the "Russian millionaire," Khalid al-'Azm, from his longtime ambition.

As mentioned, Nasser was intent on securing the Ba'th Party's position in Syria. In this fashion, he could enhance the ability of the Ba'thists to withstand and reverse growing Soviet influence in Syria and solidify the country's attachment to Egypt. The fact that the Egyptian troops immediately moved inland toward Aleppo only supports this assertion. Nasser and his Ba'thist allies believed that they could help their cause in elections scheduled to be held soon in Aleppo by staging a dramatic "rescue," with the possibility of changing the view of most Aleppans toward Egypt and thus providing more votes for Ba'thist candidates. It is not surprising that the Egyptians and Ba'thists exaggerated the Turkish threat, giving plenty of air time to the purported Turkish battle cry "On to Aleppo!" Nasser and the Ba'thists, as well as the conservatives, were clearly concerned about Communist advances in Syria (particularly prevalent in northern Syria, including Aleppo) and the concomitant increase in Soviet influence.[30] The Ba'th Party had allied itself with the Communists to combat imperialism and the old guard Syrian politicians; when they succeeded, with proportionately more power accruing to the Communists as Syria's relationship with the Soviet Union tightened during the crisis, the Ba'thists decided to unofficially split from the Communists and utilize Nasser's own willingness to prevent Syria from falling under the influence of the Kremlin. All of this maneuvering proved unnecessary, however, as al-'Asali, bowing to pressure from all sides, indefinitely postponed the elections, thus buying more time for the Ba'thists to figure out a way to prevent their onetime allies from leapfrogging them. The landing of Egyptian troops returned Nasser to prominence in Syria, which made Ba'thist control and union with Egypt more palatable to many and inevitable to all.

The Egyptian troop landing at Latakia took Sa'ud totally by surprise. At a loss, he could only offer to put his armed forces at Syria's disposal, but this was hopelessly outshone by Nasser's initiative, and it was clear to all that the latter was now dictating the pace and direction of the regional diplomatic game. Evidence of this came on October 16, 1957, when King Hussein informed the ambassadors of Turkey, the United States, and Britain that Jordan would fully support Syria in the event of an attack and that Syria's independence should be maintained. Iraq publicly restated its support for Syria; even the Lebanese government reportedly gave Syrian officials assurances that they would offer assistance in case of an attack.[31]

The information disseminated from Cairo also focused at this time on linking Israel and Turkey (with US support) to an alleged plot against Syria, with reports that Israeli Chief of Staff Moshe Dayan of the Israeli Defense Forces had paid a visit to Turkey to discuss such plans. Not only did Nasser effectively portray Egypt as the savior of Syria and Arabism against Turkey and the "imperialists," but also against Public Enemy No. 1, Israel, which compelled other Arab states to follow his lead. In addition, a Turkish delegation visited Saudi Arabia on October 24 as part of Turkey's support for Sa'ud's mediation; however, it cast the king in a negative light in the Arab world since he was personally negotiating with the country that Egypt had effectively portrayed as an aggressor and imperialist tool. Sa'ud had various constraints upon his diplomatic maneuvering; namely, he did not and could not detach himself completely from the United States, and his efforts therefore seemed to be slow and plodding, especially in comparison to Nasser's actions from October 13 on. The king had to walk a tightrope to maintain a balance between Arab nationalist forces, on the one hand, and the West and pro-West elements in the Arab world on the other. Nasser, however, did not have this constraint, which allowed him to take the bold and decisive step of sending his forces into Syria. Nasser also had the military wherewithal to do so; Sa'ud did not, and the only role the king could play was that of mediator. Sa'ud's fatal mistake was that he could only accomplish his objectives at Nasser's expense. This compelled Nasser to respond to the challenge in a way that Sa'ud could not, and, for all intents and purposes, the "Arab cold war" had already begun.

US-Egyptian Modus Vivendi?

The American-Syrian crisis showed on several occasions how similar objectives can sometimes make strange bedfellows. Both Egypt and the United States were very interested in keeping Syria from becoming Communist and from falling too deeply into the Soviet orbit. In fact, a confidant of Nasser informed US officials on December 11, 1957, that the Egyptian president

> had investigated recent information we [United States] had given him relative to the communist connections of [Syrian Chief of Staff Afif al-] Bizri and is now convinced Bizri [is] a communist and that something must be done about it. . . . He [Nasser] asks of us only that we keep hands off Syria for a maximum period of three months and particularly that we do nothing which could have unintentional effect of making heroes out of Bizri, [Communist Deputy] Bakdash and [pro-Soviet] Khalid Al Azm.[32]

The Egyptian official suggested that there were "several ways of attacking the Syrian problem," but the "only country with capability [to] succeed, and which can do so with minimal repercussions is Egypt. Of [the] countries primarily concerned with [the] Syrian situation, US and Egypt have greatest interest in ensuring that country [has] stable, anti-communist government."[33] On December 10, the US ambassador to Egypt, Raymond Hare, had had a conversation with a member of the inner circle of the Revolutionary Command Council (the ruling group within Egypt), 'Ali Sabri, in which the latter stated that Egypt had more reason to worry than the United States regarding the prospect of Arab nationalism taking too much of a left-hand turn, since Egypt "had to live in the area and could not escape the consequences."[34] The State Department reacted by stating that "we wish [to] avoid impeding any Egyptian efforts to bring about change and in particular appreciate considerations re[garding] Bizri, Bakdash and Azm."[35]

The three months Nasser had asked for was one more than he actually needed. The long courtship over union between Egypt and Syria was finally consummated on February 1, 1958, producing the United Arab Republic. The regional solution to the Syrian problem that Eisenhower and Dulles so desperately wanted had occurred, albeit from an unexpected source. The Eisenhower administration calculated that if it could not keep the Soviets out of Syria, it might as well trust the job to someone who could. The United States had tried just about everything short of committing US forces to keep Syria from becoming a Soviet base in the Middle East. Dulles turned to a policy of "containment-plus," keeping the "virus" from spreading out from Syria. Nasser had successfully kept the Soviets at arm's length in Egypt; maybe his stature and power in the Arab world was enough to do the same in Syria.

The US-Egyptian rapprochement did not occur overnight and, at least from the US perspective, was by default bred more out of necessity than prescience. There had been signs during the crisis that their coinciding interests vis-à-vis Syria might produce some sort of a working relationship. In early October, the State Department publicly expressed its desire for closer relations with Egypt. Egyptian press and radio comment reacted favorably to this and generally welcomed US friendship. A piece in *Al-Sha'b* stated on October 12 that Egypt "is anxious to have good relations with the United States and other states." The next day, *al-Jumhuriya* printed that "we antagonize those who antagonize us and pacify those who pacify us."

This budding cooperation was clearly evident early on at the UN debate over the Syrian situation. The Egyptian representative to the UN, Mahmoud Fawzi, apparently told UN Secretary-General Dag Hammarskjold that the Egyptians were doing their best to keep the Syrians from proceeding with their complaint in the UN General Assembly, including trying to dissuade them from insisting that an investigatory commission be sent to the Turkish border.[36] They felt the debate would not be confined to the relatively narrow Syrian-Turkish item but would expand to cover broader issues in the Middle East that could place Nasser in some rather uncomfortable diplomatic positions, especially on the Arab-Israeli front. Fawzi also told the secretary-general that he was "bitter" over how the Soviets were forcing the hand of the Syrians in the UN.[37] Indeed, Soviet guidance of Syrian actions at the UN seemed to have awakened the US and Egyptian delegations to the possibility of limited cooperation.

From the point of view of the Eisenhower administration, cooperation with Egypt became more desirable after Sa'ud's mediation had failed and Nasser had regained his paramount position in the Arab world after the landing of Egyptian troops at Latakia on October 13. Evidence of this is found in a summary record of conversations US officials had had with Fawzi. One of these stated:

> We told Fawzi in our opinion his statement . . . was restrained and we appreciated [the] tone he had struck in it. We said we believed objectives which had outlined to us for handling this item [Syrian complaint in the UN] . . . were shared by U.S. Fawzi said Egypt and U.S. share desire to see in Middle East peaceful, constructive, independent states, free from outside interference of any kind. . . . Fawzi said he appreciated our initiative and our approach which, as far as he was concerned, represented a clean slate from which to start.[38]

The Eisenhower administration began to realize what the Egyptians already knew, that is, the latter were the only ones capable of preventing an increase of Soviet influence in Syria. Fawzi's actions at the UN (and other indications from Cairo) convinced Dulles that Nasser was sincere in his desire to "save" Syria. Having exhausted all other reasonable avenues, Dulles had no choice.

Recognizing the new political balance in the Middle East, *al-Ahram* stated on November 6, 1957, that the Soviet Union "may be on its way to the conquest of space but America can certainly conquer people's hearts." For Nasser, however, he had just traded in one headache for another with his reluctant acquiescence to the union with Syria. Most Syrians saw union with Egypt as a necessary step to avoid more internal turmoil and external interference. But for Egypt and Nasser, it was a political disaster that directly contributed to the heightening tension of the Arab cold war and the environment for the outbreak of the 1967 Arab-Israeli war. Nasser's diplomatic acumen in this particular episode certainly enabled him to achieve his immediate objectives, and it had short-term positive results. But the long-term implications were ultimately negative, as it contributed to a level of responsibility and popularity that Nasser spent the rest of his tenure in power trying to live up to—and never quite reaching.

Conclusion

With Nasser's fait accompli, and lacking any alternative, Sa'ud continued to pursue his mediation policy, but its effects were much more keenly felt in the UN than in the Middle East. Blocked at the domestic level by the disclosure of the coup attempt in Syria, at the regional level by the actions of Sa'ud and Nasser, among other persons, and at the international level by the threats emanating from the Kremlin, the Eisenhower administration opted to pursue "victory" in the UN. In doing this, however, the United States had unwittingly reignited at the international level what was a diminishing crisis by early to mid-October. Sa'ud's official offer to mediate the Syrian-Turkish crisis (as it was termed at the time) actually had the effect of lessening tensions at the UN, as other Arab delegates began to support his efforts. On October 22, 1957, the UN General Assembly officially suspended debate on the Syrian-Turkish dispute pending the outcome of Sa'ud's mediation. It would come to absolutely nothing, as Syria politely rejected his intervention, but it did provide a respite in the UN that allowed the United States and the Soviet Union to reassess their positions and separately agree to just let the crisis peter out.[39] Soviet General Secretary Nikita Khrushchev realized the untenable situation in the UN in the wake of Sa'ud's efforts. His objective of deterring the Turks and the Americans from intervening in Syria had been successful, with the concomitant rise in Soviet prestige in the Arab world and influence in Syria. It was time to end the crisis before the Soviets lost at the UN much of what they had won in the Middle East. With this in mind, Khrushchev unexpectedly appeared at a reception at the Turkish Embassy in Moscow on October 29, unofficially ending the American-Syrian crisis.

Regional players had largely dictated the pace and scope of the crisis, whereas the global superpowers, especially the United States, initiated policies in a reactionary fashion that only escalated tensions to higher and more dangerous levels. The Eisenhower Doctrine signified a globalist application of foreign policy to the Middle East, focusing on the Soviet threat, something that most Arabs thought was absolutely incongruous considering the fact that Egypt had just been attacked by Britain, France, and Israel and not by the Soviet bloc or Communist forces. By remaining at, and constantly retreating to, this analytical level, US policymakers failed to appreciate the agendas of regional actors that, in many cases, had nothing to do with the East-West conflict yet set the parameters of the political dynamics of the Middle East.

In Iran, the Eisenhower administration was successful in blunting a nationalist movement that was deemed susceptible to Communist takeover; however, this did not prevent Iranian disillusionment with, and ultimately anger toward, the United States for betraying its stated principles with democracy and self-determination, a hostility that poured forth in 1979 with the added venom of twenty-six years of repression. In Syria, the United States was unable to curb the rise of leftist Arab nationalist forces and ironically found itself ultimately, and indirectly, through Nasser's sangfroid, relying on a nationalist movement to prevent the Soviet Union from expanding its position in the Middle East; the hostility engendered by a feeling of imperialist victimization nonetheless was created, severely hampering US-Syrian relations for more than a generation. The circumstances surrounding Syria during this turbulent period compelled its leaders to think in terms of national survival rather than national development, preordaining choices and options that invariably sent it down a path trodden by many other Third World nations caught in the vice of the cold war: stunted economic growth, regional conflict and hostility, and superpower confrontation.

Notes

1. For a detailed examination of this subject and the events that led up to it, see David W. Lesch, *Syria and the United States: Eisenhower's Cold War in the Middle East* (Boulder: Westview, 1992).

2. The Eisenhower Doctrine essentially offered American military and economic aid to those nations in the Middle East that requested it in order to resist the advances of other states who were, in the official opinion of the administration, dominated by "international communism."

3. On Sa'ud's relationship with the United States and his role in the American-Syrian crisis, see David W. Lesch, "The Role of Saudi Arabia in the 1957 American-Syrian Crisis," *Middle East Policy* 1, no. 3, 1992.

4. Foreign Reports, letter to John Foster Dulles from Harry Kern, February 28, 1957, John Foster Dulles Papers, Box 118, John Foster Dulles Collection, Seeley G. Mudd Library, Princeton University, Princeton, N.J.

5. Telegram from the Embassy in Saudi Arabia to the Department of State, April 11, 1957, *Foreign Relations of the United States*, vol. 8 (1955–1957) (hereinafter FRUS), at 492.

6. British Foreign Office (FO) Report, "Middle East: The Nature of the Threat and Means of Countering It" (in preparation for the Bermuda Conference with the United States in March 1957), March 8, 1957, FO 371/127755, Public Record Office, Kew Gardens, London (hereinafter PRO); Foreign Office Reports in preparation for Anglo-American talks on June 12–14, 1957, "Measures to Ensure Continued Access to Middle East Petroleum Resources," FO 371/127756, PRO; and, "Saudi Arabia and Buraimi and Their Relations to Kuwait," FO 371/127756, PRO.

7. Memorandum of a Conversation, Department of State, Washington, D.C., August 19, 1957, 3:45 p.m., FRUS 8 (1955–1957):340–341.

8. Dulles telephone call to General Twining, August 21, 1957, John Foster Dulles Papers, Telephone Calls Series, Box 7, Dwight D. Eisenhower Library, Abilene, Kans. (hereinafter DDEL).

9. Dulles to Selwyn Lloyd, August 21, 1957, Ann Whitman File, Dulles-Herter Series, Box 7, DDEL.

10. Harold Macmillan, *Riding the Storm, 1956–1959* (New York: Harper and Row, 1971), pp. 279–280.

11. Eisenhower to King Saud, August 21, 1957, Ann Whitman File, International Series, Box 42, DDEL.

12. British Foreign Office, August 23, 1957, FO 371/128224, PRO; also, Macmillan, *Riding the Storm,* 279.

13. Memorandum of a Conversation with the President, White House, Washington, D.C., August 28, 1957, FRUS 8 (1955–1957):659–660.

14. Telegram from the Department of State to the Embassy in Saudi Arabia, August 27, 1957, FRUS 8 (1955–1957):500–502.

15. Dwight D. Eisenhower, *Waging Peace, 1956–1961* (Garden City, N.Y.: Doubleday, 1965), p. 198.

16. Ibid.

17. British Consulate-Istanbul, August 25, 1957, FO 371/128224, PRO.

18. As a US official pointed out, Iraqi troops would have a much easier time penetrating Syria through Jordan than to traverse the vast desert and roadless space directly across the Syrian-Iraqi border. Memorandum of a Conversation Between the President and the Secretary of State, White House, Washington, D.C., September 2, 1957, FRUS 8 (1955–1957): 669–670.

19. British Embassy-Amman, August 28, 1957, FO 371/128225, PRO, and Eisenhower, *Waging Peace,* 200–201.

20. Eisenhower, *Waging Peace,* 200.

21. Letter from Secretary of State Dulles to Prime Minister Macmillan, September 5, 1957, FRUS 8 (1955–1957):681–682.

22. For a detailed analysis of this policy transformation, see Lesch, *Syria and the United States.* There are no "smoking-gun" documents to prove that the United States gave or was prepared to give the Turks the "green light," but there is enough circumstantial evidence as well as confirmations acquired from players who were intimately involved in the process at the time (who wish to remain anonymous), that I am convinced that the Eisenhower administration did so and that it was only Soviet threats against Turkey that prevented what could have been a very dangerous situation from developing. For a particularly revealing document on the subject, see Telegram from the Department of State to the embassy in Turkey, September 10, 1957, FRUS 8 (1955–1957):691–693.

23. On October 6, 1957, the Saudi government officially denied its acceptance of the Eisenhower Doctrine, countering what had been taken for granted in diplomatic circles since Sa'ud's visit to Washington in February, even though the king never publicly announced his country's adherence to it.

24. Foreign Broadcast Information Service (FBIS), September 11, 1957, A2.

25. FBIS, September 16, 1957, A1.

26. *New York Times,* September 15, 1957.

27. If Syria was "lost" to Saudi Arabia, it is likely that pro-West elements would have gained in strength and possibly even assumed power (with the issues of union with Iraq and membership in the Baghdad Pact resurfacing), but there is nothing to suggest that Saudi Arabia and the United States were working together toward this goal, that is, Washington was not supportive of Sa'ud's mediation until it became useful to do so to escape from a United Nations dilemma later during the US–Syrian crisis; indeed, there exists much evidence that Riyadh and Washington were at odds with each other during most of the crisis period. See Lesch, *Syria and the United States,* 190–209.

28. Telegram from the Embassy in Egypt to the Department of State, December 11, 1957, FRUS 8 (1955–1957):744–746.

29. "Syria's Egyptian Visitors," *Economist,* October 19, 1957, 230–231.

30. Elias Murqus, a former Syrian Communist, offers an interesting criticism of the Communist Party's activities at this time. He felt its overaggressiveness vis-à-vis the Ba'th seriously damaged its chances to gain power. *Tarikh al-ahzab al-shuyu'iyya fi al-watan al-'arabi (History of the Communist Parties in the Arab World)* (Beirut: al-Jam'a al-Lubaniya, 1964), 91–92.

31. FBIS, October 17, 1957, A2.

32. Telegram from the Embassy in Egypt to the Department of State, December 11, 1957, FRUS 8 (1955–1957):744–746.

33. Ibid.

34. Ibid.

35. Telegram from the Department of State to the Embassy in Egypt, December 12, 1957, FRUS 8 (1955–1957): 746–747.

36. British United Nations (UN) Delegation-New York, October 16, 1957, FO 371/128242, PRO.

37. British UN Delegation-New York, October 18, 1957, FO 371/128242, PRO. The US delegate at the UN, Henry Cabot Lodge, told Dulles that "Bitar is here and is lonely and overwhelmed by Soviet overtures and would like to talk with someone from the West." Telephone Call from Lodge to Dulles, October 2, 1957, 5:40 p.m., John Foster Dulles Papers, Telephone Calls Series, Box 7, DDEL.

38. Telegram from the Mission at the United Nations to the Department of State, October 24, 1957, FRUS 8 (1955–1957):728–729.

39. British UN Delegation-New York, October 28, 1957, FO 371/128244, PRO.

8

US Policy and Military Intervention in the 1958 Lebanon Crisis

Erika Alin

The administration of President Dwight D. Eisenhower regarded the 1958 civil crisis in Lebanon as a microcosm of the threat to Western influence emanating from the spread of Soviet communism and Arab nationalism in the Middle East during the 1950s. In analyzing Lebanon's disturbances, it focused on the regional and international contexts and repercussions of the crisis, attributing the crisis to external interference in Lebanese affairs by Egyptian and Syrian Arab nationalists. It feared that a major consequence of the crisis would be a reduction of Western influence in Lebanon and the coming to power of an Arab nationalist leadership in Beirut that would reorient Lebanon's foreign policy away from the West and in the direction of nonalignment and closer relations with Moscow. At a time when US officials believed that Western interests were being challenged not only in Lebanon but throughout the Middle East, the administration feared that a change in the Lebanese government could prove deleterious to the US position in the region.

Concerned with the potentially negative regional and international repercussions of the Lebanon crisis, the United States adopted a public posture of firm support for the pro-Western Lebanese government. It publicly declared that it was ready to use military force to secure Lebanon's political integrity and, following the July 14 overthrow of the pro-Western government of Iraq, dispatched military forces to Beirut to prevent a violent and/or radical change in the country's government and to deter further challenges to Western interests in the Middle East.

Yet even as the Eisenhower administration publicly responded resolutely to the crisis, privately it had reservations regarding both the nature of the challenge to Western interests presented by developments in Lebanon as well as the need for and effectiveness of US military action to resolve the crisis. Despite its emphasis on the external Communist and Arab nationalist challenges to Lebanon, it recognized that Lebanese tensions were partly rooted in domestic conditions and events particular to that country. And, though it was convinced that the US standing in the cold war required a firm demonstration of commitment to Lebanon's pro-Western government—including the potential use of force—it also realized that Lebanese developments were only indirectly related to the US-Soviet struggle. It also generally believed that the crisis could be resolved without the use of US force. Consequently, US policy toward Lebanese developments in 1958 was marked by ambiguity. As the crisis evolved during the spring and early summer, the Eisenhower administration adopted a wait-and-see posture, publicly announcing its support for Lebanon's pro-Western government yet remaining reluctant to act militarily. This posture, however, came to an abrupt end with the July 14 coup in Iraq, which dramatically raised US fears concerning the stability of pro-Western governments in the region, including that of Lebanon.

US-Lebanese Relations, 1953–1957

The Eisenhower administration regarded Lebanon as an important political asset to its Middle East policy. Lebanon, a former French mandate, had a history of friendly relations with the West. US-Lebanese ties had grown following World War II with the expansion of US business and political interests in the Middle East and the emergence of Beirut as a financial and commercial center in the area. During the mid-1950s, Lebanon's president, Camille Chamoun, grew increasingly supportive of US regional initiatives despite the growing popular appeal of Arab nationalism both in and outside of Lebanon. Furthermore, whereas many Arab countries in the late 1940s and early 1950s experienced domestic crises and upheavals, Lebanon's political system—dominated by the Christian community—seemed to augur well for continued Western influence and relative political stability. Lebanon's significance for US Middle East policy was premised on its role as a stable counterpoint to the growing, nationalist inspired, anti-Western orientation of most Arab states at the time and as a center for US political and commercial operations in the region.

US officials believed that many Lebanese government officials during Chamoun's initial year in the presidency were "extremely friendly" to the United States. Yet they were not unaware of the potential for growing domestic challenges to Lebanon's "pro-Western neutrality." A spring 1953 Middle East mission headed by Secretary of State John Foster Dulles had concluded that even pro-Western Lebanese officials were reluctant to pursue closer relations with the United States until regional issues that contributed to anti-Western sentiments among Lebanese and other Arabs, such as the Palestine problem and the British presence in the Suez Canal Zone, had been addressed.[1] Over the next several years, regional developments, especially Nasser's assumption of power in Egypt, the emergence of the pro-Western Baghdad Pact defense alliance, and the growing appeal of the Arab nationalist movement following the 1956 Suez crisis, increased popular criticism of the West in Lebanon. Such developments also contributed to a growing sectarian-based polarization on foreign policy issues among Lebanese.

At the center of the political controversy in Lebanon was the conviction held by many Lebanese that their influence within the country's political system was being challenged by the activities and allegiances of the country's other sectarian communities. The 1943 so-called National Pact, which provided the basis for Lebanon's political system, had aimed to balance political influence among the country's major sects—especially the politically dominant Maronite Christians and Sunni Muslims—and to prevent these communities from entering into external alliances that could upset the domestic political balance.[2] During the mid- and late 1950s, many Lebanese Muslims believed that the political balance mandated by the pact was being violated, directly or indirectly, by President Chamoun. At the domestic level, Chamoun attempted to diminish the influence of politicians opposed to his policies—especially traditional communal leaders—and to increase the authority of the country's Christian presidency; at the foreign policy level, he sought to move Lebanon closer to the West.[3] Lebanese Christians, in turn, especially Maronites, feared that Muslims, increasingly influenced by Arab nationalist sentiments, wanted to incorporate Lebanon into a pan-Arab Muslim political union.

Sectarian political, social, and economic differences among Lebanese had predated Chamoun's presidency. They were, however, exacerbated by Chamoun's policies and by regional developments during the 1950s. Following the 1956 Suez crisis, the Lebanese government's increasingly pro-Western orientation found support primarily among Christians, whereas pan-Arab allegiances were to be found primarily, but by no means exclusively, among the country's Muslim population.[4]

During the mid-1950s, as Arab nationalist allegiances increased among Lebanese Muslims, US officials began to grow "concern[ed] over political developments in Lebanon and [the] possible consolidation [of] opposition to Chamoun."[5] Partly in order to reduce domestic criticism of his policies and gain time to consolidate his political position, Chamoun altered the composition of the Lebanese cabinet to better correspond to growing Arab nationalist sentiments in the country. In September 1955, he replaced the pro-Western prime minister, Sami Solh, with Rashid Karami, a supporter of closer relations with Egypt and especially Syria. Officials at the US embassy in Beirut feared that Karami's policies would "not be favorable to United States interests" and that the new cabinet would align Lebanon with the Egyptian, Syrian, and Saudi Arabian axis that had emerged as a counteralliance to the pro-Western Baghdad Pact.[6] In March 1956, yet another Lebanese cabinet, this time under the leadership of Abdullah Yafi, announced that Lebanon would remain neutral in the cold war and would improve its relations with Syria.[7]

Although US embassy officials recognized that these cabinet changes represented tactical political moves by Chamoun, they were also aware that Chamoun himself was not entirely satisfied with US policies toward Lebanon or the Arab world as a whole. Even as the Lebanese leader credited the Eisenhower administration with demonstrating a greater interest in Arab affairs than had previous US governments, he criticized it for not having "arrived at a correct solution to Arab problems," such as the Palestine issue. He also believed that the administration's emphasis, in its bilateral relations as well as overall regional policy, on the positions of Arab states in the cold war was not effectively supported by a "firm [and] planned policy" to counter Communist challenges and especially to assist pro-Western leaders in the region, the absence of which, he claimed, was evident in the U.S. refusal to provide Lebanon with arms for even a "minimum posture of defense."[8]

During the mid-1950s, the Eisenhower administration expressed concern not only with the growing criticism of Chamoun's government from Arab nationalist Lebanese, and with Chamoun's decision to counter such pressure by according prominent government posts to Arab nationalists, but also with what it perceived as an expansion of Communist activities in Lebanon. By the early 1950s, according to the US Department of State, Beirut had become "a center for the propagation and dissemination of communist propaganda in the Near East."[9] The US embassy, during the administration's early years, reported extensively on Communist recruitment efforts among Lebanese students, women, and Palestinian refugees. It believed that the "inaction, indifference, and even appeasement" of the Chamoun government had contributed to an escalation of Communist activities in the country. Chamoun had permitted Communists to assume a greater public role, refused—embassy and State Department officials complained—to try suspected Communists "in a more energetic manner," and rejected US requests for firmer measures against Communist meetings and street demonstrations.[10]

Although US officials were concerned with Communist involvement in Lebanon, they generally recognized that most Lebanese did not support communism as an ideology but rather used it as a practical means of expressing dissent. They also subsequently recognized that Communists were not a major factor in Lebanon's escalating troubles during 1957 and early 1958.[11] Although Communists shared the anti-Chamoun sentiments of Lebanese Arab nationalists, according to State Department and embassy officials, the Lebanese "Communist Party has not sought to subvert or overturn the Lebanese government" and "none of the [anti-Chamoun] opposition parties or religious groups in Lebanon have seriously entertained offers of communist collaboration."[12]

The appointment of Arab nationalists to prominent cabinet posts in late 1955 and early 1956 provided Chamoun with a political respite that enabled him to begin, in late 1956, to reassert his control over Lebanon's domestic and foreign policies. Following the British-French-Israeli attack on Egypt in the Suez crisis, Chamoun refused to suspend relations with Britain or France, a position that was opposed by many Lebanese Muslims and provoked the resignation of Prime Minister Yafi. Chamoun subsequently reinstated the pro-Western Sami Solh as prime minister and appointed the pro-US Charles Malik as foreign minister. Embassy officials regarded these cabinet changes as a "pronounced defeat for Syria and for Nasser" in Lebanon.[13]

The expansion of pan-Arab popular sentiments among Lebanese Muslims as well as other Arabs following the Suez crisis convinced Chamoun to strengthen Lebanon's relations with the West, the historical protector of the country's Christian community. The Lebanese government accepted the January 1957 Eisenhower Doctrine, under which the United States committed itself to defending Middle East countries against Communist aggression, becoming the only Arab state to officially do so.[14] Most Lebanese Christians supported the government's position toward the Eisenhower Doctrine; Muslims generally opposed it. Chamoun's acceptance of the US initiative, therefore, increased sectarian-based polarization on foreign policy issues among Lebanese.

In April 1957, largely in anticipation of parliamentary elections scheduled to be held in Lebanon in June, anti-Chamoun politicians established a United National Front, which subsequently became the principal vehicle for coordinating opposition to the government during the period leading up to the 1958 crisis. The National Front was led by prominent Muslim politicians but also included several of Chamoun's Christian opponents and competitors for the presidency. As the June parliamentary elections approached, US concerns regarding Lebanon's future orientation increased. Since Chamoun's six-year presidential term would expire in September 1958, the parliament elected in 1957 would select a successor president the following year. US officials feared that anti-Chamoun and pro-Arab nationalist politicians, if elected to the parliament, would choose an anti-Western president. They believed, in the embassy's words, that electoral "defeat of the political grouping now in power would severely damage U.S. interests and could swing Lebanon into [the] Syrian-Egyptian fold."[15]

As the Eisenhower administration became concerned with the potential impact of the 1957 parliamentary elections on Lebanon's future foreign policy orientation, as the US Central Intelligence Agency (CIA) recognized, the anti-Chamoun opposition formed an "uneasy coalition" that, even if elected to the parliament, would probably "not be effective unless it is able to construct a binding control over its various factions . . . [and] it is doubtful that such control will be achieved."[16] US intelligence reports indicated that it was uncertain whether anti-Chamoun candidates, even if elected, could sustain the political cohesion required to significantly change Lebanon's foreign policies, especially since "the opposition . . . has no common objective other than forcing Chamoun from office."[17] Nevertheless, the Eisenhower administration remained concerned about the potential election outcome. It provided covert financial support to the campaigns of pro-Chamoun candidates, in part to counteract the impact of Egyptian, Syrian, and Saudi support for opposition candidates.[18]

The magnitude of the victory enjoyed by Chamoun supporters in the parliamentary elections caused even US intelligence officials to express surprise.[19] The election outcome was viewed in Washington as a victory over Nasserism in Lebanon. Yet within Lebanon the elections were accompanied by reports of government fraud and US interference, which added to the conviction of opposition politicians that Chamoun was attempting, with US support, to perpetuate his political position at their expense. The cabinet that was formed following the elections consisted almost exclusively of Chamoun supporters and was headed by the pro-Western Solh. The new parliament, devoid of several prominent Muslim politicians who had been defeated in the elections, did not accurately reflect the political sentiments of a large segment of the Lebanese population. The National Front refused to recognize the election outcome and sporadic violence erupted in the country.

US Policy and the Escalating Crisis

During the spring and early summer of 1958, tensions in Lebanon escalated in response to both regional and domestic political developments. These developments included the February 1 unification of Egypt and Syria into the United Arab Republic (UAR)—welcomed by many Lebanese Muslims as the beginning of a pan-Arab political union but feared by many Christians—as well as, at the domestic level, heightened speculations that Chamoun intended to remain in the presidency beyond the expiration of his constitutional term in 1958. During the second week of May, the Lebanese opposition began an armed insurrection against the government, prompting President Chamoun to make the first of three inquiries to the Eisenhower administration, between mid-May and the July 15 US intervention, aimed at determining whether the United States was prepared to militarily intervene in Lebanon.

By late spring 1958, the possibility of Chamoun seeking a second presidential term, in contravention of the one-consecutive-term limit of the Lebanese constitution, had become a key political grievance among Lebanese opposition leaders. Such leaders feared that, if he was reelected Chamoun would deprive them of political influence for another six years and continue strengthening the country's pro-Western posture. Although Chamoun never publicly stated his intention to seek reelection, he implied on several occasions in conversations with US officials that he was considering doing so.[20] The Eisenhower administration doubted that any presidential successor to Chamoun would continue Lebanon's open support for Western policies in the region. During the early spring of 1958, it believed, as indicated by the State Department, that "the only hope for preserving Lebanon's international posture" lay with supporting possible efforts by Chamoun to seek election to a second presidential term.[21] As Ambassador Robert McClintock later recalled, "at one time we had indicated our full support for his re-election," yet "of course we could not say this publicly and our official line would be one of assiduous refusal to meddle in Lebanese politics."[22]

Prior to the initial May 13 White House meeting on the Lebanon crisis, the Eisenhower administration therefore leaned in the direction of supporting a second presidential term for Chamoun. However, when the opposition initiated an armed revolt against the Lebanese government in mid-May, a growing recognition developed among US officials as to the extent of anti-Chamoun sentiments held by many Lebanese. US officials increasingly realized that a reelection campaign by Chamoun could escalate the civil disturbances and, given the Lebanese leader's close alignment with the United States, increase anti-Western sentiments in Lebanon. Following the real onset of the crisis, consequently, they generally preferred that Chamoun step down at the expiration of his term. By mid-May, Eisenhower had become convinced that "the thing for him [Chamoun] to do is announce that he is not going to do any running" for a second term.[23] US officials now preferred that a presidential candidate be found who would only marginally compromise Lebanon's relations with the West while gaining the support of Muslim and Arab nationalist Lebanese.

The Eisenhower administration, however, was reluctant to hurt its relations with the pro-Western Chamoun, especially given its uncertainty regarding the eventual outcome of the crisis. It therefore left open in its communications with Chamoun the possibility that, under certain conditions, it might tacitly support him or, more likely, look the other way should he attempt to extend his presidential tenure. The United States, as Dulles noted in mid-June, "[wa]s not concerned with [Lebanese] constitutional factors and would not object if, after this crisis is solved, he [Chamoun] wished to stay on as President."[24] Given indications that Chamoun perceived US support as important in deciding whether or not to seek a second presidential term, Washington's reluctance to clearly communicate its concerns over the reelection issue undoubtedly contributed to the Lebanese leader's failure, throughout the spring and early summer, to definitively state publicly that he would not seek reelection. This failure in turn contributed to the continuation of the civil crisis.

During the second week of May, antigovernment riots erupted in the Lebanese coastal town of Tripoli, triggered by the murder of an anti-Chamoun newspaper editor. The Eisenhower administration publicly blamed the riots on external Arab nationalist and local Communist instigation. It pointed to "indirect aggression" against Lebanon by the UAR and stated that it had "no doubt" that Communists had "fann[ed] the flames" of the riots and, as Eisenhower notes in his memoirs, "that Chamoun's uneasiness was the result of one more communist provocation."[25] Privately, however, as earlier indicated, many administration officials recognized that Communists were not directly involved in Lebanon's civil disturbances.

Moreover, they were aware that the crisis was partly rooted in Lebanon's unique sectarian political structure and in Chamoun's controversial policies. According to the CIA, Chamoun's policies had alienated a diverse array of Lebanese, including many who were not anti-Western.[26] State Department and intelligence officials noted that Lebanon's sectarian political balance would remain vulnerable to disruption by regional developments, particularly Arab nationalism, and—in the CIA's words—did "not believe that the present political-religious balance, with its slight edge in favor of the Christians, can long be maintained in Lebanon."[27] The domestic sources of the Lebanon crisis were also emphasized in numerous dispatches by Ambassador McClintock.[28] Yet even as US officials were aware that the internal Lebanese political situation was "extraordinarily complex," they tended to underestimate the extent to which domestic factors contributed to opposition to Chamoun's government. They also tended to subordinate a serious consideration of ways to encourage Chamoun to address such factors to the primary objective of ensuring that the crisis did not diminish Western influence in Lebanon or the Arab world. In accordance with the latter objective, the administration emphasized public support for Chamoun and the need to halt external, particularly Egyptian and Arab nationalist, involvement in Lebanon's affairs.

In response to the opposition insurrection against the Lebanese government, President Chamoun requested, on May 13, that the United States—as well as Britain and France—inform him how it would respond to a Lebanese request for external assistance, possibly in the form of military intervention. On May 13, Eisenhower convened the first White House meeting on the Lebanon crisis. During this and subsequent discussions US officials weighed the implications of using force in Lebanon. They recognized that military action could have considerable negative repercussions for US relations with Arab, Muslim, and Third World countries and that it could enable Moscow to score a propaganda victory in the cold war. They feared that, in order to protest an intervention Arab states would close the Suez Canal and suspend oil shipments to the West, threatening "a new and major oil crisis" for the Western alliance. Finally, they doubted that military action would either resolve the Lebanon crisis or guarantee Lebanon's pro-Western orientation.

Although the administration harbored reservations regarding the implications of the use of military force in Lebanon, it was also concerned that, unless it demonstrated a firm commitment to defending Lebanon's pro-Western orientation, US credibility would be questioned around the world. According to Eisenhower, although it was necessary to consider the liabilities of military action, the United States "had to take into account the apparently much larger problems which would arise if the Lebanese needed our intervention and we did not respond."[29] Both Eisenhower and Dulles were concerned that mounting challenges to pro-Western governments worldwide in the mid-1950s were creating the perception that closer relations with the Soviet Union were the wave of the future for Third World countries. Accordingly, Dulles, at the May 13 meeting, "reviewed current Communist methods of warfare throughout the world."[30] Given this global context within which the administration analyzed Lebanese developments, military action was viewed as an important means of sending a deterrent signal to anti-Western forces in the Middle East and elsewhere. Following the May 13 meeting, the Eisenhower administration informed Chamoun and made a public announcement indicating that it was prepared to consider dispatching military forces to Lebanon. US combat forces were placed in a state of readiness.

Despite its determined public posture, the administration's actual response to Lebanese developments during the late spring and early summer continued to reflect a certain ambivalence regarding both the nature and appropriate resolution of the crisis. On the one hand, the administration was convinced that the US position in the cold war required firm action in support of Chamoun's pro-Western government. On the other, it recognized that military pressure and/or action could have negative consequences for US interests—as it had experienced in the previous year's crisis with Syria—and, further, might not be needed to resolve the situation. Since it believed that "almost any course that the United States could pursue would impose a heavy cost,"[31] it basically preferred to avoid taking definitive action and, instead, let the crisis run its course in the hope that Chamoun would assert his control over the situation and/or that the contending Lebanese factions would work out a political compromise of their own accord.

According to Dulles, the United States, following the May 13 meeting, made no commitment to Chamoun beyond "the possibility of moving in troops to protect U.S. life and property if that should prove necessary" as well as aiding Lebanon in developing its military assistance program.[32] Washington had indicated that it would consider intervention if and when it determined that the situation warranted such action but not automatically in response to a Lebanese request. Key officials from the Department of State, the Department of Defense, and the CIA believed that it was important to "de-emphasize the prospect of military action" and attempt to "induce Chamoun to find a solution to the internal political problem."[33] Dulles noted, in mid-June, that there could be "no satisfactory solution to the Lebanese problem except through the lawful government's working one out with all possible assistance except armed intervention."[34]

In accordance with its belief that the Lebanon crisis could and should be resolved domestically, the Eisenhower administration, in mid-May, outlined conditions that had to be met by Lebanon before it would sanction military action. Such conditions could preclude, or at least delay, the need for military action; yet they could also establish a political framework for such action should it eventually be required. The administration made clear that it would not intervene to maintain Chamoun in power for a second presidential term (though privately US officials continued not to object to Chamoun's remaining in the presidency once the crisis had been resolved); that, concurrent with a request for US intervention, Lebanon would have to file an official complaint of its grievances regarding external Arab nationalist/ UAR interference in its affairs with the United Nations (UN) Security Council; and that, prior to an intervention, it would have to secure support for such action from at least two other Arab states. Chamoun was also informed that, should he ultimately request US intervention, such a request would have to be premised on the need for US action to protect US citizens in Lebanon and to preserve the country's independence and integrity.

Specifically, any request for US military action was to avoid references to the 1957 Eisenhower Doctrine. Although the administration feared that growing Nasserist influence could move Lebanon away from the West and toward the Soviet bloc, it recognized that "there has not occurred 'armed aggression from a country controlled by international communism'" against Lebanon.[35] The Eisenhower Doctrine was ambiguous on the circumstances justifying US military action—it failed, among other things, to clearly distinguish Communist from nationalist activities, the latter of which were not legally subject to US action under the doctrine—and the UAR was neither "controlled by international communism" nor engaged in "armed aggression" against Lebanon.[36] In legally justifying the intervention, the administration subsequently emphasized Lebanon's right to collective self-defense under Article 51 of the UN Charter, arguing that although Lebanon had not been subject to a direct foreign armed attack as required for action under the charter, UAR subversion and "indirect aggression" could be viewed as tantamount to such an attack. It also emphasized that the Lebanese government had explicitly requested US military action and that the United States had a right to protect its citizens in Lebanon.

During mid- and late May, various Lebanese groups and personalities attempted to mediate the crisis, proposing, among other things, that a caretaker government headed by the commander of the Lebanese army, General Fuad Shihab, be formed until elections for a successor president were held. General Shihab was widely respected among opposition leaders and Lebanese Muslims, partly because he regarded the crisis as a domestic dispute over Chamoun's reelection and rejected requests by Chamoun to order the armed forces to quell the civil disturbances. Efforts by Lebanese parties to mediate the crisis, however, stalemated. The opposition demanded Chamoun's early resignation and continued to incite civil disturbances. Chamoun, meanwhile, continued to refuse to clarify his position on the reelection issue. On May 22, furthermore, the Lebanese government submitted a complaint of UAR interference in Lebanon's affairs to the UN Security Council, thereby heightening opposition fears that Chamoun was seeking external support, especially from the United States, to remain in the presidency.

On June 15, in response to reports that opposition forces planned to take over the Lebanese presidential palace, Chamoun again asked the Eisenhower administration how it would respond to a request for US intervention. Both Eisenhower and Dulles believed that Chamoun was now "closer than ever" to requesting external assistance.[37] Eisenhower, in response, convened the second top level policy meeting on the Lebanon crisis, following which the United States reiterated its readiness to consider intervention. By mid-June, the Lebanese government had satisfied US conditions for an intervention, having submitted a complaint to the UN Security Council, received support for military action from Jordan and Iraq, and, through the Solh cabinet, announced that an amendment of the constitution's reelection clause would not be introduced to the parliament.

US officials remained convinced that US credibility in the cold war could be jeopardized by a failure to support the pro-Western Lebanese government; yet they continued to prefer a nonmilitary resolution to the crisis. Eisenhower, at the time, had "little, if any, enthusiasm" for military intervention. The potential liabilities of intervention led administration officials to speculate, at the June 15 meeting, on alternative ways of providing military support to strengthen the Lebanese government's position short of direct military action, including the formation of a multinational UN force. None of these suggestions, however, were seriously pursued. By mid-June, with the Lebanese government having fulfilled US conditions for an intervention, the administration recognized that, even though it believed that the crisis should be resolved without US involvement, it would be hardpressed to justify a failure to respond to a "properly worded" Lebanese request for military action.

Moreover, it feared that Chamoun in fact preferred external military action to domestic initiatives, whether military or political, to resolve the crisis. Dulles believed that Chamoun had to be "disabuse[d] . . . of any thought that he has a blank check from us with regard to military intervention."[38] The administration was convinced that, militarily, "the regular Lebanese army can and will deal with" the crisis by suppressing opposition activities.[39] US officials expressed confusion as to why Chamoun neither effectively used the Lebanese armed forces to quell the disturbances nor replaced General Shihab with a commander prepared to do so. They recognized some of the reasons for Shihab's opposition to involving the army in the disturbances, as well as for Chamoun's reluctance to order the former to do so, including that such involvement could cause a sectarian split in the army and, according to Dulles, that any move by Chamoun to dismiss Shihab could trigger a military coup.[40] Yet the administration nevertheless tended to regard Chamoun's failure to secure army involvement as evidence that the Lebanese leader was reluctant to take the necessary domestic measures to resolve the crisis.

It also questioned why Chamoun was not trying harder to put an end to the controversial reelection issue and, specifically, why he continued to refuse to make a public statement indicating that he would not seek a second term (which he would not do until June 30). Eisenhower believed that Chamoun had made a "political error" in not publicly foreclosing his reelection at an earlier date. In addition, according to Dulles, Chamoun had not made a "loud and effective" case for his government's position, especially the contention that the crisis was the result of UAR interference, to the Lebanese public. The United States believed that Chamoun's failure to seriously attempt to win support for his government's position within Lebanon and, more generally, to gain control over the crisis—either through political or military means—increased both the potential need for US intervention to resolve the crisis and the political as well as possible military complications of such action should it eventually be required.[41]

Chamoun's preference for close relations with the West, and the perceived threat of Arab nationalism in Lebanon, encouraged the Lebanese president to look outside of Lebanon for assistance. Chamoun appeared confident that the United States would automatically intervene if requested to do so. His confidence can be attributed, in part, to the fact that the Eisenhower administration, despite privately and, at times, publicly encouraging the Lebanese government to find a political solution to the crisis, remained reluctant to communicate to Chamoun its reservations regarding his handling of the crisis and to clearly make US military action contingent on evidence that Chamoun had seriously pursued domestic policies intended to resolve the crisis. Instead, the administration essentially deferred to Chamoun's preferences regarding how Lebanese developments should be handled. Dulles believed, as did many other Washington officials, that the United States "should not destroy Chamoun's heart or courage by pressing him to compromise with the opposition" and "should not offer him specific advice with regard to political moves which he might make within Lebanon."[42]

The Intervention and Its Aftermath

On July 14, the Eisenhower administration ordered 14,000 US troops to Lebanon. The immediate impetus for the intervention came from the overthrow of the pro-Western government of Iraq, which heightened US fears concerning the security of pro-Western governments throughout the Middle East. Eisenhower believed, upon receiving news of the Iraqi coup, that the United States was facing its "last chance to do something" to end challenges to pro-Western governments and Western interests in the region. Within the context of the cold war, the administration feared that a failure to respond decisively to developments in Iraq would send a signal of US weakness that could have repercussions for the West's political and military positions worldwide.

On July 14, Chamoun, fearing that the Iraqi coup would embolden the Lebanese opposition, requested US military intervention, in response to which Eisenhower convened, on the same day, the third and fourth White House meetings on the Lebanon crisis. Even before the morning meeting, Eisenhower's "mind was practically made up" concerning the need for intervention.[43] From having maintained a wait-and-see posture toward the use of force throughout the spring and early summer, the administration, within hours following the Iraqi coup, came to see an intervention as the only means of securing the political stability and integrity of the Lebanese state and, even more important, of deterring further challenges to pro-Western countries in the Middle East. In the minds of US officials, the need to act firmly and quickly in response to the Iraqi coup overrode earlier concerns regarding both the necessity and effectiveness of the use of force to resolve the Lebanon crisis.[44]

Lebanese reaction to the landing of US marines on the beaches of Beirut reflected preexisting political loyalties. Many Christians welcomed the action, even though a significant number opposed Chamoun's appeal for external assistance. Government supporters and the opposition initially believed that US troops had been sent to Lebanon to prolong Chamoun's tenure, and many Christians, including Chamoun and foreign minister Malik, were reportedly disappointed with the failure of US troops to more actively support the Lebanese government's position.[45] According to Dulles, the Lebanese government remained "anxious to drag us into this [crisis] in a bigger way" by securing US troop support for the defeat and/or complete disarming of the opposition.[46] Most Lebanese Muslims condemned the intervention, fearing that the United States intended both to uphold Chamoun's tenure and to use Lebanon as a base for intervening in Jordan and possibly also Iraq. Although opposition leaders protested the intervention, they sought to avoid clashes between their armed supporters and US troops, believing that Chamoun wanted to provoke such clashes in order to prompt direct US troop support for his presidency.[47] Overall, as US embassy officials recognized, few prominent Lebanese politicians, whether Muslim or Christian, expressed public support for the intervention.[48]

One day following the arrival of US forces in Lebanon, the Eisenhower administration dispatched Deputy Undersecretary of State Robert Murphy to Beirut. During the month that he remained in the Middle East, Murphy, despite initial administration denials, played a central role in mediating the political compromise that resulted in General Shihab's election to the Lebanese presidency on July 31. Following his arrival in Beirut, Murphy communicated to Washington his analysis of the domestic context of the Lebanon crisis.

In terms of the overriding objective of deterring further challenges to Western interests in the Middle East, US officials believed that the use of military force had been successful, at least in the short term. The Soviet Union did not respond militarily to the intervention. Indeed, most high-ranking US officials, including Eisenhower, had become convinced during the months prior to the intervention that neither Moscow nor Cairo would respond militarily to US action in Lebanon and that such action consequently would not carry significant military risks for the United States.[49] If, prior to the intervention, the administration had been preoccupied with the regional and international dimensions of the crisis, the absence of further immediate challenges to Western regional interests following the intervention convinced it both to limit its military action to Lebanon and to attempt, through Ambassador Murphy, to address what had earlier been considered a second-order concern, that is, the domestic political sources of the crisis. A compromise settlement, capable of at least partially satisfying the demands of Lebanese nationalists, could now minimize the negative regional political fallout from the intervention.

On July 31, after a period of considerable political uncertainty, General Shihab was elected by the parliament to succeed Chamoun. The Eisenhower administration had not openly supported any particular candidate in the political process leading up to Shihab's election and, in order not to be perceived as attempting to influence the elections, Murphy left Lebanon on July 30. However, Murphy's extensive rounds of mediation had played an important role in generating agreement on a presidential successor.[50] Despite continued concerns regarding Shihab's political leanings, especially his relations with Nasser, Dulles subsequently noted that the general's election "was probably the most favorable result under the complicated circumstances existing in Lebanon, particularly since the opposition had voted for Shihab."[51] On September 24, Shihab was inaugurated as president of Lebanon and, one month later, the last US forces withdrew from the country.[52]

Within Lebanon, an easing of political tensions occurred following the presidential election, which was accompanied by a relaxation of tensions between Lebanon and the UAR—since Nasser had generally supported Shihab's election—as well as between the United States and the UAR. Internationally, in late July and early August, the UN became the arena for a diplomatic contest between the United States and the Soviet Union that culminated in the convening of a special session of the UN General Assembly on the Middle East on August 13. Eisenhower's address to the assembly was intended to create the public perception that the United States had used force in Lebanon based on sound political and legal principles and that it was interested in improving its relations with Arab countries.

Within Lebanon, Chamoun's departure from the presidency and the subsequent reintegration of opposition leaders into the political system partially removed a principal grievance that had contributed to the escalation of anti-American sentiments among Lebanese Muslims during the mid-1950s. However, many Lebanese and other Arabs had regarded the intervention as an illegal interference in Lebanon's domestic affairs and had viewed US policy throughout the crisis as favoring Chamoun. The intervention, therefore, contributed to the perception, both within Lebanon and the wider Arab world, that the United States "to some extent bec[a]me identified along with the British and French as 'imperialists'" prepared to intervene militarily to secure its interests in the Middle East.[53] Lebanese attitudes toward the United States following the intervention also continued to be affected by the same factors that offended the nationalist sentiments of Arabs in general, such as US support for Israel. Partly as a result of continued anti-Western and pro-Arab nationalist sentiments among many Lebanese, as well as of Shihab's own preferences for a more neutral Lebanese international posture, the CIA accurately predicted, in October 1958, that Lebanon was likely to depart from its pro-Western orientation and move "in the direction of neutralism and accommodation with pan-Arab nationalism."[54]

Conclusion

By sending US troops to Lebanon, the Eisenhower administration sought to uphold Western interests in the Middle East against the perceived challenge of Arab nationalism and, to a lesser extent, communism. During the mid-1950s, the administration had attempted to curtail the spread of anti-Western political forces in the region by supporting pro-Western Arab governments, such as Chamoun's, and encouraging Arab states, through the Eisenhower Doctrine, to align with the West in the cold war. At the same time, however, it had recognized that its efforts to weaken the Arab nationalist movement and to bind Arab states to the West were alienating Arab public opinion and encouraging Arab leaders to pursue closer ties with the Soviet Union. In the wake of the Suez crisis, it had become more sensitive to the nuanced context of local and regional politics and had attempted to pursue a more conciliatory posture toward Arab nationalism. It had refrained from supporting its Western allies' aggression against Egypt in 1956 and from publicly denouncing the 1957 formation of the UAR. Its experiences in the 1957 Syrian crisis had, in addition, resulted in a greater recognition of the potentially negative consequences of US efforts to intervene too directly in domestic Arab political developments, contributing to its subsequent reluctance to become militarily involved in the Lebanese situation prior to the July 14 Iraqi coup.

The events of the summer of 1958 (the Lebanon crisis, the unexpected overthrow of the pro-Western Iraqi government, and the conviction of US officials that only the resort to military force had prevented a further deterioration in Western influence in the Arab world) increased the Eisenhower administration's recognition that safeguarding long-term US interests in the Middle East would require "winning the minds of the Arab peoples." The administration's concern to avoid alienating

Arab nationalist public sentiment had encouraged it, following the arrival of US forces in Lebanon, to support a compromise political settlement capable of partially satisfying the demands of pro-Arab nationalist Lebanese and to propose, through Eisenhower's August address to the UN General Assembly, US contributions to an economic development fund for the Arab world.[55] Yet even though sensitive to the need to improve US-Arab relations, the Eisenhower administration's policy toward the 1958 crisis had remained premised on the perception that Arab nationalist and Western interests stood poised against one another in the Middle East.

Notes

1. US Department of State (hereinafter DOS) Position Paper, May 5, 1953, *Foreign Relations of the United States* (hereinafter FRUS) 9 (1953–1955).

2. The pact distributes political offices in accordance with a sectarian formula, premised on demographic information from the 1932 census, under which the country's president must be a Maronite Christian, the prime minister a Sunni Muslim, and the speaker of the parliament a Shi'a Muslim, and states that Christians should refrain from calling on Western countries to defend their interests and that, although Lebanon has an "Arab face," Muslims should not attempt to politically unify the country with other Arab states.

3. Chamoun, who had initially pursued relatively neutral regional and international policies, had attained the presidency in September 1952 during a political crisis revolving around former President Bishara al-Khoury's election to a second presidential term. Once in office, Chamoun attempted to diminish the political influence of Lebanon's traditional communal leaders, many of whom had supported his bid for the presidency, and also instituted economic policies perceived by many such leaders as neglecting the predominantly rural regions of their constituents. See Abdo I. Baaklini, *Legislative and Political Development: Lebanon, 1842–1972* (Durham, N.C.: Duke University Press, 1976), 144; Michael C. Hudson, *The Precarious Republic: Modernization in Lebanon* (New York: Random House, 1968), 105–107 and 275; and Wade R. Goria, *Sovereignty and Leadership in Lebanon, 1943–1976* (London: Ithaca Press, 1985), 29.

4. Differences remained within both the Christian and Muslim communities between the political positions of, for instance, Maronite and Greek Orthodox Christians and Sunni and Shi'a Muslims. Chamoun also had influential rivals among Christian politicians. Attitudes toward the Baghdad Pact were particularly illustrative of the emerging controversy over Lebanon's foreign alignment during the mid-1950s. Muslims generally opposed the pro-Western defense alliance. Chamoun, in contrast, reportedly indicated, in April 1955, that "there would be no delay in the Lebanese decision to adhere to the Turco-Iraqi [later Baghdad] Pact" provided that the United States reaffirmed its support of the defense arrangement. See Daily Intelligence Abstracts, April 8, 1955, Box 11, Operations Coordinating Board (hereinafter OCB) Central File Series, White House Office NSC Staff Papers, Eisenhower Library, and Leila M.T. Meo, *Lebanon: Improbable Nation, A Study in Political Development* (Bloomington: Indiana University Press, 1965), 97. By late 1954, a loose coalition of anti-Chamoun politicians had emerged and, in December 1954, a congress of "Muslim parties, associations, and organizations" submitted a list of demands to Prime Minister Solh, focusing on a more equitable distribution of government posts among the country's sects; a constitutional amendment balancing the authority of the country's president, prime minister, and parliamentary speaker; the formation of an economic union between Lebanon and Syria; and

the preservation of the country's Arab character. Fahim I. Qubain, *Crisis in Lebanon* (Washington, D.C.: Middle East Institute, 1961), 32–36.

5. Undersecretary of State Herbert Hoover Jr., DOS to Embassy in Beirut, October 28, 1955, FRUS 13 (1955–1957).

6. Embassy in Beirut to DOS, Telegram 151, October 17, 1955, 783A.21/10–1755, DOS Central Files, National Archives.

7. Embassy in Beirut to DOS, Telegram 409, March 29, 1956, 783A.13/4–456, DOS Central Files, National Archives.

8. Embassy in Beirut to DOS, Telegram 1508, May 28, 1956, 783A.11/5–2356, DOS Central Files, National Archives, and Intelligence Notes, July 9, 1956, Box 11, OCB Central File Series, White House Office NSC Staff Papers, Eisenhower Library.

9. *World Strength of the Communist Party Organizations,* Annual Report 10, DOS Bureau of Intelligence and Research (Washington, D.C.: DOS, 1958). See also M. S. Agwani, *Communism in the Arab East* (New York: Asia Publishing House, 1969), 106.

10. "Sino-Soviet Bloc Activities in Lebanon," Research and Analysis Report 7260, May 24, 1956, DOS Bureau of Intelligence and Research, Lot 58 D 776, DOS INR Files, National Archives; Embassy in Beirut to DOS, Telegram 1, July 1, 1953, 783A.001/7–153; and Telegram 623, April 6, 1954, 783A.00/4–254, DOS Central Files, National Archives.

11. See "Political Trends in Lebanon," Research and Analysis Report 7286, July 5, 1956, DOS Bureau of Intelligence and Research, Lot 58 D 776, DOS INR Files, and Embassy in Beirut to the US Information Agency (hereinafter USIA), TOUSI 326, May 19, 1958, Box 1, Record Group 59, General Records of DOS, National Archives.

12. Embassy in Beirut to DOS, Telegram 623, April 6, 1954, 783A.00/4–254, and "Sino-Soviet Bloc Activities in Lebanon," Research and Analysis Report 7260, May 24, 1956, DOS Office of Intelligence Research, DOS Central Files, National Archives.

13. William Rountree to J. F. Dulles, January 12, 1957, FRUS 13 (1955–1957).

14. Under the doctrine, Lebanon also received $10 million and $2.2 million in grant economic and military aid. American officials acknowledged that such aid was difficult to justify on economic grounds but believed that it could "make of Lebanon an example of U.S.-Arab cooperation." Briefing Materials Prepared for the Richards Mission to the Middle East, 1956–1957, Record Group 59, Lot File No. 57D 616, DOS General Records, National Archives, and James P. Richards to J. F. Dulles, March 16, 1957, and "Operation Plan for Lebanon," OCB Report, June 31, 1957, FRUS 13 (1955–1957).

15. Embassy in Beirut to DOS, March 16, 1957, FRUS 13 (1955–1957).

16. "Assessment of the Political Situation in Lebanon," July 15, 1957, Central Intelligence Agency Action Copy, DA IN 38166, declassified documents, Central Intelligence Agency.

17. "Consequences of Possible U.S. Courses of Action Respecting Lebanon," June 5, 1958, Special National Intelligence Estimate (hereinafter SNIE) SNIE 36.4–58, declassified documents, Central Intelligence Agency.

18. Memorandum of Conversation, Charles Malik and Dwight D. Eisenhower, February 6, 1957, Box 34, International Series, Ann Whitman File, Eisenhower Library.

19. "Results of the Elections in Northern Lebanon," July 9, 1957, Central Intelligence Agency Action Copy DA IN 36 202, declassified documents, Central Intelligence Agency.

20. In late 1957, he had informed then US Ambassador Charles Heath that, save for himself, no viable presidential aspirant existed who would preserve Lebanon's pro-Western alignment. During the spring of 1958, he attempted, more directly, to ascertain the US position on his possible reelection in conversations with Ambassador McClintock, who had noted already upon arriving in Lebanon in January that "Chamoun would probably prefer

for personal reasons to continue in power." Embassy in Beirut to DOS, Telegram 2203, December 30, 1957, 783A.11/12–3057, DOS Central Files, National Archives, and Memorandum from Officer in Charge of Lebanon-Syria Affairs (Waggoner) to Director of the Office of Near Eastern Affairs (Rockwell), January 17, 1958, FRUS 11 (1958).

21. DOS to Embassy in Beirut, Telegram 3709, May 7, 1958, 783A.00/5–758, DOS Central Files, National Archives.

22. Embassy in Beirut to DOS, Telegram 654, May 12, 1958, 783A.00/5–1258, DOS Central Files, National Archives, and Embassy in Beirut to DOS, July 10, 1958, FRUS 11 (1958). The CIA, in early April, indicated that Chamoun—who "actually enjoys the prospect of a bout with the opposition"—probably could outmaneuver his domestic opponents if he chose to seek reelection as a result of his own "extraordinary qualities of force, energy, and courage" and of serious divisions among opposition leaders regarding an acceptable successor presidential candidate. "Assessment of the Political Situation in Lebanon," April 4, 1958, Central Intelligence Agency Action Copy DA IN 106001, declassified documents, Central Intelligence Agency.

23. Memorandum of Telephone Conversation Between the President and the Secretary, May 14, 1958, FRUS 11 (1958).

24. Memorandum of Conversation, DOS, June 18, 1958, FRUS 11 (1958).

25. Dulles statement in *Department of State Bulletin* 38 (June 9, 1958), *U.S. News and World Report,* July 25, 1958, and Eisenhower, *Waging Peace,* 266.

26. "The Lebanese Crisis," June 14, 1958, SNIE 36.4–1–58, Central Intelligence Agency.

27. "Political Crisis in Lebanon," Report 7784m, April 15, 1958, DOS Office of Intelligence Research and Analysis, quoted in H. W. Brands Jr., *Cold Warriors: Eisenhower's Generation and American Foreign Policy* (New York: Columbia University Press, 1988), 101; and "Consequences of Possible U.S. Courses of Action Respecting Lebanon," June 5, 1958, SNIE 36.4–58, declassified documents, Central Intelligence Agency.

28. See, for example, Embassy in Beirut to DOS, February 21, 1958, and Embassy in Beirut to DOS, June 2, 1958, FRUS 11 (1958).

29. Memorandum of Conversation with the President, May 13, 1958, Box 6, White House Memoranda Series, J. F. Dulles Papers, Eisenhower Library.

30. Ibid.

31. Staff Notes, June 23, 1958, Box 33, Eisenhower Diary Series, Ann Whitman File, Eisenhower Library, and Eisenhower, *Waging Peace,* 274.

32. Memorandum of Telephone Conversation, J. F. Dulles and John Reston, May 19, 1958, Box 8, Telephone Call Series, J. F. Dulles Papers, Eisenhower Library.

33. D. J. Decker (Joint Middle East Planning Committee of the Joint Chiefs of Staff) to Chief of Naval Operations (Burke) Regarding Meeting at DOS, May 19, 1958, FRUS 11 (1958).

34. Memorandum of Conversation, DOS, June 18, 1958, FRUS 11 (1958).

35. Outgoing Telegram to President Chamoun, May 13, 1958, Drafting Office Copy, Box 16, J. F. Dulles Chronological Series, J. F. Dulles Papers, Eisenhower Library.

36. Yet in order to uphold the relevance of a doctrine it had only a year earlier proclaimed, US officials wanted to bring an intervention "into context of the [Eisenhower] Doctrine at least to some extent" by making reference to the declaration of the Mansfield amendment to the doctrine that the independence and integrity of Middle East countries was vital to US interests. Memorandum of Conversation with the President, May 13, 1958, Box 6, White House Memoranda Series, J. F. Dulles Papers, Eisenhower Library, and Dulles, as quoted in *New York Times,* May 21, 1958.

37. Memorandum of Telephone Conversation, J. F. Dulles and Dwight D. Eisenhower, June 14, 1958, Box 12, Telephone Calls Series, J. F. Dulles Papers, Eisenhower Library.

38. Memorandum of Conversation, DOS, June 18, 1958, FRUS 11 (1958).

39. DOS to Embassy in Beirut, Telegram 4890, June 19, 1958, Box 34 (2), International Series, Ann Whitman File, Eisenhower Library.

40. "The Lebanese Crisis," June 14, 1958, SNIE 36.4–1–58, Central Intelligence Agency, and "Political Crisis in Lebanon," quoted from Brands, *Cold Warriors,* p. 85, and Memorandum of Conversation with the President, June 15, 1958, Box 33, DDE Diary Series, Ann Whitman File, Eisenhower Library.

41. Both John Foster Dulles and CIA Director Allen Dulles feared that, if Lebanon's political tensions remained unaddressed, "by the time Chamoun asks, if he does, for armed intervention the situation would have deteriorated to the point where it will be difficult to do it." Memorandum of Telephone Conversation, J. F. Dulles and Allen Dulles, June 20, 1958, Telephone Call Series, J. F. Dulles Papers, Eisenhower Library.

42. Memorandum of Conversation, DOS, June 18, 1958, FRUS 11 (1958), and DOS to Embassy in Beirut, Telegram 4890, June 19, 1958, Lebanon (2), Dulles-Herter Series, Ann Whitman File, Eisenhower Library.

43. Eisenhower, *Waging Peace,* 270. Administration advisers, such as Special Assistant for National Security Council Affairs Robert Cutler, concurred that the "president knew exactly what he meant to do" at the morning meeting. Robert Cutler, *No Time for Rest* (Boston: Little, Brown, 1965), 363.

44. In the initial uncertainty surrounding the Iraqi coup, Dulles believed that there was a strong possibility "that force would be used to preserve access to Middle East oil," an access that Eisenhower had also authorized the use of "all necessary means" to safeguard. Memorandum of Conference with the President, July 20, 1958, Staff Memos-July 1958, Box 35, DDE Diary Series, Ann Whitman File, Eisenhower Library. Yet in the absence of further immediate challenges to Western interests following US troop arrival in Beirut, the administration resisted pressure by Britain that it join in intervening in Jordan on July 17.

45. Robert Murphy, *Diplomat Among Warriors* (Garden City, N. Y.: Doubleday, 1964), 404.

46. Memorandum of Telephone Conversation, J. F. Dulles and Dwight D. Eisenhower, July 19, 1958, Telephone Call Series, J. F. Dulles Papers, Eisenhower Library.

47. Embassy in Beirut to DOS, Telegram 617, July 22, 1958, 783A.00/7–2258, DOS Central Files, National Archives.

48. Embassy in Beirut to DOS, Telegram 533, July 19, 1958, 783A.00/7–1958, DOS Central Files, National Archives.

49. Nevertheless, the Joint Chiefs of Staff—as well as a few administration advisers—were less optimistic regarding the probable Soviet reaction and also feared hostile US troop contact with the Lebanese army. Dulles indicated that "the military are reluctant. . . . They say Lebanon exhausts their possibilities." See Barry M. Blechman and Stephen S. Kaplan, *Force Without War: U.S. Armed Forces as a Political Instrument* (Washington, D.C.: Brookings Institution, 1978), 232, and Memorandum of Telephone Conversation, J. F. Dulles and Richard Nixon, July 15, 1958, Box 8, Telephone Call Series, J. F. Dulles Papers, Eisenhower Library.

50. The United States had made it known that it was committed to resolving the successor issue. Once Shihab had appeared capable of gaining sufficient votes for election, moreover, the United States had been widely rumored to also back the Lebanese general and had sought to ensure that Lebanese Christians—who generally regarded Shihab as sympathetic to the opposition—accepted his candidacy. Lebanese Christians, Foreign Minister Malik commented,

were convinced that the United States was "pushing" Shihab in the elections. Embassy in Beirut to DOS, July 30, 1958, FRUS 11 (1958).

51. 374th Meeting of the NSC, July 31, 1958, Box 10, NSC Series, Ann Whitman File, Eisenhower Library. Although several administration officials had initially described Shihab as a pro-Western and apolitical military leader, Shihab's refusal to involve the Lebanese army in the crisis led them to question his motives; CIA officials in particular regarded him as too "busy dabbling in politics" and having "ambitions of his own for the presidency." NSC Staff Notes, June 23, 1958, Box 33, DDE Diary Series, Ann Whitman File, Eisenhower Library, and 366th Meeting of the NSC, May 22, 1958, Box 10, NSC Series, Ann Whitman File, Eisenhower Library.

52. Shihab's initial cabinet, headed by former Tripoli opposition leader Rashid Karami, had been rejected by pro-Chamoun politicians, who supported a public strike to protest its partisan composition, resulting in a resumption of civil disturbances. Eventually a "National Salvation Cabinet" was formed that on October 17 received a vote of confidence from the parliament.

53. Embassy in Cairo to DOS, Telegram 2149, January 23, 1959, 783A.5411/1–2359, DOS Central Files, National Archives.

54. "Developments in the Aftermath of U.S. and U.K. Troop Withdrawals," October 28, 1958, declassified documents, Central Intelligence Agency.

55. Commenting on the Arab reaction to his development fund proposal, Eisenhower lamented that US officials had "perhaps presumed too much to assume that we knew what it was that the Arabs wanted." Although most Arab leaders did not openly criticize his UN speech, many resented not having been consulted concerning the development fund proposal, believed that the League of Arab States and not the United Nations should administer the fund, and, in any case, insisted that the United States and Britain had to withdraw from Lebanon and Jordan before they would discuss details on how the proposal could be implemented.

9

The United States and Nasserist Pan-Arabism

Malik Mufti

In this chapter I shall argue that US Middle East policy from the mid-1950s to the early 1960s consisted primarily of safeguarding US interests by accommodating the populist pan-Arabism of Egyptian President Gamal 'Abd al-Nasser. After its initial attempt (1955–1956) to bring together all regional actors in a grand pro-US alliance collapsed, Washington watched with dismay as Soviet influence appeared to advance, first in Syria and then in Iraq. Nasser successfully played on these fears to enlist US support for his regional ambitions from 1958 to 1962. Around 1963, however, when Nasser himself became a threat to its interests, the United States started building up his pro-Western rivals in Israel, Jordan, and Saudi Arabia while entrusting the campaign of liquidating the remnants of Arab communism to the Ba'th Party in Syria and Iraq.

Washington's Initial Four-Pronged Policy

US interests in the Middle East can be boiled down to two strategic objectives, both of which emerged after World War II. First, the United States was intent on keeping Saudi Arabia and its smaller oil-rich neighbors securely under the US umbrella; and second, it wanted to prevent the expansion of Soviet influence in the Arab world. Initially—during the period roughly from 1947 to 1955—Washington relied on a four-pronged policy approach to accomplish those objectives. First, it sought to maintain the regional status quo by opposing the pan-Arab ambitions of the Hashemites in Baghdad and Amman—particularly given their Hijazi roots. As a 1950 US Department of State paper on Syrian-Iraqi union put it at the time: "There would thus be no contribution to United States interests in giving encouragement to the movement, and any suggestion of intervention by this Government in favor of [a] union [of Arab states] would undoubtedly incur deep resentment among peoples of the Near East, particularly in Saudi Arabia where U.S. strategic interests are of vital importance."[1]

Second, Washington decided instead to support, wherever possible, leaders whose populist nationalism gave them credibility in their peoples' eyes but whose visions did not extend beyond modern reforms within their countries. In other words, US support went to anti-Communists whose pan-Arab rhetoric remained just that. In Syria, this policy resulted in US support first for Colonel Husni Za'im when he seized power in March 1949, then for Colonel Adib al-Shishakli, who succeeded in his coup in December of the same year. Shishakli turned out to be a relatively competent dictator who seemed to fit the US bill well.

In Egypt, the Americans pinned even greater hopes on Colonel Gamal 'Abd al-Nasser and his fellow officers who overthrew the monarchy in 1952. Contacts between the two sides predated the coup and intensified significantly during the years immediately following it. During this time, Nasser enlisted Washington's support for his fledgling regime and for its struggle to free Egypt from lingering British influence by convincing the Americans that his interests and theirs coincided on most issues. In the fall of 1954, for example, "Colonel Nasser declared that Egypt was basically inclined toward the West and that Russia and communism represented the only conceivable danger to Egypt's security."[2] For its part, Washington forced Israel to suspend its diversion of Jordan River waters, by temporarily suspending aid in October 1953, brokering a final Anglo-Egyptian agreement signed on October 19, 1954, and concluding an economic assistance agreement with Egypt on November 6, 1954. A State Department paper, prepared in 1966, recalled nostalgically: "U.S. economic assistance during the sunny early years of the Nasser regime, 1952–1956, amounted to $86 million."[3]

US support continued even after Nasser—having consolidated his hold on power—delivered his famous speech of July 23, 1954, which outlined Cairo's new foreign policy orientation: Henceforth, his government would abandon its isolationist outlook and strive for Arab solidarity under Egyptian leadership. Thus, Wilbur Crane Eveland, a US intelligence operative in the region at the time, remembers that US Central Intelligence Agency (CIA) propaganda experts were kept busy during late 1954 "dreaming up ways to popularize Nasser's government in Egypt and the Arab world."[4] They apparently went to unusual lengths to maintain Nasser's nationalist credibility. According to another operative involved in those events:

> While the "straights" in Washington were increasingly displeased with the anti-American content of Nasser's public utterances and the anti-American propaganda that poured out of Radio Cairo . . . can you guess who was writing a goodly portion of the material? We were. . . . We took pains to make it subtly counter-productive, of course, and we included a lot of patent nonsense, but we kept virtually in control of its production. We even had Paul Linebarger, perhaps the greatest "black" propagandist who ever lived, come to Egypt to coach the Egyptian-American team that turned out the stuff.[5]

The third element of US policy during this period envisaged bringing all the "progressive" but pro-Western Arab regimes that could be sustained into a regional anti-Soviet alliance modeled on the North Atlantic Treaty Organization (NATO). The fourth and final element was a logical extension of this third objective: Avoid regional conflicts that would weaken the alliance, such as those that would pit members against one another and force Washington to choose sides, thereby creating opportunities for Moscow to gain influence.

Collapse of the Four-Pronged Strategy

Unfortunately for the United States, its four-pronged strategy soon fell victim to the conflicting objectives of other regional actors. Nasser, for one, realized that the optimal strategy for him would be to play the two superpowers off one another and to extend Egyptian influence abroad, even if that brought him into conflict with other US allies. Iraq's Hashemites still harbored dreams of ruling a greater Arab homeland, dreams that of course conflicted with Nasser's hegemonic dream. In this they received limited backing from the British, who viewed Iraq as the linchpin to their own regional ambitions and were therefore willing to support the extension of Hashemite influence—primarily through the Baghdad Pact—so long as it did not result in actual border changes (for example, with Kuwait). The Saudis, who initially welcomed Nasser's foray into Arab politics as a counterweight to their nemeses, the Hashemites, gradually began to fear Egyptian expansionism as well.

Most decisively, Israel's concern about the close relationship between Washington and Cairo led it to pursue an aggressive policy culminating in the Gaza raid of February 28, 1955, its first major engagement with Egypt since 1948 and a humiliating blow to Nasser's prestige. The raid scuttled Washington's attempts to focus regional attention on the Soviet threat, brought the Arab-Israeli conflict to the fore, and initiated an arms race that forced Washington to choose sides among friends in the Middle East. Thus, Israel succeeded in its primary objective of driving a wedge between Cairo and Washington. When Nasser's subsequent request for US weapons received a negative response, he announced six months later that he would be purchasing arms from the Soviet bloc instead. Further setbacks, such as the Aswan Dam financing dispute and the failure (despite private lip service by both sides)[6] of a secret US attempt to mediate the dispute between Egypt and Israel in early 1956, led US Secretary of State John Foster Dulles to conclude:

> In view of the negative outcome of our efforts to bring Colonel Nasser to adopt a policy of conciliation toward Israel, we should, I believe, now adjust certain of our Near Eastern policies, as indicated below. The primary purpose would be to let Colonel Nasser realize that he cannot cooperate as he is doing with the Soviet Union and at the same time enjoy most-favored-nation treatment from the United States. We would want for the time being to avoid any open break which would throw Nasser irrevocably into a Soviet satellite status and we would want to leave Nasser a bridge back to good relations with the West if he so desires.[7]

Estrangement, 1956–1958

The adjustments that Secretary of State Dulles eventually specified for President Dwight D. Eisenhower established a pattern that would be repeated whenever the United States sought to discipline Nasser: freeze economic aid to Egypt, extend support to Nasser's Arab rivals, and draw closer to Israel. Thus, in addition to withdrawing its offer to finance the Aswan High dam, Washington halted PL–480 food shipments and other assistance in 1956. It also expressed greater public support for the Baghdad Pact (without actually joining it), as well as the pro-Western governments of Sudan, Libya, Lebanon, and Jordan. Finally, although the United States continued to refrain from providing arms to Israel directly, it now encouraged other Western governments to do so.[8] As Dulles indicated, however, US officials did not want to back Nasser too far into a corner because they still held hope that he would become a cooperative ally. Hence they rejected repeated British invitations to join the Baghdad Pact. More significantly, of course, hence also they refused to back Britain and France in their ill-conceived collusion with Israel during the 1956 Suez crisis.

Eisenhower had begun musing about the need for an Arab counterweight to Nasser even before Suez. Now—with Nasserist radicalism developing into an irresistible force that destabilized the governments of Syria, Lebanon, Jordan, and Iraq itself—he referred to him as "an evil influence" and argued the need "to build up an Arab rival . . . to capture the imagination of the Arab world."[9] After an early candidate, Saudi Arabia's King Sa'ud, proved deficient in the personal and ideological attributes necessary for such a role, however, US officials decided to take things into their own hands. In accordance with the Eisenhower Doctrine (enunciated in January 1957, the doctrine was a policy generally designed to halt Communist expansion in the Middle East, specifically to isolate and reduce Nasser's power), the new approach envisaged a series of bilateral security arrangements with individual states rather than relying on one key ally to act as regional policeman. Saudi Arabia, Jordan, and Iraq responded positively, and US officials concluded the next (and last) step was to bring Syria into line, thereby isolating Nasser and dashing his hopes of parlaying his influence into a negotiating chip with which to play Moscow and Washington off one another. Then, or so the rosy scenario continued, the ensuing network of moderate Arab states would make peace with Israel and come together in an anti-Communist alliance under US leadership.

But bringing Syria into line turned out to be problematic. A power struggle that pitted the pro-Egyptian Ba'th Party against an increasingly pro-Soviet faction headed by Khalid al-'Azm caused the US National Security Council (NSC) to place Syria "in the dangerous category"[10] and to initiate a series of covert operations aimed at reversing Syria's leftward lurch. As is well known, the failure of those plots only strengthened pro-Communist elements in the Syrian military, led by new Chief of Staff 'Afif al-Bizri. The mood in Washington now shifted from concern to panic. Dulles in particular became convinced that a Communist takeover of Syria was imminent. Four days after Bizri's appointment, he concluded that "there is now little hope of correction from within and . . . we must think in terms of . . . external assets."[11]

Accordingly, Dulles sent his deputy, Loy Henderson, to Ankara on August 24, 1957, for talks with Turkish, Iraqi, and Jordanian leaders. Henderson expressed his government's support for unspecified Iraqi or Jordanian "action" against Syria and promised that it would block any interference by the Soviet Union, Egypt, or Israel. He did set one condition however: In order to allay the concerns of the Saudis and others, it had to be clear that the proposed action "[did] not aim at the unification of Syria and Iraq" and that the goal was only "the return to power in Syria of a truly independent leadership." Iraq's rulers had to agree to the stipulation.[12] This point is worth underlining: Even though Washington was extremely fearful of a Communist takeover in Syria, it remained unwilling to countenance any Hashemite action that aimed at revising the regional status quo. As Dulles once reiterated to his underlings, "No success achieved in Syria could possibly compensate for the loss of Saudi Arabia."[13]

As described in more detail elsewhere in this book (see especially Chapter 7, by David Lesch), Iraq and Jordan felt unable to mount an unprovoked military attack on a fellow Arab state, so soon after Suez anyway. Turkey therefore took the lead, massing troops on the Syrian border and carrying out threatening maneuvers all through September.[14] This, however, unleashed a storm of indignation in the Arab world, further tarnishing Washington's image and providing Moscow with a new opportunity to portray itself as the champion of Arab nationalism—and the Third World. Soviet Premier Nikolay Bulganin warned Ankara on September 13 that armed conflict in Syria "would not be limited to that area alone."[15] One week later, two Soviet warships arrived at the Syrian port of Latakia amid great popular fanfare, and Turkey was forced to back off. Suddenly, just as the crisis was winding down into a Soviet propaganda coup, Nasser stepped into the breach. Units of the Egyptian army arrived in Latakia on October 13 and took up positions to "defend" Syria in case of an attack. It was a brilliant stroke. On the one hand, his prestige and popularity as the nemesis of imperialism soared to new heights in Syria and throughout the Arab world. On the other hand, the Soviet Union had gained so much sympathy in Syria during the preceding weeks that Nasser could credibly justify his intervention to the United States as the only way of dampening pro-Communist fervor there.[16]

Sure enough, a report prepared by the commander of US naval forces in the Mediterranean welcomed the Egyptian military landing in Latakia, viewing it as likely "to bolster Pan-Arabism and check Syrian drift into Soviet orbit." The report went on: "'If you can't lick them join them' and Nasser probably better than any prospective replacement anyway."[17] There would be many more twists and turns in the US-Egyptian relationship, but the convergence of interests in Latakia set a precedent and strengthened those officials in Washington who wanted to abandon the attempt to find alternatives to Nasser.

The UAR and the Iraqi Coup

Still, not everyone was convinced—certainly not John Foster Dulles. When Syria and Egypt announced their unification under the flag of the United Arab Republic (UAR) in January 1958, for example, he interpreted it as a plot masterminded by Moscow, telling an emergency session of the Baghdad Pact Council held in Ankara on January 28 and 29 that the "union between Syria and Egypt would be dangerous to all our interests and if we remained passive it would expand and would shortly take in Jordan and Lebanon and ultimately Saudi Arabia and Iraq leaving us with a single Arab State ostensibly under Nasser but ultimately under Soviet control. It was clear that we ought to oppose such a union."[18]

It is instructive, however, that when Iraq's Hashemites—acutely aware of the mortal peril posed to them by the UAR—agitated for effective countermeasures, neither Britain nor the United States would hear of it. Thus, Iraqi Crown Prince 'Abd al-Ilah insisted to the British ambassador in late February that to save the monarchy it would be necessary to incorporate Kuwait into the hastily arranged "Arab Federation" of Iraq and Jordan—"both on economic grounds and because of the moral effect"—and "to bring over Syria, by the use of force if there was no other way."[19] Later, Iraqi Prime Minister Nuri Sa'id caused considerable alarm in London by drawing up a memorandum threatening to annex half of Kuwait's territory unless it joined the Arab Federation at once,[20] but to no avail. Britain's ambassador assured his government that he was doing all he could to prevent the Iraqis "from taking any rash step over Syria or Kuwait,"[21] and John Foster Dulles fretted about "Nuri's recent intemperate statements."[22] The matter became moot on July 14, 1958, when Iraqi military leaders overthrew the Iraqi government in a coup and slaughtered its Hashemite leadership.

In the final analysis, both Britain and the United States continued to view Hashemite pan-Arabism as a threat to their interests in the oil-producing shaykhdoms of the Arabian Peninsula. Even John Foster Dulles, paranoid as he was about the Communist "threat" in Syria and elsewhere, never allowed this concern to overshadow the greater strategic objective of maintaining US hegemony over the oil lanes. He put it to the National Security Council this way, in response to an earlier proposal that the United States might discretely encourage the "ultimate union of Arab countries in the Arabian peninsula": "If the policy on the supply of oil from the Arab states to Western Europe were made uniform as a result of the unification of the Arab states, [the intervening portion of the quote is censored] the threat to the vital oil supply of Western Europe from the Near East would become critical."[23] Dulles added that he "was not saying that the State Department opposed moves in the direction of Arab unity; but the State Department wanted to be very careful that we did not end up by uniting the Arab states against the United States and the West."[24] Although Washington might have liked to see the Hashemites in Iraq and Jordan thwart Nasser's newly formed UAR, in short, it would not allow them to do so at the cost of creating a new political entity that could potentially threaten the US protectorates in the Arabian Peninsula.

Nevertheless, 'Abd al-Karim Qasim's sudden Iraqi coup took Washington aback. CIA Director Allen Dulles (the secretary's brother) told Eisenhower that "the hand of Nasser in these developments is very evident" and added that if the coup "succeeds, it seems almost inevitable that a chain reaction will set in which will doom the governments of Iraq, Jordan, Saudi Arabia, Turkey and Iran."[25] Accordingly, US troops were landed in Lebanon to prop up the Christian Maronite government already besieged by pro-UAR rebels, and British forces arrived in Jordan to stabilize the situation there. Ten days after the Iraqi coup, John Foster Dulles was still arguing that "the real authority behind the Government of Iraq was being exercised by Nasser, and behind Nasser by the USSR."[26]

In fact Qasim initially went out of his way to project a moderate stance: refusing to join the UAR; adopting a hostile stance toward Nasser; dropping all claims on Kuwait (whose emir was one of the first to congratulate him); and abiding by the 50–50 profit-sharing arrangement with foreign oil companies that the Hashemites had long been trying to overturn. As a result, when the new dictator managed to foil two Egyptian-backed plots to overthrow him in late 1958, he apparently did so with some assistance from Britain, which continued to view Nasser as the greater threat to its regional interests.[27] Qasim certainly appreciated the helping hand. According to Britain's ambassador: "He said he wanted to assure me that he wished friendship with Britain to stand fast and continued, with some emphasis, 'I will even say that not even friendship with any Arab country shall interfere with it.'"[28]

But the Americans reached a different conclusion than the British: Qasim's growing reliance on the Iraqi Communist Party (ICP) in his struggle against his domestic opponents induced Washington to replace its hostility toward Nasser with a new phase of close cooperation.

Anti-Communist Cooperation and NSC 5820/1, 1958–1963

Evidence of Washington's renewed tilt toward Nasser could be found even before the Iraqi coup. Egypt's union with Syria and the ensuing wave of pan-Arab enthusiasm that swept the region greatly impressed US officials, prompting them to conclude that "Western interests will be served by placing US-UAR relations on a more normal basis" and to resume limited economic assistance to Egypt.[29] After Qasim's coup and his growing association with the ICP, however, the pro-Nasser chorus became deafening. US Information Agency Director George Allen, for example, argued for a renewed alliance with Nasser even if it meant abandoning allies such as King Hussein: "We must adjust to the tide of Arab nationalism, and must do so before the hotheads get control in every country."[30] Eisenhower balked at Allen's more extreme suggestions, but even he could be heard musing, "Since we are about to get thrown out of the area, we might as well believe in Arab nationalism."[31]

A split developed within the Eisenhower administration regarding the extent to which it should accommodate Nasser. The Department of Defense and Department of Treasury argued that Washington should merely "accept pan-Arab nationalism, of which Nasser is the symbol" and seek to normalize relations with him only as head of the UAR. But the State Department and CIA—representing the majority opin-ion—wanted to go further, suggesting that the United States actively "accept and seek to work with radical pan-Arab nationalism," even to the extent of cooperating with Nasser on "certain area-wide problems."[32]

In the end their arguments prevailed, and the result was NSC 5820/1, a water-shed National Security Council report dated November 4, 1958, that formed the basis of US Middle East policy for the next three years. It began by acknowledging that "the prevention of further Soviet penetration of the Near East and progress in solving Near Eastern problems depends on the degree to which the United States is able to work more closely with Arab nationalism."[33] Securing Washington's "pri-mary objectives" in the region—foremost the "denial of the area to Soviet domina-tion" and secondarily the "continued availability of sufficient Near Eastern oil to meet vital Western European requirements on reasonable terms"[34]—required the United States to "deal with Nasser as head of the UAR on specific problems and is-sues, area-wide as well as local, affecting the UAR's legitimate interests."[35] And though NSC 5820/1 warned against accepting Nasser's hegemony over the entire Arab world, it also recognized that "too direct efforts on our part to stimulate de-velopments lessening the predominant position of Nasser might be counter-productive."[36]

Nasser's regional rivals received short shrift in NSC 5820/1. US support for Saudi Arabia would remain intact, of course, but even there the report acknowl-edged the "reduced influence of King Saud" and called for strengthening "United States influence and understanding among groups in Saudi Arabia from which ele-ments of leadership may emerge, particularly in the armed forces and the middle level Saudi Arabian Government officials."[37] As to Jordan, NSC 5820/1 had more drastic recommendations: "Recognizing that the indefinite continuance of Jordan's present political status has been rendered unrealistic by recent developments [seek] to bring about peaceful evolution of Jordan's political status . . . including partition, absorption, or internal political realignment."[38] And though Washington continued to support the preservation of Israel "in its essentials, we believe that Israel's contin-ued existence as a sovereign state depends on its willingness to become a finite and accepted part of the Near East nation-state system."[39]

NSC 5820/1 remained a controversial document, and both Defense and Trea-sury felt obliged to put their dissenting opinions on record. John Foster Dulles also continued to argue—against his own department—that it went too far in appeasing Nasser at the expense of more important allies such as Britain. But the secretary of state was dying of cancer and would soon leave office. As Qasim increasingly tied his fate to that of the Communists, fewer and fewer voices would be heard opposing the tilt toward the UAR.

Egyptian Opportunism

Nasser's case was greatly helped by the reception accorded in Baghdad to William Rountree, the US assistant secretary of state who visited the region in December

1958. Rountree endured volleys of rotten vegetables and trash thrown at his motorcade by angry Iraqi crowds only to receive a cool and perfunctory reception from Qasim himself. The shrewd Egyptians gave him a warmer welcome, and when he returned to Washington, Rountree reported that they were "showing a real concern over Communist penetration of the Middle East" and that "we can work with Nasser on the Iraqi situation."[40] The desk officer for Iraq at the State Department told Britain's ambassador after Rountree's trip that the "only hope for retrieving the situation now [seems?] to lie in the army acting under the inspiration of Arab nationalism of a pro-United Arab Republic and anti-Communist kind. This need not mean a takeover by the United Arab Republic."[41]

In fact, Nasser had been preparing the ground for a rapprochement with the United States for some time. He had already purged Bizri and his pro-Communist officers within weeks of the UAR's creation in an effort to earn the Syrian business community's trust as well as to defuse the ideological challenge posed by communism to his brand of radicalism—a challenge that grew particularly acute after the coup in Iraq and the subsequent rise of ICP influence there. It was partly in order to nip this threat in the bud and partly to curry US favor that Nasser launched his anti-Communist campaign in earnest with a vitriolic speech in Port Sa'id on December 23, 1958. Many party members lost their lives during the days that followed, and hundreds more were thrown into prison. A second wave of arrests in March liquidated the Communists as a political force in the UAR altogether.

In Iraq, by contrast, the Communist advance seemed inexorable. The crushing of an Egyptian-backed revolt in Mosul in March 1959, followed by extensive purges of Arab nationalists, strengthened the ICP still further. As the party gained control of one professional association after another, as its armed militia grew to 25,000 members by May 1959, and as it began to infiltrate the army itself, even Qasim started to worry. Every time he tried to rein in the Communists, however, a resurgence of Nasserist and Ba'thist opposition would force him to turn to them once again. Thus, a crackdown on the ICP after a particularly grisly outbreak of class warfare in Kirkuk in July 1959 ended in October after a Ba'thist attempt on the president's life.

British officials continued to insist that Qasim represented the best hope of preventing an all-out Communist takeover in Iraq and pointed to the strongly anti-Communist sentiments of senior military officers,[42] but the Americans remained far less sanguine. Mosul and the ICP's subsequent gains dispelled any remaining doubts about the reorientation outlined in NSC 5820/1 and led CIA Director Allen Dulles to describe the Iraqi situation as "the most dangerous in the world today."[43] Another US official captured the mood of helpless frustration that gripped Washington during this period by observing that "we sit and watch unfolding events which seem to point inevitably to Soviet domination of Iraq, acknowledging, I am afraid, an inability to do anything about it. It is almost like watching a movie whose end we will not like but which we are committed to see."[44]

Nasser astutely fueled Washington's anxiety. He told reporters, for example, that he had "reliable information" of a Soviet master plot to create a "red fertile crescent"—

a Communist federation encompassing Iraq, Syria, Jordan, Lebanon, and Kuwait. Only Egypt, he implied, blocked the path of this fiendish plan. Not surprisingly, relations with Moscow deteriorated. Three days after the collapse of the Mosul revolt, Soviet General Secretary Nikita Khrushchev declared, "Nasser wants to annex Iraq. As I see it he is a hot-headed young man who has taken on more than he can manage." Nasser retaliated on March 20 by denouncing communism and accusing Khrushchev of "intervention in our affairs."[45]

Nasser's strategy paid off: The loss of Soviet support was more than offset by the advantages of a renewed alliance with Washington, where the initial trepidation concerning Nasser's role in Iraq gave way—much as it had in Syria in 1957—to a sense of enormous relief. An NSC report listed some of those advantages: $125 million in special assistance and surplus commodity sales in 1959; additional export guarantees and loans; US backing for a $56 million Egyptian loan request to the International Bank for Redevelopment and Development (the IBRD, or World Bank); and in "support of the UAR's anti-communist propaganda offensive . . . grant aid for the purchase of newsprint and . . . basic anti-communist material for use by UAR press and radio." Perhaps most important for Nasser, the report added: "Consistent with our recognition of the lack of any desirable alternatives for Syria's future and our understanding that continuance of the present trend in US-UAR relations will depend, in part, on our willingness to assist Nasser in his Syrian economic objectives, we have given special attention to DLF loan applications for the Syrian region."[46]

Both sides clearly understood the quid pro quo involved: It was spelled out by a State Department paper in mid-April 1959: "While we have not directly linked with Nasser's present campaign against communism the steps we have recently taken to aid Egypt, there is no doubt that Nasser knows that we have taken these steps as a sign of approval of his current campaign and that they have emboldened him in his anti-communist efforts."[47]

US Reservations

Washington's renewed affinity with Nasser alarmed those who resented the spread of his influence. Britain, Turkey, Saudi Arabia, Jordan, and Israel all felt that US support for Nasser's subversive campaign against Iraq was tilting the regional balance of power too far in his favor. Turkey had warned from the beginning that it would take military action if the Egyptians tried to bring Iraq into the UAR and made threatening moves along its southern borders both after the Mosul revolt in March 1959 and following the failed attempt on Qasim's life in October. In December, Foreign Minister Fatin Rustu Zorlu confided his fears to the British ambassador: "He believed that the C.I.A. were dickering with the idea that the situation in Iraq was so precarious that Egypt ought to be ready to do something about it in case things went completely wrong. He even thought it possible that some hint of this thinking might be available to the Egyptians."[48]

Saudi Arabia, already embarrassed by the revelation in March 1958 that King Sa'ud had financed an assassination plot against Nasser, also kept up steady pressure on Washington to do something about Nasser's growing influence in Arab politics. King Hussein of Jordan, for his part, tried to put himself forward as a viable alternative to Nasserism and communism in both Syria and Iraq. A skirmish involving armored vehicles on the Jordanian-Syrian border occurred in late April 1959, and in August the British embassy in Amman got wind of a coup plot in Syria that the Jordanians were at least aware of.[49] On the Iraqi side, Hussein was just as assertive. Asked by an interviewer in October whether he would consider invading Iraq, he responded by saying "we would do everything we could to save Iraq from Communism" and that the "showdown" was now imminent.[50] There were reports of tension on the Jordanian-Iraqi border as well later in the month.

But US officials, believing that King Hussein could not hope to compete with either Nasser or the Communists for the allegiance of the Arab masses, categorically refused to support his initiatives. As a State Department official told one of his British counterparts, "There could be no question of a Hashemite restoration either in Iraq or Syria."[51] Quite the contrary: The British embassy in Amman reported on April 24, 1959, that the US military attaché and his assistant had been "touting pro-Nasser views round the various offices" much to the consternation of the Jordanian government.[52] This at a time of ongoing clashes along the Jordanian-Syrian border—and just five months after UAR jets tried to shoot down Hussein's plane. In a conversation with a Canadian diplomat, Nasser once again evoked the Communist bogeyman: "Nasser said categorically that King Hussein's idea of intervening militarily with Arab Legion in Iraq was profoundly unwise. Quote it could ruin everything unquote. It might have some effect in the short term and locally, but the implication that there might be a Hashemite restoration would inevitably play into the hands of the Communists, who would be quick to exploit it."[53] Washington concurred. Not only did US officials oppose Hussein's revisionist pan-Arab ambitions, they even "cautioned" him against "provocative acts" directed at the UAR.[54] Hussein abandoned his efforts in August 1960 after a bomb placed by UAR operatives killed Prime Minister Hazza' al-Majali and ten other Jordanians in Amman.

US officials tried to allay the concerns of their other allies by assuring them that the UAR had no further expansionist ambitions and by pointing out that "Nasser's recent attacks on Communism had done more to stay the advance of Communism in the Middle East than anything the Western Powers could have achieved in years of work."[55] Still, it became evident even to Washington that the excessive reliance on Nasser was growing increasingly problematic: Freed of almost all restraints, he was antagonizing his neighbors to the point where any one of them—Turkey, Jordan, Israel, Saudi Arabia, or Iraq itself—might lash out in a dangerously unpredictable fashion.

The dilemma confronting Washington was the same one it had faced since 1955: to find a credible anti-Communist movement that was not a mere vehicle for Egyptian expansionism. Some other version of radical pan-Arabism seemed the only answer, reflected in a conclusion suggested by Eisenhower in the aftermath of the Iraqi coup: "If we could somehow bring about a separation of Syria from Egypt and thereafter a union of Syria with Iraq, this might prove very useful."[56] Qasim, with his narrow popular base and his dependence on the ICP, would clearly not do. Neither would Hussein's Hashemite alternative, since Washington doubted it could work and feared the consequences for its hegemony in Saudi Arabia and the Persian Gulf if it did.

The Syrian Secession

Deliverance came on September 28, 1961, when a group of Syrian officers mounted a coup d'état and effected Syria's secession from the UAR. The implications of this devastating blow to Nasser's prestige for US-Egyptian relations were not lost on the foreign policy team of the newly elected president, John F. Kennedy. Robert Komer of the NSC observed just five days after the secession: "I am convinced that recent events may present us with the best opportunity since 1954 for a limited marriage of convenience with the guy who I think is still, and will remain, the Mister Big of the Arab World."[57] Kennedy's special envoy, Chester Bowles, fleshed out Komer's observation in a telegram from Cairo in early 1962:

> I believe the time has come for a change of emphasis in our dealings with the UAR in general and with Nasser in particular. If Nasser were now riding high he might view any effort by us to establish a new relationship as an act of weakness. However, Nasser is deeply conscious of the serious problems which now face him and his regime. . . . Under these circumstances I believe that a skillful, sophisticated, sensitive effort to establish a more affirmative relationship is called for. Furthermore, I believe that Nasser is likely to meet us more than half way.[58]

During the winter of 1961–1962, then, Nasser's stock in Washington rose still further, bolstered largely by his diminished ability to provoke other US allies in the Middle East after Syria's secession, but also in part by the Kennedy administration's generally more tolerant attitude toward Third World radicalism. In practical terms this meant increased assistance for Egypt's now seriously ailing economy, including a three-year PL–480 agreement signed in 1962 for the sale of about $430 million worth of surplus foods. In return, Nasser agreed to maintain his anti-Communist stance and—as he put it in 1961 to the new US ambassador, John S. Badeau—to cooperate with the United States in keeping "the Israeli-Arab question 'in the icebox' while devoting themselves to the development of mutual interests."[59] As a result, Badeau could report at the onset of 1964 that "the United States now wields more influence in the Near East than it has at any time since 1955."[60] Yet even before Badeau penned those words, the US-Egyptian relationship had already begun the inexorable process of disintegration that would culminate when Nasser, in his desperation and folly, took a final, fatal step in 1967, which brought his world crashing down around him.

Breakdown, 1963–1967

Exactly two months after Badeau's rosy assessment, Nasser complained to visiting US Assistant Secretary of State Phillip Talbot that "he could not accept . . . Talbot's presentation that U.S. Middle East policy had not changed since the death of President Kennedy."[61] One year later Nasser's envoy in Washington, Mustafa Kamel, also dated the downturn in bilateral relations to the transition from the Kennedy to the Lyndon B. Johnson administrations: "In late 1963, primarily as result of Yemen problem but possibly also as effect of US-Soviet détente, Kamel said Egyptians had sensed slow-down in US aid."[62]

The Egyptians were not imagining things, although the change in fact predated Kennedy's assassination. Its roots lay in the weakening of Nasser's regional influence following the Syrian secession. Whereas the events of 1958 convinced US officials that even the appearance of opposing Nasser would harm their fundamental interests, by 1962 the picture had changed dramatically. In Saudi Arabia, Crown Prince Faisal—now the effective ruler—coupled domestic reform with a foreign policy that did not shrink as readily from confrontations with Nasser. Syria's secessionist regime, wobbly as it was, enjoyed good relations with the United States while trading bitter public invectives with Egypt. Qasim of Iraq, his economy in ruins, found himself bogged down in a Kurdish revolt that conveniently broke out just weeks after his ill-considered bid for Kuwait in June 1961 (which may have received some US backing). His relations with Nasser were, if anything, worse than those of the Saudis and Syrians. Even King Hussein of Jordan proved more resilient and durable than NSC 5820/1 had predicted, and now he too engaged in a spirited propaganda battle with the Egyptian leader. Nasser's isolation gave Washington leverage to diversify its regional assets by strengthening its ties with countries such as Saudi Arabia, Jordan, and, above all, Israel—all of which began receiving significantly increased levels of US military aid during the early 1960s. As Secretary of State Dean Rusk observed on August 7, 1962: "An extensive and intensive review of our policy toward Israel has been conducted in recent months. . . . The relatively high standing of the United States among the Arabs, while still fragile, provides us with a minor degree of maneuvering room in terms of adjustments in policy with respect to Israel."[63]

Twelve days later a presidential envoy informed Israeli leaders that Kennedy had approved Hawk missile sales to their country, initiating a process that would see US military assistance to Israel soar from $44.2 million in 1963 to $995.3 million by 1968.[64] Domestic political considerations undoubtedly played a role in this shift—both Kennedy and Johnson were far more sensitive to the pro-Israeli feelings of the US Jewish community than Eisenhower had been—but they cannot be understood in isolation from the strategic imperative: "to reinforce Israel as a counterweight to Nasser in case he misused or abused American assistance to him."[65] No wonder Nasser's high expectations in late 1961 regarding his new rapprochement with the United States gave way so quickly to disappointment.

As 1963 rolled by, moreover, Washington's "minor degree of maneuvering room" expanded considerably. Ba'thist coups in Iraq (8 February) and Syria (8 March) at

In any case, US aid to Egypt dried up once again and Nasser retaliated in characteristic style—lambasting the United States as "leader of the imperialist camp" and vowing to remain in Yemen "until the British-American-Saudi danger is completely removed" and threatening to resume bombing of Saudi border towns.[71] Nes in Cairo mused gloomily on May 11, 1967: "We seem to have driven Nasser to a degree of irrationality bordering on madness, fed, of course, by the frustrations and fears generated by his failures domestic and foreign. Our debate here revolves around where he will strike next—Libya, Lebanon?"[72] But Nasser, woefully underestimating the ferocity of Israel's determination to crush him and deluding himself that Washington still cared enough to rescue him from disaster, chose instead to roll the dice in Sinai.

Conclusion

John Foster Dulles once summarized Washington's attitude toward Arab nationalism by likening it to "an overflowing stream—you cannot stand in front of it and oppose it frontally, but you must try to keep it in bounds. We must try to prevent lasting damage to our interests in the Near East until events deflate the great Nasser hero myth."[73] And that is precisely what the Americans did. Despite some false steps, they ultimately succeeded in keeping Arab nationalism in bounds, and in doing so they achieved their two fundamental strategic objectives: maintaining control over the oil fields and denying the region to the Soviets. When Hashemite pan-Arabism threatened Saudi Arabia or Kuwait, Washington helped build up a counterweight in Cairo. When Nasser in turn got too big for his britches, Washington neutralized him by sanctioning the rise of the Ba'thists in Syria and Iraq and by letting Israel out of the icebox (where it had moved neither toward resolution of Arab issues nor toward war).

The competence of US Middle East policy during the period in question is often faulted. Eisenhower and Dulles in particular have been roundly criticized (including in this volume) for their clumsy covert operations and for their tendency to see Soviet plots everywhere. Some of this criticism is fair. But in most really crucial respects they were right: They were correct that a "Hashemite solution" in Syria in 1956–1958 would have been—from the standpoint of US hegemonic interests—a cure worse than the disease. Despite a little initial confusion, they did finally recognize that Nasser was a useful ally against the 'Azm-Bizri-Bakdash bloc in Syria; there was a real Communist threat in Iraq after 1958; and given the popular mood of the time, Nasser was in fact the only viable counterweight.

Similarly, there is a long tradition of criticism that blames the breakdown in US-Egyptian relations during the early 1960s on the receptivity of Presidents Kennedy and (especially) Johnson to lobbying by domestic supporters of Israel. But this criticism erroneously assumes that the rationale for close US ties to Nasser—which existed under Eisenhower—continued to exist after 1961. This chapter has tried to show that it did not. Kennedy and Johnson were more responsive to their Jewish electorates largely because they could afford to be.

It made sense for the Americans to use Nasser so long as he was useful to them, just as it made sense for them to drop him when he outlived his usefulness. If there is blame to be assigned, it must fall squarely on Nasser's shoulders: It was he who failed to comprehend the magnitude of the change in his strategic relationship with the United States during the early 1960s; it was he who indulged in demagoguery and reckless foreign adventures rather than addressing the pressing problems confronting Egypt's society and economy; and it was he who chose to give the Israelis the excuse they needed to destroy him in 1967.

At the end of the day the Arab world remained divided, Saudi Arabia and the other oil-rich protectorates huddled safely under the US umbrella, and the Soviets were no closer to breaking Washington's regional hegemony. This may not have been the optimum solution for advocates of Arab nationalism, but by the standard of US national interests, it must be reckoned a great foreign policy success.

Notes

1. "The Political Union of Syria and Iraq," 25 April 1960. US Declassified Documents Reference System (Washington, D.C.: Carrollton Press, 1975), microfiche (hereinafter USDD) 1975:26H.

2. George Lenczowski, *The Middle East in World Affairs* (Ithaca: Cornell University Press, 1980), p. 527.

3. Department of State Paper: "US-U.A.R. Relations," 20 [?] February 1966. USDD–1982:000982.

4. Wilbur Crane Eveland, *Ropes of Sand: America's Failure in the Middle East* (London: W. W. Norton, 1980), p. 103.

5. Miles Copeland, *The Game Player: Memoirs of the CIA's Original Political Operative* (London: Aurum Press, 1989), p. 167.

6. Nasser wrote to Eisenhower on 6 February 1956 that "in the interest of peace Egypt recognizes the desirability of seeking to eliminate the tensions between the Arab States and Israel." USDD 1981:192C.

7. Memorandum from Dulles to Eisenhower, 28 March 1956. USDD–1989:001511.

8. Washington allowed France to divert NATO military equipment to Israel in the spring of 1956. Dulles also asked Canada to supply Israel with F–86 aircraft. Dulles Telegram from Paris, 3 May 1956; USDD–1987:000714.

9. Eisenhower Message to Dulles, 12 December 1956. USDD–1989:003548.

10. National Security Council (NSC) Progress Report: "United States Objectives and Policies with Respect to the Near East," 2 November 1955. USDD–1988:001022, p. 3.

11. Dulles Telegram to Selwyn Lloyd, 21 August 1957. USDD–1987:002090.

12. See the notes of Rafiq 'Aref, the Iraqi chief of staff who attended the talks, in *Mahkamat al-Sha'b, Al-Muhadarat al-Rasmiyya li-Jalasat al-Mahkama al-'Askariyya al-'Ulya al-Khassa (The People's Court: Official Proceedings of the Sessions of the Special Higher Military Court)* (Baghdad: Mudiriyyat Matba'at al-Hukuma, 1959–1962), vol. 4, pp. 1516–1519.

13. Quoted in Eveland, *Ropes of Sand*, p. 181.

14. For a detailed analysis of this episode, see Chapter 7 by David Lesch in this volume. See also his *Syria and the United States: Eisenhower's Cold War in the Middle East* (Boulder: Westview Press, 1992).

15. Quoted in Patrick Seale, *The Struggle for Syria: A Study of Post-War Arab Politics, 1945–1958* (New Haven: Yale University Press, 1965), p. 300.

16. For more on Nasser's actions during the American-Syrian crisis, see David W. Lesch, "Gamal 'Abd al-Nasser and an Example of Diplomatic Acumen," *Middle Eastern Studies* 31(2) (April 1995), pp. 384–396.

17. Appendix to a Memorandum by the Chief of Naval Operations for the Joint Chiefs of Staff on "Middle East Policy," dated 7 November 1957. USDD–1984: 000135, pp. 3096–3097.

18. Summary of Dulles's comments reported by Secretary of State Sir J. Bowker in Ankara to the Foreign Office on 28 January 1958. British Foreign Office Documents (hereinafter BFOD) FO371/134386/VY10316/10.

19. Report from Michael Wright in Baghdad on his conversation with Crown Prince 'Abd al-Ilah on 25 February 1958. BFOD:FO371/134198/VQ1015/18.

20. See F. Hoyer Millar's Foreign Office Minute of 25 June 1958 on the talks with Nuri in London. BFOD:FO371/134219/VQ1051/19.

21. Letter from Wright to London, 23 June 1958. BFOD:FO371/134198/VQ1015/49.

22. US Department of State, "Memorandum of Conversation," dated 15 June 1958. USDD–1981:371B.

23. Briefing Note dated 21 January 1958 on the suggestions of the Planning Board of the National Security Council. USDD–1985:000640, p. 2.

24. Summary of the discussion at the 353rd meeting of the NSC, 30 January 1958. USDD–1990:000328, p. 8.

25. "Memorandum of Conference with the President," 14 July 1958. USDD–1993:002371.

26. Memorandum of the discussion at the 373rd meeting of the NSC, 25 July 1958. USDD–1990:000330, p. 3.

27. See, for example, the observation by Britain's ambassador in Ankara in early January 1959 that "we took certain action in favour of Qasim in regard to the recent plot in Iraq." BFOD:FO371/140956/EQ1071/1.

28. Cable from Ambassador Wright in Baghdad to the British Foreign Office, 24 November 1958. BFOD:FO371/133090/EQ1051/69.

29. "Background Paper" dated 9 June 1958 for Eisenhower's meeting with British Prime Minister Harold Macmillan. USDD–1988:001568. Among the steps taken to "normalize" US-UAR relations between January and July 1958: removal of export restrictions on civilian items such as aircraft spare parts; reinstitution of an "Exchange of Persons" program; and release of $400,000 (frozen since 1956) road-building and communications equipment.

30. Summary of the 373rd NSC meeting on 24 July 1958. USDD–1990:000330, p. 6.

31. Summary of the 374th NSC meeting on 31 July 1958. USDD–1990:000331, p. 11.

32. "Briefing Notes" for the NSC meeting of 21 August 1958. USDD–1990:000352, p. 3; and 16 October 1958. USDD–990:000332, p. 2.

33. "NSC 5820/1: U.S. Policy Toward the Near East," 4 November 1958. USDD–1980:386B, p. 2.

34. Ibid., p. 3.

35. Ibid., p. 10.

36. Ibid.

37. Ibid., p. 11. Two years later, Sa'ud would be effectively overthrown by his more reformist brother, Faisal.

38. Ibid., pp. 11–12.

39. Ibid., p. 9.

40. "Memorandum of Conference" dated 23 December 1958. USDD–1983:001435.

41. Cable from Ambassador H. Caccia in Washington to the Foreign Office, 18 December 1958. BFOD:FO371/133086/EQ10345/7.

42. See, for example, Humphrey Trevelyan's report of 19 January 1960 to Selwyn Lloyd on the political situation in Iraq. BFOD:FO371/149841/EQ1015/10.

43. Interview in the *New York Times*, 29 April 1959, quoted in Hanna Batatu, *The Old Social Classes and the Revolutionary Movements of Iraq: A Study of Iraq's Old Landed and Commercial Classes and of Its Communists, Ba'thists, and Free Officers* (Princeton: Princeton University Press, 1978), p. 899.

44. Note by Gordon Gray, special assistant to the president for national security affairs, 1 April 1959. USDD–1984:000586.

45. See Mohamed Hassanein Heikal, *Sphinx and Commissar: The Rise and Fall of Soviet Influence in the Arab World* (New York: Harper and Row, 1978), p. 107.

46. Operations Coordinating Board (OCB) Report on the Near East, 3 February 1960, pp. 6–7. USDD–1984:002567.

47. "The Situation in Iraq: Policy the United States Should Follow to Prevent Communism from Establishing Control of the Country," 15 [?] April 1959. USDD–1992:002638.

48. Cable from Ambassador Burrows in Ankara to the Foreign Office, 12 December 1959. BFOD:FO371/140959/EQ1071/70.

49. See the Cable dated 5 August 1959 from Amman to the Foreign Office (BFOD:FO371/ 141900/VG1017/9), as well as a later dispatch from the Canadian Embassy in Cairo reporting the arrest of fourteen officers in Syria on conspiracy charges. 22 September 1959, BFOD:FO371/141900/VG1017/12.

50. Quoted in a dispatch from the British Embassy in Baghdad on 3 November 1959. BFOD:FO371/140958/EQ1071/52(D).

51. Letter from Burrows to London, 23 May 1959. BFOD:FO371/140957/EQ1071/31.

52. Ibid., BFOD:FO371/140957/EQ1071/28.

53. Report dated 20 October 1959 from Arnold Smith in Cairo to the Canadian Foreign Ministry. BFOD:FO371/141903/VG10110/36.

54. At least that is what Deputy Undersecretary of State Raymond Hare told Nasser in New York on 30 September 1960. USDD–1984:002431.

55. Ambassador Burrows's account of remarks made by a US State Department official to Turkish Foreign Minister Zorlu. Cable from Ankara to the Foreign Office on 23 May 1959. BFOD:FO371/140957/EQ1071/31. Stuart Rockwell, director of the State Department's Office of Near Eastern Affairs, explained his government's position to the British envoy by saying, "He did not think there was any serious danger of overt military intervention by the U.A.R. This being so he thought that it would be unwise to urge moderation on Nasser," since the United States did not wish to be seen as supporting communism against Arab nationalism. Cable from Ambassador Caccia in Washington to the Foreign Office, 19 March 1959. BFOD:FO371/ 140937/EQ10316/96.

56. Memorandum of the discussion at the 383rd meeting of the NSC, dated 17 October 1958. USDD–1990:000332, p. 8.

57. Memorandum from Komer to McGeorge Bundy and Walt Rostow. USDD–1991:001643.

58. Bowles Telegram dated 21 February 1962. USDD–I:454A.

59. Badeau Letter to President Johnson, 3 January 1964. USDD–1976:274C, p. 4.

60. Ibid., p. 3.

61. "Nasir's Comments on His Meeting with Assistant Secretary Talbot," CIA cable, 3 March 1964. USDD–1976:12B.

62. Outgoing State Department telegram dated 12 January 1965 summarizing a meeting between Kamel and Secretary of State Dean Rusk four days before. USDD–1982:002580.

63. "Review of United States Policy Toward Israel," State Department memorandum to the President, 7 August 1962. USDD–1992:003242.

64. Steven L. Spiegel, *The Other Arab-Israeli Conflict: Making America's Middle East Policy, from Truman to Reagan* (Chicago: University of Chicago Press, 1985), p. 135.

65. Nadav Safran, *Israel: The Embattled Ally* (Cambridge: Belknap Press of Harvard University Press, 1981), p. 374.

66. Interviews conducted by author in Damascus, 22 July 1991.

67. Nadav Safran, *From War to War: The Arab-Israeli Confrontation, 1948–1967* (New York: Pegasus, 1969), p. 135.

68. Quoted in Spiegel, *The Other Arab-Israeli Conflict,* p. 122.

69. "Current Status of U.S.-U.A.R. Relations," 12 August 1966. USDD–1980:323B.

70. Letter from Nes to Rodger P. Davies at the State Department, 17 October 1966. USDD–1985:001635.

71. "Nasser's May 2 Speech," State Department memorandum dated 4 May 1967. USDD–1993:001379.

72. Letter from Nes to Rodger P. Davies at the State Department, 11 May 1967. USDD–1985:002605.

73. Memorandum summarizing the discussion at the 374th National Security Council meeting on 31 July 1958. USDD–1990:000331, p. 7.

Part Two

Arab-Israeli War and Peace

10

The 1967 Arab-Israeli War
US Actions and Arab Perceptions

Fawaz A. Gerges

On more than one level the June 1967 Arab-Israeli war (also known as the Six Day War) was a watershed in the recent history of the Middle East. In particular, the confrontation radically transformed the nature of regional politics and the relationship between local states and the superpowers. On the one hand, the Arab-Israeli dispute became the most dominant single foreign policy issue in the external relations of the Arab states. The main focus of regional instability shifted from inter-Arab politics to Arab-Israeli interactions. The war also set the stage for the contemporary Arab-Israeli peace process. For the previous ten years, the dispute between Israel and the Arabs had been kept in the "icebox," moving neither toward resolution nor toward war.[1] In this sense, the Six Day War was a catalyst that forced Israel and the Arabs as well as their superpower patrons to participate in the quest for peace. On the other hand, the bloody escalation of the Arab-Israeli conflict made local players much more dependent on their superpower allies. As a result, the Arab-Israeli conflict became increasingly entangled in the US-Soviet cold war rivalry. Thus, bipolarity on the international stage was reflected on the regional level. The increased reliance of the local states on the superpowers restricted their freedom of action and compromised their independence.

This chapter examines the impact of the 1967 Arab-Israeli war on Arab nationalist perceptions regarding the input that the United States had in the crisis, in order to examine how these perceptions influenced Arab attitudes toward the US and Soviet roles in the peace process. I will argue that the Six Day War had a devastating, negative impact on Arab views regarding the US role, as well as on Arab beliefs in the efficacy of the Soviet Union and its reliability as a superpower ally. Although Arab nationalists, particularly in Egypt, were highly critical and suspicious of President Lyndon B. Johnson, they recognized the indispensable and preponderant role of Washington in the post–1967 peace process. They believed the United States wielded much influence over its client—Israel—and held most of the cards in the peace process.

In contrast, Arab rulers, and not just Egyptian President Gamal 'Abd al-Nasser, became conscious of the limited nature of Soviet power and prestige in world politics. Their experiences with the Soviet Union during the 1967 crisis convinced them that Moscow did not have the means or the will to defend the Arabs. This belated realization played a decisive role in the mellowing of Egyptian radicalism during the post-1967 period and, one might venture to claim, in the revolutionary reorientation of Egyptian foreign policy throughout the 1970s.

Thus, this chapter must address several critical questions: How did the Arab confrontational states, particularly Egypt, respond to their crushing defeat at the hands of Israel in June 1967? How did they perceive the role of the superpowers in the war, and did their perceptions of the two contrasting superpower positions influence their behavior toward the peace process? What was the impact of the US-Soviet rivalry on the dynamics of peacemaking? Why did President Johnson abandon previous US support for the 1949 armistice regime, and how did this radical change in US policy complicate the quest for peace? To what extent did the dramatic alteration in the regional balance of power inhibit both Israel and Arab rulers' willingness and ability to compromise? In this sense, did the 1967 war sow the seeds of a bloodier conflagration in the Middle East?

Arab Perceptions of the US Role in the 1967 Arab-Israeli War

The polarization of the Arab-Israeli conflict along East-West lines was directly related to the crushing defeat of the Arab states in 1967 and their perceptions that the United States had colluded with Israel to destroy the "revolutionary Arab regimes which had refused to be a part of the Western sphere of influence."[2] Nasser, the leading Arab nationalist, believed that his regime was the main target of the US-sponsored Israeli attack. He told Mohamed Heikal, a confidant of his, that Johnson succeeded in "trapping us." As for Nasser, this collusion entailed a complex set of political and diplomatic tricks and maneuvers. Moreover, the Egyptian leadership—not just Nasser—believed that the Johnson administration indirectly colluded with Israel by covering its flanks and neutralizing the Soviet Union and by deliberately deceiving Egypt and lulling it into a state of complacency.[3]

The Egyptians pointed to the fact that although the United States had secured from Egypt a commitment not to fire first, it failed to extract a similar pledge from Israel. They said that Egypt was under overwhelming pressure by the United States and the Soviet Union not to fire first. They argued that the Johnson administration impressed on Soviet leaders the urgent need to call upon its Egyptian ally to desist from any military adventure. To show his goodwill, Nasser declared publicly that he would not be the one to initiate hostilities. He said he was given the impression that Israel had also committed itself not to shoot first.[4]

Little wonder, then, that the Arab nationalists were very bitter after Israel's preemptive strike on June 5. They felt overwhelming resentment and anger for the

Johnson administration, fueled initially by official Egyptian and Jordanian accusations that the United States had participated alongside Israel in the first air attacks against the Arab forces.[5] Although unfounded, these accusations served to confirm a widely held Arab stereotype of US hostility. In particular, the Egyptians felt deceived by the United States; they also believed that the United States had involved the Soviets subconsciously in its strategy to mislead Egypt.

Nasser asserted that the US government helped Israel in several ways by providing it with intelligence and weapons. For example, Israel's attack on the USS *Liberty*—a US intelligence ship stationed off the Sinai coast on June 8—convinced the Egyptian leader of Johnson's complicity: the *Liberty* supplied Israel with critical intelligence about Egyptian military installations. In this context, Nasser claimed that Johnson had known and had approved of Israeli war plans in advance. As Nasser put it, the US role in the war was a continuation of its shutting off of aid to Egypt: Having failed to subdue Egypt through economic warfare, Johnson instigated Israel to use physical force instead.[6] Nasser said the United States "must be made to feel the brunt of its collusion with Israel. We must bring the weight of mobilized Arab anger to bear on her. The severing of relations is imperative."[7] This perception, or rather misperception, was shared by all the confrontation Arab states (most importantly, Egypt, Syria, and Iraq), which promptly broke diplomatic relations with Washington.

To understand the rationale behind Arab perceptions, one has to focus on the nature of the relationship between the Johnson administration and the Arab nationalist forces, particularly on the steady deterioration of US-Egyptian relations since the end of 1964. The gradual suspension of US food aid to Egypt beginning in 1965, coupled with the direct supply of arms to Israel and other conservative states in the area, embittered Egyptian leaders and convinced them that Johnson was not only determined to humiliate and starve their country to death, but also was working closely with their regional enemies to overthrow the revolutionary Arab governments.[8] In September 1965 the Egyptian ambassador to Washington informed a senior US diplomat that the Egyptian leadership believed that the US Central Intelligence Agency (CIA) was seeking to topple the Nasser regime.[9]

By the end of 1966 Nasser seemed to have lost hope for US policy, viewed as irredeemably pro-Israeli and anti-Egyptian.[10] The mood in Washington was equally hostile: "We're not angry [with Nasser]; we're fed up," wrote Harold Saunders, a key National Security Council (NSC) official dealing with the Middle East.[11] The US ambassador to Egypt, Lucius Battle, also said that a good deal of uncertainty and tension and a general sense of discouragement existed in US-Egyptian relations. The two countries, asserted the ambassador, were on a "slippery slope headed toward confrontation of the 1957–58 type." He warned his superiors in Washington to bear in mind that they were approaching a watershed in their relationship with Egypt.[12]

The Arab View of the US Role in the Peace Process

The general Arab view of the US role in the 1967 war and in the subsequent peace process should be studied squarely within this polarized context of suspicion and distrust. The Arab nationalists had no faith in the Johnson administration to act as a neutral mediator in the quest for peace. To them, an identity of interests existed between the White House and Israel, manifesting itself in Johnson's unequivocal support of Israel in the United Nations (UN) General Assembly and Security Council and subsequent actions, which were designed to ensure Israel's military superiority over all its Arab neighbors.[13] Arab rulers had a fixation with the United States that, in their opinion, determined questions of war and peace in the Middle East. They failed to appreciate the complexity of US-Israeli relations and the wide degree of autonomy that Israeli leaders exercised in their ceaseless quest for absolute security.

In both 1956 and 1967, Nasser and his Arab counterparts did not consider seriously the possibility that Israel, by manipulating the polarized international system, was capable of acting on its own in the pursuit of its national interests, with or without superpower collusion. Israel was simply seen as an instrument and agent of the Western powers and imperialism, performing at the behest of its masters; Israel was not working for itself alone but was serving as a US tool to dominate the Arab world. In the words of Algerian President Houari Boumedienne, "Israel played a secondary role in the 1967 war. The battle was American, and only the performance was Israeli." Likewise, Nasser said that the United States—not Israel—was the main party with which to discuss the occupation of Arab territories.[14] Although some of this was merely hyperbole, Arab politicians really believed that the United States held the key to war and peace in the region. Reading the recollections, speeches, and some minutes of the meetings of Arab officials, one gets the impression that Johnson had the power and the means to force Israel to withdraw to the prewar borders but did not want to employ them.[15]

Despite the vehemence of his attack on US policy, Nasser was in no position to confront the United States in the region. When the dust settled over the desert, Nasser found the bulk of his army destroyed, the Sinai occupied, his coffers empty, and his political career in jeopardy. Unlike the war of 1956, Nasser could not turn a military defeat into a political victory. In fact, the Six Day War was markedly different from the Suez crisis. In 1956 Nasser could rightly claim that Egyptian capabilities were no match for the combined forces of Britain, France, and Israel. In spite of his efforts, Nasser could not repeat the same political performance in 1967. The "most powerful state in the Middle East" had been decisively beaten and humiliated by a young, vigorous, and small nation.

As a result, Nasser's status and position in the Arab world were weakened as well. With the totality of defeat, Nasser's long-term goal of constructing a new Arab order disappeared. Undermined were the symbols and ideas of secular Arab nationalism that had served as the building blocks for this order. The revolutionary ideal was discredited in Arab politics. In inter-Arab relations, the overall balance of forces shifted dramatically in favor of the Arab conservatives, who held the power of the purse and who shaped the politics of the inter-Arab state system during the post-1967 period.

Furthermore, the Arab nationalists could no longer rely on the sympathy of world public opinion or on the active intervention of the superpowers. They did not understand the changed international situation in the late 1960s. The United States was bogged down in Vietnam and was not terribly focused on the Middle East. Likewise preoccupied at home and abroad, the Kremlin leadership was building bridges to the West in the hope of gaining economic and political concessions. The Soviets were against a war in the Middle East that might involve them in a direct clash with the United States (and thus endanger their new approach to the West).[16] The Arab radicals were mistaken in their assumption that the Soviets would intervene in a Middle East war. Such thinking was symptomatic of the prevailing, pervasive tendency of the regional actors to inflate their own importance. After the 1967 war, Nasser told his colleagues that he had not weighed carefully the changes in Soviet foreign policy after the death of Soviet leader Nikita Khrushchev.[17]

More significant to the Kremlin leadership were the nuclear stalemate with the United States and the perennial question of international security. In the Six Day War, US and Soviet policymakers communicated at the highest levels to contain the conflict and to prevent its spread and expansion. They exerted considerable pressures on their local allies to accept a cease-fire. Although the war was short, the superpowers used the hotline more than once to clarify any misunderstanding that might force them into an unwanted confrontation. In the aftermath of the war, top US and Soviet officials held talks to try to find a political solution.[18]

Although the Soviets were critical of Israel's actions in June 1967 and were supportive of the Arabs, they did not take concrete measures—except to promise to resupply arms—to help their friends. The Soviets could not even offer their Arab allies much support in the UN Security Council because of US objections to any resolution stipulating that Israel withdraw behind the 1949 armistice lines.[19] It was not until June 10 that the Soviet Union took drastic steps to halt the Israeli advance on the Syrian front. According to Johnson, Soviet Premier Alexei Kosygin used the hotline to inform him that as the result of Israel's ignoring all UN Security Council resolutions for a cease-fire, a very crucial moment had arrived. Kosygin foresaw the risk of a "grave catastrophe" unless Israel unconditionally terminated its military operations within the next few hours. Otherwise, the Soviet premier warned that his government would take all "necessary actions, including military." In addition, the Soviet Union severed diplomatic relations with Israel and threatened to take stronger measures unless the latter ceased hostilities immediately.[20]

Although he recognized that the Soviet Union was sensitive about its special relationship with Syria, Johnson said that he was determined to resist Soviet intrusion in the Middle East. His immediate response was to issue orders to the US Navy Sixth Fleet to move closer to the Syrian coast so as to send a warning signal to the Kremlin: "There are times when the wisdom and rightness of a President's judgment are critically important. We were at such a moment. The Soviets had made a decision. I had to respond."[21]

But neither the United States nor the Soviet Union had the stomach for a clash. The Soviets knew that pressure from the US government was the only way to stop an Israeli advance deep into Syria. Their warning to Johnson was designed to impress upon him the need to halt Tel Aviv's march toward Damascus. Soviet calculations proved correct. According to senior Israeli officials, on June 10 the Johnson administration informed its ally that the situation had reached a dangerous point and that Soviet intervention was no longer inconceivable. Israel agreed to a cease-fire on the same day, following the occupation of the Syrian Golan Heights.[22]

A crisis between the superpowers was thus averted. Their high-level contacts had effectively prevented an open clash between them. As the CIA put it, the Soviet Union had no intention of intervening militarily in the war and so did what it could to avoid confrontation. Another major concern of the Kremlin leadership, argued a CIA intelligence assessment, was to forestall a disastrous Arab defeat that would make the Kremlin the target of Arab criticisms.[23] As a superpower, the Soviet Union was more concerned about its relationship with the United States than with any abstract obligations to its regional partners. The logic of superpower politics took priority over other interests.

Given the ambivalent position of the Soviet Union, one would have expected Nasser to swallow his pride and mend fences with the Johnson administration. In the case of the Suez conflict, Nasser knew that it was the United States rather than the Soviet Union that ultimately forced the tripartite coalition to cease fire and withdraw. In 1967, however, Nasser believed that Johnson unleashed Israel's military action against Egypt to topple his progressive regime. Unlike Eisenhower, who played the leading and most effective role in thwarting the tripartite aggression, Nasser asserted that Johnson played a decisive role in Israel's swift victory over the Arabs.[24]

By using the last weapon in his arsenal—severing diplomatic relations with the US government—and by his accusations against the United States, Nasser embittered Johnson and made him more determined to prevent Nasser from regaining a position of pan-Arab leadership. The US president made it clear that the United States "could not afford to repeat the temporary and hasty arrangements" between Egypt and Israel after Suez. Johnson now had the opportunity to try a different approach, by supporting Israel's hold on the newly occupied territories pending Arab consent to make peace with Israel.[25]

Indeed, as soon as the fighting started, Johnson, as former Ambassador Richard Parker puts it, "showed a clear and lasting bias in favor of Israel and a disregard for the public commitments he and his administration had made to oppose aggression from any quarter."[26] The United States became more closely allied with Israel in opposition to vital Arab interests. The extremely pro-Israeli stand of US public opinion, coupled with Arab hostility and Johnson's dislike of Nasser, enabled Johnson to adopt a policy of "unquestioning support for Israel."[27] The extent of the Arab defeat took US officials by surprise. They had expected Israel to win but were unsure about the duration or immediate results of an Arab-Israeli contest. On the first day of the war, the uncertainty and uneasiness of the administration were reflected in its call for all combatants to work for a cease-fire and return to old positions before the start of hostilities.[28]

The US stand changed dramatically, however, as soon as the completeness of Israel's victory became known. In a memorandum to the president on June 7, his special assistant, Walt Rostow, wrote that the Israeli victory created new conditions that the US government quickly should move to exploit. The following day Rostow warned that the greatest risk would be to fail to appreciate the political consequences of Israel's military triumph. He summarized the US official position as being opposed to any UN resolution that would require Israel to concede war gains except in return for an Arab-Israeli final settlement.[29] No doubt Rostow was fully aware that the new bargaining situation created by the war was asymmetrical.

The Johnson administration hoped to use the new asymmetrical situation to extract peace treaties and recognition of Israel's existence from the Arabs. Some US officials argued that the humiliating defeat of Egypt and Syria provided the United States with a golden opportunity to take "big" political measures in the region, since "Soviet policy was in ruins."[30] Even before the war was over the administration had concluded that Nasser's fate was sealed. US diplomats in the field were certain that a general anti-Nasser convulsion would shake Egypt and the Arab world; indeed that the domestic survival of his regime was in doubt, as was the allegiance of other Arab states.[31]

US intelligence agencies also believed that the Egyptian leader's days were numbered, and they began to think seriously about the post-Nasser era. Likewise, the US Department of State thought that the fall of Nasser's regime would lead not only to the reestablishment of US relations with Egypt, but also to the resurrection of US interests in the whole Arab arena.[32] The dominant view in Washington was that no quick palliative solutions or temporizing compromises should be accepted. In the words of the undersecretary of state for political affairs, Averell Harriman, the United States would never have another opportunity as propitious to deal with the underlying problems besetting this turbulent region—"so vital to our own and Western Europe's security."[33] Ironically, Nasser interpreted the US position as motivated by a desire to freeze the present situation, hoping that his regime, along with all revolutionary Arab regimes, "would fall, to be replaced by another more receptive to U.S. interests, or alternatively to instill utter despair in us, driving us to make peace with Israel on its conditions."[34]

The basic outlines of US long-term strategy were defined as follows: (1) cessation of hostilities between Israel and its Arab neighbors; (2) Arab recognition of Israel; (3) support of moderate Arab forces—the leader of which was Saudi Arabia—at the expense of the Arab radicals: Egypt, Syria, and Iraq; (4) a bigger role for Turkey and Iran in the Middle East; (5) regional arms control arrangements; and (6) a new mechanism for social and economic development.[35] In US eyes, the denouement of the war provided a great opportunity to solve the festering Arab-Israeli conflict and to redraw the political map of the region. A central element in this strategy was to cut Nasser's prestige and influence in the Arab world and revise regional political alignments.

Achievement of this objective would require the active involvement of Turkey, Iran, and Israel. For a decade these states had campaigned hard to become integral players in the inter-Arab state subsystem. According to an intelligence assessment by the CIA, before the war Israel had hoped to construct a loose coalition of Iran, Turkey, Iraqi and Syrian Kurds, and moderate Arabs. It follows that the primary

Israeli war aim was the destruction of Nasser as the leader of the pan-Arab national-ist movement. If that goal could be achieved, Israeli officials assumed that Israel, Turkey, and Iran would become the dominant regional actors by representing an overwhelming balance of military power.[36]

In the aftermath of the war, both Israel and Iran lobbied the US government to support more substantial roles for them in the area. Israeli officials informed their US counterparts that their victory over the Arabs created new opportunities to build a more viable order in the Middle East. They argued further that the United States and its regional allies would be the main beneficiaries of this order.[37] The shah of Iran also informed the Johnson administration that "Nasser must be elimi-nated as otherwise he [could] again inflame Arab sentiments." Iran would be more than pleased, he added, to play a more active part and to be a solid pillar in the re gion, as Japan did in the Far East.[38] (Indeed, some time later, the Nixon Doctrine of 1969 envisaged hegemonic roles for Iran in the Gulf and Israel in the Fertile Crescent. President Richard M. Nixon and his assistant for national security, Henry Kissinger, saw Iran and Israel as the policemen and the protectors of US in-terests in the region.)[39]

These arguments impressed the Johnson administration, which accepted Tel Aviv's view that no withdrawal should take place except in return for a peace agree-ment. Johnson placed the major responsibility for the war on Egypt and refused to pressure Israel to concede any territories, as Eisenhower did in 1957. He said Israel must be accepted as a reality in the area and must be recognized by the Arabs.[40] Johnson spelled out five principles that were essential to peace: (1) the recognized right to national life (for all parties to the dispute); (2) justice for the (Palestinian) refugees; (3) innocent maritime passage (through the Suez Canal and the Strait of Tiran); (4) limiting the arms race (in the region between Arabs and Israelis); and (5) political independence and territorial integrity (for all). Both the Israelis and the Arabs saw Johnson's Five Great Principles of Peace as wholly supporting Israel. The convergence of interests between the United States and Israel was almost complete, marking the beginning of a special relationship between the two countries.[41] Thus, the Six Day War brought about a major shift in US policy toward the Middle East.[42] The president and his aides decided not to return to the old, failed policy supporting the 1949 armistice regime. This attitude explained the administration's posture of distant reserve toward the question of Arab-Israeli peace.[43]

The Arab View of the Soviet Role

Given their perceptions of an unholy US-Israeli alliance, the Arab confrontation states—Egypt, Syria, and Iraq, with the exception of Jordan—felt compelled to turn to the Soviet Union for political and military support. They recognized, however, the limited nature of Soviet power and influence.[44] The Soviet failure to provide di-rect military assistance to the Arabs had important repercussions on Soviet-Arab re-lations. Egyptian, Iraqi, and Algerian leaders were disappointed with the lack of tangible Soviet assistance. They suspected the Soviets of either being "scared of the

Americans" or of having sacrificed their Arab allies on the altar of détente with Washington. Egyptian officials criticized the Soviet Union for actually playing the role demanded of it by Johnson during the crisis in May and June; some senior Egyptian officials were skeptical about the value of Moscow as a friend, whereas others even suspected a collusion between the United States and the Soviet Union. Arab rulers realized that the security requirements of their superpower ally vis-à-vis the United States took priority over Middle East regional concerns.[45]

This realization convinced the Arabs that their alliance with the Soviet Union was tactical rather than strategic. In this context, the Six Day War marked a watershed in Arab-Soviet relations. The Arabs questioned the nature of their alliance with the Kremlin; though Israel enjoyed full protection by the United States, the Arabs did not receive an equal Soviet commitment.[46] It could be argued that one of the main reasons for the decline of Soviet influence in the Arab world in the early 1970s lay in Arab perceptions of Moscow's stand during the war.

Yet despite the feeling of abandonment and indignation, Nasser and the other Arab nationalists could not afford a final divorce from the Communist giant—especially after they cut their political links with the United States and Great Britain. The Soviet Union became their last refuge. Nasser believed that the regional and global configuration of forces were in US and Israeli favor, thus he needed Soviet military and political support to rebuild his military and to counterbalance US and Israeli hegemony. Immediately after the war Nasser moved swiftly to end the ill feeling that was souring Arab-Soviet relations. Nasser publicly praised Kremlin leaders for their political, economic, and military assistance. He informed Soviet officials that he wanted to strengthen and deepen Egyptian-Soviet relations and that he was ready to sign any pact to organize and structure the relationship between their two countries on a more permanent basis.[47] Moscow's deepening involvement with Egypt and Syria took the Arab-Israeli conflict still deeper into the cold war rivalry between the superpowers. The Arab-Israeli dispute became a global-military-strategic problem, not a regional-political problem.[48] The peace process thus became entangled in the web of great power politics.

To the Soviets, the immediate results of the war must have been gratifying. Nasser's crushing defeat humbled him, and he became more receptive to Soviet requests. No longer could he afford to challenge Moscow's influence in the region, as he had in 1959; this reassured the Soviets. By regulating the flow of arms to Egypt and Syria, the Kremlin would have a greater impact on their policies. Nasser was left in no doubt as to Moscow's preference for a peaceful solution to the Arab-Israeli conflict.[49] Time and again, the Soviets would procrastinate and decline to supply their Arab friends with offensive weapons. The war had taught the Soviets the need to exercise more control over their regional allies, and the war's aftermath enabled them to do so. In the next three years the question of arms deliveries became one of the most effective clubs the Soviets wielded over the Arabs.[50]

The Egyptians were frustrated with their treatment by the Kremlin. In fact, Anwar Sadat described the period after the war as a clash between Egypt and the Soviet Union.[51] In the long run, Soviet behavior bred suspicion and bitterness in Arab ranks, especially in Egypt. Sadat claimed that one of the reasons motivating Nasser to accept the 1970 Rogers Initiative—a peace initiative by US Secretary of State William Rogers—was Nasser's belief that the Soviet Union was a "hopeless case."[52] Hence, it was a only matter of time before the Egyptians would rebel against what they perceived to be Soviet heavy-handedness.

In the short term, Soviet political and material influence increased considerably in the Arab world. Soviet leaders kept their promise to restore lost Arab inventories, with the exception of offensive weapons. Soviet military personnel also were sent in increasing numbers to Cairo and Damascus to assist in defense of deep strategic and industrial targets. However, the flourishing Soviet presence in the region was tactical and temporary, the product of a devastating upheaval that left Egypt, the nerve center of the Arab order, with few international options to pursue. The Arabs could not help comparing US support of Israel with the Kremlin's lukewarm commitment to the Arabs. Thus, the seeds of mistrust and suspicion had been sown in Arab-Soviet relations. Although Nasser could not distance himself from his Soviet ally, he eventually reopened his relationship with the United States, and by the time of his death from natural causes in 1970 he had come to recognize the indispensable role of Washington in the peace process. Sadat claimed that Nasser had told him that "whether we like it or not, all the cards of this game [i.e., the Arab-Israeli conflict] are in America's hands. It's high time we talked and allowed the U.S.A. to take part in this."[53]

Although Sadat's account is exaggerated and self-serving it is also important, as it foreshadows the future direction of US-Egyptian relations. More than once Nasser tested the degree of US commitment to a balanced approach to the Middle East crisis. For example, following Richard Nixon's election to the presidency in 1968, Nasser decided to make a fresh start with the United States by initiating a dialogue with the new US leader. In fact, Nasser and Jordan's King Hussein informed Nixon that they were prepared to accept a diplomatic solution with Israel and that they were constrained neither by Syria's opposition nor by opposition from other Arab radicals. Egyptian Prime Minister Mahmoud Fawzi also told Nixon privately that as part of a regional settlement Israel would have freedom of navigation in the Suez Canal. The Egyptians hoped that the Nixon administration would reciprocate by adopting evenhanded policies toward the Arabs and the Israelis. They were disappointed, however, with the lack of a positive US response. According to scholar William Quandt, Kissinger was not persuaded. Thus, the Nixon administration did not change its attitude and maintained close ties with Israel by preserving Israel's military superiority over Arab neighbors without pressing its leaders to withdraw from recently occupied Arab territories.[54]

Nasser still thought that Nixon—unlike Johnson—could play a positive role in the Arab-Israeli conflict. In May 1970, the Egyptian leader personally appealed to Nixon to adopt an evenhanded policy and become actively engaged in the quest for peace. He said Egypt had not given up on the United States, despite US military and political support to Israel: The United States must either order Israel to withdraw from the recently occupied territories or, if it was unable to go that far, refrain from extending any further assistance to Israel as long as the latter occupied Arab lands. Although Egypt and the United States did not have diplomatic relations, Nasser said this did not prevent the two countries from cooperating to achieve peace.[55] According to Sadat, this appeal to Nixon implied a desire on Nasser's part to pursue a political course of action.[56] Although Nixon responded to the appeal, and Rogers in fact outlined a peace initiative, Nasser and the United States could not overcome differences. It would take Nasser's successor (ironically, that turned out to be Sadat) and other new leaders to revive the old connection with the United States—at the sole expense of the Kremlin.

The Khartoum Summit

Nasser accepted the convening of a summit of Arab heads of state in Khartoum, Sudan, at the end of August 1967. As to the Arab militants—Syria, Iraq, Algeria, and the Palestine Liberation Organization (PLO)—it was their feeling that a counteroffensive was urgently needed to stem the tide of US advance in the region. In their view, the termination of diplomatic relations with the United States was not adequate to force it to change its policy. Thus, the Syrians, Algerians, Iraqis, and Palestinians called for a complete boycott of the United States and for a strategic alliance with the Soviet Union. They argued that the peace process would lead to Arab surrender and a US-Israeli dictate. On the regional level, they advanced the idea of a popular war against Israel and of a revolutionary crusade against the conservative Arab regimes. The Syrian rulers, in particular, took an anti-Western posture and poured abuse on reactionary Arab regimes that had remained on the sidelines during the latest round of Arab-Israeli hostilities. Syria boycotted the Khartoum Summit because it refused to accept Arab reaction as a partner.[57]

However, the clarification of the Soviet position played a decisive role in Nasser's decision to accept the convening of the summit. Its purpose was to define a collective Arab strategy toward Israel and the West. In Khartoum, Nasser joined the Arab moderates in supporting a political rather than military solution to the Arab-Israeli conflict. They also agreed to keep the dialogue with the West, and they opposed the militants' proposal to suspend Arab oil production.[58] An oil embargo, Nasser argued, would harm Arab economies more than those of the West and would almost certainly antagonize the West. Nasser's new realism manifested itself in his unwillingness to ask the conservative Arab regimes to sever diplomatic relations with the US government. He also informed Jordan's King Hussein that he was free to pursue a separate negotiated settlement—including signing a defense treaty with the United States—to recover the West Bank and Jerusalem.[59]

Nasser's behavior was designed not only to mend his fences with the Arab conservatives, but also to keep open lines of communication with the United States. He said he wanted to give the United States an opportunity to prove to its few remaining Arab friends that it was serious about reducing its total alignment with Israel. Nasser was not convinced by the arguments of the militants to cut all links with Washington. The war and its aftermath made the Egyptian leader acutely aware of the influential weight of the United States in the region. As Nasser himself put it, "Political positions cannot be built on myths but facts. We do not want and cannot fight America." Thus, the Egyptian leader asked Saudi King Faisal to serve as his channel of communication with the Johnson administration.[60]

Nasser parted company with the Arab radicals on the Arab-Israeli conflict itself: He was not impressed by their call for a total war against the Jewish state. He knew full well that the regional balance of power favored Israel, which had won the sympathy and respect of world public opinion and a decisive edge in international diplomacy. Nasser also took into account the superpower agreement to resolve the problem by political means. Moreover, as mentioned previously, both the Soviet Union and the nonaligned movement informed the Arabs that they would prefer to see a peaceful way out of the Arab-Israeli labyrinth.[61]

For all these reasons, the Egyptian president joined the moderates in Khartoum in support of a political rather than military solution to the conflict. This fact should not be confused by the summit's three declarations on Israel "no peace, no negotiations, no recognition." The Sudanese premier noted that the three no's were adopted as an instrumental response, a political gesture, to the uncompromising stand of the PLO. Afterward, Nasser, Hussein, and other Arab officials made it clear both publicly and privately that they were prepared to live in peace with Israel in return for Israel's complete withdrawal from Arab territories occupied in 1967 and for a just solution to the Palestine problem. The summit, noted Hussein, empowered Egypt and Jordan to seek a political solution. In particular, Hussein was convinced that a political solution was the only feasible option open to the Arabs. This belief led him to coordinate his efforts with the United States as well as to serve as a link between the United States and Egypt.[62]

It was within this spirit that Egypt and Jordan accepted UN Security Council Resolution 242, which was adopted unanimously by the major powers in November 1967. This resolution called for the withdrawal of Israeli armed forces from territories—not "the" territories—occupied in the recent conflict and the termination of the state belligerency between Israel and its Arab neighbors.[63]

Nasser subsequently accused Johnson of supporting Israel in resisting the implementation of the terms of Resolution 242; instead the Johnson administration applied considerable political pressure in an attempt to force Egypt (and Jordan) into a separate peace settlement with Israel: The basis of any agreement with Egypt centered on total Israeli withdrawal from all occupied Egyptian territories in return for Egypt terminating the state of war with Israel. Nasser refused to conclude a separate deal with Israel and called for a comprehensive solution: "The issue is not only about withdrawal from Sinai. It is much bigger than that. The issue is to be or not to be." To Nasser, accepting a separate agreement with Israel meant coming to terms with the reality of defeat and abandoning the core of the Arab policy upon which he had built his political career.[64]

The Egyptians were angered when Johnson started to develop intimate ties with Tel Aviv. They believed that Johnson's actions were not only confined to safeguarding Israel, but also assisting it in its occupation of Arab lands. To Nasser and his colleagues, the US president was pushing Egypt to depend further upon the Soviet Union for military, economic, and political support. Egyptian Foreign Minister Mahmoud Riad said that Nasser felt puzzled by the element of self-destruction in US policy that was driving the Arabs into Soviet arms: "The United States leaves us no choice."[65] Egyptian leaders could not understand the radical change in the US position toward the peace process after the 1967 war, especially Johnson's abandonment of previous US support for the 1949 armistice regime. They believed that the US-Israeli drive aimed at "forcing Egypt to accept the fait accompli in the hope that the Arab area would surrender to U.S. and Israeli demands."[66]

This was another attempt by Johnson, asserted Nasser, to humiliate the Arabs, thus adversely affecting US-Arab relations. By the end of 1967, given Nasser's perception of Johnson's hostility, he had concluded that the peace process was dead as long as the balance of power favored Israel; it was only by restoring this imbalance that the United States would be induced to reassess its position. Nasser said that redressing the imbalance, and escalating military pressure, would have a radical impact on the whole Middle East situation, particularly on the positions of the superpowers, and would convince the superpowers of the need to stop maneuvering and to act decisively. Thus, Nasser's subsequent choice of a "war of attrition" can be seen as a result of the lack of progress toward a political settlement in the two years after the 1967 war and of his desire to break the political and military stalemate, something Anwar Sadat would do as well in 1973.[67]

Conclusion

Although the Six Day War set the stage for the Middle East peace process, it did not motivate or force Israel and the Arabs to reach a compromise. Israel's overwhelming victory over the Arabs brought about a radical shift in the regional balance of power in its favor. This shift in the configuration of forces, coupled with the strong pro-Israeli position of the US government, hardened the position of the two antagonists. Although most Arab rulers declared their readiness to live in peace with their Jewish neighbor, none of the Arab confrontational states—except for Jordan—was willing to conclude formal peace treaties with Israel. They were very weak militarily for any risky initiative on the diplomatic front. For Nasser and his Arab counterparts, to give the sort of commitments the United States and Israel were demanding would have meant accepting the reality of defeat, thus endangering the very survival of their regimes. Furthermore, despite their rude awakening in June 1967, Arab leaders were not yet ready to come to terms with Israel; they were still prisoners of their historical fears and prejudices.

Israel, on the other hand, was a satisfied power. As a result of their swift victory over the Arabs, Israeli officials demanded a high price for their withdrawal from some, but not all, of the recently occupied Arab territories. Given the disarray, fragmentation, and impotence of the Arab world and unwavering US support, some Israeli elements believed that they could indefinitely hold on to the occupied Arab territories. By the time UN Resolution 242 was passed, Israel was no longer interested in exchanging land for commitments of any kind from the Arabs. As the then deputy assistant secretary of state for Near Eastern affairs, Rodger Davies, put it: "Israel's appetite had grown with the eating."[68]

The diplomatic stalemate in the Middle East was directly related to the deepening polarization of the Arab-Israeli conflict along East-West lines. As mentioned previously, Arab nationalist perceptions of US involvement in the 1967 war influenced their attitudes toward the US role in the peace process. They believed that the Johnson administration had colluded with Israel against the forces of Arab nationalism. Subsequent US abandonment of its previous support for the 1949 armistice regime reinforced the widely held Arab view of US hostility.

As a result, Arab nationalists did not trust the United States to act as a neutral mediator in the quest for peace; they turned instead to the Soviet Union for political and military succor—despite their recognition of the limited nature of Soviet power—hoping to redress the regional imbalance. Moscow's further involvement with Egypt and Syria took the Middle East crisis still deeper into the cold war rivalry between the superpowers. The entanglement of the Arab-Israeli conflict in the web of great power politics complicated the peace process and made Israel and the Arabs less willing to compromise. Thus, far from being a catalyst for peace, the 1967 war sowed the seeds of yet another bloody conflagration in the region.

Notes

I want to thank former Ambassador Richard Parker, Professor William Quandt, Dr. Avi Shlaim, and Professor Chris Taylor for reading and commenting on an earlier version of this chapter.

1. William B. Quandt, *Peace Process: American Diplomacy and the Arab-Israeli Conflict Since 1967* (Washington, D.C.: Brookings Institution and University of California Press, 1993), p. 1.

2. *Wataiq 'Abdel-Nasser: Khutab, ahadit, tasrihat: Yanayir 1967–Disember 1968 [Abdel-Nasser's Documents; Speeches, Discussions, and Declarations, January 1967–December 1968]* (Cairo: Markaz al-dirasat al-siyasiya wa al-istratijiya bi Al-Ahram, 1973), p. 246 (hereinafter this series will be referred to as *Wataiq Nasser, 1967–1968*). Shortly after the war, Nasser told his colleague, Vice-President Zakaria Muhieddin, that Johnson was determined to get rid of Nasser. See Tharwat Akasha, *Mudhakkirati fi al-siyasa wa al-thaqafa [My Memoirs in Politics and in Culture]*, vol. 2 (Cairo: Maktaba al-madbuli, 1988), pp. 490, 501–502.

3. *Wataiq Nasser, 1967–1968*, p. 226; Mahmoud Riad, *The Struggle for Peace in the Middle East* (London: Quartet Books, 1981), pp. 36–37; Mohamed Heikal, *1967: Sanawat al-galayan, Harb al-talateen sana [1967: The Years of Upheaval, the Thirty Years War]*, vol. 1 (Cairo: Markaz Al-Ahram litarjama wa al-nashr, 1988), p. 846.

4. *Wataiq Nasser, 1967–1968*, p. 226; Riad, *The Struggle for Peace in the Middle East*, pp. 36–37; Heikal, *1967: Sanawat al-galayan*, p. 846; Mohamed Heikal, *Nasser: The Cairo Documents* (London: New English Library, 1972), p. 219.

5. H. M. King Hussein, *Harbuna ma'a Israil [Our War with Israel]* (Beirut: Dar al-nahar lilnashr, 1968), pp. 67–69.

6. Beginning in 1965, Johnson applied economic pressure against Nasser by reducing the flow of foreign aid to Egypt. *Wataiq Nasser, 1967–1968*, pp. 226, 243–248; Lieutenant Gen-

eral Salah al-Din al-Hadidi, *Shahid ila harb sab'a wa sitteen [Witness to the 1967 War]* (Cairo: Maktaba al-madbuli, 1974), p. 180. Diya al-Din Baybars, *Al-asrar al-sakhsiya li 'Abd al-Nasser [The Personal Secrets of Nasser as Told by Mahmoud al-Jayar]* (Cairo: Maktaba al-madbuli, 1976), p. 165; Ahmed Hamroush, *Qissa taura 23 Yulio: Karif 'Abd al-Nasser [The Story of the 23 July Revolution: The Autumn of 'Abd al-Nasser]*, vol. 5 (Cairo: Maktaba al-madbuli, 1984), pp. 138–139, 141; Mahmoud Riad, *Mudhakkirat: America wa al-'arab [Memoirs: America and the Arabs]*, vol. 3 (Beirut: Dar al-Mustaqbal al-'Arabi, 1986), pp. 40–42; Mohamed Heikal, *1967: Al-infijar, Harb al-talateen sana' [1967: The Explosion, the Thirty Years War]*, vol. 3 (Cairo: Markaz Al-Ahram liltarjama wa al-nashr, 1990), pp. 756, 846, 876.

7. Riad, *The Struggle for Peace in the Middle East,* p. 25.

8. *Wataiq Nasser, 1967–1968,* p. 336; Abdel Meguid Farid, *Min muhadarat ijtima'at 'Abd al-Nasser al-'arabiya was duwaliya [From the Minutes of 'Abd al-Nasser's Arab and International Meetings, 1967–1970]* (Beirut: Mu'assasa al-abhat al-'arabiya, 1979), pp. 120–121; Hamroush, *Qissa taura 23 Yulio,* vol. 5, pp. 82–83; Ahmed Youssef Ahmed, *Al-dawr al-Misri fi al-Yaman, 1962–1967 [The Egyptian Role in Yemen, 1962–1967]* (Cairo: Al-Hai'a al-Misriya al-amma ilkitab, 1981), p. 319.

9. US Department of State, Memorandum of Conversation, Subject: US-U.A.R. Relations, 17 September 1965, in *The Lyndon B. Johnson National Security Files, the Middle East: National Security Files, 1963–1969* (Frederick, Md.: University Publications of America, 1989), reel 8 of 8 (hereinafter, this series will be referred to as *LBJ Files*).

10. Riad, *The Struggle for Peace in the Middle East,* p. 16; Tom Little, *Modern Egypt* (London: Ernest Benn, 1967), p. 231; Hamroush, *Qissa taura 23 Yulio,* vol. 5, pp. 83–84, 94; Mohamed Heikal, *Sphinx and Commissar: The Rise and Fall of Soviet Influence in the Arab World* (London: Collins, 1978), pp. 161–162, 165–167.

11. Hal Saunders, Recommend Clearing Cable from Hare to Battle with Added Final Sentence, 4 June 1966, in *LBJ Files,* reel 8 of 8.

12. Cairo to Secretary of State, No. 3062, 25 May 1966 [sections one and two of two], in ibid.

13. Mohammed Fawzi, *Harb october am 1973: Dirasa was durus [The October War of 1973: A Study and Lessons]* (Beirut: Dar al-Mustaqbal al-'arabi, 1988), p. 5; Riad, *The Struggle for Peace in the Middle East,* p. 27; Mohamed Hafez Ismael, *Amin Misr al-quami fi asr al-tahadiyat [Egyptian National Security in the Challenging Age]* (Cairo: Markaz Al-Ahram lilnashr, 1987), p. 125.

14. *Wataiq Nasser, 1967–1968,* p. 495; Heikal, *1967: Al-infijar,* pp. 914, 933; Mohamed Heikal, *The Road to Ramadan: The Inside Story of How the Arabs Prepared For and Almost Won the October War of 1973* (India: Natraj Publishers, 1981), p. 47; Riad, *The Struggle for Peace in the Middle East,* pp. 76–77.

15. Riad, *The Struggle for Peace in the Middle East,* pp. 25, 37, 39. Riad, *Mudhakkirat,* vol. 3, p. 45.

16. Robert Stephens, *Nasser: A Political Biography* (Middlesex, England: Penguin, 1971), p. 521; Richard Parker, "The June War: Whose Conspiracy?" *Journal of Palestine Studies* 21(4) (Summer 1992), pp. 15–17; Abdel-Latif A. Baghdadi, *Mudhakirat [Memoirs],* vol. 2 (Cairo: Al-maktab al-Misri al-hadit, 1977), p. 277.

17. Heikal, *1967: Al-infijar,* pp. 725, 733, 895; Baghdadi, *Mudhakirat [Memoirs],* vol. 2, pp. 275–276.

18. Draft Message to Chairman Kosygin, 8 June 1967, in *LBJ Files,* reel 1 of 8; Lyndon B. Johnson, *The Vantage Point: Perspectives of the Presidency, 1963–1969* (New York: Holt, Rinehart, and Winston, 1971), p. 298.

19. Memorandum for Mr. Rostow: The Security Council Meeting of 6 and 7 June 1967, in *LBJ Files,* reel 1 of 8.

20. The states of Eastern Europe, with the exception of Romania, also broke off diplomatic relations with Tel Aviv. Pravda, 10 June 1967; Johnson, *The Vantage Point,* p. 302; Moshe Dayan, *Story of My Life* (London: Weidenfeld and Nicolson, 1976), p. 304; Abba Eban, *An Autobiography* (London: Weidenfeld and Nicolson, 1977), p. 423.

21.Johnson, *The Vantage Point,* p. 302.

22. The weight of evidence indicates that Washington turned a blind eye toward Israel's offensive campaign against Syria. Israel's foreign minister at the time, Abba Eban, noted that some US officials informed him that Syria should not be allowed to escape injury. On June 8 these officials were worried lest the UN Security Council adopt a cease-fire resolution, thus leaving Syria off the hook. During the debate on whether to storm the Golan Heights, Eban told the Israeli cabinet that Washington would be delighted if Syria were beaten. Declassified US documents also show that US officials hoped that Israel would "go fast enough" to create a "de facto" situation on the Syrian front before the UN Security Council passed a cease-fire resolution. The USS *Liberty* incident, however, indicates that the Johnson administration did not sanction Israel's attack on Syria. We still do not know the whole story behind Israel's attack on this US-flagged intelligence-gathering ship in the eastern Mediterranean, killing thirty-four men, although some believe it was a deliberate attempt by Israel to keep Washington in the dark as to its intentions vis-à-vis the Golan Heights rather than an accident, as the Israelis claim. The recently declassified US documents do not provide any critical insights as to Israel's motives. For evidence on the US stand toward the Golan issue, see Walt Rostow to President, 6 June 1967, in *LBJ Files,* reel 1 of 8. See also Eban, *An Autobiography,* pp. 421–422; William B. Quandt, *Decade of Decisions: American Policy Toward the Arab-Israeli Conflict, 1967–1976* (Berkeley: University of California Press, 1977), p. 63; Steven L. Spiegel, *The Other Arab-Israeli Conflict: Making America's Middle East Policy, from Truman to Reagan* (Chicago: University of Chicago Press, 1985), p. 151; Dayan, *Story of My Life,* p. 304.

23. US Central Intelligence Agency (CIA), Memorandum for Walt W. Rostow, Subject: Objectives of the Middle East Combatants and the USSR, 6 June 1967, in *LBJ Files,* reel 1 of 8.

24. *Majmu'at Khutab wa tasrihat wa bayanat al-ra'is Gamal Abdel-Nasser, 23 Yulio 1952 1958 [The Collected Speeches, Declarations, and Statements of President Gamal 'Abd al Nasser, 23 July 1952–1958],* vol. 1 (Cairo: Hai'a al ist'lamat, n.d.), p. 617; *Wataiq Nasser, 1967–1968,* pp. 226, 243–248; Riad, *The Struggle for Peace in the Middle East,* p. 37; Sa'id Mar'iy, *Awraq siyasiya: Min'azma Mars ila al-naksa [Political Papers: From the March Crisis to the Disaster]* (Cairo: Al-maktab al-Misri al-hadit, 1978), p. 362; Salah Nasr, *Abdel-Nasser wa tajriba al-wahda [Nasser and the Unity Experience]* (Cairo: Al-watan al-'arabi, 1976), vol. 1, p. 281; Heikal, *1967: Al-infijar,* p. 846; Heikal, *Sphinx and Commissar,* p. 72.

25. During his first meeting with King Hussein after the war, President Johnson informed his guest that he was "angry" with Egypt. H. M. King Hussein, *Mahammati kamalik [My Profession as King]* (Jordan: Al-sirka al-'arabiya iltiba'a wa nashr, 1978), p. 221. See also Hussein, *Harbuna ma'a Israil,* p. 95; Johnson, *The Vantage Point,* p. 303; Quandt, *Peace Process,* pp. 51, 54, 62; and Stephens, *Nasser: A Political Biography,* p. 522.

26. Richard B. Parker, *The Politics of Miscalculation in the Middle East* (Bloomington: Indiana University Press, 1993), p. 121.

27. Quandt, *Peace Process,* p. 61; Parker, *The Politics of Miscalculation,* p. 129; Robert Stookey, *America and the Arab States: An Uneasy Encounter* (London: John Wiley, 1975), p. 217.

28. Harriman to the President and Secretary of State, No. 19914, 6 June 1967, in *LBJ Files,* reel 1 of 8.

29. Walt Rostow to the President, No. 299, 7 June 1967; and Department of State to Embassy Paris, No. 209550, 8 June 1967, in ibid.

30. Department of State to Embassy Tehran, Subject: Middle East Crisis, No. 209086, 7 June 1967, in ibid.

31. Cairo to Secretary of State, No. 3292, 7 June 1967, in ibid.

32. Ibid. CIA, Memorandum for Walt W. Rostow, 6 June 1967; and Department of State, Subject: Middle East Crisis, Embassy Tehran, No. 209086, 7 June 1967, in ibid.

33. Harriman to the President, No. 6577, 8 June 1967; and Department of State to Embassy London, No. 208887, 7 June 1967, in ibid.

34. Riad, *The Struggle for Peace in the Middle East,* p. 83; Riad, *Mudhakkirat,* vol. 3, p. 73; *Wataiq Nasser, 1967–1968,* p. 306; Amin Huweidi, *Hurub Abdel-Nasser ['Abd al-Nasser's Wars]* (Cairo: Dar al-mauqif al-'arabi, 1982), p. 149.

35. Walt Rostow to the President, No. 299, 7 June 1967; Department of State to Embassy London, No. 208887, 7 June 1967; and NSC Memorandum for Walt Rostow, Subject: Reactions to Your Paper of 7 June 1967, 8 June 1967, *LBJ Files,* reel 1 of 8.

36. Richard Helms, CIA, to Walt Rostow, Subject: Israeli Objectives in the Current Crisis—Soviet Policy Miscalculation, 6 June 1967, in ibid.

37. Embassy Tel Aviv to Secretary of State, No. 3998, 7 June 1967, in ibid.

38. Department of State to Embassy Tehran, Subject: Middle East Crisis, No. 209086, 7 June 1967; and Harriman to the President, No. 6577, 8 June 1967, in ibid.

39. Henry Kissinger, *White House Years* (Boston: Little, Brown, 1979), p. 1262; George Lenczowski, *American Presidents and the Middle East* (Durham, N.C.: Duke University Press, 1990), pp. 116–140; Quandt, *Decade of Decisions,* p. 9.

40. Johnson, *The Vantage Point,* pp. 303–304; and Quandt, *Peace Process,* p. 55.

41. David Kimche and Dan Bawly, *The Sandstorm, the Arab-Israeli War of June 1967: Prelude and Aftermath* (New York: Stein and Day, 1968), pp. 279, 281; Riad, *The Struggle for Peace in the Middle East,* pp. 39, 55; Quandt, *Decade of Decisions,* p. 64.

42. Strong US support of Israel in the post-Nixon Doctrine and post-Jordanian civil war period was not as big a shift in US foreign policy as popularly thought. All that Nixon did was to carry further the change in US policy toward Israel that was inaugurated by Johnson after the 1967 war.

43. NSC, Memorandum for Walt Rostow, 8 June 1967, *LBJ Files,* reel 1 of 8. Quandt, *Peace Process,* pp. 54, 57.

44. *Wataiq Nasser, 1967–1968,* pp. 221, 226, 242–243; Baghdadi, *Mudhakirat [Memoirs],* pp. 274–275, 298–299.

45. *Wataiq Nasser, 1967–1968,* pp. 221, 226, 242–243; Heikal, *1967: Al-infijar,* p. 754; Cairo to Secretary of State, No. 3292, 7 June 1967; Soviet Objectives in the Middle East, No. 41, 2 January 1968, *LBJ Files,* reels 1 and 7 of 8 respectively; Riad, *The Struggle for Peace in the Middle East,* pp. 29–30, 36–37; Riad, *Mudhakkirat,* vol. 2, p. 46; Hamroush, *Qissa taura 23 Yulio,* vol. 5, pp. 126–163, 188–189; Heikal, *Sphinx and Commissar,* p. 181; Stephens, *Nasser: A Political Biography,* p. 511.

46. Anwar *Sadat, In Search of Identity: An Autobiography* (London: Collins, 1978), pp. 172–173; Munir Hafez, "Al-tarik al-sirri lihukm Gamal Abdel-Nasser," *Rose al-Yusif,* No. 2498, 26 April 1976, pp. 22–23; Baghdadi, *Mudhakirat [Memoirs],* vol. 2, p. 298; Anouar Abdel-Malek, *Egypt: Military Society, the Army Regime, the Left, and Social Change Under Nasser,* trans. Charles Markmann (New York: Random House, 1968), viii; Heikal, *Sphinx*

and Commissar, p. 191; Heikal, *1967: Al-infijar,* pp. 773, 916–918; Hamroush, *Qissa taura 23 Yulio,* vol. 5, p. 186.

47. *Wataiq Nasser, 1967–1968,* pp. 261, 268; Riad, *The Struggle for Peace in the Middle East,* pp. 42–45; Farid, *Min muhadarat,* pp. 29–30, 34, 41; Fawzi, *Harb october am 1973,* pp. 189, 194–195; Heikal, *Sphinx and Commissar,* p. 193; Hamroush, *Qissa taura 23 Yulio,* vol. 5, p. 186.

48. Stookey, *America and the Arab States,* p. 215.

49. Riad, *The Struggle for Peace in the Middle East,* pp. 49–50, 84; Farid, *Min muhadarat,* pp. 40, 52, 54–61; Fawzi, *Harb october am 1973,* p. 346; Heikal, *1967: Al-infijar,* pp. 788, 914; Heikal, *Sphinx and Commissar,* pp. 185–188; Huweidi, *Hurub Abdel-Nasser,* p. 150; Hamroush, *Qissa taura 23 Yulio,* p. 288.

50. Heikal, *1967: Al-infijar,* pp. 896, 912–913, 936; Heikal, *Sphinx and Commissar,* p. 195; Riad, *The Struggle for Peace in the Middle East,* p. 48; Sadat, *In Search of Identity,* pp. 181, 196.

51. Cited in Sadat, *In Search of Identity,* pp. 187, 197; Heikal, *Sphinx and Commissar,* pp. 193–194

52. Sadat, *In Search of Identity,* p. 199. The Rogers Initiative was a limited diplomatic initiative designed to convince the Israelis and Egyptians to "stop shooting" and "start talking." The US-proposed cease-fire went into effect in August 1970.

53. Ibid., p. 198.

54. *Wataiq Nasser: Khutab, ahadit, tasrihat: Yanayir 1969–Siptember 1970 [Nasser's Documents: Speeches, Discussions, and Declarations, January 1969-September 1970]* (Cairo: Markaz al-dirasat al-siyasiya wa al-istratijiya bi Al-Ahram, 1973), p. 303 (hereinafter, this series will be referred to as *Wataiq Nasser, 1969–1970*); Riad, *The Struggle for Peace in the Middle East,* pp. 94, 96; Heikal, *Sphinx and Commissar,* p. 198; Quandt, *Peace Process,* p. 77.

55. *Wataiq Nasser, 1969–1970,* pp. 371–372.

56. Sadat, *In Search of Identity,* p. 198.

57. T. Petran, *Syria* (London: Ernest Benn, 1972), p. 201. Syrian rulers were silent, however, about their own procrastination and passivity during the first two days of fighting and about their slow response to Egyptian and Jordanian urgent appeals for help. On June 6, in its report on the military situation on the Israeli-Jordanian front, the US embassy in Jordan made note of Syria's poor response — the "bare minimum to help out since [the] beginning of the conflict." See Amman to Department of State, No. 4098, 6 June 1967, *LBJ Files,* reel 1 of 8. This stand should be measured against the fact that since the early 1960s, Damascus had been pushing the Arab world toward an armed confrontation with Israel. The behavior of the Syrian leaders, writes Patrick Seale, could be explained by the scale and speed of the war that caught them off-balance and mentally unprepared for Israel's all-out, highly mobile blitzkrieg. Patrick Seale, *Asad of Syria* (London: I. B. Tauris, 1988), pp. 138–139, 144; Majid Khadduri, *Republican Iraq: A Study of Iraqi Politics Since the Revolution of 1958* (London: Oxford University Press, 1969), p. 291; Marion Farouk-Sluglett and Peter Sluglett, *Iraq Since 1958: From Revolution to Dictatorship* (London: KPI, 1987), p. 100; Hamroush, *Qissa taura 23 Yulio,* p. 202; Riad, *The Struggle for Peace in the Middle East,* p. 55; Stephens, *Nasser: A Political Biography,* p. 521.

58. Farid, *Min muhadarat,* p. 81; Hussein, *Harbuna,* p. 97; Heikal, *1967: Al infijar,* pp. 932, 935; Stookey, *America and the Arab States,* p. 213.

59. Hussein insisted, however, on a collective Arab strategy toward the question of peace with Israel. Riad, *Mudhakkirat,* vol. 3, pp. 47–48; Hussein, *Mahammati kamalik,* p. 228.

60. A few months earlier Nasser had asked his prime minister to discuss with US officials the possibility of a peaceful solution to the Arab-Israeli conflict. The head of the Egyptian intelligence was also told to maintain contacts with the CIA. In November 1967, Nasser publicly declared that Egypt was talking to the United States because "we could not let anger determine our policy." *Wataiq Nasser, 1967–1968,* pp. 248, 288; Farid, *Min muhadarat,* p. 98; Riad, *Mudhakkirat,* p. 50; Hamroush, *Qissa taura 23 Yulio,* pp. 288–289, 342–343.

61. Mohamed Ahmed Mahgoub, *Democracy on Trial: Reflections on Arab and African Affairs* (London: Andre Deutsch, 1974), p. 145; Riad, *The Struggle for Peace in the Middle East,* p. 54.

62. Mahgoub, *Democracy on Trial,* p. 146; United Arab Republic, No. 41, 2 January 1968, *LBJ Files,* reel 7 of 8; *Wataiq Nasser, 1967–1968,* pp. 289–290; Hussein, *Harbuna,* p. 97; *Majmu'at khutab al-malik Hussein: 25 'ammn min al-tarikh, 1952–1977 [The Collected Speeches of King Hussein: 25 Years of History, 1952–1977],* vol. 1 (London: Samir Mutawi's Company for Publication, 1978), p. 662; Wasfi Tal, *Kitabat fi al-qadaya al-'arabiya [Writings on Arab Issues]* (Jordan: Dar al-liwa lisihafa wa nashr, 1980), p. 486; Saad Abu Wardiya, *'Amaliya itiakad al-qarar fi siyasa al-Urdunn al-kharijiya [The Making of Jordan's Foreign Policy]* (Jordan: Daira al-taqafa wa al-funun, 1983), p. 251; Peter Snow, *Hussein: A Biography* (London: Barrie and Jenkins, 1972), pp. 198, 251; Riad, *The Struggle for Peace in the Middle East,* pp. 38, 53–56; Farid, *Min muhadarat,* p. 92; Hamroush, *Qissa taura 23 Yulio,* pp. 235, 244; Stephens, *Nasser: A Political Biography,* p. 523.

63. Although the French text included the definite article, its absence from the English text was partly to preserve ambiguity and partly a product of US pressure in the United Nations. The removal of the definite article affected later interpretations of UN Resolution 242, especially by the Israelis.

64. *Wataiq Nasser, 1967–1968,* pp. 429, 481, 590; *Wataiq Nasser, 1969–1970,* p. 301; Riad, *The Struggle for Peace in the Middle East,* pp. 91–92; Riad, *Mudhakkirat,* pp. 76, 80, 94, 103; Mohammed Fawzi, *Mudhakkirat al-Fariq awwal Mohammed Fawzi: Harb al-talat sanawat, 1967–1970* (Damascus: Tlasdar, 1986), p. 202; Huweidi, *Hurub Abdel-Nasser,* p. 152.

65. Riad, *The Struggle for Peace in the Middle East,* pp. 25, 38, 77; Fawzi, *Harb al-talat sanawat,* p. 192; Heikal, *1967: Al-infijar,* p. 887.

66. *Wataiq Nasser, 1967–1968,* p. 498; Riad, *The Struggle for Peace in the Middle East,* p. 39.

67. As a result of the stalemate in the diplomatic arena, the situation deteriorated significantly in the Middle East in spring 1969. Fighting erupted along the Suez Canal, and in April Nasser announced the abrogation of the cease-fire, signaling the onset of the War of Attrition, which lasted until the Rogers Initiative cease-fire in August 1970. *Wataiq Nasser, 1967–1968,* pp. 289–290; Riad, *The Struggle for Peace in the Middle East,* pp. 75, 77–78, 88, 101; Huweidi, *Hurub Abdel-Nasser,* p. 147; Heikal, *1967: Al-infijar,* p. 937; Heikal, *Sphinx and Commissar,* pp. 191–192; Heikal, *The Road to Ramadan,* p. 56; Stephens, *Nasser: A Political Biography,* p. 518.

68. Cited in Parker, *The Politics of Miscalculation in the Middle East,* p. 128.

11

Flawed Strategies and Missed Signals
Crisis Bargaining Between the Superpowers, October 1973

Janice Gross Stein

On the night of October 24, 1973, the Soviet Union proposed joint military intervention with the United States to end the fighting that had begun when Egypt and Syria attacked Israel eighteen days earlier. After intense fighting, as well as massive Soviet and US airlifts of military supplies to the belligerents (the Soviet Union to Egypt and Syria, the United States to Israel), the Egyptian army was in a perilous position. Israel's forces had crossed the Suez Canal and, despite a cease-fire ordered by the United Nations (UN) Security Council, had advanced to cut off Egypt's Third Army. Moscow warned that if joint US-Soviet action were impossible, it would consider taking unilateral action to halt Israel's military offensive. In response, the United States alerted its nuclear and conventional forces worldwide in an attempt to deter Soviet military intervention. The superpowers found themselves in a dangerous confrontation.

The crisis had developed when least expected, after Soviet General Secretary Leonid Brezhnev and US Secretary of State Henry Kissinger had jointly negotiated the terms of a cease-fire on October 23. Both leaders wanted to stop the fighting and to avoid a crisis between their countries. Moreover, they shared the same tactical objectives: In the wake of Israel's stunning battlefield successes, the United States now fully shared the Soviet Union's interest in ending the war before the Egyptian Third Army was destroyed. Brezhnev and Kissinger were also in constant communication with each other. Under these conditions, no crisis should have occurred. Yet, despite shared objectives and an agreement negotiated between Moscow and Washington, a serious crisis erupted, one that ended in confrontation.

Good bargaining might have averted the crisis and avoided the confrontation, since the zone of agreement between the United States and the Soviet Union was really very wide. At the least, bargaining strategies that read intentions more or less accurately and were signaled clearly could have minimized the damage from a confrontation. Bargaining should certainly not exacerbate the crisis and create the confrontation. Yet both Soviet and US strategies made the crisis more, not less, difficult to manage, contributed heavily to the confrontation, and did long-term damage to the relationship. Bargaining by both superpowers in 1973 was deeply flawed and potentially dangerous. This chapter explores Soviet and US strategies at the end of the 1973 Arab-Israeli war as a textbook case of inappropriate bargaining.

The Context of the Conflict

Egypt and Syria launched a surprise attack against Israel on October 6, 1973. President Anwar Sadat of Egypt decided to go to war because he had lost hope that negotiation could successfully address the issue of Israel's occupation of the Sinai Peninsula. He felt his diplomatic overtures regarding an agreement over the Sinai in the few years preceding the war had been ignored by both Israel and the United States, and therefore he believed that war was his only recourse to reactivate diplomacy and improve his bargaining position. Israel's control of the Sinai, the Golan, the West Bank, and the Gaza Strip emerged from the 1967 Arab-Israeli war, which was precipitated by Egypt's expulsion of a UN peacekeeping force (in place since the end of the 1956 Suez crisis) and a blockade of the Strait of Tiran.

The fighting on both fronts was intense. Israel's army, caught by surprise, took several days to launch a counteroffensive, and it succeeded only after very heavy fighting pushed Syria's army back across the cease-fire lines. The Soviet leadership, anticipating serious Syrian and Egyptian military losses, began a massive airlift and sea lift to its allies, and US President Richard M. Nixon and Secretary of State Kissinger, after an agonizing debate, decided to match the Soviet airlift with a US airlift to Israel. The choice was so difficult because Kissinger was determined to seize the opportunity provided by the war to fracture the Soviet-Egyptian alliance and position the United States as the linchpin of postwar negotiations between Egypt and Israel (and simultaneously not endanger the primary administration foreign policy focus, i.e., détente; however, both superpowers became, through the airlifts, implicated in the war through their respective client-states in the region).

Once assured of resupply, Israel's armies went on the offensive against Egypt and penetrated Egyptian lines on the western bank of the Suez Canal. As the threat to Egypt grew, Brezhnev invited Kissinger to Moscow to negotiate a cease-fire resolution to be put before the UN Security Council. When the cease-fire went into effect, there were no UN observers in the field to determine the positions of both belligerents. A few hours after Egypt and Israel accepted the cease-fire Brezhnev and Kissinger had negotiated, fighting renewed on October 23. Egypt and Israel each accused the other of violating the cease-fire first, but the Israel Defense Forces (IDF) clearly took advantage of the violations to complete the encirclement of the Egyptian Third Army.

In Moscow the crisis developed in two phases. As fighting continued on October 23 and 24, Brezhnev anticipated a catastrophic military defeat of Egypt and a concomitant blow to the reputation of the Soviet Union as ally and arms supplier to the Third World. The road to Cairo was undefended and Egypt was on the verge of military disaster. Brezhnev also felt pressed for time. By October 24, the Soviet Union had only hours to prevent an Egyptian defeat. Here too, his sense of urgency was grounded in reality.

The second phase of the crisis began for Soviet leaders after the United States alerted its forces worldwide. Brezhnev and the Politburo were surprised and angered by the US alert; they met on October 25 for eight hours, in an angry and tense session. In this final phase of the confrontation, Politburo members did not worry about an intentional attack by the United States. Nevertheless, they were intensely angered and greatly disappointed by the US action and seriously concerned about the possibility of inadvertent escalation.

In Washington, the crisis also developed in two distinct but related phases, each following the other in rapid succession. In both phases, US officials perceived a threat, but the nature of the threat changed rapidly under the pressure of events during the course of thirty-six hours. Within hours after his return from Tel Aviv on the morning of October 23, Kissinger learned of the cease-fire violations and received an urgent message from Brezhnev. He worried about the consequences of the destruction of the Egyptian Third Army for US relations with Egypt—and with the Soviet Union. "The Egyptian Third Army on the east bank of the Canal was totally cut off," Kissinger explained. "A crisis was upon us."[1]

Nixon and Kissinger knew that the destruction of the Egyptian Third Army was unacceptable to Moscow. They also shared the Soviet objective of preventing an Egyptian defeat because it would seriously compromise their central objective of creating a postwar political monopoly. Kissinger not only understood Soviet constraints, he shared the estimate regarding the limited time available before the Egyptian Third Army would collapse. From early on October 23 until the evening of October 24, Kissinger identified a threat to US objectives, empathized with Soviet concerns, and considered it urgent to halt Israel's offensive.

Once Brezhnev proposed joint intervention and then warned that he would consider acting alone if necessary to stop the fighting, the nature of the crisis changed dramatically. Kissinger framed the problem as a threat not only to US interests in the Middle East but to US interests worldwide. If the United States backed down, he believed, its bargaining reputation in future encounters with the Soviet Union would be fundamentally compromised.[2] From Washington's perspective, the crisis was now primarily in the US-Soviet relationship. Kissinger, unlike his Soviet counterparts, did not worry about the risk of inadvertent escalation but focused on the threat to the US reputation for resolve.

Although they considered the risk of war to be low, Kissinger and his colleagues in the White House Situation Room nevertheless felt an acute sense of urgency. If the Soviet Union intended to send troops, they would do so in a matter of hours. They had very limited time to find an appropriate way to signal their determination to resist any deployment of Soviet forces in the Middle East. Although leaders in

Moscow and Washington felt pressed for different reasons, the sense of urgency was real and shared, though not equally, in both capitals.

US Compellence

I begin with an analysis of US bargaining with Israel. Thirty-six hours elapsed between reports of the first violations of the cease-fire and Kissinger's receipt of Brezhnev's letter on the night of October 24. Initially, Kissinger made a less than vigorous effort to compel Israel to hold its hand. By October 24, however, *before* Brezhnev issued his threat, Washington tried vigorously to compel Israel to stop the fighting. US compellence succeeded, but it was too late. The threat to the Egyptian Third Army had provoked Brezhnev to raise the specter of unilateral intervention. There was also a fundamental ambiguity in US strategy: As the United States repeatedly warned Israel against the "destruction" of the Third Army and urged an immediate end to the fighting, it tacitly acquiesced in its encirclement. And an encircled Third Army was a ticking time bomb.

On October 23, Kissinger learned from Israel that all roads to the Egyptian Third Army had been cut. He immediately tried to arrange a second cease-fire through the United Nations in collaboration with Moscow. Israeli Prime Minister Golda Meir, in a "blistering communication," informed Kissinger that Israel would not comply with or even discuss the proposed resolution.[3] Kissinger did not threaten Israel but persisted, over its objections, in negotiating a second cease-fire. He noted that it called for a return to a line that "we had carefully not specified."[4] In so doing, he signaled Jerusalem that the United States was willing to tolerate, at least for the moment, an IDF encirclement of the Egyptian Third Army.[5]

When Kissinger learned of renewed fighting early on the morning of October 24, he made a vigorous effort to compel Israel to observe the cease-fire. He threatened to leave Israel alone if its actions provoked Soviet intervention.[6] In an effort to underline the seriousness of US intent, Kissinger asked Alexander Haig, the president's chief of staff, to call Israel's ambassador in the United States, Simcha Dinitz, to demand, on behalf of the president, an immediate end to offensive military action by Israel.[7] Israel's response was positive but laced with ambiguity: The IDF was trying to absorb Egyptian fire without responding, it would not try to advance, and Israel would keep the US ambassador in Israel, Kenneth Keating, fully informed "in a further effort to calm the Secretary and demonstrate Israeli good intentions."[8]

Even though US efforts to stop the fighting succeeded, the trapped Egyptian Third Army was still at risk because it had nearly exhausted its food, water, and medical supplies. By the time Ambassador Dinitz assured Kissinger that the fighting had stopped, desperate Egyptian President Anwar Sadat had already made his request for joint action by the United States and the Soviet Union.

Thus, US compellence worked, but it was too little and too late to do any good. Although Israel had promised not to advance any further, Kissinger observed that "this [the Israeli reply] left open the possibility of a war of attrition designed to use up Egyptian supplies and force the surrender of the Third Army."9 The United States had not yet tried seriously to compel Jerusalem to permit food and medical supplies for the Third Army through their lines. Joseph Sisco, assistant secretary of state for Near Eastern and South Asian affairs, explained why the United States concentrated so heavily on an end to the fighting:

> We put enormous pressure on Israel on October 23 and 24. We pressed first on the ceasefire, then on the siege of Suez City, and finally on the encirclement of the Third Army. We pressed hardest on the ceasefire, because that was the first priority: We wanted to stop the fighting. The distinction among the three issues was not that sharp in our minds. We concentrated on what we had to accomplish urgently. We succeeded in stopping the fighting by the afternoon of October 24.[10]

Shortage of time and fast-moving events on the battlefield led Kissinger to concentrate on the urgent and difficult task at hand.

It is not surprising, then, that it took the extraordinary threat from the United States to abandon Israel to face Soviet intervention alone to compel Jerusalem to halt its military operations. Even then, the United States achieved only the first of several objectives. Kissinger understood that he was asking Israel to exchange a tangible gain on the battlefield for a vague US promise about a peace process in the future and acknowledged how difficult it was for Israel's cabinet to see the logic of this kind of concession.[11] Given his understanding of the forces propelling Israel's behavior, it is surprising that he expected to succeed in compelling Israel to observe the cease-fire before it had consolidated its military victory. Despite its dependence on the United States for military and diplomatic support, Tel Aviv framed the conflict very differently than did Washington. The Israeli leaders used every resource at their disposal to secure the military victory they and their population desperately wanted. Under these conditions, only an extraordinary effort would permit US compellence to succeed.

The Soviet Resort to Compellence

On October 24 at 9:35 p.m. Washington time, Ambassador Anatoliy Dobrynin, the Soviet envoy to Washington, called Kissinger with an urgent letter from Brezhnev. Dobrynin read Kissinger the most important passages:

> Let us together, the USSR and the United States, urgently dispatch to Egypt the Soviet and American military contingents, to insure the implementation of the decision of the Security Council of October 22 and 23 concerning the cessation of fire and of all military activities and also of our understanding with you on the guarantee of the implementation of the decisions of the Security Council. . . . It is necessary to adhere without delay. I will say it straight that if you find it impossible to act jointly with us in this matter, we should be faced with the necessity urgently to consider the question of taking appropriate steps unilaterally. We cannot allow arbitrariness on the part of Israel.[12]

When Brezhnev sent his letter to Nixon, there was significant activity by Soviet paratroops and naval forces. On October 23, Moscow ordered two of its amphibious ships, which had been anchored off the coast of Syria, to steam for Egypt.[13] Early the next morning, a Soviet helicopter carrier and two destroyers were moved from their positions off Crete to relieve the Soviet anticarrier group covering the USS Independence. Four Soviet airborne divisions were on ready-to-move status and an in-flight command post was also established in the southern Soviet Union.[14] Preparations were made for the imminent departure of several airborne units, and transport aircraft were loaded. Communications nets surged with activity, and flight plans for the next day were changed.[15] The Soviet Union also halted its airlift to Egypt, thereby freeing significant numbers of transport aircraft.[16]

Soviet officials all agree that Brezhnev's proposal of joint US-Soviet military action was a serious signal, for the appeal to the United States was genuine. However, it was based on a misunderstanding that grew directly out of the drafting of the cease-fire agreement, with an attached memorandum of understanding, by Foreign Minister Andrei Gromyko and Kissinger in Moscow. The third clause of the draft cease-fire resolution provided for negotiations "under appropriate auspices." To clarify the meaning of the phrase, Gromyko and Kissinger also prepared an additional document that was not made public. The document read:

> It is understood that the phrase "under appropriate auspices" in Point 3 of the resolution shall mean that the negotiations between the parties concerned will take place with the active participation of the United States and the Soviet Union at the beginning, and thereafter, in the course of negotiations when key issues of a settlement are dealt with. Throughout the entire process of negotiation, the United States and the Soviet Union will in any case maintain the closest contact with each other and the negotiating parties.[17]

Brezhnev did not see either the private document, which was initialed by Gromyko and Kissinger, or the final text of the cease-fire resolution, which was drafted hurriedly by Kissinger, Sisco, and Gromyko and quickly cabled from Moscow to the United Nations and to Cairo and Damascus. President Sadat interpreted "appropriate auspices" as a US-Soviet guarantee to enforce the cease-fire if necessary.[18] The Soviet Ambassador to Egypt, Vladimir Vinogradov, reported Sadat's understanding that the United States and the Soviet Union had "guaranteed" the cease-fire to Moscow.

The confusion arose when the Politburo met on October 23 to discuss the appropriate response to the continued violations of the cease-fire. At the meeting, members of the Politburo argued that the agreement reached in Moscow "obligated" the United States and the Soviet Union to take the steps necessary to implement the resolution that had been adopted by the UN Security Council. Victor Israelian, then the head of the Department of International Organization in the Soviet Foreign Ministry, was present at almost all the Politburo meetings and took detailed notes. He explained:

The formula "under appropriate auspices" was interpreted as joint action by the USA and the USSR to guarantee the ceasefire in the Near East. For instance, [Prime Minister Alexei] Kosygin suggested at the Politburo meeting that a joint Soviet-American team of military officials should be sent to observe the ceasefire. His idea was that this group should include 200 or 250 observers from each of the two states. Kosygin was supported by Ustinov. They thought that this step should be agreed upon with the Americans and that the Americans should be reminded that, when Kissinger visited Moscow, an agreement was reached to "act as guarantors."[19]

The interpretation given the critical clause by Brezhnev and Kosygin did not go unchallenged at the Politburo meeting. Gromyko explained how the term "under appropriate auspices" had been interpreted in the document that he and Kissinger had initialed. He insisted that the dispatch of Soviet and US personnel would require approval by the UN Security Council; most likely, China would veto such a resolution. Besides, Gromyko added, there were already UN personnel in Cairo.[20]

Kosygin irritably dismissed Gromyko's objections: "That's all formalities. They [the UN Truce Supervisory Organization personnel] are dead souls," he insisted. "The fact is that both we and the Americans committed ourselves to carrying out the Security Council decision and we should proceed from that assumption. Action is needed."[21] Brezhnev was adamant that the United States and the Soviet Union should cooperate in sending military personnel as "guarantors" of the cease-fire. At his urging, the Politburo agreed to make this suggestion to the United States.[22]

Thus, Brezhnev was signaling a serious intent to cooperate in enforcing an end to the fighting. He hoped that the United States and the Soviet Union would act together to enforce the cease-fire as the capstone of détente. The first part of his letter to Nixon was not a threat but an offer of collaboration based on what he thought was a joint understanding of their responsibilities. As bizarre as the proposal would sound in Washington, collective enforcement action was considered realistic in Moscow.[23]

The last sentence of Brezhnev's letter to Nixon is more controversial. Brezhnev warned that "if you find it impossible to act jointly with us in this matter, we should be faced with the necessity urgently to consider the question of taking appropriate steps unilaterally."[24] Brezhnev did not explicitly threaten the use of military force, but his tone was menacing. This sentence was not in the original draft of the letter prepared for Brezhnev by Gromyko. Brezhnev added the warning at the last moment before the letter was sent.[25]

There is debate about the course that Brezhnev would have followed if the United States rejected the proposal for joint action. There is good evidence that Brezhnev was bluffing, that he was not prepared to act unilaterally and send Soviet forces to Egypt. Some Soviet officials considered that the Soviet Union would actually have sent forces if the fighting had not stopped. Vadim Zagladin, who was deputy director of the International Relations Department of the Central Committee, reported that Soviet leaders considered military intervention in the Cairo region.[26] Anatoliy Gromyko, who was in the Soviet Embassy in Washington on

October 24, was more cautious: "The Soviet Union seriously considered intervention. The plan was to send troops to the Cairo region. We would have put a cordon around Cairo. On the other hand, we were anxious not to get involved in the fighting. Some of my colleagues might say that this [Brezhnev's letter] was only a form of political pressure."[27] General Yuri Yakovlevich Kirshin of the Red Army confirmed that military leaders were asked to prepare contingency plans for the optimum use of Soviet paratroopers.[28]

Soviet officials with more detailed knowledge of the Politburo meeting deny that the Soviet Union would have sent troops to Cairo. They insist that Brezhnev's threat was a bluff. Ambassador Dobrynin, who was in Washington on October 24 but in close contact with Soviet leaders, doubted that the Soviet Union would have sent troops.[29] Georgi Kornienko, head of the US desk in the Soviet Foreign Ministry and one of the four members of the special working group drafted to work with the Politburo, was adamant: "I am absolutely certain that there were no plans to send Soviet forces to the Middle East. They were put on alert to put pressure on the Americans."[30] Israelian insists that the warning was a bluff, that the Soviet Union had no intention whatsoever of sending troops to Egypt: "Kulikov [the chief of staff of the military] opposed sending any officers there. He opposed sending even observers without a disengagement of Israeli and Egyptian forces. Members of the Politburo had not the slightest desire, on any level, to send forces. There might have been some contingency planning by the military, but there was no intention to send forces."[31]

At the Politburo meeting on October 23, there was no discussion whatsoever of sending regular forces, only military observers. The Politburo did not meet on October 24, before Brezhnev's letter was sent, nor did it discuss his message after the fact. Gromyko drafted the message for Brezhnev and the two walked and talked with a few colleagues in the corridor.[32] "It was not a considered decision," Israelian explained. "No formal decision was ever made by the Politburo to threaten military intervention. Brezhnev added the threat to put pressure on Nixon to get the fighting stopped. He wanted to put pressure on the United States. He thought it was a clever thing to do."[33]

The threat to consider unilateral action to stabilize the cease-fire was the last in a series of steps taken by the Soviet Union, all with a common political purpose. In the first instance, Brezhnev hoped that joint action with the United States would end the fighting. The threat that the Soviet Union might act alone was added at the last moment to signal to the United States the seriousness of Soviet interests at stake. Brezhnev hoped that if joint action were impossible, the threat that the Soviet Union would consider sending forces would be enough to compel the United States to stop Israel, that the visible preparation of Soviet troops and his warning would succeed in stabilizing the cease-fire and remove the danger to Cairo.

Brezhnev acted in response to four reinforcing considerations: the failure of intensive negotiations with the United States to stop the fighting; the need to safeguard the political position of proponents of détente at home; the reputation of the Soviet Union as a reliable ally; and the multiplicative effect of anger fueled by a sharp sense of betrayal. Counteracting these pressures was a keen appreciation of the risks of any deployment of forces and the desire to avoid a confrontation with the United States.

The first three motives are obvious and easily understood. Brezhnev's decision was also motivated by fury at what he considered to be Kissinger's duplicity. Brezhnev, prone to intensely emotional reactions, suspected—wrongly—that Kissinger had deliberately deceived him and encouraged Israel to violate the cease-fire. Soviet officials, in interviews, referred again and again to Brezhnev's acute sense of betrayal and anger on October 24. Dobrynin described Brezhnev's reaction in vivid detail: "He was very emotional. He felt deceived by Nixon and Kissinger. I was worried about our relations with the United States and worried that Brezhnev's anger with Nixon and Kissinger would lead him to do something rash."[34] Kosygin was also infuriated. At the Politburo meeting on October 25, he charged that "Kissinger visited Moscow, lied to us, went to Tel Aviv, and fraternized with the Israeli people."[35] Israelian recalled that "the fact that the United States refused to cooperate in regulating the Near-Eastern crisis irritated us and made us suspect that Kissinger was acting behind the back of the Soviet Union."[36] Soviet officials felt especially betrayed because they thought that Kissinger had violated the rules of the game that had been mutually agreed upon during the meeting in Moscow.

The pressures acting on Brezhnev could well have led him to decide to send forces to Egypt if Israel did not halt its military offensive and Cairo became directly threatened. The Soviet Union certainly had the capability to move forces quickly to Cairo West Airfield. Soviet General Alexander Ivanovich Vladimirov insists that had the Soviet Union wanted to send paratroops to Egypt, it would have taken very little time; four paratroop divisions were at full readiness and needed only twenty-four-hour notice before they could board transport aircraft for deployment.[37] The Soviet Union did not have the airlift capability for four divisions, but some movement of troops could have begun quickly.[38]

Soviet leaders, however, were sensitive to the risks of escalation and confrontation that could grow out of a deployment of Soviet conventional forces in Egypt. "Of course, it was a situation of the utmost danger," explained Anatoliy Gromyko. "The possibility that the Soviet Union would be involved in military action was real. . . . There was a real possibility of escalation, the consequences of which I cannot envisage."[39] Brezhnev worried about the escalation that could result from any deployment of Soviet troops. His fear of escalation led him to reject any Soviet military involvement in the fighting. As soon as the war began, he repeatedly made his opposition to the dispatch of Soviet troops clear to his colleagues in the Politburo and to President Sadat. It is very likely that when Brezhnev added that last threatening sentence to an otherwise temperate draft message, he was driven by anger and intense emotion. Anxious about the fate of Egypt, despairing of diplomacy, and angry at Kissinger's alleged deceit—yet fearful of the escalatory consequences of unilateral intervention—Brezhnev decided first to propose joint intervention, and then to bargain through bluff. He saw no alternative.[40]

Brezhnev miscalculated badly. His attempt at compellence did not accomplish his immediate or long-term political purposes. The United States misread the message intended and responded with a worldwide alert to signal its own resolve. The Soviet threat failed utterly to elicit the desired response.

The US Resort to Deterrence

The United States responded to the Soviet threat with a worldwide alert of its forces.[41] At 11:41 p.m., about an hour after the meeting began in the White House Situation Room, Admiral Thomas Moorer, the chairman of the Joint Chiefs of Staff, issued orders to all military commands to increase readiness to Defense Condition III (DEFCON III).[42] At 12:20 a.m. on October 25, US intelligence reported that eight Soviet Antonov–22 transport planes were scheduled to fly from Budapest to Egypt within the next few hours and that elements of the East German armed forces had been alerted. In response, the 82nd Airborne Division was ordered to be ready to deploy within four hours. At 12:25 a.m., the aircraft carrier Franklin Delano Roosevelt was sent to the eastern Mediterranean and the carrier John F. Kennedy, with its task force, was ordered to move at full speed from the Atlantic to the Mediterranean.[43]

Those who participated in the meeting in the White House Situation Room on the night of October 24 were divided in their estimate of Soviet intentions. Some thought the Soviet Union was bluffing; others thought that Moscow would send a limited number of forces to Egypt. Brezhnev's letter and the intelligence data on Soviet military preparations were consistent with both a bluff and a serious intent to deploy forces in the Middle East.

These differences were not important as to the appropriate response chosen by US officials. Those who thought that the Soviet Union might deploy a limited number of forces were determined to deny the Soviet Union political and military opportunity in the Middle East. Those who thought that the Soviet Union was bluffing also accepted the necessity of an alert. Secretary of Defense James Schlesinger, Moorer, and Haig agreed with Kissinger that an alert was the appropriate response to Brezhnev's challenge. Schlesinger argued that even if the probability of Soviet military action were low, the United States must demonstrate that it could act firmly.[44]

The alert served two purposes. If the Soviet Union was indeed intent upon unilateral military action, the alert's immediate objective would be to deter the Soviet deployment. The Nixon administration determined to deny Moscow this opportunity to introduce military forces into the Middle East. Secondarily, the alert was designed to bank resolve and build reputation for future bargaining. If Brezhnev was bluffing, the alert would "educate" the Soviet leadership. It was imperative to demonstrate resolve to convince Brezhnev that the United States could not be coerced by Moscow. Washington wanted to demonstrate resolve firmly, visibly, and quickly. Everyone present at the White House meeting agreed quickly on the necessity of an immediate, highly visible signal that would be noticed rapidly by Soviet leaders and would either "shock" them into abandoning any intention to intervene with military force or would call their bluff.[45]

The worldwide alert was a singularly inappropriate signal on the part of the United States. It was ineffective, potentially dangerous, and ill-considered. It was inherently ineffective because in the context of the Middle East any kind of nuclear threat was disproportionate and not credible. It was potentially dangerous because it moved up the ladder of escalation and increased the risk of confrontation with the Soviet Union. Even more alarming, US leaders made their decision with little attention to the technical and operational requirements of the alert, its risks, or its likely consequences. The alert was chosen in haste, with little consideration either of its capacity to deter Soviet military intervention or of the alternative measures that might have constituted an effective signal with a reduced risk of escalation.

The alert of the 82nd Airborne was also not a carefully crafted signal. William Quandt, then on the staff of the US National Security Council, provides a detailed—and vivid—description of the decision in the White House.

> Later that night, we got a fragment of a message, the tail end of a message, suggesting the imminent arrival of Soviet forces at Cairo West airfield. Kissinger was frantic. He ordered Atherton [the deputy assistant secretary of state for Near Eastern and South Asian affairs] and me to draft a plan to send U.S. troops to the Middle East, immediately, but not to Israel. Atherton and I were bewildered. Where would the forces go? Kissinger replied that he did not know, but that the forces could not go to Israel, but that a plan was to be prepared immediately to deploy forces in the Middle East. This was the only time that Atherton and I were totally confused. We could not conceive of how to meet the request.[46]

After he briefed the president early the next morning, Kissinger recalls, "Nixon was determined to match any Soviet troop buildup in the area."[47] When asked what kind of conventional military action he wanted, Kissinger replied: "We would have put down the 82nd Airborne if the Soviets had sent forces. We never got to that point. We never discussed it. It would have been very dangerous. That's why you get paid, for doing the dangerous jobs."[48]

The possibility of failure of this deterrence received no serious attention, and no contingency plans were in place. There was no discussion of where US troops were to be deployed, nor of the likelihood of combat with Soviet forces. "We had no plan for blocking [Soviet] intervention," confirms Peter Rodman, then special assistant to Kissinger. "We didn't think about it."[49] Thus, instead of considering the consequences and their options should deterrence fail, US leaders merely hoped that deterrence would succeed.

If the Soviet Union had sent forces to Egypt, and the United States had responded with a conventional deployment of its own, even limited encounters between the two forces in the context of a worldwide alert could easily have escalated to a broadening of the conflict. The Soviet Union might have mobilized additional forces in response. Under this not-so-unlikely scenario, the worldwide alert could have worked against the localization and termination of the fighting in the Middle East—the principal objective of both Moscow and Washington.

The Irrelevance and Relevance of Deterrence

"The Soviets subsided," Kissinger claims, "as soon as we showed our teeth."[50] His argument suggests that despite strategic and conventional parity, and despite an acute domestic crisis in Washington (that being the Watergate scandal), the US strategy had persuaded Soviet leaders that Nixon was willing to risk war to block unilateral intervention by Moscow.[51] Soviet leaders purportedly reevaluated the likely costs of intervention, changed their minds, and decided not to send troops to Egypt.

If deterrence is to work, the leaders who are considering military action must change course because they reconsider the likely costs and consequences in the face of the threatened deterrent. Even *before* the United States alerted its forces, however, Brezhnev had no intention of sending Soviet forces to Egypt. As early as October 8, he instructed Ambassador Vinogradov to emphasize Soviet determination not to become involved in the fighting.[52] Again, this time on October 15, during the Politburo meeting, Brezhnev warned Kosygin against misleading Sadat. Although the Soviet government was willing to continue military support to Egypt on a large scale, it would "under no circumstances participate directly in the war."[53] Brezhnev's threat to consider unilateral action was a bluff, issued in frustration at the failure of diplomacy to stop the fighting and in anger at what Brezhnev considered Kissinger's duplicity. Since Brezhnev had no intention of sending forces, deterrence could not have changed his mind. At best, it was irrelevant.

The consequences of the US strategy were not irrelevant. Soviet leaders were genuinely bewildered by the alert; they could not decipher the US "signal." They were also provoked and deeply angered by an action that they could not understand. Shortly after Soviet intelligence picked up signs of the alert, Brezhnev convened the Politburo early on the morning of October 25. The meeting was attended by almost all members, and discussion continued for more than eight hours. General Kulikov began with a briefing on the US alert, including the alert of strategic nuclear forces.

Members of the Politburo had great difficulty interpreting the political intent of the alert. "They could not understand it," Israelian explained. "They asked: 'Are they [the Americans] crazy? The Americans say we threaten them, but how did they get this idea?'"[54] Gromyko was advised by Kornienko, Mikhail Sytenko, who then headed the Department of the Near East, and Israelian that the US reaction was provoked by the last sentence of Brezhnev's letter to Nixon.[55] Brezhnev was incredulous when this explanation was suggested at the Politburo meeting. "Could this be the reason?" he asked. "Could Nixon choose an alert based on this one sentence? But this man Nixon knows that I stopped the airlift as a demonstration of my willingness to cooperate."[56]

Soviet officials were divided in their assessments of the causes and purposes of the alert. Brezhnev thought that Nixon had ordered the alert to demonstrate that he was as courageous as John F. Kennedy—the strong man in a crisis.[57] This interpretation was widely shared by Politburo members. "It seemed to the Politburo," Israelian recalled, "that Nixon's decision was determined mainly by domestic politics. In a situation of growing emotions surrounding Watergate, Nixon had to demonstrate that he was a 'strong president' and that the United States needed him."[58] Many Soviet officials saw the alert as so inconsistent with the ongoing negotiations and the frequent communications between the two capitals that they could find no explanation other than Watergate. The preeminent Soviet expert on US politics, Georgi Arbatov, put it bluntly: "The American alert was designed for home consumption."[59]

However, not all senior officials agreed that the alert was largely a response to Watergate. Kornienko, who was present as an aide to Gromyko at the Politburo meeting, thought that the alert was designed to intimidate the Soviet leadership: "The DEFCON III alert was taken seriously in Moscow. Some of us saw it as an attempt to intimidate us from sending forces to the Middle East. The alert was not dismissed as a response to Watergate. We took it seriously."[60] Dobrynin thought that the alert was intended to intimidate the Soviet Union and to demonstrate resolve for US public opinion.[61]

Irrespective of their conclusions as to the purposes of the alert, Brezhnev and other members of the Politburo were "very emotional, very angry," according to Israelian. "There was no feeling of fear, but of great disappointment and anger."[62] According to Dobrynin, Brezhnev was so emotional because he "felt deceived by Nixon and Kissinger." Dobrynin was concerned "that Brezhnev's anger with Nixon and Kissinger would lead him to do something rash. I was furious, too."[63]

Thus, Politburo members debated the appropriate response to the alert within a highly charged emotional atmosphere. A significant minority supported a military response to the US "provocation." Marshal Andrei Grechko acknowledged that a large-scale mobilization of forces would be very expensive, yet he still recommended the mobilization of 50,000 to 75,000 troops in Ukraine and the northern Caucasus.[64] Dmitri Ustinov, then secretary of the Central Committee in charge of defense production; Andrei Kirilenko, a loyal Brezhnev supporter; K. F. Katushev, responsible for liaison with ruling Communist parties; Yuri Andropov, then head of KGB, the Soviet intelligence agency; and Kosygin all supported the mobilization of some Soviet forces in response to the alert. "We should respond to mobilization," Andropov argued, "by mobilization."[65] Ustinov thought that Soviet forces should be mobilized without public announcement.

Marshal Grechko also urged the Politburo to order the 1,500 Soviet soldiers in Syria to occupy the Golan Heights. "In the past," he exclaimed, "we have never asked anybody if we could send our troops and we can do the same now."[66] His proposal clearly was not a response to the desperate plight of the Egyptian Third Army but a reaction to what he considered a US attempt at intimidation.

Gromyko, Kirilenko, and Kosygin spoke vigorously against the proposal to involve Soviet troops in the fighting. "We shall send two divisions to the Near East,"

Kosygin argued, "and in response the Americans will send two divisions as well. If we send five divisions, the Americans will send their five. . . . Today nobody can be frightened by anybody. The United States will not start a war and we have no reason to start a war."[67] Kosygin dismissed the US threat as not credible. He did not oppose Soviet involvement in the Middle East because he was intimidated by the United States but rather because of the futility of Soviet intervention.

The discussion grew more heated until the usually silent Brezhnev finally put the question: "Comrades, if we do not react at all, if we do not respond to the American mobilization, what will happen?"[68] Nikolai Podgorny, who formally held the office of president of the Soviet Union, Gromyko, and Boris Ponomarev, who headed the International Department of the Central Committee, agreed that Soviet interests would not suffer if Moscow decided not to respond to the US alert with its own military measures. These officials agreed with the general secretary that the crisis in US-Soviet relations should be resolved by political rather than military measures.

The Politburo then discussed the possibility of sending Gromyko immediately to Washington to confer personally with Nixon. Kosygin recommended that Gromyko express Moscow's bewilderment at the US alert and discuss the possibility of sending Soviet and US observers to monitor observance of the cease-fire. Kosygin's proposal to signal Soviet interest in a cooperative solution in this highly visible manner received no support in the Politburo. In fact, Brezhnev argued that to send a representative to Washington after the United States had alerted its forces would be interpreted as "weakness."[69] He rejected any Soviet attempt at reassurance in the face of the US attempt at deterrence.

In an emotional speech, Brezhnev summarized the Soviet Union's eventual response to the US alert: "The Americans say we threaten them," he said, "but they are lying to us."[70] Thus, he insisted again that the Soviet Union had given the United States no grounds to alert its forces and that a Soviet mobilization in response would accomplish nothing. In strong language, Brezhnev reemphasized his opposition to any preparatory military measures.

The US attempt at deterrence provoked anger, disappointment, and bitterness among Soviet leaders. What US officials regarded as a signal of resolve, Soviet officials interpreted as an attempt to intimidate or a response based on domestic political weakness. Bewildered and angered, a significant group within the Politburo proposed the mobilization of Soviet forces *in response* to the alert. Although Brezhnev opposed a military response, he too could not understand the intent of the alert. Angered by the alert, he rejected a proposal that Gromyko attempt to reassure Nixon personally of Soviet intentions, even though Soviet intentions were benign. Thus, the US strategy had made the confrontation more difficult to resolve. Following the Politburo meeting, Brezhnev wrote to President Nixon that although the Soviet Union had chosen not to respond with military measures, the US action was unprovoked and not conducive to the relaxation of international tensions.[71] Under a different leader, the Politburo might well have chosen differently.

The Failure of Soviet Compellence

The Soviet strategy of threatening unilateral intervention if the fighting did not stop in the Middle East might well have resolved the crisis. In a nutshell, Brezhnev was trying to compel the United States to press Israel to stop the fighting. Once the cease-fire was stabilized and the safety of the Egyptian Third Army was assured, the crisis would most likely have ended. We have already shown how Soviet bargaining provoked escalation by leading the United States to issue a worldwide military alert. The evidence also suggests that the Soviet threat did not resolve the crisis. Like its US counterpart, it was both irrelevant and provocative.

By the time Brezhnev's letter arrived in Washington the fighting had stopped. Ironically, Brezhnev's threat only interrupted the US efforts to compel Israel to allow food and medical supplies to reach the trapped Egyptian Third Army. Kissinger, who had been actively trying to prevent the destruction of the Third Army, stopped pressing Israel immediately after he received Brezhnev's letter on the evening of October 24; he did not resume these efforts until the following morning—after it was apparent that the crisis between the United States and the Soviet Union would be resolved. Kissinger then pressed Israel to permit nonmilitary supplies to reach the Third Army despite the fact that Brezhnev had made no such demand in his letter. By the time the United States finally extracted a commitment from Israel on October 26 to permit a one-time convoy to reach the Third Army, the crisis was over.

The critical period was the thirteen hours from 7:00 p.m. on October 24, when Dobrynin first informed Kissinger of Brezhnev's letter, until 8:00 a.m. the next morning, when President Sadat withdrew his request for intervention by Soviet and US forces. It seemed unlikely to Kissinger that Moscow would send forces without Egyptian consent. During that period, Kissinger met several times with Israel's ambassador to Washington but made no request that Israel break its encirclement of the Third Army. Instead, Israel's leaders received a request from Kissinger for a contingency plan to destroy the Third Army. In the face of the Soviet threat, Kissinger subtly encouraged Israel to consider escalating military action. When asked directly long after the crisis was over, Kissinger confirmed his refusal to be coerced: "The Soviet threat backfired. Only after the Russians caved in, did I turn on the Israelis. After the Soviets threatened, I asked the Israelis to develop an option to defeat the Third Army. Only after I knew that the Russians were caving in, did I press the Israelis really hard on Friday [October 25]."[72]

The United States responded to Soviet strategy by redefining the problem as a test of US resolve and ceased its attempts to compel its ally, Israel.[73] It might be argued that Soviet compellence nevertheless increased US incentives to coerce Israel once the crisis between Moscow and Washington passed. The evidence does not sustain this argument. The United States had tried to compel Israel to observe the cease-fire before the Soviet Union issued its threat. Nixon and Kissinger had also decided—again, before the Soviet ultimatum—that they would not permit the destruction of the Egyptian Third Army.[74] Kissinger had also begun his attempt to coerce Israel to permit the resupply of the Third Army before the Soviet Union raised the issue with the United States. And Nixon and Kissinger also worried about a confrontation with Moscow before Brezhnev sent his letter. Thus, the evidence suggests strongly that the United States would have compelled Israel to accept a cease-fire and allow resupply of the Third Army even in the absence of a Soviet threat because of its overriding interest in establishing a relationship with Egypt that would endure after the war was over.

The Soviet attempt at compellence was not only unnecessary but also irrelevant, poorly constructed, and counterproductive: Soviet leaders did not have real-time battlefield intelligence and were unaware that the fighting had stopped by the time Brezhnev's letter arrived in Washington; Brezhnev's threat was poorly constructed in that it did not raise the critical issue of the supply of the trapped Third Army; it was counterproductive because it interrupted the US attempt to coerce Israel. Soviet bargaining provoked precisely the responses it had wanted to prevent: an interruption of US efforts to save the Egyptian Third Army and a worldwide alert of US forces that threatened the confrontation that Brezhnev wanted above all to avoid.

The Crisis Is Resolved

When the Soviet Union decided not to respond to the US alert with military measures, the process of escalation stopped. A halt in escalation was necessary but insufficient to resolve the crisis. To settle the crisis, the Soviet Union had to withdraw its threat to consider unilateral military intervention. Brezhnev did so implicitly on October 25 when he accepted Nixon's offer to send US and Soviet observers to monitor the cease-fire. Later that day, the Soviet ambassador to the United Nations supported a resolution in the UN Security Council (Resolution 340) to dispatch a peacekeeping force that, by convention, excluded Soviet and US forces.

"It was not the military threat," according to Anatoliy Gromyko, "but diplomacy that finally found a solution."[75] As Brezhnev was concluding his emotional speech at the Politburo meeting, Konstantin Chernenko, acting informally as secretary to the Politburo, passed to him the text of Nixon's letter (actually drafted by Henry Kissinger). Brezhnev read the long letter aloud to the Politburo, emphasizing what he considered two particularly conciliatory phrases: "I agree with you that our understanding to act jointly for peace is one of the highest value and that we should implement that understanding in this complex situation"; and, "In the spirit of our agreements this is the time not for acting unilaterally, but in harmony and with cool heads."[76] Nixon's proposal provided the Politburo with a face-saving opportunity to end the crisis without confrontation. It was accepted "with relief," and the Politburo ended its meeting.[77]

Several important considerations help to explain Soviet acceptance of a political solution to the crisis. Foremost, Soviet leaders did not consider the stakes in the Middle East to be worth the risk of confrontation and war. When Politburo members began their first meeting after the US alert, the first issue they discussed was whether the Soviet Union was prepared to confront the United States and fight a large-scale war. Despite the differences within the Politburo, the unanimous answer was "no." Kosygin put it bluntly: "It is not reasonable to become involved in a war with the United States because of Egypt and Syria."[78] Andropov, Kirilenko, Ponomarev, Gromyko, Kosygin, and Grechko all made essentially the same point.[79]

The belief that the Soviet relationship with Egypt and Syria was not worth a war with the United States was widespread. "Nobody shared Arab war aims," Israelian said. "Sadat was not Castro. Our relationship with him was not the same."[80] Although the reputation and the interests of the Soviet Union were heavily engaged in Egypt, the Soviet-Egyptian relationship had long been troubled.[81] The Politburo was angered by Egyptian military incompetence, by Sadat's expulsion of Soviet military advisers, and by his failure to heed its advice. Soviet stakes in the region were high but tempered by ideological, military, and personal differences between Arab and Soviet leaders. The Politburo was therefore not prepared to risk a US-Soviet confrontation to save Sadat. Even after he listened to a pessimistic evaluation of Egypt's military situation, Brezhnev said to his colleagues: "We must tell Sadat, 'We were right. We sympathize with you but we can't reverse the results of your military operations.'"[82]

A second consideration was the importance Brezhnev personally attached to good relations with the United States. Brezhnev considered détente the outstanding accomplishment of his foreign policy. Even before the alert, Brezhnev recognized that a deployment of Soviet forces in Egypt would seriously complicate the Soviet relationship with the United States. He therefore strongly preferred a diplomatic solution within the framework that he had negotiated with Kissinger when Kissinger had come to Moscow.

In large part because Brezhnev prided himself on his personal relationship with the US president, he was deeply angered by "Nixon's action." Anger can lead to ill-considered and risky actions because people who are emotionally aroused are less likely to think through the consequences of their choices. In this case, the Soviet Union did not do so because of the impact of crosscutting emotions. Although Brezhnev was angered and disappointed by the US alert, he was also angry with Sadat for consistently ignoring Soviet advice. Anger pulled in opposite directions. These crosscutting emotions moderated Brezhnev's reaction and reduced the impact of his anger at the United States. He was therefore able to temper his response.

One other factor contributed significantly to the resolution of the crisis. There was an important asymmetry in the perceptions of Moscow and Washington as to the actual risks of war. Leaders in Moscow worried about a confrontation between Soviet military forces and those of Israel if Soviet troops were sent to Egypt. They feared that a Soviet-Israeli conflict could easily escalate into a wider engagement that could draw in the United States. Politburo members worried that actions they might take might lead inadvertently to war. "The steps we take," Kirilenko urged, "should not lead to war."[83]

Analysts who argue today that the crisis was resolved because the United States manipulated the risk of war miss the fundamental point.[84] Soviet leaders worried about the risk of war as a consequence of *their* military deployment, *before* the US alert. Their evaluation of the risks of war worked in favor of crisis resolution. It served as a powerful incentive to search actively for a political solution and as a brake on a military response to the US alert. However, US leaders did not consider the risk of war and confrontation with Soviet forces to be significant even after their alert. Fortunately, the asymmetrical pattern of the fear of war worked in favor of crisis resolution. Soviet leaders, who worried seriously about escalation, had to make the critical decision about a response to the US alert.

Conclusion

Bargaining is usually ineffective when the two sides maintain radically different understandings of the context. As to the US-Soviet bargaining in 1973, messages were framed in one context and interpreted in another. It is not surprising that the interpretation of critical signals bore no relationship to the intentions of the signal senders. Attempts both to demonstrate resolve and to cooperate failed. Signals had a nearly random, hit-and-miss effect. The crisis, as we have seen, was resolved in spite of the bargaining strategies of both superpowers.

To the extent that bargaining had any impact, it was largely negative because of the way it reinforced Soviet images of the United States as unreliable, unpredictable, and duplicitous—and US images of the Soviet Union as aggressive and treacherous. Ironically, the bargaining process between the two superpowers not only failed to resolve the crisis but damaged the long-term relationship between them. Inappropriate strategies triggered a self-reinforcing cycle of conflict that led to the progressive deterioration of the relationship between the superpowers for the remainder of the decade.

After the 1973 Arab-Israeli war, Brezhnev and the proponents of détente faced a growing barrage of criticism from colleagues who alleged that the United States had tricked the Soviet leadership and used the war as a cover to exclude the Soviet Union from Egypt. Although Kissinger had not engaged in any deliberate deception of the Soviet leadership during the war, he seized the opportunity after the war to initiate a process of negotiation between Egypt and Israel that led to two successive disengagement agreements and culminated ultimately in the Camp David accords in 1978 and the subsequent Egyptian-Israeli peace treaty in 1979. The Soviet Union was almost entirely excluded from this process. Although the United States achieved its strategic objectives in the heartland of the Middle East and successfully moved the two most powerful parties in the region to a peace agreement, flawed bargaining during the crisis of October 1973 marked the beginning of the end of détente between the superpowers. Suspicion and distrust weakened the advocates of détente in both Moscow and Washington and contributed to a "second cold war" between the United States and the Soviet Union that would last for more than a decade.

Notes

1. Henry Kissinger, *Years of Upheaval* (Boston: Little, Brown, 1972), p. 571.
2. Henry Kissinger, interview by author, New York, 19 June 1991.

3. Kissinger, *Years of Upheaval*, p. 573.

4. Ibid.

5. Former member of Prime Minister Meir's staff, interview by author, April 1988.

6. In his book, Kissinger wrote: "It was clear that if we let this go on, a confrontation with the Soviets was inevitable. . . . I told Dinitz [Israel's ambassador to Washington] that the art of foreign policy was to know when to clinch one's victories. There were limits beyond which we could not go, with all our friendship for Israel, and one of them was to make the leader of another superpower look like an idiot. I said to Dinitz that if Sadat asked the Soviets, as he had us, to enforce the cease-fire with their own troops, Israel would have out-smarted itself." Kissinger, *Years of Upheaval*, p. 576.

7. Hanoch Bartov, in his *Dado—Arbaim Ve'Shmoneh Shanim V'Esraim Yom (Dado—48 Years and Twenty Days)*, 2 vols. (Tel Aviv: Ma'ariv Book Guild, 1978), vol. 1, p. 592, reports that every five minutes that morning, calls were coming in from the White House warning Israel to stop its offensive. Israel was informed that Kissinger was boiling with rage. This biography of General David Elazar, the chief of staff of the Israeli Defense Forces (IDF) during the war, is based on the private papers of the chief of staff, which are not yet publicly available.

8. Cited by Kissinger, *Years of Upheaval*, p. 579.

9. Ibid.

10. Joseph Sisco, interview by author, Washington, 17 April 1991.

11. Kissinger, *Years of Upheaval*, p. 573.

12. Cited by Kissinger, ibid., p. 583.

13. Galia Golan, "Soviet Decisionmaking in the Yom Kippur War," in Jiri Valenta and William Potter, eds., *Soviet Decisionmaking for National Security* (London: George Allen and Unwin, 1984), pp. 185–217; and Bradford Dismukes and James McConnell, *Soviet Naval Diplomacy* (New York: Pergamon Press, 1979), p. 203.

14. There is some controversy as to how many airborne divisions were moved to the status of ready-for-combat that day. All seven divisions had been on alert since October 11, but some analysts claim that only one airborne division moved to ready-to-move status on 24 October. See Raymond Garthoff, *Détente and Confrontation: American-Soviet Relations from Nixon to Reagan* (Washington, D.C.: Brookings Institution, 1985), pp. 377–378, n. 68. Hart maintains that three of the seven divisions were placed on ready to move status on 10 October and the remaining four early on 24 October. See Douglas M. Hart, "Soviet Approaches to Crisis Management: The Military Dimension," *Survival* 26(5) (September–October 1984), pp. 214–222.

15. Hart, "Soviet Approaches to Crisis Management."

16. The Politburo was not told of these military measures. When he was asked at the Politburo meeting on 25 October about Soviet military movements, Marshal Andrei Grechko, responsible for defense, responded that they were routine military maneuvers. Victor Israelian, interview by author, State College, Pa., 8 January 1992. Evgeny Pyrlin, the deputy director of the Middle East division in the Soviet Foreign Ministry in 1973, confirms that during the October War, "Grechko frequently replied to questions from his Politburo colleagues, 'I just informed Comrade Brezhnev about this,' and all questions became useless. As a rule the Minister of Defense was authorized to order military actions short of the mobilization of reserves and the reinforcement of armored and air divisions. To be frank, Mr. Grechko as the Minister of Defense had wide liberty of action and sometimes didn't inform the political leadership of the details." Evgeny Pyrlin, "Some Observations (Memoirs) About

the Arab-Israeli War (1973)," unpublished memorandum commissioned for this project, Moscow, August 1992, p. 5. Andrei Alexandrov-Agentov, a senior aide to Brezhnev in 1973, explained that "Brezhnev liked and trusted Grechko. Very often, Grechko, confident of Brezhnev's trust, authorized measures of military preparedness without Brezhnev's knowledge or approval. He had a free hand." Andrei M. Alexandrov-Agentov, interview by author, Moscow, 19 August 1992. Alexandrov was a career diplomat whom Brezhnev had borrowed from the Ministry of Foreign Affairs when he became chairman of the Presidium of the Supreme Soviet.

17. Victor Israelian, personal communication, 9 March 1992.

18. Victor Israelian, interview by author, State College, Pa., 8 January 1992. In his message to Kissinger on 23 October, Sadat asked the United States to "intervene effectively, even if that necessitates the use of forces, in order to guarantee the full implementation of the cease-fire resolution in accordance with the joint US-USSR agreement." Cited by Kissinger, *Years of Upheaval,* p. 574.

19. Victor Israelian, "The Kremlin: October 1973," unpublished monograph, p. 22.

20. Ibid., p. 23.

21. Ibid., p. 21, and personal communication, 9 March 1992.

22. Israelian, "The Kremlin: October 1973," p. 23.

23. Vadim Zagladin (then deputy director of the International Relations Department of the Central Committee), interview by author, Moscow, 18 May 1989.

24. Cited by Kissinger, *Years of Upheaval,* p. 583.

25. Victor Israelian, interview by author, State College, Pa., 8 January 1992.

26. Vadim Zagladin, interview by author, Moscow, 18 May 1989.

27. Anatoliy Gromyko, interview by author, Moscow, 18 May 1989.

28. General Yuri Yakovlevich Kirshin, interview by author, Moscow, 17 December 1992.

29. Dobrynin, interview by author, Moscow, 17 December 1992.

30. Georgi Kornienko, interview by author, Moscow, 17 December 1991.

31. Victor Israelian, interview by author, State College, Pa., 8 January 1992.

32. Israelian is not certain how this last sentence was inserted. "It is difficult for me to say to whom this idea belonged originally. It is possible that it was born during one of Brezhnev's lobby interviews with his closest colleagues from the Politburo and was immediately put into the message." Israelian, "The Kremlin: October 1973," p. 24.

33. Victor Israelian, interview by author, State College, Pa., 8 January 1992.

34. Anatoliy Dobrynin, interview by author, Moscow, 17 December 1991.

35. Israelian, "The Kremlin: October 1973," p. 27.

36. Ibid., p. 23.

37. General Alexander Ivanovich Vladimirov, interview by author, Moscow, 18 December 1991. William Colby, director of the CIA in 1973, insists that Soviet forces did not need much coordination with Egypt to deploy. "They had a mission there. All they needed was landing times at Cairo West and they could have gotten those at the last moment." William Colby, telephone interview by author, 11 January 1992. On the other hand, Admiral Nikolai Amelko, deputy chief of the Soviet navy in 1973, argued that the deployment of paratroopers would have required air, logistical, and marine support, which would have required some coordination and time. No such request was made to the Soviet navy in October 1973. Admiral Nikolai N. Amelko, interview by author, Moscow, 18 December 1991.

38. Raymond Garthoff, personal communication, 9 July 1992. Garthoff estimates that it would have taken a considerable length of time to move the full four divisions.

39. Anatoliy Gromyko, interview by author, Moscow, 18 May 1989.

40. Alexander Kislov, Deputy Director of IMEMO, interview by author, Moscow, 18 May 1989. Garthoff, *Détente and Confrontation,* p. 383, concurs with this interpretation of Brezhnev's intentions.

41. Secretary of Defense James Schlesinger and Secretary of State Kissinger made the decision to alert US forces, in consultation with the director of the CIA, William Colby, the chairman of the Joint Chiefs of Staff, Admiral Thomas Moorer, and the president's chief of staff, Alexander Haig, who was with the president in his personal quarters. Present as well in the Situation Room of the White House were the deputy assistant to the president for National Security Affairs, General Brent Scowcroft, and Commander Jonathan T. Howe, the military assistant to the secretary of state at the National Security Council.

42. President Nixon did not participate in the discussions, was not informed of the alert when it was ordered, and only approved the alert retroactively at about 3 a.m. on the morning of 25 October. Overwhelmed by the growing scandal of Watergate, the president was reportedly drunk and exhausted upstairs in his personal quarters in the White House. *Inquiring into the Military Alert Invoked on October 24, 1973,* 93rd Congress, House of Representatives, Report 93–970 (Washington, D.C.: US Government Printing Office, 14 April 1974, 74–09780), p. 3.

43. Barry M. Blechman and Douglas M. Hart, "The Political Utility of Nuclear Weapons: The 1973 Middle East Crisis," *International Security* 7(1) (Summer 1982), pp. 132–156; Garthoff, *Détente and Confrontation,* p. 379; and Kissinger, *Years of Upheaval,* pp. 587–589. At 3:30 a.m., sixty US B–52 bombers were ordered back to the United States from Guam. This had been a long-standing objective of the Pentagon, but the State Department had objected to a visible reduction of the US commitment in Southeast Asia. Under the rubric of the DEFCON III alert, the Pentagon ordered their return.

44. Steven L. Spiegel, *The Other Arab-Israeli Conflict: Making America's Middle East Policy, from Truman to Reagan* (Chicago: University of Chicago Press, 1985), citing interview of Schlesinger, p. 264. William Colby confirmed that "nobody had any problems. Schlesinger and Moorer went along. They had no problems with it." William Colby, telephone interview by author, 11 January 1992.

45. Kissinger, *Years of Upheaval,* p. 584.

46. Interviews conducted by author. William Quandt, Washington, D.C., 7 December 1988; and Alfred (Roy) Atherton, Washington, D.C., 15 March 1990.

47. Kissinger, *Years of Upheaval,* p. 593.

48. Henry Kissinger, interview by author, New York, 19 June 1991.

49. Peter Rodman, interview by author, Washington, D.C., 24 April 1991.

50. Kissinger, *Years of Upheaval,* p. 980.

51. For an explicit version of this argument, see Blechman and Hart, "The Political Utility of Nuclear Weapons," pp. 151–152.

52. Israelian, "The Kremlin: October 1973," pp. 5–6.

53. Ibid., pp. 13–14.

54. Ibid., p. 29.

55. Victor Israelian, interview by author, State College, Pa., 9 January 1992.

56. Ibid.

57. Ibid.

58. Israelian, "The Kremlin: October 1973," p. 26.

59. Georgi Arbatov, interview by author, Moscow, May 19, 1989. Kissinger also had worried about the impact of Watergate but for quite different reasons. At the meeting in the Sit-

uation Room of the White House on the night of 24 October, he and his advisers speculated about whether the Soviet Union would have challenged a "functioning" president. His concern about the weakness of the president made Kissinger all the more intent on signaling resolve through a worldwide alert. "We are at a point of maximum weakness," Kissinger said, "but if we knuckle under now we are in real trouble. . . . We will have to contend with the charge in the domestic media that we provoked this. The real charge is that we provoked this by being soft." Kissinger, *Years of Upheaval,* p. 589. It was not only the US media but most of the Soviet leadership that accused Nixon and Kissinger of manipulating domestic politics. The Politburo, however, did not see the domestic crisis in Washington as a weakness to exploit but as a source of American irresponsibility.

60. Georgi Kornienko, interview by author, Moscow, 17 December 1991.

61. Anatoliy Dobrynin, interview by author, Moscow, 17 December 1991.

62. Victor Israelian, interview by author, State College, Pa., 9 January 1992.

63. Anatoliy Dobrynin, interview by author, Moscow, 17 December 1991.

64. The Soviet alert system is designed to allow conventional alert readiness to be raised to high level without alerting any strategic nuclear forces. Joseph J. Kruzel, "Military Alerts and Diplomatic Signals," in Ellen P. Stern, ed., *The Limits of Military Intervention* (Beverly Hills, Calif.: Sage, 1977), pp. 83–89, 98.

65. Israelian, "The Kremlin: October 1973," p. 27.

66. Ibid.

67. Ibid.

68. Ibid., p. 28; and Victor Israelian, interview by author, State College, Pa., 9 January 1992.

69. Israelian, "The Kremlin: October 1973," p. 28. Gromyko also did not want to go to Washington.

70. Ibid., p. 29.

71. Israelian, "The Kremlin: October 1973," p. 28; also cited by Kissinger, *Years of Upheaval,* p. 608.

72. Henry Kissinger, interview by author, New York, 19 June 1991.

73. Garthoff concurs that the alert and the Brezhnev letter that prompted it did not end the crisis or resolve the situation. He argues that the Brezhnev letter did not serve to reinforce US readiness to curb Israel, which was in any case the product of US policy, but slowed it down. See Garthoff, *Détente and Confrontation,* pp. 380 and 383.

74. On 23 October, Nixon and Kissinger had decided to prevent the destruction of the Third Army and Kissinger had so informed Israel. Kissinger, *Years of Upheaval,* pp. 571, 573; and William Quandt, *Decade of Decisions: American Policy Toward the Arab-Israel Conflict* (Berkeley: University of California Press, 1977), p. 194.

75. Anatoliy Gromyko, interview by author, Moscow, 18 May 1989.

76. Israelian, "The Kremlin: October 1973," pp. 29–30.

77. Ibid., p. 30.

78. Ibid., p. 26.

79. Ibid.

80. Victor Israelian, interview by author, State College, Pa., 8 January 1992.

81. Leonid Zamyatin, an official of the Ministry of Foreign Affairs who subsequently headed the TASS news agency, put the relationship in context: "Egyptian-Soviet relations began to deteriorate under Nasser, who was pro-Soviet in his foreign policy but repressive toward Communists at home. We had even lower expectations of Sadat because of our dealings with him when he was in charge of the Aswan Dam project. He was a pain in the neck,

always trying to renegotiate contracts. We became more cautious." Leonid Zamyatin, interview by author, Moscow, 16 December 1991.

82. Israelian, "The Kremlin: October 1973," p. 29.

83. Ibid., p. 26.

84. Blechman and Hart, "The Political Utility of Nuclear Weapons," pp. 132–156.

12

The United States and Israel

The Nature of a Special Relationship

Bernard Reich

In a press conference on May 12, 1977, US President Jimmy Carter said, "We have a special relationship with Israel. It's absolutely crucial that no one in our country or around the world ever doubt that our number-one commitment in the Middle East is to protect the right of Israel to exist, to exist permanently, and to exist in peace. It's a special relationship."[1] In February 1993, US Secretary of State Warren Christopher observed that the "relationship between the United States and Israel is a special relationship for special reasons. It is based upon shared interests, shared values, and a shared commitment to democracy, pluralism and respect for the individual." In spring 1994 President Bill Clinton suggested that, in working for peace in the Middle East, a first pillar is the security of Israel.

This perspective tends to "confirm" the Arab view, in the wake of the 1967 Six Day War, that there existed a special and exclusive US-Israeli relationship. But these statements are more than political rhetoric or platitude; they are reflective and representative of hundreds of such statements over time. Nevertheless, there is much that the statements do not say, and though there is a broad-scale commitment on the part of the United States at a very significant level, as in any relationship of this sort there are also areas of discord.

The US-Israeli relationship is not the exclusive one that is often portrayed by Arab spokesmen and others advocating a different orientation to Israel in US policy. This became increasingly clear in both the Clinton and Bush administrations—the former during the efforts to implement the Oslo accords and the latter with its two-state "vision" and the "Road Map" for a final settlement of the Israeli-Palestinian conflict. Although there was a period of exclusivity favoring Israel following the events of the Six Day War, this lack of a dual relationship began to change after the Yom Kippur War of 1973.[2] It was also during the Yom Kippur War that a massive US airlift of ammunition and military equipment proved essential to Israel in its response to the Egyptian and Syrian military attacks. By 1977 and the inauguration of

Jimmy Carter into office, there had begun a period in which Arab (especially Egyptian) views were factored into the process and affected US policy. Some of the Arab states (but not yet the Palestinians and the Palestine Liberation Organization [PLO]) became increasingly important from a foreign policy perspective because they were seen as moving in a general direction toward peace. Thus, there was a change from exclusivity to dual-factor diplomacy.

However, the generalized image of a "positive only" US-Israeli relationship ignores the fact that within that linkage there is, has been, and probably will continue to be dissonance on a wide range of issues, both procedural and substantive. As in any relationship, there is a certain frustration when one actor does not perform in the way that the other would prefer. One actor might be obstinate and problematic, and the decisionmakers involved may have difficult personalities. An example: In the spring and summer of 1990 in Israel (with the fall of the national unity government and the efforts by Labor Party leader Shimon Peres to form a government and the ultimate success of Yitzhak Shamir of the Likud Party in doing so), clear US preferences were reflected in the public and private comments of the senior policymakers and decisionmakers in the George H. W. Bush administration; the United States was not a disinterested, dispassionate, and uninvolved observer. Although a direct effort to affect the situation cannot be identified from the record, there was a clear view of US preferences. Moreover, the US position probably played a role in the ultimate selection of Labor's Yitzhak Rabin as the new prime minister and the formation of a new government under his leadership in 1992. In a similar way, Israeli ambassadors have also made clear, although disowning any efforts to do so, their views concerning preferred policymakers and policies in the United States.

An additional, important political factor in the US-Israeli relationship has been the US Congress. Congress plays a role in the relationship, although it is limited by constitutional and practical factors. It is a crucial actor on such matters as aid, including what (economic and military assistance, loans or grants, and so on), how much, and to whom. Not only is Congress a crucial element in determining what aid Israel gets, it also helps to determine which Arab parties (such as Hamas after its election victory in 2005) do not receive aid. Its role goes beyond the formal allocation of aid, with its views on central issues and seemingly unrelated matters often connected to the Israel factor.[3] Congressional concerns about a Jewish state can be traced back to at least 1922, when Congress unanimously supported the Balfour Declaration (which President Woodrow Wilson had endorsed earlier) in the Lodge-Fish Resolution. The positive perception of public opinion toward Israel reflected in Congress continues to be manifested in substantial levels of economic and military assistance and related policy decisions that favor Israel.

However, the positive elements in the relationship, as well as the overall cordial and congruent nature of the partners' concerns and policies in the region, have not prevented negative factors from manifesting themselves. When President Jimmy Carter, Egyptian President Anwar Sadat, and Israeli Prime Minister Menachem Begin met at Camp David in September 1978, there was discord on many elements of the March 1979 Egyptian-Israeli peace treaty despite the ultimate agreements; some

issues were left for later clarification and resolution. During the subsequent autonomy negotiations, which began in May 1979, agreement was reached on some issues
but not on the major questions.

During the administrations of Prime Ministers Menachem Begin and Yitzhak
Shamir, there were disagreements between the United States and Israel on a wide
range of issues, including Israel's bombing of the Osirak nuclear reactor in Iraq
(1981), the Israeli annexation of the Golan Heights (1981), its bombing of PLO facilities in Beirut (1982), the war in Lebanon (1982), the Sabra and Shatila camp
massacres (1982), the Jonathan Pollard espionage affair, and Israeli involvement in
the Iran-Contra arms-for-hostages deal. There were questions about the *intifada* and
Israel's response to it (which also led to image problems for Israel in the United
States and the questioning of its methods) as well as Israel's reaction to the plan offered by US Secretary of State George P. Shultz and assorted efforts in 1988 to deal
with these and related matters.

There have been disagreements on the deportation of Palestinians (whether in
large numbers or small) from the occupied territories and on the building of Israeli
settlements in disputed territory. These were particularly acerbic during the tenures
of George H. W. Bush and Yitzhak Shamir. There was, and is, policy dissonance as
to the status of Jerusalem; the United States retains its embassy in Tel Aviv and does
not accept Israel's unilateral declaration of Jerusalem as its capital. This remains the
case despite the fact that the Jerusalem Embassy Relocation Act of 1995 requires the
move of the US Embassy from Tel Aviv to Jerusalem. Other legislation also reflects
some ambiguity on this matter in US law and policy. And there have been broader
policy questions on such matters as the sale of AWACS (airborne warning and control system) aircraft to Saudi Arabia during the administration of Ronald Reagan,
the establishment of a dialogue between the United States and the PLO in 1988,
and Arab terrorism and the appropriate Israeli response to it over an extended
period. During George H. W. Bush's tenure, tensions emerged over Israel's role (or,
more properly, non-role) in the 1991 Gulf war as well as discord over the subsequent Madrid peace conference (1991).

The framework within which the United States and Israel have interacted with
each other has changed over time, and policies perforce have changed to reflect the
altered environment. The US-Israeli relationship had its origins during the time that
the United States and Soviet Union competed for supremacy following World War
II. Both superpowers courted Israel in their efforts to incorporate new states into
their spheres of influence. Israel was seen as a valuable prize in the newly important,
oil-rich Middle East. Nevertheless, within the US government there was substantial
disagreement concerning the appropriate policy, and US support for the Jewish state
was a presidential decision, often opposed by the senior bureaucrats in the departments of state and defense. Today, the US-Israeli relationship operates within the
confines of a new world order in which there is neither an alternative superpower nor
US-Soviet competition to curry the favor of states or regional groupings.

A second factor is to be found in the perspectives of a small country confronting
a large country, both of which see the world through a different lens. The United

States is a superpower with global interests affected by the residue of the cold war; Israeli interests are more regional and narrow, and there are more "life-and-death" issues.

The United States and Israel have been linked in a complex and multifaceted special relationship that had its origins prior to the establishment of the Jewish state in 1948 and that has focused on continuing US support for the survival, security, and well-being of Israel. But its content has varied over time. During the first decades after Israel's independence the relationship was grounded primarily in humanitarian concerns, in religious and historical links, and in a moral-emotional-political arena. The United States remained aloof from Israel in the strategic-military sector. The United States and Israel developed a diplomatic-political relationship that focused on the need to resolve the Arab-Israeli conflict, but though they agreed on the general concept, they often differed on the precise means for achieving that end. Despite a growing positive connection between the two states, especially after the 1967 Six Day War, appreciation of the linkage, especially in the strategic sphere, remained limited.

Relations Between the Carter Administration and Israel

The accession of both Jimmy Carter and Menachem Begin to office in 1977 inaugurated a new period in the relationship, characterized often by increased public tension and recrimination. Egyptian President Anwar Sadat's peace initiative also reduced the exclusivity of the US-Israeli relationship that had been established after 1967 as a consequence of Soviet policy and the ruptures of relations between some Arab states and the United States.

The Carter and Begin administrations became divided over numerous issues that directly affected the US-Israeli relationship. They were in accord in some aspects, however, as on the need to achieve peace and foster the security of Israel. Yet they would often disagree on the methods and mechanisms best suited to achieving those goals, the preferred end results, and the modalities that best served national interests. There were questions regarding the poor personal chemistry between policymakers on both sides as well. Senior US and Israeli officials were not always compatible, and this affected the countries' ever-evolving relationship. Mutual dislike and mistrust extended beyond Carter and Begin into the Reagan administration; the United States was unhappy with Begin and his successor, Yitzhak Shamir, and Israel had strong anxieties about Secretary of Defense Caspar Weinberger and his policies. There were disagreements concerning the nature of the situation in the region, often focusing on alternative intelligence estimates of the threat to Israel's national security.

The Carter tenure was filled with episodes of discord between the United States and Israel that generated numerous efforts by each power to influence the policies of the other. Israel's major success was in connection with the October 1, 1977, US-Soviet joint communiqué. Although proclaimed with great fanfare by the Carter administration, Israel was able to secure abandonment of the communiqué within a matter of days by mobilizing Israel's traditional supporters in the US Jewish community and non-Jewish supporters in Congress and elsewhere. It took advantage of strong public sympathy for Israel as well as strong public views against re-involvement of the Soviet Union in the peace process.

The Carter administration had its most noteworthy success in effecting change in the Israeli position at Camp David and in the Egyptian-Israeli peace treaty. The main techniques included high risk/high visibility presidential involvement and Carter's suggestion that Israel could not allow the failure of this president, who might then transfer the blame to Israel in Congress and public opinion. Israel was also influenced by the administration's continuing economic and military assistance.

The Reagan Tenure

Ronald Reagan came to office with a very different perception of Israel and its importance. His campaign rhetoric concerning Israel went beyond the customary pledges of friendship, suggesting strong and consistent support for Israel and its perspective regarding the Arab-Israeli conflict. He saw Israel as an important ally and an asset in the struggle against the Soviet Union. He was opposed to dealing with the PLO until that organization dramatically changed its policies by renouncing terrorism, accepting United Nations Security Council Resolution 242, and acknowledging Israel's right to exist (which it eventually did in 1988). This pro-Israel perspective was retained and reiterated after he took office.

The US-Israeli relationship during the eight years Reagan held office was generally characterized by close positive ties, but there were also specific, divergent interpretations regarding the regional situation, the peace process, and Israel's security needs. Israel bombed an Iraqi nuclear reactor near Baghdad and PLO positions in Beirut during the summer of 1981, and it took action on other issues when it believed its national interest was at stake—even when it understood this would lead to clashes with the United States. The United States strongly opposed the raid on the Iraqi reactor, questioned the Beirut bombings, and postponed the delivery of previously contracted F-16 aircraft to Israel. Other issues emerged, including disputes about settlements in the territories occupied by Israel in the 1967 war and Israel's concern about a perceived pro-Saudi tendency in US policy manifested, in part, by arms supplied to Saudi Arabia, including F-15 enhancements and AWACS. Israeli anxiety was heightened when the Reagan administration suggested that a proposal to resolve the Arab-Israeli conflict put forward by then Crown Prince Fahd of Saudi Arabia (the so-called Fahd Plan) in August 1981, which Israel had rejected, had some merit.

Reagan sought to reassure Israel that the United States remained committed in helping it to retain its military and technological advantages over the Arab states. In fact, Israel was drawn to a Reagan administration proposal of cooperation, and on November 30, 1981, the United States and Israel signed a Memorandum of Understanding on Strategic Cooperation (MOU) in which the parties recognized the need to enhance strategic cooperation to deter threats to the region from the Soviet

Union. For the Begin government, it represented an important achievement, suggesting an improved relationship with the United States, and it mitigated some of the negative effects of US sales of AWACS and other advanced weapons systems to Saudi Arabia. But this positive aura soon dissipated when Israel decided in December 1981 to alter the status of the Golan Heights by extending the law, jurisdiction, and administration of Israel to that area. The action generated swift negative reactions in Washington, including US support for a UN resolution of condemnation and the suspension of the MOU. Israel was stunned by the extent of the US reaction; Israel's strongly negative response included Begin's castigation of the US ambassador to Israel.

Although Israel's Golan decision exacerbated tensions, the turning point was Israel's 1982 invasion of Lebanon, which called into question the links between the United States and Israel and led to clashes over the nature and extent of Israel's military actions and the US effort to ensure the PLO's evacuation from Beirut. US forces, which had been withdrawn from Beirut following the PLO's evacuation, returned there after the massacres of Palestinians by Lebanese Phalangists at the Shatila and Sabra camps in September 1982, leading to the burdensome involvement of US marines in the turmoil of Lebanon.

The war also precipitated the Reagan "fresh start" initiative of September 1, 1982, which sought to reinvigorate the Arab-Israeli peace process by taking advantage of the opportunities presented by the new situation in Lebanon. Israel, which was not consulted in advance, saw the proposals as detrimental because they departed from the conceptual framework of Camp David and seemed to determine prematurely the outcome of negotiations on several points, including the status of Jerusalem and the futures of the West Bank and Gaza. There were other concerns as well, and these led Israel to reject the initiative. That action, coupled with the refugee camp massacres, resulted in a sharp deterioration in Israel's standing in US public opinion and in further disagreements with the Reagan administration, causing months of rancor. However, by the summer of 1983 the US-Israeli relationship reverted to its earlier positive levels as a consequence of Israel's Kahan Commission's report (which found Israel bore indirect responsibility for the Shatila and Sabra massacres), the failure of Jordan's King Hussein to join the peace process, the increase in Soviet involvement in Syria, the signing of the US-promoted Lebanon-Israel agreement of May 17, 1983, and the Syrian-Soviet opposition to it. The United States and Israel appeared linked by a congruence of policy that included recognition of Israel's strategic anti-Soviet value, their mutual desire for peaceful resolution of the Arab-Israeli conflict, as well as a parallelism concerning Lebanon and the future of that country. This comported well with Reagan's initial perceptions of Israel and presaged a period of positive relations, given tangible expression at the end of November 1983, when President Reagan and Prime Minister Yitzhak Shamir reached agreement on closer strategic cooperation.

Israel and the United States worked together to bring about the May 17, 1983, agreement between Israel and Lebanon that dealt with shaping the Lebanese government in conjunction with Israeli withdrawal and an eventual Israeli-Lebanese peace treaty. (The agreement was never implemented due to Syrian opposition and the opposition of Syrian-supported groups in Lebanon; indeed, Syria, and through it the USSR as perceived in Washington, was excluded from the May 17, 1983, negotiations and resented it.) At the same time, the major issues of discord in the relationship, which centered on the West Bank and Gaza and the Reagan "fresh start" initiative, were not addressed in any meaningful way. There was an air of good feeling that pervaded both the executive and legislative branches of the US government.

Reagan faced other difficult times. The Pollard affair became a prominent issue.[4] Although this intelligence disaster captured headlines in both countries, had some short-term repercussions, and remains on the US-Israel agenda, it has had little tangible or lasting effect on overall relations. A much more serious issue was the US effort to secure the release of its hostages in Lebanon through arms sales to Iran, which erupted, in November 1986, into a public scandal that became known as the Iran-Contra affair. This infamous chapter in US history involved active Israeli participation in the planning and execution of some operations of the US National Security Council and demonstrated the high level of strategic cooperation between the two governments during the Reagan administration.

Although interaction ranged over a variety of issues, both countries placed an overarching focus on the peace process throughout Reagan's second term. The concept of an international peace conference became more central during 1987, although little progress was made toward convening such a conference. Israel and the United States agreed on two prerequisites for Soviet participation: the regularization of Soviet Jewish emigration, and the restoration of Soviet ties with Israel broken at the time of the 1967 Six Day War.

The onset of the Palestinian *intifada* in December 1987 led to public disagreement over the methods employed by Israel to contain the violence and restore law and order. Israel's use of live ammunition provoked protests by the State Department as early as January 1988. Israel's deportation of Palestinian civilians charged with inciting the demonstrations led the United States to vote in favor of a UN resolution calling on Israel to refrain from "such harsh measures [which] are unnecessary to maintain order." Although the State Department minimized the significance of the US vote, describing it as a disagreement among friends that did not affect the broader relationship, this was the first time since 1981 that the United States had voted for a resolution critical of Israel. Secretary of State Shultz referred to US support for Israel as "unshakable." As the violence continued and the United States launched the Shultz initiative to seek an accord, however, tensions continued to grow.

Despite this setback, the Reagan administration marked a time of substantial and unprecedented growth in relations. Ronald Reagan saw Israel as a strategic asset, but there were other positive factors—a free-trade arrangement, intelligence exchanges, and high-level joint groups on political-military and related issues—as well as the more prosaic intercourse of a relationship between two friendly states. US economic and military assistance reached $3 billion per annum in essentially all grant aid, and special grants helped Israel to deal with particular economic problems. Strategic cooperation between the United States and Israel reached new levels during this period, and on April 21, 1988 (in the Jewish calendar, the fortieth anniversary of Israel's independence), the two states signed a memorandum of agreement that institutionalized the emerging strategic relationship. Growing links in the military sphere involved joint military exercises, sales and purchases of equipment, training, and related activities. Israel had also gained status as a Major Non-NATO Ally.

With the November 1988 decision of the Palestine National Council (PNC) in Algiers to declare the establishment of a Palestinian state, the policy environment changed dramatically, with repercussions for President George H. W. Bush and his administration. This declaration was accompanied by ambiguous statements concerning the peace process, Israel, and terrorism. However, on December 14, 1988, in a press conference in Geneva, PLO leader Yasser Arafat read the script articulating a change in PLO views toward Israel and the Arab-Israeli conflict, renouncing terrorism, recognizing Israel's right to exist, and accepting UNSC Resolutions 242 and 338. Arafat thereby met the conditions for beginning a dialogue between the United States and the PLO that had first been enunciated by then Secretary of State Henry Kissinger. The same day as the Algiers statement, Secretary of State George Shultz formally announced, "The United States is prepared for a substantive dialogue with PLO representatives." The US Ambassador to Tunisia, Robert Pelletreau, was designated as the only authorized channel for that dialogue. This official opening helped the incoming Bush administration to avoid what might have been a difficult issue; at the same time, it moved the process to another level. Skepticism remained, and the administration sought to reassure Israel that "those who believe that American policy is about to undergo a basic shift merely because we have begun to talk with the PLO are completely mistaken."

The George H. W. Bush Tenure

President George H. W. Bush took office in January 1989 with no long-range strategic plan or specific policies for the Arab-Israeli issue or the Gulf region of the Middle East. The end of the cold war, the implosion of the Soviet Union, the collapse of the Warsaw Pact, and the emerging new democracies in eastern Europe preoccupied the administration and Congress and entranced the media and public. The Iran-Iraq war had given way to a cease-fire, the departure of Soviet troops altered the hostilities in Afghanistan, and a dialogue with the PLO, established in the last days of the Reagan administration, continued. Within the context of a changing international system the Middle East was not a high national priority.

Much of Bush's first year in office was marked by a coolness on various issues, especially those relating to the peace process. Broad-scale concord, on such matters as the need for peace through direct negotiations, and specific-issue discord, for instance on questions relating to a land-for-peace exchange and related themes, increasingly seemed to be the measure of the US-Israel dialogue. Nevertheless, substantial US economic and military aid to Israel continued.

During the first year and a half of the Bush administration, Israel and the United States were preoccupied with the effort to begin a negotiating process between Israel and the Palestinians. Bush administration frustration with the Yitzhak Shamir government was obvious in its preference for a Shimon Peres–led government after a successful vote of no-confidence terminated the tenure of the Israeli government in the spring of 1990 and in its voiced concerns about the prospects for peace after Shamir succeeded in constructing a new government in June 1990. The peace process was moribund when the Iraqis invaded Kuwait in August 1990, attributable (at least in the eyes of the Bush administration) in large measure to the policies of the Shamir government in Israel.

During the Gulf crisis and the war against Iraq, Israel was relegated to a marginal role. Its position as a strategic asset seemed diminished, and there was a widespread view in the Bush administration that Israel was not tactically relevant to potential actions in the Arabian Peninsula and the Persian Gulf. During the crisis, Israel did not serve as a staging area for forces nor as a storage depot for military materiel, nor was it utilized for medical emergencies. There was a conscious US effort to build a broad-based international force with an Arab component to oppose Saddam Hussein and to distance Israel from any such activity. Israel was not to be used as a tool to break the coalition. From the outset Israel was concerned that it was not part of the coalition. There was no publicly identified role for Israel, given US objectives in the crisis, although the Israelis did endorse the firm and rapid US reaction to Iraq.

When Iraq bombarded Israel with scud missiles, however, the United States was prompted to take a more determined stance with Israel. Responding to the entreaties of President Bush, Israel refrained from taking military action against Iraq. Other factors swayed Israel against taking reprisals, including the arrival of US Patriot missile batteries and US cajoling in a crucial telephone conversation between President Bush and Prime Minister Shamir. The visit of Deputy Secretary of State Lawrence Eagleburger to Israel was especially important.

The resumption of the Arab-Israeli peace process in the aftermath of the Gulf war revived traditional Israeli concerns about the United States as something less than a wholly supportive and reliable ally. This was further complicated by the chemistry (or the lack thereof) between US and Israeli leaders and by concerns about specific Bush administration policies. Differences before the Gulf war were exacerbated by developments afterward when the United States pressed for movement on an Arab-Israeli peace process even as Israel remained unconvinced that the Arab world was ready to move in that direction. Within several months of the Gulf war cease-fire, the US-Israeli relationship was again characterized by discord and tension, and much of the newly created goodwill was dissipated by disagreements over the modalities and substance of the peace process and other matters. Tensions developed as the Bush administration appeared to link proposed housing loan guarantees, essential to the settling of Soviet Jews in Israel, to Israel's actions on settlements in the West Bank and Gaza Strip and its responsiveness to the peace process. In testimony before the US House Subcommittee on Foreign Operations of the Appropriations Committee on May 22, 1991, Secretary of State James Baker observed,

"I don't think that there is any bigger obstacle to peace than the settlement activity that continues not only unabated but at an enhanced pace." In the autumn of 1991 tensions became public when Bush asked Congress to postpone consideration of Israel's request for US guarantees of $10 billion in loans. Ultimately, the administration placed conditions on the loan guarantees that were impossible for the government of Israel to accept, and the matter was dropped in the spring of 1992 with recriminations by both sides.

The Bush administration clearly favored the Labor Party over Likud (and Yitzhak Rabin or Shimon Peres over Yitzhak Shamir), both in 1990 (during the period of the vote of no-confidence and the formation of a new Israeli government in June) and in the 1992 Knesset elections. Despite numerous denials and claims to the contrary, the Bush administration and the Shamir government were not harmonious on many of the issues central to peace in the Middle East. The outcome of the June 1992 elections in Israel, with Yitzhak Rabin replacing Shamir as prime minister, was welcomed by the Bush administration as a significant and positive factor that would alter the regional situation, the prospects for progress in the Arab-Israeli peace process, and the nature of the US-Israeli relationship. In late June 1992 Secretary of State Baker called for a quick resumption of Middle East peace talks, reflecting the administration's view that the elections had resulted in the demise of a hard-line Likud government and thereby facilitated the prospects for success in the peace negotiations. They saw the onus now falling upon the Palestinians and other Arabs to make serious compromises and proposals for peace.

At the same time, the overall tenor of US-Israeli relations improved, and tensions were relieved. During a US visit by Rabin in August 1992, the prime minister and Bush focused on resuming the positive aspects of the US-Israeli relationship. Bush noted that the visit was an important one, and "the meetings were also significant for the tone of the discussions. Our time together can best be described as a consultation between close friends and strategic partners." The two leaders announced that they had reached an accord, with the Bush administration supporting loan guarantees for Israel. President Bush noted that "we understand the position [of the Rabin government concerning settlement construction] and all I will say is that I salute this change. We salute what the Prime Minister is trying to do. We understand his position. He understands our position. And obviously, we would not be going forward with this loan guarantee if we did not salute the change."

US determination to see the Arab-Israeli peace process through was stressed by Bush in a speech to a joint session of Congress on March 6, 1991: "A comprehensive peace must be grounded in United Nations Security Council Resolutions 242 and 338 and the principle of territory for peace. This must provide for Israel's security and recognition, and at the same time for legitimate Palestinian political rights. Anything else would fail the twin tests of fairness and security."[5] Baker's visits to the Middle East in the spring and early summer of 1991 made it clear that there was no agreement among the concerned parties to convene a conference between the Arab states and Israel that would lead to bilateral negotiations between Israel and the bordering states still at war with Israel. The issues in contention included the venue of a conference (whether in the region or elsewhere), what powers and authority it would have (whether primarily ceremonial or substantive in nature), under whose auspices it should be conducted (whether the United Nations would be a factor), which Palestinians and other Arabs could and would attend, and what prior commitments must be made by the participants.

Eventually, Baker convened the Madrid peace conference at the end of October 1991. The conference was attended reluctantly by the parties, who retained substantial concerns about its nature and expected little of value to come from it. The conference did not achieve a substantive breakthrough, although it eliminated the procedural barriers to direct bilateral negotiations between Israel and its immediate neighbors when the Israeli and the Syrian, Egyptian, Lebanese, and Jordanian-Palestinian delegations met at an opening public session and an official plenary session and delivered speeches and responses. Bilateral negotiations between Israel and each of the Arab delegations followed.

The Madrid conference was followed by bilateral talks in Washington later in 1991, talks that directly or indirectly contributed to the September 1993 Israel-PLO Declaration of Principles, the October 1994 Israeli-Jordanian peace, and Israeli-Syrian talks focusing on the Golan Heights. The first rounds achieved accord on non-substantive matters, primarily the time and venue of future meetings. Progress was measured primarily by the continuation of the process rather than by significant achievements on the substantive issues in dispute. The wide gap between the Israeli and Arab positions was not narrowed in these initial encounters, and it could not be bridged by outside actors (such as the United States and the former Soviet Union). The United States adhered to its role as facilitator and sought not to intervene on substantive matters. It was not a party to the bilateral talks, and its representatives were not in the room or at the negotiating table, although it did meet separately with the parties and heard their views.

In the bilateral negotiations the Israeli-Palestinian and Israeli-Syrian negotiations were the most central and most difficult. In the case of both Jordan and Lebanon the general perception at the time was that agreements would be relatively easy to achieve, although these would have to await the resolution of the Syrian and Palestinian talks. In the case of Syria the central issue was peace and security and the future of the Golan Heights, with little likelihood of compromise in the short term. In the Israeli-Palestinian discussions the disagreement centered on the Palestinian desire for self-government and the Israeli opposition to that goal. Compromise was elusive, as the positions were mutually exclusive. However, Israeli proposals for Palestinian elections in the territories and the reality of the situation in the region suggested areas for continued negotiation, ultimately leading to the Oslo bilateral negotiations that resulted in the signing of the Israel-PLO Declaration of Principles on the White House lawn in September 1993.

A related and parallel process included multilateral discussions on several regional issues and an initial organizing conference convened in Moscow in January 1992. The goal was to achieve progress on important regional issues, even without a political solution, which would reinforce the earlier bilateral negotiations. The five permanent members of the UN Security Council and a number of other important powers (including the European Community and Japan) were represented in Moscow. Despite some initial difficulties over the question of Palestinian participation and representation, the talks continued to fortify the bilateral process.

Despite the achievements symbolized by the Madrid conference and the subsequent bilateral and multilateral discussions, by the time of the Israeli and US elections in 1992 no substantive breakthrough had occurred and no specific achievement (beyond continuation of the process) had been accomplished. Nevertheless, the Baker team seemed optimistic in the spring of 1992; although the differences between the parties were still wide, they would eventually narrow, and then it would be possible to bridge the gaps. Policy under the Clinton administration continued to emphasize the US role of facilitator.

The Clinton Tenure

The accession of the Clinton administration to office in 1993 and of the Rabin government in 1992 provided the basis for a continuation of the relationship, but in a more positive mode, with strong and improving personal and country-to-country relations focusing on the Madrid-inaugurated Arab-Israeli peace process. The United States reassured Israel that the US commitment to its security would be sustained. And a strong positive personal relationship seemed to develop between the American president and his Israeli prime minister counterpart.

The relationship between Clinton and Rabin continued to grow closer and became more intimate as the peace process, begun at Madrid and amplified by Oslo, continued to make progress. Each achievement seemed to be marked by an added positive glow to both the personal chemistry and the political accord between the two partners. The unusual nature of this relationship was revealed when Rabin was assassinated in November 1995. Clinton appeared to be personally moved by the death of his peace partner and issued the famous statement "Shalom, chaver" (goodbye, friend), which struck close to the heart of their dealings. The substantial size and level of the US delegation to the funeral was essentially unprecedented, but it reaffirmed the connection between the two states and reflected the close personal ties forged between the two leaders.

The success of Benjamin Netanyahu in his race against Shimon Peres (Rabin's foreign minister and alter ego in the peace process) in the first-ever popular election of a prime minister in Israel in the spring of 1996 illustrated again the unusual nature of the connection. The Clinton administration, seeking continuity in the peace process, clearly preferred that Shimon Peres succeed. Some noted that the Clinton team all but campaigned for Peres (and some of Peres's opponents argued that the US government had gotten involved in Israeli domestic affairs). Despite the outcome, the relationship endured, and the United States continued to support Israel's security and quest for peace. There was a lack of personal chemistry between Clinton and Netanyahu, but many in the Republican-dominated US Congress endorsed Netanyahu's approach.

The period of Netanyahu's tenure in some ways resembled that of Menachem Begin in the relationship between the United States and Israel on the issues of the peace process. The Clinton administration continued to press for progress on the peace process begun at Madrid and expanded in Oslo and by subsequent Israeli accords with the Palestinians and with Jordan. The prime minister of Israel, reflecting a skepticism of the Palestinian position and a deep-seated concern for an arrangement that would ensure Israel's security as well as a personal goal of ensuring the stability of his governing coalition and, hence, his position in office, acted with considerable deliberation and pursued a pace seen by the Clinton administration as far too slow. Clashes of position were reflected in numerous public (and private) conflicts between the two parties. By the middle of 1998 the Clinton administration presented an "ultimatum" to Israel that was ignored and then faded from public view. The two states pursued the peace process and clashed with each other. But the administration often was not backed by Congress, which seemed more sympathetic to the Netanyahu approach and position and provided public and private positive reinforcement to the Israeli government.

These episodes and others in the Clinton tenure reflected the themes that marked the Carter-Begin relationship and characterized the broader relationship between the United States and Israel, which centered on endurance and continuity in the quest for peace and Israeli security and on discord concerning the means and procedures (as well as some of the content) of the process to best achieve those ends.

The election of Ehud Barak as prime minister of Israel in May 1999 brought to power a native-born Israeli whose professional experience was as a military officer in the Israel Defense Forces (IDF). Barak's election was seen in the Clinton administration, and elsewhere, as an opportunity for peacemaking to resume and make progress; expectations were high that he would be a prime minister in the mold of Rabin, his mentor and friend. Barak set out on an ambitious diplomatic program and, with Yasser Arafat, set February 12, 2000, as the target date for preparing a framework agreement for an Israeli-Palestinian permanent peace settlement, the completion of which was to occur by September 12, 2000. Israelis and Palestinians had a large number of meetings, and there was extensive involvement by the United States.

The Clinton administration, by choice and through developments, maintained the Middle East peace process at the center of its policy world. From the outset, the Clinton administration was engaged at its most senior levels in the bilateral and multilateral negotiation process. Negotiations between Israel and the Palestinians resumed soon after Barak's election, but little progress was made.

As the Clinton administration entered its final year in office, accelerated efforts suggested a possible tripartite summit involving Clinton, Barak, and Arafat. But the parties were far apart. The objective of the negotiations in July 2000 at Camp David (generally referred to as Camp David II) was to put together a package that Barak believed would generate acceptance and recognition from the Palestinians, which had eluded Israelis to that point, on the basis of a two-peoples, two-state solution within the region. But this was not to be. Arafat rejected the Barak proposals, left the negotiating table, and thereby provided the basis for the al-Aqsa *intifada,* which soon brought violence to the area. The Clinton tenure ended without an Israeli-Palestinian peace accord and with the area engulfed in violence.

George W. Bush and Sharon

A month after George W. Bush was elected president in November 2000, Ehud Barak announced his resignation as prime minister to seek a renewed mandate to pursue peace with the Palestinians. In the special prime ministerial election held on February 6, 2001, Ariel Sharon defeated Barak in a landslide victory with 62.7 percent of the vote. Bush congratulated Sharon, saying, "Our bilateral relationship is rock solid, as is the US commitment to Israel's security."

In his inaugural speech to the Knesset on March 7, 2001, Prime Minister Ariel Sharon, like his predecessors, remarked on the importance of the special relationship between the United States and Israel. "We shall work toward deepening our special relations with our great friend and ally, the United States."

The ascension of George W. Bush to the presidency and the election of Ariel Sharon as prime minister of Israel brought an end to the Oslo peace process in which President Clinton had been personally very active. Bush initially had a "hands-off" policy toward the Arab-Israeli problem, wary of investing the kind of political capital Clinton had spent for such a meager return. Sharon and Bush would establish their own "special" connection. Significantly, while the Bush administration called for an end to Arab-Israeli violence and initially put the onus on Arafat to publicly call for the termination of violence, it signaled its determination to be less active, suggesting it would not emulate the Clinton administration's deep involvement in the details of the conflict.

By early spring 2001 the position of the new Bush administration had begun to emerge, and it seemed to dovetail with the program of the Sharon government. Assistant Secretary of State Edward A. Walker Jr, in testimony before the Subcommittee on Middle East and South Asia of the Committee on International Relations of the House of Representatives on March 29, 2001, noted: "Our country has vital strategic and economic interests in the region, and we believe that these interests will best be served by a peace that can be embraced by Israelis, Palestinians, and the region as a whole. We also have a vital and strategic interest in the survival and well-being of Israel."

At the annual policy conference of the American Israel Public Affairs Committee (AIPAC), Secretary of State Colin Powell, while articulating the administration's laissez-faire stance on the peace process, disparaged Arafat, noting: "Leaders have the responsibility to denounce violence, strip it of legitimacy, stop it. . . . [T]he United States stands ready to assist, not insist." Exactly one decade earlier, on March 19, 1991, then Chairman of the Joint Chiefs of Staff Powell had declared before the same group: "We have stood with Israel since the day of its founding. We have stood with Israel throughout its history. We have demonstrated again and again that our roots are intertwined, as they are with all nations who share our beliefs in openness and democracy. So let there be no question that America will stand by Israel in the future." On March 19, 2001, Powell repeated those words: "I am proud to say that these words remain true." He further declared:

> There is a special friendship linking America with Israel, just as George Bush said before your conference one year ago when he was a governor of the state of Texas. I stand here today to emphasize this friendship another time. It includes all sides of life. This strong relationship ranges from areas of politics and economics to areas of security and culture. This relationship between two democratic systems will continue strong like a rock. It represents an unconditional relationship, deep-rooted and broad, a link built upon history, interests, values and ideologies. We are resolved in maintaining this special relationship with Israel and the Israeli people. We realize that Israel exists in a region of extreme danger. Therefore we will work and examine means to consolidate our valuable strategic cooperation with Israel in order to protect its military superiority.

Bush enlisted Sharon's support in developing a national missile defense shield, and Sharon was happy to oblige given that Israel was the target of several rogue states. Furthermore, 87 senators and 209 representatives in Congress joined Sharon in pushing Bush to not invite Arafat to the White House, to close the PLO's Washington office, and to cut US aid to the Palestinian Authority until Arafat publicly called for an end to violence against Israel. As violence continued to flare between Israelis and Palestinians after Sharon's election, efforts to halt it, to restore confidence between the parties, and to resume negotiations became the core of US efforts to facilitate a peace process between Israel and the Palestinians.

The situation was dramatically altered by the September 11, 2001, attacks on the United States. The Bush administration worked to create an international coalition to respond to terrorism, focusing on Osama bin Laden and the al-Qa'ida movement. Al-Qa'ida's terrorist attack on the United States had the effect of postponing any new US efforts on the Arab-Israeli conflict and redirecting the Bush administration's priorities into leading the country in a war on global terror, particularly against Islamic extremism in the Middle East. The United States could now identify with Israel in profound new ways, having experienced terrorist attacks on its homeland for the first time, and it could empathize with Israel's decision to strike unilaterally against terrorists. At the same time, Osama bin Laden continued to link the attacks to the plight of the Palestinians and attributed that to unequivocal US support for Israel—a view widely accepted in the Arab and Muslim worlds.

In a press conference on October 11, 2001, President Bush noted that his administration would continue to focus on resolution of the Arab-Israeli conflict within the context of continued US-Israeli friendship. At the same time, he noted: "I also stated the other day that if we ever get into the . . . process, where we can start discussing a political solution in the Middle East, that I believe there ought to be a Palestinian state, the boundaries of which will be negotiated by the parties so long as the Palestinian state recognizes the right of Israel to exist, and will treat Israel with respect, and will be peaceful on her borders." But negotiations for an end to violence and to achieve resolution of the Arab-Israeli conflict were held hostage to the continued violence that erupted in the wake of the failure of the Camp David talks.

A year after the termination of the Middle East peace process launched at Madrid, the new efforts seemed to be moving in the opposite direction. Arafat was unwilling or unable to halt Palestinian terrorism and violence against Israelis, thereby incurring Israeli responses and US concern, frustration, and disappointment. In late January 2002, Bush publicly expressed his disappointment in Arafat for his involvement in an arms shipment that could escalate Palestinian violence against Israel and for his failure to prevent terrorism. Despite US sympathy and empathy for Israel, and a strong bond on many matters, the United States proved unable to stop the cycle of violence, restore confidence, and get the Israelis and Palestinians back to the negotiating table.

Infuriated by Arafat's rhetoric and inaction, the United States generally viewed Israel's acts against Palestinian terrorists as defensive and placed the burden on Arafat to stop the violence. It could hardly do otherwise given that by the end of 2001 the United States had ousted the Taliban from power in Afghanistan for harboring al-Qa'ida terrorists. "Obviously Israel has the right to defend itself, and the president understands that clearly," White House spokesman Ari Fleischer said on December 3, 2001.

On December 12, 2001, the Israeli Security Cabinet determined that Arafat was responsible for deadly attacks against Israel and stated, "Arafat is no longer relevant." The Bush administration soon adopted a similar position, and in June 2002, Bush called on the Palestinian people to "elect new leaders, leaders not compromised by terror."

The ensuing period was marked by Arafat's continued failure to lead the Palestinians to substantive peace negotiations and by the inability of Mahmoud Abbas, his successor, to make progress. The United States was increasingly preoccupied by the global war on terrorism and the war in Iraq—both issues that reaffirmed many of the positive factors in the US-Israel relationship. In this environment, Prime Minister Ariel Sharon launched a plan for the unilateral withdrawal of all Israelis from the Gaza Strip, which Sharon outlined in a visit to Washington. On April 14, 2004, in a joint news conference at the White House, Bush recognized Israel's right to retain some territory and settlements in the West Bank. Bush called Sharon's plan both "historic" and "courageous." The implementation of the Sharon unilateral withdrawal was hailed by the Bush administration as a very positive step forward.

Sharon's forming of the new Kadima political party in late 2005 and the call for parliamentary elections in early 2006 raised some questions about the progress of the peace effort and the nature of the US-Israel relationship in the second Bush term.

In the aftermath of Sharon's stroke and incapacity, Ehud Olmert became prime minister of Israel in March 2006. In a telephone call in early January 2006, Bush reiterated his intention to continue implementing Sharon's vision for advancing the peace process in the region. The Hamas victory in the Palestinian elections later that month raised additional concerns. These were summarized by Bush in remarks on May 4, 2006:

> As you know, I'm a strong believer in democracy and free elections, but that does not mean we have to support elected officials who are not committed to peace. Hamas has made it clear that they do not acknowledge the right of Israel to exist, and I've made it clear that so long as that's their policy, we will have no contact with the leaders of Hamas. Hamas must accept the demands of the international community to recognize Israel, disarm and reject terrorism, and stop blocking the path to peace.

As in earlier periods, the US-Israeli relationship did not change significantly.

On February 1, 2006, President George W. Bush said that the United States would rise to Israel's defense against Iran if needed and denounced the president of Iran for "menacing talk" against Israel. In an interview aboard Air Force One, Bush said, "I am concerned about a person that, one, tries to rewrite the history of the Holocaust, and two, has made it clear that his intentions are to destroy Israel. . . . Israel is a solid ally of the United States; we will rise to Israel's defense if need be." When asked if he meant that the United States would rise to Israel's defense militarily, Bush replied, "You bet, we'll defend Israel."

Bush and Sharon had established a firm relationship based on a strong opposition to terrorism of the type the United States faced, especially after 9/11, and with which Israel could empathize because of its being a target of terrorism for much of its existence. The congruence of their approach to dealing with this threat moved the two leaders closer together over the years, but there were elements of discord on the peace process. Sharon was not enthralled by the Road Map, and Bush expected more concessions from Israel toward the Palestinians.

Endurance and Continuity

Israel's special relationship with the United States—revolving around a shared ideology and positive perception and sentiment evident in public opinion and official statements and manifest in political and diplomatic support and tangible military and economic assistance—has not been enshrined in a legally binding commitment joining the two in a formal alliance. Despite the extensive links that have developed, the widespread belief in the existence of the commitment, and the assurances contained in various specific agreements, the exact nature and extent of the US commitment to Israel remains imprecise. Israel has no mutual security treaty with the United States, nor is it a member of any alliance system requiring the United States to take up arms automatically on its behalf.

The US commitment to Israel has taken the generalized form of presidential statements (rather than formal documents), which have reaffirmed the US interest in supporting the political independence and territorial integrity of all Middle East states, including Israel.

It has largely been assumed by the United States and Israel that the United States would come to Israel's assistance should it be gravely threatened; this perception has become particularly apparent during times of crisis. Despite this perception and the general feeling in Washington (and elsewhere) that the United States would take action if required, there is no assurance that this would be the case. Israeli leaders continue to be interested in military and economic assistance as the primary tangible expression of the US commitment and have been particularly cautious about potential US participation in a conflict. Thus, the exact role of the United States in support of Israel, beyond diplomatic and political action and military and economic assistance, is undefined.

The United States is today an indispensable if not fully dependable ally. It provides Israel, through one form or another, with economic (governmental and private), technical, military, political, diplomatic, and moral support. Indeed, Israel is the largest recipient of US aid. It is seen as the ultimate resource against potential enemies, it is the source of Israel's sophisticated military hardware, and its interest in lasting peace is central to the Arab-Israeli peace process. Although there is this substantive relationship, there is also an Israeli reluctance, bred of history, to abdicate security to another party's judgment and action. Israel will continue to follow its own course on threat and security.

The two states maintain a remarkable degree of congruence on broad policy goals. The policy consensus includes the need to prevent war, at both the regional and international levels, the need to resolve the Arab-Israeli conflict, and the need to maintain Israel's existence and security and to help provide for its economic well-being. At the same time, however, there will continue to be a divergence of interests that derives from a difference of perspective and overall policy environment. The United States has broader concerns resulting from its global obligations, whereas Israel's perspective is conditioned by its more restricted environment and lesser responsibilities. Israel's horizon is more narrowly defined and essentially limited to the survival of the state and a concern for Jewish communities and individuals that goes beyond the frontiers of the Jewish state.

Despite the generally positive nature of the relationship since 1948, Israelis tend to recall a series of negative episodes as well. They highlight the 1947 arms embargo and the subsequent refusal to provide military equipment or other assistance during the War of Independence and the period that followed; Dulles's aid suspensions and general unfriendliness; US actions in connection with the Suez war of 1956 and Israel's subsequent withdrawal from the Sinai Peninsula and the Gaza Strip; and the disappointing lack of action by the United States just prior to the Six Day War in support of its 1957 pledge concerning freedom of passage for Israeli shipping in the Strait of Tiran. In 1967—the year of the Six Day War with Egypt—Israel ultimately decided that the United States would not act unilaterally and that multilateral action would not succeed. Israel determined its need to act alone and estimated that the United States would not object to or seek to prevent its action, and when Israel decided to go to war, it did not consult or inform the United States.

There has also been a divergence on methods and techniques employed, as well as discord on specific issues. During the Six Day War there was a clash over Israel's mistaken attack on the US intelligence ship USS *Liberty*. In May 1968 there was disagreement over Israel's control of the islands of Tiran and Sanafir. The United States and Israel disagreed on the matter of reprisals by Israel in response to Arab *fedayeen* (literally, "self-sacrificers") actions and on the limits placed on the refugees from the West Bank in the wake of the Six Day War. There was major disagreement concerning the value of a great power to resolve the Arab-Israeli conflict, Israel's need for military supplies, and the status of the occupied territories. They have differed over the construction of settlements in the occupied territories and whether they are legal and whether they are in fact obstacles to peace. They have argued over Israel's desire for significant changes in the pre–Six Day War armistice lines as contrasted with the US perspective that there be "insubstantial alterations" or "minor modifications." The two states will continue to hold divergent views on the several elements of the Palestinian issue, particularly the West Bank's future, the rights of the Palestinians, and the delineation of a Palestinian homeland, entity, or state. These differences became increasingly obvious in the Carter and Reagan administrations.

In many respects, the issue of Jerusalem has highlighted the areas of discord. The United States has supported the Partition Plan designation of Jerusalem as a separate entity and has stressed the international character of the city while refusing to recognize unilateral actions by any state affecting its future. The United States refuses to move its embassy to Jerusalem and maintains it in Tel Aviv. (Although both the House and Senate overwhelmingly passed bills in October 1995 to move the embassy to Jerusalem by 1997, President Clinton did not do so because it might disrupt the peace negotiations, and President Bush has followed a similar course.) This stance has placed the two states in conflicting positions continuously from 1947 to the present, since Israel has declared Jerusalem to be the capital of the state and has insisted on the reunification of the city since the Six Day War. The increase in Israel's dependence on the United States and the areas of policy discord suggest possible reemployment of various forms of pressure utilized previously, including the withholding of economic aid as in the mid-1950s, military aid decisions and delivery slowdowns since 1967 (such as the slow response to Israeli requests during the 1973 war), joining in United Nations censures, moral persuasion, private and open presidential letters, and similar devices.

The general consensus on major issues does not ensure agreement on all aspects or specifics of each problem. As the dialogue has increasingly focused on details, rather than broad areas of agreement, there have been disturbances in the relationship. Israel and the United States understand that this is inevitable but seek to minimize the areas of discord. Strains in the relationship are probably inevitable given the extensive nature of the issues considered in the dialogue. Foreign Minister Yitzhak Shamir described the situation to the Knesset in these terms in September 1982:

Our relations with the United States are of a special character. Between our two nations there is a deep friendship based on common values and identical interests. At the same time differences between our two countries crop up occasionally, chiefly on the subject of our borders and how to defend our security. These differences of opinion are natural; they stem from changing conditions, and they express our independence and our separate needs. . . . Israel is a difficult ally, but a faithful and reliable one. We are certain that what we have in common with the United States is permanent and deep while our disagreements are ephemeral. The permanent will overcome the ephemeral.

In presenting his government to the Knesset in July 1992, Prime Minister Yitzhak Rabin defined the relationship in these terms: "Sharing with us in the making of peace will also be the United States, whose friendship and special closeness we prize. We shall spare no effort to strengthen and improve the special relationship we have with the one power in the world. Of course we shall avail ourselves of its advice, but the decisions will be ours alone, of Israel as a sovereign and independent state."

Changing administrations in Washington and governments in Jerusalem have all affected the nature and content of the links between the United States and Israel within the broad parameters of the enduring special relationship. The broad patterns of concord on the more strategic and existential issues are accompanied by disagreement on the specifics of many of the elements of the Arab-Israeli conflict and on the means to achieve congruent objectives.

At Israel's birth the United States seemed to be a dispassionate, almost uninterested, midwife—its role was essential and unconventional but also unpredictable and hotly debated in US policy circles. Today, decades later, some of the policy debate continues, and there are periods of tension in the relationship. Some of this reflects personality and related differences between US and Israeli leaders. But there is little doubt about the overall nature of US support for its small and still embattled ally.

In remarks at the American Jewish Committee's Centennial Dinner, on May 4, 2006, George W. Bush summed up the relationship in these terms:

My administration shares a strong commitment with the AJC to make sure relations between Israel and America remain strong. We have so much in common. We're both young countries born of struggle and sacrifice. We're both founded by immigrants escaping religious persecution. We have both established vibrant democracies built on the rule of law and open markets. We're both founded on certain basic beliefs, that God watches over the affairs of men, and that freedom is the Almighty God's gift to every man and woman on the face of this earth. These ties have made us natural allies, and these ties will never be broken. America's commitment to Israel's security is strong, enduring, and unshakable.[6]

Notes

1. *New York Times,* May 13, 1977.

2. To a great extent this was a consequence of the rupture of diplomatic relations by major Arab states with the United States, and much of what was seen of the region from Washington was viewed through an Israeli prism rather than an Arab perspective, and it was difficult for the Arab states to gain the sympathy and understanding of the American people.

3. An example of the latter is found in the confirmation hearings of Strobe Talbott as deputy secretary of state, when congressional queries and votes tended to focus on what Talbott had written more than a decade earlier on the Arab-Israeli conflict, when he was seen as critical of Israel.

4. Jonathan Jay Pollard, a US Navy intelligence analyst, was arrested in November 1985 and charged with spying. Pollard pleaded guilty in June 1986. Israel denied that its senior officials had knowledge of or had approved any espionage activities against the United States. Shimon Peres apologized and promised a full investigation.

5. The full text is in the *New York Times,* March 7, 1991.

6. On March 20, 2006, in answering a question after a speaking engagement at City Club in Cleveland, Ohio, Bush said: "The threat from Iran is, of course, their stated objective to destroy our strong ally Israel. That's a threat, a serious threat. It's a threat to world peace; it's a threat, in essence, to a strong alliance. I made it clear, I'll make it clear again, that we will use military might to protect our ally, Israel."

13

The US-PLO Relationship
From Dialogue to the White House Lawn

JoAnn A. DiGeorgio-Lutz

On September 13, 1993, Yasser Arafat, in his capacity as chairman of the Executive Committee of the Palestine Liberation Organization (PLO), stood on the White House lawn to witness the signing of the Declaration of Principles (DOP) and the mutual recognition between Israel and the PLO. Even though the administration of President Bill Clinton had endeavored to reap some diplomatic profit from the event, the only accolade that the United States could claim was its role as master of ceremonies; Arafat's unprecedented appearance at the White House did not occur as a result of a constructive US-PLO relationship. In fact, Arafat bypassed US diplomacy altogether when he unilaterally took a diplomatic detour through Oslo, Norway, to reach a principled agreement with the Israeli government. This occurred even as Palestinian negotiators participated at the Washington rounds of bilateral talks that began under the George H. W. Bush administration after the convening of the Madrid conference in October 1991. Arafat's deliberate removal of Washington from the Oslo equation begs the question as to why the PLO leader opted for an alternative strategy despite the implicit recognition of the Palestinian negotiators as PLO arbitrators during the latter stages of the bilateral talks.

In order to answer that question, this chapter examines the precarious nature of the US-PLO relationship from the viewpoint of the PLO. Such an approach deviates from conventional themes that generally emphasize the US-PLO connection from the perspective of US diplomacy, particularly as it relates to the broader Arab-Israeli conflict.[1] Scholarly efforts do not always uncover the myriad dynamics that contribute to the formation of PLO foreign policy, especially toward the United States. Moreover, an understanding of the factors that shape PLO foreign policy helps dispel some of the misperceptions that persist about the organization and provides some insight into the formation of its overall foreign policy behavior.

Characteristics of PLO Foreign Policy

Much like any state actor, the PLO is subject to a set of factors that influence the formation and direction of its foreign policy. In addition to regional and international dynamics that often necessitate a foreign policy decision, there are three separate political bodies within the PLO that participate in the foreign policy process, bodies that parallel the executive and legislative branches of governments of states. Those bodies are the Palestine National Council (the PNC—the PLO's "parliament-in-exile"), the Executive Committee (which functions as the "supreme executive authority of the PLO"), and the Central Council (originally established by the 7th PNC to serve as an intermediary between the organization's executive structure and the PNC when the latter is not in session). Also contributing to the foreign policy process is the interplay among the PLO's various guerrilla groups, which causes a bureaucratic political effect. In a broad sense, these groups act like political parties that influence foreign policy through their support or rejection of a particular strategy or goal. Bureaucratic politics remained a key element of PLO foreign policy throughout the 1970s and early 1980s, when consensus decisionmaking was the organizational rule and the PLO's constituency was anchored in the Diaspora. However, the PLO's adoption of majority-rule decisionmaking in 1984, followed by the voluntary withdrawal of key guerrilla groups from power-sharing positions and the leadership's subsequent turn to the Occupied Territories as the backbone of its legitimacy, led to an erosion of bureaucratic politics as the primary mechanism driving foreign policy. This decline helped pave the way for Arafat to assume a commanding role in the foreign policy process.

This notion—that a constituency shapes foreign policy—is probably more acute for PLO leaders than for most state actors because the PLO does not exercise direct control over people; the PLO's "constituency" is located in the Diaspora and in the Occupied Territories of the West Bank and Gaza. The continued legitimacy of the PLO and its leadership requires that they take into consideration the aspirations and demands of that constituency. Prior to the 1982 Israeli invasion of Lebanon and the subsequent expulsion of the PLO from Beirut, the organization primarily aspired to meet the demands of Diaspora Palestinians. After 1982 and the loss of its military presence in Lebanon, however, the PLO redirected its attention toward the West Bank and Gaza as the mainstay of its constituency. Since the *intifada*, and especially since the Gulf war, the leadership of the PLO has increased its focus on the Occupied Territories as the primary determinant of its foreign policy to the exclusion of the Diaspora Palestinians, especially those residing in refugee camps. This is partly because of the activities of the Islamic Resistance Movement, or Hamas, which not only rejects the secular-based policies of the PLO but also poses a credible challenge to the continued political viability of the organization and its leadership.

The PLO, like many decisionmaking bodies, evaluates its foreign policy based on the feedback it receives regarding the success or failure of a particular tactic or goal. Furthermore, the presence of a threat or opportunity also serves as a mechanism for gauging the direction of its foreign policy behavior. PLO leadership perceives any attempt to marginalize the organization's right to act as the legitimate representative of the Palestinian people as a threat. Conversely, it views any situation in which it can initiate content and direction of PLO foreign policy and maintain an independent role in the process as an opportunity. Whenever the PLO leadership is able to retain the initiative, it is more likely to pursue pragmatic policies characterized by political accommodation and concessions.

Two additional, general features can be noted about the nature of PLO foreign policy. First, what often appears as a dramatic change in policy is actually the culmination of a series of evolutionary modifications that have occurred over time. For example, a study of PNC resolutions reveals that the PLO gradually modified its use of armed struggle as the exclusive means to achieve strategic objectives.[2] What the organization considered to be the sole means to liberate Palestine in 1968 was changed to a principal means in 1971 and was foremost by 1974, culminating in the renunciation of armed struggle altogether by 1988. Additionally, the same study reveals that the PLO has modified its strategic goals over the years, moving from the goal of total liberation of Palestine in 1968 to acceptance of the Gaza-Jericho First Plan in 1993.[3]

The second feature is the leadership's persistent demand that it retain the initiative over foreign policy based on the organization's authority to act as the sole, legitimate representative of the Palestinian people.[4] Since 1968, the PLO leadership has historically refused to accept a subservient or secondary role by its sustained rejection of any attempt to impose upon the organization externally mandated foreign policy agendas.[5]

Climate of Opportunity

Toward the end of the Reagan presidency an opportunistic political climate emerged that provided the PLO leadership an occasion to launch a more moderate, realistic course of foreign policy. By the 18th PNC (April 1987), the PLO had reunified its previously disaffected bureaucratic groups and reasserted its commitment to United Nations (UN) General Assembly Resolution 38/58, which called for, among other things, an international conference on the Middle East with equal PLO participation.[6]

The PLO gained an additional opportunity shortly after the outbreak of the *intifada* in December 1987. Because the uprising marked the first time that Palestinians had taken matters into their own hands independent of the PLO, the organization's legitimacy faced a potential threat. The leadership of the PLO, however, quickly transformed the *intifada* into an opportunity that allowed it to reassert the organization's leadership role and to direct the course of events in the Occupied Territories.

The international environment was also marked by significant changes. The demise of the cold war was accompanied by the Soviet Union's return to the Middle East as a moderator of peace. By 1988, the reentry of the Soviet Union into the region, coupled with media attention given to the *intifada* and the resulting public outcry in support of the Palestinians, obliged Reagan's secretary of state, George Shultz, to revitalize the Arab-Israeli peace talks. This led to the May 1988 Shultz initiative, which featured the long-standing US goal of a comprehensive settlement to the Arab-Israeli conflict based procedurally on bilateral talks and substantively on UN Security Council Resolutions 242 and 338. Also, according to the Shultz initiative, only the legitimate rather than national rights of the Palestinians would be addressed. Because there would be no direct role for the PLO in the peace process, Palestinian participation would be linked exclusively with that of Jordan.[7]

The US preference for bilateral talks consequent to an international conference that would only serve to launch negotiations stood in contrast to the PLO's predilection for a sustained international forum as a means to achieve a negotiated settlement. Despite these procedural differences, the substantive aims of the United States were not entirely inconsistent with PLO objectives. Since 1983, PNC resolutions indicated that the PLO had gradually narrowed the basis of its rejection of Resolutions 242 and 338. If congruency between the PLO and Washington could be established on a substantive level, then perhaps their respective procedural differences could also be overcome in the future.

Moreover, because the PLO leadership was interested in broadening the organization's foreign policy agenda to include more moderate and less revolutionary behaviors to achieve its political objectives, it was not averse to granting concessions, provided it retain the initiative in the formation and direction of that policy. By 1988, moderates within the PLO were contemplating the possibility of openly pursuing a two-state solution to the Israeli-Palestinian conflict as the more attainable and realistic goal. The PLO responded to the Shultz initiative by circulating a position paper authored by an aide to Arafat, Bassam Abu Sharif, to the international media prior to the Algiers Arab summit conference in early June 1988. In the position paper, Abu Sharif acknowledged that the PLO had already accepted Resolutions 242 and 338. The organization's reluctance to state this "unconditionally" however, had been the failure on the part of the resolutions to address the "national rights of the Palestinian people, including their democratic right to self-expression and their national right to self-determination."[8] With the publication of the Abu Sharif paper, the PLO indirectly signaled to Washington that it might be willing to compromise and recognize the state of Israel in exchange for a direct role in any international peace conference.

Even though these signals did not elicit the response from Washington that the PLO leadership may have hoped for, they did not go unnoticed by the organization's bureaucratic factions and Palestinian constituency in the Occupied Territories. Although both the Democratic Front (DFLP) and the Popular Front for the Liberation of Palestine (PFLP) apparently rejected what appeared to be a unilateral move on the part of Arafat at the expense of the organization's decisionmaking institutions, the constituency of the Occupied Territories signaled its approval for the chairman's diplomatic offensive and a new foreign policy role for the PLO grounded in pragmatism.[9]

On July 31, 1988, Jordan's King Hussein announced that Jordan was relinquishing legal and administrative ties to the West Bank, which created an opportunity for the PLO leadership in the form of political space. That provided Arafat with ample room to pursue a diplomatic offensive. His thinking was guided by the observation that the effective removal of Jordan from the West Bank political equation meant that any settlement of the West Bank's territorial status would now have to include an active role for the PLO. Capitalizing on the opportunity provided by Jordan, Arafat launched a unilateral campaign to secure international and regional support for a pragmatic two-state territorial solution. Speaking before the European Parliament on September 12, 1988, Arafat indicated the PLO's willingness to negotiate with Israel either on the basis of all relevant UN resolutions or on the isolated basis of UN Resolutions 242 and 338—provided that Israel accept the Palestinian right to self-determination. Arafat also reaffirmed the PLO's commitment to the 1985 Cairo Declaration, in which he condemned terrorism.[10]

The political environment grew more opportunistic as private channels of diplomacy were being explored through Sweden about the possibility of a US Jewish-PLO initiative that could potentially lead to an Israel-PLO dialogue. The Swedish efforts served to activate the initiative developed by PLO and US representatives Mohamed Rabie and William B. Quandt that detailed conditions for a US-PLO dialogue. These events subsequently engaged Secretary of State Shultz and set the stage for the development of the US-PLO dialogue.[11]

The results of the November 1988 US presidential election and the Israeli parliamentary elections (which brought to power a Likud-led coalition without Labor sharing in the premiership), provided additional impetus for the PLO to push forward. Arafat's public sentiment about the PLO's more pragmatic goal of a two-state territorial solution and moderate foreign policy required a measure of official endorsement. That endorsement was made official at the historic 19th PNC (November 1988) in which the PLO explicitly accepted UN General Assembly Resolution 181 and Security Council Resolutions 242 and 338. In addition, the political resolutions adopted at this PNC did not assign any role for armed struggle as a means to achieve Palestinian political objectives, nor was there any reference to the 1968 Palestine National Charter. Instead, the resolutions endorsed by the PNC rejected "terrorism in all its forms," including state terrorism. Even though the language of the resolutions failed to satisfy Shultz, Arafat accommodated the United States at a press conference shortly after the 19th PNC in which he clarified certain ambiguous points. Arafat furthered clarified his position in an address to the UN General Assembly, which met in Geneva on December 13, 1988, following Shultz's refusal to grant the PLO chairman a visa to address the General Assembly in New York. Because the PLO was on the initiating end of its own foreign policy, Arafat was able to finally satisfy Shultz and "renounced" terrorism at a December 14 press conference without significant bureaucratic backlash.

In theory, the PLO had opened the diplomatic door to new foreign policy opportunities when it satisfied Washington's three demands as preconditions for a dialogue. Those demands were the recognition of Israel's right to exist, acceptance of Resolutions 242 and 338, and the "renouncement" of terrorism. The PLO leadership met those demands in a political climate of opportunity in which the leadership maintained the initiative in the selection of its foreign policy behavior. The PLO's willingness to accommodate Washington paid off when the outgoing Reagan administration announced in December 1988 that the United States was now prepared to commence a "substantive dialogue" with the PLO. This announcement also marked a major shift in US policy toward the PLO.[12]

Although the new dialogue's procedural conditions were limited to contacts with the US ambassador to Tunisia, Robert Pelletreau, the substance of that dialogue would be left for the newly elected Bush administration to define. Subsequently, it would produce little in terms of diplomatic gains for the PLO.

A Change in the Political Climate

During the first round of US-PLO talks, held in Tunis on December 16, 1988, differences surfaced over procedural issues regarding the peace process. The United States insisted on direct, bilateral Arab-Israeli negotiations as part of any peace process. The PLO, however, was not willing to compromise on this point because its preference had always been for an international conference that would include Soviet participation as a means to counter US support for Israel. Moreover, bilateral talks seemed pointless as long as the Israeli government maintained its policy of refusing to negotiate with the PLO. The leadership of the PLO expressed cautious optimism about the status of its newfound relationship with the United States despite the pressures on Arafat from bureaucratic factions, including elements from within his own faction, Fatah, to halt concessionary practices.

The incoming George H. W. Bush administration heralded the possibility of a successful US-PLO relationship because it represented the first US government that was on speaking terms with all the parties to the conflict. However, the potential for a collapse in the newly established US-PLO relationship also existed. The Bush administration assumed office with the same long-standing convictions and policies regarding the Arab-Israeli conflict that characterized preceding US presidential administrations.[13]

By March 1989, the PLO leadership began to signal the possibility that the dialogue might be headed toward failure. Senior PLO officials expressed their disappointment over the substance of the dialogue, which failed to move beyond lectures on terrorism.[14] As a result, several areas of disagreement between the United States and the PLO were left unresolved. Those differences centered around Washington's insistence that the PLO curb the violence of the *intifada,* that the organization cease its military activities in southern Lebanon, and that procedural conditions for the convening of peace talks involve direct bilateral talks. Even though the PLO leadership's assessment of the dialogue remained somewhat sanguine, there was a growing conviction among the leadership that the PLO had granted enough concessions and that "time was running short."[15] Pressures from the PLO's bureaucratic groups, in combination with a growing discontent in the Occupied Territories, limited Arafat's ability to take unilateral steps to meet Washington's demands.

At a meeting of the PLO's Central Council, the representatives of all the PLO's bureaucratic factions granted Arafat a powerful mandate on April 8, 1989, when they unanimously designated him Palestine's first president. Despite this show of political support, the bureaucratic factions criticized Arafat's unilateral style of leadership, his compromising statements toward the United States, and continued Israeli-Palestinian contacts, which threatened to bypass the PLO.[16] The effect of those criticisms temporarily dampened Arafat's ability to act independently.

Regional dynamics constrained Arafat even further as the political environment began to change from opportunistic to threat driven when Israeli Prime Minister Yitzhak Shamir announced his election plan as part of the Israeli initiative for peace.[17] One of the features of the Shamir Plan called for West Bank and Gaza elections as the means for Palestinians to select representatives to conduct negotiations for a transitional period of Palestinian self-rule. This transitional period would precede future negotiations for a permanent solution for the Occupied Territories that precluded the possibility of a two-state solution. Moreover, the Shamir Plan explicitly stated that the government of Israel would not negotiate with the PLO.

The PLO leadership began to perceive that it was losing the initiative in both the formation and course of its foreign policy. These perceptions proved correct when Egyptian President Hosni Mubarak submitted his version of how the Israeli elections should be conducted. When Mubarak's ten points were rejected by the Israeli cabinet, US Secretary of State James Baker submitted his "Five-Point Framework" as a preliminary step to bolster Shamir's election plan.[18] Neither Mubarak's ten points nor Baker's five mentioned any role for the PLO.

By 1990 the PLO was compelled to conduct its foreign policy in an international environment that threatened to corner the organization into a subservient role in the peace process. Washington had effectively marginalized the PLO by insisting that it extend to Egypt the right to name a Palestinian delegation to conduct peace talks with the Israelis. Although the United States jeopardized the PLO's right to act as sole legitimate representative of the Palestinian people, the PLO leadership endeavored to maintain this right by offering a compromise solution. The PLO would accept a limitation of its legitimate right to act a sole spokesperson for the Palestinians provided that it be allowed to name its own representatives.

As the United States effectively pushed the PLO into a subservient role, its leadership faced growing internal pressures. In addition to pressure directed at Arafat from the various bureaucratic factions to fall back on a more militant approach, Palestinians in the Occupied Territories began to signal their growing frustration over the PLO's continued conciliatory policy toward Washington. The PLO leadership could no longer ignore the growing frustration of its West Bank and Gaza constituency. Regional dynamics began to force the organization to respond to the cues and demands it received from the Occupied Territories at the expense of formal contacts with the West.

Alignment with Iraq

Frustration in the Occupied Territories began to mount during the course of the *intifada*. Already into its third year, the uprising had not succeeded in ending Israeli occupation. The Palestinians also began to express their dissatisfaction with the lack of progress in the US-PLO dialogue. There was a growing disillusionment among inhabitants of the Occupied Territories that the PLO policy of continually accommodating US demands had yet to produce any tangible results. The Palestinians in the West Bank and Gaza needed some measure of relief. That relief was temporarily satisfied with the re-entry of Iraq into the regional political equation.

A renewed sense of optimism developed among Palestinians in the Occupied Territories during Saddam Hussein's February 1990 visit to Jordan to mark the first anniversary of the Arab Cooperation Council, an economic union forged among Jordan, Iraq, and the PLO. In a speech transmitted over Jordanian television and broadcast throughout the Occupied Territories, Saddam Hussein essentially condemned the West for its unwavering support of Israel and called upon all Arabs to unite in the struggle against the United States. Reacting to Saddam's speech, inhabitants of the West Bank and Gaza Strip began to pin their hopes on Iraq as the new power in the region that could liberate them from the yoke of Israeli occupation.

Political dynamics both inside and outside the Occupied Territories pushed Arafat into taking a nonretractable, hard-line position vis-à-vis the West. Inside the Occupied Territories, increased Israeli settlement activity along with Palestinian concern over the policies of the Likud government (which proved to be more hard-line than the previous Labor-Likud coalition), coupled with the influx of Soviet Jews, fueled both discontent and despair. In Gaza, severe economic pressures, in addition to the renewed threat of expulsions when the far-right Moledet Party gained seats in the new Israeli government, added to Palestinian despair.[19] The PLO also had to consider the increased activities of Hamas in both Gaza and the West Bank.

In the aftermath of the foiled May 30, 1990, raid on an Israeli beach by members of the Palestine Liberation Front (PLF), Washington pressured Arafat to condemn the PLF leader of the attack, Abu 'Abbas. With a growing belief that renewed violence, or a return to armed struggle, might be the only solution for the Palestinian dilemma, the PLO leadership was faced with a decision: Bow to US pressures to punish Abu 'Abbas as a condition for maintaining a one-sided dialogue or heed the growing discontent in the Occupied Territories over the PLO's continued accommodationist behavior toward the West. In June 1990, when Arafat refused to punish Abu 'Abbas, the United States suspended its eighteen-month dialogue with the PLO.

Following the Iraqi invasion of Kuwait in August 1990, demonstrations in support of Saddam Hussein broke out in the Occupied Territories. One of the driving mechanisms behind the public support of Saddam was the "linkage-issue," in which the Iraqi withdrawal from Kuwait was conditional upon the Israeli withdrawal from the West Bank and Gaza. Hamas was particularly active during this time, distributing leaflets in the territories that called on all Palestinians to take their struggle to Israeli soil and for Baghdad to attack Tel Aviv if the West attacked Iraq.[20] Even though the PLO was attempting to distance itself from its alignment with Iraq, it could not ignore the grassroots support that Palestinians expressed for Saddam without risking its legitimacy in the eyes of its primary constituency. In addition to pro-Iraqi demonstrations, the Palestinians held strikes to protest the US military presence in the Gulf, responding to an event that had transformed itself from a regional dispute into an international conflict.[21]

At the international level, the US veto of a proposed UN resolution calling for an observer force in the Occupied Territories following the Rishon Le Zion killings in Gaza in May 1990 and the inability of the PLO to pressure the UN Security Council to condemn the Haram al-Sharif murders of October 1990 in harsher terms contributed to the PLO's closer alignment with Iraq. The PLO leadership had no other option but to accept the position imposed on it by regional events and its constituency in the Occupied Territories and align with the Iraqi camp during the Gulf war. The PLO paid a heavy price for its decision not to side with the US led coalition against Saddam Hussein. The effect of that decision left the PLO politically and financially isolated in the postwar environment that promised a new world order in the Middle East.

The Postwar Environment

Following the Gulf war, President Bush announced that the United States was prepared to pursue a peaceful settlement of the Arab-Israeli conflict. The PLO, however, found itself without a direct role in the proposed peace conference initiated by the United States. What appeared to be a combined US, Arab, and Israeli attempt to bypass the PLO (and Arafat in particular) was met with a measure of resistance by Palestinians. The PLO's main card continued to be the legitimacy and support it received from its constituency in the Occupied Territories.

A renewed but limited opportunity presented itself when the United States announced that a Palestinian delegation would be allowed to attend the peace conference jointly sponsored by the United States and Soviet Union, scheduled to convene at Madrid. The only remaining question was the role that the PLO would exercise in the process. Operating through a Palestinian delegation, the PLO presented Secretary of State Baker with a list of questions when he met with Palestinian representatives Faisal Husseini, Hanan Ashrawi, and Zakariya al-Agha in Jerusalem on July 21, 1991. Among the points that the PLO wanted clarified was the exact role it would be allowed to exercise in the upcoming peace process.[22]

Although no direct role for the PLO was forthcoming, its leadership was willing to operate behind the scenes provided that Washington give its assurance that the peace conference would be based on Resolution 242. The PLO, however, still insisted on its right to appoint Palestinian delegates to the conference. The 20th PNC convened in Algiers in September 1991 and formally endorsed Palestinian participation at the Madrid conference. The PLO's willingness to exercise a limited role in the peace process was partly the result of its weakened position following the Gulf war. PLO thinking was guided by the belief that participation, albeit indirect, could help break the organization's diplomatic isolation. In addition, the collapse of the Soviet Union in August 1991 translated into the loss of a valuable counterweight to US hegemony. In essence, the organization was left without any effective alternatives. On October 13, 1991, the PLO Executive Committee gave its approval for a joint Palestinian-Jordanian delegation.

On October 18, 1991, the United States sent an official invitation to the Palestinian delegation from the Occupied Territories to attend the Madrid conference. Included in the invitation were Washington's three demands for Palestinian participation: no PLO officials, no Palestinians from outside the Occupied Territories, no Palestinians from Jerusalem.[23]

In the absence of an official role for the PLO, Arafat endorsed the attendance of the Palestinian negotiating team. Perceptions among the Palestinian negotiators at the start of the conference rested on the belief that the United States was finally committed to work for a fair and equitable solution to the Israeli-Palestinian conflict. This line of thought rested on the conviction that the demise of the cold war had lessened Israel's strategic importance to the United States. By the end of the first round of bilateral talks, however, the Palestinian negotiators' initial optimism had faded. In a December 1991 press conference held in Jerusalem, the delegates concluded that the continued success of the peace process would require the active participation of the United States. In their view, a stronger US role was needed, especially since Israel demonstrated a lack of commitment to the peace process, evidenced by the Jewish state's refusal to negotiate separately with the Palestinian delegation.

Despite the lack of a strong US role and the absence of any tangible gains, the PLO continued to endorse Palestinian participation in the subsequent rounds of the conference. In retrospect, the PLO's approach to this process leading up to the signing of the Declaration of Principles can be divided into two distinct phases: the Shamir phase and the Rabin phase.

The Shamir Phase

The Shamir phase produced a minor PLO policy success in that it marked the first time that Palestinians were officially seated at the negotiating table with the other parties to the conflict. Notwithstanding this public relations success, the terms of Palestinian participation had situated the negotiators at an unfair disadvantage vis-à-vis the other negotiating teams. In terms of this disadvantage, the PLO had no other choice but to accept a restricted delegation in lieu of a visible role because Israel had effectively set the terms.[24]

Also, the initial optimism held by the Palestinian negotiating team at the start of the conference soon gave way to frustration and dwindling public support, especially among the inhabitants of the Occupied Territories. In their assessment of the first round, the Palestinian negotiators expressed the belief that the United States was not exercising an impartial role. Moreover, the talks had failed to yield the momentum that Secretary of State Baker believed would be generated merely by bringing the parties to the negotiating table.[25] It should be noted, however, that it was never the intention of the United States to impose a solution on the parties to the conflict. Instead, the United States viewed its role in the peace process as a "catalyst" that would merely bring the parties together by ironing out procedural differences rather than concentrate on substantive affairs.[26]

As the peace rounds progressed, opposition against continued Palestinian participation came from Hamas and the Damascus-based Palestine National Salvation Front (PNSF), which comprised various PLO bureaucratic factions. Discontent also existed over Israel's policy of continued settlement activity, the increase in human rights violations, and a growing economic crisis. The United States regained a measure of credibility among the Palestinians when President Bush linked the issue of Israel's $10 billion loan guarantee request to a halt in additional settlement building. This small opportunity, however, soon faded as the reality of the talks continued to leave the Palestinians without any concrete gains.

Israel's rejection of the Palestinian proposal for self-rule and the change in the status of the West Bank and Gaza—from occupied lands to disputed lands—necessitated a change in PLO strategy. Part of that centered around discussions regarding possible confederation with Jordan, which triggered an internal debate that threatened to divide the negotiating team. The core of this debate was the issue of whether to achieve Palestinian statehood before or after confederation. In an effort to quell disagreement, Arafat's political adviser, Nabil Sha'th, stated that any plans for confederation automatically presupposed the existence of an independent Palestinian state in accordance with the resolutions adopted by the 19th PNC (1988).[27]

In May 1992, the PLO Central Council endorsed the organization's continued participation in the peace process despite the barrage of criticisms from the bureaucratic factions.[28] Particularly vocal were representatives of the PFLP and Nayef Hawatma's faction of the DFLP, which charged that the PLO's current negotiating strategy had not only sidestepped the issue of the 1948 refugees but also failed to expand the terms of PLO participation to include Palestinians from East Jerusalem at the multilateral rounds. Moreover, the bureaucratic groups accused the PLO leadership of failing to bring to a halt Israel's settlement activities.[29]

The Rabin Phase

The PLO responded to the formation of the new Israeli government in July 1992 under the premiership of Yitzhak Rabin with a mixture of relief and caution. The Labor Party's victory at the polls offered some measure of relief from the hard-line policies of the Likud regime. For many Palestinians, however, the memory of Rabin's "iron-fist" policy at the start of the *intifada* provoked caution. Moreover, any optimism the Palestinians might have held at the start of this phase dissolved following Rabin's July 13 inaugural address to the Israeli Knesset, in which he outlined Labor's basic policy.[30] Included in this policy was an offer of Palestinian autonomy, along the lines of the Camp David accords, without the possibility of statehood. Rabin was also emphatic about the nonnegotiable status of Jerusalem. Additionally, the prime minister alluded to a distinction between security and political settlements when he noted that Israel would continue its settlement activity in areas "along the confrontation lines due to their security importance."

As the peace talks progressed, Arafat came under increasing pressure from the bureaucratic members of the PNSF, including Hamas, to withdraw from the peace process altogether. The PLO leader was further constrained when the United States announced in November 1992 its approval of the $10 billion in loan guarantees to Israel. Israel's expulsion of 417 alleged Hamas supporters in December 1992 granted the PLO an opportunity to temporarily withdraw from the peace process in the face of mounting bureaucratic pressures. Despite the brief moment of internal unity sparked by the deportations, the PLO was unable to prevail and hold out for a total return of the deportees as a condition to its returning to the talks. Aside from the opposition voiced by the bureaucratic groups, members of the PLO's negotiating team, including chief negotiator Haydar Abd al-Shafi, threatened to resign if Arafat did not reject Rabin's initial offer to return 100 deportees.

The change in US presidential administrations (Democrats regained the White House in January 1993 with the election of Bill Clinton) signaled the possibility of a return to a climate of opportunity for the PLO. Clinton's apparent interest in maintaining the peace process along with his pledge to commit the United States to work as a "full partner" portended an opportunity for the PLO to regain the initiative at the negotiating table. However, Clinton's key appointments, as well as his refusal to press Israel to abide by UN Security Council Resolution 799 (which both condemned the deportations of the 417 Islamic activists and called for their immediate return), damaged the credibility of the United States to act as a "fair partner" in the peace process.

Because history affords one an invaluable look at the past, it is understandable now why Arafat insisted on continued Palestinian participation during these rounds of the peace process despite growing pressures to withdraw. At the PLO internal level, the issue of the deportations, rising apathy in the Occupied Territories, the loss of employment, the severe economic crisis that resulted from Israel's closure of the West Bank and Gaza, the increase in human rights violations, and the gains made by Hamas played heavily on Arafat's continued leadership. Externally, bureaucratic opposition to Arafat's unilateral style of leadership, the financial unreliability of Arab regimes, as well as talk of possible Israeli-Syrian rapprochement further constrained the leadership of the PLO from regaining the initiative over its foreign policy. In light of these pressures, Arafat seized upon the opportunity that the newly opened Oslo channel had afforded.

During the Rabin phase Arafat sidestepped Washington and opted for private rather than public channels of diplomacy. The factors that precipitated Arafat's detour through Oslo are not exceedingly complex. They do, however, underscore the PLO's consideration of the Occupied Territories as the primary mechanism guiding the formation of foreign policy along with Arafat's undaunted determination to re-tain the initiative over the outcome of PLO policy despite mounting opposition to his leadership.

From Public to Private Channels of Diplomacy

As Palestinian negotiators maintained a public diplomatic appearance in Washing-ton, Arafat simultaneously embarked on a private diplomatic gamble by giving the green light to one of his top aides, Abu Alaa, to pursue the back-channel approach through Oslo in search of a separate agreement with the Israelis.[31]

The PLO's foreign policy "success" at Oslo is the result of the opportunities that the closed nature of diplomacy provided. The opportunities afforded by the Oslo channel essentially removed the constraints placed on Arafat's ability to act in a pub-lic diplomatic forum. Moreover, the nature of private diplomacy allowed him to po-sition the PLO on the initiating rather than receiving end of foreign policy. In this type of environment, the PLO is more open to compromise and accommodation, evidenced by the stipulations to which Arafat had to agree prior to Israel's final ac-ceptance of the Declaration of Principles.

Critics of Arafat maintain that he negotiated away the rights of Diaspora Pales-tinians, particularly the 1948 refugees' right to return, in deference to the Occupied Territories. In addition, Arafat's agreement to postpone discussion on the status of Jerusalem and his inability to resolve the settlement issue have intensified the oppo-sition to his leadership. The DFLP keenly observed that the PLO under Arafat rep-resents only some, rather than all, Palestinians. However, since the outbreak of the *intifada* and the rise of Hamas as a credible threat, it is not difficult to understand Arafat's isolated preoccupation with the West Bank and Gaza to the detriment of the organization's Diaspora constituency.

Opportunities and Obstacles

The Declaration of Principles served for a time to temporize the situation in the Oc-cupied Territories; however, Arafat's leadership remained in jeopardy because of lack of progress in implementing the phases of the accord and a significant upgrading of the standard of living for the Islamist Palestinian group in the Occupied Territories, especially in the Gaza Strip. The Islamist Palestinian group, Hamas, galvanized and led the opposition to Arafat's approach. The challenge to his chairmanship intensi-fied following the additional concessions he provided Israel in Cairo on February 14, 1994, as a means to facilitate the implementation of the Gaza-Jericho First Plan. Arafat's foremost predicament was his need to rebuild internal unity in order to forge a consensus for his incremental approach to solving the Israeli-Palestinian con-flict. After the massacre at Hebron on February 24, 1994, Arafat took a more hard-line approach by insisting that the issue of the Israeli settlements be addressed as a precondition for returning to the negotiating table. Although he retained the initiative for the moment, Arafat was not operating in a climate of political opportunity. Instead, the political environment remained essentially threat-driven.

Although there appeared to be some measure of consensus among the PLO's bureaucratic groups and constituencies for the organization's approach, Arafat's ability to maintain the initiative depended in part on continued progress. However, despite continued progress in negotiations with Israel to implement the Declaration of Principles, such as the September 28, 1995, self-rule accord (which provided for the withdrawal of Israeli troops from the West Bank, therefore extending limited autonomy to the area under the PLO, as well as calling for Palestinian elections in January 1996), the dynamics at the time indicated that unless Arafat provided some measure of economic and political relief to the PLO's West Bank and Gaza constituency, there would be a return to the militant roles that served the organization well in its earlier stages of development—an approach long abandoned by the PLO's more moderate leadership but, as evidenced by the al-Aqsa *intifada,* one that was adopted after September 2000, especially by the younger generation of Palestinians frustrated by the lack of success by the elder leadership and emboldened by the Hizbollah example in south Lebanon.

It is tempting to explain the deadlock in the talks during the Netanyahu years (1996–1999) by reciting the all-too-familiar litany of Israeli transgressions and persistent demands that the PLO/PA (Palestinian Authority) leadership was responsible for keeping the process at a standstill. Moreover, it is equally inviting to lay blame on the unwillingness of the United States to exert more influence on the Likud-led coalition government of Benjamin Netanyahu to implement the second-phase redeployment of troops in the West Bank by withdrawing from at least an additional 13 percent of the area—a compromise figure proposed by the United States. However, notwithstanding such factors as Israeli settlement expansion in the Har Homa area of East Jerusalem, increased housing demolitions, and Palestinian land expropriation alongside the seemingly ineffectual foreign policy of the Clinton administration in the region, the PLO/PA leadership was more in need of a modification in its own approach to peace rather than waiting for its counterparts to forge change. Specifically, the PLO/PA leadership needed to reevaluate its outmoded foreign policy behavior that was primarily based on pragmatism. Although this type of behavior served the organization well in the late 1980s and seemingly throughout the early 1990s, pragmatism was not able to foster greater Palestinian political support in either Washington, D.C., or Tel Aviv. Moreover, with the untimely assassination of Prime Minister Rabin in November 1995 and the narrow electoral loss of Labor's acting prime minister, Shimon Peres, to a Likud-led government under Prime Minister Netanyahu in May 1996, Arafat essentially lost two negotiating partners who were committed to peace and receptive to this type of policy approach. Additionally, given the complex Palestinian domestic political environment that also shapes the peace process, it is little wonder that Arafat's pragmatic foreign policy endured in the absence of an opportunistic political climate in which Arafat could take an initiatory role and advance Palestinian political and economic goals.

Instead, Arafat took his policy of pragmatism and dropped it on the doorstep of the Clinton administration in what was apparently a vain hope that the United States would resolve the problem. However, this type of foreign policy behavior was neither pragmatic nor capable of fostering an opportunistic political environment for the PLO leadership. Instead, this approach was subservient and conciliatory because it located the PLO leadership on the receiving end rather than the initiatory side of the foreign policy process. If the past is prologue, this pattern of behavior was reminiscent of the approach to foreign policy that the organization was forced to adopt following the 1991 Gulf war and the subsequent rounds of the Madrid peace talks. Ultimately, it was the lack of progress during those talks that led Arafat to pursue private rather than public forums of diplomacy in which he initiated accommodation and compromise to reach an agreement with Israel that resulted in the Declaration of Principles.

However, the environment in which Arafat was attempting to steer the Palestinian people toward statehood in the latter half of the 1990s was not the same political arena as the 1991 post–Gulf war setting. For one, the Israeli leadership was neither amenable nor politically able to seek compromise and accommodation with the Palestinians. Benjamin Netanyahu's and Ariel Sharon's version of the peace process seemed based on a strategy of delaying as long as possible any further Israeli redeployment in the West Bank. In addition to offering Arafat withdrawal figures that left the Palestinian president little room for compromise, Netanyahu proposed an Israeli referendum on the subject of withdrawal.

Another factor that changed after the Gulf war was the nature of Palestinian domestic politics. Arafat's penchant for unilateral decisionmaking in private diplomatic forums was not compatible with the openness of a democratic system that, at least electorally, made its formal appearance in the Occupied Territories. In January 1996, Palestinian voters elected Arafat to the office of the presidency of the PA along with a mandate for maintaining the peace process with Israel through diplomacy. Even though, at that time, public opinion in the West Bank and Gaza remained supportive of continued negotiations with Israel over the use of more unconventional forms of participation, there was a corresponding deterioration of the economic situation among Palestinians that tended to reverse this trend.[32]

To maintain the status quo of pursuing peace, Arafat had to walk a fine line between pragmatism and conciliation. The distinction between the two was a matter of perception. Whereas the United States cautiously approved the 21st PNC's (April 1996) decision to amend clauses in the Palestine National Charter that questioned the legitimacy of Israel as a state, critics of the decision charge that it was an empty act of conciliation for which the Palestinians received nothing in return. In the deadlock of the peace process, perceptions, alongside economic and political realities among the PLO/PA's constituency and disaffected groups, mattered considerably. Particularly key were the democratic undercurrents among a growing disaffected constituency that could wave ballots of political accountability at their "elected" leaders should Arafat's pragmatic conciliation fail to produce tangible results. The members of the Palestine Legislative Council (PLC) seemed to understand the dynamics of representative democracy more than Arafat; for example, in 1996, amid allegations of corruption and lack of progress in the peace process, members of the PLC threatened to call for a vote of no-confidence against Arafat's administration. The PLC decided to postpone this action for a few weeks, pending Arafat's voluntary offer to reshuffle his self-rule cabinet.

Among the PLO/PA's disaffected groups, the DFLP remained steadfast in its unwillingness to endorse the government created by Oslo and, along with the PFLP, advocated a reformulation of PLO strategy that seemingly did not include compromise. However, the more tenacious threat to Arafat's leadership and the peace process in general remained the suicide bombings and other anti-Israeli militant activities being carried out by Islamic Jihad and Hamas (the bombings carried out by Hamas in Israel in early 1996 are evidence of this fact).

In the year preceding Netanyahu's electoral defeat in May 1999, the peace process once again remained at a virtual standstill. Arafat delivered his all-too-familiar mantra that consisted of calling on the Israeli government to implement the previous US-brokered initiative by withdrawing from an additional 13 percent in the West Bank while simultaneously pleading with the Clinton administration to revive the stalled talks. Clinton responded in his typical Washington style by dispatching Dennis Ross, US Special Envoy to the Middle East, for yet another round of what would eventually prove to be futile diplomacy. Because the Clinton administration never provided Ross with any viable options for use as leverage against Israeli inflexibility, his main task appeared to consist of extracting additional concessions from Arafat along with promises for a renewed US-backed initiative for peace. When viewed in hindsight, the US–PLO/PA relationship throughout the Clinton administration exhibited a cyclical pattern of foreign policy stalemate followed by periodic breakthroughs. Furthermore, hindsight suggests that this was precisely the Clinton administration's intended approach to foreign policy as a player in the post-Oslo negotiations and especially during the last two years of Clinton's presidency.

On the part of the PLO/PA, Arafat's overreliance on the Clinton administration to sustain progress toward a shrinking vision of Palestinian statehood amid expanded settlement building began to resemble the dependency role that was reminiscent of the PLO's early years prior to Arafat's ascent. Moreover, Arafat's misguided foreign policy based entirely on conciliation unwillingly failed to foresee, let alone prevent, the return and reimposition of subservient role behavior vis-à-vis the PA's ostensible partners in peace. The effects of his outmoded foreign policy, coupled with rising domestic discontent, laid the groundwork for the al-Aqsa *intifada* that began in late September 2000.

As noted earlier in this chapter, feedback is an important component of the foreign policy process. One of the defining characteristics of the PLO's pre-Oslo approach to foreign policy was the particular attention that Arafat gave to this important variable as a factor determining the content and direction of foreign policy. However, in the post-Oslo environment, it appears that Arafat developed amnesia. In October 1998, the players in the peace process, including the late King Hussein of Jordan, assembled once more under US auspices at the Wye

River Plantation to hammer out yet another agreement on the final status talks. Arafat, under growing domestic pressure, hoped to secure the release of 2,200 Palestinian prisoners held in Israeli jails, along with further Israeli redeployment in the West Bank, and to ensure an end to Israel's continued land confiscation, housing demolition, and settlement building. Ariel Sharon, Israel's newly appointed foreign minister, insisted on further changes to the PLO's charter, a reduction in the size of the Palestinian police force, the confiscation of all illegal weapons, and the arrest and extradition of those waging attacks against Israelis.[33]

Despite the intensity of the negotiations, the partial agreement on security that the parties agreed to at Wye was fated to fail for a number of reasons. In the first place, feedback from previously signed agreements should have signaled to Arafat that Netanyahu had no intention of actually implementing the accord. In the absence of any foreign policy adjustment, the only real negotiating chip that Arafat could bring to Wye was the impractical threat of declaring a Palestinian state on May 5, 1999. The change to the PLO charter should have been a non-issue, because in 1996 the 21st PNC convened in Gaza to abrogate those sections of the PLO's national charter that were contrary to the letters exchanged between Israel and the PLO back in 1993. Furthermore, Arafat either miscalculated Clinton's intentions or overlooked the linkage between US domestic politics and Clinton's foreign policy agenda at Wye. On the domestic front, with midterm congressional elections only weeks away, Clinton needed a foreign policy success to soothe his domestic woes following the just-released Starr report that came on the heels of the Lewinsky scandal and the fallout from his decision in August to launch cruise missile strikes at targets in Sudan and Afghanistan in retaliation for the US embassy bombings in Kenya and Tanzania. Absent from Arafat's plate was any innovation or adjustment in PLO/PA foreign policy that may have allowed him to capitalize on this situation in an effort to counter Israeli intransigence and to advance Palestinian goals. Instead, conciliation and growing subservience once again determined the outcome for the PLO/PA.

Israeli elections in May 1999 brought Ehud Barak to power as prime minister. Despite the change from Likud to Labor, Barak would continue the delay tactics of his predecessor and initiate a new wave of West Bank settlement building. Even though Barak professed his commitment to reaching a final agreement with the Palestinians, the prime minister's conditions as a basis of negotiation contrasted with the PLO/PA's goals and objectives. Barak insisted that Israel would not return to the pre-1967 borders; that a united Jerusalem remained Israel's eternal capital; and that the settlements would remain under Israeli sovereignty.[34] If foreign policy is a learning process, then it should have become apparent to Arafat that the PLO/PA's foreign policy goals were consistently being shortchanged throughout the entire post-Oslo peace process. That alone should have necessitated either an adjustment in strategy or a change in the goals.

After more than six years' experience working with the Clinton administration, Arafat should have been able to accurately assess the US-PLO relationship relative to the US-Israel "special relationship." However, this would prove not to be the case.

By November 1999, following a round of summits, the Clinton administration once again found itself revitalizing the peace process for what presumably was to be the start of the final status talks. However, the "Framework Agreement" referred to by both Clinton and Barak merely shifted the deadline for final status talks to February 2000. This would be followed by a full agreement the following September, just prior to the November US presidential elections. Yet when the parties met in Ramallah on November 8, 1999, the PLO/PA negotiating team was dealt a major blow: Barak had announced to his cabinet on the previous day that UN Security Council Resolution 242 did not apply to the West Bank and Gaza and that settlement building would be expanded. Barak's instructions to the Framework Agreement negotiators at Ramallah merely reiterated the conditions he had set down previously as a basis for further negotiation, only now they were christened the "five red lines."[35] The chief negotiator for the Palestinians at Ramallah, Yasser Abd Rabboo, essentially played the conciliatory role, particularly when he yielded to Israel's right to claim their own interpretation of Resolution 242.

One question remains: Why did Arafat not recognize the reimposition of subservient role behavior and abandon conciliation in the absence of tangible gains by modifying PLO/PA foreign policy at this crucial juncture? Furthermore, what role choices did Arafat have at this juncture? Despite Arafat's assertion to the Arab world that the PLO/PA would not make further concessions, he was unable to excite a broader regional role in the peace process. Nor did Arafat attempt to reinvigorate the independent role by pursuing a possible back channel approach within the EU, where he generally enjoyed a wide measure of support. Instead, Arafat once again pinned his hopes on a greater US role in the peace process in the obstinate belief that the US would pressure Israel into conceding to Palestinian demands—a role that Clinton was not about to play.

Perhaps the key to understanding this dilemma resides in the Occupied Territories. Despite the PLO/PA's subservience in the peace process, public opinion in the West Bank and Gaza toward the peace process rose in December 1999 following the Framework Agreement talks, whereas opposition to the process declined. Moreover, Palestinian support for armed attacks against Israelis experienced a significant drop, from 45 percent in June 1999 to 36 percent in December, despite the harsh realities of daily life in the territories.[36] As noted earlier, Arafat remained under intense pressure to deliver some form of a Palestinian state in order to quell domestic dissent and mounting opposition to his rule. History has shown us that when Arafat was located on the receiving end of foreign policy, there was a loss of innovation in foreign policy.

Previous solutions to this dilemma consisted of reinvigorating the PLO's independent role; however, Arafat was not able to exercise this option while directing foreign policy from within the Occupied Territories. Moreover, pragmatism was no longer a policy option, given the dwindling benefits of such a role, and further conciliation could only lead to increased subservience. In many ways it is not difficult to comprehend why blame for failing to move forward in the peace process and the escalation of violence in both Israel and the Occupied Territories has fallen squarely on Arafat's misguided foreign policy.

On July 5, 2000, President Clinton announced a summit meeting that would convene on July 11 at Camp David in an eleventh-hour effort to move the peace process forward. Just days prior to Clinton's announcement, the PLO's Central Council met in Gaza and issued a communiqué authorizing Arafat to take whatever steps were necessary to ensure the realization of a Palestinian state by September 13.[37] Additionally, the Central Council's communiqué would form the basis of Arafat's negotiating position at Camp David and consisted of the following points, which were antithetical to Barak's previously stated "red lines": the right of return for Palestinian refugees or "adequate" compensation; Israel's adherence to UN Resolutions 242 and 338; the removal of Israeli settlements; and East Jerusalem as the capital of an independent Palestinian state. However, despite the concessions made by both sides, Camp David failed following Arafat's refusal to accept a demographic solution to the problem of Jerusalem's status that would have left the Palestinians with only "religious" sovereignty over Haram al-Sharif. It is generally known that Palestinians would rather have no agreement whatsoever with Israel than an agreement that gives them a state without East Jerusalem.[38] Hence, it came as no surprise that Ariel Sharon's provocative September 28 visit to Haram al-Sharif and Israel's severe military response to Palestinian protests triggered the outbreak of the al-Aqsa *intifada*.

In November 2000, under the threat of a US veto, the PLO/PA failed to get UN support for a peacekeeping force in the Occupied Territories. However, there was consensus for the formation of a fact-finding commission to investigate the violence as well as Israel's security concerns, which would be chaired by former US Senator George Mitchell. The committee submitted its findings, subsequently known as the "Mitchell Report," in April 2001. The committee concluded, inter alia, that their findings were consistent with the Palestinian perspective:

> The current crisis is the outgrowth of the consequences of Israel's illegal occupation of Palestinian territories, its systematic abuses of international humanitarian law, and its unwillingness to implement those measures agreed upon with the Palestinians over the last seven years designed to mitigate the worst of those consequences.[39]

Throughout the remaining few weeks of his presidency, Clinton made a last attempt to salvage the peace process. By this time the PLO/PA negotiators openly expressed the "pointless" nature of the talks.[40] In the meantime, armed resistance against Israelis by Palestinian popular resistance forces and Islamic Jihad suicide bombers increased, upcoming elections for prime minister in Israel portended to bring Sharon to power, and the change in US leadership would bring closure to one US-PLO relationship without any guarantee that the incoming US president would open another.

In January 2001, the mantle of the presidency passed to George W. Bush and his Republican-led administration. This change did not augur well for Arafat, given Bush's inexperience and his questionable interest in foreign affairs. Despite the continuation of the al-Aqsa *intifada*, Bush indicated that he would not take a forward role in brokering peace. In March, the United States demonstrated its lack of commitment to promoting peace by vetoing a UN Security Council resolution to establish a UN observer mission. Instead, Bush dispatched CIA Director George Tenet to the Occupied Territories in June to negotiate a cease-fire plan that was lambasted by both Hamas and Islamic Jihad for its failure to address the root of the violence.

Prior to the September 11, 2001, terrorist attacks against the United States, Arafat did not publicly call for an end to the violence, and speculation abounded that he was not able to quell the uprising because he had lost his leadership role. Despite Arafat's public statement condemning the September 11 attacks and his calls for a cease-fire and self-restraint among the Palestinians in the face of Israeli aggression, the nature of the attacks on the United States would change the political equation dramatically. The terrorist strikes on the World Trade Center and the Pentagon did not bode well for the Palestinian people; when televised images of Palestinians celebrating the attacks were broadcast around the world, public aversion to their cause followed. Nor did it aid their cause in any way when a video of Osama bin Laden referenced the Palestinian plight.

Unlike the *intifada* of December 1987 in which the PLO was able to reassert its leadership role over its constituency in the Occupied Territories, Arafat had not been directing the course of events. For Ariel Sharon, the events of September 11 allowed him to redefine Israel's policy of political assassinations, military incursions into Palestinian towns, aerial bombings, and the bulldozing of Palestinian lands from one designed to quell the violence associated with the al-Aqsa *intifada* into a policy to combat Palestinian terrorism against Israel. Additionally, the resumption of suicide bombing attacks committed inside Israel by Islamic Jihad in October 2001 and by Hamas in December 2001, along with the PFLP's killing of Rehavam Ze'evi on October 17 in retaliation against Israel's August targeted assassination of PFLP General Secretary Abu Ali Mustapha in Ramallah, seriously weakened Arafat's authority on the domestic front to bring an end to the violence. Both Israel and the United States placed full responsibility for ending the violence on Arafat. However, the only thing that Arafat had to offer the Palestinians in exchange for a halt to the violence was a temporary reprieve against Israel's siege and continued occupation. On December 12, 2001, Sharon's cabinet defined a new role for Arafat when it proclaimed him to be "irrelevant," yet the Palestinian leader was still expected to direct his police force to arrest suspected Palestinian terrorists and to end the violence against Israel. Arafat's public appeals to Hamas and Islamic Jihad were not effective and 2002 would witness an increase in suicide attacks both within Israel and in the Occupied Territories. Israel's professed retaliation against terrorist attacks ultimately led to a reoccupation of the Gaza Strip and Palestinian West Bank towns, including Ramallah, in which Operation Defensive Shield would leave Arafat trapped and "totally isolated" in his compound. With the PLO/PA structures in the Occupied Territories near collapse, Saudi Arabia's Crown Prince Abdallah announced an initiative for peace in February that was presented to the Arab League and subsequently adopted at their meeting in Beirut. In what would later be dubbed the Saudi Plan, Abdallah offered full

Arab normalization of relations with Israel in exchange for Israeli's full withdrawal from the territories it captured in the 1967 war.

As Sharon's cabinet discussed the possibility of "removing" Arafat, Bush's solution to the problem was not unlike his predecessor's; he dispatched his special envoy, Anthony Zinni, to the region to secure a cease-fire. As the violence intensified, the UN Security Council passed Resolution 1397 on March 12, with Syria abstaining, which called for an immediate end to the violence. Although the resolution is noteworthy because its preamble affirms the creation of a Palestinian state, it failed to address the root cause of the violence, namely, the occupation. The weakness of the resolution was confirmed two weeks later when the UN Security Council met again on March 30 and adopted Resolution 1402, following additional suicide attacks in Israel and the continued assault on Arafat's compound in Ramallah. Even though Resolution 1402 called for the implementation of Resolution 1397, along with an Israeli withdrawal from Palestinian cities, the absence of will among the international community to enforce Israeli compliance or set a timetable for withdrawal further intensified the situation.

With Arafat essentially cordoned in Ramallah, the Israeli army invaded the Jenin refugee camp in early April and laid siege to the camp in its effort to root out "terrorists." Outcries of a massacre in Jenin prompted the passage of UN Security Council Resolution 1405 on April 19, which authorized the UN Secretary General Kofi Annan to "develop accurate information regarding recent events in the Jenin refugee camp through a fact-finding 'team.'" Annan's efforts would be hamstrung, as the team encountered repeated delays in entering Jenin, owing to diplomatic deadlock over the actual composition and mandate of the team. Because the resolution was prompted by serious humanitarian concerns, the United States could not politically afford to exercise its veto power over the resolution. Instead, the United States maintained its public concern for the humanitarian dimension of the Jenin crisis, while demonstrating its support for Israel by backing a watered-down resolution that avoided the formation of a fact-finding "mission," preferring instead a "team" with considerably less, if any, authority to draw conclusions over what had transpired.[41] In exchange for the US-backed version of the resolution, which allowed Israel to escape public condemnation for its actions in Jenin, the Israeli cabinet accepted on April 28 a US proposal that would allow Arafat to emerge from his compound. However, this proposal was not a charitable act on the part of the Bush administration; President Bush had begun to publicly speak out against the chairman, blaming him personally for the failure to establish a Palestinian state, while hailing Sharon as a "man of peace," and the PLFP members who were confined with Arafat, among them Ahmed Saadat, were transferred to a jail in Jericho, where they would be monitored by US and British security personnel until their fate could be settled by Israel and the PA.[42]

Sharon's agreement to this proposal gained him an invitation from Bush to the White House, but while Arafat's physical survival was a tentative certainty, his political survival was in serious doubt. As Bush and Sharon met in Washington, the Israeli prime minister reiterated that he would not discuss peace until Palestinian violence ended and Arafat was removed from power. Further succumbing to US pressure, Arafat gave his approval for an agreement to end the siege of the Church of the Nativity, which meant either exile or confinement to Gaza for most of the Palestinians inside the compound.

In a weakened attempt to reassert his authority, Arafat called for reforms in the PA and new elections in the near future. If Arafat was banking on being able to exercise a role other than subservience by accepting responsibility for past mistakes and calling for broad PA reforms, he was mistaken. The content and direction of PLO/PA policy relative to Israel would now be formulated by the Bush administration under the auspices of the Quartet, which included the United States, the European Union, Russia, and the UN. In what would become a prelude to the "Road Map," Bush's speech on June 24, 2002, spelled out the necessary conditions that the Palestinians must meet if they aspired to "provisional" statehood. In addition to ending terrorism and a complete cessation of Palestinian violence, Bush also endorsed regime change in the PA; he essentially told the Palestinian people that they needed "new and different leadership," though he did not mention Arafat specifically.[43] As Bush was laying out his myopic vision of a conditional Palestinian state, Israel began construction of the separation wall on confiscated Palestinian lands, and its re-occupation of the West Bank towns of Nablus, Jenin, Qalqilya, Tulkarm, Ramallah, and Bethlehem, and later Hebron, became more entrenched.

Although there was supposed to be an international effort to draft a document that would lead to a permanent two-state solution, it was the US draft that was circulated among the members of the Quartet as well as Sharon and the PA. Owing to the numerous objections raised by Sharon on the draft document, finalization did not take place in time for the scheduled meeting of the Quartet in December 2002. The Bush administration sought delays until after the February 2003 Israeli elections, which subsequently returned Sharon to power. Additionally, the Bush administration delayed finalizing the Road Map until the conclusion of what it thought would be a quick war in Iraq, which began in March 2003. Liberating the Iraqi people from Saddam Hussein would tie in nicely with the Bush administration's broader vision of Middle East peace predicated on freedom and democracy. The Road Map also had to wait until a "credible" prime minister was appointed by the PA, a leader who could curb the violence of Hamas and usher in reforms. Although the PLO/PA was willing to surrender to US demands, Hamas had no intention of exercising an accommodationist or subservient role vis-à-vis the United States and would not end the violence without reciprocal guarantees from Israel. Despite Egypt's attempts to coordinate talks between Hamas and Fatah toward the end of 2002 and to forge a "unilateral truce" on a trial basis as a means to test Israeli intentions, Hamas refused to cooperate.[44]

In March, the PLO's Central Council approved the creation of the position of prime minister and accepted Arafat's nominee, Mahmoud Abbas, secretary general of the PLO, to fill the post. Even though Abbas was subsequently confirmed by the PLC as prime minister, Arafat remained PLO chairman and was responsible for foreign policy and "national security." Abbas's formal duties were limited to governance and the maintenance of public order in the self-rule areas. Abbas was thought to lack a popular base of support both within the Occupied Territories and among the Diaspora, and his legitimacy rested on the fact that he was a founding member of Fatah and appointed by Arafat. Yet Bush publicly approved of the "new leader" and hoped to release the Road Map once Abbas formed a new cabinet.

Even though Abbas was not successful in bridging the divide among Hamas, Islamic Jihad, and the PFLP by inviting them to participate in his new government, his more difficult challenge would be fostering internal unity within the ranks of his own faction, Fatah, over his reshuffling of the PA cabinet, which excluded posts for several Arafat loyalists. Abbas assuaged the divide between the younger generation, who grew up under occupation, and the old guard within Fatah. Both factions recognized that short term conciliation and a return to the process of peace talks would reveal Sharon's true intentions. Had Abbas not been an architect of the PLO's Oslo process, this assumption would have bordered on naïveté. As expected, Sharon's April 13 interview in *Ha'aretz* foreshadowed his dismissive view of Abbas and his tentative support of the Road Map when he indicated that there were "principles" that Washington would have to agree to before the Road Map was formally announced.[45] Without any viable alternative to initiate a process, Abbas formally embraced the Road Map at Sharm el-Sheikh in June 2003. The US inclusion of most of Sharon's principles in the final version not only destined the document to failure but would weaken an already conciliatory Abbas, while politically strengthening Hamas and its unambiguous program based on "resistance."

Officially titled "A Performance-Based Road Map to a Permanent Two-State Solution to the Israeli-Palestinian Conflict," the Road Map was significant because it marked the first time that the UN had been directly involved in peace negotiations. However, both the substance and prospects for the Road Map's implementation were seriously flawed. The plan was laid out in three phases, and the first phase, which would last through May 2003, called on the Palestinians to "undertake comprehensive political reform in preparation for statehood," which would be built upon the drafting of a new constitution and "free, fair, and open elections." With respect to security, the first phase demanded that both Israel and Palestinians end violence, but it was the Palestinians who were directed to end "terrorism" and dismantle their infrastructure.[46]

Throughout the six months of phase two, the Palestinians could expect a state with "provisional borders and attributes of sovereignty," as theoretically spelled out in the new constitution that would already be drafted at this time. Moreover, it asserted that the means of attaining this goal were to be predicated on a leadership that would act "decisively against terror" and commit to the mechanisms and substance of democracy, whose performance would be judged by a "consensus" of the Quartet. It is here that the fault lines were drawn. The Bush administration missed the mark completely with its assumption that the Palestinians in the Occupied Territories valued *democratic* freedom over freedom from occupation. Nowhere does the Road Map mention that the root cause of the violence against Israel stems from the occupation. Moreover, if the Bush administration was banking on Abbas's ability to deliver "democracy" as a precondition for a provisional state, they either misunderstood or ignored Abbas's intentions behind his acceptance of the Road Map.

The third phase, which would culminate in 2005, was supposed to produce a permanent status resolution on the issues of borders, the status of Jerusalem, Palestinian refugees, and Jewish settlements. Even though UN Security Council Resolutions 242, 338, and the more recent 1397 would form the basis of the final resolution, the PLO/PA in 1999 had conceded to Israel under Barak the right to Israel's own interpretation of 242 and its non-applicability to the West Bank and Gaza Strip. Hence, the PLO/PA was under no illusion that just because Resolution 242 was included in the Road Map that it actually meant that Israel would withdraw to the pre-1967 borders, especially given the path of the separation wall. Lastly, on the issue of the Palestinian refugees, the Road Map does not specifically mention UN General Assembly Resolution 194 or other instruments of international law that uphold the Palestinian refugees' right of return. The Road Map calls for an "agreed, fair, and realistic solution to the refugee issue"—absent any reference to a *just* solution.[47] Although Sharon wanted a clause in which the PLO/PA would have to abrogate the right of return for refugees, *Ha'aretz* reported that Washington did not agree with Sharon on this point.[48] Conciliation on the issue of the refugees by any PLO/PA leader has its limits. Abbas, and perhaps Washington, recognized that all too well. Throughout the Oslo period, as Arafat repeatedly weakened the refugees' *political* rights, he understood that the PLO's legitimacy as representative of all Palestinians would never allow him to abrogate their *legal* rights. That Abbas didn't press Washington for stronger language on the refugees (and other issues) as a condition for his acceptance of the Road Map established his political limitations relative to his Israeli counterpart. It also reflected his somewhat pragmatic assessment that the suicide bombings and other violent attacks carried out by Hamas, Islamic Jihad, the al-Aqsa Martyrs Brigade, and others were ultimately no match against the Israeli Defense Forces, which would account for his repeated calls to end the violence. Focused more on the need to generate a process to halt the retaliatory devastation in the Occupied Territories, Abbas had no other choice but to pragmatically choose a subservient role as a way out of the impasse. The fundamental difference between Abbas and Arafat was that Arafat would have extracted concessions for his subservience, such as securing the release of Palestinian prisoners held in Israeli jails, whereas Abbas could not.

For Abbas, accepting the Road Map proved easier than implementing its provisions. Abbas's June speech at Aqaba, in which he announced that the *intifada* must end and denounced terrorism against Israel, only reinforced his subservience to the United States. He was fiercely criticized by Hamas for what he didn't say at Aqaba, such as his failure to affirm the rights of the refugees and the importance of Jerusalem. Israel's attempted assassination of Dr. Rantisi just days after the Sharm el-Sheikh and Aqaba summits seriously eroded support for Abbas's policy. It was Egypt that would help broker a three-month truce between Hamas and Islamic Jihad that lasted barely seven weeks. Less than three months following his acceptance of the Road Map, Abbas tendered his resignation, and he was replaced by Ahmed

Qurai. The collapse of the cease-fire, along with Sharon's December announcement at the Herzilya conference indicating that Israel would impose its own solution on the Palestinians in the form of unilateral disengagement, ensured that the Road Map would become a diplomatic memory. Qurai, powerless to engage the United States or to arrange a meeting with Sharon, once again looked to Egypt to negotiate a truce. Qurai soon proved incapable of charting a viable foreign policy owing to growing disorder within the PLO/PA and the rising popular discontent over his failure to address the wanton destruction inflicted on the Occupied Territories.

Instead, it was Hamas that articulated a consistent position by insisting that Israel end targeted assassinations, arrests, and incursions into the Occupied Territories as a condition for stopping attacks against civilians inside Israel. The Bush administration was equally "disengaged," as Bush became preoccupied with the war in Iraq, the revelation that no weapons of mass destruction were found in Iraq, and his own presidential re-election campaign.

The year 2003 came to a close with the International Court of Justice (ICJ) agreeing to give an advisory opinion on the separation wall at the request of the UN General Assembly. The wall or "security fence" constructed by Israel is intended to prevent Palestinian attacks emanating from the West Bank. The ICJ set January 30, 2004, as the deadline for the submission of written briefs and February 23 for oral arguments. Because of the PLO's observer status at the UN, Palestinians were allowed to take part in the ICJ's proceedings. The ICJ issued its nonbinding opinion on July 9, ruling that segments of the wall that were built on Occupied Territory violated international law and therefore should be removed or not built. Even though the Palestinians achieved a political victory with the ICJ's ruling, Sharon was not compliant, and construction on the wall continued.

Within the span of one month, Israel assassinated two prominent Hamas leaders: Sheik Yasin, the organization's quadriplegic spiritual leader was targeted on March 22, and Abdel Aziz Rantisi, who emerged as Hamas's official spokesperson, on April 17. Despite international criticism of Yasin's assassination, the UN Security Council failed to pass a resolution condemning Israel for this extrajudicial act because of a US veto. The assassinations, however, allowed Hamas to unify its program around several core goals that would define its role precisely and lead to a rise in popularity among Palestinians in the Occupied Territories. These goals included the use of armed resistance to liberate the West Bank and Gaza Strip, the rejection of any cease-fire without reciprocal guarantees by Israel, and a willingness to accept an interim solution ending hostilities provisional upon Israel's full withdrawal from the Occupied Territories. These core goals and their accompanying roles, such as armed struggle, independence, and pragmatism without conciliation, were familiar to Palestinians because they were roles that the PLO adopted—but shelved—years ago. Hamas's unwillingness to compromise on its goal of ending the occupation widened its base of support at the expense of the Fatah-led PLO/PA. Sharon's meeting with Bush in April 2004 and his announcement that he was willing to make "painful concessions" and to disengage from the Gaza Strip reinforced the primacy of Hamas's goal of armed struggle over the illusion of negotiations as a means to end the Israeli occupation. From Hamas's viewpoint, Israel's willingness to withdraw from the Gaza Strip meant that armed resistance was effective.[49] Additionally, Bush's support for Sharon's plan and the assurances that he provided Sharon at their April meeting dissolved any expectation on the part of the PLO/PA that the United States was even remotely committed to the Road Map. Bush's guarantee that he would not support a return of the refugees to homes or land inside Israel and that "existing population centers" (settlements) in the West Bank would remain under Israeli sovereignty effectively undercut the work of two previous US administrations (George H. W. Bush and Bill Clinton) to engage the Palestinians in a negotiated settlement of the Israeli-Palestinian conflict.

As the Abu Ghraib prison abuse scandal began to preoccupy the Bush administration and with the other members of the Quartet signaling their support for the disengagement plan, Israel launched Operation Rainbow in the Gaza Strip, aimed at clearing out Palestinian militants before the withdrawal. Palestinian anger at the carnage inflicted was aimed at Qurai, who was meeting with Secretary of State Colin Powell and National Security Advisor Condoleezza Rice. The United States was no longer interested in reiterating demands that Palestinians curb violence as a precondition for resuming talks; instead Qurai was informed that the Bush administration supported Sharon's disengagement plan, while Powell absurdly stated that Bush would still adhere to the guidelines of the Road Map and supported a two-state solution.[50]

On October 29, 2004, the critically ill Arafat left Ramallah for a Paris hospital but not before authorizing Abbas to assume the responsibilities of the PLO and Fatah in the West Bank and Gaza Strip. On Tuesday, November 2, Bush narrowly won reelection, and on November 10, Arafat died in a hospital in Paris. The following day, the PLO Executive Committee voted for Abbas to assume the position of PLO chairman, and plans were set in motion to hold PA presidential elections within two months. In a prelude to the upcoming PA presidential elections, Abbas, Fatah's official presidential candidate, along with Qurai, met with Syrian President Bashar al-Asad to hold reconciliation talks. They also traveled to Lebanon to meet with President Emile Lahoud and to visit refugee camps that are Fatah strongholds, where they vowed to uphold the right of return.[51] On January 9, 2005, Abbas won the PA presidential election with 62 percent of the vote but without the participation of Hamas or Islamic Jihad. Following his swearing in a week later, Abbas reappointed Qurai as his prime minister, declared his intent to hold elections for the legislature in the summer, and called for talks with Sharon to move beyond the Road Map and in the direction of final status talks.

Abbas's electoral victory renewed interest by the Bush administration in once again becoming engaged in the peace process. Purportedly, Washington's turnaround and Bush's willingness to consider Abbas a "partner for peace" was based on the 1995 Beilin–Abu Mazen unsigned agreement that had formed the basis of Clinton's "generous offer" at Camp David, which Arafat adamantly rejected. Bush assumed that because Arafat was no longer an obstacle, Abbas would be a compliant partner in promoting the Road Map while simultaneously supporting Sharon's grand designs. In an editorial published shortly after the PA presidential elections, Abbas's counterpart to the agreement, Yossi Beilin, praised Abbas as a man committed to achieving peace and ending violence. However, Beilin cautioned that Abbas's success hinged on the willingness of the United States, Europe, and Israel to become fully engaged in the peace process. Beilin stressed that the United States must do more than articulate rhetorical support for a Road Map with artificial deadlines and that the Bush administration needed to be actively involved, with clear "political vision." Beilin further urged Sharon to halt his brutal occupation tactics and to stop behaving as if Arafat were still his negotiating partner; otherwise, Israel would lose a valuable opportunity.[52]

In May 2005, Bush welcomed Abbas to the White House. In contrast to his support for Sharon's plan, Bush affirmed that "changes to the 1949 armistice lines" would have to be decided at the bargaining table, but he stopped short of providing the Palestinian president with a written guarantee that Washington was fully committed to a renewed peace process once the Israeli disengagement from Gaza was completed. The Bush administration clearly missed an opportunity to work with the more pragmatic and conciliatory Abbas. Acting with carte blanche at their June meeting, Sharon ignored Abbas's demands for more concessions other than token gestures like the release of Palestinian prisoners whose sentences were about to end. In August 2005, Israel completed the evacuation of its settler population from the Gaza Strip. But disengagement did not mean an end to the occupation; Israel still controlled both sea and air space, as well as travel in and out of the Gaza Strip, which was difficult if not impossible.[53] Additionally, Israel made it clear that reoccupation remained an Israeli prerogative if Palestinian terrorist attacks resumed.

As the Bush administration's justification for the continued war in Iraq became predicated on democracy, Palestinians were preparing for the January 25, 2006, PLC elections. Hamas's decision to participate in the democratic process under the Change and Reform Party sounded alarm bells in Washington. In December 2005, the Quartet released a statement demanding that the PA immediately institute legislation that prohibited the participation of any party that did not recognize Israel's right to exist and renounce violence.[54]

The elections occurred against a backdrop of sheer civil, economic, and political decay in the Occupied Territories. The aggressive extension of the separation wall built on confiscated Palestinian land isolated communities from each other. Israelis continued to build new settlements in the West Bank and increased check points. There were renewed allegations of corruption in the PA. Palestinian housing demolitions continued unabated, and there were few prospects for a viable Palestinian state. Despite significant US efforts—including campaign contributions—to produce an electoral victory for Fatah, Hamas's win should not have come as a surprise to US officials. Even though the Change and Reform Party of Hamas won in free and fair elections—a US benchmark of democratic progress for the region—the United States refused to accept Hamas's victory, citing Hamas as a terrorist organization that refuses to recognize Israel's right to exist. Like the PLO, Hamas initially relied on armed struggle in its pursuit of Palestinian liberation, and like the PLO,

Hamas has also shown its ability to exercise a range of roles, which has ensured its long-term political survival.

While many hailed the election as historic, the circumstances in the post-election environment are equally historic. First, Hamas has demonstrated its willingness to accommodate other Palestinian factions by including them in the new cabinet. Yet, Hamas has also insisted on exercising an independent role and refuses to be bound by past agreements between the PLO and Israel. It also refuses to recognize the PLO as the sole legitimate representative of the Palestinian people.

History has often demonstrated that the struggle for independence is rarely won at the negotiating table; instead, it is usually won after a long and protracted armed struggle—now often defined as terrorism. Presently, it appears that the Palestinians in the West Bank and Gaza Strip are acting as the determinants of PLO/PA foreign policy in the absence of political support at the regional and international level. With their votes for Hamas, they have redirected foreign policy away from sub-servience and back toward independent armed struggle. However, within this new political landscape, Washington and the PLO have an excellent opportunity to create a new US-PLO relationship. Although Abbas remains president of the PA, as chairman of the Executive Committee of the PLO he can reassert the PLO's representative role by taking the struggle for liberation once again "outside" the Occupied Territories and reestablishing the organization's commitment to its Diaspora constituency. However, the PLO's long-term viability will depend on its ability to deliver to both constituent groups a viable Palestinian state without further compromise on the issues of the status of Jerusalem, the refugees' right of return, and Israeli settlements in the West Bank as well as significant financial commitments to rebuild the devastated Gaza Strip. Their success could hinge on a possible lame-duck president with a willingness to ensure Israeli compliance through a strengthened US-PLO relationship that affirms the legitimacy of the PLO and once again opens the White House door to its leadership.

Notes

1. See, for example, William B. Quandt, *Decade of Decisions: American Policy Toward the Arab-Israeli Conflict, 1967–1976* (Berkeley: University of California Press, 1977); William B. Quandt, *Peace Process: American Diplomacy and the Arab-Israeli Conflict Since 1967* (Washington, D.C.: Brookings Institution and University of California Press, 1993); George Lenczowski, *American Presidents and the Middle East* (Durham, N.C.: Duke University Press, 1990); Steven L. Spiegel, *The Other Arab-Israeli Conflict: Making America's Middle East Policy from Truman to Reagan* (Chicago: University of Chicago Press, 1985).

2. See JoAnn A. DiGeorgio-Lutz, "A Role Modification Model: The Foreign Policy of the Palestine Liberation Organization, 1964–1981," Ph.D. diss., University of North Texas, Denton, Texas, 1993.

3. For example, modifications in the PLO's strategic goals include the idea of establishing a secular democratic state following the total liberation of Israel formulated at the 6th PNC (September 1969), the establishment of a national authority at the 12th PNC (1974), the PLO's failure to mention the goal of total liberation at the 14th PNC (1979), possible

confederation plans with Jordan at the 16th PNC (1983), acceptance of a two-state solution at the 19th PNC (1988), and the Gaza-Jericho First Plan in 1993, which has not been endorsed by the PNC.

4. This role was formally given to the PLO at the 1974 October Arab Summit at Rabat, which unanimously endorsed the PLO as the rightful spokesperson for all Palestinians. Resolution 2 affirmed "the right of the Palestinian people to establish an independent national authority under the command of the Palestine Liberation Organization, the sole legitimate representative of the Palestinians in any Palestinian territory that is liberated." For the full text, see document 308 in *International Documents on Palestine* (Beirut: Institute for Palestine Studies; and Kuwait: University of Kuwait Press, 1974).

5. The PLO has characteristically refused external attempts to impose strategic as well as tactical behaviors on the organization. Some examples include their rejection of the 1970 US-sponsored Rogers Plan, the United Arab Kingdom Plan initiated by Jordan in 1972, Anwar Sadat's government-in-exile scheme of 1972, and the initial refusal to submit to the US demand to "renounce" terrorism in 1988.

6. See *United Nations Resolutions on Palestine and the Arab-Israeli Conflict,* vol. 3 (Washington, D.C.: Institute for Palestine Studies, 1982–1986).

7. For a lengthy discussion of the Reagan administration and its reactionary policies to international events, see Nasser Aruri, "The United States and Palestine: Reagan's Legacy to Bush," *Journal of Palestine Studies* 18, 3 (1989):3–22. See also Cheryl A. Rubenberg, "The US-PLO Dialogue: Continuity or Change in American Policy," *Arab Studies Quarterly* 11, 4 (1989):1–48.

8. For the full text of the paper, see Bassam Abu Sharif, "Prospects of a Palestinian-Israeli Settlement," Algiers, 7 June 1988. Reprinted in *Journal of Palestine Studies* 28, 1 (1999):272–275. See also *New York Times,* 22 June 1988.

9. *Middle East International,* 8 July 1988.

10. See "A Call for Peace," PLO Chairman Yasser Arafat's speech to the European Parliament, Strasbourg, France, 13 September 1988. Reprinted in *Return* 1, 3 (1993):34–39.

11. See Mohamed Rabie, "The US Dialogue: The Swedish Connection," *Journal of Palestine Studies* 21, 4 (1991):54–66.

12. The US pledge not to negotiate or recognize the PLO is spelled out in the "Memorandum of Agreement Between the United States and Israel Regarding the Reconvening of the Geneva Conference," which was signed by US Secretary of State Henry Kissinger and Israeli Deputy Prime Minister and Minister of Foreign Affairs Yigal Allon on 1 September 1975. The text of the memorandum was released by the US Senate Committee on Foreign Relations on 3 October 1975. For the full text, see document 150, p. 267, in *International Documents on Palestine, 1975.* Although the first two conditions for not recognizing or negotiating with the PLO were attached to the Sinai II disengagement agreements, the third condition, that is, the renouncement of terrorism, was a stipulation imposed by the Reagan administration.

13. See Muhammad Hallaj, "The PLO's Peace Offensive: False Start or New Beginning?" *Middle East International,* 3 February 1989.

14. *Christian Science Monitor,* 24 March 1989.

15. Ibid.

16. See Lamis Andoni, "The PLO: President Arafat Under Fire," *Middle East International,* 14 April 1989.

17. See "Israeli Government Election Plan," Jerusalem, 14 May 1989, reprinted in *Journal of Palestine Studies* 29, 1 (2000):145–148.

18. See "Egypt's Ten-Point Response to Israel's Election Plan," Cairo, 2 July 1989, reprinted in *Journal of Palestine Studies* 29, 1 (2000):144–145. "Secretary of State James Baker's Five-Point Framework of an Israeli-Palestinian Dialogue," Washington, D.C., 10 October 1989, reprinted in *Journal of Palestine Studies* 29, 1 (2000):169–170.

19. For an examination of the conditions in Gaza leading up to the Gulf war, see Sara Roy, "The Political Economy of Despair: Changing Political and Economic Realities in the Gaza Strip," *Journal of Palestine Studies* 20, 4 (1991):58–69.

20. *Washington Times,* 14 August 1990.

21. *Middle East Times,* 11 September 1990.

22. *Middle East International,* 2 August 1991.

23. *Al-Fajr,* 9 December 1991.

24. See interview with Abdel al-Shafi, *Al-Fajr,* 2 August 1992.

25. For an extended analysis of the first five rounds, see Herbert C. Kelman, "How to Create a Momentum for the Israeli-Palestinian Negotiations," *Journal of Palestine Studies* 22, 1 (1993):1–38.

26. *New York Times,* 26 October 1991.

27. Foreign Broadcast Information Service, 16 March 1992.

28. See "PLO Central Council, Statement on the Peace Process," Tunis, 10 May 1992 (excerpts), reprinted in *Journal of Palestine Studies* 21, 4 (1991):149–153.

29. *Middle East International,* 15 May 1992.

30. See "Prime Minister Yitzhak Rabin, Inaugural Address to Thirteenth Knesset," Jerusalem, 13 July 1992, reprinted in *Journal of Palestine Studies* 22, 1 (1992):146–150.

31. See Mark Perry and Daniel Shapiro, "Navigating the Oslo Channel: Breakthrough in the Peace Talks," *Middle East Insight* 9, 6 (1994):9–27.

32. CPRS (Center for Palestine Research and Studies) opinion poll, 6–9 March 1997, 10–12 April 1997, reprinted in *Journal of Palestine Studies* 26, 4 (1997):130–131.

33. *The Jerusalem Times* V(246), 23 October 1998; *The Jerusalem Times* V(248), 6 November 1998.

34. Joel Beinin, "The Oslo Process—Back on Track?" *Middle East Report and Information Project (MERIP),* Press Information Note 8, 1999.

35. Lamis Andoni, "Final Status Talks Off to a Non-Start," *Middle East International,* 12 November 1999, Peretz Kidron, "Israel's Tough Parameters," *Middle East International,* 12 November 2000.

36. CPRS opinion polls, 3–5 June 1999, 2–4 December 1999, 27–31 January 2000, http://www.cprs-palestine.org.

37. Graham Usher, "The 'Make or Break' Summit?" *Middle East International,* 14 July 2000; see also Graham Usher, "Camp David: The American Bridge," *Middle East International,* 28 July 2000.

38. Shibley Telhami, "Camp David II: Assumptions and Consequences," *Current History,* January 2001.

39. See "Official Response of the Palestine Liberation Organization to the Final Report of the Sharm El Sheik Fact-Finding Committee (Mitchell Report)," 15 May 2001, reprinted by the Islamic Association of Palestine, http://www.iap.org/articles/sharm.htm.

40. *Middle East International,* 22 December 2000.

41. Graham Usher, "The Battle for Jenin Camp," *Middle East International,* 3 May 2002.

42. "Chronology: 16 February–15 May 2002," *Journal of Palestine Studies* 31, 4 (2002):199–221.

43. Kathleen Christison, "'All Those Old Issues': George W. Bush and the Palestinian-Israeli Conflict," *Journal of Palestine Studies* 33, 2 (2004):36–50.

44. Khaled Hroub, "Hamas After Shaykh Yasin and Rantisi," *Journal of Palestine Studies* 33, 4 (2004):21–38.

45. Graham Usher, "Enter Abbas," *Middle East International*, 18 April 2003.

46. U S Department of State, "A Performance-Based Road Map to a Permanent Two-State Solution to the Israeli-Palestinian Conflict," Washington, D.C., 30 April 2003.

47. Ibid.

48. "Israel's Road Map Reservations," *Ha'aretz* (Jerusalem), 27 May 2003.

49. Mohammed Omer, "Hamas Scores Majorities in Gaza Municipal Council Elections," *Washington Report on Middle East Affairs* 24, 5 (2005):14.

50. Lamis Adoni, "Quray's Failed Mission," *Middle East International,* 28 May 2004.

51. Michele K. Esposito, "Chronology, 16 August 15 November 2004," *Journal of Palestine Studies* 34, 2 (2004):217–240.

52. Yossi Beilin, "Help Abbas Succeed," www.washingtonpost.com, 14 January 2005.

53. Sara Roy, "Praying with Their Eyes Closed: Reflections on the Disengagement from Gaza," 2005, www.palestine-studies.org.

54. "Quartet Dictates to PNA Conditions for Parliamentary Candidates; PNA Should Codify in Law Renunciation of Violence, Recognition of Israel," 29 December 2005, Palestine Media Center, www.palestine-pmc.com.

14

From Madrid and Oslo to Camp David

The United States and the
Arab-Israeli Conflict, 1991–2001

Jeremy Pressman

From 1991 to 2001, Arab-Israeli relations were characterized by diplomatic triumphs as well as familiar problems. The multilateral peace conference at Madrid, the secret Oslo negotiations and agreement, the return of Palestine Liberation Organization (PLO) leaders to historic Palestine, and Israel's disengagement from Gaza all seemed to herald an era in which the contentious aftermath of the 1967 war might finally be addressed and resolved. Yet bus bombings, checkpoints, and most importantly, the second Palestinian uprising *(intifada)* reminded all the participants that neither side had abandoned the use of force in its relations with the other.

Throughout the 1990s, first under President George H. W. Bush (1989–1993), a Republican, and then under President Bill Clinton (1993–2001), a Democrat, the United States remained deeply involved in Arab-Israeli relations. In 1991, the Bush administration capitalized on major changes in regional and world politics to jumpstart the peace process at Madrid. US officials sought to negotiate agreements and then shepherd their implementation through intensive involvement in negotiating details and logistics. Secretaries of State James Baker III, Warren Christopher, and Madeleine Albright expended great effort on the issue and frequently met with Arab and Israeli officials; they often traveled to the region to further negotiations. President Clinton regularly hosted the Israeli prime minister and the PLO chairman, Yasser Arafat, at the White House. He traveled to Geneva to meet with Syrian President Hafiz al-Asad in January 1994, and the presidents met again in March 2000 when Clinton thought an Israeli-Syrian deal was likely. When the second *intifada* erupted in late 2000, US diplomats unsuccessfully worked to bring it to an end.

US diplomatic efforts from 1991–2001 came the closest yet to achieving the long-sought-after American goal of a comprehensive Arab-Israeli peace, but in the end the conflict was not resolved. Israel and Jordan inked a peace deal, and the fact that Israel now has signed peace treaties with two of its neighbors was in part due to Washington's diplomatic diligence. But Israeli-Palestinian agreements collapsed in violence despite enormous US investments in the peace process. Moreover, Israel and Syria came close to signing an agreement in 1999–2000, but they could not bridge the last differences over the exact border delineation of an Israeli withdrawal from the Golan Heights. A wide range of political and procedural errors blocked the achievement of both agreements. Near the end of Clinton's presidency, the Arab-Israeli negotiating failures at Shepherdstown, Geneva, and Camp David were part of a disappointing conclusion to ten years of talks. The US inability to contain the second *intifada* only reinforced the distance between the American interest in a comprehensive peace and the reality on the ground.

Throughout this period, Israeli prime ministers were either cognizant of the importance of US-Israeli ties or paid the price for challenging Washington. The three Israeli leaders from the left-wing Labor Party—Yitzhak Rabin, Shimon Peres, and Ehud Barak—had fewer problems because their efforts to advance the peace process dovetailed with US interests. The challenge was for right-wing Likud Party leaders—Yitzhak Shamir and Benjamin Netanyahu. In 1992, Shamir's re-election bid suffered from the US-Israeli fight over loan guarantees and Israeli settlements. In 1999, Netanyahu's record of undermining the peace process led to strains in the US-Israeli relationship.

In the next section, I describe changes in the international and regional distribution of power that opened the door to Arab-Israeli diplomacy. I then address the Oslo agreements (1993, 1995) and some of the specific reasons why the Israeli-Palestinian process failed. I consider the tenures of Benjamin Netanyahu and Ehud Barak, the failed Camp David summit (2000), and the Clinton Plan and final talks at Taba, Egypt, in January 2001. In the closing section, I consider four broader explanations for why Israeli-Palestinian and Israeli-Syrian talks never led to peace agreements. I conclude that political and procedural factors, not conflicting objectives or violent opposition, best explain the failures.

Shifting Power: The Pathway to Madrid

After shifts in the global and regional distribution of power set the stage for the Arab-Israeli peace talks of the 1990s, the United States played an important role in bringing the parties together for diplomatic talks. The end of the cold war and the 1991 Persian Gulf war eliminated the Arab military option against Israel. Whether the military option meant attacking Israel or trying to acquire parity in the arms race, the Arab side's only hope was based on Soviet military and financial support. Only Soviet support could give the Arab armies access to weapons that could meet US/Israeli weapons on the battlefield. Only Soviet subsidies and aid could facilitate the Iraqi and Syrian purchase of such weapons.[1]

The Soviet decision in 1987 to stop subsidizing Syrian arms sales strongly reinforced the trend that had started when Egypt made peace with Israel in 1978–1979 and thereby greatly reduced the possibility of a coordinated Arab attack against Israel. After the reformist Soviet leader Mikhail Gorbachev told Syrian President Hafiz al-Asad of the change in Soviet policy, Syria dropped its pursuit of strategic parity with Israel; Damascus had no choice. The Arab side could still resort to violence through guerrilla war and terrorism through proxies, but it could not seriously challenge Israel in the conventional military arena. Since that time, the only Arab strikes against Israel have been by substate actors such as Hamas, Lebanon's Hizbollah, Palestinian Islamic Jihad, and various factions of the Palestine Liberation Organization (PLO).

The Soviet decision was followed in 1991 by the expulsion of Iraq from Kuwait by a US-led coalition. Not only did the United States reverse Iraq's occupation of Kuwait, but it also destroyed a significant amount of Iraqi arms. The UN Security Council (UNSC) sanctioned the creation and enforcement of "no-fly zones" in southern and northern Iraq where Iraqi aircraft were barred. UN inspectors traveled around Iraq and sought evidence of nonconventional weapons; they destroyed Iraqi weapons stocks and equipment. US forces remained stationed in Saudi Arabia, the Persian Gulf waters, and in smaller Gulf states. Iraq was contained, and the possibility of Iraqi soldiers joining other Arab forces for an attempt from the east to cut Israel in half was gone (though the Israeli fear of an attack on its eastern front lingered).

Taken together, the end of the cold war and the Persian Gulf war meant the Arab side lacked the numbers and the external support to match Israel in the strategic realm. This did not guarantee a turn toward diplomacy, but it did make such a possibility much more likely.

The end of the cold war and, ultimately, the collapse of the Soviet Union, did not dampen US interests in achieving a comprehensive settlement of the Arab-Israeli conflict. One might have expected that the demise of the only other superpower and long-time US rival for power and influence in the Middle East might have eased US concerns about Arab-Israeli disagreements. Yet the Bush and Clinton administrations, which governed in the period between the cold war and the al-Qa'ida threat, nonetheless invested heavily in regional diplomacy. The United States remained dependent on Middle East oil, and the continuance of the Arab-Israeli conflict complicated US relations with Arab oil exporters; at a minimum, the possibility of another Arab oil embargo emerging after a future Arab-Israeli clash could not be wholly dismissed. Furthermore, Israel's security remained a central US commitment. Arab-Israeli peace agreements made Israel more secure and reduced the likelihood of a demand for US political or military intervention in a crisis situation similar to the wars in 1967 and 1973.

The United States, then, exploited the opening created by changes in the global and regional balance of power to bring about the first multilateral Arab-Israeli peace conference since the 1970s. The US effort, led by Secretary of State James Baker III, sought to bring together Israel and its neighboring Arab rivals—Jordan, Lebanon, and Syria.[2] In part, the United States was indebted to Syria for its membership in the anti-Iraq coalition. The PLO was not invited; instead, the Jordanian delegation, which included Palestinians from the occupied territories, was seen as representing both Jordan and the Palestinian people. During the summer of 1991, after intense US diplomatic lobbying, all the key parties agreed to attend a conference. The opening meeting was held in Madrid, Spain, from October 30 to November 1, 1991. It produced no breakthroughs and largely served as a forum for the public repetition of uncompromising positions.

The Madrid talks were followed by two types of negotiations, bilateral and multilateral, but the negotiations soon stalled.[3] The bilateral talks consisted of Israeli-Syrian, Israeli-Lebanese, and Israeli-Jordanian meetings and were usually held in Washington. With the collapse of the Soviet Union in December 1991, the United States was the sole superpower, and officials hoped to use US primacy to advance the cause of Middle East peace, leveraging its predominant position in the region and the goodwill it had generated by liberating Kuwait in the Gulf war earlier in the year. The talks, however, devolved into dueling press conferences at which the respective diplomats commented on the lack of progress after each day's sessions.

The Oslo Agreements

In 1993, as the bilateral talks dragged on, Israeli Prime Minister Yitzhak Rabin and PLO Chairman Yasser Arafat both signed off on secret unofficial talks in Oslo, Norway. Rabin did not expect much to come of the talks and probably saw them as a pet project of Shimon Peres, his foreign minister, and Yossi Beilin, deputy foreign minister.[4] Yet in August 1993, the two sides initialed a breakthrough agreement, what soon became known as the Declaration of Principles. Unlike most of the other diplomatic milestones during this period, the United States was not involved in the Oslo talks because Norway initiated and hosted the meetings. Both parties wanted to shun the inevitable attention commensurate with US involvement, and for Israel, it has always been an objective to deal one-on-one with Arab parties in negotiations, where it can maximize its leverage and avoid American pressure to make unwanted concessions.

In the June 1992 elections, Rabin had promised a breakthrough with the Palestinians. At a meeting of the Labor Party's central committee in March 1992, for instance, Rabin suggested a time frame of six to nine months for reaching an autonomy agreement.[5] Rabin believed that resolving the Israeli-Palestinian conflict in the short term would help Israel both avoid antagonism from potential strategic threats such as Iran in the long term and lock in US support for Israel.

Arafat was struggling to come to terms with the impact of the first *intifada* and the Gulf war. The PLO backed Iraq, the losing side in the Gulf war; Arab Gulf financial support dried up as a result. By 1992–1993, the *intifada* had slowed and lost some of its popular character and appeal. Arafat was still on the outside of the occupied territories, while younger Palestinian leaders on the inside had established a vibrant institutional infrastructure. In order to sustain Palestinian daily life and resistance to the occupation during the first *intifada,* Palestinians developed a range of political and social welfare organizations. To Tunis-based PLO leaders, these new organizations were potential rival centers of political power.

The Declaration of Principles (DOP), signed on the White House lawn on September 13, 1993, launched the public phase of the Oslo process. That the DOP was signed on the White House lawn was a testament to how quickly the United States recognized the potential value of the agreement. Washington had not been involved in negotiating the deal, but Clinton officials used the White House ceremony to signal US backing for the agreement as well as to indicate that henceforth US diplomatic muscle would support the implementation of the agreement. The parties themselves also probably recognized the value of the United States as a future guarantor, broker, and funder.

The DOP did not resolve the core Israeli-Palestinian issues such as the future status of Jerusalem, Israeli settlements, or Palestinian refugees. Nor did it explicitly call for a Palestinian state alongside Israel or a freeze on Israeli settlement building in the occupied territories. Israeli Foreign Minister Shimon Peres, on flying to California and presenting the Oslo agreement to Secretary Christopher and Dennis Ross in August 1993, explained why: "The logic, Peres stressed, was to build a network of cooperation so that the harder issues would become resolvable in a very different climate."[6]

Instead of dealing with these "harder issues," the DOP set up a five-year transitional period in which Israel would gradually redeploy from the Gaza Strip and West Bank, starting with Gaza and the West Bank city of Jericho. Further withdrawals were contingent on security matters, as explained in the DOP: "Further redeployments to specified locations will be gradually implemented commensurate with the assumption of responsibility for public order and internal security by the Palestinian police. . . ." The Palestinians would develop a quasi-government, the Palestinian Interim Self-Government Authority (later known more simply as the Palestinian Authority), hold elections, and develop a "strong police force." Talks on the most difficult issues, "permanent status negotiations," would start by the beginning of the third year of the transitional period. Permanent or final status issues included core disputes over "Jerusalem, refugees, settlements, security arrangements, [and] borders." Article XV created nonviolent mechanisms for resolving disputes.

The Israelis withdrew from Jericho and much of Gaza in mid-1994, and Arafat and many other Tunis-based PLO leaders entered Gaza. This brought Arafat and the leaders of the PLO back into the center of Palestinian politics and gained the PLO legitimacy with the United States. After concern about marginalization and financial troubles, the PLO saw the DOP, however imperfect, as an opportunity for gaining political power and fiscal support. PLO acceptance was a sign of the movement's weakness, not strength.

Meanwhile, Israel and Jordan signed a peace treaty on October 26, 1994, after years of clandestine elite ties. Israeli leaders and Jordan's Hashemite monarchy had long met in secret. Yet because the majority of Jordan's population was Palestinian, Jordan had been unwilling to reach a public agreement with Israel prior to an Israeli-Palestinian breakthrough. The Oslo agreement changed the environment and gave Jordan the political cover it needed to solidify cooperative relations with Israel as well as regain the good graces of Washington after tacitly backing Iraq in the

1991 Gulf war. The United States helped facilitate the treaty, but Israel and Jordan had no fundamental disagreements and needed only limited outside assistance.

Rabin's election also ushered in an intensive period of Israeli-Syrian contacts from 1993 to 1995. It was a period in which the United States played an active role, and Israelis and Syrians made progress on a number of practical issues. The two sides traded diplomatic phrases: Rabin said "the depth of the withdrawal will reflect the depth of peace." In May 1993, Asad offered "full peace for full withdrawal." In 1993–1994, Rabin secretly agreed to a full Israeli withdrawal from the Golan Heights to the June 4, 1967, line, though exactly how to delineate that line remained a point of debate. US officials carried messages between Rabin and Asad just before Rabin opted for the Oslo (Israeli-Palestinian) track in August 1993. At a meeting with Clinton in Geneva on January 16, 1994, Asad spoke of a strategic decision for peace and "a new era of security and stability in which normal, peaceful relations among all shall dawn anew." Clinton traveled to Damascus in October of the same year, and Christopher frequently met with Asad and Rabin as well. In June 1995, the United States hosted the Israeli and Syrian chiefs of staff in Washington for talks on security matters at which a good deal of progress was made.[7]

Meanwhile, on September 28, 1995, the Israelis and Palestinians signed a second major agreement that detailed additional territorial changes in the West Bank. The agreement, Oslo II, created three types of West Bank land: Area A under Palestinian security and civil control, Area B under Palestinian civil control and Israeli security control, and Area C under Israeli security and civil rule. The territorial withdrawals of Oslo II proceeded slowly and were never fully implemented. The sides repeatedly disagreed on the exact size, timing, and location of agreed-upon withdrawals, but Israel was the ruling power so it had the final say. By the outbreak of the second *intifada* in September 2000, the majority of the West Bank, including all Israeli settlements, remained as Area C. About 17 percent of the West Bank was Area A and another 23 percent was Area B.[8]

Unlike the first Oslo agreement, Oslo II was partially the result of intensive US diplomacy, though not of the level of the late 1990s and 2000. Secretary of State Christopher and, in later years, Secretary of State Albright, were willing to spend time and political capital nailing down Israeli-Palestinian agreements. US diplomats, including Martin Indyk, Aaron David Miller, and Dennis Ross, moderated, cajoled, proposed, and persuaded until the Arabs and Israelis found common ground on issues both large and small. At times, US diplomats called on other American officials, such as CIA Director George Tenet, to play a role with one or both sides.

From 1993 to 2001, the Oslo process proceeded more slowly than planned and ultimately failed to lead to a final resolution of the conflict. At the popular level, neither Palestinian expectations of freedom of movement, economic improvement, and statehood nor Israeli hopes for peace, security, and a normal life were met. Expectations had been high. At the DOP signing ceremony in 1993, Arafat expressed Palestinian hopes: "My people are hoping that this agreement which we are signing today marks the beginning of the end of a chapter of pain and suffering which has lasted throughout this century . . . [and that it] will usher in an age of peace, coexistence, and equal rights."9 Rabin sought a break with the past: "We wish to open a new chapter in the sad book of our lives together, a chapter of mutual recognition, of good neighborliness, of mutual respect, of understanding. We hope to embark on a new era in the history of the Middle East."10 These unmet expectations, especially on the Palestinian side, fueled growing disenchantment with the Oslo talks and greater sympathy for confrontational and violent policies that eventually crystallized into the second *intifada*.

In particular, the Oslo process suffered from four developments. First, some Palestinian groups, including Hamas and the Palestinian Islamic Jihad, attacked and killed Israeli civilians. To Israelis, terrorist bus bombings inside pre-1967 Israel suggested that they were not safe personally and that the process was not leading to normalization and peaceful relations. The wave of bus bombings in February–March 1996, for instance, killed and wounded hundreds of Israelis and contributed to the defeat of Prime Minister Shimon Peres in the May 1996 elections.

Second, some Israeli Jewish settlers used terrorist violence against Palestinians, mostly in the West Bank. The first Hamas suicide bombings came after an Israeli settler killed twenty-nine Palestinians at the Ibrahimi Mosque in Hebron on February 25, 1994. Most of the settler attacks, however, were less dramatic and often resulted in injury and property destruction rather than death. Yet when coupled with the civilian casualties from Israel Defense Forces (IDF) counter-terror operations, they had a corrosive effect on Palestinian views of Israeli intentions.

Third, Israel continued to massively develop the West Bank settlements, including building a network of Jewish-only bypass roads that crisscrossed the West Bank. From 1993 to 2000, the number of Israeli settlers increased by at least 117 percent in Gaza and at least 46 percent in the West Bank (not including East Jerusalem where settler growth was also large).11 In the 1990s, Israel stopped authorizing new settlements but still allowed the building of new "neighborhoods" for existing settlements. Israeli settlers also proceeded to set up tens of unauthorized outposts, a practice that mushroomed after Ariel Sharon became prime minister in 2001.12

Fourth, Israel used collective punishment, such as checkpoints, home demolitions, closure and curfews, bureaucratic procedures, and targeted assassinations to advance its security objectives. For example, approximately 670 Palestinian homes in the West Bank (including Jerusalem) were destroyed from September 1993 to June 1998.13 Israel also implemented a policy of revoking permission to live in Jerusalem from Palestinians who could not prove the center of their life was in Jerusalem; Palestinians had to prove that their work, family, education, and housing centered on Jerusalem rather than elsewhere in the West Bank or abroad. Over 1,600 Palestinians and their families were removed in this way from 1996 to 1998, according to Israeli officials.14 Palestinians often rejected Israel's security justifications for these policies and instead highlighted Israel's desire for continued control of the West Bank. A process Palestinians thought would lead to the end of the occupation instead seemed to be leading to its intensification.

While Washington was deeply involved in the negotiations, the United States refrained from coercing either party. With one exception in the 1990s, the United States did not provide aid directly to the Palestinian Authority, so it could not threaten to withhold aid if the PLO or PA failed to fulfill their commitments.[15] Although Israeli settlement expansion was changing the reality on the ground in the West Bank and undermining Palestinian support for the Oslo process, the United States did not exert significant pressure. The United States deducted the costs of settlement expansion from multi-billion-dollar loan guarantees Israel had secured from the United States, but this was a marginal punishment that had a limited practical effect. With only a few exceptions, the United States has long been reluctant to threaten Israel.[16]

On November 4, 1995, Israeli Prime Minister Yitzhak Rabin was assassinated by an Israeli Jew. The killing deeply affected the personal chemistry of US-Israeli relations. Clinton and Rabin had developed a warm relationship in the first years of Clinton's presidency; the young president enjoyed interactions with Rabin, an older, seasoned politician. Reflecting on Rabin's death, Clinton later wrote, "We had become friends in that unique way people do when they are in a struggle that they believe is great and good . . . . I had come to love him as I had rarely loved another man."[17] At Rabin's funeral, Clinton's comment "shalom chaver" (goodbye friend) captured their friendship and came to embody the profound sense of shock and loss felt by many Israelis. Although Arafat was also a frequent visitor to the White House, the relationship between Clinton and Arafat, though cordial, lacked the personal chemistry of the Clinton-Rabin ties.

Netanyahu and Barak

The Rabin assassination exacerbated Israeli-Palestinian problems. Not only was Rabin gone, but he was replaced six months later by Benjamin "Bibi" Netanyahu, who campaigned against the Oslo process. A wave of Palestinian bus bombings in February–March 1996—a response to Israel's assassination of Palestinian bomb maker Yahya Ayash in January—had the effect of reinforcing Netanyahu's criticism of Rabin's replacement, Shimon Peres.

With Netanyahu's electoral victory, the United States was then challenged with the task of getting a harsh opponent of the Oslo process to implement it and continue negotiations. Some agreements were signed, such as the Hebron Protocol (January 15, 1997) and the Wye agreement (October 23, 1998), but Bibi's overall stance further undermined Israeli-Palestinian relations. US officials worked hard to keep Netanyahu's government committed to the Oslo agreements, but in doing so they usually gave some ground as the contents of past agreements were renegotiated. The Hebron agreement (1997), for instance, relaxed the expectations contained in the Oslo II agreement (1995) for further Israeli withdrawals from parts of the West Bank. As Israel slowed the negotiations and the pace of the withdrawals, Netanyahu's relations with both Arafat and Clinton became strained.

The Wye agreement was classic US-led Middle East diplomacy and typified US efforts in 1996–1999 to keep the peace process afloat, but the agreement's actual impact was limited. The United States invited Arafat and Netanyahu to the Wye River Plantation in Maryland for intensive discussions. Clinton, along with the terminally ill King Hussein of Jordan, worked at an agreement until the two parties signed a deal on West Bank land, Palestinian prisoner releases, the Palestinian charter, and other issues. The agreement led to some modest progress, but relations quickly soured. Clinton traveled to Israel and Gaza in December 1998 to try to aid the faltering process.

The Israeli government changed again when the left-leaning Labor Party and Ehud Barak defeated Netanyahu and his Likud Party in elections on May 17, 1999. Although Barak signed an Israeli-Palestinian protocol at Sharm el-Sheikh, Egypt, in September 1999, he chose to first move aggressively on the Israeli-Syrian front. Despite Palestinian concern, the United States backed Barak's focus on Syria. The United States finally hoped to capitalize on the commitment of Yitzhak Rabin and his successors to withdraw from the Golan Heights to the June 4, 1967 line, the line that Syria demanded in order to sign an agreement.

After high-level talks in December 1999, Israeli and Syrian negotiators met in Shepherdstown, West Virginia, in January 2000. Barak was concerned about opposition in Israel to a full withdrawal, and the talks failed. In March 2000, Syria thought it had a US commitment that Israel would agree to the June 4, 1967 line, as opposed to the 1923 international boundary or other possible borders. Asad and Clinton met in Geneva expecting a momentous breakthrough, but the meeting immediately broke down when it became clear that Israel was proposing a modified version of the June 4, 1967 line. Barak, with US knowledge, decided not to offer Syria a complete return to the June 4, 1967 line, and so the two sides failed to come to an agreement.[18] Having failed to secure an agreement with Syria, in which Barak also hoped to come to an agreement regarding Lebanon, Israel unilaterally withdrew its soldiers from southern Lebanon in May 2000. On June 10, 2000, Asad died.

During the first part of Barak's term, Palestinian attacks on Israelis nearly ceased. Israeli-Palestinian security cooperation and Palestinian hopes that Barak's new government would lead to a two-state breakthrough combined to usher in greater quiet in Israel. In 1999 and the first ten months of 2000, only seven Israelis were killed in terror attacks—including just one inside pre-1967 Israel.[19] According to Ami Ayalon, the head of Israel's Shin Bet at the time, Palestinian political hope led to a drop in Palestinian mass support for violence and an increased willingness on the part of Palestinian security personnel to combat it.[20] Some have argued that Israel squandered this period of Israeli-Palestinian calm by focusing on Syria instead of pursuing high-level Israeli-Palestinian talks.

Camp David Summit

In the spring of 2000, during Clinton's last year in office, Barak turned his attention to the Palestinian track after the failure with Syria. Perhaps hoping to recapture the Scandinavian magic of Oslo, the two sides held secret talks in Stockholm, Sweden, to deal with the core issues, but these negotiations broke up inconclusively after word of the talks leaked to the media. Israel soon decided to pursue a high-level, high-stakes summit to resolve the conflict. Barak, long a skeptic of Oslo's incrementalism, felt this was the only way to test whether Arafat would commit to a final agreement instead of offering only more interim steps and indecision. Palestinian leaders resisted in part because they feared the intensity of joint American-Israeli pressure in a closed summit, but US cajoling caused Palestinian leaders to set aside their concerns. President Clinton announced on July 5, 2000, that Israeli and Palestinian delegations had agreed to join him at his presidential retreat, Camp David.

Many explanations have been offered for the failure of the American-Israeli-Palestinian summit of July 11–25, 2000, but all parties contributed to its demise. The conventional wisdom that Israel made a generous offer and the Palestinian negotiators rejected it out of hand is not backed up by the evidentiary record.[21]

The United States made a number of procedural errors. Washington pressured a reluctant Palestinian leadership to attend, promised not to blame the Palestinians if the summit failed, and then reneged on that promise. US diplomats had not lobbied other Arab leaders to support Palestinian concessions on Jerusalem and did not have a workable fall-back plan for the summit should an overall agreement prove impossible. After meeting Israeli-Palestinian resistance, US officials quickly backed away from tabling written drafts of compromise language on sticky issues. At least in hindsight, the gap between Israel and the Palestinians on all the core issues entering the summit was wider than one would want coming into a meeting at the highest levels.

Israel attended the talks with unrealistic expectations about the Palestinian bottom line. During the summit, Israel rejected Palestinian sovereignty in the Arab parts of East Jerusalem and limited the Palestinian territory in the West Bank to two or three noncontiguous chunks of, at most, 91–92 percent (and by other measures as little as 77 percent) of the entire West Bank.[22] Why Israel thought the Palestinians would accept this package is a lingering historical puzzle. In general, Barak often seemed to assume he knew best and could compel others to follow his lead, but this approach failed at Camp David, much as it did on other issues during his short tenure as Israeli prime minister. At the summit itself, he did not engage Arafat, even though Arafat would have to sign off on any of the central Palestinian concessions on Jerusalem and refugees that were needed to strike a deal. Some Israeli and US diplomats also mistakenly thought that the unofficial final status agreement negotiated in 1995 between Palestinian Mahmoud Abbas and Israeli Yossi Beilin, known as the Beilin–Abu Mazen agreement, could serve as a rough blueprint for the summit.

Palestinian negotiators operated from a defensive position, fearful that Israel and the United States would try to compel them to accept the unacceptable. The Palestinians were largely reactive and never tabled a detailed proposal that went much beyond international law and UN resolutions. Contrary to many claims, however, the Palestinians did present a map of the West Bank proposing the Israeli annexation of 2–3 percent of the West Bank. The delegation was beset by power struggles, as was common under Arafat's long rule of the Palestinian national movement. Arafat's rejection of a key aspect of Jewish history—the site of the ancient Jewish temple in Jerusalem's Old City—undermined his credibility.

Some promising ideas solidified at the summit, however. The Palestinians agreed to the idea of swapping land for a few major settlement blocs in the West Bank that Israel wanted to annex, though how narrow or expansive such blocs should be remained a contested issue. Israel's idea of dividing Jerusalem was a breakthrough, even if Israel did not offer Palestinian sovereignty in all Arab areas in East Jerusalem. As they had indicated in prior negotiations, the Palestinians were willing to allow Israeli sovereignty in Jewish neighborhoods of East Jerusalem.

After the summit, quiet talks continued into August and September 2000, but just as the United States was about to present its own plan, the second *intifada* erupted.[23] Ariel Sharon, then the leader of the Israeli parliamentary opposition, visited the Temple Mount in Jerusalem on September 28, and Palestinian protests broke out and escalated. The Tanzim, an offshoot of the nationalist Fatah movement, welcomed the confrontation as a way to compel by force what Israel refused to give up at the negotiating table: control of the West Bank. The IDF, as planned, responded to the Palestinian protests with massive force, hoping that this would quickly quell the rioting. It had the opposite effect, and by the end of October 2000, Israeli forces had killed 116 Palestinians compared with 11 Israeli dead.[24] Once the fighting was underway, Arafat felt the Palestinians could gain further regional and international support and thereby put pressure on Israel if the fighting continued; top Palestinian leaders did little to restrain Palestinian fighters. A Clinton-led summit of leaders at Sharm el-Sheikh in mid-October 2000 and other diplomatic efforts to end the violence failed.

The Clinton Plan and Taba

On December 23, 2000, President Bill Clinton brought together negotiators from both sides and finally presented a US plan for a two-state solution. His proposal, the Clinton Plan, called for Palestinian sovereignty in Gaza and about 97 percent of the West Bank.[25] Palestinian refugees could stay in their host countries, return to the Palestinian state, or settle in small areas of land handed over by Israel as compensation for Israeli territorial annexations in the West Bank. Though Israel would annex settlement blocs in the West Bank, more isolated settlements would presumably be dismantled. Israel and third-party states could also choose to absorb some Palestinian refugees, but they were not required to do so.

Clinton called for a division of Jerusalem with Palestinian sovereignty in the Arab areas of East Jerusalem, and Israeli sovereignty in West Jerusalem and the Jewish areas of the east side. He offered two possible compromises for Jerusalem's Temple Mount (Muslims call it the Haram al-Sharif, or Noble Sanctuary), a location holy to both Jews and Muslims. The Clinton Plan also dealt with security matters. In order to pressure the parties, the United States insisted that the plan would only be considered a valid proposal until Clinton left office on January 20, 2001. The plan's continuing relevance today testifies to the bankruptcy of this idea.

The Israeli government accepted the plan but offered reservations. Privately, Barak sent Clinton a long and still-classified letter detailing his concerns, including misgivings about the refugee formulation.[26] In public, Barak rejected Clinton's call for Palestinian sovereignty over the Temple Mount/Haram al-Sharif. In practice, this meant a rejection of Clinton's compromise for sovereignty in the holy sites.

The Palestinian response has been the subject of much controversy, but it too was a technical acceptance with significant reservations. Arafat accepted the plan on January 2, 2001, in a face-to-face meeting with Clinton but offered reservations. Arafat accepted Israel's sovereignty over the central Jewish holy site known as the Wailing Wall but not over the entire ancient temple wall of which it is a part; he objected to Israeli use of West Bank airspace; and he requested a different framework for dealing with Palestinian refugees.[27]

The Clinton Plan was closely followed by Israeli-Palestinian negotiations at Taba, Egypt, during January 21–27, 2001. According to most participants and observers, the talks were substantive, and the parties made progress,[28] although the United States was not involved at a time when strong US mediation could have been very helpful. The negotiators issued an optimistic concluding statement: "The sides declare that they have never been closer to reaching an agreement, and it is thus our shared belief that the remaining gaps could be bridged with the resumption of negotiations following the Israeli elections."

On February 6, Ariel Sharon defeated Ehud Barak in Israeli elections. Upon taking office, Prime Minister Sharon chose not to engage in high-level talks, and the George W. Bush administration, itself having just come to power on January 20, accepted that approach.

Because both the Israeli-Syrian and Israeli-Palestinian negotiations ended in failure, the discussions that took place concerning a deeper US strategic role in the Arab-Israeli arena have been overlooked. Had the Israeli-Syrian negotiations gone differently, for instance, US monitors and peacekeepers might have been sent to the Golan Heights to supervise an Israeli-Syrian deal. The United States also agreed to a request from Arafat for US peacekeepers in the Jordan Valley. In July 2002, two years after the Camp David summit, Bruce Riedel, a former member of the US National Security Council staff, revealed that at the summit Israel proposed "a formal mutual defense agreement including a commitment by the United States to come to the assistance of Israel in the event of attack in the future, enshrined in a treaty to be ratified by the Congress and the Knesset." Israel also wanted the United States to include Israel under the US nuclear umbrella. Israel's draft treaty was an expansion of discussions that had focused on the Israeli-Syrian talks. At Camp David, Israel also sought billions of dollars for new arms and access to advanced US military technology such as Tomahawk cruise missiles and F-22 aircraft.[29]

The Failure of the Peace Process

Why did the Israeli-Palestinian and Israeli-Syrian negotiations fail to lead to final peace agreements? In a broad sense, why did the Arab-Israeli peace process of

1993–2001 fail? In this concluding section, I consider four possible explanations and find that political and procedural mistakes, including missteps by Washington, doomed the talks.[30] The claim that one or more parties did not want a peace agreement is the least persuasive explanation despite its widespread popularity.

The actors did not want peace. One or more of the parties to the conflict did not actually want peace, so the failure of the talks helped them achieve their true objectives. Participation in the process was a ruse, perhaps to appease the United States and the international community. Negotiators could talk forever without actually reaching a final agreement that would require real sacrifice in exchange for concrete gains. The Palestinians did not want peace; they wanted a single Palestinian state in place of Israel. Israel did not want peace but rather the occupation and annexation of the West Bank, Gaza, and the Golan Heights. Syria would never accept normal, peaceful relations with Israel.

The evidence does not support this claim. Israel, Syria, and the Palestinians invested massive diplomatic energy and political resources in the process. Each expended great amounts of political capital domestically in order to pursue the negotiations; they took risks in the domestic arena that might undermine their hold on power. All agreed to policies that would not be popular at home. For example, Israel agreed to the division of Jerusalem and withdrawal from the Golan Heights; the Palestinians agreed to allow Israeli annexation of some settlements in Jerusalem and elsewhere in the West Bank; and Syria accepted normalization with Israel. When Israel recognized that the offer at Camp David had been insufficient, they continued to negotiate (as did the Palestinians). Barak's government paid the ultimate political price: It fell apart over a deal with the Palestinians. When Asad came to Geneva to meet with Clinton in March 2000, the Syrian delegation was massive, because Asad expected to need many officials to iron out all the details of the peace agreement. Israel's offer at the Camp David summit was imperfect for Palestinians only because they truly believed they would be bound by the agreement. If instead they had hoped to use the new state of Palestine as a springboard for a military attack on Israel, the difference between receiving 92 percent or 97 percent of the West Bank and many other stipulations would not have mattered.[31]

One caveat to the idea that Israelis and Palestinians are ready to compromise on all the core issues is that the negotiators do not have a clear solution to the problem of who would control the Temple Mount/Haram al-Sharif in Jerusalem. While the contours of an agreement on all the other issues are clear, the division of this sacred area is still unsettled.

Procedural errors undermined the negotiations. On the Israeli-Palestinian track, the way in which the process was constructed and carried out led to its failure. The initial terms of the 1993 Declaration of Principles were too favorable toward Israel. With no explicit mention of a Palestinian state or a settlement freeze, the agreement was bound to run into trouble. The process was too gradual, and this left opponents much time and many opportunities to thwart the drive toward peace. It was driven by elites, and this left out the Israeli and Palestinian publics. They were never conditioned to accept the compromises that would be needed. Along the way, as I noted above with the US performance at the Camp David summit, the handling of the actual negotiations was frequently botched. Everyone wanted an agreement, but the pathway was too rocky and ill conceived.

While much of this critique is accurate in terms of identifying the shortcomings of the Oslo process, it implicitly suggests that a balanced, rapid process with both leader and popular participation was a realistic possibility in 1993. It was not. Israel's general power advantage translated into a negotiating advantage, one that Israel, like any state in that position, would not willingly give up. Conditioning one's people is difficult without telegraphing to the other negotiating party in advance the concessions one will accept. Negotiators hold concessions close to their chests; they try not to broadcast them in public.

Furthermore, the gradualism of the Oslo process was the only approach likely to gain sufficient Israeli and Palestinian support so that it could be sustained. A more rapid move to a two-state solution on the June 4, 1967 lines would never have gotten off the ground. In part, the gradualism itself makes possible the post-hoc view that Oslo was too gradual. Everyone has come to expect much more than what, in 1993, seemed like a monumental leap. In other words, the Oslo breakthrough conditioned people on both sides to be able to expect much more—a more lasting rapprochement—and therefore makes the initial approach seem misguided.

This explanation has mostly focused on the Israeli-Palestinian track, but the Israeli-Syrian process may also have suffered. First, the competition for Israeli and US attention between the two negotiating tracks slowed the talks. The best example was probably in August 1993 when Rabin weighed talks with Syria against the Oslo track and chose the latter at the (temporary) expense of the former. Second, Israel and Syria did not engage in consistent high-level negotiations. Months often went by without much interaction. The United States could have done more to speed up the Israeli-Syrian process, a claim that carries over to the next explanation.

Despite some limitations, then, the wide array of procedural mistakes and political decisions is the best explanation of the failure to reach agreements. Israelis, Palestinians, and Syrians were close, but they tripped themselves up, and the United States, the central mediator, failed to steer them in the right diplomatic direction on too many occasions. The problems were not just at Camp David or Geneva in 2000 but ran throughout the entire period. In the next section, I address the US failings more specifically. But while I treat the second and third explanations separately, they fit together quite well.

The United States was too passive. The United States failed to do its job as mediator, facilitator, and enforcer. The United States failed to monitor the parties and sanction actors who failed to uphold their agreed-upon commitments. During Clinton's first term, William Quandt argues that Washington could have forced the pace of all the negotiations rather than letting the talks drag and risk squandering a window of opportunity. He further claims that the United States did not always press Netanyahu when the Israeli government was ambivalent about the Oslo process.[32] The United States convened meetings at the highest level only to see them fail at Shepherdstown, Geneva, and Camp David. By the time the top leaders reached such meetings, US officials should have ensured that the odds of failure were low.

Another version of the idea that US failings stalled the drive for peace is that the United States should have coerced Israel in order to advance the process. Israel was the more powerful party, and only US efforts could counterbalance Israel's advantage and lead to an equitably structured negotiating framework. If the Oslo process failed in part because Israel could dictate the terms of the DOP and continue settlement expansion, the only leverage resided in Washington. The second alternative, then, to the gradual process as it unfolded was a process with a much stronger US role. But this is not just about the opening of the talks; it also would have required a strenuous US policy along the way to ensure success.

Still, for this to have been a viable US approach, one would have to completely ignore a core tenet of US policy: strong Israeli-US relations. As noted earlier, the United States has generally been unwilling to coerce Israel with sanctions or other material threats. Israel has many domestic supporters, including many elected and appointed officials, who balk at pressuring Israel and criticize presidential administrations who contemplate a coercive approach.

The opponents of the process bested supporters. On the Israeli-Palestinian track, the peace process failed because opponents used violence to dash euphoric expectations and prevent the timely implementation of agreements. Most terrorist attacks led to a temporal delay in the negotiations and caused supporters to question where this process was really headed. Israeli settlers who rejected territorial compromise continued to build and expand, often with the support of sectors within the Israeli government. In short, opponents used political and military means to thwart the diplomatic process. Israel and certainly Palestinians are not unitary actors; those opposed to compromise have plenty of avenues for undermining the process.

On the Israeli-Syrian front, little evidence has emerged from Syria that opponents of a deal with Israel undermined Hafiz al-Asad's strategic decision for a peace. On the Israeli side, segments of the Israeli public that opposed withdrawal from the Golan Heights spoke out and used the domestic political process to build momentum against the Rabin government. In a crucial domestic political challenge, a handful of members of parliament broke with Rabin over the Golan issue.

On the Israeli-Palestinian front, violent opponents were a major impediment, but they were an impediment all parties could have expected. Actors seeking to end a conflict regularly face opponents, and they must be able to manage such challenges. To place primary blame for the negotiating failure on the heads of opponents is to let off too easily the organizers and governments. The violence was greatly damaging, but leaders need to anticipate it and minimize the damage to the political process. In a sense, the procedural explanation is more persuasive because it subsumes the issue of addressing opposition attacks on diplomacy. Perhaps only a robust, resilient, well-managed process could have succeeded, and this is where US officials came up short. The United States is left with a good amount of material upon which to build the next time around, but Washington had hoped for much more than a recipe book for future Arab-Israeli talks.

Notes

I would like to thank Robert Blecher, Arie Kacowicz, and Henry Krisch for thoughtful comments on an earlier draft. I presented a version of this chapter at the annual conference of the International Studies Association in March 2006.

1. In theory, an alternative to Soviet funding for arms would have been financial support from the Arab Gulf states. But with the end of the cold war, those states did not step in to replace Soviet support.

2. Egypt and Israel had signed a peace treaty in 1979.

3. The multilateral negotiations included five working groups with participants from both inside and outside the Middle East: arms control and regional security, environmental issues, refugees, regional economic development, and water.

4. On Rabin's dismissive attitude, see David Makovsky, *Making Peace with the PLO: The Rabin Government's Road to the Oslo Accord* (Boulder: Westview, 1996), pp. 27 and 51. On the Oslo process more generally, see Graham Usher, *Palestine in Crisis: The Struggle for Peace and Political Independence After Oslo* (London and Chicago: Pluto Press in association with Transnational Institute and Middle East Research & Information Project, 1997); Geoffrey Kemp and Jeremy Pressman, *Point of No Return: The Deadly Struggle for Middle East Peace* (Washington, DC: Brookings Press, 1997); Uri Savir, *The Process: 1,100 Days That Changed the Middle East* (New York: Random House, 1998); Mahmud Abbas (Abu Mazen), *Through Secret Channels* (Reading, UK: Garnet, 1995); and Yossi Beilin, *Touching Peace: From the Oslo Accord to a Final Agreement* (London: Weidenfeld & Nicolson, 1999).

5. Efraim Inbar, "Labor's Return to Power," in *Israel at the Polls, 1992,* ed. Daniel J. Elazar and Shmuel Sandler (Lanham, Md. Rowman & Littlefield, 1995), pp. 27–43, at p. 35.

6. Dennis Ross, *The Missing Peace: The Inside Story of the Fight for Middle East Peace* (New York: Farrar, Straus and Giroux, 2004), p. 116.

7. On Israeli-Syrian relations during these years, see Ross, *The Missing Peace;* Sadik al-Azm, "The View from Damascus," *New York Review of Books* 47, no. 10, June 15, 2000; and Itamar Rabinovich, *The Brink of Peace: The Israeli-Syrian Negotiations* (Princeton: Princeton University Press, 1998).

8. A separate territorial regime was developed in the West Bank city of Hebron.

9. Declaration of Principles on Interim Self-Government Arrangements, Texts and Speeches, the White House, Washington, 13 September 1993," *Israel's Foreign Relations: Selected Documents,* Volume 13–14: 1992–1994, http://www.israel-mfa.gov.il/mfa/go.asp?MFAH0jhk0.

10. http://www.mfa.gov.il/MFA/Archive/Peace+Process/1993/Remarks+by+PM+Yitzhak+Rabin+at+Signing+of+DOP+-+13.htm, accessed February 22, 2006.

11. The Foundation for Middle East Peace (fmep.org), citing the statistical abstract of Israel, puts the 1993 figures at 3,000 (Gaza) and 117,000 (West Bank). The foundation's November-December 2000 report, citing Israeli Ministry of Interior officials on July 28, 2000, puts the Gaza figure for 2000 at 6,700. The foundation's September-October 2000 report puts the West Bank at 200,000. For 2000, the CIA World Factbook puts the figures at 6,500 and 171,000, respectively.

12. By unauthorized, I mean that the Israeli government did not formally authorize them, though arms of the government provided support. To most of the world, outposts and settlements in the West Bank (including East Jerusalem) are both illegal under international law.

13. The Palestinian Society for the Protection of Human Rights & the Environment (LAW), "House Demolitions since the Oslo Agreement," http://www.lawsociety.org/Reports/reports/1998/hdlist.html.

14. Human Rights Watch, *World Report 1999*, http://www.hrw.org/hrw/world-report99/mideast/israel.html. See also "Israel 'quietly deporting' Palestinians," *BBC News* (online), September 15, 1998.

15. Jeremy M. Sharp, "US Aid to the Palestinians," *CRS Report for Congress*, February 2, 2006, p. 4.

16. The exceptions include policies in the Dwight D. Eisenhower administration following the Suez War in 1957; the initial intent, perhaps, of the Ford administration's "reassessment" in 1975; and the Bush-Baker-Shamir loan guarantee debate in 1991–1992.

17. Bill Clinton, *My Life* (New York: Alfred A. Knopf, 2004), p. 679.

18. For more on Barak and the Israeli-Syrian process, see Jeremy Pressman, "Lost Opportunities," *Boston Review* 29, no. 6, December 2004-January 2005, pp. 44–46, http://bostonreview.net/BR29.6/pressman.html (book review of Dennis Ross's *The Missing Peace*). See also Charles Enderlin, *Shattered Dreams: The Failure of the Peace Process in the Middle East, 1995–2002* (New York: Other Press, 2003); Frederic C. Hof, "The Line of June 4, 1967," *Middle East Insight*, September-October 1999, pp. 17–23; and Akiva Eldar, "Who never misses an opportunity to miss an opportunity?" *Ha'aretz,* August 12, 2003.

19. "Fatalities in the First Intifada," http://www.btselem.org/English/Statistics/First_Intifada_Tables.asp, accessed January 9, 2006,

20. "New Tries for Mideast Peace," *New York Times,* October 31, 2003.

21. Jeremy Pressman, "Visions in Collision: What Happened at Camp David and Taba?" *International Security* 28, no. 2 (Fall 2003), pp. 5–43. See also Enderlin, *Shattered Dreams;* Ross, *The Missing Peace;* and Clayton E. Swisher, *The Truth About Camp David: The Untold Story About the Collapse of the Middle East Peace Process* (New York: Nation Books, 2004).

22. Pressman, "Visions in Collision," p. 17. For more on differences among the Israeli negotiators during the Oslo years, see Arie Kacowicz, "Rashomon in Jerusalem: Mapping the Israeli Negotiators' Positions on the Israeli-Palestinian Peace Process, 1993–2001," *International Studies Perspectives* 6 (2005), pp. 252–273.

23. Jeremy Pressman, "The Second Intifada: An Early Look at the Background and Causes of Israeli-Palestinian Conflict," *Journal of Conflict Studies* 22, no. 2 (Fall 2003), pp. 114–141.

24. "Fatalities," http://www.btselem.org/english/Statistics/Casualties.asp, accessed December 1, 2005. The best article on the Israeli belief that force would end, not escalate, the confrontation is Ben Kaspit, "Israel is not a state that has an army but rather an army that has a state attached to it," *Ma'ariv*, September 6, 2002, pp. 8–11, 32 of Rosh Hashanah supplement; and Ben Kaspit, "The Army Will Decide and Approve," *Ma'ariv*, September 13, 2002, pp. 6–10 of sabbath supplement (in Hebrew but English translations available on the Web).

25. I have used 97 percent as shorthand for more complex details. The plan called for 94–96 percent of the West Bank plus an additional land swap of 1–3 percent. By land swap, the negotiators meant that a small amount of pre-1967 Israel, equal to 1–3 percent of the area of the West Bank, would be annexed by the new Palestinian state in exchange for the areas of the West Bank annexed to Israel.

26. For some of the contents of Barak's letter, see Gilead Sher, *The Israeli-Palestinian Peace Negotiations, 1999–2001: Within Reach* (New York: Routledge, 2006), pp. 206–207.

27. Ross, *The Missing Peace*, p. 11. For Arafat's reservations letter to Clinton, see Clayton E. Swisher, *The Truth About Camp David*, 399–401. The Palestinian Negotiations Support

Unit (NSU) also wrote a letter. See http://www.nad-plo.org/inner.php?view=nego_nego_clinton_nclinton2p, accessed March 21, 2006.

28. Pressman, "Visions in Collision," pp. 21–22.

29. Bruce Riedel, "Camp David—The US-Israeli Bargain," bitterlemons.org, July 15, 2002, edition 26, http://www.bitterlemons.org/previous/bl150702ed26extra.html, accessed March 9, 2006.

30. One additional explanation is that Rabin's assassination blocked peace. In relation to the Israeli-Syrian talks, see Yoav Stern, "Report: Bishara acted as Syria-Israel mediator in 1990s talks," *Ha'aretz*, March 17, 2006. Stern quotes from an interview that former Syrian Vice-President Abed al-Halim Haddam gave to the Israeli newspaper *A-Sinara:* "Syria was ready for peace. As for Israel, it seemed like Israel was ready for it but he [Rabin] was killed."

31. For instance, minutes from a PLO central council meeting in October 2000 revealed, according to a press report, "readiness to give up 3 percent of the West Bank in a territorial exchange, as well as readiness to recognize Israeli sovereignty in the Jewish Quarter [of Jerusalem's Old City]." The minutes asserted the right of return for refugees, but, quoting the document, "there's nothing against providing compensation" instead. Israel captured and released the document. See Akiva Eldar, "Trite of return or the refugees problem," *Ha'aretz*, June 26, 2003.

32. William Quandt, *Peace Process* (Berkeley: University of California Press; and Washington, DC: Brookings Institution Press, 2001), pp. 339 and 352.

15

The Bush Administration and the Arab-Israeli Conflict

The First Term and Beyond

Robert O. Freedman

Introduction

The basic factors that have influenced the Bush administration in its policy toward the Arab-Israeli conflict are clear now that George W. Bush has completed his first four-year term and is well into his second. First, after initially wishing to keep a "hands-off" policy toward the Arab-Israeli conflict, in part because of President Clinton's failures in that area, the Bush administration pursued an activist policy on four different occasions—only to see its policy initiatives fail, primarily because of outbreaks of Palestinian terrorism. Second, the al-Qa'ida terrorist attack on the United States on September 11, 2001, had a defining impact on the Bush administration. This worked to the disadvantage of the Palestinians because by June 2002, Palestinian leader Yasser Arafat's links to terrorism had made him persona non grata to the Bush administration. Third, serious divisions at the top of the Bush administration, especially the split between Secretary of State Colin Powell on the one hand and Secretary of Defense Donald Rumsfeld and Vice President Richard Cheney on the other created a certain amount of incoherence in the administration's Middle East policy. Fourth, the US effort to build an alliance to wage war against Iraq significantly influenced its policy toward the Arab-Israeli conflict. Finally, the administration's effort to seek support among evangelical Christians and American Jews also affected administration policy and was an increasingly important factor as the 2004 elections approached.

The Clinton Legacy

From Rabin to Netanyahu

The failure of the Clinton administration to make significant breakthroughs in the Israeli-Palestinian conflict, despite a major personal effort by Clinton, was a factor that influenced the Bush administration initially to maintain a hands-off policy toward the conflict, along with the general "I'm not Clinton" approach of the early Bush presidency. Having seen Clinton try and fail to achieve Palestinian-Israeli agreements in July, October, and December 2000, Bush had little desire to invest his limited political capital in trying to resolve the conflict.

Clinton, despite his failures in 2000, had a mixed record in Arab-Israeli peacemaking.[1] In his first presidential term (1993–1996), Clinton served essentially as a cheerleader for the Oslo I (1993) and Oslo II (1995) Israeli-Palestinian agreements and for the Israeli-Jordanian peace agreement (1994), which were negotiated by the parties themselves with Israeli Prime Minister Yitzhak Rabin spearheading the diplomacy. By the late summer of 1996, however, Clinton was forced to take a more activist approach. Following the assassination of Rabin, and the electoral defeat of his successor and new Labor party leader Shimon Peres, Israel's newly elected prime minister, Likud leader Benjamin Netanyahu, who had a tougher attitude toward the Palestinians, decided to secretly open the Hasmonean Tunnel linking the Via Dolorosa to the plaza adjoining the Temple Mount/Haram in Jerusalem, an action Palestinians believed infringed upon their administrative authority of the Haram al-Asharif. In response, the Palestinians erupted in rioting and 70 people were killed, 55 Palestinians and 15 Israelis. Clinton managed to quell the violence by convening a meeting in Washington of Netanyahu, Arafat, and King Hussein of Jordan. However, by this time what little trust had existed between Netanyahu and Arafat had dissipated, and Clinton had to entrust his special envoy, Dennis Ross, with the responsibility for negotiating an agreement for dividing Hebron in January 1997. Following the Hebron agreement, negotiations stagnated, in part because Clinton was bogged down by the Lewinsky affair, until October 1998 when Clinton used his personal prestige to directly negotiate an agreement between Arafat and Netanyahu to move the peace process forward, in what became known as the Wye Agreement (after the town on Maryland's eastern shore where the agreement was negotiated). Under the Wye Agreement, Israel was to withdraw from an additional 13.1 percent of West Bank land and transfer an additional 14.2 percent of land jointly controlled by Israel and the Palestinians to exclusive Palestinian control. In return Arafat promised to eliminate the twenty-six articles in the Palestinian charter calling for Israel's destruction, to prohibit all forms of incitement to violence, and to suppress terrorism.[2] Unfortunately the agreement quickly fell apart, in part because of a series of Palestinian terrorist attacks against Israelis, including the attempt to set off a bomb in the Mahaneh Yehudah Market in Jerusalem. This led to the unraveling of the Netanyahu government, and new elections were held on May 17, 1999. These brought to power the new Labor party leader Ehud Barak who decisively defeated Netanyahu in the Israeli elections 56–44 percent and who brought a burst of optimism to the peace process.

The Policies of Ehud Barak and the Outbreak of the al-Aqsa Intifada

When Barak took office he switched the direction of Israel's peace policy from the Palestinian track to the Syrian track and received positive signals from Syria. Barak must have also thought that peace with Syria, which basically involved only territorial issues, could be more easily achieved than peace with the Palestinians, where negotiations had yet to deal with the highly sensitive issues of the sovereignty of Jerusalem and the plight of Palestinian refugees. Needless to say, the Palestinian leadership took a dim view of the shift in priorities, as well as Barak's decision to allow the continued expansion of Jewish settlements on the West Bank, which Barak permitted to keep the National Religious party, whose constituency included the West Bank settlers, in his coalition. The expansion took place primarily in areas near Jerusalem, in cities like Maaleh Adumim, which Barak hoped to annex. For his part, Clinton went along with Barak's peace process priority and invested a great deal of his personal prestige, including a meeting with Syria's president, Hafiz al-Asad, in Geneva in March 2000, to try to obtain a breakthrough in negotiations.[3] Despite Clinton's best efforts, however, an agreement with Syria was not achieved, in part because of a dispute over Syria's claim to territory on the northeast shore of the Sea of Galilee, and in part because of Asad's rapidly deteriorating health (he died a few months after meeting Clinton in Geneva).

Barak then sought to politically outflank the Syrians by arranging a unilateral pullout from southern Lebanon in May 2000. Asad had been manipulating Hezbollah attacks against Israeli forces in southern Lebanon, and occasional rocket attacks into Israel proper, as a means of pressuring Israel to be more flexible in its negotiations with Syria. Indeed, just such an escalation of fighting had occurred following the collapse of the Syrian-Israeli talks in February 1996. By unilaterally withdrawing from southern Lebanon without a peace treaty, Barak may have hoped to avoid a repetition of these events, while gaining support in the international community, including the United States, which had long pressed for such a pullback. Unfortunately for Barak, regardless of the support he received from the international community, he set a precedent for withdrawing under fire—without an agreement—from a territory occupied by Israeli troops. This lesson was not lost on a number of Palestinians who felt that if Israel could be made to withdraw from Lebanon under fire, it could also be made to pull out of at least the West Bank and Gaza under similar pressure.[4]

Following the failure of the Syrian talks, Barak turned back to the Palestinian track. After initial discussions between the two sides in May, Barak pushed for a summit in July in the United States where, at one stroke, all the remaining final status issues, including those that had not yet been seriously discussed, such as the status of Jerusalem and the refugee problem, could be settled and a peace agreement achieved. Clinton went along with Barak's plan and devoted two weeks of scarce presidential time to the summit, which became known as Camp David II. There have been many different explanations for the failure of the Camp David II summit, with even members of the same delegation disagreeing as to the causes of the failure.

Those sympathetic to Arafat blame Barak's negotiating style, his "take it or leave it" attitude, and his unwillingness to meet what they felt were even the minimum needs of the Palestinians. Those sympathetic to Barak note that he offered unheard-of Israeli concessions, including giving up all of Gaza, 92 percent of the West Bank and dividing Jerusalem, which threatened the viability of his coalition government, especially on the issue of Jerusalem, which Israel thus far had contended was to remain united under Israeli control. It was also felt by Barak's sympathizers that Arafat, by rejecting the Israeli concessions and demanding the return of the more than 3 million Palestinian refugees to Israel proper (which would have destroyed Israel as a Jewish state),[5] and by denying the existence of the Jewish temples on the Temple Mount/Haram and making no counteroffers, had demonstrated that he was not a serious partner for peace. Following the failed summit, Clinton took Barak's side in the debate over who was responsible for the failure, thereby alienating Arafat. Arafat also fared badly in the court of Western opinion, including in western Europe where the Palestinian leader was blamed for the failure to reach an agreement. In addition to shouldering the international disapproval for the failure to reach an agreement, Arafat was criticized by Palestinians for his heavy-handed authoritarian ways and the corrupt practices within the Palestinian Authority. Arafat counterattacked, claiming he had defended the interests of the world's Muslims at Camp David by not making concessions on the Temple Mount/Haram. He also stepped up the military training given to Palestinian youth in special military camps, perhaps assuming that in the aftermath of the failure to reach a peace agreement, the only alternative was renewed conflict.

And conflict did come in late September 2000, following the visit of the new Likud leader, Ariel Sharon, accompanied by more than 1,000 Israeli police, to the Temple Mount/Haram, a move linked to internal Israeli politics, as Netanyahu had begun to challenge Sharon's leadership of the Likud party. Palestinian rioting broke out, for which the Israeli police were ill prepared. As Palestinian casualties rose, the *intifada* ("uprising") spread, and soon both the West Bank and Gaza had erupted. The causes of the *intifada* (often referred to as the "second *intifada*" or "al-Aqsa *intifada*"—named for the mosque at the site visited by Sharon) are as much in dispute as the causes of the failure of Camp David II, as Palestinians and Israelis have very different narratives on the issue. For the Palestinians the uprising was the result of rising frustration over continued Israeli settlement expansion and the failure of the Oslo process to give them what they demanded; Sharon's visit to the Temple Mount/Haram was simply the straw that broke the camel's back. For Israelis, it was an attempt by Arafat to get by force what he could not get by negotiations, an effort to win back international public opinion by again becoming the Palestinian David to Israel's Goliath, as Palestinian casualties rose more quickly than Israeli. Many Israelis also believed that Arafat was applying the lesson learned in Lebanon, forcing Israel to withdraw through the use of not only stones, as in the first *intifada* (1987), but also gunfire and mortar attacks, as the Palestinians turned the weapons they had been given by the Israelis under the Oslo process against their one-time peace partners.[6] Many also suspected that Arafat, whether he planned the *intifada* or not, was exploiting it to divert attention from Palestinian criticism of his authoritarian and corrupt practices.

Whatever the cause of the *intifada,* President Clinton sought to quell it, much as he had done after the eruption of violence in 1996 following Netanyahu's opening of the Hasmonean Tunnel. Consequently, he convened a summit with both Arafat and Barak at Sharm al-Shaykh on October 16, 2000, and proposed an investigatory commission to analyze the causes of the conflict. The commission was headed by former US Senator George Mitchell, who had been Clinton's special envoy to the conflict between Protestants and Catholics in Northern Ireland, and who was the father of the "Good Friday" agreement.

Unfortunately for Clinton, despite Arafat's pledge at Sharm al-Shaykh to stop the violence,[7] the task proved either beyond his will or beyond his ability to achieve, and not only did the *intifada* continue, but the violence escalated. Clinton tried again in December, preparing, with the help of Dennis Ross and his colleagues, an American plan to settle all the final status issues, including the most heavily disputed issues of Jerusalem's sovereignty and the so-called "right of return" of Palestinian refugees. Essentially, Clinton proposed some major trade-offs: the withdrawal of Israel from 95 percent of the West Bank; the compensation of Palestinians with Israeli territory near Gaza; the establishment of East Jerusalem as the capital of the new Palestinian state; and the partitioning of the Temple Mount/Haram area, with the Temple Mount/Haram going to the Palestinians, and the Jewish quarter of the Old City and Western Wall going to Israel, and a passage to both through the Armenian quarter. On the issue of the Palestinian right of return, Clinton's plan called for the vast majority of refugees to go to the new Palestinian state.[8]

Barak was willing to accept the plan even though he knew that with Israeli elections looming on February 7 (which he would lose badly to Ariel Sharon), he would run into problems with the Israeli electorate. For his part, Arafat added so many conditions to his acceptance of the Clinton plan that he, in fact, rejected it, once again confirming to most Israelis that the Palestinian leader was not really interested in peace. To make matters worse, several members of his entourage made disparaging comments about Clinton—rather poor payment for the president's near-Herculean efforts to bring about an Israeli-Palestinian peace agreement.

The Bush Administration

From the Inauguration to 9/11

Incoming US President George W. Bush had witnessed the massive investment of political capital by President Clinton in trying to secure an Israeli-Palestinian peace agreement and took note of the very meager return on that investment. Even if Bush had had the inclination to actively pursue an Arab-Israeli settlement, a quick assessment of Clinton's record would have given him pause. Adding to Bush's hesitation was his extremely narrow victory in the November 2000 elections. Bush had lost the popular vote to Al Gore and had only eked out a very controversial victory over Gore in the Electoral College after a divided Supreme Court ruled against a hotly disputed vote recount in Florida. In addition, the Republicans had suffered major losses in the US Senate in the fall 2000 election, maintaining control by only a one-vote margin. Several months later, even that one-vote margin slipped away when a liberal Republican defected from his party. Furthermore, Bush faced an economic downturn. In sum, even if he had been inclined to undertake a major new Middle East peace initiative, which he was not, the overall domestic political situation in the United States appeared to preclude any such initiative.

When the Bush administration took office on January 20, it took a long time to get its senior-level executives in place, especially those in the Middle East section of the Department of State; an assistant secretary of state was not approved until late May. Compounding problems, the administration was beset by an extraordinary number of public disagreements over such issues as whether to strengthen sanctions against Iraq (Secretary of State Colin Powell) or weaken them (Vice President Richard Cheney), whether to take a more aggressive military stance against Iraq (Secretary of Defense Rumsfeld and Deputy Secretary of Defense Wolfowitz–yes; Powell–no), whether to pull US peacekeeping forces out of the multinational force in the Sinai (Rumsfeld–yes; Powell–no), whether to pursue negotiations with North Korea (Powell–yes; Bush–no); whether to pull US forces out of Balkan peacekeeping missions (Powell–no; Rumsfeld–yes), and whether to drill in the Arctic National Wildlife Refuge (Environmental Protection Agency head Christine Todd Whitman–no; Bush–yes) to mention only a few of the disputes.[9] These types of disputes were to persist throughout all four years of the administration, creating problems of incoherence and inconsistency in US policy in the Middle East as well as elsewhere in the world.

Another problem the administration had to deal with was the significant degree of optimism in the Arab world, especially among Palestinians, that Bush, following in the steps of his father, who had clashed openly with then Israeli Prime Minister Yitzhak Shamir, as well as with Sharon, would take a much tougher stance toward Israel than Clinton had done. In this, they were sorely mistaken. Initially, Bush followed essentially a "not Clinton" policy and refused to get personally involved in trying to settle the conflict. Secretary of State Powell repeatedly emphasized the primary responsibility of the parties themselves to solve the conflict. "We will facilitate, but at the end of the day, it will have to be the parties in the region who will have to find the solution."[10]

In this, perhaps, they were hoping for a return to the situation that prevailed during the Oslo I and Oslo II agreements, which were negotiated directly between Israelis and Palestinians without significant US intervention. The Bush administration followed up its word with deeds that emphasized the new "hands-off" policy. Thus, when special Middle East envoy Dennis Ross retired in January 2001, no replacement was named, and it was not until late May, with the Israeli-Palestinian conflict rapidly escalating, that a "special assistant" for the Middle East, William Burns, was appointed. Second, the United States did not send a representative to the Israeli-Palestinian negotiations at Taba, which took place at the end of January, just before the February 7, 2001, Israeli elections.[11] Third, the United States ended CIA mediation efforts between Israel and the Palestinians, which had begun as part of the Wye Agreement of October 1998. Finally, much to the displeasure of the Palestinians, Bush supported the Israeli position that the offers made by Israel's Labor government at Camp David II and at Taba were "off the table," after the new Israeli government, headed by Likud leader Ariel Sharon, was elected on February 7, 2001.

Despite the effort to play down the US role in the Arab-Israeli conflict, the first foreign trip undertaken by the newly appointed US Secretary of State was to the Middle East. Powell's purpose, however, was not to deal directly with the al-Aqsa *intifada,* but rather to convince the Arab states to support his plans for "smart sanctions" against Iraq. However, his Arab hosts, including not only Egypt and Jordan, Kuwait and Saudi Arabia, but also Syria, had a different priority, and they urged the Bush administration to become actively involved in settling the Arab-Israeli conflict. For his part, Powell called for a renewal of peace talks after a reduction in violence—not the total cessation of violence demanded by Sharon.[12] However, Powell was to move closer to the Israeli position several weeks later.

On the eve of the Sharon visit to Washington in mid-March 2001, Powell gave a major speech on the Middle East to a conference of the pro-Israeli AIPAC lobbying organization. In it, he moved to support Sharon's position on the violence, noting that the starting point for talks had to be the end of violence. In a clear slap at Arafat, Powell publicly stated that "leaders have the responsibility to denounce violence, strip it of legitimacy [and] stop it." Powell also repeated the Bush administration's position that the United States would assist but not impose a peace agreement: "The US stands ready to assist, not insist. Peace arrived at voluntarily by the partners themselves is likely to prove more robust . . . than a peace widely viewed as developed by others, or worse yet, imposed."[13]

When Sharon met with Bush several days later, he was again reassured that the United States would facilitate, not force, the peace process. Bush also sought to enlist Sharon in his campaign to develop a national missile defense system, something the Israeli leader, whose country was a prime target of such "rogue" states as Iran and Iraq, was only too happy to agree to. Sharon, for his part, pressed Bush not to invite Arafat to the White House unless he publicly called for an end to the violence, a request endorsed by nearly 300 members of Congress (87 senators and 209 House members), who also called on Bush to close the Washington office of the Palestine Liberation Organization (PLO) and to cut US aid to the Palestinian Authority (PA) if the violence did not cease.[14]

Yet the Sharon visit, as successful as it was, was not without its problems. On the eve of the visit, Sharon had authorized the construction of more Jewish housing in the East Jerusalem suburb of Har Homa, near Bethlehem, a development criticized by State Department spokesman Richard Boucher as a unilateral act "not contributing to peace and stability."[15] In addition, Secretary of Defense Rumsfeld, apparently oblivious to the escalating conflict between Israel and the Palestinians, which had caused a resultant deterioration in Israeli-Egyptian relations, told Sharon that the

United States wanted to withdraw US forces serving as peacekeepers in the multinational force in the Sinai Desert.[16]

Still, the Sharon visit was clearly a success and marked a high point in the US-Israeli relationship for the new Israeli leader, who had been severely criticized by previous US administrations. At the end of March, the United States vetoed a United Nations Security Council resolution calling for a UN observer force on the West Bank and Gaza as "unbalanced and unworkable,"[17] and Bush, in a news conference, took the strongest anti-Palestinian position of the administration to this point: "The Palestinian Authority should speak out publicly and forcibly in a language that the Palestinian people [understand] to condemn violence and terrorism. . . . The signal I am sending to the Palestinians is stop the violence and I can't make it any more clear."[18]

Although Egyptian President Hosni Mubarak and King Abdullah II of Jordan called for a more active US role during their visits to Washington in late March and early April, the Bush administration continued to insist that the Israelis and Palestinians had to bear the primary responsibility for coming to an agreement. Unfortunately for Bush, however, an upsurge of Israeli-Palestinian fighting called into question the US strategy.

Following the successful Sharon visit to Washington, Arafat shifted the strategy of the Palestinian *intifada.* Given the disparity of forces between Israel and the Palestinians, Arafat's only hope for achieving political gains was to mobilize not only Arab support for the Palestinian cause (the Arab leaders had been rather fickle supporters in the past and remained so) but also the European Union, Russia, and if at all possible, the United States. As things stood, the United States was solidly behind Sharon, so Arafat escalated the fighting in an apparent attempt to precipitate an Israeli response that would compel both the European Union and the United States to take action. Thus, the Palestinians began to fire mortars not just at Israeli settlements in Gaza but also into Israel proper. This indeed brought a major Israeli response, with Israeli forces invading the section of Gaza from which the mortars had been fired into Israel. Israeli Brigadier General Yair Naveh seemed to play into Arafat's hands by stating that Israel would stay there "as long as it takes—days, weeks, months." Powell termed the Israeli action "excessive and disproportionate," and the Israeli forces soon withdrew, seemingly under US pressure. Nonetheless, Powell also blamed the Palestinians for precipitating the Israeli attack with "provocative" mortar attacks on Israeli territory.[19] The United States also disappointed Israel when the State Department's annual terrorist report did not brand the PA as a terrorist organization for its role in fostering the *intifada* (and the terrorist bombings that were a part of it). Instead, the report noted only that the Israeli government had accused the PA of facilitating terrorist attacks.[20]

Meanwhile, as Palestinian mortar and other attacks against Israel continued to increase, Israel stepped up its retaliatory raids into Palestinian Authority–controlled territories in Gaza, although it quickly withdrew each time. The United States condemned both the attacks and Israel's retaliatory efforts with State Department spokesman Boucher noting that the Israeli responses represented "a serious escalation that causes concern that makes it harder to resolve this." Boucher also criticized the Palestinians who "have to immediately end provocative acts of violence."[21] Meanwhile, possibly as a response to Palestinian actions, Sharon once again began to push settlement expansion claiming that the West Bank and Gaza were not "occupied" territory, but "disputed" territory.[22] This prompted the expected denunciation from the State Department (which mirrored criticism from the left of the Israeli political spectrum): "This activity risks further inflaming the already volatile situation in the region and is provocative."[23]

As the fighting escalated further, with terrorist attacks by Palestinians being responded to by increasingly severe Israeli reprisals, including the use, for the first time, of Israeli jet fighters to bombard Palestinian positions, the Bush administration seemed hard-pressed to respond to the situation. The only hope for the administration appeared to be the completion of the Mitchell Report in mid-May, which provided the administration a diplomatic framework on which to base its Middle East position.

Conceived at the Sharm al-Shaykh summit in October 2000 as a device to determine the causes of the al-Aqsa *intifada* and find ways to bring the fighting to a halt, the report was delivered by a commission headed by former US Senator George Mitchell. The report, which did not assign blame to either side for starting the *intifada,* instead described each side's reasons for blaming the other for the outbreak and continuation of the uprising. It also listed a series of steps the Israelis and Palestinians should take to resume negotiations.[24] These recommendations included, in order: (1) a 100 percent effort to stop the violence; (2) the immediate resumption of security cooperation; (3) the exchange of confidence-building measures; and (4) the speedy return to serious negotiations. In many ways the Mitchell Report was supportive of the Israeli position in the conflict; it called for a cease-fire before negotiations, for the PA to condemn incitement and denounce terrorism and arrest terrorists, and for the PA to prevent gunmen from using Palestinian-populated areas to fire upon Israeli-populated areas and Israeli military positions. It also did not blame Sharon's visit to the Temple Mount/Haram for precipitating the *intifada.* On the negative side, as far as Israeli Prime Minister Sharon was concerned, was the call to freeze all settlement activity, including "natural growth," as a necessary confidence-building measure. (Israel has always held to the position that the future of the settlements was a "final status" issue to be negotiated by the two sides.)

On balance, it was a report that was quite sympathetic to the Israeli position, and Sharon, while having reservations about the settlement issue, agreed to order a cease-fire and called on Israeli forces not to fire upon Palestinians unless fired upon. For their part, the Palestinians, while also accepting the report in principle, made their formal acceptance contingent upon Israel stopping the building of settlements.

Palestinian deeds, however, did not follow their words, as a series of terrorist attacks were mounted against Israel in Hadera and Jerusalem, along with the killing of Jews in the West Bank and Gaza, which the PA could not, or would not, stop. Meanwhile, Powell, who warmly praised the Mitchell Report, appointed a "special assistant" to help implement it. William Burns, the US ambassador to Jordan, who had been nominated to become the Assistant Secretary of State for Near Eastern Affairs, was given the task of trying to establish a "time line" of Israeli and Palestinian confidence-building measures that might bring about the unconditional cease-fire deemed an absolute necessity by the Mitchell Report.[25] Nevertheless, despite the appointment of Burns and subsequent efforts to secure a resumption of security cooperation between the Israelis and Palestinians, Powell continued to echo the administration theme that the United States would not directly intervene, as had the Clinton administration, to put forth its own solution to the conflict. Powell asserted that the United States was not ready to get involved in shuttle diplomacy or sensitive final status issues.

This stance changed with the Dolphinarium suicide bombing in June 2001 that killed twenty-one people, mostly teenagers. With Israeli Prime Minister Sharon under heavy pressure not only to terminate the cease-fire induced by the Mitchell Plan but also to launch a massive attack on the Palestinian leadership, Arafat, who had held back from accepting a cease fire, finally endorsed it. In part, this was due to pressure from Bush who strongly condemned the bombing, stating: "I condemn in the strongest terms the heinous terrorist attack in Tel Aviv this Sabbath evening. There is no justification for senseless attacks against innocent civilians. This illustrates the urgent need for an immediate, unconditional cessation of violence." Bush also called on Arafat "to condemn this act and call for an immediate cease-fire."[26] Arafat's condemnation of the terrorist act and his call for a cease-fire were also due to heavy pressure from German Foreign Minister Joshka Fischer, who indicated that the terrorist act had cost the Palestinians dearly in public opinion not only in the United States but also in Europe.[27] Bush followed Arafat's call for a cease-fire by sending CIA chief George Tenet to the Middle East to consolidate the cease-fire, something that was achieved, on paper at least, on June 13, 2001.

Almost immediately, however, the cease-fire began to break down as Arafat could not, or would not, prevent further attacks on Israel; neither Hamas leader Abdel Aziz Rantisi nor Fatah leader Marwan Barghouti supported the cease-fire.[28] To prevent the situation from deteriorating further Bush sent Secretary of State Powell to the Middle East. Powell's visit came after an open disagreement between Sharon, who was visiting the United States, and President Bush, with Bush, perhaps accenting the positive, stating "progress had been made toward controlling the violence" and Sharon saying that mediation would not work so long as the shooting continued.[29] In any case, the Powell trip proved to be a failure, as violence not only continued but escalated during the summer, with drive-by shootings of Israeli settlers, mortar firing into Jewish settlements in Gaza and into Gilo, a suburb of Jerusalem occupied after the 1967 war, and several suicide bombings, including one in a pizza parlor in Jerusalem that killed fifteen Israelis along with the suicide bomber.

Sharon responded to these attacks both militarily and diplomatically. On the diplomatic front, he went to France, Italy, and Germany in early July, seeking to convince the Europeans to pressure Arafat to halt the attacks on Israel, much as Fischer had pressured the Palestinian leader to agree to a cease-fire after the Dolphinarium bombing. But Sharon was not successful in his quest, hearing from Gerhard

Schroeder, the chancellor of Germany—Israel's best friend in Europe—that the Mitchell Report should be implemented, even if the violence had not come to a halt.[30] With the United States again taking a hands-off policy following the failure of the Powell mission, and with Europe unwilling to bring the desired diplomatic pressure on Arafat, Sharon turned to intensified military force, as a war of attrition intensified between Israelis and Palestinians. The Israeli actions not only included incursions into Palestinian territory and the takeover of Orient House, the de facto Palestinian headquarters in East Jerusalem, but also assassinations of Palestinians suspected by Israel of planning terrorist attacks, including at the end of August the leader of the Popular Front for the Liberation of Palestine, Abu Ali Mustafa.

US reaction to the Israeli assassination policy was mixed. State Department spokesman Richard Boucher condemned it, stating "Israel needs to understand that targeted killings of Palestinians don't end the violence but are only inflaming an already volatile situation and making it much harder to restore calm."[31] Taking an opposing view was Vice President Cheney, who had stated on FOX-TV in early August, "If you've got an organization that had plotted or is plotting, some kind of suicide bomber attack, for example, and they have hard evidence of who it is and where they're located, I think there's some justification in their trying to protect themselves by preempting."[32] Meanwhile, President Bush, who had used US influence at the United Nations to block the approval of an anti-Israeli resolution for international monitors in the region, remained adamant that Arafat must "put 100 percent effort into stopping the terrorist activity" before the beginning of peace talks and "do a better job of quashing violence."[33] With diplomacy frozen, the Palestinian-Israeli conflict intensified. Despite calls by America's Arab allies, like Egypt, for the United States to take a more active role because Arafat could not stop the violence on his own, and "America is the only sponsor of the peace process," and the outspoken French Foreign Minister Hubert Vedrine, caustically comparing Bush to Pontius Pilate, washing his hands of the Middle East, the United States remained on the diplomatic sidelines.[34] This situation changed dramatically, however, after the terrorist attacks on the World Trade Center in New York and the Pentagon in Washington on September 11, 2001.

US Policy from 9/11 to the Karine A Incident

Immediately after the terrorist attacks on the World Trade Center and the Pentagon, the United States changed its "hands-off" policy toward the Israeli-Palestinian conflict and sought to build a coalition, including Muslim states, against Osama bin Laden and his al-Qa'ida terrorist organization. In an effort to gain Arab support, the United States announced its support of a Palestinian state and exercised a considerable amount of pressure on Sharon to agree to a meeting between Israeli Foreign Minister Shimon Peres and Arafat to establish yet another cease-fire, despite the fact that Palestinian violence had not stopped as Sharon had demanded as the price for talks. Since the violence continued after the talks, including a terrorist bombing in Jerusalem and an attack on a Jewish settlement in Gaza, there was some question as to the long-term effect of the Peres-Arafat meeting—and the US strategy. Frustrated by this policy, Sharon called it the equivalent of British and French policy at the 1938 Munich Conference when Czechoslovakia had been sold out to the Nazis. His comments drew a retort from the White House press secretary, Ari Fleischer, who called them "unacceptable."[35] Although Sharon later apologized, claiming his words were misinterpreted, the basic issue remained unresolved and was a cause of friction in US-Israeli relations, albeit only a temporary one.

Meanwhile, Palestinian attacks on Israel escalated, and so did retaliation by the Israeli army. In the latter part of October, Israeli cabinet minister Rehavam Zeevi was assassinated in a Jerusalem hotel, and this precipitated a move by the Israeli army into six major Palestinian cities to search for the assassins, because, as Sharon asserted, Arafat continued to refuse to arrest Palestinians who attacked Israelis. The Israelis also stepped up their policy of killing or capturing suspected terrorists. Israelis compared their actions to that of the United States in Afghanistan, arguing that just as the United States was justified in attacking the Taliban for harboring the al-Qa'ida terrorists, so too was Israel justified in invading Palestinian areas to search for terrorists.[36]

The State Department, however, had a different view. State Department spokesman Philip Reeker, noting the Palestinian casualties resulting from the Israeli incursions, declared that Israeli forces "should be withdrawn immediately from all Palestinian-controlled areas. We deeply regret and deplore Israeli defense force actions that had killed numerous Palestinian civilians over the weekend." He also stated that Israel should abstain from further incursions.[37] President Bush, separating himself from the State Department, was a bit milder in his criticism, stating, "I would hope that Israelis would move their troops as quickly as possible." Bush balanced the criticism of Israel, however, with criticism of Arafat: "We continue to call upon Chairman Arafat to do everything he can to bring the killer to justice. It is very important that he arrest the person who did this act—and continue to arrest those who would disrupt and harm Israeli citizens. He must show the resolve necessary to bring peace to the region."[38]

This, however, was to be the low point in the US-Israeli relationship through the end of 2001. Beginning in November, the United States scored a series of military victories in Afghanistan, as Secretary of Defense Donald Rumsfeld's military activities took precedence over Colin Powell's limited success in coalition building.[39] As the Taliban fled one city after another in Afghanistan, often leaving operational equipment such as tanks behind, they became increasingly discredited, as did Osama bin Laden, whose call for the Muslim world to rise up against the United States received little active support from Muslims.

In this atmosphere of military victory, the United States embarked on a two-fold strategy. The first, to try to reinvigorate the Israeli-Palestinian peace process, was warmly greeted by its European allies and by pro-US governments in the Arab world. The second strategy, to threaten to carry the war from Afghanistan to other supporters of terror, especially Iraq, met with far less support. However, as I discuss below, the US efforts to build a coalition for an invasion of Iraq significantly influenced its policy toward the Arab-Israeli conflict.

The US effort to invigorate the Israeli-Palestine peace process began with a speech by President Bush at the United Nations in November 2001, where he said, "We are working for the day when two states—Israel and Palestine—live peacefully together within secure and recognized boundaries." However, in a clear warning to Arafat to crack down on terrorists, he also added: "Peace will come when all have sworn off forever incitement, violence, and terror. There is no such thing as a good terrorist."[40] Bush also pointedly did not meet Arafat at the United Nations as National Security Advisor Condoleezza Rice noted, "You cannot help us with al-Qaʻida, and hug Hezbollah or Hamas. And so the President makes that clear to Mr. Arafat."[41] The United States backed up Rice's words by adding Hamas, Islamic Jihad, and Hezbollah to the post–September 11 terrorist list.

The next step in the US peace effort came on November 19 with a major speech by Secretary of State Colin Powell on the US view of a solution to the Israeli-Palestinian conflict.[42] In his speech Powell strongly condemned Palestinian terrorism, noting that the al-Aqsa *intifada* was now mired in "self-defeating violence." He also stated that although the US believed that there should be a two-state solution to the conflict, with two states, Palestine and Israel, living side by side in secure and recognized borders, the Palestinians must make a 100 percent effort to stop terrorism, and for this actions, not words, were required, and terrorists must be arrested. He emphasized that "no wrong can ever justify the murder of the innocent," that terror and violence must stop now, and that Palestinians must realize their goals by negotiations, not violence. He further asserted, possibly in response to Arafat's call for the more than 3 million Palestinian refugees to return to Israel, a development that would have upset Israel's demographic balance, that the Palestinians must accept the legitimacy of Israel as a Jewish state.

While emphasizing that the United States and Israel were closely "bound together by democratic tradition" and that the United States had an "enduring and iron-clad commitment to Israeli security," Powell indicated that Israel, too, had to make concessions for peace to be possible. These included a stop to settlement expansion and an end to the occupation of the West Bank and Gaza, which "causes humiliation and the killing of innocents." In conclusion, he stated that the United States would do everything it could to facilitate the peace process "but at the end of the day the peoples have to make peace"—a position very similar to the one Powell held when he joined the cabinet nearly a year earlier.

In order to implement the US vision of peace outlined by Powell, in addition to promises of economic aid, Assistant Secretary of State William Burns and former Marine General Anthony Zinni were dispatched to meet with Israeli and Palestinian delegations to reach a cease-fire that would lay the basis for the resumption of peace negotiations. In an effort to facilitate the Zinni mission, President Bush put his personal prestige on the line by writing to five important Arab leaders, King Abdullah II of Jordan, Egyptian President Hosni Mubarak, King Mohammed VI of Morocco,

Saudi Crown Prince Abdullah (who had publicly praised Powell's speech), and President Ben-Ali of Tunisia, asking for their help in persuading "the Palestinian leadership to take action to end violence and get the peace process back on track."[43] For his part, Zinni stated that his goal was the achievement of a cease-fire, which would allow for the implementation of the Mitchell Plan, and the former Marine general asserted that he would stay in the region "as long as needed" to complete his mission.[44] Unfortunately for Zinni, it was an ill-fated mission that left not only the peace process but also US-Palestinian relations close to collapse.

On November 27, soon after Zinni's arrival, two Palestinian terrorists, one of whom was a member of Arafat's Fatah organization (the other was from Islamic Jihad), killed three Israelis and wounded thirty others in Afulah, a town in northern Israel. Zinni responded to the violence in a balanced way, stating: "This is why we need a cease-fire. Both sides have suffered too much."[45] Zinni then met with Arafat, asking him to end the violence, but even as they were meeting, Palestinian gunmen fired at the Israeli Jerusalem neighborhood of Gilo from the neighboring Palestinian suburb of Beit Jala—despite an explicit promise by Palestinian leaders not to do so in October.[46] The next day three more Israelis were killed as a suicide bomber exploded a bomb on a public bus near the Israeli city of Hadera.[47] This time Zinni's response was much stronger: "The groups that do this are clearly trying to make my mission fail. There's no justification, no rationale, no sets of conditions that will ever make terrorist acts a right way to respond."[48] Zinni's words, however, did not stem the tide of terrorism. Two days later suicide bombers killed ten Israeli teenagers who had gathered at the Ben Yehudah pedestrian mall in Jerusalem. This time Arafat condemned the attacks, stressing not the loss of life by Israel but the negative political effect the suicide bombers were having on the Palestinian world image: "The goal of the attacks has been to destroy the American peace efforts. These attacks cause great damage to our people in international public opinion and the Palestinian Authority will do everything in its power to catch those responsible. It pays its condolences to the Israeli people."[49]

By now, Zinni was furious, as he saw his mission literally going up in flames. "Those responsible for planning and carrying out these attacks must be found and brought to justice. This is an urgent task and there can be no delay or excuses for not acting decisively. The deepest evil one can imagine is to attack young people and children."[50] President Bush, whose prestige had been put on the line by the Zinni mission, also responded strongly. "Now more than ever Chairman Arafat and the Palestinian Authority must demonstrate through their actions, and not merely their words, their commitment to fight terror."[51]

Even President Bush's urgent pleas, however, did not stop the terrorist attacks; one day later, fifteen Israelis were killed in a suicide bomber attack on an Israeli bus in Haifa. While Powell, Bush, and Zinni had asserted that nothing justified such terrorist attacks, Hamas, the organization responsible for the bus bombing, justified it as "the natural retaliation by a people slaughtered day and night, whose dignity is humiliated by the Zionist enemy."[52] This time when Israel retaliated against the Palestinian Authority, the United States did not respond critically. Sharon ordered the destruction of Arafat's helicopters and the airport runway in Gaza—in a symbolic blow to Arafat's position as a leader who traveled the world—and also attacked PA security headquarters on the West Bank and Gaza, while also reimposing closure on the major Palestinian cities on the West Bank from which Israel had withdrawn as a goodwill gesture to the United States when Zinni began his visit. Presidential spokesman Ari Fleischer noted, "Obviously Israel has the right to defend herself, and the President understands that clearly."[53] The administration also reiterated its demand that Arafat find and imprison the terrorists: "The President thinks it is very important that Palestinian jails not only have bars on the front, but no longer have revolving doors at the back."[54]

As the pressure built, Arafat began to arrest some terrorists, but far fewer than either the United States or Israel demanded. Meanwhile, yet another Palestine suicide bomber struck in Haifa, blowing himself up on a bus, and three days later, ten Israelis were killed when Hamas detonated bombs under a bus in the West Bank and shot passengers as they tried to flee.[55] An exasperated Israeli government announced, "Chairman Arafat has made himself irrelevant as far as Israel is concerned" and declared that it was breaking all contact with him.[56] Then, as a further blow to Arafat, Israeli tanks surrounded his compound in Ramallah, and Israeli troops blew up the main transmission tower of the Palestine Broadcasting Company while also hitting offices of Arafat's Fatah organization in Gaza, Ramallah, and Jenin.[57] Meanwhile, it was clear that the United Sates, and especially President Bush, was thoroughly exasperated with Arafat, who had done nothing to prevent Palestinian terrorists from destroying the mission of General Zinni, on which Bush had staked his personal prestige. While US Secretary of State Colin Powell stated diplomatically that the United States "really can't give up hope, we can't walk away from this, the stakes are too high," Powell also warned that Hamas was "more likely to destroy the Palestinian cause than to destroy the State of Israel" and stated that the "burden" was on Arafat to stop the spiral of violence.[58]

Arafat seemed to get the message, if rather belatedly, from US political pressure and from Israeli military retaliation. On December 16, he called for an immediate cease-fire, condemning both suicide attacks and the launching of mortar attacks.[59] Nonetheless, the Palestinian leader did not root out the Hamas and Islamic Jihad organizations from Gaza and the West Bank but rather negotiated a tenuous truce with them (a tactic later repeated by Mahmoud Abbas in June 2003), something that was clearly unsatisfactory to the Israeli government. Arafat was kept penned up in Ramallah by Israeli tanks, and in a further blow to his prestige, he was prohibited from leaving his compound to attend Christmas services in Bethlehem.

While promising that the United States would remain involved in mediating the Israeli-Palestinian conflict, Powell nonetheless returned Zinni to the United States (so much for Zinni saying he would stay as long as necessary to solve the crisis).[60] Powell himself now turned his attention toward trying to prevent a war between India and Pakistan, both of whom had nuclear weapons, following a December 13 attack on the Indian legislature by Muslim terrorists who India claimed were backed by Pakistan.[61]

Three weeks after Arafat's call for a cease-fire, Israeli forces captured a ship in the Red Sea, the *Karine A,* that held fifty tons of concealed weapons, including C-4 explosives and Katyusha rockets—clearly weapons of terrorism. Arafat's initial denial that the Palestinian Authority had anything to do with the vessel further undermined his credibility, both in Israel and the United States.[62] In response to heavy pressure by the United States, he eventually arrested several of the Palestinian officials involved, including a major general in his own security forces and an officer in the Palestinian Authority's naval police.[63]

Meanwhile Hamas broke the truce by attacking an Israeli military outpost in Gaza, killing four Israeli soldiers and claiming the attack was retaliation for Israel's seizure of the weapons ship.[64] Israel's response was not long in coming. First, it hit a series of Palestinian naval targets, setting a fuel depot and a barracks on fire and destroying a number of boats docked in Gaza. It also destroyed a large number of Palestinian homes in a refugee camp, which it claimed gave cover to the Hamas attacker. Finally, it ripped up the runway of the Palestinian airport in Gaza as yet another symbolic act against Arafat, although the action drew criticism from European Union officials since the EU had paid for construction of the airport.[65] By contrast, Powell called the Israeli actions defensive in nature and warned Arafat that if he did not take action against those involved in the arms smuggling, it would "complicate enormously" relations between Arafat and the United States.[66]

Following the Hamas attack and the Israeli reprisal, the violence escalated even further. Israeli forces killed Raed Karmi, a Palestinian Fatah militia leader who had killed a number of Israelis in previous months.[67] Palestinian terrorists linked to Arafat's own Tanzim militia responded by killing six Israeli civilians and wounding more than thirty at a Bat Mitzvah party in the Israeli town of Hadera.[68] The Israeli response was to move its tanks to within one hundred meters of Arafat's compound in Ramallah and then to destroy the main Palestinian radio transmitter.[69] Meanwhile, Colin Powell, having sensed that the atmosphere was not conducive for another visit by General Zinni, had already called off Zinni's upcoming visit to the Middle East.[70]

Thus ended the first year of the Bush administration's efforts to resolve the Israeli-Palestinian conflict. Despite two major US efforts, one in June and one in November-December 2001, Palestinian terrorism, which Arafat was either unable or, more likely, unwilling to control (he had long used terrorism as a political weapon), had sabotaged US efforts to resolve the Palestinian-Israeli conflict. This pattern continued over the next three years as the Bush administration made two additional attempts to resolve the conflict, one in March-April 2002 and another with the publication of the "Road Map" in April 2003.

From the Karine A Incident to
President Bush's Speech of June 24, 2002

Following the failure of the Zinni mission and the *Karine A* incident, the United States again pulled back from active involvement in the Arab-Israeli peacemaking process. Violence between the two sides, however, continued to rise. In mid-February 2002, Ahmed Qurei (also known as Abu Ala), the head of the Palestinian Legislative Council (and who would later become Palestinian prime minister), tried to stop the escalation on the Palestinian side, making an appeal for de-escalation: "Let's be honest. Everyone who visits us or we visit them holds the same opinion—the Palestinians are the source of the tension. I believe that we must also consider the rightward shift that Israeli public opinion has taken. Some of the actions that harm us need to stop."[71] Ahmed Qurei, however, was not running the Palestinian Authority; Arafat was. The fighting continued to escalate, despite a tentative peace plan worked out by Ahmed Qurei and former Israeli Prime Minister Shimon Peres calling for a cease-fire and the declaration of a Palestinian state whose borders would be worked out within a year.[72] Another effort to make peace came from Saudi Crown Prince Abdullah, who in an apparent trial balloon, told *New York Times* Middle East specialist Thomas Friedman that he was confident that if Israel withdrew to the June 4, 1967, borders, all twenty-two members of the Arab League would normalize relations with Israel.[73]

Despite these efforts at resolving the conflict, Palestinian suicide bombings and Israeli reprisals continued. Although the United States deplored the rising violence, there appeared to be little it could do to stop it. Indeed, in a remarkably frank interview with the *New York Times* on February 28, 2002, Colin Powell stated: "We have not put it [the search for an Arab-Israeli peace agreement] on the back burner. What that [US engagement] usually means is 'Go and force the Israelis to do something.' That's what many people think when they say 'Get more engaged' or 'You're standing on the sidelines. You haven't made Israel blink in the face of the violence.'" Powell also praised the Saudi peace plan but said it was something that had to be "fleshed out," further noting that Vice President Cheney would undertake this task during his March 2002 visit to the Middle East.[74]

Although the primary purpose of the Cheney visit was not to "flesh out" the Crown Prince's peace plan but to build support for a planned US attack on Iraq, Vice President Cheney was met with strong Arab calls for the United States to work out a solution to the Israeli-Palestinian conflict before engaging in a war with Iraq. This apparently convinced President Bush to send Zinni back for another try at achieving a cease-fire. To facilitate the Zinni visit, Sharon made a major concession by lifting his demand for the passage of seven days without violence before talks could resume. The atmosphere of the Zinni visit was further improved by the announcement that the peace plan suggested by Saudi Arabia would be introduced at the Arab summit scheduled for the end of March in Beirut. To help reinforce the momentum for peace, the United States pushed for a new UN Security Council resolution, Resolution 1397, on March 13, 2002, which called for a two-state solution to the Israeli-Palestinian conflict; the end of violence, incitement, and terrorism; and the resumption of negotiations based on the Tenet and Mitchell plans.[75]

Unfortunately, the diplomatic momentum for peace was shattered by another series of Palestinian terrorist attacks just as Zinni was seeking to consolidate a cease-fire and the Arab summit was taking place in Beirut. On March 27, the first night of the Jewish holiday of Passover, twenty-nine Jews were murdered, and more than one hundred were wounded at a Passover seder in the coastal resort town of Netanya. This was followed by suicide bombings in Jerusalem, Tel Aviv, and Haifa over the next three days, which resulted in the deaths of an additional seventeen people and the wounding of eighty-four. These events precipitated an Israeli attack on Arafat's compound in Ramallah, which was followed by a sweep into the major Palestinian cities of the West Bank in what Sharon called Operation Defensive Shield.

As these events were unfolding, the United States at first strongly backed Israel, with Powell noting, "Sharon made concessions, while Arafat backed terrorism."[76] Then, when mass demonstrations broke out in the Arab world, which may have worried Bush as he stepped up his preparations for an attack on Iraq, the president decided to once again involve the United States. In a major speech on April 4, after first denouncing terrorism and pointedly noting that "the chairman of the Palestinian Authority has not consistently opposed or confronted terrorists nor has he renounced terror as he agreed to do at Oslo," Bush called for the Israelis to withdraw from the West Bank cities they were occupying.[77] Bush also announced that he was sending Powell to the Middle East to work out a cease-fire. Several days later, the president urged the Israelis to withdraw "without delay,"[78] but then he ran into a firestorm of domestic criticism for pressuring Israel. First, the neoconservatives, who were the intellectual lifeblood of the administration, attacked Bush for urging Sharon to withdraw, claiming the Israeli leader was fighting terrorism just as the United States was fighting terrorism after 9/11. Then the evangelical Christians, who are a large and energetic base of Bush's core constituency, also attacked Bush for pressuring Israel.[79] Third, on April 15, 250,000 people convened on the Mall in Washington, a demonstration organized by the US Jewish community, which also included evangelical Christians among its speakers. The message of the rally was that the United States should support Israel's fight against Palestinian terrorism. Finally, the administration was severely criticized by members of Congress, including Republican leader Tom DeLay, a strong friend of Israel.[80]

Another factor prompting Bush to change his position was Arafat's continued sponsorship of terrorism. When Arafat's wife came out in support of suicide bombings as a legitimate form of resistance against Israeli occupation, and the Israelis gave the United States documents showing Arafat not only had tolerated terrorism but had helped finance it, Bush further turned against the Palestinian leader. On May 26, while on a state visit to Russia, Bush noted that Arafat "hasn't delivered. He had a chance to secure the peace as a result of the hard work of President Clinton and he didn't. He had a chance to fight terrorism and he hasn't."[81]

As Palestinian terrorist attacks continued to proliferate, Sharon, who had pulled Israeli forces out of the cities of the West Bank in May 2002, sent them back in June, this time to minimal criticism from the United States. Indeed, in a major speech on June 24, Bush called for "a new and different Palestinian leadership" so that a Palestinian state could be born.

In the most anti-Arafat speech in his presidency, Bush stated:

I call on the Palestinian people to elect new leaders, leaders not compromised by terror. I call upon them to build a practicing democracy, based on tolerance and liberty. If the Palestinian people actively pursue these goals, America and the world will actively support their efforts. If the Palestinian people meet these goals, they will be able to reach agreement with Israel and Egypt and Jordan on security and other arrangements for independence. And when the Palestinian people have new leaders, new institutions, and new security arrangements with their neighbors, the United States of America will support the creation of a Palestinian state whose borders and certain aspects of its sovereignty will be provisional until resolved as part of a final settlement in the Middle East.

Today, Palestinian authorities are encouraging, not opposing, terrorism. This is unacceptable and the United States will not support the establishment of a Palestinian state until its leaders engage in a sustained fight against the terrorists and dismantle their infrastructure. This will require an externally supervised effort to rebuild and reform the Palestinian security services. The security system must have clear lines of authority and accountability and a unified chain of command.[82]

President Bush then called on Israel to respond to a new Palestinian leadership when it was formed:

As new Palestinian institutions and new leaders emerge, demonstrating real performance on reform, I expect Israel to respond and work toward a final status agreement. With intensive security and effort by all, this agreement could be reached within three years from now. And I and my country will actively lead toward that goal . . . .

As we make progress toward security, Israeli forces need to withdraw fully to positions they held prior to September 28, 2000. And consistent with the recommendations of the Mitchell Committee, Israeli settlement activity in the occupied territories must stop.[83]

While chiding the Israelis somewhat on settlement activity, the brunt of the president's ire was clearly on Arafat, and with this speech Bush formally joined Sharon in ruling out Arafat as a partner in the peace process.

Pitfalls Along the Road to Peace: US Policy from July 2002 to October 2003

Following the June 24 speech, US foreign policy in the Middle East had two main objectives. The first was to work with the European Union, Russia, and the United Nations as part of a "Quartet" to fashion a "Road Map" leading to a Palestinian-Israeli peace settlement. The second was to build a large coalition to prepare for war with Iraq.

In designing the Road Map with the EU, Russia, and the UN, the Bush administration faced a major problem. Although the United States had written off Arafat as a suitable partner for peace, as had Israel, the other three members of the Quartet had not, and this caused problems in subsequent Quartet diplomacy. In addition, the presentation of the Road Map, which the Quartet began planning in July 2002, was delayed on numerous occasions and was not made public until the completion of the major combat phase of the Anglo-American war on Iraq at the end of April 2003. As a result, many cynical, and not so cynical, Middle East observers felt that the Road Map was aimed at merely assuaging the Arabs while the Bush administration was preparing to attack Iraq.[84] Indeed, in the run-up to the war in September 2002, when the Israelis laid siege to Arafat's compound in Ramallah following a series of brutal suicide bombings, the United States chose to abstain on, rather than veto, a UN resolution condemning the Israeli action, with Condoleezza Rice reportedly telling the Israeli government that the United States expected a speedy resolution of the siege because it "doesn't help" US efforts to galvanize support for the campaign against Iraq.[85]

In any case, following delays on account of the Israeli elections of January 2003 (in which Sharon's Likud party scored an impressive victory) and the war against Iraq, which began in late March, the Road Map was finally published on April 30, 2003. At the time, it appeared that Bush, spurred on by his ally British Prime Minister Tony Blair, wanted to prove his critics wrong by demonstrating that he was genuinely interested in an Israeli-Palestinian peace agreement. According to the Road Map, which the Bush administration announced with great fanfare,[86] the Palestinians, in phase one of the three-phase plan leading to a Palestinian state, had to "declare an unequivocal end to violence and terrorism and end incitement against Israel and undertake visible efforts on the ground to arrest, disrupt, and restrain individuals and groups conducting and planning attacks on Israelis anywhere." Second, the Palestinians had to appoint an "empowered" prime minister and establish a government based on a strong parliamentary democracy and cabinet and have only three security services, which would report to the empowered prime minister. By these measures, the United States hoped to weaken, if not eliminate, Arafat's power base and in his place create an "empowered" prime minister who would be a proper partner for peace. For their part, Israel, under phase one of the Road Map, had to refrain from deportation, attacks on civilians, and the confiscation or demolition of Palestinian homes and property, and as the "comprehensive security performance" of the Palestinians moved forward, the Israeli military had to "withdraw progressively" from areas occupied since September 28, 2000, dismantle settlement outposts erected since March 2001, and "freeze all settlement activity (including natural growth of settlements)."

With Bush at the peak of his international influence, as a result of the overwhelming military victory in Iraq, Arafat was compelled to accede to the Road Map's demands to create the post of prime minister, to which senior Palestinian leader Mahmoud Abbas, also known as Abu Mazen, was appointed. Yet this appointment appeared to be a ploy; it soon became evident that Mahmoud Abbas was not the "empowered" prime minister the United States had in mind, since Arafat retained control over most of the Palestinian security forces. Apparently, the United

States had overlooked this fact in the hope that Abbas, who, unlike Arafat, had never been demonized by either Sharon or the Israeli public, had sufficient power to be a credible negotiating partner for Israel. Although the Palestinian Authority accepted the Road Map, Hamas, Islamic Jihad, the al-Aqsa Martyrs Brigade, and the Tanzim did not. Israel, albeit with a number of reservations, also accepted it. When the Road Map was published, it was attacked by eighty-eight US senators, who asserted that the Road Map's position against Palestinian terrorism was not as strong as that in Bush's statement of June 24, 2002.[87]

President Bush again invested his personal prestige in an effort to gain Arab support for the Road Map, meeting with King Abdullah II of Jordan, Crown Prince Abdullah of Saudi Arabia, Hosni Mubarak of Egypt, King Hamad al-Khalifa of Bahrain, and Mahmoud Abbas at the seaside resort of Sharm al-Shaykh in Egypt. The following day, he met with Sharon and Abbas in Aqaba, Jordan. While the meetings were strong on photo opportunities, not much progress was made on achieving a cease-fire on the ground. Palestinian terrorist attacks, followed by Israeli reprisals, continued until June 29, 2003, when Abbas succeeded in eliciting a ninety-day Hudna, or truce from the leaders of Hamas, the Tanzim, and Islamic Jihad, though not from the al-Aqsa Martyrs Brigade.

Although Israeli military leaders worried that the terrorist groups would use the ninety-day period to rebuild their forces and armaments (especially the Qassem rockets that had been fired into Israel from Gaza), Sharon proved willing to take a chance on the Hudna. He called for the withdrawal of Israeli forces from northern Gaza and Bethlehem, the closing of some checkpoints hindering traffic between Palestinian villages and cities, the shutdown of some illegal outposts on the West Bank (although other outposts were set up), the release of some Palestinian prisoners (though far fewer than the Palestinians wanted), including an elderly terrorist who had killed fourteen Israelis in 1975, and the loosening of work restrictions on Palestinians.

President Bush sought to move the peace process forward by meeting with both Abbas and Sharon in Washington in July 2000, although differences over Israel's construction of its security wall proved to be problematic during Bush's talks with the two leaders.[88] Meanwhile, during the Hudna, attacks on Israel continued, including the murder of Israeli civilians, although the number of attacks was down significantly from the period preceding the Hudna. In addition, Abbas worked to lessen anti-Israeli incitement, painting over some of the anti-Israeli slogans displayed on walls in Gaza. However, the key demand of both Bush and the Israelis—that Abu Mazen crack down on the terrorists—was not met, primarily because Arafat refused to allow it. Nonetheless, Abbas tried to convince the United States that he could negotiate a permanent truce with the terrorist groups. While some in the US State Department seemed to be willing to go along with Abbas on this, Sharon was not, and as attacks on Israelis continued during the Hudna, Sharon decided to retaliate by attacking Hamas and Islamic Jihad terrorists who were seen as responsible. Then, on August 19, less than two months into the Hudna, a terrorist attack in Jerusalem killed twenty one Israelis, including a number of children. In

response, Sharon stepped up his attacks on the terrorists, which led Hamas to declare an end to the Hudna.

The end of the Hudna jeopardized Abbas's position (he eventually resigned on September 6, 2003), as did an unwise appeal by Powell directly to Arafat to help Abbas
end the violence. This statement by Powell, perhaps borne of desperation, seemed to
undermine Bush's (and Sharon's) attempt to isolate Arafat. The end of the Hudna and
the resignation of Mahmoud Abbas (he was replaced by Ahmed Qurei, also known as
Abu Ala) appeared to bring the Road Map to a halt, if not to a dead end. Indeed, in
mid-September 2003, following Bush's talks with Jordan's King Abdullah, in which
the US president strongly condemned Arafat for the failure of the Israeli-Palestinian
peace process, Condoleezza Rice stated that the peace process was in a "lull," while the
United States waited to see if Qurei could bring the terrorist groups under control.[89]

Recognizing his weak position vis-à-vis Arafat, Qurei demanded concessions
from Sharon before he would agree to resume negotiations, something Sharon refused to do. Nonetheless, fearing international pressure in the forthcoming negotiations—Yossi Beilin's Geneva Plan had begun to get positive reactions in Europe and
the United States—Sharon decided to move unilaterally and by doing so would set
the tone for Arab-Israeli diplomacy in the fourth year of the Bush administration's
first term.[90]

The Sharon Disengagement Initiative,
November 2003–November 2004

In pursuing his initiative, Sharon adopted a two-pronged approach. First, he moved
to speed up construction of the security fence separating Israel from the West Bank.
Second, he announced that Israel was moving toward a unilateral withdrawal from
Gaza. These initiatives posed both problems and opportunities for the United
States. The fence, as initially conceived by Sharon, veered from the 1967 borders
and took in large swaths of Palestinian land—something that appeared to prejudge
a peace settlement. While Sharon justified the fence in terms of protection from suicide bombers and claimed it could be moved if negotiations ever got underway and
reached a satisfactory peace settlement, US officials were not fully convinced. Moreover, any unilateral move from Gaza could pave the way for chaos, a civil war, or
even a possible Hamas takeover of the region—certainly not the outcome the
United States wanted. On the other hand, an Israeli withdrawal from Gaza, including the Jewish settlements there, could be seen as a major step along the Road Map
to peace, which the Bush administration could point to as a diplomatic victory for
the United States just as the 2004 election campaign heated up. Consequently, there
was a steady stream of diplomatic traffic back and forth across the Atlantic beginning in November 2003, as the United States and Israel sought to coordinate their
positions on Sharon's unilateral moves, with the United States seeking to get Israel
to add the dismantling of West Bank settlements to the Gaza initiative.[91]

Making matters more difficult for the Bush administration was the growing
guerrilla war it faced in Iraq, replete with mortar attacks, car bombs, and suicide

bombers—just as the United States planned to hand over sovereignty to the Iraqis in June 2004. Indeed, Secretary of State Powell noted the Iraqi connection to the Arab-Israeli conflict in a speech to the Senate in February 2003: "We fully understand that this conflict between the Palestinians and the Israelis is a source of a great deal of the anti-American feelings that exist in that part of the world and does affect what we're doing in Iraq."[92]

Powell went on to note:

> We are following closely Mr. Sharon's proposals of recent weeks about evacuating the settlements in Gaza and what we have said to the Israelis: that's interesting, we want the settlements closed; we want to know exactly how they're going to—how that's going to be done, and where will those settlers go, and how does it affect settlement activity in the West Bank. We have to understand the total picture.[93]

However, Powell, in a speech at Princeton University several days later, acknowledged the difficulties the United States had in pressuring Israel: "It is difficult for us . . . to put this kind of pressure on the Israeli side as long as terrorism is seen as a legitimate political act on the part of the Palestinians. It is not—it can't be, not in this post 9/11 age."[94]

By the end of February 2004, the Israelis had begun to describe their plan as an "interim arrangement." Israeli ambassador to the United States Daniel Ayalon went further and stated that once the Sharon plan was implemented, the peace process would be in a "parking place." Israel, he noted, was "filling in our parts of the puzzle. When the Palestinians do their part of the puzzle that would be the basis for moving onto the next stage."[95] The United States seemed to at least buy into the Israeli strategy with a "senior Bush administration official" noting the US hope that the withdrawal would "re-energize" political and other reforms on the Palestinian side.[96]

Meanwhile, of course, there remained tactical issues for the United States and Israel to work out. Thus, Washington took a dim view of reports that Sharon planned to move the Gaza settlers into settlements on the West Bank. The United States was also pressing Israel to move the security fence closer to the 1967 border. For his part, Sharon sought US support for a number of his positions, including the following:

1. a cessation of negotiations and work on diplomatic initiatives with the Palestinian Authority until the PA leadership (Arafat) was replaced;
2. US agreement for construction in major Jewish settlement areas such as Gush Etzion, Maaleh Adumim, and Ariel;
3. US agreement for a strong Israeli military response should terror attacks be launched from regions where Israel had withdrawn troops and settlements.[97]

As Sharon was putting forth his initiatives, the European Union sought, albeit without much success, to get Sharon to put the plan into EU parameters, asserting that (1) Sharon's plan should supplement the Road Map, not replace it; (2) the separation fence should promote the realization of the formula of two states, Israel and

Palestine; (3) there should be no movement of Gaza settlers to West Bank settlements; (4) the disengagement plan should be coordinated with the Palestinian Authority rather than making it a unilateral step; and (5) Israel should help in the Gaza Strip's recovery after its withdrawal. The EU also suggested that an international police force should be deployed in areas vacated by the Israelis, a suggestion quickly repudiated by Israeli Foreign Minister Silvan Shalom, who asserted that international peacekeepers would stop Israel from pursuing terrorists.[98]

But it was the United States, not the European Union, that mattered to Sharon, and throughout the first quarter of 2004 he undertook detailed negotiations with the Bush administration over his disengagement agreement. Under US pressure (and that of the Israeli Supreme Court), Sharon agreed to move the security fence closer to the 1949 armistice line, and according to Israeli ambassador to the United States Daniel Ayalon, Sharon also agreed to add four settlements in the northern part of the West Bank to his disengagement plan.[99]

The end result of the bargaining was a meeting between Sharon and Bush in Washington in mid-April 2004 that was structured not only to reinforce the Sharon disengagement initiative but also to help each leader politically. Thus Bush went a very long way to supporting Sharon's policies. Not only did he welcome Sharon's disengagement plan as "real progress" and assert that the United States was "strongly committed" to Israel's well-being as a Jewish state within "secure and defensible borders," he went on to reject any Palestinian "right of return" to Israel, stating: "It seems clear that an agreed just, fair, and realistic framework for a solution to the Palestinian refugee issue as part of any final status agreement will need to be found through the establishment of a Palestinian state, and the settling of Palestinian refugees there, rather than in Israel."[100]

Bush also reinforced Israel's position that it would not fully return to the 1949 armistice lines and that any final agreement would have to reflect the settlements Israel had built since 1967, stating: "In light of new realities on the ground, including already existing population centers, it is unrealistic to expect that the outcome of final status negotiations will be a full and complete return to the armistice lines of 1949."

Finally, Bush reaffirmed Israel's right to self-defense against terrorism, noting, "Israel will retain its right to defend itself against terrorism including to take action against terrorist organizations." This not only endorsed Israel's right to go back into Gaza to fight terrorism but also implicitly endorsed Israel's strategy of assassinating the leaders of Hamas, a process that continued during the spring and summer of 2004.

In his meeting with Sharon, Bush also made a number of gestures to the Palestinians. Not only did he reaffirm his commitment to a two-state solution to the Israeli-Palestinian conflict and called for Israel to freeze settlement activity and remove unauthorized outposts, but he also put limits on Israel's security wall, asserting: "As the government of Israel has stated, the barrier being erected by Israel should be a security rather than a political barrier, should be temporary, and therefore not prejudice any final status issues including final borders, and its route should take into account, consistent with security needs, its impact on Palestinians not engaged in terrorist activities." Nonetheless, returning to the theme he had emphasized since 9/11, Bush demanded that the Palestinians "act decisively against terror, including sustained, targeted, and effective operations to stop terrorism and dismantle terrorist capabilities and infrastructure."

It is clear that Sharon had scored a great diplomatic success with his visit, and he heaped lavish praise on President Bush. After noting that the disengagement plan "can be an important contribution" to the president's Road Map for peace, he went on to state: "You have proven, Mr. President, your ongoing, deep, and sincere friendship to the State of Israel and to the Jewish people. . . . In all these years, I have never met a leader as committed as you are Mr. President, to the struggle for freedom and the need to confront terrorism wherever it exists."

Needless to say, for a president now deeply engaged in an election campaign against John Kerry, a liberal senator from Massachusetts, who normally could expect to get the vast majority of Jewish votes, Sharon's words were extremely helpful to Bush, especially in pivotal states like Florida with its large Jewish population.

While Bush benefited from Sharon's political support (he went on to win Florida by a significant margin with support from Jewish voters), Sharon did not reap a similar benefit from his trip to Washington. Despite the warm embrace by Bush, Sharon lost a Likud Central Committee vote by a 60–40 margin on the disengagement plan and faced a rebellion in his own party leadership because of the disengagement initiative. Sharon, however, continued to move forward with it, gaining support from Israel's Labor and Meretz (Yahad) parties, although he faced increasing opposition within the Likud, where the opponents of disengagement also fought against the inclusion of Labor into the ruling coalition, a development that became possible in June 2004 when Sharon was not indicted by Israel's attorney general on an alleged bribery charge.[101]

While Sharon was battling his domestic opponents, Bush was building international support for Sharon's disengagement plan. In May 2004, he got the Quartet meeting at the UN to endorse the plan as a "rare moment of opportunity in the search for peace in the Middle East," and in early June the administration obtained the support of the G-8 nations. The G-8 meeting endorsed the Bush anti-terrorist platform, urging a rebuilding of the Palestinian Authority security services "so that they enforce the rule of law, mount effective opposition against all forms of terrorism, and report to an empowered Interior Minister and Prime Minister."[102]

In the summer and early fall, while facing a rising insurgency in Iraq and an increasingly close presidential race, Bush continued to enthusiastically support Sharon's disengagement plan. Yet Sharon encountered problems from his cabinet and his party in preparing the legislation to implement it. Some in the settler movement, and the Israeli rabbis who supported them, called for religious soldiers to disobey orders to uproot the settlements.

In his speech to the United Nations in September, President Bush repeated his main themes, calling on Israel to impose a settlement freeze and dismantle unauthorized outposts, while denouncing Palestinian terrorism and calling for a new

Palestinian leadership: "Peace will not be achieved by Palestinian rulers who intimidate opposition, tolerate corruption, and maintain ties to terrorist groups. . . . Those who would lead a new Palestinian state should adopt peaceful means to achieve the rights of their people and create the reformed institutions of a stable democracy."[103] He also called on the Arab states to end incitement, to cut off public and private funding for terrorism, and establish normal relations with Israel and called on world leaders to "withdraw all favor and support from any Palestinian ruler who fails his people and betrays their cause."

As Bush was denouncing Palestinian terrorism, Israel was stepping up its efforts to destroy the terrorist infrastructure in Gaza so that neither Hamas nor Islamic Jihad could claim they had forced Israel out of Gaza, as Hezbollah had done to Israel in South Lebanon. A second goal for Sharon appeared to be to demonstrate to his Likud opponents that he remained "tough on terrorism." These efforts culminated in a major military operation in late September called "Days of Repentance," which was precipitated by Qassem rocket attacks from Gaza, which killed two young Israeli children in the town of Sderot, near Gaza. The operation lasted seventeen days, during which more than one hundred Palestinians, primarily but not exclusively terrorists, were killed.

Not unexpectedly, Arafat sought to mobilize Arab and world opposition to the Israeli action, and a resolution was introduced into the UN Security Council to condemn the Israeli incursion into Gaza. While the US State Department, in commenting on the Israeli move, stressed that Israel had the right to self-defense, it also stated that the Israeli military forces should seek to "minimize the humanitarian consequences of their actions."[104] The United States nonetheless vetoed the UN resolution, calling it "lopsided and unbalanced because it failed to mention the Palestinian rocket attacks that triggered the action."[105]

As the United States and Israel coordinated their actions in the run-up to both the US election of November 2 and to the votes in the Israeli parliament in late October and early November on disengagement, a problem emerged in early October 2004. Dov Weinglass, Sharon's former chief of staff and a major interlocutor in the US-Israeli talks on disengagement, gave an interview in the Israeli newspaper *Ha'aretz* in which he appeared to argue that Sharon's disengagement plan, far from being an important step on Bush's Road Map to an Israeli-Palestinian peace agreement, would, in fact, freeze the peace process, placing it into "formaldehyde—with the blessing of both the Congress and the Administration."[106] While Weinglass's comments may have been aimed at assuaging the rising opposition to the disengagement plan within the Likud party, they were viewed negatively by the United States. State Department spokesman Adam Ereli responded to Weinglass by stating, "Our understanding is that Israel is committed to the Road Map and to the president's three-stage solution."[107] Sharon also quickly repudiated Weinglass's comments, and the mini-crisis in US-Israeli relations ended.

As Sharon's disengagement efforts continued (with the help of the Labor party he would win two major votes, one in support of the disengagement in principle, and another on compensation for the uprooted settlers),[108] Bush continued to woo the

Jewish community during what virtually all the polls predicted was an extremely close presidential race between Bush and Senator John Kerry. Thus, not only did he strongly support Sharon on the disengagement plan, but the Bush administration sent a twenty-six-page booklet, titled "President George W. Bush—A Friend of the American Jewish Community," to American Jewish organizations, stressing Bush's commitment to the state of Israel and to the world Jewish community. Prominent themes in the booklet were Bush's opposition to terrorism aimed at Israel and his opposition to PLO leader Yasser Arafat. The booklet stated, "For Yasser Arafat the message has been clear. While he was a frequent White House guest during the last Administration, he has never been granted a meeting with President Bush."[109] In another effort to court Jewish support, Bush reportedly overrode State Department opposition to create an office at the State Department to monitor the rising tide of anti-Semitism around the world. Perhaps reflecting on the political nature of the proposed office, an unnamed State Department official told the *Washington Times:* "It's more of a bureaucratic nuisance than a real problem. We are not going to fight a bill that has gained such political momentum."[110] Finally, on the eve of the US presidential election, Bush sent National Security Advisor Condoleezza Rice to address the American-Israel Public Affairs Committee (AIPAC) meeting in Florida. The very fact of her presence, despite an ongoing FBI investigation of a Pentagon analyst who allegedly passed secrets to AIPAC, underlined the great importance the Bush administration placed on getting Jewish support in the election.[111]

Bush won the 2004 election by 3.5 million votes. The election and the almost simultaneous serious illness and subsequent death of PLO leader Yasser Arafat provide a useful point of departure for analyzing the policy of the Bush administration toward the Arab-Israeli conflict during its first term.

Conclusion

There are three major conclusions that can be drawn from this examination of the first four years of the Bush administration's policy toward the Arab-Israeli conflict. First, after an initial reluctance to get directly involved in Arab-Israeli peacemaking, having witnessed the failure of the efforts of his predecessor Bill Clinton, Bush was nonetheless drawn into the peacemaking process on four different occasions. The first was in June 2001, when, following the Dolphinarium suicide bombing by a Palestinian terrorist, Arafat felt compelled to accede to the Mitchell Report's call for a cease-fire. Bush sent both CIA Director George Tenet and Secretary of State Colin Powell to solidify the cease-fire, only to see it evaporate because Arafat was unwilling to crack down on the Palestinian terrorist groups that opposed it.

The second US effort, in which Bush invested considerably more of his personal prestige, came after 9/11 when the US president sought to expedite a two-state solution to the Israeli-Palestinian conflict not only through a major speech to the UN but also by sending General Anthony Zinni, the former US Centcom commander, to work out a Palestinian-Israeli cease-fire. This, too, foundered on Palestinian terrorism, as no sooner had Zinni arrived than he was met by a series of Palestinian terrorist attacks that torpedoed his mission. Arafat, despite his 40,000-man army, proved unwilling to prevent these attacks or even crack down on the terrorist groups after the attacks were perpetrated. With Bush now dedicating his presidency to the fight against terrorism, Arafat's support of terrorism—reinforced by the *Karine A* incident—de-legitimated him in the eyes of the American president.

The third US effort occurred in March-April 2002, as Bush was seeking to build a coalition for the invasion of Iraq. Zinni was again sent to secure a cease-fire, but then came a particularly horrendous suicide bombing at a Passover seder in Netanya and other bombings in Israeli cities. In response, Israeli Prime Minister Sharon sent the Israeli army into the major cities of the West Bank. Bush responded by dispatching Secretary of State Powell to the region to try again for a cease-fire, only to once again meet failure.

The final effort came after the successful conclusion to the major military phase of the war in Iraq in April 2003. At that time the Quartet published the long-awaited Road Map for an Israeli Palestinian peace, aimed at weakening Arafat through the creation of an "empowered" Palestinian prime minister with control of all the Palestinian security forces. However, the Road Map foundered on two shoals. The first was Arafat's unwillingness to cede full power to his prime minister, Mahmoud Abbas, and the second was the continuation of Palestinian terrorist attacks against Israel, which Abbas, due to a lack of power, proved unable to prevent, and which Arafat was unwilling to stop. Thus, all four of the US peacemaking efforts failed, primarily because of Palestinian terrorism.

It was the failure of these peacemaking attempts, the de-legitimization of Arafat as a "partner for peace" by both Bush and Sharon, and the approaching US elections that appear to have motivated Bush to endorse Sharon's disengagement plan and give the Israeli prime minister solid backing on key issues in the Israeli-Palestinian dispute, such as negating any Palestinian refugee "right of return" to Israel, supporting Israeli desires to include large settlement blocs in Israel in any final settlement, and approving Israel's military efforts against Palestinian terrorism. In return, Sharon agreed to dismantle settlements on the West Bank as well as Gaza and to endorse the Bush position that the barrier being constructed on the West Bank was a security fence not a political one and hence could be moved in any final agreement. Sharon also agreed to move the fence closer to the 1949 armistice lines. Bush then sought to win international support for the Sharon disengagement initiative, convincing first the Quartet and then the group of G-8 nations to endorse it.

A second conclusion that can be drawn from this study is that external events have had a significant influence on US policymaking toward the Israeli-Palestinian conflict, primarily in the area of pressuring Israel to make concessions to the Palestinians. Thus, after 9/11, when the United States was trying to forge a worldwide coalition, including Muslims, to confront al-Qa'ida, Israel was pressured into resuming negotiations with the Palestinians even though Palestinian attacks on Israelis had not ceased. Then, following a string of Palestinian suicide attacks in March-April 2002, when Israel reoccupied the major cities of the West Bank, Bush, fearing an Arab backlash that would hinder his efforts to confront Iraq, urged Israel to withdraw from the Palestinian cities "without delay." A similar US motive appeared to underlie the US decision to abstain on, rather than veto, a September 2002 UN Security Council resolution calling on Israel to lift the siege of Arafat's compound, which had been imposed following another series of Palestinian suicide bombings against Israel.

A final conclusion relates to the importance of domestic politics in the Bush administration's policymaking. Following his razor-thin victory in the 2000 presidential elections, Bush had to be concerned about 2004. Consequently, whenever he heavily pressured Israel, as in April 2002 when he called on Israel to withdraw from Palestinian West Bank cities, which Israel had occupied following a series of Palestinian suicide bombings, Bush ran into a firestorm of domestic criticism to which he had to be sensitive. These included large majorities in both houses of Congress who argued, as did the neoconservatives in the administration itself, that Israel was fighting terrorism just as the United States was doing in Afghanistan. Another major source of support for Israel came from evangelical Christians and their congressional allies, including the very influential Republican congressman Tom Delay. Finally, the vast majority of the American Jewish community, driven rightward by the al-Aqsa *intifada* and the murder of numerous Israeli civilians, rallied around Sharon. Given the potential closeness of the 2004 presidential election and the location of large Jewish communities in key electoral states, especially Florida, Bush could not afford to alienate the Jews, whom he wished to win over from their long-time association with the Democratic party. Indeed, in the six months preceding the election, Bush stepped up his support for Sharon, not only endorsing his unilateral disengagement plan and supporting Israeli military attacks in Gaza against Hamas terrorists but also vetoing a UNSC resolution critical of Israel for its anti-terrorist actions in Gaza during a prolonged military intervention in late September and early October 2004. He also sought to outdo his Democratic rival John Kerry in demonstrating his support for Israel by continuing to blast Arafat and also by establishing an office at the US State Department to combat anti-Semitism.

In looking to the future it should be noted that two of the central factors in the Bush administration's policy toward the Arab-Israeli conflict seem to have changed significantly. First, the death of Arafat could remove the central obstacle to the resumption of talks between Israel and the Palestinian Authority, because the two leading contenders for the succession, Mahmoud Abbas and Ahmed Qurei, have not been demonized by the United States or the Israeli public as Arafat has been. Under these circumstances the United States could play an important mediating role between them and Israel during the disengagement from Gaza. Assuming they are able to consolidate power, and one is not tempted to play Hamas and Islamic Jihad against the other with the result that the terrorist groups would not be suppressed, there would be a real opportunity for the Bush administration to move the peace process forward. Nonetheless, it is far too early in the Palestinian succession process to determine whether this is a viable possibility.

Second, having won reelection, Bush is in a stronger position vis-à-vis the constituencies that put him into power. Nonetheless, given the fact that it took victories in Florida and Ohio, states with sizeable Jewish populations, to enable Bush to win in the Electoral College, and given the desire of Republican leaders to increase the size of the Republican majority throughout the country, it is possible that the Bush administration may not press Israel any more in the second term than it did in the first. On the other hand, President Bush's friend and key ally in the war in Iraq, British Prime Minister Tony Blair, will be up for reelection in 2005, and Blair, in an effort to satisfy the disgruntled left-wing of his Labor party, has urged Bush to take a more active role in securing an Israeli-Palestinian peace agreement. As mentioned above, the expected demise of Arafat may make this easier for Bush to do. Nonetheless, at this point one can only speculate about whether the Bush administration will be more activist in seeking an Arab-Israeli settlement in the second term than in the first.

Epilogue

In the aftermath of the death of Arafat and the reelection victory of George W. Bush, the situation initially appeared to improve, as far as US policy in the Middle East was concerned. First, the replacement of Colin Powell by Condoleezza Rice as US Secretary of State added a great deal of coherence to US policy, as the old rifts between the Department of State, on the one hand, and the White House and the Department of Defense, on the other, were minimized. In addition, as the influence of Defense Secretary Donald Rumsfeld's declined with the increase in problems in Iraq, Rice became the unquestioned spokesperson on foreign policy for the administration. Second, the US democratization plan for the Middle East appeared to score some major triumphs with democratic elections being successfully held in Iraq, Lebanon, and the Palestinian Authority (PA). In the PA, an election was held to choose the successor to Yasser Arafat, and in what international observers considered a fair and democratic election, Mahmoud Abbas, who had earlier served a brief term as Palestinian prime minister under the Road Map, was elected. What made Abbas such an appealing candidate for the United States was the fact that he regularly had denounced terrorism as inimical to Palestinian interests. Thus, with the Abbas election, the two main strands of US post-9/11 Middle East policy—the fight against terrorism and support for democratization—came together, and it was not long before Abbas was welcomed to the White House with full pomp and ceremony—a privilege that had been denied to Arafat, whom the Bush administration saw as closely linked to terrorism. And, in order to help Abbas strengthen his position in the PA, the United States dispatched Lt. General William Ward to reorganize the Palestinian armed forces and James Wolfensohn, the former head of the World Bank, to help develop the Palestinian economy. Unfortunately, neither proved to be very effective. Ward was never able to transform the disparate Palestinian military groupings into an effective fighting force, and he was replaced by Major General Keith Dayton. As far as Wolfensohn was concerned, despite his heroic efforts—including the use of his personal funds to facilitate the purchase by the Palestinians of Israeli greenhouses in Gaza—the Palestinian economy remained in a chaotic condition.

Although US-Palestinian relations got off to a good start after the election of Abbas, the new Palestinian leader took a risky gamble in March 2005 when, in an effort to achieve harmony among the contending Palestinian forces, he signed an agreement with Hamas and several other Palestinian organizations (with the exception of Islamic Jihad) that in return for a cease-fire with Israel, the only mode of interaction among the Palestinians would be "dialogue." This ran counter to Israeli and American calls for Abbas to crack down on Hamas and the other Palestinian terrorist organizations. This issue became particularly pressing as Israel prepared for its disengagement from Palestinian territories during the summer of 2005, which involved the pull-out of Israeli settlements and military forces from Gaza and the pullout of Israeli settlements from the Northern West Bank. Although Hamas had signed the cease-fire agreement, Islamic Jihad had not, and there were concerns that the Iranian-supported organization might disrupt the Israeli disengagement. While this proved not to be the case, Islamic Jihad did undertake a number of terrorist attacks against Israel in 2005 and 2006, and the Israeli government responded with "targeted killings" (assassinations) of Islamic Jihad operatives.

In order to facilitate the Israeli disengagement, Secretary of State Rice helped to negotiate a number of agreements between Israel and the PA, including one to haul away debris from the destroyed Jewish settlements (the PA had demanded the destruction) and another on the modus operandi of the crossing points between Gaza and Egypt and between Gaza and Israel. The disengagement went relatively smoothly, despite the protests of Jewish settlers in Gaza. The next issue to arise was the election for the Palestinian Legislative Council (PLC). Abbas had postponed the elections from their original July 2005 date to January 2006, in part so he could get political credit for the Israeli withdrawal, and in part because he could not settle the rifts between the old and young guards of his Fatah organization.

A key issue in the elections was whether Hamas would run, and if so, under what conditions. Israeli Prime Minister Ariel Sharon initially opposed Hamas participation in the elections, citing the Oslo accord requirement that no "racist" party could run in the elections, and since Hamas continued to call for the destruction of Israel, it was clearly racist. Only if Hamas renounced terrorism and recognized Israel's right to exist, should it be allowed to run, Sharon asserted. The United States, however, took a contrary position. In part because forbidding Hamas to participate would hurt the US democratization plan for the Middle East, and in part because Abbas had promised to finally crack down on Hamas after the PLC elections, Rice exerted heavy pressure on Sharon to allow Hamas participation. The Israeli leader, perhaps preoccupied with Israeli domestic politics (he had broken away from his Likud party and formed the new Kadima party in November 2005, four months before the Israeli parliamentary elections) gave in to US pressure. It was a decision that both the United States and Israel would come to regret.

Capitalizing on Fatah's corruption, the PA's inability to provide law and order in the West Bank and Gaza, and the continued divisions between Fatah's old and young guards, Hamas swept to victory in the January 25, 2006, PLC elections. Hamas representatives were quick to claim that their victory was due to their policy of "resistance" against Israel. The Hamas victory created a major dilemma for the United States, as its two main policies in the Middle East—the war against terror and support for democratization—had now come into direct conflict with each other, as Hamas, a terrorist organization utilizing democratic means, had taken control of the Palestinian legislature and a Hamas leader, Ismail Haniyeh, had become the new Palestinian prime minister. Israel faced a different challenge. By the time of the Hamas election victory, Sharon, who had suffered a severe stroke in early January 2006, was no longer Israel's prime minister. He was replaced by his Kadima colleague, Ehud Olmert, who now, as acting prime minister, not only had to prepare his new party for the March 28 Israeli elections (in which his party won the most seats, and Olmert was able to piece together a coalition government) but also had to deal with Hamas as the new leadership of the Palestinians. Olmert quickly decided that Israel would have nothing to do with Hamas unless it changed its policies toward Israel, a position embraced by most of the Israeli political spectrum. For her part, Rice quickly convened the diplomatic Quartet (the United States, European Union, United Nations, and Russia), which agreed not to have any dealings with the Hamas-led Palestinian government until Hamas renounced terrorism, agreed to recognize Israel, and acceded to the agreements signed between Israel and the PLO, including Oslo I, Oslo II, and the Road Map. Russia, however, soon broke with the Quartet consensus by inviting a Hamas delegation for an official visit to Moscow. In April 2006, after the United States and the European Union saw no change in Hamas policy and therefore cut all aid to the PA (except "humanitarian" assistance), Russia again broke ranks with its Quartet colleagues by offering the PA economic assistance.

Thus, well into 2006 US policy toward the Arab-Israeli conflict appeared to be in serious disarray. The newly elected Israeli government refused to have anything to do either with Abbas (whom they claimed was ineffectual) or with the Hamas-led Palestinian government. For its part, the new Hamas government repeated its refusal to recognize Israel or make peace with it and supported as "legitimate resistance" continuing attacks on Israel, whether in the form of Qassem rockets fired from Gaza into Israel or of suicide bombings, such as the one on April 17, 2006, which claimed ten Israeli lives. Under these circumstances, the United States faces a major (and perhaps insurmountable) challenge in trying to resuscitate the Israeli-Palestinian peace process, unless the Hamas government falls. Given the fact that the Bush administration has been badly weakened by a series of political scandals (Scooter Libby, Jack Abramoff, and Tom Delay), an ineffectual response to Hurricane Katrina, which devastated New Orleans in 2005, and the ongoing war in Iraq, it is a very open question as to whether it is up to the challenge.

Notes

1. For a very useful survey of US policy during this period, see William B. Quandt, *Peace Process: American Diplomacy and the Arab-Israeli Conflict Since 1967* (Berkeley: University of California Press, 2001), ch. 11.

2. For a description of the Wye Agreement, see Barton Gellman, "Netanyahu, Arafat Sign Accord," *Washington Post*, October 24, 1998.

3. For a description of US efforts to achieve a Syrian-Israeli peace agreement, see Quandt, *Peace Process*, pp. 358–361.

4. As Arafat's national security adviser Jibril Ragoub later noted, Palestinian organizations should "learn from Hezbollah." Cited in Arnon Regular, "Militants agree to end civilian attacks, no mention of settlers," *Ha'aretz*, December 7, 2003.

5. For analyses of the failure of Camp David II, see Quandt, *Peace Process*; Ari Shavit, "End of a Journey" (interview with former Israeli Foreign Minister Shlomo Ben-Ami), *Ha'aretz* (English), October 3, 2001; Rogert Malley and Hussein Agha, "Camp David: The Tragedy of Errors," *New York Review of Books*, August 9, 2001, pp. 59–65; Ehud Barak, "It seems Israel has to wait for new Palestinian leadership," *International Herald Tribune*, July 31, 2001; Alain Gresh, "The Middle East: How the peace was lost," *LeMonde Diplomatique,* September 2001, pp. 1, 8–9; Barry Rubin, "The Region," Besa@mail.biu.ac.il, June 25, 2001; and Bassam Abu-Sharif, "A call to Israel to understand what the Palestinian want," ipcri@ipcri.org, September 14, 2001. For a balanced view, see Madeleine Albright, *Madam Secretary: A Memoir* (New York: Mirimax Books, 2003), ch. 28. See also the memoirs of Bill Clinton, *My Life* (New York: Knopf, 2004); and Dennis Ross, *The Missing Peace* (New York: Farrar, Straus and Giroux, 2004.)

6. For a different view of the "Lessons of Lebanon," see Roula Khalaf, "Misleading Ghosts of Lebanese Resistance," *Financial Times,* August 16, 2001.

7. Quandt, *Peace Process,* p. 370.

8. Ibid., p. 371.

9. This was especially true in administration policy toward Iraq. See John Newhouse, "Sidetracked by the State-Defense split," *Washington Post* (Outlook section), October 5, 2003; James Drummond, "Iraqi minister blames failures on US infighting," *Financial Times*, November 12, 2003; Dana Priest, "Senators say Bush needs to take control," *Washington Post,* October 13, 2003; and Bill Sammon, "Bush vows he's 'in charge,'" *Washington Times,* October 14, 2003.

10. Cited in Dana Milbank, "Powell vows US will match foes," *Washington Post,* December 17, 2000.

11. See Mathew Burger, "Middle East talks held in Taba—without the United States," *Washington Jewish Week,* January 25, 2001.

12. "Colin Powell's Conversion," editorial, *Washington Times,* February 28, 2001; Alan Sipress, "Powell urges cooperation in ending Middle East violence," *Washington Post,* February 26, 2001.

13. Cited in Roula Khalaf, "Powell sets out Bush line on Middle East," *Financial Times*, March 20, 2001.

14. Alan Sipress, "Lawmakers criticize Palestinians," *Washington Post,* April 6, 2001.

15. Alan Sipress, "Bush assures Sharon on US role in talks," *Washington Post,* March 21, 2001.

16. Cited in Jane Perlez, "Rumsfeld seeks to withdraw American troops from Sinai," *New York Times*, April 19, 2001.

17. Barbara Crosette, "US vetoes U.N. Council bid on Palestinian force," *New York Times*, March 29, 2001.

18. Cited in Ben Barber, "Bush presses Arafat to stop violence," *Washington Post,* March 30, 2001.

19. Alan Sipress, "Worried US issues rebuke to Israelis," *Washington Post,* April 18, 2001.

20. Marc Lacey, "Attacks were up last year US terrorism report says," *New York Times,* May 1, 2001.

21. Cited in Ben Barber, "Israel refuses to halt settlement building," *Washington Times,* May 8, 2001.

22. Cited in Mike O'Connor, "Sharon promises to continue expansion in West Bank, Gaza," *Washington Post,* May 9, 2001.

23. Cited in Associated Press report, "Settlement allocation cut after US protests," *Jerusalem Post,* May 10, 2001.

24. For the text of the Mitchell Report, see *Ha'aretz* (English edition), May 6, 2001.

25. Jane Perlez, "US widens role in Mideast crisis, sending an envoy," *New York Times,* May 22, 2001.

26. Cited in Lee Hockstader, "Bombing kills at least 17 at Tel-Aviv Club," *Washington Post,* June 2, 2001.

27. Cited in Deborah Sontag, "Arafat calls for cease-fire, deploring Tel-Aviv attacks," *New York Times,* June 3, 2001.

28. Cited in Dan Ephron, "Israelis, Palestinians, agree to cease-fire," *Washington Times,* June 13, 2001.

29. Cited in William A. Orme, Jr., "Shockwave in Israel over Bush's comment," *New York Times,* June 28, 2001.

30. Herb Keinon, "Playing Europe," *Ha'aretz* (English), July 6, 2001.

31. Jane Perlez, "US says killings by Israel inflame Middle East conflict," *New York Times,* August 28, 2001.

32. Cited in Mark Lavie, "Cheney backs Israel assassination policy," *Sidney Morning Herald,* August 4–5, 2001.

33. Cited in Melissa Radler, "US backs Israel at U.N., opposes international monitors," *Jerusalem Post,* August 21, 2001.

34. Cited in Reuters Report, "Egypt leader joins Arab chorus pressing US on its Middle East role," *New York Times,* August 27, 2001.

35. Cited in Aluf Benn, "Sharon calls Powell after White House blasts PM comments," *Ha'aretz* (English), October 5, 2001.

36. See Eli Kintsch, "'US vs. Israel' Blip say Jewish groups," *Forward,* October 26, 2001.

37. Daniel Milbank and Lee Hockstadter, "Israel incursion strains relations," *Washington Post,* October 24, 2001.

38. Tim Weiner, "Israel rebuffs US demand to end its West Bank raids," *New York Times,* October 24, 2001.

39. For an analysis of US military progress in Afghanistan, see Thom Shanker, "Conduct of war is redefined by success of Special Forces," *New York Times,* January 21, 2002.

40. For the text of Bush's speech, see the *New York Times,* November 12, 2001. See also Serge Schmemann, "Arafat thankful for Bush remark about 'Palestine,'" *New York Times,* November 12, 2001.

41. Cited in Bill Sammon, "Bush will not meet with Arafat," *Washington Times,* November 9, 2001.

42. For the text of Powell's speech, see "United States position on terrorists and peace in the Middle East," November 19, 2001, www.state.gov/secretary/rm/2001/6219.htm.

43. Janine Zacharia, "Bush asking Arab nations to pitch in for a secure peace," *Jerusalem Post,* November 25, 2001.

44. Aluf Ben, "Zinni to PM: I will stay as long as needed to fulfill my mission," *Ha'aretz,* November 27, 2001.

45. Cited in *New York Times,* November 28, 2001.

46. See James Bennet, "US envoy meets Arafat and asks for end of violence," *New York Times,* November 29, 2001.

47. Avi Machlis, "Israeli bus blast casts shadow on peace process," *Financial Times,* November 30, 2001.

48. Joel Greenberg, "Envoy to Middle East assails Palestinian militants," *New York Times,* December 1, 2001.

49. Cited in Lee Hockstadter, "Bomber in bus kills 15 in Israel," *Washington Post,* December 3, 2001.

50. Ibid.

51. Cited in Peter Herman, "Terrorists kill at least 15 in Israel," *Baltimore Sun,* December 2, 2001.

52. Cited in Lee Hockstadter, "Bomber on bus kills 15 in Israel," *Washington Post,* December 3, 2001.

53. Cited in James Bennet, "Israelis strike Arafat's bases," *New York Times,* December 4, 2001.

54. Cited in Bill Sammon and Ben Barber, "US takes harder line on Arafat," *Washington Times,* December 4, 2001.

55. Joel Greenberg, "More violence jolts ME truce efforts," *New York Times,* December 10, 2001.

56. Cited in James Bennet and Joel Greenberg, "Israel breaks with Arafat after Palestinian assault on bus in West Bank kills 10," *New York Times,* December 13, 2001.

57. Tracy Wilkinson, "Israel pounds Palestinian Authority," *Los Angeles Times,* December 14, 2001.

58. Cited in Ha'aretz Service and Agencies, "Powell: US will not abandon its role in Mideast mediation," December 13, 2001; and Peter Slevin and Lee Hockstadter, "US hangs on in Middle East: 'Stakes 'too high' to pull out, Powell says," *Washington Post,* December 13, 2001.

59. Clyde Haberman, "Arafat demands halt in attacks against Israelis," *New York Times,* December 7, 2001.

60. Aluf Benn, "US envoy recalled to Washington; meets Egypt's Mubarak," *Ha'aretz,* December 16, 2001.

61. Alan Sipress, "Musharaf urged to calm South Asia: US asks Pakistani leader to act against Islamic militants," *Washington Post,* January 12, 2002.

62. For a discussion of this point, see David Frum, *The Right Man: The Surprise Presidency of George W. Bush* (New York: Random House, 2003), p. 256. Frum was a speechwriter for Bush from January 2001 to February 2002. See also Bob Woodward, *Bush at War* (New York: Simon & Schuster, 2002), p. 297.

63. Lee Hockstadter, "Arafat arrests three in arms incident," *Washington Post,* January 12, 2002.

64. Mary Curtius, "Hamas takes responsibility for attack," *Los Angeles Times,* January 10, 2002.

65. Margot Dudkevich, "Navy destroys PA boats and installations," *Jerusalem Post,* January 13, 2002.

66. Cited in "Powell: IDF actions are defensive response," *Jerusalem Post News Agencies,* January 13, 2002.

67. David Rudge, "Defense Minister Ben-Eliezer: Tanzim terrorist had been planning more murders," *Jerusalem Post,* January 16, 2002.

68. David Rattner, "Hadera victims buried on Friday," *Ha'aretz,* January 20, 2002.

69. Amos Harel, "IDF plans to hit more PA targets, Voice of Palestine Radio torched in Ramallah, police bombed in Tulkarm," *Ha'aretz,* January 20, 2002.

70. Aluf Benn, "US decides to postpone Zinni's return; Sources cite failures to implement full cease-fire," *Ha'aretz,* January 15, 2002.

71. Cited in Daniel Solidman, "Abu Ala: PA needs to restore Israeli belief in peace," *Ha'aretz,* February 17, 2002.

72. Cited in *Baltimore Sun,* February 13, 2002.

73. Thomas Friedman, "An intriguing signal from the Saudi Crown Prince," *New York Times,* February 17, 2002.

74. Todd S. Purdum, "Powell says US will grab chances at Middle East peace," *New York Times,* February 28, 2002.

75. The text of UNSC Resolution 1397 is on the United Nations Web site.

76. For Powell's comments, see "Excerpts from Powell's news conference of March 29, 2002," *New York Times,* March 30, 2002. See also Tracy Wilkinson, "Israel corners a defiant Arafat," *Los Angeles Times,* March 30, 2002.

77. Woodward, *Bush at War,* p. 34.

78. Ibid.

79. Israel has been carefully cultivating the support of evangelical Christians. The Israeli ambassador to the United States, Daniel Ayalon, regularly visits evangelical churches to thank them for their support, which he has called "so important in this day and age." Cited in James Morrison, "Israel gives thanks," *Washington Times* (Embassy Row), November 27, 2003. See also James Morrison, "Praying for Israel," *Washington Times* (Embassy Row), October 28, 2003, citing Ayalon speaking in an evangelical church in Tampa, Florida, where he stated, "The American Christian community is a bedrock of support for the State of Israel and its people."

80. Howard Kohr, Executive Director of AIPAC, has called DeLay, the former House majority leader, "one of the more important, resolute, and outspoken supporters of Israel." Cited in Juliet Eilperin, "Mideast rises on DeLay's agenda," *Washington Post,* October 16, 2003.

81. Cited in "Bush slams Arafat but sees 'new attitude' in some PA leaders," *Ha'aretz,* May 26, 2002.

82. For the text of the Bush speech, see the *Washington Post,* June 25, 2002.

83. Ibid.

84. The skepticism was reinforced in December 2002 when neoconservative Elliot Abrams was made Condoleezza Rice's deputy on the National Security Council for Arab-Israeli affairs. For a view of the evolving thinking of Abrams and his relationship with other neoconservatives, see Connie Bruck, "Back roads: How serious is the Bush Administration about creating a Palestinian state?" *New Yorker,* December 15, 2003.

85. Cited in Aluf Benn, "US telling PM that the Muqata siege undermining plans for Iraq," *Ha'aretz,* September 29, 2002.

86. The text of the Road Map is found on the US Department of State Web site, April 30, 2003.

87. For the text of the letter of the eighty-eight senators, see *Journal of Palestine Studies* 32, no. 4 (Summer 2003):185.

88. See Elaine Monaghan, "Bush praises Palestinian leader's courage," *Times of London,* July 26, 2003; Guy Dunmore, "Bush attacks Israelis for building of West Bank wall," *Financial Times,* July 26, 2003; and Brian Knowlton, "Sharon meets with Bush but says security fence will still go up," *International Herald Tribune,* July 30, 2003.

89. Cited in report by Mark Mathews, "Bush pulls back from Middle East peace effort," *Baltimore Sun,* September 19, 2003. See also Mike Allen, "Bush blames Arafat for stalled road map," *Washington Post,* September 19, 2003; and Elizabeth Bumiller, "Bush admits Mideast plan is stalled and blames Arafat," *New York Times,* September 19, 2003.

90. See Yossi Beilin, *The Path to Geneva: The Quest for a Permanent Agreement, 1994–2004* (New York: RDV Books, 2004), Appendix 5. See also Robert O. Freedman, "Sharon: The Evolution of a Security Hawk," *Midstream,* May-June 2004.

91. Nicholas Kralev, "White House urged West Bank action," *Washington Times,* August 13, 2004.

92. Cited in Ron Kampus, "Election year aberration: White House presses Israel on Gaza withdrawal plan," *Washington Jewish Week,* February 26, 2004.

93. Ibid.

94. Ibid.

95. Cited in Glenn Kessler, "Interim plan from Israel may receive US backing," *Washington Post,* February 26, 2004.

96. Cited in "US urges Israel to work with Arabs in any pull-out," *New York Times,* February 26, 2004.

97. Cited in Aluf Benn, "Israel proposes fence revision to Washington," *Ha'aretz,* February 29, 2004.

98. Ibid.

99. Kralev, "White House urged West Bank action."

100. This and subsequent quotations are taken from *Ha'aretz,* April 15, 2004.

101. Labor had refused to join the coalition while Sharon was under the threat of indictment.

102. Cited in Adam Sharon, "G-8 backs Sharon Plan," *Jerusalem Post,* June 11, 2004.

103. Bush's UN speech was reprinted in the *New York Times,* September 22, 2004.

104. Cited in Cox News Service, "Israel steps up raids in Gaza," *Baltimore Sun,* October 3, 2004.

105. Cited in Colum Lynch, "US vetoes UN resolution" *Washington Post,* October 6, 2004.

106. Cited in Greg Myre, "Israeli aide hints that Gaza exit would freeze peace plan," *New York Times,* October 7, 2004.

107. Cited in Harvey Morris, "Key Sharon adviser says Gaza plan is hindrance to Palestinian state," *Financial Times,* October 7, 2004. See also Ari Shavit, "Top PM aide: Gaza plan aims to freeze the peace process," *Ha'aretz,* October 6, 2004.

108. Steven Erlanger, "Lawmakers back Sharon on plan for leaving Gaza," *New York Times,* October 27, 2004.

109. Cited in Nathan Guttman, "President Bush woos the Jewish vote," *Ha'aretz,* August 12, 2004.

110. Cited in Nicholas Kralev, "Anti-Semitism office planned at State Department," *Washington Times,* October 14, 2004. See also "State Department opposes anti-Semitism bill," *Washington Post,* October 14, 2004.

111. Cited in Nathan Guttman, "Kerry and Bush send in top guns to woo AIPAC," *Ha'aretz,* October 26, 2004.

Part Three

Gulf Wars

16

The United States in the Persian Gulf
From Twin Pillars to Dual Containment

Gary Sick

The United States arrived reluctantly as an active player in the Persian Gulf, but after a quarter-century of resistance, turmoil, and false starts, it emerged as the unquestioned military and political power in the region. In some respects this was merely the story of how the United States slowly reconciled itself to assume the role originated by the British in the nineteenth century. British interests, however, were never identical to US interests, and the underpinnings of US policy by the turn of the century bore little resemblance to the classic British defense of its eastern lines of communication.

The interests of the United States in the Persian Gulf region have been very simple and consistent: first, to ensure access by the industrialized world to the vast oil resources of the region; and second, to prevent any hostile power from acquiring political or military control over those resources. Throughout the cold war, the most immediate threat was the Soviet Union; after the Soviet collapse, Iran and Iraq became the primary targets of US containment efforts.

Other objectives, such as preserving the stability and independence of the Gulf states or containing the threat of Islamic fundamentalism, were derivative concerns and were implicit in the two grand themes of oil and containment. Preoccupation with the security of Israel was a driving factor in US Middle East policy for half a century, and developments in the Arab-Israel arena sporadically influenced US policies in the Persian Gulf (and vice versa). Especially after the end of the cold war, the Israeli factor began to assume much greater importance in the formulation of US policy in the Gulf.

The slow unfolding of US policy contributed to (and occasionally was the victim of) the development of the modern Persian Gulf. This chapter focuses on a few key turning points, where seemingly unrelated US policy choices eventually resolved themselves into a surprisingly coherent strategic posture.

The Twin Pillar Policy

Prior to World War II, US involvement in the Persian Gulf was minimal. The first sustained encounter with the region was in the nineteenth century, in the days of the great clipper ships.[1] The Persian Gulf and Indian Ocean were regarded as a British preserve, and US political, commercial, and military contact with the region was extremely rare.[2]

The US Middle East Command was established during World War II to oversee the supply route of war materiel to the Soviet Union. Its 40,000 US troops constituted the largest US deployment to the region from that time until Operation Desert Storm in 1991. The small US naval contingent (Middle East Force) that was established in 1947 relied on British hospitality at Jufair on Bahrain Island.

The British announcement in 1968 that it intended to withdraw from its historic position east of Suez came as an unwelcome shock in Washington, which had long relied on the British presence as an essential component of its Soviet containment strategy along the immense arc from the Suez Canal to the Malacca Straits. It also came at the worst possible moment, since US forces were increasingly strained by commitments in Vietnam and Southeast Asia.

The Nixon administration undertook a major review of US Persian Gulf policy when it took office in 1969. This was part of a global effort to redefine US security interests at a time of competing demands on US military forces and a growing reluctance by the American public to support what were seen as potentially costly foreign commitments. The result of this effort was the Nixon Doctrine, which placed primary reliance on security cooperation with regional states as a means of protecting US interests around the world. In the Gulf, it was decided to rely heavily on the two key states of Iran and Saudi Arabia, a strategy that quickly became known as the "Twin Pillar policy."[3]

From the beginning, it was recognized that Iran would be the more substantial of the two "pillars" because of its size, its military capabilities, its physical juxtaposition between the Soviet Union and the Persian Gulf, and the willingness of the shah (unlike the Arab states of the region) to cooperate openly with the United States on security matters. This very special relationship between Washington and Tehran was sealed in May 1972 during the visit to Tehran of President Nixon and his national security adviser, Henry Kissinger.

In two and one-half hours of conversations over two days, a deal was struck in which the United States agreed to increase the numbers of uniformed advisers in Iran and guaranteed the shah access to some of the most sophisticated nonnuclear technology in the US military arsenal. The shah, in return, agreed to accept a key role in protecting Western interests in the Persian Gulf region. All of this was summed up with startling candor at the end of the meetings, when President Nixon looked across the table to the shah and said simply, "Protect me."[4]

This moment was the culmination of several decades of tumultuous political relations between the United States and Iran. In 1953, the Eisenhower administration had carried out a "countercoup" that restored the shah to the throne and ended the political career of nationalist leader Muhammad Mussadiq.[5] By this act, the United States at once lost its political innocence with regard to Iran and guaranteed that it would be held permanently responsible—at least by Iranian popular opinion—for the Iranian ruler's excesses and cruelties. In 1963, a fiery religious leader, Ruhollah Khomeini, led the opposition to a bill that, among other things, extended diplomatic protection to American military advisers. This rebellion, which in retrospect was a rehearsal for the revolution of 1978–1979, led to Khomeini's fourteen-year exile. Although most Americans were scarcely aware of this incident, the Iranian opposition was convinced that the shah was acting on behalf of the United States.

The agreement between President Nixon and the shah in 1972 transformed the previous client relationship. Iran was on the brink of becoming a major power in the oil market and now had free access to the US arsenal of modern weaponry. This was formally acknowledged when Iran agreed to become the protector of US interests in the region, and the shah increasingly felt emboldened to lecture his great power ally on politics, economics, and strategy. The United States in turn reduced its intelligence coverage of Iran's internal politics and relied on the shah for assistance in putting down the Marxist rebellion in Dhofar, for an assured energy supply at the time of the oil embargo of 1973, and for support in political and military operations in the Middle East and Africa as well as Vietnam.

This role reversal went almost unnoticed in the Persian Gulf and elsewhere, however. In Iran, the image of a compliant shah responding to orders dictated in Washington remained vividly implanted in the national psyche. As a consequence, when the revolution exploded in the late 1970s, the United States had the worst of both worlds. It had relinquished much of its independent capacity to assess and influence Iran's internal politics, but it was popularly suspected of orchestrating every move by the shah's regime.

The Twin Pillar policy also involved a tripartite covert action with Israel to destabilize Iraq by supporting a Kurdish rebellion against Baghdad. This plan was adopted in May 1972 during the Nixon-Kissinger visit; it collapsed in 1975 when the shah unilaterally came to an agreement with Saddam Hussein and abandoned the Kurds. It established a precedent for viewing the Persian Gulf as an extension of the Arab-Israel conflict and for US-Israeli cooperation in the region.[6]

The collapse of the shah's regime in February 1979 was the death knell for the US Twin Pillar policy. From the beginning, the policy had been predicated on a close personal relationship with the shah. With his departure and the arrival of a hostile Islamist regime in Tehran, the United States was left strategically naked in the Persian Gulf, with no safety net.

The Carter Doctrine

This blow was compounded in February 1979 by reports of an incipient invasion of North Yemen by its avowedly Marxist neighbor to the south. This event, coming in the wake of the Marxist coup in Afghanistan in April 1978, the conclusion of the Ethiopian-Soviet treaty in November 1978, the fall of the shah, and the assassination of US Ambassador Adolph Dubs in Kabul in February 1979, created the impression that the United States had lost all capacity to influence regional events. That impression was strengthened when Turkey and Pakistan followed Iran in withdrawing from the Central Treaty Organization in March.

Washington responded by dispatching a carrier task force to the Arabian Sea and by rushing emergency military aid to Yemen and the airborne warning and control system, or AWACS, to Saudi Arabia. The United States also undertook a systematic effort to develop a new "strategic framework" for the Persian Gulf. By the end of 1979, the outlines of a strategy had been sketched in, including initial identification of US forces for a rapid deployment force and preliminary discussions with Oman, Kenya, and Somalia about possible use of facilities. Nevertheless, when the US embassy in Tehran was attacked in November, a high-level review of US military capabilities drew the sobering conclusion that US ability to influence events in the region was extremely limited. In late November, when there were serious fears that the US hostages were in danger of being killed, a second aircraft carrier was sent to the area and two additional destroyers were assigned to the Middle East Force.

The Soviet invasion of Afghanistan just before Christmas in 1979 reawakened fears of a Soviet drive to the Persian Gulf and Indian Ocean. The practical effect of the Soviet invasion was to terminate the efforts of the Carter administration to seek mutual accommodation with the Soviet Union, including support for the SALT II treaty. This policy shift was articulated by Carter in his State of the Union address of January 23, 1980: "Any attempt by any outside force to gain control of the Persian Gulf region will be regarded as an assault on the vital interests of the United States of America, and such an assault will be repelled by any means necessary, including military force."

This declaration, which quickly came to be known as the Carter Doctrine, bore a remarkable resemblance to the classic statement of British policy by Lord Lansdowne in 1903, when he said the United Kingdom would "regard the establishment of a naval base, or of a fortified port, in the Persian Gulf by any other power as a very grave menace to British interests," an act that would be resisted "with all the means at our disposal."[7] The statement clearly established the United States as the protecting power of the region and effectively completed the transfer of policy responsibility in the Persian Gulf from the British to the Americans.

When Carter made this statement, it reflected US intentions rather than capabilities. By the time the Reagan administration arrived in Washington in January 1981, it would have been accurate to say that the US security structure in the Persian Gulf region was more symbol than reality—at least as measured in purely military capacity.[8] Nevertheless, it was equally apparent that the developments of 1980 marked a major threshold in the evolution of US strategy and a new conviction that this region represented a major strategic zone of US vital interests, demanding both sustained attention at the highest levels of US policymaking and direct US engagement in support of specifically US interests. That was without precedent.

The Reagan administration adopted the Carter Doctrine and over the following seven years succeeded in putting more substantial military power and organization behind its words. The Rapid Deployment Joint Task Force (RDJTF) was reorganized in 1983 as a unified command known as the Central Command, based at MacDill Air Force Base in Tampa, Florida, with earmarked forces totaling some 230,000 military personnel from the four services. Its basic mission reflected the two themes that had wound through US regional policy from the very beginning: "to assure continued access to Persian Gulf oil and to prevent the Soviets from acquiring political-military control directly or through proxies."

The Iran-Iraq War (1980–1988)

Despite the shadow of Soviet military power, all threats to oil supplies and to regional stability came not from Russia and its allies but from political developments within the region. The first of these was the Arab oil boycott at the time of the Arab-Israeli war of 1973, which nearly tripled the price of oil and sent Western economies spinning into a serious recession. The second was the Iranian revolution, and the third was the Iran-Iraq war, which Iraq launched with a massive invasion in September 1980.

The United States asserted its neutrality at the beginning of the war, then later tilted unofficially in favor of Iraq as Iran drove back the Iraqi forces and counterattacked across the border. In 1985–1986, as part of a "strategic opening" to Iran coupled with an abortive effort to free US hostages in Lebanon, the United States and Israel undertook a series of secret contacts and substantial arms transfers to Iran that effectively shifted US policy—at least at the covert level—toward Iran. When the revelation of these arrangements created consternation and threatened US relations with the friendly oil-producing states of the Gulf, the United States reversed field sharply and adopted an openly pro-Iraqi position.[9]

During much of the war, the United States and many other powers adopted a hands-off posture, content to see these two abominable regimes exhaust each other on the battlefield, particularly since the war was having relatively little impact on oil supplies or prices.[10] That nonchalance began to fade in 1985–1986 when Iran began to retaliate for Iraqi air attacks against its shipping in the Gulf by using mines and small armed boats against neutral shipping en route to Kuwait and Saudi Arabia.

In late 1986, Kuwait asked both the United States and the Soviet Union to place Kuwaiti tankers under their flag and provide protection.[11] The Soviet Union agreed to reflag three Kuwaiti tankers, and the United States quickly followed suit by reflagging eleven. The United States moved a substantial number of naval ships into or near the Gulf and began escorting tanker convoys to and from Kuwait.[12] Iran's indiscriminate use of mines led other NATO navies to send minesweepers and other escort ships to the Gulf to protect international shipping.

Although the reflagging decision was seen at the time as a temporary US response to a specific problem, in retrospect it was a fundamental turning point. For the first time since World War II, the United States assumed an operational role in the defense of the Persian Gulf, with all that implied in terms of development of infrastructure, doctrine, coordination with NATO allies, and direct collaboration with the Arab states on the southern littoral. President Reagan's military intervention thus confirmed President Carter's assertion that the Gulf was of vital interest to the United States and that the United States was prepared to use military force in pursuit of that interest. Although the Carter Doctrine addressed the prospective threat from the Soviet Union, its first major implementation involved a regional state, anticipating the massive international coalition that repelled Iraq's occupation of Kuwait in January 1991.

From War to War

United Nations (UN) Security Council Resolution 598 was passed unanimously by the Security Council on July 20, 1987, calling for an immediate cease-fire between Iran and Iraq. This set off a full year of acrimonious debate, punctuated by sporadic missile bombardments of cities and further attacks on oil tankers.[13] A new element in this escalation of the war was the expanded use of chemical weapons by Iraq against civilian targets. Iraq had used poison gas extensively in earlier campaigns, but the targets had been Iranian military forces. On the evening of March 16, 1988, Iraq conducted two bombing raids against the village of Halabjah, which Iranian forces were about to enter. The bombs caught the local Iraqi Kurdish villagers in their homes and in the street, killing at least 2,000 civilians. The UN dispatched an investigating team that confirmed the atrocity. But Iraq was unrepentant. Foreign Minister Tariq 'Aziz wrote to the UN secretary-general that "in their legitimate, moral, and internationally approved self-defense, our people are determined to use all available abilities and means against the criminal invaders."[14] In fact, in the succeeding months, Iraq used poison gas more frequently and against a wider range of targets, including civilians, than at any previous time in the war. The UN Security Council passed Resolution 612 on May 9, 1988, mandating an immediate end to the use of chemical weapons in the war and holding out the prospect of sanctions against violators, but it had no effect.

During this same period, the Soviet Union announced its intention to withdraw its military forces from Afghanistan by the end of 1988. This resulted in the signing of an accord between Afghanistan and Pakistan on April 14 in Geneva, with the United States and the Soviet Union as co-guarantors.

Throughout this period, political cohesion in Iran was breaking down, and the continued use of mines in the Gulf set off a new round of clashes with US forces.[15] Iraq went on the offensive against Iran's disorganized and disheartened military forces, recapturing the Fao Peninsula in a lightning attack on April 18, then proceeding to push back Iranian forces all along the front. In mid-May, apparently with assistance from Saudi Arabia, Iraq carried out a devastating attack on the Iranian oil transfer site at Larak Island in the southern Gulf, destroying five ships, including the world's largest supertanker.[16] Antiwar sentiment began to appear openly in demonstrations in major Iranian cities. And most disturbing of all for the divided leadership, persuasive evidence began to accumulate that Khomeini was severely ill and virtually incapacitated.

On July 3, a commercial Iranian aircraft was shot down by the USS *Vincennes,* killing all 290 passengers and crew. This terrible accident, coming at the end of a seemingly endless series of defeats, underscored the despair of Iran's position. On July 18, the Iranian foreign minister sent a letter to the UN secretary-general formally accepting Resolution 598. Two days later, Khomeini sent a "message to the nation," read by an announcer, associating himself with the decision, which, he said, was "more deadly than taking poison."[17]

Iraq was taken by surprise and initially resisted accepting a cease-fire, while continuing its mopping up operations. Iraq also continued to demonstrate a contemptuous disregard for the Security Council and for world opinion on the use of chemical weapons. A UN investigative team presented its report to the Security Council on August 1, finding that "chemical weapons continue to be used on an intensive scale" by Iraq. Only hours later, Iraq launched a massive chemical bombing attack on the Iranian town of Oshnoviyeh. However, as international pressure mounted, Saddam Hussein finally agreed to accept a cease-fire on August 6. A UN observer force was rushed to the region, and a cease-fire went into effect on August 20, 1988.

The end of the war provided an opportunity for the George H. W. Bush administration to reconsider its support for Saddam Hussein in the wake of revelations about Iraq's use of chemical weapons against its own population, the genocidal Anfal campaign against the Kurds, and Iraq's efforts to develop nuclear weapons and other weapons of mass destruction. The policy of limited cooperation with Iraq, however, remained intact. This policy became an embarrassment after the defeat of Iraq in the 1991 Gulf war, when claims were leveled that the US government had chosen to ignore warnings that agricultural credits might have been diverted to the purchase of military equipment. The most sensational charges of criminal responsibility were never substantiated, and the so-called Iraqgate scandal faded after the 1992 US presidential elections. However, documents made available to the Congress and the media did demonstrate persuasively that the Bush administration had pursued a largely uncritical policy toward Iraq during the period between the end of the Iran-Iraq war and the Iraqi invasion of Kuwait.[18]

At a minimum, this policy of tolerance and inattentiveness may have contributed to a false sense of security on the part of Saddam Hussein as he prepared to invade his neighbor to the south. The US ambassador to Baghdad, April Glaspie, was widely criticized for failing to warn Saddam Hussein about the possible consequences of an attack, but any fair-minded review of the record would reveal that she was accurately reflecting the policy of the president and secretary of state during this interwar period.[19]

The Second Gulf War

When Iraqi forces crossed the border into Kuwait at 1 A.M. on the morning of August 2, 1990, they set in motion a series of events that would transform US policy in the Persian Gulf. It marked a turning point in US relations with the Arab states of the Gulf, as pointed out by Shafeeq Ghabra and F. Gregory Gause III elsewhere in this volume. The cooperation between the United States and the Soviet Union on a matter of high strategy and military policy, which would have been unthinkable only a few years earlier, marked the undeniable end of the cold war.[20] The successful creation of a very large international coalition under the auspices of the UN and under the direct leadership of the United States aroused expectations for both the UN and peacekeeping, some of which was expressed in President George H. W. Bush's use of the phrase "a new world order" in relation to the Gulf intervention.[21]

The eventual use of missiles by Iraq against Israel underscored the relationship between the Arab-Israel conflict and Gulf policy more clearly than at any time since the oil embargo of 1973. The immediate imposition of a draconian sanctions regime against Iraq, and its continuation over a period of many years, demonstrated both the extent and limitations of collective nonviolent coercion by the international community. The combined use of air power, lightning-fast ground mobility, and high-tech weapons—many for the first time in combat—in a computerized battlefield environment wrote a new chapter in the conduct of modern warfare and raised some troubling new questions.[22] The media, and especially television, brought these events into the world's living rooms with an intimacy and immediacy that may have been unprecedented in its universality.

Saddam Hussein's forces were ejected from Kuwait with minimal combat casualties.[23] On March 3, US General Norman Schwartzkopf met with an Iraqi military delegation at Safwan airfield in southern Iraq, and the Iraqis quickly agreed to allied terms. Almost immediately, revolts against Saddam Hussein's regime broke out among the Kurds in northern Iraq and among the Shi'a in southern Iraq. Initially President Bush declared that Iraq was violating the terms of the cease-fire by using military helicopters to put down the revolts. He reversed himself almost immediately, however, stating that "using helicopters like this to put down one's own people does not add to the stability of the area. . . . We are not in there trying to impose a solution inside Iraq."[24]

The distinction was critical. Over the following weeks, Iraqi forces brutally suppressed the uprisings and arguably preserved Saddam Hussein's position of power. The rationale for the change was spelled out two weeks later by White House spokesman Marlin Fitzwater, who noted, "There is no interest in the coalition in further military operations." Arab officials, he said, were advising Washington: "Let Hussein deal with this, then the dust will settle and he's going to have to pay the piper for the war over Kuwait. Or at least that is what we are counting on."[25]

In an interview with David Frost, General Schwarzkopf said he was "suckered" by the Iraqis into agreeing to permit helicopters to fly, ostensibly to move top officials between cities, when they really intended to use helicopter gunships against the rebels.[26] Five years later, also in an interview with David Frost, George H. W. Bush commented on Saddam Hussein and the postwar situation: "I miscalculated. . . . I thought he'd be gone." With regard to the Safwan meeting, Bush noted, "I think he took us by surprise. . . . We might have handled the flying of helicopters differently. . . . So I think there's room for some ex post facto criticism here."[27]

Whatever the rationale, the US decision to permit Saddam Hussein to use advanced weaponry to suppress the internal revolts after the war made the United States an accessory after the fact to a massacre and ensured, whether inadvertently or not, that Saddam Hussein would retain power in Iraq. When the extent of the repression became known, and as Kurdish refugees began flooding across the border into Turkey, the United States, together with France and Great Britain, established so-called no-fly zones in the north and south. This gesture undoubtedly saved some lives and effectively prevented Saddam Hussein from reestablishing total control over the Kurdish territories. It was, however, much too late to save the many thousands of Iraqis who had spontaneously attacked the symbols of Ba'thist rule in the weeks after the allied victory.

The Clinton Administration and Dual Containment[28]

On May 18, 1993, two months after President Clinton took office, Martin Indyk of the National Security Council staff spelled out the broad outlines of what he called America's "dual containment" policy in the Persian Gulf.[29] Traditionally, the United States had pursued a policy of balancing Iran and Iraq against each other as a means of maintaining a degree of regional stability and to protect the smaller oil-rich Arab states on the southern side of the Gulf. That was the purpose of the Twin Pillar policy, and it was implicit in subsequent tilts toward Iraq and (briefly) Iran during the Iran-Iraq war. Indyk, however, proclaimed the policy bankrupt and rejected it "because we don't need to rely on one to balance the other." Iraq was boxed in by UN sanctions, Iran was nearly prostrate after the eight-year war with Iraq, and the United States was the predominant power in the Persian Gulf with the "means to counter both the Iraqi and Iranian regimes."[30]

Iraq

The objective of the policy with regard to Iraq was to sustain the coalition that had defeated the armies of Saddam Hussein in Operation Desert Storm and to ensure that Iraq complied with all United Nations resolutions. The United States characterized the existing regime in Iraq as criminal and irredeemable and favored maintaining the sanctions until Saddam Hussein was gone.[31] This position created difficulties with other members of the UN Security Council, since Article 22 of the enabling Resolution 687 specified that the sanctions would be lifted once Iraq had eliminated and accounted for all of its weapons of mass destruction.

In the years after the adoption of the policy, the United States reportedly bud-geted approximately $15 million per year for covert actions to destabilize the Sad-dam Hussein regime and for support of various Iraqi opposition groups.[32] The US Central Intelligence Agency attempted to organize several operations to depose Sad-dam Hussein, including a major covert action just before the Clinton administra-tion took office and at least two others in 1995 and 1996.[33] These operations were unsuccessful.

There was very little debate in the United States about the desirability—even the necessity—of maintaining strict sanctions against the government of Saddam Hus-sein. The substantial American consensus in favor of severe sanctions could be at-tributed in large measure to the Iraqi leader himself. The nature of his attack on Kuwait, the looting and killing and burning that followed, his ruthless suppression of dissent, his near-genocidal tactics against his own people, the discovery that he was much closer to having nuclear and chemical weapons than had been supposed, his systematic obstruction of UN investigations including physical interference and mass falsification of documents, and his continued military forays and threats when-ever he believed he could get away with it—all of these firmly implanted an image of utter evil and constant threat. That image underscored and reinforced US insis-tence on what was the most elaborate network of sanctions ever imposed on a mem-ber state of the UN.

There was, however, considerable sympathy in the United States for the plight of the people of Iraq, who bore the worst of the brunt of two wars and stringent eco-nomic sanctions. This popular concern was no doubt a factor in the US decision to acquiesce in the limited sale of Iraqi oil under terms negotiated by the UN in 1996.[34] The United States insisted, however, that the misery of the Iraqi people was directly attributable to Saddam Hussein, who callously used the deprivation of his own people as a bargaining chip.[35]

In June 1993 and in September 1996, the United States launched cruise missiles against targets in Iraq. The first case was retaliation for evidence of an Iraqi plot to assassinate former President George H. W. Bush in Kuwait. The second was in retal-iation for Iraqi ground force incursions in northern Iraq in cooperation with the Kurdish Democratic Party.[36] On several occasions, the United States surged military forces into the region in response to Iraqi threats or failure to comply with UN Spe-cial Commission (UNSCOM) inspections. In February 1998, the United States ap-peared to be poised for a massive strike against Iraq, when it refused to permit in-spection of presidential sites. That crisis was resolved only when the UN secretary-general, Kofi Annan, went to Baghdad and negotiated a memorandum of understanding with the Iraqi president.[37]

The bottom line, however, was that the United States, with significant help from a number of friends, allies, and the UN Security Council, was generally successful in keeping Saddam Hussein in what Secretary of State Madeleine Albright called a "strategic box." By mid-1998, this policy was losing support from the Arab states, which felt that the Iraqi people were being unfairly punished for the misbehavior of their rulers, and from states such as Russia, France, and China that had major political and financial interests in Iraq. The international consensus was preserved, however, primarily because of the unrelenting intransigence and belligerence of the Iraqi leader.

Iran

The other target of dual containment, Iran, posed a very different set of problems. The dual containment policy called for Iran to (1) cease its support of international terrorism and subversion, (2) end its violent opposition to the Arab-Israel peace talks, and (3) halt efforts to acquire weapons of mass destruction. President Bush had made a hopeful reference to Iran in his Inaugural Address in January 1989, saying, "Goodwill begets goodwill. Good faith can be a spiral that endlessly moves on."[38] However, there was no talk of goodwill by the Clinton administration. Instead, US officials developed a special vocabulary in which Iran was routinely branded as a "rogue," "terrorist," "outlaw," or "backlash" state. This relentless drumfire of attacks—the mirror image of Iranian depictions of the United States as the "Great Satan"—had its effects in the media, in the Congress, in the public, and in the attitudes of lower-level bureaucrats. With a Democrat in the White House and the Republicans in control of the Congress, a domestic political contest developed over which party could be most vigorous in promoting US policies to deal with Iran.

The debate was galvanized in 1995 when the US oil company Conoco announced that it had signed a $1 billion contract with Iran to develop the Sirri gas field in the Persian Gulf. Although perfectly legal, the prospect that this deal would breach the wall of containment around Iran generated such a wave of outrage that the company was forced to renounce it. The Congress and the American-Israel Public Affairs Committee (AIPAC) began preparing legislation that would end all trade with Iran and punish any corporations that engaged in investments there. President Clinton, who was preparing for his reelection campaign, quickly preempted this by issuing two executive orders that made it illegal for American oil companies to operate in Iran and established penalties for any US citizen or corporation doing business with Iran.[39] Both decisions were announced by senior administration officials before major Jewish organizations. The US business community, apparently intimidated by the public outcry, remained silent on the matter.[40]

This process was replayed in presidential election year 1996. The Congress prepared a bill that would impose sanctions on any foreign corporation that invested $20 million or more in the Iranian oil and gas sector. Libya was later added on the floor of the Senate, and the bill became known as the Iran-Libya Sanctions Act (ILSA). Although the bill was certain to create serious problems with America's allies, the Congress saw ILSA as an opportunity to take a public stand against terrorism. The bill passed 415-0 and was signed into law by President Clinton.

In May 1997, Seyyed Mohammed Khatami was elected to a four-year term as president of Iran in a stunning electoral surprise. He conducted a grassroots campaign on the issues of rule of law, civil society, and dialogue among competing ideologies. His campaign struck a resonant chord with the Iranian population, particularly among women and the burgeoning population of young people, many of whom had no memory of the ancient regime. Paired against the well-known speaker of the Majlis (parliament), who represented revolutionary orthodoxy, Khatami attracted the largest number of voters in Iranian history and won a decisive victory with 69 percent of the vote. He carried all of the urban centers in Iran and virtually every province. In August, his reformist cabinet was accepted without exception by the Majlis.

Although Khatami was widely regarded as a candidate of domestic issues, it was his foreign policy moves that attracted the most attention during the first year of his term. In December 1997, Iran played host to the Organization of the Islamic Conference, where it won plaudits for its conciliatory positions and moderation. Iran called for closer cooperation with the UN, an institution it had shunned as a Western tool after the revolution. Iran began a concerted effort to improve its relations with Saudi Arabia and its other Arab neighbors in the Persian Gulf region, with some substantial initial success.

In January 1998, Khatami made an unprecedented "Address to the American People" in the form of an interview on CNN.[41] He praised the achievements of American civilization, went as far as an Iranian politician could go in expressing regret for the hostage crisis, and spelled out very clearly Iran's positions on all of the major issues of concern to the United States.

> On terrorism: "Any form of killing of innocent men and women who are not involved in confrontations is terrorism. It must be condemned, and we, in our turn, condemn every form of it in the world."
>
> On the peace process: "We have declared our opposition to the Middle East peace process, because we believe it will not succeed. At the same time, we have clearly said that we don't intend to impose our views on others or to stand in their way."
>
> On weapons of mass destruction: "We are not a nuclear power and do not intend to become one."

Washington responded to the Khatami initiative cautiously but generally positively.[42] The United States toned down its rhetoric and took some small steps to improve relations. But problems remained. Less than sixty days after Khatami took office, the French oil company Total, together with state-owned partners Gazprom of Russia and Petronas of Malaysia, concluded a $2 billion deal to develop an Iranian gas field. These negotiations, which had been underway since Conoco withdrew in 1995, placed Total and its partners in apparent violation of ILSA, which mandated US sanctions against any company investing more than $20 million in the Iranian oil and gas sector.[43]

In May 1998, the United States announced that it would waive the provisions of ILSA on grounds of national security. That decision was due almost entirely to pressure from America's European allies, but it was nevertheless received positively in

Tehran.[44] The United States also announced a major redeployment of its Persian Gulf forces, sharply reducing the number of ships and aircraft permanently stationed in the region. This was due primarily to cost factors and personnel pressures, but again it was received positively by Tehran. There was growing awareness among Washington strategists that the initial assumption that the United States alone could confront both Iran and Iraq may have been exaggerated. At a minimum, as the threat from Iran appeared to be declining, the United States could ill afford to deliberately cultivate enemies.

On June 17, 1998, Secretary of State Albright delivered a major speech that responded almost point by point to the issues that Khatami had addressed in his interview six months earlier.[45] The speech was notable for its conciliatory tone and for the absence of the rhetoric that had characterized US statements about Iran over the previous five years. The speech offered no specific new policies or initiatives, but it held out the prospect for a new beginning:

> We are ready to explore further ways to build mutual confidence and avoid misunderstandings. The Islamic Republic should consider parallel steps. If such a process can be initiated and sustained in a way that addresses the concerns of both sides, then we in the United States can see the prospect of a very different relationship. As the wall of mistrust comes down, we can develop with the Islamic Republic, when it is ready, a road map leading to normal relations. Obviously, two decades of mistrust cannot be erased overnight. The gap between us remains wide. But it is time to test the possibilities for bridging this gap.[46]

Conclusion

By the end of the twentieth century, the United States had become a Persian Gulf power in its own right. Its political, military, and economic footprint in the region was greater even than the governments of the region themselves. Its role as security guarantor was not in doubt, and its prestige and influence were at their zenith.

Less clear was what the future might hold, and how the United States might choose to exercise its power in its new role as the sole superpower. History provided no reliable guidance. For more than a half century, the United States experimented, often clumsily, with stratagems of all sorts in a variety of circumstances. In the end, as in the cold war, its interests were preserved, and it emerged as the dominant power. The challenge for the future would be to blend military power with diplomacy in a region that could no longer be sequestered from the broader issues of the Middle East, international politics, and the global economy.

Notes

1. These early contacts led to a treaty with the sultanate of Muscat and Oman in 1833, which is still recalled on occasions of state with Oman.

2. The following comments draw on the author's article "The Evolution of US Strategy Toward the Indian Ocean and Persian Gulf Regions," in *The Great Game: Rivalry in the Persian Gulf and South Asia,* ed. Alvin Z. Rubinstein (New York: Praeger, 1983), pp. 49–80.

3. For a more detailed account of this period, see Michael A. Palmer, *Guardians of the Gulf: The Growth of American Involvement in the Persian Gulf, 1833–1991* (New York: Free Press, 1992).

4. A detailed account of this episode and its implications can be found in Gary Sick, *All Fall Down: America's Tragic Encounter with Iran* (New York: Random House, 1985), pp. 14ff.

5. See Chapter 3 by Mark Gasiorowski in this volume.

6. For a more detailed account, see James A. Bill, *The Eagle and the Lion: The Tragedy of American-Iranian Relations* (New Haven, Conn.: Yale University Press), 1988, pp. 204–208. Israel had a well-developed strategy, known as the Doctrine of the Periphery, to outflank its hostile Arab neighbors by promoting relations with non-Arab states on the fringes of the conflict. In the case of Iran, this took the form of a very close strategic relationship for more than twenty years.

7. Cited in J. C. Hurewitz, *The Persian Gulf After Iran's Revolution,* Foreign Policy Association Headline Series 244, April 1979, p. 22.

8. Former Secretary of Defense James Schlesinger drew attention to this fact in an article questioning whether the RDJTF was rapid, deployable, or even a force. See "Rapid(?) Deployment(?) Force(?)," *Washington Post,* September 24, 1980.

9. For a detailed examination of this episode, see Theodore Draper, *A Very Thin Line: The Iran-Contra Affair* (New York: Hill and Wang, 1991).

10. The casualty figures for the Iran-Iraq war are often exaggerated. Mohsen Rafiqdust, the former head of the Iranian Revolutionary Guard Force, told Robert Fisk of the *Independent* (June 25, 1995) that 220,000 Iranians were killed and 400,000 wounded during the Iran-Iraq war. That is roughly consistent with Iranian official statements and with independent Western estimates. Iraq has never published any figures on its losses, but Amatzia Baram, a specialist on Iraq at Haifa University, has estimated that 150,000 Iraqis were killed (*Jerusalem Quarterly* 49 [Winter 1989], pp. 85–86). If the standard ratio of two wounded for every man killed is applied, Iraq may have had 300,000 wounded. Thus, an informed estimate of total losses on both sides would equal approximately 370,000 killed and some 700,000 wounded, which is imprecise but plausible. In the case of Iraq, this casualty level is roughly comparable to US losses in the Civil War.

11. See Chapter 17 by Shafeeq Ghabra in this volume.

12. The substantial deployment of US forces to the Gulf was hastened—as was congressional approval—by the Iraqi missile attack on the USS *Stark* on May 17, 1987. Although the buildup was intended to counter Iran, the Iraqi attack galvanized public attention and underlined the threat to shipping in the Gulf.

13. Iraq was much better equipped than Iran, and it fired three to four missiles to every Iranian missile. The only confirmed use of poison gas was by Iraq—against Iranian troop formations and some civilian sites in Kurdish territory. For a more detailed examination of this armed negotiation, see Gary Sick, "Slouching Toward Settlement: The Internationalization of the Iran-Iraq War, 1987–88," in *Neither East Nor West: Iran, the Soviet Union, and the United States,* ed. Nikki Keddie and Mark Gasiorowski (New Haven, Conn.: Yale University Press, 1990), pp. 219–246.

14. Letter to the secretary-general of March 28 (*FBIS,* March 30, 1988).

15. One mine struck the USS *Samuel B. Roberts,* and on April 18, 1988, US forces hit two Iranian oil platforms, Nasr (near Sirri Island) and Salman (in the joint Iran-Oman Lavan

field), cutting Iran's oil production by some 50,000 barrels per day. In the same action, two Iranian frigates were sunk, another was severely damaged, and four gunboats were damaged or sunk. In 1996, Iran brought a suit against the United States in the International Court of Justice seeking compensation for the loss of the oil platforms on the grounds that the attacks were a violation of international law and contrary to the terms of existing US-Iranian agreements.

16. The bitter dispute between Iran and Saudi Arabia over Iran's participation in the annual *hajj* deepened the distrust between these two states. Saudi Arabia stepped up its direct support for Iraq, apparently permitting Iraqi aircraft to utilize Saudi airfields during raids on Iranian oil facilities in the southern Gulf. On April 26, 1988, Saudi Arabia broke diplomatic relations with Iran.

17. *FBIS,* July 21, 1988. On July 25, Khomeini made a six-minute appearance on television from the balcony of his residence. He appeared extremely frail and did not speak.

18. For example, see Murray Waas and Douglas Frantz, "US Gave Data to Iraq Three Months Before Invasion; Persian Gulf: Documents Show Intelligence Sharing with Baghdad Lasted Longer Than Previously Indicated," *Los Angeles Times,* March 10, 1992, p. 1 (one of a series of investigative reports). See also "News Conference, Rep. Jack Brooks (D–TX) Rep. Charles Schumer (D–NY): Special Prosecutor Criminal Dealings with Iraq Prior to Iraqi Invasion of Kuwait," *Federal News Service,* July 9, 1992.

19. A verbatim text of Glaspie's meeting with Saddam Hussein on July 25, 1990, was later released by the Iraqi government and was published by the *New York Times* on September 23, 1990, p. 19. Glaspie, in testimony before the Senate Foreign Relations Committee on March 20, 1991, characterized the transcript as about 80 percent accurate, but with some key passages edited out.

20. See Chapter 15 by Robert O. Freedman and Chapter 22 by Georgiy Mirsky in this volume.

21. Speech by President Bush from the Oval Office, January 16, 1991, two hours after the bombing campaign against Iraqi positions had begun.

22. See, for example, "Needless Deaths in the Gulf War: Civilian Casualties During the Air Campaign and Violations of the Laws of War," *Middle East Watch Report,* Human Rights Watch, New York, November 1991.

23. According to official counts, allied deaths were 146 Americans (35 by friendly fire) 24 British (9 by American fire), 2 Frenchmen, 1 Italian, and 39 among various Arab allies. Baghdad has never given an official count of its casualties, but postwar analyses concluded that Iraq's uniformed losses were far smaller than previously estimated, perhaps as low as 1,500 deaths. Estimates of civilian casualties were uncertain and varied greatly from one observer to another. See John G. Heidenrich, "The Gulf War: How Many Iraqis Died?" *Foreign Policy* 90 (Spring 1993), pp. 108–125. The Associated Press on March 9, 1993, provided an overview of the various estimates.

24. *New York Times,* March 15, 1991, p. 13.

25. *New York Times,* March 27, 1991, pp. 1, 9.

26. *New York Times,* March 28, 1991, pp. 1, 18.

27. *Dow Jones News,* January 15, 1996.

28. The following analysis draws extensively on the author's article "Rethinking Dual Containment," *Survival: The IISS Quarterly* 40, no. 1 (Spring 1998), pp. 5–32.

29. Martin Indyk, "The Clinton Administration's Approach to the Middle East," Keynote Address to the Soref Symposium on "Challenges to US Interests in the Middle East: Obstacles and Opportunities," *Proceedings of the Washington Institute for Near East Policy,* May

18–19, 1993, pp. 1–8. Martin Indyk at the time of this speech had just joined the National Security Council staff. He later became the US ambassador to Israel and then assistant secretary of state for Near East affairs.

30. Indyk, "The Clinton Administration's Approach to the Middle East," p. 4.

31. See, for example, the remarks by Secretary of State Madeleine K. Albright at Georgetown University, Washington, D.C., March 26, 1997, as released by the Office of the Spokesman, US Department of State.

32. Elaine Sciolino, "CIA Asks Congress for Money to Rein in Iraq and Iran," *New York Times,* April 12, 1995, p. 1.

33. All of these operations were publicly confirmed after the event by former senior officials of the US government. See Don Oberdorfer, "US Had Covert Plan to Oust Iraq's Saddam, Bush Adviser Asserts; Effort to Remove Leader Came 'Pretty Close,'" *Washington Post,* January 20, 1993, p. 1; and ABC News, "Unfinished Business—the CIA and Saddam Hussein," transcript no. 97062601-j13, June 26, 1997. There have also been detailed reports in the *Los Angeles Times, New York Times,* and other media.

34. Initially, Iraq was permitted to sell up to $2 billion of oil in two 90-day periods after each authorization. The first sales began on December 10, 1995. In 1998, the terms were extended to permit total sales of $4.5 billion—more than the Iraqis were physically capable of producing, given the low price of oil at the time. The sales contracts were monitored closely by the UN, and the proceeds were allotted to humanitarian relief and repayment of claims from the war and to cover UN expenses in Iraq.

35. United Nations Special Commissioner Rolf Ekeus estimated that Iraq deliberately deprived itself of more than $100 billion in revenues by refusing to cooperate with UN weapons inspections. See "For the Record," *Washington Post,* January 31, 1997.

36. This attack was particularly controversial since the targets were in the south and unrelated to the ground attack in the north.

37. See "Memorandum of Understanding Between the United Nations and the Republic of Iraq," *Associated Press,* February 24, 1998.

38. See the text of the Inaugural Address in the *New York Times,* January 21, 1989, p. 10. Iran welcomed this remark and responded by helping to free the US hostages in Lebanon. It is a sore point with Iran that this gesture, in their view, was never reciprocated by the United States.

39. See Executive Order 12957 of March 15, 1995, and Executive Order 12959 of May 6, 1995.

40. For a detailed analysis of the politics associated with the developments of Iranian sanctions, see Laurie Lande, "Second Thoughts," *International Economy,* May-June 1997, pp. 44–49.

41. The transcript of this interview with Iranian President Mohammed Khatami was posted on the CNN Web site immediately after it was aired on January 7, 1998. Large portions of the text were published in a number of newspapers the following day.

42. Even before the Khatami election, many senior policy observers and former US officials were calling for changes in the dual containment strategy. These voices included two former national security advisers, a former secretary of defense, three former assistant secretaries of state for Near East affairs, and the former commander of US forces in the Persian Gulf, among others.

43. The trigger level had been reduced automatically from $40 million to $20 million on the first anniversary of the legislation in August 1997.

44. The European Union threatened to take the case to the World Trade Organization if the United States imposed sanctions on the French company, on grounds that the US policy was in violation of international trade agreements.

45. Secretary of State Madeleine K. Albright, Remarks at 1998 Asia Society Dinner, Waldorf-Astoria Hotel, New York, New York, June 17, 1998, as released by the Office of the Spokesman, June 18, 1998, US Department of State.

46. Ibid.

17

Closing the Distance
Kuwait and the United States in the Persian Gulf

Shafeeq N. Ghabra

US interests in Kuwait, a country the size of New Jersey with a population of 800,000 Kuwaitis and 1,670,000 non-Kuwaitis, evolved over an extended period of time.[1] In 1990–1991, as a result of the Persian Gulf war, the United States indisputably became the most important foreign power in the region, succeeding Great Britain, which had completed its disengagement from the area in the early 1970s. The war not only laid the foundation for a more active US policy in the region but also transformed Kuwait's foreign policy objectives and priorities.

After the war, Kuwait moved from a hesitant and distant relationship with the United States to security and cooperation engagement. This new relationship manifested itself in Kuwait becoming the only country to grant US forces permission to launch a land attack into Iraq from its territory in spring 2003. Kuwait also provided necessary logistics to help the US-led invasion in the effort to transform Iraq. This chapter traces the development of US-Kuwaiti relations within the context of US policy toward the Gulf and examines the nature of this bilateral relationship, its irritants, and the challenges confronting it in the post-9/11 era.

Early US-Kuwaiti Relations

Shaykh Mubarak al-Sabah, the ruler of Kuwait during the early part of the twentieth century, was on a visit to Basra in 1910 when he asked Dr. Binitt, a US missionary with a clinic in Basra, to treat his daughter and come work in Kuwait. Thus began the American Hospital, a clinic and missionary operation that remained in use until the 1950s.[2] Over the years, the clinic became a symbol of US goodwill, but beyond that, Kuwait remained a British autonomous protectorate. In accordance with an agreement signed with Great Britain in 1899, Kuwait committed to denying foreigners concessions within its territory unless the British consented, and agreed not to lease any land or deal with a foreign power without British approval.[3]

Some two decades later, in 1923, Shaykh Ahmad al-Jabir al-Sabah, emir of Kuwait from 1920 to 1950, began negotiations with the Anglo-Iranian Oil Company for Kuwait's first oil concession. The emir continued to put off a final decision, however, because he wanted to strike the best deal possible by bringing US companies into the bidding. Meanwhile, he, along with the founder of Saudi Arabia, King 'Abd al-'Aziz Al Sa'ud (or Ibn Sa'ud), granted a concession to Major Holmes of Eastern and General Syndicate (EGS) to explore the Neutral Zone, at the time a territory that Kuwait and Saudi Arabia shared. The emir was pleased when the US-based Gulf Oil Corporation acquired EGS operations in the Gulf in 1927. Shaykh Ahmad was convinced that a better deal could be achieved by negotiating with Gulf Oil and that the company's representative "had no political aspirations, being purely commercial as had been proved in Bahrain."[4] He expressed disappointment in the "British treatment of Kuwait[i] interests" at the Ojair conference in 1922, when some Kuwaiti territory was granted to Ibn Sa'ud.[5]

After negotiations spanning 1928 to 1934, Shaykh Ahmad managed to convince Anglo-Iranian and Gulf Oil to form the Kuwait Oil Company (KOC). He then signed Kuwait's first oil concession, emerging "as the prime architect of the 1934 agreement and the vast benefits it has brought to Kuwait."[6] According to 'Abd al-Rahman al-Atiqi, Kuwait's minister of oil and finance from 1967 to 1975, although Kuwait needed cash, it had intentionally waited as British companies reached agreements with Bahrain, Iran, and Iraq. Ahmad then used to his advantage the British desire to limit US involvement in the region.[7] Kuwait would use a similar approach in foreign affairs by devising a policy to balance forces in a way that allowed it to maintain some latitude and freedom of movement.

Regional Shifts and the Dilemma of a Small State

Until Independence in 1961, Kuwait's political relationship with the United States involved little more than the operation of a consulate, which oversaw the few commercial ties between the two countries. Even after independence, Kuwait held little interest for the United States, as US policy in the Gulf centered primarily around Iran and Saudi Arabia.[8] Meanwhile, Kuwait, being a small state, obsessed about remaining independent of the neighboring larger countries of Iran, Iraq, and Saudi Arabia. It did not, however, seek outside commitments from major powers for security. Instead, Kuwait compensated by seeking the protection of an informal "Arab umbrella."

At the time, anti-Western sentiments ran high in the region, and independence movements and their effects abounded. A policy of close ties with such powers as the United States or Britain would have been unpopular if not suicidal, so Kuwait safeguarded its independence by committing to involvement in Arab affairs and using its wealth to maintain Arab backing.[9] After all, Arab allies—Egypt and Saudi Arabia in particular—had prevented Iraq from invading Kuwait in 1961, when it became independent. That incident proved influential in Kuwait adopting a policy of pan-Arabism and solidarity with Arab causes.

Kuwaiti policy neatly overlapped with the populist pan-Arabist trends percolating through the region. This pan-Arabist component naturally committed Kuwait to Arab causes and issues, the most important of which was the Arab-Israeli conflict. The 1967 Arab-Israeli war intensified criticism of US policy in the region, building on the revolutionary rhetoric that had emanated from Egypt, Iraq, and Syria during the 1950s and early 1960s. While supporting the broad concept of pan-Arabism and being in the forefront of financial support for development projects in the Arab world, Kuwaiti policy at the same time required that it maintain neutrality in inter Arab conflicts and differences.[10]

Kuwait became one of the most active states in the Office of the Boycott of the League of Arab States against Israel. When the United States suggested as its ambassador to Kuwait someone who worked as a counselor in Jerusalem, Kuwait refused to accept him.[11] Other factors also served to distance the United States from Kuwait, including the actions of the Organization of the Petroleum Exporting Countries (OPEC) and its 1971 negotiations with US companies over oil pricing. That year, OPEC raised prices by 29 cents per barrel, despite President Richard M. Nixon's attempts to prevent the increase. In response, the United States devalued the dollar. The 1973 Arab-Israeli war exacerbated tensions, resulting in OPEC further increasing oil prices. In addition to participating in such alliances, Kuwait also supported policies adopted by the nonaligned movement and the United Nations (UN) that were typically inimical to US interests and wishes.

Kuwait did, however, have a vested interest in cordial relations with the United States. Kuwait eschewed communism and conducted most of its economic affairs with Western countries; it also held huge investments predominantly in Europe and the United States. Such strong ties with the US economy meant that a decline or collapse of the US dollar could have tremendous ramifications for Kuwait. These economic interests laid the groundwork, despite the 1967 war, for the first official visit by a Kuwaiti emir to the United States, in December 1968. Within the Kuwaiti government and among the ruling Sabah family, there had always been members advocating better US-Kuwaiti relations. Nevertheless, the US position on the Arab-Israeli conflict always clouded relations.[12]

Although Kuwaiti foreign investments and business deals were conducted primarily in the West, Kuwaiti politics remained oriented toward the internal and external pan-Arabist and anti-Western currents prevalent in the region. The dual nature of Kuwaiti policy is reflected in the fact that the government had to publicly distance itself from the United States even as it sent most of its students and huge sums of money to the United States and Western Europe. This constant conflict among local, regional, and international interests continued to characterize US-Kuwaiti relations until August 1990. A similar dilemma, on various levels, also affected US relations with the other Arab Gulf states.

Vacuum in the Gulf

As the British began to withdraw from the Gulf in the late 1960s and early 1970s, it looked as if full independence had finally arrived in the region. Full of self-assurance, Gulf Arabs believed that they could protect their resources and the region by themselves. OPEC's power after the 1973 Arab-Israeli war served to boost their confidence.

For the United States, the petroleum resources of the Gulf had greatly increased the region's significance during the cold war. The US policy of maintaining stability there emerged to ensure the easy access to and safe transport of oil from the region while keeping the Soviets at bay. After the British withdrawal, the United States turned to Iran to fill the vacuum left in its wake. Thus it developed the so-called twin pillars policy of using Iranian muscle and Saudi money to maintain regional balance.[13]

The Nixon Doctrine, outlined in the 1970 State of the Union address, informed the twin pillars policy. The doctrine reflected a hesitant superpower attempting to limit its involvement in areas of potential conflict. This policy, a result of US experiences in the Vietnam War, had ramifications in the Gulf for both friend and foe.[14]

The shah of Iran recognized the reluctance of the United States and took seriously his "mandate" to police the region. He wanted no major US role in the area, and he said as much in 1972 in a press conference statement opposing a US naval presence in Bahrain.[15] At the same time, from 1971 to 1979 the shah aided US policy objectives and supplied Israel with 50 percent of its oil needs. The Israelis, meanwhile, supported arms shipments to Iran to counterbalance Iraq.[16]

With the collapse of the shah of Iran's government in 1979, the United States found itself with only one "pillar" standing, that is, Saudi Arabia. The failure of the twin pillars policy motivated US policymakers to develop contingency plans for responding to crises in the Gulf.[17] Alert to the possibility of dangers ahead, in January 1980 President Jimmy Carter set out the Carter Doctrine, which replaced the Nixon Doctrine as the blueprint for US involvement in the region. According to the new doctrine, developed in response to the Soviet invasion of Afghanistan in late 1979, the United States would not tolerate any attempt by an outside force to gain control of the Gulf region. The United States would use all means necessary, including military force, to repel such an effort.[18]

The Carter Doctrine reiterated the importance of the region's oil supply to the United States, especially given the diminishing US share of world production. In 1938, the United States had produced 62 percent of the world's oil. By 1955, however, 80 percent of all new oil discoveries were in the Middle East, and by 1962 the United States was importing 2 million barrels per day. That figure more than doubled to 5 million barrels per day by 1973. Demand continued to rise as discoveries in the United States declined. European dependence on oil was even greater. In 1962, Europe imported 37 percent of its oil needs, and in 1972 it imported 60 percent. Japan imported 73 percent of its needs in 1972.[19] During the 1980s, it became apparent that Iran, Iraq, Kuwait, Saudi Arabia, and the United Arab Emirates

(UAE) would be among the few producers of oil in the next century. These countries would also be responsible for most increases in production as well as new discoveries. (Two-thirds of the world's proven oil reserves are located in the region.)

The assassination of Egyptian president Anwar Sadat in October 1981, the bombing of the US Marines barracks in Beirut in October 1983, and the subsequent US shelling of Lebanese positions and raids on Syrian targets in Lebanon created an overall impression of US weakness and a lack of resolve in implementing the Carter Doctrine (or any other doctrine for that matter). When the Reagan administration attempted to sell arms to Gulf states, they ran into problems with Congress. During the 1980s, the administration had difficulty getting congressional approval for defense packages for Saudi Arabia and Kuwait. In the end, the arms appropriations that passed required intense lobbying, and severe cuts were made in the original packages.[20]

During the 1980s, Gulf rulers considered a large US military presence in the region to be a danger to themselves. Fearful of regional and domestic reactions, they blocked efforts at US infrastructural buildups in the area. Only Egypt and Oman allowed the pre-positioning of weapons and munitions, with operations kept at a minimum. Kuwait opposed the pre-positioning of US equipment and arms in the Gulf, especially during the Iran-Iraq war, sensing that it would add to regional tensions.[21]

Kuwaiti Neutrality and the Reflagging of Tankers

Kuwait and most of the other Gulf states were taken by surprise when Iraq invaded Iran in 1980 to quell internal Shi'a dissent and assert its hegemony in the Gulf. The Saudis in particular were furious that Iraqi president Saddam Hussein had not consulted with them prior to his decision to go to war. They also did not like the fact that he later asked for financial assistance when the war bogged down. It was not clear at the time how the conflict would be resolved, and few anticipated that Iraq would later pose a serious threat to the security of the entire region.

Apprehension created by the advances of an Iranian counteroffensive in 1983 contributed to the reversal of Kuwaiti policy from one of neutrality to one supportive of Iraq. Fearful of Iran as a semi-revolutionary power, the Gulf states, in addition to Egypt and Jordan, provided Iraq with logistics, money, and weapons. According to Abdullah Bisharah, former secretary-general of the Gulf Cooperation Council (GCC), such support was thought to be the only way to contain revolutionary Iran, which increasingly threatened the security of Kuwait by supporting clandestine groups that bombed several targets in Kuwait and attempted to assassinate the emir.[22]

When Iran began attacking Kuwaiti oil tankers in the Gulf in 1985, Kuwait recognized the need to improve its ties with the United States, other Western powers, and the Soviet Union. Stopping the war and ending Iranian attacks on Gulf shipping became a political and security priority. At one point in 1986, Kuwaiti oil production fell to 300,000 barrels per day, as opposed to 2 million earlier in 1986.[23] The war threatened Kuwait's economic lifeline.

Reflagging Kuwaiti tankers appeared to be the only way to engage other countries in protecting Kuwaiti shipping. Used primarily to avoid high taxes, reflagging was common in the world of commercial shipping. Under US law, any ship under the US flag is entitled to protection by the US Navy. According to Su'ud al-Usaymi, Kuwait's state minister for foreign affairs during this period, the Kuwaiti government decided to make use of this avenue and approached the United States and the Soviet Union during May and June 1986. The Reagan administration initially declined Kuwait's request, apologizing on the grounds that the operation was too risky and that US law prohibited such an undertaking. The Soviets, however, accepted within five days of the initial contact. As a Kuwaiti technical delegation negotiated details with the Soviets in Moscow, the United States reevaluated its decision and agreed to join the reflagging effort. The Kuwaiti government's leaking of information regarding negotiations in Moscow played some role in the change in US policy in July 1987.[24] The United States also recognized that it needed to shore up its relations with the Arab states of the Gulf after the embarrassing revelation of the Iran-contra affair. Under the arrangement negotiated, the US Navy escorted Kuwaiti tankers (registered as American ships with US flags) until they reached Kuwaiti waters.[25]

The reflagging effort represented the first step in security cooperation between the United States and Kuwait, although Kuwait tried to maintain its neutrality by keeping the operation purely on the level of a business arrangement. When the United States asked the Kuwaitis to supply fuel to its vessels protecting the tankers, Kuwait, to prevent US ships from docking and US personnel from coming ashore, provided fuel through tankers rented from Gulf states; the United States was also given the use of a floating dock in Gulf waters. When the United States requested the use of port facilities, Kuwait refused for fear that it would create problems with Kuwaiti rejectionists and with other nations of the Middle East.

These fears were confirmed when students at Kuwait University voiced strong opposition to the reflagging operation. The students barely mentioned the Soviet reflagging effort, choosing instead to focus on the US role, characterizing it as imperialist.[26] Their reaction stemmed in part from the US position on the Arab-Israeli conflict and the overall US Middle East policy. Similar opposition was widespread among university faculty and Kuwaiti opposition groups. With the Kuwaiti parliament having been dissolved in 1986, any government policy engaging a foreign power was viewed skeptically and seen as a possible step toward the revival of Western imperialism.

During the reflagging effort, the Kuwaiti oil ministry and the US Navy cooperated on several issues, and the ministry, headed by Ali al-Khalifa al-Sabah, lobbied for stepping up US-Kuwaiti relations. In addition to involvement in the actual shipping operations, the Kuwaiti petroleum sector funded research on the detection of incoming Iranian missiles, leading to the installation of mirrored solar panels on boats in Kuwaiti ports to lure the missiles away from their targets.[27] As a result of the reflagging, US-Kuwaiti relations improved and were strengthened. Both sides agreed on the need to end the Iraq-Iran war, the carnage in Lebanon, and terrorist activities.

Between 1985 and 1988, individuals linked to Iran hijacked five Kuwaiti airplanes. Bombings of Kuwaiti targets and the US and French embassies in the country affected the Kuwaiti government's outlook and encouraged it to pursue better relations with the United States. In July 1988, Crown Prince Sa'ad Al-Abdulla visited Washington. (During the visit, Iran accepted a UN-brokered cease-fire with Iraq.) In April 1990, US ambassador Nathaniel Howell sent a telegram stating that Kuwait had admitted publicly, for the first time, the presence of a US warship in its port.[28] Although Kuwaitis perceived relations with the United States as improving, the US assessment proved to be quite different. According to a highly knowledgeable US source,

> The reflagging did not improve relations with Kuwait. We had no better relations with Kuwait other than the relations created with the Ministry of Oil. For example, the State Department did not feel we had better relations with the Kuwaiti foreign ministry. Even our military office in Kuwait was small and limited in its program. During the reflagging, Kuwait would not discuss security issues in the region with the United States. Kuwait remained as pan-Arab as it could. In the UN, the situation continued by which Kuwait condemns the United States on a whole range of issues.[29]

From Reserved Cooperation to Dependency

The assumptions and perceptions of Americans and Kuwaitis regarding their relationship contributed to the lack of any serious cooperation during events leading up to the 1990–1991 Gulf crisis and war. The US lack of preparedness for dealing with a major crisis in the Gulf, and its history of foreign involvement from Vietnam to Iran to Lebanon, made more serious cooperation unappealing in a region historically inhospitable to foreign intervention. Even when the United States shared intelligence with Kuwait during the Iran-Iraq war, the Kuwaitis did not always trust its accuracy.

As for Saddam Hussein, the US shift toward Iraq was, of course, a result of its failed policy vis-à-vis the shah. Washington, however, overplayed its hand in its efforts to contain Iran during the 1980s. Saddam became the new guarantor of Gulf security, replacing the felled Iranian pillar, even as his army used chemical weapons against Iraq's Kurdish population.[30] When the US Senate voted for tough sanctions against Iraq, the Reagan administration responded with a lobbying effort against them, ultimately rendering them useless.[31]

Despite some negative analyses from specialists on Iraq, reports of the government's barbarity, and the potential for confrontation with the United States, Washington continued to turn a blind eye.[32] Once the Iran-Iraq war ended, the United States continued to support Saddam, including forwarding billions of dollars in agricultural loan guarantees and other assistance to Iraq.[33] Distracted by the fall of communism in Eastern Europe in 1989, the United States lost focus on Gulf security and a bankrupt Iraq. A group of Kuwaiti officials in the foreign ministry, however, began devising a new regional policy. Among the issues discussed was how Iraq would occupy its 1 million idle soldiers. According to Su'ud al-Usaymi, "No one dared to think, however, that Iraq would under any circumstances attack Kuwait. These thoughts remained unexplored for fear that supporters of Iraq and sympathizers in the foreign ministry and in society at-large would view discussions of such as treasonous or anti-Arab."[34]

Once the Gulf crisis began in mid-July 1990, the United States and Kuwait were uncertain on how to respond. Kuwait ran for the Arab umbrella, this time represented by the mediation of King Fahd of Saudi Arabia, President Hosni Mubarak of Egypt, Yasser Arafat of the Palestine Liberation Organization (PLO), and King Hussein of Jordan. Arab mediation merely provided a false feeling of security among Kuwaitis and US officials that the crisis would quickly pass. The record leading up to the fateful audience of US ambassador April Glaspie with Saddam Hussein and to Assistant Secretary of State John Kelly's announcement that no security arrangements existed between the United States and Kuwait brought to the forefront the difficulties of interpreting messages, signals, and policies in a world of conflict. To quote Glaspie, "We foolishly did not realize [that Saddam] was stupid."[35] One official in the State Department discussed the situation with his supervisor days before the crisis, musing, "What if Iraq invaded Kuwait? What will we say if it happens, what will we tell our superiors whom we keep telling nothing will happen?" With such thinking, the dearth of US-Kuwaiti cooperation surrounding such a crisis is not surprising.[36]

Iraq had contested Kuwaiti oil drilling along their border and opposed (in a letter to the Arab League) Kuwaiti oil overproduction, but neither elicited a serious response from any quarter. It was not the first crisis in inter-Arab relations, so why worry? The previous two decades had witnessed crises between the two Yemens, Jordan and Syria, and Egypt and Libya. Arab mediators and Kuwaiti leaders believed that Iraq was pressuring Kuwait in order to gain financial support and land in the Gulf. Kuwait was willing to discuss financial issues but stood firm against relinquishing control of any of its land. Furthermore, Kuwait anticipated that in return for having provided Iraq with financial aid, the Iraqis would agree to demarcate their border. This is what Kuwait hoped to achieve in a meeting in Jeddah, where the two sides met to resolve the crisis on August 1, 1990. In addition, from Kuwait's point of view, the amount of support it had provided Iraq during the war with Iran, in the form of much-needed logistical materials and billions of dollars in aid, should have earned it at least a modicum of goodwill in Iraq. Not so.

In Jeddah, the Kuwaitis found themselves on the defensive. They had hoped for a peaceful end to the crisis over their border demarcation and sovereignty over the islands of Bubiyan and Warba, which Iraq wanted for better access to the Gulf. Kuwait ultimately rejected Iraq's demand for land because not to do so would jeopardize its sovereignty. Like many crises throughout history, the possibility of preventing an escalation got lost in the traffic of mixed messages and misunderstood intentions.

Consequences of Invasion

It took an event of the magnitude of the Iraqi invasion for the Kuwaiti government to recognize the extent of its security requirements and to force the United States to take major steps to protect its interests in the Gulf. Kuwaitis realized that only US power could change the course of events for the better. Once Iraq moved across the border, the US commitment to maintaining the stability of the Gulf region became synonymous with maintaining the independence of Kuwait.

The invasion moved the US-Kuwaiti relationship to a new phase, as diplomats of the two countries discussed, through various channels, ways to address the invasion. Information provided by the Kuwaiti resistance created additional channels for greater cooperation. The United States, in moving against Iraq in the context of an international effort and through the support of UN Security Council Resolutions 773 and 833 (concerning Kuwait's boundaries with Iraq), defined its security needs in the region.[37]

The major role played by US companies in the rebuilding of Kuwait attested to the new US-Kuwaiti relationship. The reconstruction effort involved reestablishing communications, electricity, and petrochemical facilities and operations, with US firms receiving more than $5 billion in contracts from the Kuwaiti government. The US Army Corps of Engineers supervised much of the initial phases of reconstruction, and Bechtel worked as the major contractor. US exports to Kuwait in 1992 totaled some $1.5 billion.[38]

During the 1990s, Kuwaiti foreign policy became more sensitive to US interests; Kuwait dispatched soldiers to Somalia, provided financial support to Bosnia, and lifted the secondary boycott against Israel. Kuwait's votes in the United Nations were also more closely aligned with US votes than in the past.[39] Kuwait abstained from the UN vote concerning efforts to repeal or retain the resolution defining Zionism as racism. In addition, the mutual interest of Kuwait and the United States in seeing that Iraq comply with UN Security Council resolutions increased cooperation between them. This was reflected in Kuwait's agreement to the establishment of a Voice of America relay station on its territory. Moreover, the attitude adopted by Kuwait on the issues of democratization and human rights also had a positive effect on relations.

Kuwaiti participation in US programs rose remarkably after the war. Delegations from Kuwaiti government ministries traveled to the United States for training, especially in the fields of information, television, internal security, and investigation. Kuwait also donated land and paid construction costs for the new US embassy there. A May 1994 visit to the United States by a delegation of Kuwaiti members of parliament, headed by Speaker Ahmad al-Sa'dun, reflected the general trend in relations.

Kuwait did not, however, follow in lockstep with the United States. For example, it did not lift the primary embargo against Israel. That measure, Kuwait argued, was part of an Arab League decision, and it could not break with the consensus on this matter. In addition, the assistance provided by Egypt, Saudi Arabia, and Syria against the Iraqi invasion and occupation made Kuwait sensitive to the position of these states. Kuwait—always aware of its small size and made acutely aware of it by the Iraqi invasion—became even more anxious to avoid unnecessary confrontations in the Arab world. This led Kuwait to take a somewhat passive stance in the multilateral talks on the Arab-Israeli peace process. At the same time, however, Kuwait attended the Doha economic summit attended by Israel in 1997, despite Egyptian, Saudi, and Syrian pressure to boycott it.

On another level, US-Kuwaiti "cultural relations" continue to move essentially in one direction—from the United States to Kuwait. America Plus, CNN, NBC, movies, Web sites, cafés, department stores, and fast-food restaurants all symbolize the Americanization of Kuwait's younger generation. Kuwaitis recognize this trend as part of globalization and, therefore, have not erected huge barriers to this cultural interaction. At the same time, however, they remain wary of losing their cultural identity and would like to make the cultural relationship more of a two-way street. It is perhaps in response to such cultural identity issues that Islamists in Kuwait, as elsewhere in the Arab world, have gained ground politically and have played an increasingly important role in the country's elected parliament since 1992.

Military Cooperation

On August 2, 1990, Kuwaitis came face-to-face with their vulnerability and smallness. The Iraqi invasion provided an important lesson for Kuwaiti policymakers: Without a reliable security umbrella, Kuwait could not survive. Singapore, Taiwan, and other small states around the world had moved to protect themselves through security arrangements with major powers. As a result of the Iraqi invasion, Kuwait and the United States entered into a ten-year military defense pact, essentially acknowledging a US security commitment to Kuwait.[40] In the pact, signed in September 1991, the United States did not agree to "guarantee" Kuwaiti security, because that would have required that the arrangement be ratified by the US Senate. Instead, the agreement points up the significance of US power in maintaining the region's balance and the US role as successor to Great Britain as the Gulf's protector.

The agreement allows the United States to pre-position weapons in Kuwait, train Kuwaiti forces, and conduct joint maneuvers with the Kuwaiti military.[41] The agreement's clauses also provide for sales of arms (including F-18s) and cost sharing. (There are no restrictions on the technology that can be sold to Kuwait.) Another part of the agreement details the role of the US presence in Gulf waters. In this context, Kuwait provides logistics for a US naval presence, including facilities at Kuwaiti ports. The size of the pre-positioning operation, in addition to Kuwaiti units, was estimated to be more than sufficient for managing various scenarios of aggression across Kuwait's border. The Kuwaiti government pays for all in-country costs, such as maintenance, fuel, and food.[42] As a result of the 1994 crisis, when Iraq again adopted a threatening posture, Kuwait and the United States agreed to add to its existing forces twenty-four fighter aircraft and to maintain a larger US troop contingent, approximately 1,300, reinforced occasionally by US Marine units.[43]

Kuwait's aim since 1991 has been to create a small elite force as part of its effort to develop a credible military option. This requires establishing brigades that are integrated into a new air force based on the US military doctrine of using mobile forces that utilize a technological edge to deal with a larger invading force. New, more credible officers have been promoted to leadership positions in the Kuwaiti military, and morale is higher today than it previously had been.[44] In comparing Kuwaiti forces to other forces in the Gulf, US officials confirm a high level of seriousness and commitment throughout the Kuwaiti armed services. The ability to use new technology and coordinate weapons has improved dramatically since 1994.[45] On another positive note, the Kuwaiti armed forces, which normally stood at 17,000, reached 34,000 in 2002.

From the early 1990s until 2003, Kuwait based its military options on a potential threat from the Iraqi Republican Guard, in particular from four main tank divisions that could spearhead an invasion. Kuwait had achieved some of its goals concerning such a scenario before the overthrow of the Iraqi government in 2003 in the US-led invasion. The new situation in Iraq, however, necessarily calls for a revision of Kuwaiti doctrine. In the process, the issues of terrorism and cross-border arms smuggling demand more attention and in the future may require Kuwait to consider creating a stronger police force and a smaller army. Kuwait has no chance against Iran or any other large country, but its military cooperation with the United States, in the context of the renewal of its ten-year agreement with Washington, provides it with an element of deterrence. Strengthening security relations and cooperation with the United States appears to be Kuwait's best defensive option for the foreseeable future.

In the area of military cooperation, other Gulf states also entered into defense agreements with the United States after the end of the 1991 war. Bahrain accepted an agreement in July 1992. Qatar did the same in 1992 and, just prior to the 2003 invasion of Iraq, became a strategic base of command for the US military after a Saudi decision required the United States to remove its troops from the kingdom. Saudi Arabia's remaining agreements with the United States primarily concern air defense. Oman had agreed to a facility-access agreement prior to 1990.

Kuwait has also signed defense agreements with Great Britain, France, and Russia, but none of these include pre-positioning arrangements.[46] Kuwait further secured its border with Iraq by digging a deep, wide trench in the demilitarized zone and erecting an electrical fence along the entire 215-kilometer stretch. Nineteen posts monitor the barrier, which is about seven meters wide. This arrangement helps protect against smuggling as well as attack.[47]

Security Dilemmas and Other Problems

The change of regime in Iraq in 2003 and the tensions over Iran's nuclear program continue to make the Gulf a potentially dangerous place for a small, though wealthy, state like Kuwait. Iran has 70 million people (expected to increase to 120 million by 2030) and is undergoing a military buildup.[48] The election and reelection of Mohammad Khatami as president in 1996 and 2001 provided some hope that relations with Iran would improve and, more important, that US-Iranian relations would become less hostile. The failure of the reform movement and the election of the conservative Ahmadinejad to the presidency in 2005, however, only served to fuel new tensions.

Civil strife and deterioration have unfortunately become the norm in Iraq, making the difficult task of constructing a new Iraq an even more daunting endeavor than it earlier appeared. Reaching agreements that will satisfy the Kurdish, Shi'a, and Sunni communities is proving to be incredibly problematic. Kuwait, like other countries of the Gulf, is home to both Shi'a and Sunni populations, so the handling (and mishandling) of political sectarian strife in Iraq holds implications for it as well.

Future Iraqi governments, after the stabilization of the country, will find it difficult to accept the financial and territorial demands of the deposed Ba'thist regime. More disturbing still for the Gulf states is the thought that any Iraqi government that appears to acquiesce to the terms makes itself vulnerable to elements determined to wipe the slate clean and, as Saddam Hussein said when tearing up the 1975 Algiers accord with Iran, "to restore the lost honor of Greater Iraq."[49]

Setbacks for the US military in Iraq have raised questions about the staying power of the United States in the Gulf. There is no guarantee that Washington will continue to invest in Iraq if the crisis there continues without reaching an acceptable degree of stability. On the other hand, a US-friendly government in Iraq could lead to future bilateral cooperation on any number of issues.[50]

Commitments in other regions may pose an additional problem for future US administrations. For example, the United States had to transfer personnel and ships from the Gulf region to Somalia in January 1993. At the same time, it needed to deal with Iraqi violations of the "no-fly" zones, which again became problematic in the late 1990s. The situation currently in Iraq does not bode well for the ability of the United States to engage in major military conflict elsewhere should the need arise. Given the possibility of additional pressures surfacing, the United States must find new ways of dealing with security in the Gulf.[51] These pressures and issues may force the United States to consider developing multilateral regional security arrangements that possibly include reaching some sort of understanding with Iran.

President George H. W. Bush had hoped to establish an effective regional security organization in the Gulf after the war. It was thought that the GCC, together with Syria and Egypt, might provide the elements of it. The Damascus declaration of March 1991 lent the impression that an Arab peace force would be formed.[52] The problem, however, was that Kuwait and the other Gulf states were not sure about Syrian-Egyptian intentions in the long term. They also favored a more direct security arrangement with Washington, believing that route to be more reliable. After all, anything could happen in Egypt, and the odds were not good for betting on the future of Syrian policy. The Gulf states appreciated Iran's anti-Saddam stand during the Gulf crisis of 1991, but the Damascus accord had antagonized Tehran, which viewed it as another attempt to isolate it.[53]

With the failure of an Arab deterrent force to emerge, in October 1991 Oman floated the idea of a 100,000-man Gulf force, but the plan failed to receive the attention it deserved at a GCC summit in Kuwait in December 1991. The same reasons behind the rejection of the Arab military component of the Damascus declaration motivated the Gulf states to dismiss the Omani plan. In the latter case, the states feared dominance by Saudi Arabia and constraints on individual states' decisionmaking. Traditional obsessions with sovereignty and autonomy made such a plan unacceptable. Its demise came at the climax of territorial disputes between Qatar and Saudi Arabia and between Qatar and Bahrain. Furthermore, Iran had control of three islands claimed by the United Arab Emirates, adding to tensions and reminding the other Gulf states of Iran's presence (and of not wanting to do anything that might upset Tehran). Although the similarity of the GCC states' economies and political systems draws them together to repel common dangers, this is not enough to unify them. Local nationalism remains a driving force in Gulf politics even in times of peace.[54] It is to the credit of the GCC governments that they have addressed the border issues among them.

Kuwait's reliance on its arrangements with the United States for its defense and the recognition that no Gulf state possesses the means to defend itself alone led to disappointment at the executive and legislative levels of the US government in the lack of progress along regional security lines.[55] Washington actually liked the Omani idea for an Arab force.[56] A December 1993 GCC summit resulted in an agreement to build an army of 25,000 men, but some of the conditions needed for acceptance of the plan hampered the creation of an effective force. There is no common training or unified military doctrine or command, and the several armies that would compose it take orders from their own states. On the positive side, the force could help with defense in the Gulf, but the United States must still supervise that capability.

Rough Edges

Because of the US role in driving Iraqi forces from Kuwait and in providing security for it, Congress became extremely sensitive to any Kuwaiti action that smelled of ingratitude. US officials viewed as provocative a statement in 1992 by Abdul-Aziz Masa'id, former speaker of the Kuwaiti parliament, in which he minimized the US role in the liberation of Kuwait and instead focused on the role of friendly Arab forces. Furthermore, when the secondary boycott of Israel was not immediately lifted after the war, despite Kuwaiti promises to do so, it elicited an angry reaction from members of Congress. (It was lifted in 1993.)[57]

Despite such rough spots, the United States still sought Kuwaiti support for its policies in the Gulf, such as encouraging Arab-Israeli multilateral talks and progress in matters pertaining to democracy and human rights.[58] Arms sales are another potential flash point. Some members of Congress object to arms sales as a matter of principle, whereas others object out of concern that the weapons could be used against Israel. Congress often raises these issues and, if not satisfied, can delay or prevent a deal from being approved.

Kuwait policymakers must always factor the dynamics of internal US debate and decisionmaking processes into the two countries' relations. The need to be part of the US debate on the Middle East is of obvious importance. Not unlike Israel, Kuwait feels the need to stress its usefulness and importance in the international arena in the eyes of the United States. This forces Kuwait to be sensitive to the priorities of each administration; it was especially attuned to US policy after the attacks by Islamic extremists on the Pentagon and the World Trade Center in September 2001. So while Kuwait may seek to influence some US priorities, it must also cooperate with the administration on aspects of US strategy in the region. This policy dance must be managed creatively, without jeopardizing Kuwaiti political independence or regional interests. Examples of important policy arenas include issues at the United Nations and in other international agencies; human rights issues in Kuwait and in the region; policy toward Iraq; policy toward Islamic extremism, Islamic charities, and terrorism; and so on.

The peace process in the 1990s offers two good examples of policy actions that led to a US-Kuwaiti disconnect. The tenuous relationship between Kuwait and the PLO, because of the PLO's standing with Iraq during the Gulf crisis and war, made Kuwait hesitant to engage on the issue. Although the government of Kuwait publicly supported the Oslo accords, the parliament, with a strong Islamist majority, took an opposing position. This prevented Kuwait from making a contribution at a Washington fund-raising meeting in October 1993. When Kuwait later made a financial contribution of $25 million to the Palestinians, few took notice. Political support and financial assistance were important to the United States as the peace process struggled to get off the ground. In another example, Bahrain, Oman, and Qatar agreed to host the multilateral peace negotiations (after Oslo), but Kuwait hesitated, not wanting to make such a decision without Saudi and Syrian consent. Finally, the dual containment policy of the Clinton administration, which sought to contain both Iraq and Iran simultaneously, provides yet another example of policy discord. Kuwait fully supported the US policy of containing Iraq, but it also felt the need for dialogue and some kind of a relationship with Iran. These issues, among others, seemed at times to adversely affect the relationship between the United States and Kuwait.

Dialogue between the United States and Kuwait is limited. Kuwaiti leaders seldom visit the United States to engage the White House, the Pentagon, or Congress in discussions about Kuwait's needs and perceptions. A cultural gap in styles between American and Kuwaiti leaders seems to be at least partially responsible for this state of affairs. In addition to improving government-to-government relations, Kuwait also must learn the ins and outs of nongovernmental organizations (NGOs), including human rights groups, universities, and the media, which play important roles in US governance. Their positions and reactions can sometimes tie the hands of an administration or force it to change course. Work is also needed in the other direction, that is, through visits to Kuwait by prominent US congressional representatives, university professors, journalists, and human rights groups.

I had a chance to communicate many of the thoughts and ideas expressed in this article about improving relations when I was director of the Kuwait Information Office (KIO) in Washington, D.C., between 1998 and 2002. Proactively, with a team of KIO members, I built ongoing relationships with members of Congress, think tanks, the media, and various government agencies. I was also able to reach out to many of the cultural, media, and political centers throughout the country while traveling to speak on behalf of Kuwaitis and on Gulf and other Arab issues. This approach distinguished the KIO from other Arab information offices during that time. Such an engaging approach had always been missing from Arab outreach, and this particular experience proved to be rewarding.

The KIO did not depend on a public relations company or consulting firm to polish its image or make its case to the public and officials. On the contrary, it relied heavily on its very qualified and motivated staff. The KIO built good relations with major newspapers and TV stations, and as director, I appeared as a commentator on dozens of programs across the country. For most Arab diplomats and representatives, accepting the challenge to publicly debate positions and take questions had been a rare experience.

As noted, Kuwait was the only country that allowed the United States to send troops into Iraq from its territory in 2003. This operation moved the US-Kuwait relationship to a higher level of strategic partnership. Kuwait did so in the context of its special relationship with the United States and lingering reservations about the intentions of Saddam Hussein. In 2005, Kuwait granted women the right to vote and the right to be elected to the parliament. Also in 2005, Kuwait set out to increase economic cooperation with the United States, proposing future hearings on a free trade zone and the possibility of a treaty on trade. Much of the interdependence of tomorrow lies in economic cooperation today.

Conclusion

Kuwaitis' opinions of US actions during the Iraqi invasion and occupation of Kuwait are overwhelmingly positive. Because of this, Kuwaitis feel that they have a special relationship with the United States. This was made clear in Kuwait's sympathetic public response to Americans following the al-Qaʻida attacks in 2001. Many Kuwaitis visited the US embassy to express their sorrow. Kuwait was one of the first countries to express its condolences in advertisements in major US newspapers as well as those directed at Congress and the military. Kuwait was also among the first nations to publicly state its willingness to join the fight against terror and extremism.

The arm's-length relationship that characterized US-Kuwaiti relations prior to the 1991 Persian Gulf war is no longer a viable option. In the relationship between the United States and Kuwait—a superpower and a very small state—Kuwait will sometimes feel pressured, which may strain relations, but Kuwait will always try to resolve matters in the context of friendship and cooperation. For example, after the attacks of September 11, the Kuwaiti government announced new regulations on Islamic charities and other groups operating in Kuwait. The move irritated conservative sectors of society, because the government's action against Islamists' power bases resulted from US demands. It heightened tensions between liberals and Islamists, but liberals and other supporters of the US effort in Afghanistan regained ground as images arrived of Afghans celebrating the overthrow of the Taliban.

The United States revealed the depth of its commitment to the Gulf in 1990–1991. Because it cannot afford to ignore the region, the United States must find a reliable mechanism for ongoing engagement, supervision, and security. This is vital; otherwise the United States will find itself dragged unprepared into new conflicts in the area. Kuwait needs to balance its defensive capability by assuming more responsibility for it. In order to do so, it must invest in its development and within the GCC devise group defense and contingency plans. This should be done in coordination with the United States and other coalition partners, in an arrangement whereby US involvement is limited to pre-positioning and naval and air defense.

The long-term policy commitment of the United States in the region is aimed at preventing regional instability, political upheavals, adventurism, and chaos that threaten the flow of oil or places substantial oil reserves under the control of a hostile government. Today, it is also focused on preventing terrorism and challenging Islamic extremism. Long-term issues—including rebuilding a stable Iraq, addressing the possibility of a nuclear Iran, potential instability in Arab monarchies, arms buildups, economic development and cooperation, human rights, and democratization—will continue to pose challenges to the United States in the region. Friendly relations and agreements with the GCC states will be important in confronting these challenges and in maintaining the flow of oil at reasonable prices. In this context, US relations with Kuwait are an important part of the vision for a more stable region.

There exists the possibility, however, that events and shifting regional priorities will emerge to weaken the US-Kuwaiti relationship. If Kuwait outlives its political usefulness in the region, then US interest in it will diminish. Regional political realities may in the long run force the United States to compromise with whatever leadership emerges in Iraq or other regional powers on issues of interest to Kuwait. This may affect Kuwaiti oil revenues, commerce, and regional standing. To counter any deterioration in US-Kuwaiti ties, Kuwait must build its relationship with the United States on a level deeper and more meaningful than simple state-to-state relations. It is Kuwait's role, in the midst of its security dilemma, to explain in the American context its goals, its culture, its democratic processes, and its economic vision. The difficult mission for Kuwait is to increase understanding in Congress; to build a relationship with relevant NGOs, human rights groups, and the media; and to create strong ties to intellectual circles.

Kuwaiti society has shown tremendous resiliency dating back to the 1750s. This has been evident in every major crisis since Mubarak al-Sabah established an alliance with Great Britain to protect the country from the Ottomans in 1899.[59] The ability to adapt to and create policies and structures needed to survive may be Kuwait's most important asset in facing the challenges ahead.

Notes

1. Kuwait Ministry of Planning, Central Statistical Office, *Estimated Population, 1997–1998*, published in *al-Qabas*, 5 January 1998, p. 2.

2. Abdul Malik Khalaf al-Tammimi, *al-Tabshir fi Mantiqat al-Khalij al-'Arabi: Dirasah fi al-Tarikh al-Ijtima'I wa al-Siyasi* [Missionaries in the Arabian Gulf: A Study in Its Political and Social History] (Cyprus: Dar al-Shabab, 1988), pp. 60–61.

3. Jill Crystal, *Kuwait: The Transformation of an Oil State* (Boulder: Westview, 1992), pp. 12–13.

4. Archibald H. T. Chisholm, *The First Kuwait Oil Concession Agreement: A Record of Negotiations, 1911–1934* (London: Frank Cass, 1975), p. 14.

5. Ibid., p. 82.

6. Ibid.

7. 'Abd al-Rahman al-Atiqi, interview by the author, Kuwait, June 1993. Al-Atiqi was a consultant to the emir of Kuwait.

8. According to the 1965 census, Kuwait at independence had a population of approximately 180,000 citizens and some 250,000 non-Kuwaitis.

9. See the excellent and comprehensive work of 'Abd al-Ridda Assiri, *Al-Kuwayt fi al-Siyasah al-Duwaliyyah al-Mu'asirah* [Kuwait in Contemporary International Politics] (Kuwait: Jamiat al-Kuwayt, n.d.), p. 135.

10. 'Abd al-Rahman al-Atiqi, interview by the author, June 1993.

11. It was not until 1990 that an American arriving at Kuwait's airport with an Israeli stamp in his or her passport could enter the country.

12. 'Abd al-Rahman al-Atiqi, interview by the author, June 1993.

13. Michael A. Palmer, *Guardians of the Gulf: A History of America's Expanding Role in the Persian Gulf, 1833–1992* (New York: Free Press, 1993), p. 89.

14. Ibid., p. 87.

15. Ibid., p. 90.

16. Thomas McNaugher, *Arms and Oil: US Military Strategy and the Persian Gulf* (Washington, D.C.: Brookings Institution, 1985), p. 17.

17. Ibid.

18. Palmer, *Guardians of the Gulf*, p. 106.

19. McNaugher, *Arms and Oil*, pp. 3–4.

20. Palmer, *Guardians of the Gulf*, p. 121.

21. Su'ud al-Usaymi, former minister of justice and former state minister for foreign affairs, interview by the author, Kuwait, May 1993.

22. Abdullah Bisharah, former secretary-general of the Gulf Cooperation Council, interview by the author, Kuwait, June 1993.

23. Su'ud al-Usaymi, interview by the author, May 1993.

24. Ibid.

25. The administration also engaged in the reflagging in order to shore up relations with the Arab states after the Iran-contra affair revealed that the Reagan administration had illegally sold arms to Iran in the hope of engineering the return of US hostages held in Lebanon.

US actions violated the US-devised Operation Staunch Arms embargo against Iran, among other things.

26. Ibid.

27. K, a US official in charge of major aspects of the reflagging operation who asked not to be identified, interview by the author, Washington, D.C., summer 1993.

28. Ibid.

29. M, a US official involved in US-Kuwaiti relations during the reflagging operation and afterward, interview by the author, Washington, D.C., summer 1993.

30. Paul A. Gigot, "A Great American Screw-Up: The US and Iraq, 1980–1990," *National Interest,* Winter 1990, p. 4.

31. Ibid., p. 6. The Senate voted 87-0 to impose sanctions on Iraq after the chemical attacks on the Kurds.

32. Ibid.

33. Documents detailing the sales of defense-related items to Iraq were altered by the administration of George H. W. Bush before they were provided to the Government Operations Subcommittee on Commerce, Consumer and Monetary Affairs. See Caroll J. Doherty, "Panel Democrats Poised to Ask for Probe of Help to Saddam," *Congressional Quarterly,* June 6, 1992, p. 1616; and "Democrats Aim to Reignite Iraqi Aid Controversy," *Congressional Quarterly,* May 23, 1992, pp. 1457–1459. See also Alan Friedman, *Spider's Web: The Secret History of How the White House Illegally Armed Iraq* (New York: Bantam Books, 1993).

34. Su'ud al-Usaymi, interview by the author, summer 1993.

35. Pamela Fessler, "Glaspie Defends Her Actions," *Congressional Quarterly,* March 23, 1991, p. 760.

36. A and B, US officials, interviews by the author, summer 1993.

37. The United Nations ruled that the Iraq-Kuwait border be moved 600 meters in Kuwait's favor along a 200-kilometer stretch. See Charles Tripp, "The Gulf States and Iraq," *Survival* 34 (Autumn 1992), p. 54.

38. Corey D. Wright, "United States-Kuwait Business Update," *Business American,* January 25, 1993, p. 13; "To the Victor Go the Rebuilding Contracts," *Business Week,* February 18, 1991.

39. See US Department of State, "Voting Practices in the United Nations 1991," Kuwait Report to Congress Submitted Pursuant to Public Law 101-167, March 31, 1992 (Washington, D.C.: Government Printing Office, 1992).

40. This section is based on interviews with US and Kuwaiti officials in Kuwait and Washington, D.C., summer 1993. Interviewees included members of the State Department, US personnel at the American embassy in Kuwait, and members of the research staff for the US House International Affairs Committee and Senate Foreign Relations Committee. Most of those interviewed asked not to be identified.

41. US troops numbering some 2,000 were left in Kuwait for a time. In January 1993, joint exercises again turned into an alert. US troops involved in the maneuvers remained in Kuwait for several months, because of concerns about the Iraqi "no-fly" zones. In terms of equipment, the agreement established a framework for the pre-positioning of approximately 112 tanks and 1,000 vehicles, in addition to ammunition—enough materiel to equip a brigade of 6,000 soldiers. There were initially 200 Americans detailed to Kuwait for pre-positioning maintenance.

42. For information on the US-Kuwaiti defense pact, see Kenneth Katzman, "Kuwait: Current Issues" (CRS Report for Congress), *Congressional Research Service,* June 3, 1993, pp. 1–6.

43. US embassy staff and Kuwaiti military officials, interviews by the author, Kuwait, June 1998.

44. "Rebuilding the Kuwaiti Military," *International Defense Review,* 26, no. 1 (1993), pp. 157–159.

45. Kuwaiti and US military officials, interviews by the author, June 1998.

46. Tripp, "Gulf States and Iraq," p. 60.

47. Personal observations at the border of Iraq and Kuwait, June 18, 1998.

48. Paul Kennedy, *Preparing for the Twenty-First Century* (New York: Random House, 1993), p. 25.

49. Tripp, "Gulf States and Iraq," p. 60.

50. Daniel M. Pletka, director of Near East and South Asia affairs, US Senate Foreign Relations Committee Minority Staff, interview by the author, Washington, D.C., summer 1993.

51. A, US official, interview by the author, summer 1993.

52. Tripp, "Gulf States and Iraq," pp. 44–45.

53. F. Gregory Gause III, *Oil Monarchies: Domestic and Security Challenges in the Arab Gulf States* (New York: Council on Foreign Relations Press, 1994), pp. 33–134.

54. Gause, *Oil Monarchies,* p. 130.

55. C, a supervisor for activities related to the Gulf in the Clinton administration, interview by the author, summer 1993.

56. A and B, US officials, interviews, Washington, D.C., summer 1993.

57. Daniel Pletka, interview by the author, Washington, D.C., summer 1993.

58. Michael Van Dusen, senior staff director, House International Affairs Committee, interview by the author, Washington, D.C., summer 1993.

59. W. Nathaniel Howell, "Tragedy, Trauma and Triumph: Reclaiming Integrity and Initiative," *Victimization, Mind, and Human Interaction,* August 1993, p. 114.

18

US Input into Iraqi Decisionmaking, 1988–1990

Amatzia Baram

US-Iraqi relations reached their lowest point following the Arab-Israeli Six Day War (June 1967), when the regime of General 'Abd al-Rahman 'Arif severed diplomatic relations in protest of an alleged US-Israeli collusion in the war. Soon afterward, 'Arif considered an improvement in relations, but when the Ba'th regime came to power in July 1968 it reversed the process, and relations with the United States hit rock bottom again. In 1972, Iraq and the Soviet Union signed an Accord of Friendship and Cooperation, but two years later the relationship changed: After the 1973 Yom Kippur War (also known as the Arab-Israeli war of 1973 or the Ramadan War) and oil crisis, Iraq's economic priorities took precedence over ideological concerns, and relations with the West (though not with the United States) improved, at the expense of those with the Soviet Union. US-Iraqi tension eased somewhat as a result of US Secretary of State Henry Kissinger's mediation between the shah of Iran and Saddam Hussein, which led to the March 1975 Iraqi-Iranian agreement. When Saddam cracked down on the Iraqi Communist Party in 1978, and when in December 1979 he criticized the Soviet invasion of Afghanistan, US attention was drawn to the fact that his regime did not behave as a Soviet satellite.

On September 22, 1980, Iraq invaded Iran, planning on a swift and decisive victory in Khuzistan that would encourage the Iranian army to topple the new regime of Ayatollah Khomeini. For the record, the United States criticized the invasion, but its real attitude was very different. There were no illusions in Washington with regard to the nature of the Ba'th regime in Baghdad, but Saddam Hussein attacked a state that had taken Americans hostage and was most hostile to the United States and its allies in the region. As soon as it became clear that the Iraqi army had become entrapped in Khuzistan, the United States became concerned that the scales were tipping in favor of Iran. Saddam Hussein, too, once he realized no decisive military victory was forthcoming, turned toward cooperation with both the United

States and the USSR. To demonstrate goodwill he promised that the US mission in Iraq was to be treated as an embassy. Bilateral relations improved perceptibly, even though official diplomatic relations were resumed only in November 1984.

The first tangible sign of a thaw in relations was a US Department of State decision in March 1981 to lift a freeze on the sale to Iraq of a handful of planes. A year later the United States removed Iraq from the list of terrorist sponsor states. Once Saddam Hussein banished Abu Nidal from Baghdad, an agricultural program under the auspices of the Commodity Credit Corporation (CCC) was started between the United States and Iraq. In later years, this program became the single most important feature in US-Iraqi relations; indeed, in 1988, US credits for foodstuffs for Iraq were the largest given to any country in the world. US help to Iraq, direct and indirect, also included battlefield intelligence; Operation Staunch, designed to deprive Iran of arms; support in the United Nations (UN) for a resolution calling for a cease-fire; reflagging Kuwaiti tankers; sales of dual-use items; and, according to some, the leaking of military technology.

During the Iran-Iraq war, the US course altered little. Iraq was perceived as the weaker combatant and a useful barrier against Khomeini's expansion and influence in the Gulf; as such it deserved support from the United States. Late in 1983, the State Department urged the US Export-Import Bank (hereinafter Exim) to extend its own credits to Iraq to bolster US exports (other than foodstuffs) and the Iraqi economy, thereby reducing problems for the Iraqi government in light of the increasing deprivation of the general population. A Jordanian-Iraqi pipeline, which was never built and was also vigorously supported by the United States, was to be part of the effort to prevent an Iraqi economic collapse.

Although both economic and political cooperation were growing, relations were still far from ideal due to an unbridgeable chasm in political culture (a chasm even wider in terms of perceived interests). But as long as the war was raging the United States and Iraq clearly differentiated between what was vital and what was desirable and did not allow their differences to disrupt their priorities. There were, however, conflicting views within the US administration with regard to the desirable balance of power between Iraq and Iran and the degree of support for Iraq.

Obstacles in the US-Iraqi relationship included US support of Israel and Iraq's off-and-on support for Palestinian terrorist groups; the issue of human rights (especially the inability of the Ba'th regime to tolerate any dissent and Iraq's use of chemical weapons [CW]); and, lastly, Iraqi stockpiling of weapons of mass destruction. The relative US leniency toward Iraq's development of such weapons during the war stemmed from the perception that the Iraqis were in danger of losing the war and, as it seems, from a lack of intelligence. As demonstrated by declassified documents from 1985–1986, the US administration had very little information on the tremendous Iraqi nuclear and surface-to-surface missile efforts already under way.

US credits to Iraq were yet another potential point of friction. The administration was torn between the Departments of State, Commerce, and Agriculture, on the one hand, and Exim on the other, with the Department of the Treasury and the

Federal Reserve mostly siding with Exim. Whereas Treasury pushed for ever greater credits, the Fed had more and more misgivings. Exim's misgivings were based on an inconsistent financial relationship with the Iraqis and lessons learned from Iraqi treatment of other creditors throughout the 1980s. By 1987, Exim determined that Iraq, in view of its financial difficulties and debt-repayment practices, would cut its debt service rather than its military or civilian imports.

The State Department's assessment of Iraqi financial prospects was far more sanguine, and State strongly disagreed with officials in Defense who tried to prevent sales of dual-purpose technology to Iraq for fear of nuclear and missile technology proliferation. But the worst case of interagency rivalry and cross-purpose action during the war years was the arms-for-hostages deal with Iran in 1985–1986. The Iraqi reaction to the arms deal was very unusual. Although the Iraqi parliament and press—and a few politicians—strongly denounced the deal, President Saddam Hussein and Foreign Minister Tariq 'Aziz were remarkably restrained. Clearly, the Iraqi leadership looked into the abyss and froze in horror: As they saw it, any wrong move could have led to US-Iranian collusion and to their own destruction.

The trilateral arms deal made the Iraqis more aware of the significance of splits within the administration and more suspicious of US intentions. Yet, as disclosed by the Iraqi leadership in later years, until the end of the Iran-Iraq war they were not suspicious that the United States was still arming Iran behind Iraq's back. The public outrage in the United States following the exposure of the Iran-Contra affair, and the administration's subsequent change of course, including the reflagging of Kuwaiti tankers in the second half of 1987, were sufficient to convince the Iraqis that the United States was decisively on their side. This perception started to change again after the cease-fire in the Iran-Iraq war in August 1988.

Much has been said and written about the approach of the George Bush administration toward Iraq in the postwar period. This approach has been considered by many as too lenient, with the result that Saddam was emboldened in his defiance of the United States. For example, Alexander Haig (Secretary of State under President Ronald Reagan) noted in an interview: "The tilt policy Bush had supported during those years brought Saddam to the belief that he would not be challenged in Kuwait . . . and the consequences were a Gulf War and the outcome that the threat of Saddam is still there."[1] Others have pointed out that US diplomacy did not do all it could in the weeks leading up to the Kuwaiti invasion to prevent it. The second contention is easier to substantiate than the first.[2]

In this chapter—based on declassified US documents, public Iraqi sources, and interviews—I shall attempt to demonstrate that the United States, though not doing all it reasonably could to deter Saddam from invading Kuwait (by making clear its objection to some Iraqi policies, i.e., use of CW, proliferation threats, and so on), did enough to alert the Iraqi regime to the fact that in the medium and long terms the two countries were on an unavoidable collision course. It is my contention that by early spring 1990 two things became clear to Saddam and his ruling elite. In the first place, they realized that those in the US administration who supported continued efforts to enhance US-Iraqi cooperation were losing ground. Second, they became fully aware that if they wanted to achieve a number of national Iraqi goals, which they considered crucial to the survival and success of their regime, they were running into progressively tougher US resistance. They were also aware that the two issues were connected: It was precisely Iraq's energetic quest for its cherished national goals that progressively weakened the position of those within the administration who favored a dialogue with and assistance for Iraq. The single most important indication that the United States was changing course was the suspension of the agricultural loan guarantee system, the centerpiece of US-Iraqi economic and political relations.

There is much dispute over whether or not the Iraqi leadership truly believed its own conspiracy theory. It is my intention to show that, although this issue is not unimportant, one should be careful not to overestimate its significance. Either way, the Iraqi regime reached the conclusion that under the existing circumstances US and Iraqi interests were irreconcilable, at least in the medium and long terms. Having realized that time was running out, Saddam decided to change the rules of the game and create new circumstances under which US policy vis-à-vis Iraq could be remolded. The invasion of Kuwait was supposed to create such new circumstances. Long before the US policymakers realized it, Saddam was fully aware it was impossible to cultivate good relations with the United States while achieving his central national goals. Convinced that US reaction would go no further than a limited air attack, he decided to act preemptively.

US Diplomacy After the Iran-Iraq War: A Change of Perspective

During the Iran-Iraq war the administration's pro-Saddam position was based on Iraq's vulnerability and the fact the United States could not afford an Iraqi military defeat. Following the Iraqi victories of April-August 1988 and the cease-fire, both the outlook and the argument were transformed. The United States, it was felt and argued, could not afford a hands-off policy in regard to Iraq because the latter was far too powerful and influential. If left to its own devices, Iraq's capacity to destabilize the whole region was enormous. If, however, the United States continued or even augmented its loan guarantee programs, administration officials argued that it would enable the United States to achieve two goals: To convince Iraq to slow down its nonconventional arms production and to play a constructive role in the Middle East peace process and Gulf security. On the positive side, US policymakers felt that Iraq offered a lucrative market for US foodstuffs and, potentially, technology.[3]

This position appeared in many State Department documents beginning in the fall of 1988, but it did not appear in a major policy document until presidential National Security Directive NSD–26, formulated in the spring of 1989 and signed by President Bush on October 2 of that year. The directive stated:

Normal relations between the US and Iraq would serve our long-term interests and promote stability in both the Gulf and the Middle East. The United States government should propose economic and political incentives for Iraq to moderate its behavior and to increase our influence with Iraq. . . . [Also], we should pursue and seek to facilitate opportunities for U.S. firms to participate in the reconstruction of the Iraqi economy . . . where they do not conflict with our non-proliferation . . . objectives. . . . The U.S. should consider sales of non-lethal forms of military assistance, e.g., training courses and medical exchanges.[4]

The directive also warned that any of the following would complicate relations and that some would even lead to economic sanctions: renewed use of chemical or biological weapons, any breach by Iraq of International Atomic Energy Agency (IAEA) safeguards in its nuclear program, human rights infringements, Iraqi meddling in the affairs of foreign countries, and noncooperation over the Middle East peace process. But it seems that the directive's main emphasis was on the need to intensify cooperation. Thus, for example, when the president waived a congressional bill in January 1990 that imposed limitations on trade relations with Iraq, the "Waiver" read:

Iraq is a major military power in the Persian Gulf and increasingly influential in the Arab world. It is also an important supplier of petroleum for the U.S. market. It is in the national interest . . . to maintain existing economic and political incentives . . . to encourage Iraq to moderate its behavior and increase our ability to deal effectively with Iraq. . . . We also wish . . . to facilitate opportunities for U.S. firms to participate in the post-war reconstruction of the Iraqi economy.[5]

Similar arguments against any sanctions aimed at Iraq were brought up by Assistant Secretary of State for Near East and South Asian Affairs John Kelly in his statement to Congress in May 1990.[6] This approach, however, came under increasing criticism as US and Iraqi interests moved further and further apart following the cease-fire in the Gulf.

In March 1988, a few months before the cease-fire, the first major confrontation occurred. The Iraqi army was reported to have used CW against Kurdish civilians in Halabja, causing thousands of casualties. The United States denounced the act,[7] but Iraq was still at war and still looked vulnerable. In June both houses of Congress discussed bills condemning Iraq and calling for sanctions against it, but the bills were not passed.[8] As a sign of the administration's displeasure, in June a State Department official received Jalal Talabani, leader of the Popular Union of Kurdistan (which opposed the Iraqi regime and fought for more autonomy). To protest the official reception, Foreign Minister 'Aziz canceled a scheduled meeting in Washington with Secretary of State George Shultz. A few days later Saddam was too busy to meet Assistant Secretary of State Richard Murphy, who had just arrived in Baghdad with a message from President Reagan.[9] The Iraqi media accused the

United States of colluding with Israel and Iran to prevent Iraq from suppressing the Kurdish revolt.[10]

Yet the Iraqi side knew its limits—it still needed US support. To defuse the political tension, in July a senior Iraqi official made it clear that once the cease-fire went into effect (it occurred on August 20, 1988), the US presence in the Gulf would still be sought, at least for the time being, to "keep the Iranians under some check." Iraq also tried to allay US fears for the safety of its allies in the area by insisting that, after the war, Iraq would remain close to Jordan, Egypt, Saudi Arabia, and Kuwait: "Relations with those four countries will be the backbone of our Arab policy," a senior Iraqi official said.[11]

The crisis was over, but not for long. Three weeks after the cease-fire in the Gulf, on September 8, 1988, after apparently being prodded by the press and Congress, the State Department announced that reports of the use of poison gas against the Kurds in northern Iraq had been corroborated. In his meeting a few hours later with Iraqi Minister of State for Foreign Affairs Sa'dun Hammadi, Secretary of State Shultz surprised Hammadi by denouncing Iraq and warned that continued use of CW and abuse of "other human rights" (referring to other aspects of the campaign against the Kurds) would harm US-Iraqi relations. One day later the US Senate passed a bill that imposed widespread economic sanctions on Iraq, and on September 27 the House passed a similar (though weaker) bill. Due to jurisdictional fights over other foreign policy issues and administration objection, neither bill became law, but there was no mistaking congressional feelings toward Iraq.[12]

The State Department, however, had a very different view. Richard Murphy insisted that "we need to move quickly to ensure that our action is seen as anti-chemical weapons, not [as] anti-Iraq or pro-Iran." There is need to get "the CW genie back in the bottle" and to deal with Iraq's human rights violations, but "the U.S.-Iraqi relationship is never-the-less important to our long-term political and economic objectives in the Gulf and beyond." Iraq, Murphy pointed out, had shown signs of moderation in three areas: terrorism, the Palestine issue, and its relations with its conservative Arab neighbors (on all three, though the test-time was very short, this analysis was correct). Murphy also argued that Saddam recognized US instrumentality in facilitating Iraq-Iran peace negotiations (in reality the Iraqis were highly ambivalent about the US role), and in supplying Iraq with modern technology (not surprisingly, this was correct). Thus, Murphy felt that there was a good basis for future cooperation: "We believe that economic sanctions will be useless or counter-productive in terms of our ability to influence the Iraqis. We may want to support . . . action for broader CW purposes, as part of an effort to make an example of the Iraqis, but we should be clear in our minds that this will not produce any results in Baghdad."[13] Murphy also recommended to "continue to speak out on Iraqi human rights abuses, but without gratuitous Iraq-bashing." Finally, Murphy pointed out that although the Iraqis "have curbed their support for Palestinian terrorism," they remained "willing to use international terrorism themselves against their opponents." However, there was no recommendation to place Iraq again on the list of states sponsoring terrorism.[14]

Because US criticism over Iraq's use of CW to suppress the Kurdish revolt was perceived as a threat to one of the regime's core interests, namely, the complete eradication of Kurdish opposition and total control of the north, Baghdad's immediate response was unusually strong. On September 11, 1988, after Iraqi spokesmen angrily denied the "allegations," a mammoth demonstration was organized in front of the US embassy in Baghdad to convey the utmost indignation of the Iraqi people.[15]

A few days later the anti-American campaign was stepped up. Targeting mainly Congress, senior Iraqi officials joined in and the criticism became harsher. Fear of Iraqi victories, argued First Deputy Prime Minister Ramadan, had pushed Congress, or as he called it, "the U.S. Knesset," to try to weaken Iraq by preventing it from "clean[ing] the northern part of its homeland . . . of the traitors." Ramadan went on to say that by saving the Kurdish revolt, Congress wanted to help the Iranians in order to help Israel (which was considered Iran's ally) control the Palestinian uprising in the Occupied Territories. "To remove any delusions . . . and in order to present the true facts," Ramadan suggested, "the American Knesset [should] meet in Israel. . . . [This] would confirm that its policy serves the country in which it meets."[16] *Al-Jumhuriyya* added that the US condemnations were meant to legitimize an Israeli raid on "some Iraqi economic enterprises," apparently chemical missile or nuclear plants, recalling the Israeli raid on Iraq's atomic reactor in June 1981.[17] This fear of a new Israeli raid under a political US umbrella, though in itself unfounded, was all the same a real one.

In a diplomatic gesture designed to defuse the situation, on October 3, 1988, after a meeting at the UN in New York, the Iraqi foreign minister was reported by a State Department spokesman to have privately assured Secretary of State Shultz that Iraq held the international restrictions on chemical weapons to be applicable "to internal matters, such as dealing with its Kurdish minority, as well as external conflicts."[18]

On the economic level, however, it was business as usual, which sent mixed signals to the Iraqis. Amid all the diplomatic commotion, the Department of Agriculture (USDA) allocated to Iraq $1.05 billion in credits for 1989. By late October 1988 senior US officials and a congressional staff delegation visited Baghdad and were apparently well received.[19] In June 1989 the atmosphere of business as usual was accentuated when Saddam unexpectedly received a large delegation of US businessmen (members of the US-Iraq business forum), and told them: "It is correct that we remember the Irangate scandal [i.e., Iran-Contra]. However, we are not . . . obsessed with the complexes of the past."[20]

Thus, in mid-1989 it seemed that the worst of the crisis in US-Iraqi relations was over. Yet the degree of mutual suspicion was still such that any minor incident, like a declaration by a US official of US concern in regard to the Iraqi missile force, was immediately presented (and possibly perceived) in Baghdad as a sign of US-Israeli collusion against Iraq.[21]

US Credits to Iraq Reexamined

In November 1989, in reaction to the submission of the sanctions bills in Congress, Iraq sounded the first warning against a US decision to apply sanctions. As anticipated by Exim a few years earlier, the Iraqis threatened that if Congress stopped the loan guarantee program, Iraq might no longer repay its debt. And whereas the USDA reacted to these threats by advising "not to unnecessarily anger the Iraqis and trigger a default that could jeopardize the whole CCC program,"[22] Exim was alarmed. Indeed, old fears were rising concerning Iraq's ability and willingness to repay its debts. In two "Country Risk Analyses" issued in January and September 1989, Exim warned that almost all of Iraq's main international creditors were having problems. The Iraqis were repaying Exim and CCC in arrears but only because they were expecting larger loans. Exim reported that "because of their concerns about Iraq's financial behavior, the Fed [the Federal Reserve] and [Department of] Treasury want CCC to scale back" its program. However, by far the most ominous note Exim sounded was in regard to a newly discovered financial scandal, one connected with the Atlanta-based branch of the Italian Banca Nazionale Del Lavoro (BNL).[23]

Immediately upon the start of the investigation of BNL fraud, by the Federal Bureau of Investigation (FBI) and the US Customs Service, Treasury pointed out that both bank and Iraqi officials were suspected of more than arranging unauthorized credit in excess of $2.6 billion; the commodities involved were suspected to include "military-type technology and various controlled chemicals . . . [as well as] illegal export to Iraq of missile-related technology to be used in the Condor II project."[24] Administration worries were not limited to the unauthorized BNL loans. In an interagency meeting in October 1989 the Department of Agriculture, for the first time, expressed deep concern over the future of the CCC program. Because of this, US-Iraqi economic relations came under heavy public fire, and it was felt that it was urgently necessary to investigate three areas: diversion of CCC-guaranteed commodities during transit (for example, food for arms); illegal payments (or "kickbacks") required by Iraq of exporters in order to enter the Iraqi market; and "after-sales services," which required exporters to provide the Iraqis with trucks and other equipment free of charge. Other US government agencies also mentioned that some commodities were double and triple wholesale prices. As the USDA saw it, the investigation could "blow the roof off the CCC."[25]

Indeed, in early October 1989 an Iraqi economic team visiting Washington, D.C., reported to Foreign Minister 'Aziz, himself in the United States at the time, that the United States was ready to release only $488 million in CCC credits, less than half the $1 billion agreed upon for 1990. The foreign minister complained to Secretary of State James Baker that the CCC program was unjustifiably linked to the BNL scandal, "of which Iraq had no part." This, he pointed out, was "a set-back [in bilateral relations], and the government of Iraq is very unhappy." Baker, for his part, explained that the program was not canceled, only suspended pending further investigation. He promised to expedite treatment of the issue and added that the Federal Reserve and Treasury had demanded a thorough investigation of the BNL affair before resumption of the program.[26] By laying the responsibility on the shoulders of other agencies, Baker implied that his department was unhappy with the decision while pleading that his hands were tied. By promising an early resolution of the problem, a promise that it could not deliver, State only enhanced the impression of powerlessness.[27]

As later explained by Acting Secretary of State Lawrence Eagleburger, the State Department was still very interested in continuing the CCC program. US influence in Iraq depended on it, and such influence could help the Middle East peace process, limit missile proliferation, and influence Iraq's behavior in Lebanon.[28] Not surprisingly, the USDA was also unhappy about the suspension, as it noted in a memorandum to the White House. Because Iraq was such an important market for US staples, it pointed out that it was "eager to resolve the new credit to be offered to Iraq quickly." However, in view of the BNL investigation, in addition to the tremendous public sensitivity with regard to cooperation with Iraq, even it had to admit that "a business as usual approach seems unwise."[29]

Worse still, even after a delegation from the USDA visited Baghdad in April and found some of the allegations to be unfounded or easily correctable, the CCC program was not resumed. US Ambassador to Baghdad April Glaspie reported that there was no evidence of diversion of CCC-funded food to other countries (in return for military supplies), high prices were justified, and other aspects could be corrected. "USDA team [is] satisfied that a mutual solution can be reached to meet future program requirements," she wrote.[30]

Glaspie's cable was classified "confidential," and so it could not have been seen by the Iraqis. Yet it is clear that she signaled her optimism to the Iraqi side. Indeed, upon learning that USDA had decided to turn down the second tranche of CCC credits for Iraq on the basis of irregularities, Glaspie disclosed that she had given Iraq hope. In fact, so did the Bob Dole–led delegation of US senators (who had met with Saddam on April 12, 1990) and the investigating delegation from the USDA. Frustrated, Glaspie commented that turning down the CCC credits would send the signal that the administration had decided to join forces with those in Congress who favored sanctions. Canceling the CCC programs, she argued, would be interpreted as purely political and as part of the US conspiracy against Iraq.[31]

In fact, according to a mid-May USDA memorandum, there were two nonpolitical problems that justified the suspension: The Iraqis improperly included freight charges in the program and they demanded after-sales services.[32] But there was, of course, the as yet unresolved issue of Iraqi involvement in the BNL fraud, and there were also important *political* reasons. It has to be borne in mind that Glaspie's strong recommendation to continue the CCC program was made only a few weeks after Saddam implied his intent to use CW against Israel. The ambassador assured her superiors (erroneously, as it turned out) that "the Iraqi president, as you know, did not threaten to attack Israel. . . . His threat was . . . if Israel attacks with nuclear weapons, Iraq would use binary chemical weapons."[33] But it seems that Washington knew better (in fact, Saddam and his lieutenants continued to imply the use of chemical weapons in retaliation for a conventional Israeli attack). There were other developments that complicated matters, which were all political and not economic. But then, the CCC program itself was defined as a political tool, no less than an economic one. And so some State Department officials felt that Iraq's political behavior should not have been ignored. Thus, for example, in a letter to the secretary of state in mid-April, US official Robert Kimmitt wrote: "I continue to believe that we should oppose the second tranche [of the CCC] on *political grounds.* . . . If we go forward with CCC and Exim . . . Saddam Hussein will regard that decision as a positive political signal, which will lead him to . . . [continue] his proliferation campaign" (emphasis added).[34]

Iraqi diplomats started to threaten that Iraq would not repay its CCC debt,[35] but the program was not resumed. Even though the official announcement of the suspension was made only as late as May 21, 1990,[36] according to Iraqi sources they had anticipated this shift. Precisely as April Glaspie had predicted, rather than as a reaction to Iraqi excesses, the Iraqi side regarded (or presented) the withholding of the second tranche as a US conspiracy against it. As put by the Iraqi minister of trade to a visiting US member of Congress, it "reflect[ed] unjustified hostility toward Iraq."[37]

Indeed, Iraq's traditional suspicions of US intentions were heightened very soon after the end of the Iraq-Iran war, when the leadership decided that the US position started to shift from support to opposition. In a bizarre meeting between 'Aziz and Baker in Washington, D.C., in October 1989, 'Aziz accused US diplomats of "approaching officials in the Gulf, raising suspicion and fear regarding Iraqi intentions in the region." This, 'Aziz reported, dismayed the Iraqi government because it had been long committed to Gulf stability and to "good relations . . . particularly [with] Saudi Arabia and Kuwait." 'Aziz also complained that the United States demonstrated mistrust when it limited technological exports to Iraq, which were designed solely to develop the economy. He expressed deep concern over the postponement of the second tranche of the CCC credits and over the intention of Congress to legislate economic and political sanctions. Surrealistically, 'Aziz confided to Baker that "some American agencies" were trying to destabilize Iraq. The secretary was greatly surprised and promised to look into it but asked 'Aziz to provide him with more details. 'Aziz promised to do so but never did.[38] In later correspondence, Baker reported to 'Aziz that President Bush asked him to convey to the Iraqis "in the most direct way possible that the U.S. is not involved in any effort to weaken or destabilize Iraq. Having looked into the matter and discussed it with the president I can tell you this with the highest authority. Such an action would be completely contrary to the president's policy, which is to work to strengthen the relationship between the U.S. and Iraq whenever possible."[39]

The Iraqis were not convinced. According to a very knowledgeable insider, the Iraqi leadership felt that Secretary Baker was kept in the dark by the US intelligence community and that the plot was a very real one.[40] The meeting was not all negative: 'Aziz agreed not to subvert US policies over the Arab-Israeli conflict and Lebanon and both parties agreed to expand cooperation.[41] However, in hindsight, in October 1989 it was clear that a time bomb had already started to tick.

The single most important indication that pro-Iraqi elements within the administration were losing ground was the decision to suspend the CCC program. The reason for the Iraqi concern was twofold: The CCC program granted a breathing space of 360 days when it came to repayments for a billion dollars worth of much-needed foodstuffs; and, as Nizar Hamdun, Iraqi ambassador to the United States, explained in October 1989 to the US ambassador in Baghdad, it also helped them to boost Iraq's creditworthiness, as it indicated US confidence.[42] This aspect was of tremendous importance precisely because Iraq's creditworthiness was so low. In late 1989, however, important administration agencies were still working to revive the dying relationship. Thus, in late November, in accordance with NSD–26, the Joint Chiefs of Staff recommended a number of initiatives: exchange of army field manuals and English-language textbooks; visits by the US Central Command staff to the Iraqi armed forces; a series of medical consultative visits to discuss the rehabilitation of wounded personnel; and residency training for Iraqi personnel in a US military medical school. All of these were innocuous issues over which bilateral cooperation could do no harm. However, there were a few other issues that were somewhat more problematic: a training program on aviation safety and security; a mine countermeasure training program for the Iraqi navy; a military officer exchange program; Iraqi officers funded by the Iraqi government to attend US schools at the Staff and War College levels; an Iraqi "briefing team" to visit the United States and discuss with Staff and War Colleges personnel the lessons from the Faw campaign; and aerial reconnaissance training. The Joint Chiefs of Staff agreed with Ambassador Glaspie that "implementation of low-level, non-lethal military assistance would greatly . . . improve dialogue with and access to the senior military leadership and the government of Iraq."[43] Military cooperation with Iraq was still on the agenda as late as January 1990.[44] It is not clear whether the Iraqis were aware of these initiatives; if they were, it must have only increased their frustration because they realized that the administration was unable to deliver limited military cooperation as well.

Turning the Tide: US-Iraqi Relations in Crisis

The next events occurred in early 1990. January and February must have given the Iraqis fits due to the split personality then reflected in the US modus operandi. On January 17 President Bush applied a waiver to a resolution by the House that prohibited any Exim credits and loans to nine countries, including Iraq. The presidential waiver excluded Iraq in the national interest.[45]

Less than one month later the Voice of America (VOA) broadcast an editorial that, as it claimed, was "reflecting the views of the U.S. government." It came in the wake of the monumental changes to Eastern Europe. It analyzed the function of the secret police in the dictatorial regimes of Eastern Europe and predicted the end of police states all over the world, including in Iraq.[46]

Even though Iraq did not figure very prominently in the broadcast (indeed, Iraq's name was added only at the last moment), the timing was very sensitive because the

Iraqi leadership was aware of some similarities between its situation and that of deceased Romanian leader Nicolae Ceausescu, namely, a crisis of socioeconomic expectations and tensions between the army and the civilian leadership. It saw in the broadcast "a part of a total and organized plan [to topple the regime]." It asked for clarifications, and Washington officially apologized and informed it that the official responsible was sacked. However, Iraqi sources insist that suspicions did not subside.[47] These were further enhanced by the fact that the second tranche of the CCC credits was not forthcoming.[48] The National Security Council (NSC) and its head, General Brent Scowcroft, were doing their best to push the various government agencies to approve the second tranche, but they failed. This seems to have been transmitted to the Iraqi side.[49]

It also seems that between February and April 1990 the Iraqis concluded they could expect little from the United States in return for good behavior and, more important, that what the United States regarded as good behavior was diametrically opposed to crucial Iraqi interests. Following the VOA broadcast and a few days before an Arab Cooperation Council (ACC) summit in Baghdad, Kelly visited Baghdad and met with Saddam. We have no information as to what Kelly said in that meeting, but the Iraqi president told him that the United States was interested in a state of "no war, no peace" between Iraq and Iran.[50] Saddam's behavior following the meeting was ample proof that, contrary to Kelly's perception, he saw the meeting as the beginning of the end of the era of more-or-less normal US-Iraqi working relations.

In a speech he delivered at the summit of the ACC at the end of the month, Saddam accused the US Navy, then in the Gulf, of trying to fish in troubled waters and implied that it should evacuate the area. Ambassador Glaspie relayed to the Iraqi Foreign Ministry her country's anger. She asked for clarification (which she never received), explaining that the US Navy had been reduced already from fifty vessels in 1988 to six.[51] According to writer Sa'd Bazzaz, as the Iraqi leadership saw it, "in February 1990 the serious planning in the U.S. for an open and forceful action against Iraq . . . started. It became clear that the campaign had begun."[52] This could also be read as Iraqi realization that, conspiracy or not, the United States was determined to prevent Iraqi hegemony in the Gulf. According to 'Aziz, Iraq noticed US displeasure at Saddam's speech at the ACC Amman summit, and in mid-March, after Iraq executed London-based reporter Farzad Bazoft "because he was a spy," all hell broke loose. As Tariq 'Aziz put it, this was when Iraq started to fear a conspiracy.[53]

In his fateful meeting with Ambassador Glaspie just prior to the invasion of Kuwait, Saddam exposed the Iraqi way of thinking during the first half of 1990. According to Glaspie, he explained that there were "some circles in the U.S. government, including in the CIA [Central Intelligence Agency] and the State Department, but emphatically excluding the president and Secretary Baker, who are not friendly towards Iraq-U.S. relations. . . . Some circles are gathering information on who might be Saddam Hussein's successor." These circles, Saddam disclosed, were warning Gulf states against Iraq. These hostile circles were also working to ensure "no [economic] help would go to Iraq [meaning the CCC]." Finally, Saddam mentioned the "USIA [US Information Agency] campaign against himself and the general media assault on Iraq."[54] I was unable to verify the claim that officials were warning the Gulf states, but in his memoirs General Norman Schwarzkopf does mention that a short time before the invasion of Kuwait, he gave orders to test in a war game what he considered to be a realistic scenario "in which the enemy was not the Soviet Union [as before], but Iraq."[55] Tariq 'Aziz, too (not resorting this time to a plot theory), reports that the Iraqi leadership reached the conclusion that Washington was split between supporters and opponents of Iraq, and when such a draw exists, he implied, the pro-Israel lobby "controls the balance."[56] Although the pro-Israel lobby issue was greatly exaggerated (it was unable to prevent extensive cooperation until the BNL fraud was exposed), the splits within the administration and Congress were very real.

By March there were a few more incidents that further soured relations. In the middle of the month Iraq executed reporter Bazoft. At the end of the month the United States and Britain, in a "sting" operation, exposed an Iraqi network to smuggle munitions-list nuclear-related capacitors out of the United States through Britain to Iraq. The administration saw in it a breach of two diplomatic principles: It showed flagrant disregard for US law and it called into question Iraq's willingness to live up to its Non-Proliferation Treaty (NPT) commitments. The embassy in Baghdad was also instructed to deliver a démarche with regard to a conspiracy between an Iraqi diplomat at the UN in New York and an Iraqi expatriate in the United States to arrange for the assassination of another Iraqi expatriate in the United States.[57]

Trying to deflect congressional wrath, Kelly ignored Iraqi intentions, thus issuing a technically correct but incomplete communiqué: "We do not believe that Iraq is close to developing an atomic weapon, nor do we have any indication that Iraq has violated its NPT commitments."[58] Yet the US government was now far more suspicious than it had been in the mid-1980s. In late 1989 there was a widespread presumption on the part of the intelligence community that Iraq was "interested in acquiring a nuclear explosive capability." True, US exports of "dual use commodities for conventional military use" could still be (and were) approved.[59] Yet, as will be shown below, some high-profile attempts were made to prevent exports with non-conventional potential.

According to Baghdad radio and TV broadcasts, on April 1, 1990, Saddam made his thundering threat that, if Israel touches "one square inch of Iraqi soil . . . fire will consume half of Israel."[60] This threat was coupled by placing missile launchers at the H3 military base in western Iraq, facing Israel. According to 'Aziz, in late March, following the nuclear-detonators affair, the atmosphere reminded Iraq of the period leading to the Israeli raid of June 1981, and the Iraqi leadership felt that a "deterrent speech" was in order. This was the sole reason for Saddam's threat. To Iraq's dismay, the United States again took the speech very badly. This was when the Iraqi leadership became convinced that Washington "stopped listening to us" and "made up their minds to hit us."[61] As pointed out above, the Iraqi fear of an Israeli raid was a real one. However, this, too, could be read in a conspiracy-free manner: US anger at the threats against Israel convinced the Iraqis that any attempt to lead an Arab political front against the peace process would meet with US opposition. The State Department felt that by threatening Israel with a chemical attack Saddam reneged on the Iraqi commitment, given to Shultz a few months earlier, to adhere to the 1925 Geneva Protocol prohibiting the first use of chemical weapons. The embassy in Baghdad was instructed again to deliver a démarche concerning all these issues, including human rights. Embassy officials promised that US criticism of Iraq was not a "green light" to an Israeli attack and suggested that Iraq could ease the tension with Israel "by opening an indirect line of communications." The ambassador was asked, however, to deliver a very strict warning: "Iraq will be on a collision course with the U.S. if it continues to engage in actions that threaten the stability of the region, undermine local arms control efforts and flout U.S. laws."[62] And in another communication: "Without such measures [designed to address the aforementioned US concerns] on your part, what little support that is left in the U.S. for Iraq may further erode."[63]

The State Department also took the opportunity to deliver the same message via the five US senators visiting Baghdad. In their meeting in Mosul on April 12, Republican Senator Bob Dole, who headed the group, personally handed Saddam Hussein an official letter from the delegation warning Iraq that it must stop its nuclear, chemical, and missile "proliferation" as well as "disregard for U.S. law and human rights."[64] The Dole mission was later criticized as appeasing Saddam, as it emphasized the US wish for friendship with Iraq. But Saddam, for his part, could not have ignored the conditions for such friendship, and they were totally unacceptable to him. In fact, Saddam explicitly and forcefully rejected the US nonproliferation policy, saying, "It is the Arabs' right to own whatever weapon their enemy owns. . . . If any Arab state would have announced that it had the nuclear bomb, I myself and the Iraqis would have been the first to announce support and respect for this."[65]

What the senators put to him gently, Congress delivered forcefully. Following Saddam's threat against Israel, three bills were discussed on Capitol Hill. One was offered by Senators Daniel K. Inouye (D–Hawaii) and Robert Kasten (R–Wisc.), who proposed a total trade embargo (including a ban on travel) against Iraq. Another proposed bill was sponsored by Congressman Howard L. Berman (D–Calif.). It included, among other items, stricter limitations on exports of dual-use technology, cutting off Exim guarantees, and mandatory US objection to loans to Iraq by international bodies like the International Monetary Fund (IMF). The third proposal was a bill offered by Senator Alfonse D'Amato (R–N.Y.) to cut off all US aid to Iraq until it submitted to an international inspection of its military facilities.[66] An exasperated Senator Tom Lantos (D–Calif.) asked Kelly during testimony: "At what point will the administration recognize that this is not a nice guy?"[67] But views in the embassy in Baghdad and, more important, in the State Department were more optimistic, thus State was still against sanctions. Glaspie reported from Baghdad in late April: "Iraq has modified its behavior and policies in large part because of our diplomatic efforts."[68] John Kelly pointed out in late May to the Senate: "The government of Iraq is signaling that it wants to bring U.S.-Iraq relations back to a more positive level."[69] But Saddam was already light-years away from where the US analysts thought he was. In all probability, the decision to invade Kuwait was made only in late June,[70] but by late May the Iraqi president had clearly chosen a collision course with the United States, Britain, and Israel.

Less than a week after Kelly's upbeat assessment, at the Baghdad Arab League Summit Meeting, Saddam switched yet again. The convening of an extraordinary Arab Summit meeting in Baghdad was in itself a tremendous victory for the aggressive policies adopted by Iraq since the launch of its 'Abid space missile in early December 1989 and an admission of weakness on the part of the pro-Western Arab states. This summit witnessed a major offensive on the part of Iraq and its Arab supporters (chiefly Libya, the Palestine Liberation Organization [PLO], and Jordan) against Israel, Soviet-Jewish immigration, the United States, and, by implication, the Arab moderates. In the summit's concluding resolutions Iraq received support for its "right to take all measures that will guarantee the protection of its national security and . . . the possession of highly-developed scientific and technological means" necessary for its defense. The resolutions added that this had to be done within the framework of international law. Yet the "severe denunciation" of "the scientific and technological embargo" imposed on Iraq by the United States and Britain and of the Western media campaign "against [its] sovereignty and national security" sent a very different message; the Arabs as a collective denounced any attempt to stop Saddam's nuclear, chemical, bacteriological, and missile efforts and even defined these efforts as a positive contribution to "pan-Arab security."[71] Thus, the summit's resolutions should have been interpreted as tacit approval of Saddam's policies. All in all, these resolutions were a shocking demonstration of collective Arab folly. But this was not all.

During the closed sessions Saddam Hussein's other side was exposed when he accused some "Arab Brothers" of flooding the world oil market and bringing down prices. This, he pointed out, had caused Iraq and "the Arab nation" grave economic damages. He threatened that Iraq regarded this as an all-out war against it. He added darkly: "We have reached a point when we can no longer withstand pressure."[72] According to a senior diplomat from the Gulf who attended the summit, Saddam also demanded strong anti-American resolutions, and Egyptian President Husni Mubarak needed all his influence to prevent such resolutions. No one protested the attack on the Gulf Arabs, and the impression left was that of Arab sympathy toward Saddam's demands or, at least, reluctance to confront Iraq. This was further evidence of Iraq's new status, as well as its ability to use it to apply pressure on the Gulf states.

Just before the Baghdad summit the US administration went on record as objecting to any sanctions against Iraq. The State Department's main concerns were that sanctions (especially the Inouye-Kasten bill) "just short of a declaration of war" would damage the peace process, reintroduce Soviet influence, affect the US energy supply (675,000 barrels per day; 8 percent of all imported oil came from Iraq), and damage US exporters of foodstuffs and dual-use technology as other developed countries gladly filled the gap. Conspicuous by its absence was any particular concern about security in or policy toward the Gulf region. More generally, State claimed that the United States had already imposed severe limitations on any exports to Iraq that could be used to produce missiles and chemical and nuclear weapons. State also felt that Congress should not limit the president in his foreign policy.[73] Congressional activity was delayed for a variety of reasons, but State needed to preempt further action. "If our efforts are deemed insufficient," a senior official wrote, "Congress can be expected to enact a host of anti-Iraqi resolutions and amendments in the next session."[74]

Iraqi rage, so explicit at the Baghdad summit, resulted from the US restrictions, some of which had been imposed on Iraq since late 1989. Among them were, in addition to the suspension of the CCC program, curtailing of certain activities by the Department of Commerce to interagency consultation; rescission of the presidential waiver in regard to Exim; the beginning of a concerted international effort to break up Iraq's covert procurement networks, a campaign designed to persuade other countries (e.g., France, USSR, the Federal Republic of Germany, and Japan) to raise nuclear, missile, chemical, and biological warfare concerns directly with Iraq's Arab friends (and themselves to refrain from any exports that could be conducive to such warfare); a ban on nuclear cooperation with Iraq and on exports of technology that could be helpful for Iraq's biological weapons program; and an expansion to fifty of the list of prohibited chemicals (identified as potentially usable in chemical weapons programs), including coordination with other Western powers, including the Australia Group, to deny Iraq chemicals for its weapons industry. Also, since spring 1989, exports of biological cultures were severely curtailed.[75]

These activities were insufficient to stop the Iraqi thirst for nonconventional weapons. Indeed, some dual-purpose technology was still sold and shipped to Iraq well into 1990.[76] However, Saddam's rage displayed at the summit meeting and his remarks to the senators indicate that the US declarations of intent were more than sufficient to alert the Iraqis to the US-led effort. The restrictions were easily monitored, because they were designed to be easily monitored and they signaled that Iraq was, indeed, on a political collision course with the United States. The Iraqis knew that in 1986 the United States managed to "kill" the Condor medium-range ballistic missile program, which they hatched together with Egypt and Argentina, by leaning on the Germans and Italians.[77] The United States could do it again. All the existing evidence in Baghdad pointed in one direction, namely, that when the Ba'th regime worked to achieve national goals, it ran into US opposition; even the sympathetic officials of State and the NSC were unable to prevent US sanctions. Indeed, in terms of US nonproliferation efforts, there was consensus over the aforementioned steps and discord only in relation to some dual-use technology.

Saddam's National Goals

What were Iraq's national goals, so dear to the hearts of Saddam and his close associates and so irreconcilable with long-term US interests? One was the development and use of chemical weapons. However, this was no longer necessary, the Kurdish opposition having been crushed. Far more contentious was the issue of Iraqi ambition in the Gulf. The editor of the government daily newspaper indicated that at the end of the war with Iran, Iraq was bent on wrenching out of the Gulf Arabs "large-scale participation . . . to enable Iraq to re-build itself and to provide [for its citizens] a suitable level of social and economic comfort."[78]

In a number of meetings between Iraqi and Kuwaiti officials during the first half of 1990, Iraqi Minister of State for Foreign Affairs Hammadi demanded that the Gulf states extend to Iraq sufficient support to compensate for past war damages and enable it to rebuild its economy. As implied by the Iraqis, the demand could reach a total of $200–300 billion, a staggering amount even for the Gulf monarchies.[79] Furthermore, according to Bazzaz, the Iraqi leadership felt that there was no way the Gulf zone could "expect stability" unless the Gulf Arabs recognized Iraq's status as the "guardian brother,"[80] meaning the senior member in the GCC.

By the spring of 1990, following a number of diplomatic crises with the United States, it became clear to the Iraqi leadership that under the existing circumstances the United States would never allow Iraq to impose its will on the Gulf Arabs. There was a need, therefore, to break the spell, to create a new reality, and to present the United States with a fait accompli. Under the new circumstances Iraq would be in control of 21 percent of all the oil sold on the world markets, and Saddam hoped that the United States would have no choice but to acquiesce and bargain. This expectation was sounded loud and clear in a meeting Saddam initiated with the US chargé d'affaires, Joseph Wilson, four days after the Kuwait invasion. According to the Iraqi transcript, Saddam offered President Bush a guarantee (what he knew to have been the US chief interest in the Gulf) that oil would flow undisturbed. This was how NSD–26 defined it[81] and how it was repeated in many US diplomatic messages. Saddam's contribution to the US formula was that he would see to it that Gulf oil would be available at a "reasonable price" of $25 per barrel. In return he expected US acceptance of the annexation of Kuwait and Iraq's status as senior US ally in the Gulf.[82]

But Iraq was harboring even greater ambitions. As had become clear since December 1989, Iraq was also bent on achieving Arab leadership. Seen from this perspective Israel was not a threat but rather an asset. At a time when Arab frustration was growing due to a slowdown of the peace talks and the exodus of Soviet Jews to Israel, assuming the mantle of Arab leadership in the political struggle against Israel could secure for Iraq substantial influence in Arab minds after eight years of nonaction from other Arab states. Following Saddam's somewhat inflated promise to burn half of Israel, Arab popular enthusiasm reached amazing levels. The Iraqi president was quick to take advantage of it: Though at first explaining (to the Senate delegation) that what he had meant was only a chemical reprisal for an Israeli nuclear attack, a few days later he and his military commanders continued to imply the use of chemical warheads in retaliation for a conventional attack on any Arab country.[83] A confrontational posture vis-à-vis Israel, however, could only lead to tension with the United States. Sheltering terrorists was yet another pan-Arab asset. But here, too, when Saddam hosted again the notorious Abu 'Abbas in the spring of 1990 he was, apparently, reminded by the United States that this could further complicate matters.[84] The Iraqi ambassador's reply to US protests: "Iraq does and will continue to provide access for all Palestinians . . . seeking to liberate Palestine."[85]

Rather than briefly lower his terrorist profile, as he had done in the past, to the consternation of US diplomats Saddam instead restocked his reservoir of terrorists. To Abu 'Abbas, in June 1990 he added Abu Nidal. The United States was aware of terrorist activities planned by these men and a few other Baghdad-based groups. "Iraq should understand clearly," Glaspie was instructed to inform her interlocutors, "the U.S. would respond to any new terrorist acts."[86] The Iraqis were not impressed. A few days after the invasion the State Department reported in an internal document that "there have been increasing signs that he [Saddam] has been rebuilding Iraq's ties to terrorist groups in recent months."[87] Clearly since early 1990, when he decided to break away from his accommodationist policies, Saddam felt that he needed the additional intimidation value and prestige associated with the presence of Palestinian terrorist groups in Baghdad, and he was indifferent to US protests. A month after the invasion the State Department decided to place Iraq again on the list of state sponsors of terrorism.[88]

In June, this listing could still have affected Iraq's economic relations with the United States because it would have effectively ended all the suspended programs and Iraqi oil exports to and technology imports from the United States. But Saddam was already riding high on his way to Arab leadership and financial solvency; once he was in possession of Kuwait and its coveted treasures, a US trade embargo could be easily compensated for by trading with other Western countries. The sponsorship of Palestinian terrorism, however, was irreplaceable under the new circumstances.

Finally, as a result of its ambitions to Gulf and Arab leadership, but also because of what it perceived as a long-term threat from Iran, Iraq was determined to develop an array of nonconventional weapons and missiles. This, too, was anathema to the United States, and US diplomats delivered this message to the Iraqis and their Arab friends loud and clear. Whether the Iraqi ruling elite genuinely saw this as a part of a "U.S.-Zionist conspiracy" or whether the theory was intended only for mass consumption, the United States stood in Iraq's path toward Gulf and Arab hegemony and what it saw as its legitimate national security interests. Baghdad's conclusion was that it was getting very close to the limits of its cooperation with the United States. One thing that guaranteed Saddam success in the domestic arena was his ability to preempt and surprise unsuspecting potential rivals. Saddam had always been the first to break formation and (often literally) stab former allies in the back. The Iraqi leader decided to project these winning tactics to the foreign arena, take the Americans by surprise, and then make them an offer that they could not turn down. US diplomacy was unaware of the full significance of the indications of the changing mood in Baghdad.

On the Eve of the Invasion

In response to Saddam Hussein's implied threat, made in his July 17 speech, to use force against unspecified Arab oil producers who exceeded quotas, and in response to his furious anti-Kuwaiti letter to the Arab League, Kuwait placed its armed forces on alert but stood down by July 20 to make sure Baghdad did not interpret the alert as a provocative move that might call for a military response. By July 20, however, there were already unconfirmed reports of the movement of two divisions of the Iraqi Republican Guards to the Iraq-Kuwait border. (In fact, according to a reliable Iraqi source, troop movements toward the Kuwait border started between July 17 and July 19.)[89] Senior US officials were in touch with their Kuwaiti counterparts, assuring them of their support. The United States also made contact with Iraq to make sure that it was aware of US concern.[90]

At about 9 a.m. (Baghdad time) on July 25, the US intelligence assessment became very ominous. It revealed that three infantry divisions, an armored division, their supporting units, and additional air defense units were in place near the Kuwait border. The Iraqi force was estimated at over 75,000. However, Kuwait and the other Arab monarchies on the Gulf responded with "only minor military activity."[91]

On July 25, US sources already concluded that Saddam had the capability to conquer Kuwait within a few days. But they were at a loss as to his intentions; clearly, they lacked human intelligence from within the ruling circle. In their perplexity, US officials turned to their closest Arab allies, assuming that Saddam's Arab neighbors, due to their proximity and common cultural background, would be either more knowledgeable or intuitively more accurate in their assessments of his intentions. The king of Saudi Arabia and president of Egypt assured Washington that Saddam would not invade, arguing that "the best way to resolve an inter-Arab squabble is for the United States to avoid inflammatory words and actions."[92] Kuwait, for its part, was so scared lest it would provoke Saddam that it refrained from requesting any US military gesture.[93]

On the diplomatic level, following Saddam's July 17 speech, President Bush expressed concern and his administration spoke of reviewing its policy vis-à-vis Iraq.[94] On July 18, the State Department announced US commitments: to ensure the free flow of oil through the Strait of Hormuz; to defend the freedom of navigation in the Gulf; and to support "the individual and collective self-defense of our friends in the Gulf, with whom we have deep and long-standing ties."[95] The first two points had little to do with Kuwait; the third was intentionally vague so as not to commit the United States automatically to direct military involvement.

On July 24, Ambassador Glaspie was instructed to convey to Iraq the US concern over the security of Kuwait and the United Arab Emirates (UAE). "The implications of having oil production and pricing policy . . . enforced by Iraqi guns [are] disturbing," she told Deputy Foreign Minister Nizar Hamdun.[96] At this point it is very likely that this warning only aggravated the situation: US officials were demonstrating extreme annoyance with Saddam but were reluctant to expose their fangs.

On July 25, Ambassador Glaspie was summoned to the Foreign Ministry, only to find herself facing Saddam Hussein in person. Her conversation with Saddam is by now a proverbial example of mutual misunderstanding. The ambassador could not imagine that Saddam would be so ill-informed and rash as to conquer Kuwait

City, and she was convinced, at least since April, that Iraq was war-weary and was only concerned with reconstruction.[97] How can one explain the ambassador's optimism at the end of the meeting? It would seem that in addition to an intellectual gestalt ("the Iraqis are tired of war"), which is always difficult to break, there were two more factors. In the first place, she had been effectively isolated from Saddam and his closest circle (his cousins, half brothers, and the command of the Republican Guards). Second, in the rare interview Saddam accorded her, he intentionally sent her a double message. He may have threatened, but he also promised to try negotiations, and he assured her that Iraq was, indeed, tired of war.

As for his own assessment of the US position, Saddam made his view very clear that he did not think the United States was capable of going to war and losing 10,000 people in one battle, as Iraq had done on numerous occasions in its war against Iran. Even though Saddam and his elite recognized that Iraq was not fully prepared for an all-out war, and that it needed "two more years" to get ready (possibly meaning the time necessary in order to build its first nuclear warheads), their calculation was that Iraq was taking relatively little risk with much to gain by an invasion. As reported by Bazzaz, Iraq had a very large army that if not used for economic gains would have become a crippling economic burden; the Iraqi public became addicted to a very high oil income and thus the depressed prices of oil posed a severe danger to the regime; had it not invaded Kuwait, it would have had to conduct an uphill struggle against the overproducers, risking in the meantime major political upheavals inside the country. With a national debt of $70 billion and oil income that covered "only" 50 percent of what was believed needed, and having anyway lost the US agricultural credits (and the abundant source of credit through the Atlanta-based branch of the BNL), the situation seemed desperate enough to dictate an invasion.[98]

The ambassador did warn Saddam that "the U.S. cannot forgive the use of force." But, in reply to his friendly complaints, she also offered sympathy for Iraq's economic plight. Ignoring the inflated defense expenditures, she pointed out that Iraq deserved higher oil income. She also made her famous comment that the United States did not take a position over Arab-Arab disputes. Under different circumstances this was a good way of keeping the United States at a safe distance from inter-Arab bickering, but with four Iraqi divisions on the Kuwait border and more moving in, together with missile and air force units, this comment left Saddam with the feeling that Washington was not fully committed to the defense of Kuwait. Saddam then hinted that, if not satisfied by the Kuwaitis, he would strike a deal with Iran over the Shatt al-'Arab (the confluence of the Tigris and Euphrates Rivers that acts as a border between Iraq and Iran) and crush the Kuwaitis militarily, as he had done to Mulla Mustafa al-Barazani in 1975. Apparently, Glaspie and all those who saw her report were convinced that he was bluffing.

Saddam, for his part, claimed later that Ambassador Glaspie gave him free rein.[99] This claim does not sound credible. In the first place, Saddam had enough indications on both the diplomatic and the military levels that the United States was not indifferent to the fate of its Gulf allies. Second, he must have known that a US ambassador does not make policy. However, the US response to his threatening moves did indicate indecision and reluctance to become fully committed. Thus, for example, in Bush's July 28 cable to Ambassador Glaspie, defined as a "nondocument," the president instructed the ambassador to convey to Saddam his wish to further US-Iraqi friendship; his warning sounded too soft: "We believe that differences are best resolved by peaceful means and not by threats involving military force."[100] Two days before the invasion, Kelly announced that the United States had no defense treaty with a Gulf state and was reluctant to commit the United States to Kuwait's territorial integrity.[101] True, this announcement was made in response to a question by a member of Congress who implied that the United States should not get too involved in the dispute. It is also true that this announcement reflected the legal reality: The United States and Kuwait had no such treaty and, in fact, belabored relations had been somewhat cool for a number of years. But under the circumstances it sent the wrong signal.

The US response was, largely, the result of Saddam's disinformation campaign. Indeed, to blur his intentions Saddam also gave Egyptian President Mubarak a vague promise not to resort to arms. The exact wording of his promise later became a subject of bitter controversy.[102] But whatever the precise wording, it is sufficiently clear that Saddam intentionally sent an equivocal message. In his discussions with both Mubarak and Glaspie, he threatened that if not satisfied he would use force, but he also promised to give negotiations a chance.

How can one explain Saddam's decision to make threats and then blur them? In his meetings with Glaspie and Mubarak he urged them to apply pressure on Kuwait to concede to his demands, and he wanted them to convey his clear threats so as to increase the chances of Kuwaiti capitulation. But Saddam must have known that the chances of that occurring were slight. And so he needed to achieve a two-fold strategic goal: He was determined to avoid a repeat of the ill-fated Kuwaiti initiative of 'Abd al-Karim Qasim in June 1961. Qasim announced his intention to annex Kuwait before issuing the order to prepare an invasion; when he was ready, it was too late—the British were already there. Saddam, whose sense of history is as vivid and relevant to decisionmaking as any strategic consideration, decided to reverse the order of things.[103] To avoid a US preemptive military interference, he needed to send a peaceful message. But then, why threaten at all? Why not attack Kuwait without any warning and thus achieve complete strategic surprise? The answer to this is that Saddam needed to prepare the ground in Iraq and the Arab world in a way that would assure him mass support. Such support in Arab streets could make it difficult for moderate Arab leaders to oppose him. Without Arab support it would have been more difficult (though not impossible) for the United States to go to war.

All this, however, does not explain the Iraqi president's vague threats in his confidential conversation with Ambassador Glaspie. It seems he hoped they would not be clear enough to force the United States to make a decisive countermove. At the same time, however, he needed to gauge the US position, and he left the United States one week to react. He hoped for a feeble reaction. In fact, by sending his mixed message he invited just such a reaction. And when he got what he had asked for, he conveniently ignored the fact that this reaction had to be misleading because it was based on misleading information, which he himself had provided the United States. Finally, Saddam wanted to be able to argue later that he gave the Americans all the necessary warnings and that they chose to stay on the sidelines. This could win him domestic support in the United States. As we have seen, this is precisely what he did: As early as September 1990 Saddam instructed his embassy in Washington to publish a somewhat doctored version of his conversation with Ambassador Glaspie. In it the Iraqi threat and the ambassador's complacency are accentuated beyond what emerges from the ambassador's communications to Washington.

Conclusion

Could the United States have prevented the invasion? There is no clear answer to this question. As we have shown, one week before the invasion the Iraqi president did not think that the United States had the stomach for a major and bloody campaign. This impression was prevalent in the Arab world following the US evacuation of Vietnam and influenced its political thinking. Saddam correctly concluded that in order to drive him out of Kuwait the United States would need huge ground forces. And he did not think that the United States would be ready to expose ground troops to a war of attrition. And Saddam truly believed that this would have to be a war of attrition because he did not understand the significance of the technological gap between the two armies; thus, there is no certainty that the United States could have convinced him to stick to diplomatic means.

The United States clearly did not maximize its leverage on Iraqi policymaking. In the first place, it alarmed the Iraqi leadership by sending it repeated messages that if it did not change policy the two countries were on a collision course. However, US diplomacy did not do all it could reasonably have done to prevent the invasion. To be sure, there were limits to US deterrence: US policymakers had to leave for themselves a degree of freedom so as not to commit themselves to the defense of every square inch of Kuwaiti territory. But they could have found a diplomatic formula that would indicate to the Iraqis more emphatically that they were passing a redline. For example, they could have warned that any use of force would be regarded as a severe infringement on US interests in the Gulf and that in such case the United States would use all necessary means to defend these interests. The United States could also have moved strong naval forces into the Gulf and conducted joint maneuvers with the Kuwaitis. It seems that this was the limit, but still a realistic policy. Such a policy would have forced Saddam to think twice before he gave his army its invasion order. True, such a policy was rendered extremely difficult to implement in view of the Arab perceptions that Saddam was only trying to improve his political bargaining cards. And the Arab friends of the United States were warning against any precipitate action that might have backfired against US interests in the Gulf by feeding into the popular perception of the United States as an aggressive imperialist power taking advantage of the situation to extend its influence in the region; a proactive policy of this kind would also have undermined the legitimacy of the pro-US regimes in the Middle East that would have been inevitably linked to the action. And as long as Kuwait did not ask for joint maneuvers, the United States could only suggest it.

Finally, it is possible that by not reacting swiftly and strongly to what it considered Iraqi excesses (the use of CW; threats against allies of the United States in the Middle East; support for terrorism; development of a nonconventional arsenal), the United States left the Iraqis with the impression of short-term US indecision and thus left open a window of opportunity. Although very possibly true, at present there is not enough evidence to substantiate such a claim.

Notes

This chapter was written during my fellowship at the Woodrow Wilson International Center for Scholars, Washington, D.C., in 1993 and 1994. Data collection was also helped by research grants from the United States Institute of Peace and the Bertha Von Suttner Special Project for the Optimization of Conflict Resolution. I am indebted to all three for their invaluable assistance. My research assistant, Ms. Debbie Lincoln, made a most important contribution to this article, for which I am grateful.

1. Alan Friedman, *Spider's Web: The Secret History of How the White House Illegally Armed Iraq* (New York: Bantam Books, 1993), p. 282.

2. See, for example, Amatzia Baram, "The Iraqi Invasion of Kuwait: Decision-Making in Baghdad," in Amatzia Baram and Barry Rubin, eds., *Iraq's Road to War* (New York: St. Martin's Press, 1994), pp. 19–22.

3. It must also be remembered that the primary attentions of the Bush administration during this period (1989 to pre-August 1990) were devoted to the dramatic events unfolding in Eastern Europe—with the fall of the Berlin Wall and the end of the superpower cold war—as well as events in China that climaxed in the Tiananmen Square massacre in June 1989. This also happened during the Carter administration in its policy neglect of Iran prior to the 1979 Iranian revolution; its involvement in other events in the region (the 1979 Egyptian-Israeli peace treaty) and in the world (the SALT II negotiations with the USSR and the formal opening of diplomatic relations with China) diverted attention away from the strategic Persian Gulf region.

4. The White House, presidential documents, *Presidential Determination Number 90–7 of January 17, 1990, Application of Export-Import Bank Restrictions in Connection with Iraq,* p. 1.

5. The White House, presidential documents, *Memorandum of Justification for a Waiver of Exim Restrictions with Respect to Iraq,* January 17, 1990.

6. John H. Kelly, Assistant Secretary of State for Near Eastern and South Asian Affairs, *U.S. Relations with Iraq: Statement of Assistant Secretary Kelly Before the Senate Foreign Relations Committee,* May 23, 1990, pp. 2, 5, 10.

7. Richard Murphy, *Statement . . . Before the Sub-committee on Europe and the Middle East, House Foreign Affairs Committee,* October 13, 1988, 100th Cong., 2d sess., p. 17.

8. Pamela Fessler, "Congress' Record on Saddam: Decade of Talk, Not Action," in *Congressional Quarterly,* April 27, 1991, p. 1068; Clyde Mork, *Congress and Iraq,* 1990 (Washington, D.C., Congressional Research Service, January 3, 1992), p. 4.

9. *Wall Street Journal,* July 1, 1988. Unnamed Iraqi diplomat in *al-Anba* (Amman), June 30, 1988, *Foreign Broadcast Information Service Daily Report* (hereinafter *FBIS Daily Report*), July 5, 1988, p. 15. See also *FBIS Daily Report,* June 17 and 21, pp. 25 and 19, respectively, on articles in *al-Thawra* (Baghdad) in June threatening the United States with reprisal if such meetings continued.

10. *al-Thawra,* June 13, 1988, pp. 1, 7.

11. *Boston Globe,* July 26, 1988, p. 6.

12. Fessler, "Congress' Record on Saddam," p. 1071.

13. From Richard W. Murphy to Michael Armacost, *Action Memorandum: U.S. Policy Towards Iraq and CW Use,* September 19, 1988, pp. 1–2.

14. Ibid., p. 4. See also US Department of State, Intelligence and Research (hereinafter INR) to the Secretary of State, *Information Memorandum: U.S.-Iraqi Relations: Implication of Passage of Economic Sanctions Bill,* October 18, 1988, p. 1, pointing out that "Iraq is showing signs of adventurism throughout the Middle East" but warning that "the passage of the Sanctions Bill will undermine relations and reduce US influence on a country that . . . [is] one of the most powerful Arab nations."

15. See, for example, *Mid East Markets* (London), September 19, 1988, pp. 12–14; *Middle East Economic Survey* (Cyprus), September 19, October 3, 1988; *Middle East Economic Digest* (London) (hereinafter MEED), September 23, 1988, p. 18; *Washington Post,* September 9, 1988.

16. Deputy Prime Minister Taha Yasin Ramadan in *al-Thawra,* September 15, *FBIS Daily Report,* September 21, 1988, p. 16. See also Culture and Information Minister Jasim in *Jerusalem Post,* September 11, 1988. The accusations of collusion with Iran were fanned, no doubt, by some conciliatory words that Iran's Majlis Speaker Hasimi Rafsanjani directed toward the United States in late 1988. See, for example, *Iran News Agency* from Tehran, November 25, 1988, *FBIS Daily Report,* September 21, 1988, p. 32.

17. *al-Jumhuriyya* (Baghdad), September 19, 1988, *FBIS Daily Report,* September 22, 1988, p. 15. See also *Iraqi News Agency* (hereinafter INA) from Baghdad, October 24, 1988, *FBIS Daily Report,* October 26, 1988, p. 21; *al-Jumhuriyya,* September 16, 1988, *FBIS Daily Report,* September 20, 1988, p. 21; and see allegations, following US-Syrian discussions on the presidency of Lebanon, that the United States was conniving with Syria to support Iran against Iraq in the Geneva negotiations, *al-Thawra,* October 19, 1988, *FBIS Daily Report,* September 20, 1988, p. 22. For an accusation of US-Israeli collusion against Iraq's missile program designed to deprive Iraq of advanced technology, see INA, April 20, 1989, *FBIS Daily Report,* April 21, 1989, p. 15.

18. *Washington Post,* October 4, 1988. The Iraqis admitted the use of chemical weapons during the war, including in Halabja in March 1988, but they never admitted the use of poison gas after the cease-fire. See an interview with Vice President Taha Muhyi al-Din Ma'ruf in Paris, *Le Monde,* November 10, 1988, in *FBIS Daily Report,* November 10, 1988, p. 24.

19. INA and *Voice of the Masses* from Baghdad, October 29, 30, and 31, 1988, *FBIS Daily Report,* October 31, 1988, p. 30.

20. Baghdad Radio, June 7, 1989, in *FBIS Daily Report,* June 8, 1989, p. 25. See also Fu'ad Matar, *al-Tadamun* (Amman), July 10, 1989, *FBIS Daily Report,* July 26, 1989, pp. 19–22.

21. See an angry Iraqi attack following expressions of such concern by Assistant Secretary of Defense Richard Armitage ("The Arab nation . . . realizes well that Washington

has only been in a hostile Zionist trench"), *al-Thawra,* April 21, *FBIS Daily Report,* April 25, 1989, p.29.

22. US Department of State, *Memorandum for the Secretary: CCC Credit for Iraq,* October 11, 1989, reproduced in US House of Representatives, Committee on Banking, Finance, and Urban Affairs, *The [BNL] Scandal and . . . the [CCC] Program,* 102d Cong., 2d sess., May 21, 1992 (Washington, D.C.), part 1, p. 290 (hereinafter *The BNL Scandal and the CCC Program*).

23. *Alert Report—Iraqi Payments Situation Further Deteriorates,* Export-Import Bank of the U.S.A., Country Risk Analysis Division, January 23, 1989; Exim, *Iraq Country Review Update,* September [?] 1989.

24. Letter from US Department of the Treasury, US Customs Service, Atlanta, Georgia, to Robert L. Barr Jr., US Attorney, Northern District of Georgia, Sept. 21, 1989. Following the exposure of an Iraqi network that tried to smuggle nuclear triggers from the United States, administration officials expressed fears that the BNL funds were also used to procure such triggers. Thomas C. Baxter to Mr. Corrigan, *Office Memorandum: Lavoro,* April 5, 1990.

25. *Memorandum of Conversation: USDA Comments on Investigations of Iraq and the BNL Scandal,* October 13, 1989, p. 2; Letter from Robert Barr, US Attorney, et al., US Department of Justice, to S. Kelly, Federal Reserve Bank, Atlanta, Georgia, January 9, 1990; and see also US Department of State, *Memorandum for the Secretary,* October 11, 1989, also in *The BNL Scandal and the CCC Program,* part 1, p. 290.

26. Cable from the US Secretary of State to the Embassy, Baghdad, *Secretary's October 6 Meeting with Iraqi Foreign Minister Tariq 'Aziz,* October 13, 1989.

27. For US Department of State displeasure at the need to suspend the second tranche of the Commodity Credit Corporation (CCC) program, see, for example, US Department of State, Action Memorandum for the Secretary, *The Iraqi CCC Program,* October 26, 1989; and Glaspie assuring 'Aziz of Baker's hope that the issue "can be resolved quickly," in Letter from Embassy, Baghdad, to Secretary of State, *Tariq 'Aziz's Reply to Secretary's Letter,* October 24, 1989.

28. Letter from Lawrence Eagleburger to John Robson, Deputy Secretary of the Treasury, November 8, 1989, reproduced in *The BNL Scandal and the CCC Program,* part 2, p. 299.

29. Letter from Alan Charles Raul, Office of the General Counsel, Department of Agriculture (USDA), to Stephen I. Danzansky, Deputy Assistant to the President and Director, Office of Cabinet Affairs, The White House, including *Paper, USDA Position on Iraq,* October 30, 1989, reproduced in *The BNL Scandal and the CCC Program,* part 2, p. 239.

30. Cable from Embassy, Baghdad, to Secretary of State, *USDA Team Meetings with GOI Ministry of Trade,* April 22, 1990.

31. From an interview with a senior administration official, Washington, D.C., June 1994.

32. USDA, from Richard T. Crowder, Under Secretary for International Affairs and Commodity Programs et al., *Memorandum for Richard T. McCormack, Under Secretary of State et al., Report of Administrative Review of Iraq GSM Program,* May 16, 1990.

33. Cable from Am[erican] Embassy, Baghdad, [signed Glaspie], to Sec. State, Subject: *Hamilton Sub-Committee,* April 25, 1990.

34. [Under Secretary of State for Political Affairs] Robert Kimmitt to the Secretary, *Note: DC Meeting on Iraq,* April 17, 1990.

35. Cable from Am[erican] Embassy, Baghdad, to Sec. of State, *Iraq Minister of Trade/Finance Discusses USDA GSM Credit Guarantee Program,* July 9, 1990. In fact, apparently to avoid suspicion that they were planning a U turn in their relations with the United States, the Iraqis continued to pay their debt. The last monthly payment of $150 million was deposited on August 1, 1990. Interview with a US Department of Agriculture official, Washington, D.C., April 22, 1994.

36. USDA, Press Secretary, Office of the Secretary, *News: Administrative Review of Iraq GSM–102 Program,* May 21, 1990.

37. Glaspie, American Embassy, Baghdad, to the Sec. of State, *Public Iraqi Gestures Toward the USG,* July 3, 1990.

38. USDA, *Secretary's October 6th Meeting with . . . 'Aziz,* October 13, 1989. After the Kuwait crisis 'Aziz complained that following the Iraqi-Iranian cease-fire US officials started warning the Gulf states that Iraq was dangerous; they started levelling "false accusations" against Iraq of using poison gas against its Kurds; and the CIA started to plot to topple the regime and assassinate Saddam Hussein. 'Aziz to Viorst, *The New Yorker,* June 24, 1991, pp. 64–67; 'Aziz to *Milliyet* (Istanbul), May 30 1991, in *FBIS Daily Report,* June 4, 1991, pp. 13–14; Sa'd Bazzaz, editor of the government daily *al-Jumhuriyya, Harb Talidu Ukhra [War and the One After]* (Amman, 1992–1993), pp. 151–152.

39. From Secretary of State to Embassy, Baghdad, *Message from the Secretary to Tariq 'Aziz,* Oct. 21, 1989.

40. Bazzaz, *War and the One After,* p. 152.

41. From Secretary of State to American Embassy, Baghdad, *Tension in US-Iraqi Relations: Demarche,* April 12, 1990.

42. Interview with a senior US State Department official who dealt for a few years with Iraq during the second half of the 1980s, Washington, D.C., June 28, 1994.

43. Joint Staff, Information Service Center, USCINCCENT Macdill, to Joint Chiefs of Staff, Washington, D.C., *Proposed US-Iraqi Military Initiatives,* November 29, 1989 (in reply to suggestions from American Embassy in Baghdad from June 19, 1989).

44. From Joint Staff, Washington, D.C., to USCINCCENT Macdill. *Proposed US-Iraqi Military Initiatives,* January 3, 1990.

45. The White House, presidential documents, *Memorandum of Justification for a Waiver of Exim Restrictions with Respect to Iraq,* January 17, 1990.

46. *Voice of America,* Washington, D.C., transcript of a broadcast, February 15, 1990.

47. Bazzaz, *War and the One After,* p. 159.

48. Saddam, in his conversation with April Glaspie on July 25, 1990, *New York Times,* July 13, 1991.

49. See report of a conversation between National Security Advisor Brent Scowcroft and Iraqi Ambassador Nizar Hamdun, from the National Advisory Council to Robert Kimmitt, *National Advisory Council Meeting on Iraq CCC Program,* March 5, 1990.

50. See report of conversation from Tariq 'Aziz to Milton Viorst, in *New Yorker,* June 24, 1991, pp. 64–67.

51. Interview with a senior US diplomat, Washington, D.C., June 28, 1994. See also from Secretary of State to American Embassy, Baghdad, *Tension in US-Iraqi Relations: Demarche,* April 12, 1990.

52. Bazzaz, *War and the One After,* pp. 159–160.

53. 'Aziz to Viorst, *New Yorker,* June 24, 1991, pp. 64–67.

54. *New York Times,* July 13, 1991. See also an Iraqi threat in early July that they would not be "passive" in the face of "an anti-Iraqi campaign by . . . certain elements in the U.S. government." The main reason for the Iraqi anger was the discontinuation of the CCC program "reflect[ing] unjustified hostility towards Iraq." Cable from Glaspie, American Embassy in Baghdad, to Secretary of State, *Public Iraqi Gesture Toward the U.S. Government,* July 3, 1990.

55. General H. Norman Schwarzkopf, *It Doesn't Take a Hero* (New York: Bantam Books, 1992), p. 289.

56. 'Aziz to Viorst, *New Yorker,* June 24, 1991, pp. 64–67.

57. Interview with a senior US official, Washington, D.C., 1994.

58. John H. Kelly, *U.S. Relations with Iraq: Statement of Assistant Secretary Kelly Before the Senate Foreign Relations Committee,* May 23, 1990, p. 6.

59. US Department of State, Bureau of Oceans and International Environmental and Scientific Affairs, *Memorandum: SNEC [Subgroup on Nuclear Export Control] Cases of Interest,* November 21, 1989.

60. *Baghdad Radio and TV,* April 2, 1990.

61. 'Aziz to Viorst, *New Yorker,* June 24, 1991, pp. 64–67.

62. Secretary of State to American Embassy, Baghdad, *Tension in US-Iraqi Relations: Demarche,* April 12, 1990.

63. Secretary of State to Embassy, Baghdad, *Chemical Weapons,* April [exact date unmarked], 1990.

64. A. Jock Covey to Robert Kimmitt, *Briefing Memorandum: NSC Deputies Committee Meeting on Iraq,* White House Situation Room, April 16, 1990, p. 5. Interview with a senior US Department of State official, June 28, 1994; and Merrill W. Ruck, Rear Admiral, United States Navy, Assistant Deputy Director, Politico-Military Affairs J–5, and the Joint Staff, *Memorandum for the Record: PCC on Iraq,* April 13, 1990.

65. See the Iraqi version of the meeting, emphasizing Saddam's defiance and the conciliatory aspects of the senators' message. *al-Thawra,* April 17, 1990.

66. Fessler, "Congress' Record on Saddam," p. 1075.

67. Ibid.

68. Glaspie Cable, *Hamilton Subcommittee,* April 25, 1990.

69. John H. Kelly, *U.S. Relations with Iraq: Statement of Assistant Secretary Kelly Before the Senate Foreign Relations Committee,* May 23, 1990, p. 6.

70. Bazzaz, *War and the One After,* p. 23.

71. INA in Arabic, May 30, 1990, 12:50 p.m.

72. The speech was made on May 30, 1990, but it was broadcast only after the Iraqi-Kuwaiti dispute came out in the open on July 18, 1990. See Baghdad Radio, July 18, in FBIS, July 19, 1990, p. 21.

73. See, for example, Kelly's statement before the Senate Foreign Relations Committee, *U.S. Relations with Iraq,* May 23, 1990.

74. A. Jock Covey to Robert Kimmitt, *Briefing Memorandum: NSC Deputies Committee Meeting on Iraq,* April 16, 1990, p. 2.

75. Ibid., pp. 1ff; J. G. Mullins to W. S. Broomfield, [exact date not marked] April 1990; Kelly's statement before the Senate Foreign Relations Committee, *U.S. Relations with Iraq,* May 23, 1990; Memo from Richard Clarke to the Acting Secretary [of State Lawrence Eagleburger], *Action Memorandum, Export of Manufacturing Oven to Iraq,* July

18, 1990; Richard Murphy, *Statement . . . Before the Subcommittee on Europe and the Middle East, House Foreign Affairs Committee,* October 13, 1988, p. 18.

76. Interview with a former US Department of Defense official, Washington, D.C., July 21, 1994.

77. Ibid.

78. Bazzaz, *War and the One After,* pp. 24, 36.

79. Bazzaz, *War and the One After,* pp. 39–45. Tariq 'Aziz, speaking on Baghdad Radio, July 18, 1990, in *FBIS-Near East,* July 18, 1990, p. 23.

80. Bazzaz, *War and the One After,* pp. 24, 36.

81. Tom Gallagher, CDR, US Navy, J–5, MEAF, X–49336 (Joint Staff), *Position Paper: Heightened Tension Between Iraq-Kuwait-UAE,* prepared for [Under Secretary of Defense for Policy Paul] Wolfowitz, July 25, 1990.

82. For the Iraqi version of this conversation, see *Meeting Between President Saddam Husayn and American Charge d'Affaires Wilson on 6 August, 1990,* newsletter, Iraqi Embassy, Washington, D.C. (September 1990).

83. For the first version, see Saddam's meeting with the Dole delegation, *al Thawra,* April 17, 1990. For the "Arab" version, see, for example, General Muzahim Sa'b Hasan, Air Force Commander, Radio Monte Carlo, April 22, *FBIS Daily Report,* April 23, 1990, p. 13; Saddam, in a speech to a rally, Baghdad Radio, June 18, 1990, FBIS-NES, June 19, 1990, p. 21.

84. Glaspie Cable, *Hamilton Subcommittee,* April 25, 1990.

85. From Sec[retary of] State to Am[erican]Embassy, Baghdad, *Demarche on Abu 'Abbas,* June 20, 1990. See also from NEA and Secretary of State to American Embassy, Baghdad, *Congressional Questions for the Record,* June 21, 1990; from Secretary of State, to American Embassy, Baghdad, *Demarche on Abu 'Abbas,* June 23, 1990.

86. From Sec[retary of] State to Embassy in Baghdad et al., *Iraq and Terrorism,* June 27, 1990.

87. From Maurice D. Busby to Robert M. Kimmitt, *Information Memorandum: The Terrorist Threat from Iraq,* August 7, 1990.

88. From Katherine Shirley and John Kelly to the Acting Secretary, *Action Memorandum: Returning Iraq to the Terrorism List,* September 1, 1990.

89. Bazzaz, *War and the One After,* p. 24.

90. Colonel Gary W. Nelson, USA J–5 MEAF, *Information Paper: Iraqi Threats to Kuwait,* July 20, 1990.

91. From SSODIA/JSI–6, to SSOAU and others, *item #00407725,* July 25, 1990, 02:05.

92. Elaine Sciolino, *New York Times,* September 23, 1990, p. 18; Bob Woodward, *The Commanders* (New York: Simon & Schuster, 1991), pp. 213–215.

93. Interview with a Gulf Arab diplomat, Washington, D.C., June 15, 1994.

94. See report of the US press in *Haaretz,* July 19, 1990.

95. See US Department of State cables to US embassies in the Middle East as reproduced in *New York Times,* March 21, 1990.

96. *Washington Post,* October 21, 1992, quoting parts of the cable.

97. Glaspie Cable, *Hamilton Subcommittee,* April 25, 1990.

98. Bazzaz, *War and the One After,* pp. 23–38.

99. Saddam Hussein's interview with *Hurriyet,* February 10, 1992, in FBIS, February 13, 1992, pp. 22–23.

100. *New York Times,* April 5, 1992; *Washington Post,* October 21, 1992.

101. *New York Times,* September 23, 1990, p. 18.

102. See Amatzia Baram, "The Iraqi Invasion of Kuwait: Decision-making in Baghdad," in Amatzia Baram and Barry Rubin, eds., *Iraq's Road to War* (New York, St. Martin's Press, 1994), p. 18.

103. Bazzaz, *War and the One After,* p. 26. See also a detailed report of the reasons why Qasim failed, by the commander of Qasim's force assigned to storm Kuwait, Major General (retired) Khalil Sa'id, *al-Thawra,* August 21, 1992.

19

From "Over the Horizon" to "Into the Backyard"

The US-Saudi Relationship in the Gulf

F. Gregory Gause III

Operations Desert Shield and Desert Storm represented a turning point in the close but complicated relationship between the Kingdom of Saudi Arabia and the United States. Although the Saudis had relied on US security guarantees as an essential element of their defense policy since the 1940s, they had, at least since the 1960s, preferred to play down the military aspect of US-Saudi relations to their own public and to regional audiences in the larger Arab and Muslim worlds. And though the rulers of the kingdom did call on US military assistance in times of crisis previous to the Iraqi invasion of Kuwait, that assistance was largely limited to air and naval forces. Never before had US ground troops in such numbers been stationed in the kingdom. Never before was the Saudi regime confronted with such a stark choice in terms of declaring its ultimate reliance on the United States for its security.

This chapter sets out the essential dilemma faced by the Saudis in the security realm, explaining why the regime must rely on outside power protectors when faced with a direct threat from larger regional neighbors, despite the problems such a choice poses. It then briefly reviews the history of the US-Saudi security relationship, highlighting the tensions Riyadh has experienced in trying to maintain its defense links to Washington while asserting, for domestic and regional audiences, its independence from the United States. The background of the Saudi decision to invite US and other forces into the kingdom after Saddam Hussein's invasion of Kuwait is then discussed, along with developments in the US-Saudi relationship since the war and the potential consequences of those developments for the regime.[1]

The Saudi Defense Dilemma

The defense policy dilemma faced by the Saudi regime is the direct product of the country's oil wealth and the political strategy the regime has chosen for using that wealth. Oil makes the kingdom important to the rest of the world, but oil wealth also increases its vulnerability in a number of important ways. Most obviously, it makes Saudi Arabia a potential target for larger ambitious neighbors, as the Iraqi invasion of Kuwait clearly demonstrated. On a deeper and less obvious level, the characteristics that oil wealth has brought to domestic politics exacerbate Saudi security problems. The Saudi regime's ability to mobilize its population for defense is limited by the ethos of the particular type of rentier state the kingdom has become. Demands by the state upon citizens, like military service, are avoided because such demands could bring forth pressures for citizens to have a say in state policy. The Saudi population, small relative to potentially threatening neighbors, already complicates defense planning. Inability to utilize fully the human resources that exist compounds those complications.

A strategy of self-reliance for defense and security is both inadequate and politically troublesome for Saudi Arabia. The inadequacy of self-reliance is to some extent a simple matter of numbers. According to the 1992 census, the Saudi population was 16.9 million, of which 12.3 million were citizens.[2] Since that time, the citizen population has increased to more than 20 million. Iran's population is nearly 70 million. But numbers are not the whole story. The Saudi population is, by these statistics, not that much smaller than Iraq's. The combined population of the members of the Gulf Cooperation Council (GCC) is very close to that of Iraq. Despite the demographics, no one in 1990 suggested that the Saudis by themselves or with their GCC allies could confront the Iraqi invasion of Kuwait.

It is the political context of the states that renders a policy of self-reliance even less feasible than the numbers suggest. The mobilization of citizen manpower into the armed forces would require obligatory military service, a very real demand of the state upon its citizens (one the United States, for example, has now chosen to avoid). A ruthless and efficient authoritarian state like Iraq or Syria can extract a large proportion of its manpower from society for military purposes. States animated by revolutionary fervor, like Iran in the 1980s, or by democratic ties of loyalty between citizen and state, like Israel (for its Jewish citizens), can call upon the population for military service and receive enthusiastic answers. Saudi Arabia (and the other Gulf monarchies) lacks these kinds of mobilization abilities.

This is attributable to the type of rentier state the Saudis have chosen to build with their oil money. The Saudi "social contract" as it has developed since the early 1970s, if not before, rests upon the provision of benefits *to* citizens, not the extraction of resources (taxes and service) *from* them. Instituting a national service requirement would upset that implicit deal between state and society. In the West, the need to mobilize citizen armies contributed to pressures for popular participation in government. The ruling families in the Gulf want to avoid exacerbating the already growing demands in their societies for greater participation. Moreover, from the perspective of rulers who remember the prevalence of Arab military coups in the 1950s and 1960s, recruiting into the armed forces people whose loyalties to the regime are questionable would decrease rather than increase security.

Military recruitment strategies in the kingdom reflect these social realities. There is no military draft in Saudi Arabia; military service is voluntary. Discussions in official Saudi circles immediately after the Gulf war about doubling the size of the armed forces, which would probably entail some kind of draft or obligatory service, were shelved.[3] Military service is not among the top professions in the country in terms of social status. With economic opportunities relatively plentiful for better-educated, young, male citizens, the incentives to join the military are limited.

Moreover, there are official and unofficial barriers to military recruitment of some groups within the kingdom. Saudi Shi'a (who make up approximately 10 percent of the Saudi citizen population) rarely join the military and even more rarely advance in the officer corps, a result of government discouragement and social custom within the community.[4] There are persistent reports, unconfirmed and unconfirmable officially, that those who do not hail from Najd (Central Arabia) cannot advance in the military hierarchy and are barred from certain sensitive positions (like that of fighter pilot). Needless to say, one-half of Saudi Arabia's human resources—female citizens—are not available for military service. Taken together, these factors mean that the kingdom cannot and will not mobilize human resources for military purposes with the same efficiency as larger neighbors. Demographic, social, and political constraints combine to rule out a policy of self-reliance in security matters.

A simple comparison of Saudi Arabia to other regional powers as to the size of armed forces relative to population points out the barriers to military mobilization. In 1990 the Saudi armed forces, including active-duty National Guard forces, totaled 111,500. Iraq, with less than double the Saudi citizen population, had a military establishment at least five times as large in 1990. Syria, with roughly the same population (only 2 million greater) had a standing armed force of over 400,000 in 1991. Jordan, with less than one-half of the Saudi citizen population, had an active force of 101,000 in 1991, nearly the same size as the Saudi forces. Israel, also with less than one-half of the Saudi citizen population, had a standing force of 141,000 and a reserve force of over 500,000 in 1991.[5]

The political and demographic barriers to full utilization of the military manpower resources in the kingdom, combined with the number of potential military threats in the region, dictate that the Saudis seek outside allies. It is logical, in such a situation, that a small state should seek the most powerful ally it can in order to deter potential enemies—and win a fight, if necessary. Thus, the US-Saudi security relationship makes much sense for Riyadh. But because the nature of the security threats facing the Saudi regime are not limited to military invasion by a larger neighbor, the relationship with the United States becomes more complicated.

The lack of firm, institutionalized political links between the Saudi regime and its society opens up a new set of threats in the foreign policy sphere. It is not just military attack that the Saudi regime worries about; it also fears *political* intervention originating from abroad, based on the powerful transnational ideological platforms of pan-Arabism and Islam, aimed at stirring up its own domestic populations against it. A succession of ambitious regional figures have used propaganda and subversion, as well as military pressure, against the kingdom: Gamal 'Abd al-Nasser of Egypt in the 1950s and 1960s, Ayatollah Khomeini in the 1980s, and Saddam Hussein in 1990–1991. None of these challengers succeeded in bringing down the Saudi regime, but they all left their mark on the minds of rulers. The irony is that, having built substantial bureaucratic and coercive infrastructures, the Saudi regime is less susceptible today to this kind of foreign ideological pressure than it may have been in the past. Citizens' interests are much more focused on domestic agendas rather than on glorious but impractical transnational agendas. But it is difficult for the rulers to appreciate this change when little, if any, citizen input into the foreign policy decisionmaking process is tolerated.

Close ties with the United States open up the Saudi regime to attacks by regional enemies. Charges that the rulers have forfeited the country's independence in exchange for US protection have been staples of Arab propaganda since the 1950s. Such charges are aimed at encouraging the Saudi population to oppose the regime and shake its stability domestically. As will be discussed later, the US connection in the military sphere is disquieting to at least some part of the Saudi public, so these kinds of charges are seen by the Saudi rulers as having some potential to create domestic problems for them. This is the Saudi dilemma when it comes to relations with the United States: Military security rationales require the US link, while domestic security imperatives require that the link be as unobtrusive as possible. Walking this tightrope has not been an easy task for the Saudis.

The Background to the US-Saudi Security Relationship

US interests in Saudi Arabia began in 1933, with the granting by King 'Abd al-'Aziz of an oil concession to Standard Oil of California (SOCAL). Although SOCAL gave the king better terms than he could expect from British Petroleum, then awash with oil from Iran and Iraq, there was also a strategic element in the Saudi decision to grant the concession to a US company. Britain was the patron of the Hashemite regimes in Jordan and Iraq, rivals of the Al Sa'ud whom 'Abd al-'Aziz had ejected from Hijaz less than a decade previously. Britain was also the protecting power of the smaller Gulf and South Arabian states and directly ruled Aden. With the exception of Yemen, Saudi Arabia was surrounded in the 1930s by British power. And though 'Abd al-'Aziz was careful to maintain friendly relations with London (risking civil war in the late 1920s to stop raids by his "fanatical" Wahhabi followers, the Ikhwan, into Iraq and Transjordan), he also sought the support of other outside powers to balance British influence. Thus, his desire for some political connection to the United States is understandable.

Washington was hesitant at the beginning to respond to Saudi political overtures. It was not until World War II that US policymakers began to perceive strategic interests in the Gulf area. Even then, the region was viewed largely as a British
preserve in the global division of influence between Washington and London. In
1942 and 1943, the United States supplied lend-lease financial aid to the kingdom,
whose two main sources of revenue—oil production and pilgrimage traffic—had
been severely curtailed by the war; it did so not directly but through Great Britain.
It was only in 1944 that US aid began to go directly to Riyadh, in exchange for the
rights to use the large air base at Dhahran. The historic meeting of King 'Abd al-
'Aziz and President Franklin Roosevelt on the latter's yacht in the Great Bitter Lake
of the Suez Canal in 1945 was the first direct contact between leaders of the two
countries.

Despite this new channel, the United States continued in the late 1940s to resist
Saudi requests for a direct military alliance, which the Saudis wanted to counter the
British-backed Hashemites. Although the United States sent numerous messages to
Riyadh supporting the independence and the territorial integrity of the kingdom, a
formal alliance was ruled out. The most the United States was willing to offer in
terms of a military relationship was the supply of some equipment and the dispatch
of a training mission in 1951, in exchange for a five-year extension of the Dhahran
base rights.[6]

Even though the United States was reluctant to make a formal alliance commitment to Saudi security at this time, Washington was hardly indifferent to the kingdom. The importance of oil as a strategic commodity was underlined by the World
War II experience, and US economic and military planners began to see the Gulf as
a centrally important area in overall US strategy. Although the ambitious plans of
Harold Ickes to, in effect, nationalize US oil interests in the kingdom during the
war fell afoul of congressional and oil company opposition, Washington sought to
cement its economic relationship with Riyadh after the war by encouraging the US
oil consortium that formed the Arabian-American Oil Company (ARAMCO) to
provide more financial support to the Saudi regime. By granting the oil companies
the right to deduct from their US taxes the increased share of oil revenues they paid
to the Saudis, Washington in effect subsidized the Saudi regime, allowing the oil
companies to pay 50 percent of their oil revenues from the kingdom to Riyadh
without affecting their bottom line. The "50–50" deal, originally implemented in
Venezuela, was applied to Saudi Arabia in 1950.[7]

In the 1950s, one began to see a reversal of the pattern of Saudi desire for a close
US security relationship and US reticence to give formal defense commitments. US
military supplies to the kingdom during the 1950s were substantial (though not in
comparison to what would come later)—well over one hundred tanks of various
types and thirty-seven aircraft.[8] King Sa'ud was the first Arab leader to be received
in the White House after the announcement of the 1957 Eisenhower Doctrine,
which was aimed at containing communism in the Middle East.[9] However, the
costs to Saudi Arabia in terms of regional and domestic politics of the close relationship with the United States became more apparent as the 1960s approached. The

fall of monarchical regimes in Egypt and Iraq, in part because of domestic reactions to their close associations with Britain and British bases in those countries, brought home to the Saudis that an outside power link was not an unmitigated blessing. The pressures that built up around the rise of Gamal 'Abd al-Nasser and his brand of Arab nationalism in regional politics made association with Western powers a domestic and regional liability.

Thus, the dilemma for the Saudi leadership became acute. Just at the time when the US link became important for military security, its political ramifications became very negative. The Saudi regime walked the tightrope. Military purchases from the United States were in essence halted from 1958 to the mid-1960s, as identification with the United States became more dangerous and the regular army came to be seen as a threat to the domestic security of the regime. The lease on the US air base at Dhahran was allowed to run out without renewal in 1962 (its military usefulness to the United States for cold war purposes was much diminished with the advent of intercontinental and sea-launched ballistic missiles). However, when Egyptian air units in Yemen began to attack areas across the Saudi-Yemeni border in 1962, the Saudis requested that US fighter planes stationed at Dhahran fly demonstrative sorties over Saudi cities as a warning to Cairo.[10] In 1965 the US military supply relationship with Saudi Arabia was renewed with the supply of Hawk anti-aircraft systems.

Events in the late 1960s combined to increase US military interest in Saudi Arabia and to lessen Saudi fears of the domestic and regional consequences of their US tie. The announcement of British intent to withdraw from relationships with the smaller Gulf monarchies increased the US strategic interest in the Gulf. Still mired in Vietnam, the United States had no intention of taking on new defense commitments in any formal way in the Gulf, but US strategy was aimed at encouraging Iran, and to a lesser extent Saudi Arabia, to build up military forces (with US weaponry) and act as regional proxies for US interests. With increasing oil revenues in the early 1970s (before the price shock of 1973), Saudi Arabia's weapons purchases from the United States increased from $15.8 million in 1970 to $312.4 million in 1972.[11] With Egypt's defeat in the 1967 Arab-Israeli war and the concomitant decline in importance of Nasserist pan-Arabism in the region, the political risks of association with the United States went down. Yet, this is exactly the time that Saudi Arabia asserted its independence from the United States, in a most public and risky manner—the oil embargo and oil price increases of 1973–1974. In the minds of many Saudis, risking confrontation with the United States over Arab-Israeli issues at that time was their country's finest hour.

This brief period of confrontation with the United States quickly ended. The fourfold increase in oil prices made Saudi Arabia that much more central to US policymakers and made the United States that much more important to Saudi Arabia economically, both as a consumer of oil and as a location for Saudi investments. The new oil wealth deepened the Saudi linkages to the United States. In the military sphere Riyadh directed the vast majority of its arms spending toward the United States. US training missions instructed Saudi forces in the new weaponry. The US

Army Corps of Engineers undertook enormous building projects in the kingdom. As Saudi Arabia was now a more valuable prize, its need for an outside protector increased. In January 1979, as the Iranian revolution was unfolding, the Saudis requested a display of military support from the United States, which complied by sending a squadron of F-15s to the kingdom (though it was publicly announced that the planes would not be armed in order not to irritate the new Iranian government).[12] In October 1980, at the outbreak of the Iran-Iraq war, US AWACS (airborne warning and control system) aircraft were dispatched to the kingdom to strengthen its air defenses. Finally, with Iranian attacks on Saudi and Kuwaiti shipping growing in the 1980s, US naval forces were sent to the Gulf in 1987 to protect that shipping. Though the original request came from Kuwait, the US forces also escorted shipping bound for Saudi Arabia.

In the financial sphere, Saudi petrodollars were recycled through US (and British) banks, the Saudi government became a major purchaser of US Treasury bonds, and Saudi private wealth found investment opportunities in the United States. At an April 1993 meeting in Washington on US-Gulf business links, sponsored by the US Department of Commerce, the GCC, and the American-Gulf Chamber of Commerce, it was reported that direct Gulf investment in the United States totaled $407 billion as of the beginning of 1992.[13] As oil prices were (and still are) denominated in US dollars, the real return to Saudi Arabia of its oil sales depended on the strength of the US currency. The sinews binding the United States and the Saudi regime became stronger and more ramified as a result of the oil price increases of the 1970s.

Yet the dilemma for Saudi policymakers of the domestic and regional consequences of a close relationship, at least publicly, with the United States remained. Whereas Arab nationalist pressures might have declined in the region, the Islamic political resurgence, represented in part by the Iranian revolution, was equally hostile to a US military presence in the kingdom and equally able to address Saudi citizens over the head of their government. The Saudis would not support the Camp David accords, despite heavy US pressure to do so. When Reagan administration officials came calling in Riyadh at the beginning of 1981 to encourage Saudi Arabia to sign up for Secretary of State Alexander Haig's "strategic consensus" policy for the Middle East, with its emphasis on US military access to regional bases, the Saudis politely refused. The GCC, of which Saudi Arabia is the largest and most important member, in its first summit meeting in May 1981 declared member states' desire "for keeping the entire region free of international conflicts, particularly the presence of military fleets and foreign bases."[14] Even as the US Navy was escorting Saudi shipping in the Gulf in 1987–1988, the Saudis were very concerned to emphasize that US forces had no basing rights in the kingdom. For the Saudis, a US presence "over the horizon," close enough to come to the kingdom's aid but far away enough to avoid the political problems associated with the US connection, was the ideal situation.

This dilemma of needing the United States in the security sphere but fearing the domestic and regional consequences of public identification with the United States forms the backdrop to the Saudi decision to invite US and other foreign forces into the kingdom in early August 1990.

The US-Saudi Relationship and the Gulf War

The Saudi decision to invite hundreds of thousands of US troops, as well as other foreign units, to the kingdom was a major change in the nature of the US-Saudi relationship. It can only be understood in light of the existing relationship between Saudi Arabia and Iraq. Riyadh had supported the Iraqi war effort against Iran politically and financially. Since the end of that war in 1988, the Saudis had been unable to resume their preferred geopolitical position of rough equidistance between the two larger Gulf powers. Ideological differences with Iran remained a serious stumbling block. Although there was certainly no love in Riyadh for Saddam Hussein, there was a continuing belief that a strong Iraq was necessary to balance Iranian ambitions.

Thus, Saudi Arabia's initial response when Iraq began to raise demands against Kuwait in the summer of 1990 was to seek a negotiated settlement that would give the Iraqis some tangible gains. The Saudis were noticeably silent when Baghdad threatened Kuwait on the issue of Kuwaiti oil production, in some measure because they themselves wanted to see Kuwait abide by its OPEC production quota (OPEC being the Organization of Petroleum Exporting Countries). At the OPEC meeting of July 25–27, 1990, Kuwait agreed to cut its production to the quota level. When Iraq continued to pressure Kuwait, the Saudis and Egyptian President Hosni Mubarak joined in a mediation effort in late July that resulted in the Kuwaiti-Iraqi meeting of August 1 in the Saudi city of Jeddah, just one day before the invasion.

Circumstantial evidence indicates that although there was no detailed Saudi-Egyptian plan put forward to the parties at Jeddah, the thrust behind their mediation effort was to extract some concessions from Kuwait to mollify Saddam. Egyptian President Hosni Mubarak revealed after the invasion that he had told the Kuwaitis that they should make an offer including border modifications and financial aid to Iraq.[15] Saudi decisionmakers have not been as revealing about their stance in those days, but there are indications that Riyadh had about the same idea. The Saudis had pressured Kuwait before the invasion to reduce their oil production to their OPEC quota, as Saddam had demanded.[16] Crown Prince Hassan of Jordan told an interviewer that on August 2, King Fahd had asked King Hussein of Jordan to get the Iraqis "to withdraw to the disputed area" on the border, not completely out of Kuwait.[17] Yemeni President 'Ali 'Abdallah Salih said that on August 5 King Fahd had told him that Kuwait had been mistaken in its hard-line policy toward Iraq.[18]

Comments by Saudi Defense Minister Prince Sultan ibn 'Abd al-'Aziz in late October 1990 also give some hint as to the Saudi stand. Prince Sultan, after assuring that Saudi Arabia would not accept any solution short of unconditional Iraqi withdrawal from Kuwait and the return of the Kuwaiti government, referred to the general Saudi position on how to settle inter-Arab problems. He said that "any

Arab who has a right vis-à-vis his brother Arab must assert it, but not by means of using force. This is an undesirable thing." He indicated that Saudi Arabia "is among those who call for Arab national security, including brotherly concessions from Arab to Arab, whether such a right is established or more doubtful." He went on to say that "it is not a bad thing for any Arab country to give a brother Arab country land, or money, or access to the sea."[19] The Western press saw Sultan's remarks as a signal of Saudi willingness to compromise with Iraq.[20] However, given that the quote came directly after Sultan's direct refusal to accept anything but an unconditional Iraqi withdrawal from Kuwait, it might be more accurate to interpret his remarks as an indication of what Saudi policy was *before* the invasion, defending Saudi efforts at avoiding this crisis and indirectly criticizing the Kuwaitis for refusing to compromise.

The Saudis' sense of shock and betrayal at the Iraqi invasion reflected not only the unprecedented nature of the action but also the feeling that Saddam had reneged on a tentative agreement that the Saudis had constructed for his benefit.[21] Their perception of Saddam's ultimate intentions must have been colored by this very specific sense that the Iraqi leader could not be trusted to keep his commitments. Little else can explain the relatively quick decision by the Saudis to abandon their historical position regarding US ground forces. Although much has been made of the two-day delay in making this decision and of the hints of differences of opinion within the Saudi royal family over it, more striking is the ease with which the Saudis reversed their past aversion to an open US military presence in the kingdom and the lack of substantial opposition within the ruling elite to that policy. Even if some members of the royal family were unhappy with the decision, they did not make a public or even a quasi-public issue out of their objections. The religious establishment, which might also have been expected to oppose the deployment of US troops, officially approved the policy in a *fatwa* (religious judgment) by Shaykh 'Abdallah bin 'Abd al-'Aziz bin Baz, the senior cleric in the kingdom.[22]

Once they accepted the US military presence, the Saudis were in effect committed to the US strategy of confrontation with Saddam. Between mid-August 1990 and late February 1991 Saudi Arabia took a back seat to US political and military leaders in the crisis. During this period the regime used its propaganda organs, diplomatic weight, and financial clout to garner support within the Arab and Muslim worlds for its policy. Although attracting considerable political and some military support from other governments in the region, the regime's efforts to persuade Arab and Muslim public opinions of the legitimacy of the decision met with much less success.

As the crisis proceeded, and particularly in the postcrisis period, some of the old reservations about a high-profile US military presence in the kingdom began to resurface. In late November 1990, King Fahd, in a speech to the country, denied that Saudi Arabia had made any agreements for the permanent stationing of foreign forces in the kingdom.[23] In a statement to the press immediately after the Gulf war, Saudi Defense Minister Prince Sultan referred to a commitment on the part of the United States to withdraw its forces from the kingdom once their mission was completed.[24] In September 1991, during one of the US confrontations with Iraq over application of the United Nations (UN) resolutions, Prince Sultan expressed misgivings about the very public way in which the United States was using Saudi Arabia as a military staging area against Iraq and urged Washington to spread its deployments out to Kuwait and even to capture an airfield in Iraq itself to use as a base.[25] During subsequent US-Iraqi confrontations in October 1994 and September 1996, Sultan reiterated his reluctance to allow the United States to use Saudi facilities to stage attacks on Iraq.[26] Saudi Arabia, unlike the smaller Gulf monarchies, did not negotiate a formal defense agreement with the United States in the wake of the war.[27]

The continuing worry in the Saudi regime about limiting to the greatest extent possible the public profile of its US military connection stems from fears about the domestic consequences of that connection. It is within Islamic political currents in the kingdom that disquiet about the role of the United States is greatest. During the crisis there were some indications of discontent within religious circles about the US military presence, but manifestations of that discontent were limited.[28] After the Gulf war, indications of unease from Islamic political circles over the new relationship between the kingdom and the United States emerged more clearly. In the spring of 1991, over 400 religious officials and political activists addressed a petition to King Fahd regarding changes they wanted to see in the kingdom's policies. Although the bulk of the petition dealt with domestic issues, the signers also called on the government to avoid alliances that run counter to Islamic legitimacy and to acquire arms from a variety of sources, including the building of a domestic arms industry.[29] Both of these statements could be read as a warning about overreliance on the United States.

The clearest indication of opposition to the direction of US-Saudi relations came in a detailed, forty-six page Memorandum of Advice directed to the king in the summer of 1992 and signed by more than one hundred Islamic political activists. The bulk of the memorandum, like the shorter petition mentioned above, dealt with domestic affairs. It did, however, in much clearer terms than the other petition, challenge the foreign policy lines set down by the kingdom in the wake of the Gulf war. It called for an end to the practice of giving loans and gifts to what it termed "un-Islamic" regimes like "Ba'thist Syria and secular Egypt," pointing to the folly of funding Saddam's Iraq during its war with Iran. It said that the Gulf crisis pointed out the "lack of correspondence between the enormous military budgets and the number and capabilities of the forces" and called for expanding the army to 500,000 men (an increase of at least 400 percent), obligatory military training, the diversification of foreign arms sources, and the building of a domestic arms industry. The signers criticized the government for not supporting Islamic movements but rather providing aid to states that "wage war" against such movements, like Algeria, and called for a strengthening of relations with all Islamic tendencies, be they states, political movements, or individuals.

The signers of the memorandum were very leery of the close relations the government had with Western regimes, "which lead the assault against Islam," and particularly in "following the United States of America in most policies, relations and decisions, like the rushing into the peace process with the Jews." It urged the government to "avoid any kind of alliance or cooperation which serves imperialist goals" and to "cancel all military treaties and conventions which impinge on the sovereignty of the state and its independence in administering and arming its military." The memorandum was particularly scathing regarding the kingdom's reliance on arms supplies from the United States, a country that "gives us what it wants, denies us what it does not want us to have, exploits us in times of trouble, and bargains with us during times of calamity."[30]

In November 1995, a bomb destroyed the Riyadh office of the American training mission working with the Saudi National Guard. Five Americans and two Indian employees of the mission were killed. Four Saudis were arrested for the bombing and confessed on television to being members of the Islamic opposition. They were executed in May 1996.[31] Less than one month later, in June 1996, a car bomb exploded in front of an apartment building housing US Air Force personnel in Dhahran (in Saudi Arabia's Eastern Province). Nineteen Americans died and nearly 400 Americans, Saudis, and others were wounded. As of February 2006, there have been no convictions either in Saudi Arabia or the United States of the perpetrators of the Dhahran bombing. The American personnel, most of whom were involved in maintaining air reconnaissance of the "no-fly zone" in southern Iraq, were subsequently moved from Dhahran to an isolated desert air base south of Riyadh.[32]

These indications of domestic opposition to a high-profile US role in Saudi security plans, as well as the current indications that the regime wants to avoid inflaming that opposition, should not obscure the fact that the US-Saudi security relationship since Desert Storm has been extremely close. Between August 1990 and the end of 1992 Saudi Arabia placed weapons orders worth more than $25 billion with US arms manufacturers.[33] The centrality of Saudi arms purchases for US suppliers was made clear in the January 1994 agreement between Riyadh and five of the largest US military contractors, allowing the Saudis to stretch out payments for many of those weapons.[34] Falling oil prices and the depletion of financial reserves during Desert Storm placed fiscal constraints on the Saudi government in the 1990s, but it remained the most important foreign customer for US weapons manufacturers during that decade. Military consultations between the two countries continue at the highest levels.[35] The continuing economic importance of the kingdom for the United States was underlined by the Saudi decision in February 1994 to buy $6 billion in commercial aircraft from US rather than European companies. President Bill Clinton personally lobbied Saudi leaders, including King Fahd, on the issue.[36]

Conclusion: The Post–September 11 Relationship

Even after the experience of the Gulf war, the dilemma that characterizes Saudi relations with the United States remains. The need for a US security link is clear. Much of the reluctance to acknowledge that need before the Saudi public and the region has disappeared. Yet the Saudi leadership continues to feel at least somewhat constrained by important elements of domestic public opinion in codifying that relationship in an open military alliance or in formally and publicly permitting US military bases in the kingdom. This tension in US-Saudi relations predates Desert Storm and continues despite that extraordinary phase in the history of security ties between Washington and Riyadh. It is a permanent part of the relationship.

The permanence of this tension was underlined by the fallout for US-Saudi relations from the terrorist attacks on New York and Washington on September 11, 2001. The involvement of so many Saudis in that operation—Osama bin Laden, although stripped of his citizenship in 1994, comes from a prominent Saudi family, and fifteen of the nineteen hijackers were from the kingdom—led many in the United States to question Saudi political stability and reliability as an ally. The fact that bin Laden made his opposition to the US military presence in Saudi Arabia a centerpiece of his propaganda unnerved the Saudi rulers. They knew this issue resonated with their public. Thus, at a time when the United States expected full and open cooperation from all its allies, Saudi Arabia sought to put some public distance between itself and Washington, denying the United States use of Saudi bases for military strikes on Afghanistan.[37] Tensions rose as the media in both countries traded hostile barbs. The Iraq war of 2003 changed the strategic picture in the Gulf region, removing Washington's need to maintain substantial air force units in Saudi Arabia. In April 2003, the United States announced that it would withdraw the air force unit that had been stationed in the kingdom since the end of the Gulf war. As of July 2006, only small American military training missions remained in Saudi Arabia.

Despite those tensions, substantial Saudi-US cooperation occurred in the aftermath of September 11, including Saudi permission for the United States to coordinate the air wars over both Afghanistan in 2001 and Iraq in 2003 from a command and control center in Saudi Arabia. American special forces were also permitted to use Saudi territory as a base for operations in Iraq, though the Saudi government kept this fact from its public. Both governments insisted that the bilateral relationship remained strong, and by 2006 there were numerous indications that the crisis in the relationship produced by the September 11 attacks had passed. However, the tensions and mutual suspicions generated by this crisis reflect the continuing difficulties the Saudi rulers face regarding overt and public military cooperation with the United States.

Notes

1. Much of the material in this chapter is culled from previous work the author has done on security and political issues in the Gulf area. See F. Gregory Gause III, *Oil Monarchies: Domestic and Security Challenges in the Arab Gulf States* (New York: Council on Foreign Relations Press, 1994); "Saudi Arabia: Desert Storm and After," in *The Middle East After Iraq's Invasion of Kuwait,* ed. Robert O. Freedman (Gainesville: University Press of Florida, 1993); and "Gulf Regional Politics: Revolution, War, and Rivalry," in *Dynamics of Regional Politics: Four Systems on the Indian Ocean Rim,* ed. W. Howard Wriggins (New York: Columbia University Press, 1992).

2. Results of the Saudi census were reported in *New York Times,* December 18, 1992, p. A8. The demographic analysis firm of Birks Sinclair and Associates, publisher of the *Gulf Market Report* with long experience in the region, estimated the 1992 Saudi population to be 12.3 million, of whom 8.1 million were citizens. The Birks Sinclair estimate was cited by Roger Hardy, *Arabia After the Storm: Internal Stability of the Gulf Arab States* (London: Middle East Programme Report, Royal Institute for International Affairs, 1992).

3. See *New York Times,* October 13, 1991, pp. 1, 18; October 25, 1991, p. A9, for references to the Saudi proposals. Since that time there have been no moves to expand the size of the Saudi military.

4. Leaders of the Saudi Shi'a community addressed a petition to King Fahd in 1991. In it they complained of a "quarantine" against the entrance of Saudi Shi'a into the armed forces. Practically identical versions of this petition can be found in *Makka News,* no. 7, April 6, 1991, and in *Arabia Monitor* 1, no. 6 (July 1992). The former is published by the Organization of the Islamic Revolution in the Arabian Peninsula, an Iranian-supported exile group with a US post office box in Bowling Green, Kentucky. The latter is a monthly newsletter published in Washington by the International Committee for Human Rights in the Gulf and Arabian Peninsula. Both have apparently stopped publication as a result of an agreement between the Saudi government and Saudi Shi'a activists in late 1993. *Washington Post,* October 16, 1993, p. A15; *New York Times,* October 29, 1993, p. A11.

5. Figures taken from International Institute for Strategic Studies, *The Military Balance, 1990–91* and *The Military Balance, 1991–92* (London: Brassey's for the International Institute for Strategic Studies, 1990, 1991).

6. Nadav Safran, *Saudi Arabia: The Ceaseless Quest for Security* (Cambridge: Harvard University Press, 1985), pp. 58–69.

7. For an account both of Ickes's plans and the 50–50 deal, see Daniel Yergin, *The Prize* (New York: Simon & Schuster, 1991), chs. 20–22.

8. Safran, *Saudi Arabia,* pp. 103–104.

9. King Sa'ud of course had his own agenda, aimed at strengthening the Saudi position in the region, in backing the Eisenhower Doctrine. Those ambitions themselves led to some strains in the US-Saudi relationship. See David W. Lesch, *Syria and the United States: Eisenhower's Cold War in the Middle East* (Boulder: Westview, 1992), pp. 127–189, and David W. Lesch, "The Saudi Role in the 1957 American-Syrian Crisis," *Middle East Policy* 1, no. 3 (1992).

10. Safran, *Saudi Arabia,* pp. 92–96.

11. US Congress, House of Representatives, Committee on Foreign Affairs, Subcommittee on Near East, *New Perspectives on the Persian Gulf,* 93rd Congress, 1st Session (Washington, D.C.: Government Printing Office, 1973), p. 47.

12. Safran, *Saudi Arabia,* p. 301.

13. *al-Hayat,* April 23, 1993, p. 12.

14. R. K. Ramazani, ed., *The Gulf Cooperation Council: Record and Analysis* (Charlottesville: University Press of Virginia, 1988), doc. 9, p. 28.

15. *New York Times,* November 8, 1990, p. 14.

16. *New York Times,* July 18, 1990, pp. D1, D5; July 25, 1990, p. 8; July 27, 1990, p. 2.

17. *New York Times,* September 21, 1990, p. 1.

18. *New York Times,* October 26, 1990, p. 11.

19. *al-Hayat,* October 22, 1991, pp. 1, 7.

20. *New York Times,* October 23, 1990, p. 1; October 27, 1990, p. 4.

21. In a speech to Saudis in early January 1991, King Fahd emphasized the sense of personal betrayal he felt when he heard that Saddam had invaded Kuwait. *New York Times,* January 7, 1991, p. 10.

22. The full text of the *fatwa* can be found in *al-Sharq al-'Awsat,* August 21, 1990, p. 4.

23. *al-Sharq al-'Awsat,* November 28, 1990, p. 3.

24. *al-Hayat,* March 14, 1991, p. 1.

25. *New York Times,* September 30, 1991, p. A5.

26. Charles Aldinger, "Saudis Declined to Base US Arms," Reuters (online), November 4, 1994; "Saudi Against Hosting US Raids on Iraq," Reuters (online), September 11, 1996.

27. Personal interview with a ranking Saudi official, Jeddah, October 1992. See also *New York Times,* October 13, 1991, pp. 1, 18; October 25, 1991, p. A9.

28. See remarks by Dr. Safar al-Hawali, dean of Islamic Studies at 'Umm al-Qura University in Mecca, published by the *New York Times,* November 24, 1990, p. 21. See also *New York Times,* December 25, 1990, p. 6.

29. The author obtained a copy of the "Islamist" petition from sources in Saudi Arabia. English-language versions of this petition can be found in Foreign Broadcast Information Service—Near East and South Asia (FBIS/NESA), May 23, 1991, p. 21 (translation of a version published in the Cairo newspaper *al-Sha'b*); *Makka News,* no. 8, June 16, 1991; and Middle East Watch's *Empty Reforms: Saudi Arabia's New Basic Laws,* pp. 61–62.

30. The author obtained copies of the Memorandum of Advice in Saudi Arabia. All translations are mine. One of the copies was dated Muharram 1413, which corresponds to July 1992, indicating that it was in circulation before the fall of 1992, when Western news organizations reported on it (*New York Times,* October 8, 1992, p. A6).

31. For an interesting discussion on the background of one of those executed, see Ethan Bronner, "In Bomber's Life, Glimpse of Saudi Dissent," *Boston Globe,* July 7, 1996.

32. John C. Roper, "US Saudi Arabia Agree on Troop Move," United Press International (online), July 31, 1996.

33. Arms Control Association, "US Arms Transfers to the Middle East Since the Invasion of Kuwait—Fact Sheet," October 8, 1992 (Washington, D.C.: Arms Control Association).

34. *New York Times,* February 1, 1994, p. A6.

35. International Institute for Strategic Studies, *The Military Balance 1997/98* (Oxford: Oxford University Press, 1997), pp. 26, 140.

36. *New York Times,* February 17, 1994, p. 1.

37. *Washington Post,* January 18, 2002, p. A1.

20

The Iraq War of 2003
Why Did the United States Decide to Invade?

Steve A. Yetiv

History offers no bigger question: Why do nations choose to go to war instead of pursuing other strategies for achieving their ends? This question has been salient for ages, and it is no less germane today in trying to understand why the United States decided to invade Iraq in March of 2003.

Of course, it is too early to offer definitive answers to this question. The central documents will not be declassified for some time, and key policymakers have not yet allowed substantial on-the-record interviews. Nonetheless, it is possible to offer at least a sensible sketch of the key reasons for going to war. This chapter first describes the events leading up to the war and then considers the primary and possible secondary motivations for going to war.

The Events Preceding the 2003 War

Iraq's record of defiance was not in doubt among many nations of the world, although the decision to choose war against Iraq was controversial. Iraq had defied sixteen United Nations resolutions passed between 1991 and 2002, starting with United Nations Security Council (UNSC) Resolution 687, which was the most important. It mandated full disclosure of all of Iraq's ballistic missile stocks (above a range of 150 kilometers) and production facilities, all nuclear materials, chemical and biological weapons and facilities, and cooperation in their destruction. Paragraphs 10 through 12 required Iraq to "unconditionally undertake not to use, develop, construct, or acquire" weapons of mass destruction (WMD). UNSC Resolution 687 also forced Iraq to accept the UN-demarcated border with Kuwait, the sovereignty of Kuwaiti territory, and UN peacekeepers on the Iraq-Kuwait border.[1]

In President Bush's speech to the United Nations on September 12, 2002, he demanded that Iraq comply immediately with the previous sixteen UN resolutions.

He claimed that because Iraq was continuing to pursue the acquisition of weapons of mass destruction and missile delivery systems, it represented a "grave and gathering danger" to American and global security. He pointed out that the United Nations had struggled with Iraq for a dozen years to ensure its compliance with the demands of UNSC Resolution 687 and that Iraq defied its provisions, thus creating a credibility crisis regarding UN resolve. He held out the prospect that UN inspectors could find Saddam's WMD, but he also asserted that the United States was willing to act unilaterally, observing that it is not possible to "stand by and do nothing while dangers gather."

Washington pushed hard to pass the seventeenth resolution against Iraq on November 8, 2002. UNSC Resolution 1441 required Baghdad to admit inspectors from the UN Monitoring, Verification, and Inspection Commission and the International Atomic Energy Agency and to comply fully with all foregoing resolutions.[2] The resolution, which was passed unanimously by the UN Security Council, suggested the use of force against Iraq if it committed a "material breach" or serious infraction in its cooperation with efforts to identify and destroy its WMD capability, but the notion of "material breach" was interpreted differently among the Security Council members.

France, Russia, and China preferred to avoid war and certainly opposed war on Washington's and London's terms and timetable, yet none of the three threatened to veto Resolution 1441. However, France and, to some extent, Russia did attempt to change some of the resolution's language in order to put the brakes on a move toward war, limiting such authorization to the case of serious violations by Baghdad.[3]

For its part, Iraq moved to comply with Resolution 1441 by allowing UN inspectors back into the country and by submitting 12,000 pages and several compact discs of information to the United Nations, which supposedly described its weapons capabilities. Baghdad asserted that it lacked WMD programs and had no WMD in storage. Unfortunately, these disclosures were viewed as incomplete.

Chief UN weapons inspector Hans Blix issued a report in January 2003 that was critical of Iraq's "efforts to disarm and cooperate with UN inspectors."[4] He observed that serious questions remained about Iraq's chemical and biological weapons capability, which he believed was not accurately or fully disclosed in Iraq's report to the United Nations. Not surprisingly, the Bush administration found Iraq's lack of cooperation highly problematic. Secretary of State Colin Powell asserted that American experts had found the Iraqi declaration to the United Nations to "be anything but currently accurate, full, or complete" and that the declaration "totally fails to meet the resolution's requirements."[5] As Powell explained to the UN in his now famous appearance on February 5, 2003, "We haven't accounted for the anthrax, we haven't accounted for the botulinum, VX, both biological agents, growth media, 30,000 chemical and biological munitions."[6] Feeling the rising tide of international condemnation, Saddam responded by granting greater access to UN inspectors in Iraq. He may have thought that he could foil US efforts to gather international support for an invasion of Iraq, without revealing the fact that there were actually very few or no WMD in the country. On February 10, 2003,

Blix offered a more optimistic account of Iraq's cooperation, seeing a new "positive attitude on the part of the Iraqi regime," and asked for more time for inspections.[7]

While Russia, Germany, and France seized on Blix's report to thwart the American and British drive toward war, Washington and London proved recalcitrant. They may well have concluded that Saddam was simply engaging in more games with UN inspectors, that his track record suggested no real interest in completely ridding the country of WMD, and that inspections were therefore doomed to fail. From their perspective, if Saddam did have these weapons, he would not help UN inspectors find them, and without his help, they could remain hidden. Meanwhile, even if they did find WMD, they could not be confident that they had uncovered all of them or that, after they left, Saddam would not rebuild some of the weapons programs.

Partly as a result of this skepticism and partly because Iraq, in the view of the United States and Britain, did not meet the conditions of UN Resolution 1441 or previous UN resolutions, the United States and Britain drafted an eighteenth resolution against Iraq, which, in essence, called for war. To pass this resolution, the United States needed the support of nine of the fifteen Security Council members, while avoiding a veto by any of the four other permanent members of the Security Council. Although the Security Council had unanimously supported Resolution 1441, the underlying differences among them on going to war complicated US efforts to pass the new resolution. Russia threatened to veto it, although Moscow avoided an open breach with Washington. Russian President Vladimir Putin had supported earlier US efforts to contain and defang Iraq and had lent tentative support for war, but on a much slower timetable; he could not endorse a war that was viewed in Russia and the rest of the world as rushed or outright ill-advised.[8]

France, in particular, viewed Resolution 1441 differently, interpreting it as a warning to Iraq to comply more fully with UN inspectors, not as a *casus belli*. After France threatened to outright veto the eighteenth resolution, possibly with backing from China and Russia, the United States and Britain shifted their strategy, especially when they learned that some of the smaller countries on the UN Security Council would not support their action.

The United States and Britain offered somewhat different justifications for war, but in essence they were convinced that Iraq's violation of the previous seventeen UN resolutions gave them sufficient basis for using force. Citing this rationale, they presented Saddam, his sons, and key Iraqi elites with an ultimatum: leave the country within forty-eight hours or face war. Saddam rejected the ultimatum, possibly fearing that the United States would eventually track him down wherever he went or perhaps believing that he could survive the American-led onslaught and eventually resurrect his regime. In retrospect, it seems likely that he and his generals had plans to stand down and disperse into a guerrilla movement, with greater chances of evicting American forces from Iraq through a war of attrition. The minutes of a meeting of his top commanders, chaired by Saddam, support this interpretation.[9]

Operation Iraqi Freedom was launched against Iraq on March 19, 2003, with a massive air attack, an assault referred to with overcharged bravado as "Operation

Shock and Awe." Bombs struck their targets precisely, carrying a message that the United States was serious about change in the Middle East. Saddam's regime fell to this massive onslaught, but the security and political debris that was left in its wake would continue to bedevil the United States and its allies, who were bent on rebuilding Iraq in the Western image.

The Key Motivations for Going to War

The United States offered three key reasons for going to war.[10] Although we should not accept them uncritically, and they probably do not capture the full story of American motivations, they appear to be central to the Bush administration's decision.

First, the United States was concerned about Iraqi WMD programs. On August 14, 2002, National Security Adviser Condoleezza Rice chaired a meeting that laid out US goals in Iraq in a draft of a national security presidential directive titled "Iraq: Goals, Objectives, and Strategy." President Bush signed the directive, making it official policy, on August 29. The document emphasized the desire of the United States government to overthrow Saddam Hussein's regime in order to eliminate its WMD, to end its threat to the region, to create democracy in Iraq, and to contain the threat of a WMD attack on the United States or its allies.[11]

In June 2001, the CIA reported that although the evidence was not fully clear, it appeared that Iraq had used the period between 1998 and 2001 to rebuild prohibited WMD programs.[12] In October 2002, a special national intelligence estimate more clearly articulated those accusations: "Iraq has continued its weapons of mass destruction programs in defiance of UN resolutions and restrictions. Baghdad has chemical and biological weapons as well as missiles with ranges in excess of UN restrictions; if left unchecked, it probably will have a nuclear weapon during this decade."[13]

In one key document, President Bush warned that if the Iraqi regime were "able to produce, buy, or steal an amount of highly enriched uranium a little larger than a single softball, it could have a nuclear weapon in less than a year."[14] In September 2002, he cited a British intelligence report indicating that Iraq could launch a chemical or biological attack forty-five minutes after the order was given to do so.[15] The administration also described Iraq as capable of using WMD against the United States, a position that was not shared by the intelligence analysts who wrote the October 2002 national intelligence estimate.[16]

Senior administration officials repeatedly asserted that Iraq sought to rebuild its nuclear program and to obfuscate the existence of nuclear facilities by placing them underground or camouflaging them. In this view, inspections would not be able to detect or halt these activities, and even if they could, Iraq would resume them once the inspectors left the country.[17] In the case that Iraq did not yet possess nuclear capabilities—a scenario characterized as unlikely—the administration believed that Iraq had the intellectual infrastructure and intent to produce them. In the eyes of administration officials, that alone was enough of a threat after 9/11 to justify US action against Iraq. The administration did not trumpet this argument, however, because it was less marketable than other arguments for war.[18]

The attacks of September 11 raised the stakes high enough that the administration had a low level of tolerance for WMD in a dictator's hands, especially one with Saddam's record of aggression. Vice President Dick Cheney asserted in August 2002: "If the United States could have preempted 9/11, we would have, no question. Should we be able to prevent another, much more devastating attack, we will, no question."[19] From this perspective, irrefutable facts about Iraq's capabilities and intentions were unnecessary; Saddam had given the administration enough reason to have serious doubts about his intentions in a post-9/11 environment. As Bush asserted in his January 28, 2003, State of the Union speech, a "brutal dictator, with a history of reckless aggression, with ties to terrorism, with great potential wealth, will not be permitted to dominate a vital region and threaten the United States."[20]

President Bush described Iraq, Iran, and North Korea in his now famous January 29, 2002, State of the Union message as part of an "axis of evil" against which pre-emptive force might have to be used. Later, on September 28, 2002, Bush elaborated on the Iraq problem: "The danger to our country is grave and growing. The Iraqi regime possesses biological and chemical weapons, is rebuilding facilities to make more and . . . is seeking a nuclear bomb, and with fissile material could build one within a year."[21]

A second rationale for going to war was Iraq's purported ties to terrorism. The administration's assertion that Iraq had supported al-Qa'ida was buoyed by the fact that a majority of Americans (53 to 64 percent in an August 2002 Gallup poll) believed that Saddam was directly involved in the 9/11 attacks.[22]

Prior to the attacks of September 11, 2001, the Bush administration was not especially concerned about al-Qa'ida. Policy tended to follow that established in the Clinton administration, which had aimed to eliminate the al-Qa'ida threat not by physical deployment of forces or extensive pressure on the Taliban but rather through the use of domestic law enforcement agencies. One exception was the unsuccessful effort in President Clinton's embattled second term to assassinate bin Laden with a missile strike at an al-Qa'ida training camp in Afghanistan. The Bush administration was more fixed on the al-Qa'ida threat than the Clinton administration, yet it failed to take timely action to address it. Reflecting the broader tenor among high-level Bush administration officials, National Security Advisor Condoleezza Rice was slow to respond to suggestions made in a key memo by counter-terrorism coordinator Richard Clarke to take action against al-Qa'ida,[23] and she was subsequently accused of ignoring the threat prior to 9/11. Ironically, on September 10 she was in the process of preparing a National Security Directive on how to eliminate the terrorist threat of al-Qa'ida.[24]

After September 11, the Bush administration appeared to be concerned about, even obsessed with, the connection between WMD and terrorist organizations, as reflected in many speeches by top American officials, including Vice President Dick Cheney.[25] To what extent the Bush administration manipulated intelligence to support the war may not be fully known for some time. Yet, clearly administration officials were concerned that Iraq could be supporting transnational terrorists. Evidence for this interpretation can be found in the now famous "Downing Street memo," which summarizes discussion in a July 23, 2002, meeting of British Prime Minister Tony Blair with his top security advisers. In the memo, which is actually minutes of the meeting, the head of Britain's MI6 intelligence service reports on his high-level visit to Washington: "Bush wanted to remove Saddam through military action, justified by the conjunction of terrorism and WMD. But the intelligence and facts were being fixed around the policy."[26]

Even though the link between al-Qa'ida and Iraq was tenuous at best,[27] it was Saddam's misfortune that Iraq represented precisely what the Bush administration feared after 9/11: a dictator developing WMD with connections to terrorist groups. Bush described his post–9/11 perception of Saddam in an interview with Bob Woodward: "All his terrible features became much more threatening. Keeping Saddam in a box looked less and less feasible to me."[28] In Rumsfeld's words, "we acted because we saw the existing evidence in a new light, through the prism of our experience on September 11," a perspective that was obsessed with America's vulnerability to states with WMD and connections to terrorists.[29]

Even Secretary Powell appeared to be persuaded to some extent that Iraq posed a threat, although he may have also been playing the role of obedient soldier to the president and vice president. In his crucial speech to the UN on September 12, 2002, he warned that terrorism had been a tool used by Saddam for decades: "Saddam was a supporter of terrorism long before these terrorist networks had a name, and this support continues. The nexus of poisons and terror is new. The nexus of Iraq and terror is old. The combination is lethal."[30]

Some scholars have argued that the administration used the WMD threat to justify a war that it had decided to launch even before 9/11.[31] That is not likely. Not only did the September 11 attacks give the administration a basis for garnering public support for war, which it had previously lacked, but the strategic priorities of the administration changed dramatically after 9/11.

Indeed, having been advised in the hours following the attacks that al-Qa'ida may well have planned the attacks on New York and Washington, Donald Rumsfeld reportedly asked for the existing military plans for an invasion of Iraq; his deputy, Paul Wolfowitz, also pushed for an immediate attack on Iraq, ahead of an invasion of Afghanistan.[32] Meanwhile, President Bush asked for contingency plans to attack Iraq if it were shown that Iraq was involved in the attacks or sought to exploit the crisis for its own gain.[33] Like Wolfowitz, Bush made it known early on that he thought Iraq was involved in the 9/11 attacks,[34] and he repeated the mantra that Iraq had had long-standing ties to terrorist groups that were capable of and willing to deliver weapons of mass death.[35] His information no doubt came, in part, from the CIA. On October 7, 2002, George Tenet, then director of the Central Intelligence Agency, sent Senator Bob Graham, the chairman of the Senate Select Committee on Intelligence, unclassified information that indicated the existence of a long-term relationship between al-Qa'ida and Iraq, including "solid reporting of senior level contacts between Iraq and al-Qa'ida going back a decade."[36]

In addition to the administration's concerns about Iraq possessing WMD and having established ties with al-Qa'ida, President Bush and his advisors had a third reason for going to war with Iraq. It was their intention to topple the autocratic regime of Saddam Hussein and to democratize Iraq, so that it could then sow the seeds of democracy more broadly in the Middle East. Although the Bush administration did not initially focus on democratization as a rationale for war, it would be a mistake to assume that it was simply an afterthought.

Whereas President George H. W. Bush had been repeatedly criticized for lacking vision, his son exemplified vision, whatever one thinks of its merits, in the post-9/11 period. Although his vision may have come from the gut, it adhered to a unilinear view of history. In contrast to the cyclical view of history, which sees the afflictions of international relations repeating themselves over time, President George W. Bush held a firm belief in human progress—in this case, the democratization of a challenging region.[37]

On the evening of September 11, 2001, in the wake of the attacks in New York and Washington, well before the US decision to go to war in Iraq, Bush reassured the nation that the United States "would go forward to defend freedom and all that is good and just in our world."[38] He repeated that mantra ahead of the invasion of Iraq,[39] and he continued to repeat it throughout the long war that followed, emphasizing that the United States would support and spread democratic ideas.

The objective of democratizing Iraq and the Middle East lost traction as time wore on, especially after WMD failed to turn up in Iraq and the al-Qa'ida connection to Saddam remained elusive. This approach was a sharp break with past US foreign policy in the region. Indeed, even the Clinton administration, which was proud of its support for human rights abroad, did not attempt to launch a democratization drive in the Middle East. Secretary of State Madeleine Albright explained US restraint in this region: "We have been afraid to push too hard for democracy, especially in Arab countries. We worry, perhaps with reason, that if radical Islamists obtain power through an election, there would be no more elections . . . and instability might be created."[40] By contrast, Condoleezza Rice, who became secretary of state in early 2005, held a different view: "For sixty years, my country, the United States, pursued stability at the expense of democracy in this region here in the Middle East, and we achieved neither. Now we are taking a different course. We are supporting the democratic aspirations of all people."[41]

In the administration's view, democratization could undermine the demons that drive transnational terrorism,[42] a theme that dominated the administration's list of priorities by 2004. In his State of the Union address on February 2, 2004, President Bush urged Saudi Arabia and Egypt to "show the way toward democracy in the region."[43]

The Conceptual Motivation for War: Preemption Versus Containment

The motivations for war discussed above are insufficient to explain the decision to go to war. After all, if WMD were so threatening, why didn't the Bush administration attack North Korea, which was a far greater threat than Iraq? If fighting terrorism was the key objective, administration officials could just as easily have decided to focus on strangulating al-Qaʻida globally rather than executing regime change in Iraq, even if they believed there was a Saddam/al-Qaʻida connection. If they were concerned about WMD and terrorism, administration officials might also have decided to ratchet up their containment of Iraq with increased military, political, and economic pressures instead of invasion and occupation. Why did they choose to go to war?

Simply put, after 9/11, the Bush administration did not believe that containment would work. The perception that Iraq had WMD and connections to terrorism further drove the change in American foreign policy away from containment and toward preemption, and preemption became the conceptual basis for invading Iraq.

To be sure, prior to 9/11, the administration viewed the policy of containment as problematic. As Bush pointed out, "I was not happy with our policy," in that it was not toppling Saddam or changing his behavior, but prior to September 11, "a president could see a threat and contain it or deal with it in a variety of ways without fear of that threat materializing on our own soil."[44] That describes, roughly, the disposition of the Clinton administration, as well as that of the first Bush administration. Those earlier administrations were content with strengthening the containment effort against Saddam Hussein through "smart sanctions," which aimed to prevent Iraq from obtaining military goods, while relaxing the embargo on trade items that Iraq's people needed. Prior to 9/11, Iraq was barely mentioned by top officials, except as a potential long-term threat,[45] even though consensus had developed among them that Saddam's regime needed to be removed, and regime change had become official American policy in 1998.

After September 11, US policy toward Iraq changed dramatically from regime change through political means to regime change through the use of force.[46] The Bush doctrine of preemption was articulated in the State of the Union address on January 29, 2002, and then formally outlined in the National Security Strategy of September 2002.[47] It was based partly on the notion that deterrence and containment may not succeed, and it emphasized the need to resort in appropriate cases to preemptive measures.[48] For Paul Wolfowitz, 9/11 was the "most significant thing" that generated a change in US foreign policy, and he cited it as one of the top ten events, if not the top event, of the "last one hundred years."[49]

The United States had always practiced preemption when necessary, but it had never before been openly presented as a strategy and then used so brazenly to justify war on another country. September 11, however, altered the stakes. As President Bush put it, September 11 made it such that the "doctrine of containment just doesn't hold any water."[50] Bush asserted in a speech in Cincinnati in October 2002 that the United States had to take preemptive action because after September 11, the country could not "wait for the final proof—the smoking gun," which would come in "the form of a mushroom cloud."[51] America's threshold for terrorism had been lowered enough that Iraq became a key target for vigorous American action. Containment was a passive approach; now the United States would become much more proactive.

Regime change through the use of force was one key element of the broader policy of preemption, but the Bush administration also sought to stop terrorist attacks before they occurred through other means. Regime change was the most overt and the riskiest of these means.

Faulty Intelligence

Wars in history have often been started because of miscalculations about the strength of other actors and the threats they pose. The Bush administration's conceptual shift toward preemption and war in Iraq was driven by faulty intelligence on Iraq's WMD and connections to al-Qa'ida. It may never be fully evident to what extent the administration, or particular members within it, manipulated this intelligence to justify war, but clearly the information was important in the decision to go to war. Indeed, poor intelligence created a specter of a much greater Iraqi threat than existed; it facilitated the administration's efforts to gain domestic and, to some extent, international support for war and predisposed key officials to believe that Iraq could be rebuilt and refashioned without the extraordinary challenges that would arise in the postwar period. Accurate intelligence would have made the option of going to war less palatable and more difficult to market.

In any case, the administration insisted that it had made a sound decision based on the evidence at hand, faulty as it was, and challenged criticism that it had cooked the books for war. Reflecting the administration's position, Powell asserted that he was "disappointed" that the intelligence was not on target but that the administration had not misled the world and the American people, because government officials had believed what they said about Iraq. "We thought Iraq had stockpiles of WMD."[52]

Two major official inquiries, one by the Senate Select Committee on Intelligence in 2004 and one by the Robb-Silberman commission in March 2005, found no evidence that political pressure by the Bush administration had contributed to these intelligence failures.[53] The inquiries did find that Vice President Cheney and others had encouraged analysts to rethink their findings, but that this did not lead to different conclusions. However, the inquiries did not have access to key White House documents. Moreover, while they found that political pressure by the administration did not contribute to intelligence failures, they left open the question of the extent to which the administration exaggerated the threat from Iraq and, in particular, Iraq's ties to al-Qa'ida to justify war.[54] In fact, one February 2002 declassified document from the Defense Intelligence Agency asserted that Ibn al-Shaykh al-Libi, a top member of al-Qa'ida in American custody, had intentionally misled American debriefers about Iraq's support for al-Qa'ida and Iraqi shipments of illicit weapons to the terrorists. The administration repeatedly drew on his questionable testimony, as did Colin Powell in his February 2003 UN speech. Al-Libi withdrew his claims in 2004, but the administration's reliance on this shaky intelligence raised questions about the extent to which the administration dramatized, fabricated, or misunderstood Saddam's connection to al-Qa'ida.[55]

Other Possible Motivations for War

In addition to the motivations for war discussed thus far, we should consider several others. Many people around the world felt that the war was unnecessary. If the war was not really intended to address some imminent threat from Iraq, they thought, then what were its real aims?[56]

Oil Security and Alternatives to Saudi Energy

Millions of people in the Middle East and around the world believed that the war was about oil. According to a 2000 Pew Research Center opinion poll, 76 percent of those polled in Russia, 75 percent of those polled in France, 54 percent of those polled in Germany, and 44 percent of those polled in Great Britain believed that the war was driven by a "desire to control Iraq's oil."[57] Most Iraqis, it is fair to say, also held this view, which was prominent among both moderate and radical Islamists around the world. For his part, Osama bin Laden asserted in a 1998 interview that the Muslim world and Islam were under assault, noting that others "rob us of our wealth and of our resources and of our oil" and that "our religion is under attack."[58] This view of Americans stealing Middle Eastern oil was fairly constant in statements by al-Qa'ida and its affiliates.[59]

Although it is obvious that the United States views access to Persian Gulf oil as "vital to US and global security,"[60] little evidence exists that it has sought to steal this oil. For instance, it did not seize Iraqi oil fields or appropriate the proceeds from oil sales. However, access to oil reserves may very well have been one of the motivating factors for the invasion of Iraq.

First, the September 11 attacks created concerns about Saudi stability. Some of these concerns were rational and some were not, but they all influenced elite and general public opinion in the United States. The fact that fifteen of the nineteen hijackers came from Saudi Arabia raised questions about whether their hatred for the United States was more endemic in the kingdom than previously believed. It also raised the question of whether they attacked the United States in order to create a schism in US-Saudi relations and thus undermine the legitimacy of the Saudi regime, which may have been their primary target.

Some were concerned that elements in the Saudi regime actually supported the terrorists, suggesting the existence of a radical element within the royal family itself. Others believed that the regime had turned a blind eye to the terrorists because the religious establishment in the country made it politically difficult to confront them. If any of these explanations were credible, the future of US-Saudi relations was potentially in jeopardy.

It made sense to secure Iraq's vast oil resources if Saudi Arabia was becoming unstable. The overthrow of Saddam Hussein could put Iraq's oil production in friendlier hands, and this would give the West greater ability to maintain the flow of oil in the event of political or security problems in Saudi Arabia. Even if the Saudi regime was stable, US-Saudi tensions could mount over time, thus making Iraq more important to diversifying oil supplies.

Second, regime change could allow for higher Iraqi oil production. It is believed that Iraq has 112.5 billion barrels of known reserves, which places it second only to Saudi Arabia's 262 billion (approximately 25 percent of the world's proven oil reserves). Iraq's proven reserves are found in seventy-three fields, only one-quarter of which have been developed.[61] Other Middle East states such as Iran and Kuwait hold approximately 90 to 120 billion barrels, but those fields do not have the upward potential of Iraq's because they are already producing at a high rate. Iraq possesses 11 percent of the world's proven oil reserves, yet even at its peak production in 1979, it was producing only 5.5 percent of the world supply. Iraq's potential could have been viewed as enormous precisely because it has been hamstrung over the past twenty-five years. The Iran-Iraq war from 1980 to 1988, the 1991 Gulf war, subsequent UN sanctions, periodic American military attacks, and Saddam's own mismanagement and corruption further curtailed Iraq's potential and left its oil infrastructure in disarray.

Iraq's various conflicts with the UN resulted in a drop in oil production from an average of 2.0–2.6 million barrels per day (mb/d) from 1999 to 2001, under UN Resolution 986. Production hit a high of 2.6 mb/d in 2000 (equal to 3.4 percent of world supply) and dropped to 1.7 mb/d by August-September 2002.[62] Some analysts believed that with a totally rebuilt oil infrastructure, Iraq could have increased oil production to an estimated 6 to 12 mb/d within a decade, partly because Iraq's oil is relatively underexplored and underdeveloped.[63] In early 1990, prior to the invasion of Kuwait, Baghdad had planned to raise production and export capacity to 6 mb/d by 1996.[64] After May 1997, Iraq's oil ministry worked assiduously to produce a post-sanctions oil development plan, the latest version of which preceded the Iraq war of 2003 and had a goal of producing 6 mb/d within six years.[65]

Third, toppling Iraq's regime could have ended Iraq's threat to regional oil fields, at least in the near term. After all, Iraq's invasion of Kuwait had demonstrated that Saddam Hussein might be inclined once again to invade Kuwait or even Saudi Arabia. This was increasingly likely as international pressure and the UN sanctions began to wane, leaving Saddam greater room to maneuver in the region.[66]

These three factors may very well have contributed to the Bush administration's decision to invade Iraq. Administration officials could not have underestimated potential problems with Saudi Arabia and the importance of oil to the American and global economy. Nor could they overlook the fact that Persian Gulf oil would only become more important as other sources of oil around the world began to peak and then dry up. Just how important the oil factor was as a national security concern in the administration's decisionmaking process, compared to other motivations, is unclear and hard to assess.

Oil, Halliburton, and American Oil Companies

Although national security may have motivated an interest in Iraqi oil, another potential explanation for invading Iraq is that Vice President Cheney, and his contacts in the oil world, could have benefited from large oil contracts after Iraq was liberated by American forces. With America dominating or influencing Iraq, the United States could more effectively compete for such contracts with countries such as France, Russia, and China, who already had a foothold in the region. Not only could the United States get a bigger piece of the pie, but the size of the pie itself would expand because Iraq could produce far more oil with Saddam gone, UN sanctions lifted, and foreign investment revitalizing Iraq's oil sector.

This view of American motivation for going to war smacked of deep cynicism and may have been promoted by the administration's detractors in order to embarrass top administration officials,[67] but Cheney's previous role as CEO of Halliburton, plus the oil background of President Bush, tend to reinforce this viewpoint.[68] The Bush administration's Energy Task Force, which was headed by Cheney, presented a draft report in April 2001 that stated, among other things, that the United States should reconsider sanctions against Iran, Iraq, and Libya, because they prohibited US oil companies from doing business in "some of the most important existing and prospective petroleum-producing countries in the world."[69] Moreover, immediately prior to the invasion of Iraq in early 2003, Halliburton's subsidiary, Kellogg, Brown & Root, received a multibillion-dollar contract from the Department of Defense to repair oil fields and import consumer fuels in Iraq.[70]

It is not very likely that Cheney would have risked a national and global scandal to help a company for which he no longer worked, although he must have known that the contract would be criticized. Some have argued that he still had Halliburton stock from which he could benefit, but one would still have to argue that he would not risk a high-profile scandal for money.

Although mining Iraq's energy resources could benefit companies like Halliburton that support the infrastructure for oil production, it would not necessarily help oil producers. This is because as more oil flowed from Iraq, the price of oil would likely decrease based on simple supply/demand dynamics. Big oil companies could benefit only if the benefits that accrued to them from additional contracts in Iraq outweighed the losses they would face from decreased oil prices. Nonetheless, the factor of domestic oil and oil services companies benefiting from regime change in Iraq should be considered.

Father and Son: Personal Reasons

We might speculate that President Bush's decision to go to war in Iraq was influenced by the fact that his father evicted Saddam Hussein from Kuwait in 1991 but left him in power. In this scenario, Bush Jr invaded Iraq to finish the work that his father started. He may have sought to shore up his father's legacy by finishing off a dictator who proved to be much more resilient than his father and many others anticipated. Saddam's longevity proved to be a source of embarrassment to Bush Sr, not just because he survived the 1991 war when many thought he would fall, but because he continued to be perceived as a major threat, especially after September 11 when many people began to ask why he was not eliminated in 1991 when

Washington had the chance to do so. An invasion of Iraq could benefit the father's legacy by removing a threat that could prove to be more serious in the future if Saddam actually did have WMD and connections to terrorists. History would surely blame Bush Sr if the nuclear bombing of New York in 2015 by terrorists linked to Iraq could have been prevented had the United States marched on Baghdad and eliminated the dictator in 1991. Of course, Bush Jr could make sure that never happened by taking the matter into his own hands.

Bush Jr may have also sought to avenge Saddam's effort to assassinate his father in Kuwait in 1993 while on a visit there. In fact, he did say that Saddam Hussein was "a guy that tried to kill my dad,"[71] suggesting an overt hostility toward the dictator. We do know that loyalty runs strong in the Bush family and that Bush Jr acted as an enforcer of loyalty in his father's administration, all of which suggests that a personal motive may have influenced President Bush's decision to overthrow the regime of Saddam Hussein in 2003.

Carving His Own Path

President Bush may have also sought to set his own independent course as a determined leader rather than as a reputed follower of others. This motivation may have been reinforced by widespread criticism that it was actually Dick Cheney, one of his father's closest advisers, who ran the administration. This criticism could not have been lost on Bush and certainly not on his advisers, who may have seen a side benefit of the Iraq war in the opportunity to establish the president's credentials as a strong leader. Interestingly, when asked by Bob Woodward whether he had consulted with his father before making the decision to invade Iraq, President Bush asserted, "There is a higher Father that I appeal to," dismissing his father's role in rather unambiguous terms.

Moreover, Brent Scowcroft, his father's influential national security advisor and close friend, argued in the *Wall Street Journal* against the invasion of Iraq, asserting that containment was working well and warning that an invasion would impede the war on terrorism and destabilize the region.[72] This view may have also reflected the views of Bush Sr, who seemed unhappy with his son's decision to go to war and who had strongly opposed invading Baghdad in 1991. In any case, ignoring the advice of his father's key adviser, and possibly that of his father, suggests that he was determined to chart his own course.

Bush, God, and Religion

If Bush's father played a limited role in shaping his decisions, this was not the case for God Almighty. President Bush raised—significantly more than most presidents—the issue of religion and his relationship with God in his speeches. From his assertion on September 12, 2001, that he was in the "Lord's hands,"[73] to his constant rhetoric about the forces of good and evil, to his frequent references to the war on terrorism as a crusade,[74] Bush was prone to a religious interpretation of events.[75] His notion of "crusade" was quite different from that of most Muslims:[76] He saw it as an effort to confront evil terrorists and those who supported them, whereas Muslims tended to interpret it in terms of their difficult historical experience with the brutal Christian crusades.

In the spring of 2004 Bush referred several times to his belief that a higher source was guiding his actions. Historically, the United States had promoted the liberal tradition as a transnational set of ideas and largely kept religion out of politics. Indeed, it was an area in which the United States differed fundamentally from Islamist states. President Bush was not deviating significantly from that tradition, however, nor did the president speak for all Americans or administration officials. Nevertheless, his words were enough to raise questions in the Muslim world about a Judeo-Christian showdown with Islam. The fact that President Bush embraced Israel's leader, Ariel Sharon, added to this perception, because their close relationship fed speculation about a Zionist-Crusader conspiracy.

One might expect that Bush would be heavily criticized for his copious religious references, and to some extent he was. Yet even during the presidential election, the campaign of Senator John Kerry veered away from open criticism. Bush's religious imagery seemed to have struck a chord not only among Christian conservatives and evangelicals, who had a biblical interpretation of world events, but also among Americans who held negative views of Muslims even prior to September 11.[77]

It is possible that Bush saw Iraq through the prism of religion. The United States was a God-fearing Christian nation, and Iraq was fit for transformation. Of course, Iraq could not be Christianized, but the messianic impulse may have been part of what bolstered Bush's determination, an impulse that meshed well with his brand of American exceptionalism.

The Military-Industrial Complex

Factors particular to President Bush may have influenced the drive to war in Iraq. However, some observers, especially those inclined toward conspiracy theories, might say that the so-called military-industrial complex, whose notorious power and influence President Eisenhower warned Americans about, also had a role in the decision to go to war in Iraq. According to some thinkers, this complex of corporate and military organizations has a vested interest in going to war; wars result in high-profit military contracts, expanded military research budgets, and influence.

Invading Iraq could benefit the military-industrial complex. The armed forces could see President Bush as confirming their importance. The military-industrial complex could view the war as a ticket for producing and selling more and better weapons. The influence of the Department of Defense could rise if the armed forces performed well, and the military might stave off budget cuts and base closings and gain support for new weapons programs. And the much maligned CIA would have an important mission in the post–cold war era.

Conclusion

The Iraq war was launched in March of 2003, but US-Iraqi tensions had been building throughout the 1990s. Although the 1991 war had severely weakened Iraq, the wily dictator from Tikrit not only failed to cooperate with UN inspectors as mandated by UNSC Resolution 687 but acted as if he had WMD, which he evidently lacked. The great irony was that he may well have thought that this pretense would send a signal to his real and imagined adversaries at both the domestic and international level that he was strong, that he could deter their attacks, even punish them with retaliation if need be. Yet, by doing so, he constructed himself as the very threat that the administration of George W. Bush wanted to check and then eliminate after the September 11 attacks. In this sense, Saddam was once again acting as his worse enemy.

It is worth repeating that divining American motivations for war is academic conjecture. Still, it appears that the United States invaded Iraq chiefly because it feared WMD in the hands of a dictator and assumed the worst about Saddam's connections to terrorists. These concerns were significantly heightened and reframed by September 11. That tectonic event altered the prism through which Bush administration officials saw the world and, in particular, the potential threat posed by Iraq. This helps to explain why the United States saw Iraq so differently than did so many other countries around the world.

American fears were exacerbated by poor intelligence, which, when seen through the 9/11 prism, took on new meaning. Most likely, this intelligence was also used selectively by some officials to justify a war that the administration thought was necessary. Although 9/11 created a potential strategic rationale for going to war against Iraq, it also allowed the administration to garner public support for war. That had been lacking even after the United States made regime change in Iraq its official policy in 1998.

By eliminating Saddam's regime and refashioning Iraq, the administration could also advance democratization in the Middle East. If terrorists were hatched partly because they lived in repressive societies, democratic "shock therapy" to the region, as romantic as it sounded, might ameliorate this problem. At the same time, the United States could help secure Iraq as a hedge against post–September 11 instability in oil-rich Saudi Arabia.

Of course, we cannot rule out domestic and personal motivations for war, but they do not appear to be as important as the primary factors. After all, they had not generated war earlier, in the absence of these other critical factors.

Notes

1. For the texts of major UN resolutions adopted in 1991, see *UN Security Resolutions on Iraq: Compliance and Implementation,* Report to the Committee on Foreign Affairs by the CRS (Washington, DC: Government Printing Office, March 1992).

2. For the text of the resolution, see http://ods-dds-ny.un.org/doc/UNDOC/ GEN/N02/682/26/PDF/N0268226.pdf?OpenElement.

3. On this jockeying and for the draft of the resolution at this time, see *New York Times,* October 23, 2002.

4. Hans Blix, *An Update on Inspection,* Report of the Executive Chairman of UNMOVIC to the United Nations Security Council, New York, January 27, 2003, http://www.un.org/ Depts/unmovic/Bx27.htm.

5. See http://www.state.gov/r/pa/prs/ps/2002/16118pf.htm.

6. Powell's statement in front of the UN, excerpted in the *New York Times,* February 23, 2003.

7. Dafna Linzer, "Iraq Approves Inspectors' Use of U-2 Surveillance Planes, Iraqi Ambassador Says," Associated Press, February 6, 2003.

8. Thane Gustafson, *Changing Course? Iraq and the 'New' US-Russian Relationship* (Cambridge, MA: Cambridge Energy research Associates, 2003), 2–3.

9. See Yossef Bodansky, *The Secret History of the Iraq War* (New York: HarperCollins, 2004), 5.

10. On the war's motivations, see Lawrence Freedman, "War in Iraq: Selling the Threat," *Survival* 46, Summer 2004.

11. Bob Woodward, *Plan of Attack* (New York: Simon & Schuster, 2004), 155.

12. Cited in Freedman, "War in Iraq," 24.

13. Ibid., 5.

14. White House, "President Bush Outlines Iraqi Threat," October 7, 2002, http:// www.whitehouse.gov.

15. Remarks by President Bush on Iraq in the Rose Garden, September 26, 2002, http://www.whitehouse.gov/news/releases/2002/09/print/20020926-I.html.

16. See http://www.ceip.org/files/projects/npp/pdf/Iraq/declassifiedintellreport.pdf.

17. Kenneth Katzman, *Iraq: US Efforts to Change the Regime* (Washington, DC: Congressional Research Service, October 3, 2002), 10–11.

18. On how the war was sold, see Chaim Kaufmann, "Threat Inflation and the Failure of the Marketplace of Ideas: The Selling of the Iraq War," *International Security* 29, 2004.

19. Dick Cheney, "The Risks of Inaction Are Far Greater than the Risk of Action," Address to the 103rd National Convention of the Veterans of Foreign Wars, August 26, 2002.

20. The full text of the State of the Union address appears at http://www.gpoaccess.gov/ sou/index.html.

21. Radio Address by the President to the Nation, Office of the Press Secretary, September 28, 2002.

22. See Philip H. Gordon, "Iraq: The Transatlantic Debate," Institute for Security Studies Occasional Papers, No. 39, November 2002, 15. For an argument that this connection did exist, see Laurie Mylroie, *Bush vs. the Beltway: How the CIA and the State Department Tried to Stop the War on Terror* (New York: ReganBooks, 2003).

23. Memorandum from Richard A. Clarke to Condoleezza Rice, National Security Council, Washington, DC, January 25, 2001.

24. Bob Woodward, *Bush at War* (New York: Simon & Schuster, 2002), 34–35.

25. Dick Cheney, "Speech to the Council on Foreign Relations," Washington, DC, February 15, 2002 (www.whitehouse.gov/vicepresident/news-speeches/speeches/ vp20020215.html.

26. Downing Street memo text, http://www.downingstreetmemo.com/memo.html.

27. See Kaufmann, "Threat Inflation and the Failure of the Marketplace of Ideas." For a view that the al-Qa'ida connection to Iraq was real, see Yossef Bodansky, *The Secret History of the Iraq War* (New York: HarperCollins, 2004), ch. 3.

28. Quoted in Woodward, *Plan of Attack,* 27.

29. Testimony by Secretary of Defense Donald H. Rumsfeld, Senate Armed Services Committee, Washington, DC, July 9, 2003, http://www.defenselink.mil/speeches/2003/sp20030709-secdef0364.html.

30. Secretary of State Colin L. Powell, "Remarks to the United Nations Security Council," US Department of State, February 5, 2003, 19.

31. Some scholars argue that it did do so. See ibid.

32. See the account by former counterterrorism chief Richard Clarke, in Richard A. Clarke, *Against All Enemies: Inside America's War on Terror* (New York: Free Press, 2004), 30.

33. Testimony of National Security Advisor Condoleezza Rice, 9/11 Commission, April 8, 2004. Also, see Freedman, "War in Iraq," 18–19. Also, on the impact of 9/11, see Woodward, *Bush at War,* 34–35; "US Decision on Iraq Has Puzzling Past: Opponents of War Wonder When, How Policy Was Set," *Washington Post,* January 12, 2003.

34. Woodward, *Bush at War,* 99.

35. Radio Address by the President to the Nation, Office of the Press Secretary, December 7, 2002.

36. Letter to Senator Bob Graham, October 7, 2002.

37. On this debate, see Robert W. Merry, *Sands of Empire: Missionary Zeal, American Foreign Policy, and the Hazards of Global Ambition* (New York: Simon & Schuster, 2005).

38. "Statement by the President in His Address to the Nation," September 11, 2001.

39. For instance, see the President's Address to the American Enterprise Institute, February 26, 2003.

40. Madeleine Albright, *Madam Secretary: A Memoir* (New York: Hyperion, 2003), 416.

41. Steven R. Weisman, "Rice Urges Egyptians and Saudis to Democratize," *New York Times,* June 21, 2005, A1.

42. See "Excerpts from President Bush's Remarks at the Air Force Academy Graduation Ceremony," *New York Post,* June 3, 2004, 33.

43. *New York Times,* February 3, 2005, A1.

44. Quoted in Woodward, *Plan of Attack,* 12.

45. See Freedman, "War in Iraq," 15–16.

46. See Katzman, *Iraq: US Efforts to Change the Regime,* 7–12.

47. On this doctrine, see Lawrence Freedman, *Deterrence* (London: Polity, 2004). The full text of the State of the Union address appears at http://www.gpo.gov.Congress/sou/sou02/html.

48. See George W. Bush, "National Strategy to Combat Weapons of Mass Destruction," White House, December 2002.

49. See http://www.defenselink.mil/transcripts/2003/tr20030509-depsecdef0223.html.

50. Remarks by the President and British Prime Minister Tony Blair, White House, January 31, 2003, http://www.whitehouse.gov/news/releases/2003/01/20030131–23.html.

51. Remarks by the President on Iraq, Cincinnati, Ohio, October 7, 2002, http://www.whitehouse.gov/news/releases/2002/10/20021007–8.html.

52. Secretary of State Colin Powell on C-SPAN, December 8, 2004.

53. Select Committee on Intelligence, United States Senate, *Report on the US Intelligence Community's Prewar Intelligence Assessments on Iraq,* July 7, 2004; Commission on the Intelli-

gence Capabilities of the United States Regarding Weapons of Mass Destruction, *Report to the President of the United States,* March 31, 2005.

54. For instance, regarding Iraq's obtainment of nuclear materials from Niger. See Ambassador Joseph Wilson, *The Politics of Truth: Inside the Lies that Put the White House on Trial and Betrayed My Wife's CIA Identity* (New York: Carroll & Graf, 2005), ch. 15.

55. See Douglas Jehl, "Report Warned Bush Team About Intelligence Doubts," *New York Times,* November 6, 2005.

56. See, for instance, David Hastings Dunn, "Myths, Motivations, and 'Misunderestimations': The Bush Administration and Iraq," 79 *International Affairs,* 2003.

57. Cited in ibid., 280.

58. *Frontline* interview with Osama bin Laden, "Hunting the Enemy," May 1998.

59. See, for instance, Craig Whitlock, "Commandos Free Hostages Being Held in Saudi Arabia," *Washington Post,* May 30, 2004.

60. National Security Directive 54, White House, Washington, DC January 15, 1991. Steve A. Yetiv, *Explaining Foreign Policy: US Decision-Making and the Persian Gulf War* (Baltimore: Johns Hopkins University Press, 2004).

61. On Iraq's potential, see Vincent Lauerman, "Gulf War II: Longer-Term Implications for the World Oil Market," *Geopolitics of Energy,* April 2003.

62. Dresdner, Kleinwort, Wasserstein Research, "Oil Prices Short-Term Strength Masking Longer-Term Weakness," *World Oil Report—2002,* 2, July 24, 2002.

63. This figure represents the average of several different estimates. On Iraq's potential, see Fadhil J. Chalabi, "Iraq and the Future of World Oil," *Middle East Policy* 7, October 2000. Iraq could eventually triple its current production capacity; see EIA, *Annual Energy Outlook 2002.*

64. Issam Al-Chalabi, *Iraqi Oil Policy: Present and Future Perspectives* (Cambridge, MA: Cambridge Energy Research Associates, 2003).

65. Lauerman, "Gulf War II."

66. See John S. Duffield, "Oil and the Iraq War: How the United States Could Have Expected to Benefit, and Might Still," *Middle East Review of International Affairs* 9, June 2005.

67. On these views, see, for instance, Michael Ratner, Jennie Green, and Barbara Olshansky, *Against War in Iraq: An Anti-War Primer* (New York: Seven Stories Press, 2003).

68. On the war's motivations, see Freedman, "War in Iraq," especially page 9.

69. Quoted in Craig Unger, *House of Bush, House of Saud: The Secret Relationship Between the World's Two Most Powerful Dynasties* (New York: Scribner, 2004), 225.

70. See Erik Eckholm, "Now You See It: An Audit of KBR," *New York Times,* March 20, 2005, A4.

71. Remarks by President Bush on September 26, 2002.

72. Brent Scowcroft, "Don't Attack Saddam," *Wall Street Journal,* August 15, 2002.

73. Andrew J. Bacevich and Elizabeth H. Prodromou, "God Is Not Neutral: Religion and US Foreign Policy After 9/11," *Orbis* 48 (Winter 2004):49.

74. *New York Times,* February 15, 2003.

75. Mark Juergensmeyer, "Religious Terror and Global War," in *Understanding September 11,* ed. Craig Calhoun et al. (New York: New Press, 2002).

76. See Edward Peters, "The Firanj Are Coming—Again," *Orbis* 48 (Winter 2004):3–19.

77. See Fawaz A. Gerges, *America and Political Islam: Clash of Cultures or Clash of Interests* (Cambridge: Cambridge University Press, 1999), especially ch. 3.

21

What Went Wrong in Iraq?

Ali R. Abootalebi

As of July 2006 the conditions in Iraq are definitely not what the Bush administration had envisioned they would be when it launched its invasion of the country three years ago. At that time the administration appeared confident that the American forces "liberating" Iraq would be met with welcoming crowds of Iraqis throwing flowers and offering kisses. This euphoric entrance into Baghdad was to be followed, it was hoped, by a quick transition to a liberal secular democracy, if possible through the election of an American-friendly government composed principally of former exiles, in particular that of Ahmed Chalabi and his Iraqi National Congress (INC). With the impressive American military victory in Afghanistan and the creation of the US-friendly Karzai government in Kabul only a year earlier, it seemed the template had already been established.

However, all indications today are that the United States has not only failed to achieve its stated policy objectives in Iraq but that it has actually damaged its long-term policy goals in the Middle East region and reduced the likelihood of its victory in the "war on terror." Rather than establishing a stable democracy with a viable working economy, the invasion of Iraq has instead brought the country to the brink of sectarian civil war, intensified sectarian divisions in the Iraqi political system, undermined regional and international public support for US foreign policy, and seriously weakened the US military.

For these reasons, the invasion of Iraq in 2003 was a strategic mistake for the United States. This mistake was the result of a combination of factors—principally the neoconservative imperial hubris that had infected the Bush administration since September 11, 2001, and the lack of knowledge and understanding of Iraqi society and culture among key decisionmakers. This latter factor also played a role in the many tactical errors made by US personnel in the planning stages of the invasion and in its immediate aftermath—all of which simply compounded the strategic mistake made in the decision to go to war. These include (but are not limited to) the decision to invade with a "light" force, the lack of postwar planning, the decision to quickly disband the Iraqi military, and the absence of comprehensive communication with the Shi'a community and its leadership.

This chapter provides a comprehensive explanation of why the US invasion of Iraq was a strategic mistake and accounts for the many tactical errors that were subsequently made in its implementation.[1] No such analysis would be complete, however, without some suggestions for how a transformed US policy might succeed in extricating its forces from the country while leaving behind a government somewhat amenable to its interests. These suggestions are discussed in the conclusion.

The Iraq War as a Strategic Mistake

The Short-Sighted Neoconservative Vision

The strategic mistake of going to war with Iraq resulted from the miscalculation by President Bush that the transition to stability and democracy in the aftermath of the invasion would be relatively easy. That the president was so misled was the direct result of a number of influential policy advisers, academics, and decisionmakers, many of whom adhere to the vision of American hegemony known as neoconservatism. Though the roots of this movement date back several decades, the neoconservative movement has achieved unprecedented publicity and power in recent years through the so-called Project for a New American Century and the influence its members have gained within the Bush administration.

Individuals in positions of influence who have been part of this neoconservative movement since 2000 include Vice President Dick Cheney; Secretary of Defense Donald Rumsfeld; former Deputy Secretary of Defense Paul Wolfowitz; former Undersecretary of Defense for Policy Douglas Feith; Cheney's chief of staff, Lewis Libby; Zalmay Khalilzad (now US ambassador to Iraq); Special Assistant to the President and Senior Director for Near East and North African Affairs since 2002, Elliot Abrams; and chairman, from 2001 to 2003, of the Defence Policy Advisory Board, Richard Perle.

The neoconservative push to invade Iraq was driven by a number of policy objectives. First, there was the desire to export secular democracy and free market capitalism to Iraq and the wider Middle East. Transforming Iraq into a democracy would lessen the threat it posed to its neighbors, thus allowing for the redeployment of US troops from Saudi Arabia, where their presence near Islam's holiest sites continued to incite Muslim anger. Second, replacing the Saddam regime with a US-friendly government would end its supposed support for Islamic "terrorists" fighting Israel. Third, such a government would also aid the US goal of securing oil and gas pipelines from the Middle East, the Caucuses and Central Asia. And finally, an invasion would put an end to a twelve-year-old policy of economic sanctions and no-fly zones that were continuing to make the United States look ineffectual and weak. All of this could be achieved, they believed, through a rapid military campaign and the replacement of the Ba'thist regime with a mostly secular government composed principally of friendly exiled Iraqis.

Unable to justify the intervention on these policy objectives alone, the Bush administration appeared to fabricate a threat from Iraqi weapons of mass destruction (WMD) and to exaggerate the connections between the Saddam regime and international terrorism. Iraq's supposed WMD program was in fact limited to mainly laboratory experimentation with chemical and biological substances, and its stockpile of weapons had long been destroyed. Since the first Gulf War the United Nations' inspection teams had successfully discovered and supervised the destruction of 90 percent of these weapons, and the regime itself also disposed of its stockpiles for fear of their discovery and potential reprisal. The evidence on Iraq's nuclear activities also pointed to a rudimentary program that never really recovered after the Israeli destruction of the Osirak nuclear plant in 1981. In October 2004, the head of the Iraq Survey Group (ISG), Charles Duelfer, announced that the group had found no evidence that Iraq had produced and stockpiled any WMD since 1991, when UN sanctions were imposed.[2]

Misreading Iraqi Society and Culture

The neoconservative vision failed to take account of Iraqi culture and society and underestimated the influence of Iran. The ethnic (Arabs, Kurds, Turkmen), religious (Shi'a, Sunni), and tribal divisions in Iraq were bound to become a source of instability once the repressive central government was toppled. Islam is the religion of 97 percent of the population, divided along Shi'a, 60–65 percent, and Sunni Islam, 32–37 percent, with Christians and other minorities constituting the rest. The Arab-Kurd divide in Iraq overlaps the Sunni-Shi'a divide, as the 15–20 percent Kurdish population overwhelmingly follows Sunni Islam.[3] The Shi'a clerical leadership continues to emphasize Iraq's Islamic character instead of ethnic and class divisions. While the future of ethnic relations remains uncertain, especially in the face of Kurdish historical aspirations for independence, it is the goal of the Shi'a and Sunni clerical leadership in Iraq and in neighboring Iran to promote Iraqi unity along its Islamic identity. Indeed, given the current situation in Iraq, Islam is the only common denominator among the four main rival ethnic groups (including the small minority of Turkmen) capable of keeping Iraq unified. Secular democracy can be a very attractive solution for observers and policymakers from outside the region, as it evidently was to the Bush administration. But how can secular democracy take hold almost overnight in a society that has had entrenched religious institutions for fourteen hundred years? The experimentation with modernization elsewhere in the Middle East has usually resulted in weak societies and strong states, where power elites have continued to rule through political rhetoric and parochial sources of legitimization, including religion, personal charisma, and political repression and/or cooptation.[4] The rise of political Islam and its relative success in Iran in the mobilization and redirection of socioeconomic resources has raised hopes among sectors of the populace in Iraq and Muslims elsewhere. It is unlikely that a majority of Iraqis will abandon what is so familiar and dear—Islam—for an unknown imported ideology supported by the American and British occupiers and their cohorts among Iraq's secular elites.

A stable, pro-American regime in Iraq with an open economy would be ideal for US geostrategic and energy interests. The Bush administration had anticipated that Iraqi exiles, led by Ahmed Chalabi's Iraqi National Congress, would quickly take over after the regime in Iraq was toppled. Events soon proved otherwise, however. Meanwhile, the new US administrator in Iraq, L. Paul Bremer, set in motion the plan to deliberately dismantle the Iraqi army, privatize the Iraqi economy, and oversee lucrative economic concessions to American companies. Bremer also unsuccessfully tried to hijack Iraqi politics by pushing for elite-driven caucuses in selecting the new Iraqi leaders in January 2004.[5] Only after thousands of Iraqis, mobilized by religious clerics, demonstrated in Baghdad and elsewhere on January 19 did Bremer finally give in to direct elections for a new Iraqi government.

It is not really surprising that the United States is facing problems in Iraq. The biggest mistake has been the failure to understand the nature and the complexities of state-society relations and Islamic movements in the region, including Iraq. This is compounded by the policymakers' *deliberate* refusal to reevaluate American policy objectives in the Middle East in general. The cold war era narrowly defined American policy objectives in the Middle East in terms of cheap, accessible oil; stable, autocratic, friendly regimes; and security for the state of Israel. The only change has been that the menace of communism has been replaced with the "threat" of radical Islam, and political democracy, understood as stable governance based on electioneering, secularism, and privatization, has replaced authoritarianism. Elections and popular participation are thus good so far as they bring the favorable results. Otherwise, the Bush administration's attempt to spread democracy and freedom in the Middle East remains propaganda. And, contrary to the claim that the end of the cold war has meant "one of reduced military and economic means to influence events in the region," the United States established a military presence in Saudi Arabia and Bahrain in the 1990s and used the "Saddam scare" to become, in effect, the security guard for the Saudis, Kuwaitis, and other Persian Gulf shaykhdoms.[6]

The return of Islam to the center stage of politics and society in the Middle East is not surprising. It need not be seen as a threatening force against political stability and democracy in the region. The interplay between Islam and politics in Iraq today is over the question of "effective governance," and not whether Islam is trying to totally dominate politics or to use the democratic process to destroy democracy for the sake of an Islamic theocracy. The question really should be whether political Islam can govern and whether Islam and democracy can coexist within particular Muslim (for example, Iraqi) sociopolitical, economic, and cultural milieus. If this dilemma is not resolved, US phobia about political Islam will seriously damage its interests in Iraq and in the Middle East in general. The US invasion of Iraq was not undertaken for altruistic reasons; it was a decision based on the geopolitical interests of the United States. But the ensuing chaos in Iraq seems to be the result of strategic mistakes, miscalculations, policy blunders, and arrogance, all of which reflect a larger imbalanced and faulty policy in the Middle East.

Undermining the "War on Terrorism"

The resistance of the ex-Ba'thists, Jihadists, and nationalists to the occupation, though motivated by different agendas, has proven lethal. The Jihadists, inspired by al-Qa'ida and Salafi and Wahhabi ideologies, now consider Iraq a potential base for continuing their *jihad* against the crusading West and their Iraqi allies. The Iraqi nationalists and ex-Ba'thists, on the other hand, see their fight against occupation as a matter of Iraqi pride and lost socioeconomic resources and prestige. The insurgency has used every means available in attacks on coalition forces and Iraqi government forces with the objective of either regaining lost power (the primary motivation of the ex-Ba'thists) or setting up a new "Islamic" base to counter the US presence in Iraq and its support of "corrupt" regimes in the Arab world (the goal of the Jihadists).

The post-9/11 terrorist attack on American forces in Iraq has also revealed that al-Qa'ida is really a multinational network of dedicated radical militants from all over the Muslim world, committed to an anti-Western, and especially anti-American, campaign. The ultimate goal of al-Qa'ida is the eradication of Western influence and control over Muslim countries, especially the oil-rich Middle East. But equally important to al-Qa'ida operatives is the overthrow of "corrupt" governments in the Middle East and elsewhere in the Muslim world, who, with the support of the West, have abandoned the *will of Allah*—the establishment of just and viable Islamic governments. The US support of the "illegitimate" state of Israel in its conflict with the conquered Palestinians, the US military presence in Saudi Arabia and the Persian Gulf states and support for their corrupt regimes, and the long-standing US sanctions against innocent Iraqi people have been cited by Osama bin Laden as the fundamental reasons behind his strong anti-American stance. One observer has succinctly summarized the challenge to American foreign policy in the Middle East:

> Two groups have come under examination in the "why do they hate us?" debate that has unfolded since September 11, 2001. One comprises the perpetrators of violence and terrorism—the Osama bin Ladens, the Mohammad Attas, and some suicide bombers. They are fanatics in every sense of the word. Their interpretations of politics and Islam are so extreme that they disparage the great majority of Muslim Middle Easterners as "unbelievers." They are not going to be deterred by debate, compromise, sanctions, or even the threat of death. The challenge they pose to the United States is a security issue, a matter to be dealt with through careful police work and military action. America's resources are adequate for dealing with this threat. The vastly larger group of Muslim Middle Easterners who express anger toward the United States and evince some sympathy for bin Laden pose a far more serious challenge. This group's members are afflicted by middle-class frustrations, governed by political systems that give them no voice, and burdened by economies that offer them few opportunities. They are witnessing a conflict over land and sacred places in which they perceive the

United States as applying two standards of equity and two standards of measuring violence, each in favor of Israel. That resulting frustration and anger leads to expressions of sympathy for those who resort to violence against the United States.[7]

The Bush administration and its supporters continue to claim that Iraq has become a "graveyard" for militant Jihadists and therefore the United States remains safer today since the battleground has moved away from the homeland. However, it has become clear from various assessments by Israeli, British, and American sources that the invasion of Iraq has created a new generation of Islamic Jihadists who will continue to pose a serious threat to the United States for years to come. For example, the appearance of many "self-starter" terrorists, like the ones responsible for the attack on Madrid's public transportation system in 2004 and London's in 2005, and the Iraqi Jihadist movement, including groups like Ansar al-Sunna and the Islamic Army of Iraq, negate the claim of a Jihadist retreat in the aftermath of the Iraqi invasion.

The war in Iraq has also drawn resources away from the US-declared war on terrorism. According to the Center for Strategic and Budgetary Assessments, the United States spent $48 billion on the Iraq war in 2003, $59 billion in 2004, and $81 billion in 2005. The center predicts the figure for 2006 will balloon to $94 billion. That equates to a $1,205 bill for each of America's 78 million families, on top of the taxes they already pay.[8] More importantly, the Iraq war, as John Mueller suggests, "will have important consequences for US foreign policy for years after the last American battalion leaves Iraqi soil . . . among which could be the Bush doctrine, unilateralism, preemption, preventive war, and indispensable nationhood."[9]

There is a widespread belief among Iraqis that the US presence in Iraq is not for the sake of their "liberation" but for their oil wealth and that the US military will remain in Iraq indefinitely. A recent survey of Iraqi attitudes toward Americans indicates that

> Large majorities of Iraqis believe that the United States has no intention of ever withdrawing all its military forces from their country and that Washington's reconstruction efforts have been incompetent at best: Eighty percent of respondents said they believe the US intends to maintain permanent military bases in Iraq, including 79 percent of Shi'a Arabs, 92 percent of Sunnis, and two-thirds of Kurds, some of whose leaders have quietly suggested that Washington would be welcome to establish bases in Kurdistan in northern Iraq.[10]

Terrorism experts Peter Bergen and Alec Reynolds suggest that the war in Iraq "will generate a ferocious blowback of its own, which—as a recent classified CIA assessment predicts—could be longer and more powerful than that from Afghanistan in the 1990s and beyond."[11] This is aside from the drastic decline in popularity of the United States in the Arab and Muslim world, as indicated by various polls taken by the Pew Research center for the People and the Press, Zogby, and CNN/Gallup. According to Daniel Benjamin and Steven Simon, experts on terrorism and former members of the National Security Council under President Clinton, much of the blame for the drastic mistakes made in the invasion of Iraq and its dire consequences lies with the Bush administration.[12]

Weakening Support for US Foreign Policy at Home and Abroad

The decision to take action in Iraq should have been made by the United Nations Security Council, not made unilaterally by the United States. UN Secretary General Kofi Annan declared that the invasion of Iraq was illegal, since it contravened the UN Charter.[13] To make matters worse, later revelations entirely debunked the initial allegations by the Bush administration and British Prime Minister Tony Blair that the invasion of Iraq was justified by well-documented intelligence reports concerning weapons of mass destruction. As it turned out, intelligence reports in both Britain and the United States may have been manipulated to support the invasion, and the decision to go to war may have been driven by policy rather than facts. The "Downing Street memo," as first reported on May 1, 2005 by the *Sunday Times* of London, revealed that Blair was told by the head of Britain's MI6 intelligence service, Sir Richard Dearlove, that in 2002 the Bush administration was selectively choosing evidence that supported its case for going to war and ignoring anything to the contrary.[14] James Risen of the *New York Times* provided vital additional background to the Downing Street memo in his book *State of War.* The revelation even led to the appearance of an organization by the same name to rally American support for the impeachment of President Bush.[15]

Leaders throughout the Middle East, including traditional allies, cautioned the United States to reflect on the consequences of its "unbalanced" approach to the region (particularly vis-à-vis the Israeli-Palestinian conflict and Iraq), and public opinion in the Arab world indicated mounting resentment against perceived US hegemony and arrogance. However, the message from the White House was loud and clear: There will be no drastic changes in the overall formulation of policy preferences. Despite the flood of analyses and editorials to the contrary, the Bush administration used the occasion to portray al-Qa'ida and militant Muslims as those who hate America, without seriously contemplating those policy issues and grievances raised by not only al-Qa'ida's leadership but also the mainstream advocates of peace in the Middle East, including a just resolution of the Arab/Palestinian-Israeli conflict and the promotion of democracy instead of support for authoritarian regimes. It took the debacle in Iraq for the administration to admit that fifty years of support for authoritarian regimes in the Middle East did not make America any more secure.

The cost of the Iraq war to the American military, economy, and society itself has been substantial. The number of American soldiers dead and injured has climbed slowly and steadily, although the Iraqis have paid the brunt of the human cost of the invasion. American and coalition troops dead in Iraq as of April 1, 2006, stood at 2,314 Americans, 103 Brits, and 103 others.[16] The debate is now centered on whether the American troop presence in Iraq is helping the long-term cause of stability or whether it is a magnet for acts of violence and resistance by the insurgency.[17] By summer 2005, the Pentagon had allocated an additional $100 billion for Iraq war costs, 45 percent more than the previous year, pushing the total cost of the Iraq invasion well past $200 billion.[18] In summer 2005, the nonpartisan Congressional Research Service also reported that "since 2003, Congress had given the Defense Department $183 billion for Iraq, while appropriating an additional $25 billion to other government agencies operating in Iraq, for a total of $208 billion."[19] Others, like Nobel Laureate Joseph E. Stiglitz and Harvard budget expert Linda Bilmes, have estimated the cost of the Iraq war at $1–2 trillion, far higher than earlier estimates of $100–200 billion at the beginning of the war. The Stiglitz and Bilmes study includes such costs as the long-term medical needs of war veterans and opportunity costs involving the war.[20] Furthermore, the war in Iraq has severely damaged the American image and US capabilities worldwide, polarized the American public, and undermined civil liberties at home through the Patriot Act and legally questionable surveillance acts sanctioned by the Bush administration.

Compounding the Strategic Mistake: Tactical Errors in Planning and Implementation

Too Few Ground Troops

Soon after the initial US and UK launch of "Shock and Awe" and the ground invasion on March 20, 2006, it was clear that the number of troops committed to the operation was inadequate. The fall of Baghdad in sixteen days, on April 5, was attributed to American military strategy and technological superiority. Some elements of the Iraqi army put up stiff resistance in places like Nasariyah, but the scale of the resistance was far smaller than the expected house-to-house battle in Iraqi cities. The statute of Saddam Hussein in Firdos Square came down on April 9, but it soon became clear that the potent and deadly American military lacked the numbers to both occupy and control vast Iraqi territories. As General Franks put it, the United States had sufficient combat forces in Iraq but did not initially have enough civil affairs, military police, and other units needed to establish order after major combat was over; the issue was not the level of forces, but their composition. Reporting on General Franks's assessment, Michael Gordon of the *New York Times* asserted: "This was partly a result of difficulties in getting all of the Central Command's force requests approved quickly at the Pentagon. He also admitted that delays in obtaining funds from Congress for reconstruction efforts and the decision of many foreign governments not to send troops had contributed to the continuing turmoil in Iraq."[21] General Franks stopped short of criticizing his boss, Donald Rumsfeld, but by then the gulf between the Pentagon and the commanders on the ground on military strategy was increasingly apparent.

Others have reached similar conclusions. The generals on the ground understood what a disaster they were creating in the race to reach Baghdad, which left in its wake an entire country full of places where Saddam Hussein's loyalists could regroup and prepare to carry on a permanent war. In *Cobra II,* Michael Gordon and General Bernard Trainor underscore that the generals in the field were over-ruled by directives from Washington, where military decisions were being made by men who were guided not by reality but by their own beloved myths about Iraq and how the war was going to be won. They argue that in addition to the ac-tual war, there was an ongoing war between US field commanders, their own sen-ior commander (General Tommy Franks, the head of Central Command), and civilian leaders in Washington. Gordon and Trainor contend that the US mili-tary's quick victory came despite the strategic miscalculations of senior civilian and military leaders and that the Bush team's misjudgments made the situation in Iraq far worse than it otherwise would have been.[22] Michael Gordon observed in late 2004:

> Looking back at that crucial time, officers, administration officials, and others pro-vided an intimate and detailed account of how the postwar situation went awry. Civil-ian administrators of the Iraqi occupation raised concerns about plans to reduce American forces; intelligence agencies left American forces unprepared for the furious battles they encountered in Iraq's southern cities and did not emphasize the risks of a postwar insurgency. And senior American generals and civilians were at odds over plans to build a new Iraqi army, which was needed to impose order.[23]

Insufficient Planning

On April 14, 2003, the Pentagon declared an end to major combat operations after US forces took control of Tikrit in northern Iraq, and the commander in chief him-self announced "mission accomplished" on May 1. The question no one was asking, however, was what happened to the Iraqi army? The presumption seemed to be that the Iraqi army, facing certain destruction, had simply dissolved. But the Iraqi army had proven itself a loyal army with strong commitments to the Ba'thist ideology and the rule of the privileged Sunni Arabs. Speculations about Saddam's army making a grand stand in a battle of cities did not materialize, since the Iraqi army had learned the lessons of the first Persian Gulf war in 1991 on how deadly a direct confronta-tion with US forces can be. The Pentagon, however, had failed to anticipate and prepare for an unconventional guerrilla war. It should not have come as a surprise to the war planners that the core of the Iraqi army, the Republican Guards, would fight the invasion, but on its own terms. In the 1991 war, the Iraqi army sacrificed thou-sands of its poorly trained and equipped peasant army to slow down the American liberation of Kuwait and the occupation of southern Iraq, while the elite Republican Guards suppressed the Shi'a and Kurdish rebellion and ensured the regime's sur-vival. In October 2004 Condoleezza Rice put the blame for the insurgency prima-rily "on the fact that many Iraqi forces fled during the American push to Baghdad, only to fight another day."[24]

When Ambassador L. Paul Bremer III issued his decrees on May 16 and 23, 2003, disestablishing the Ba'th Party and disbanding Iraqi armed forces, he was fueling the resistance with additional incentives for a prolonged guerrilla resistance to the occupation. The Ba'thists had ruled over Iraq since 1968, with strong ties to tribal leaders and an iron-fist policy in suppressing Shi'a and Kurdish opposition. The Iraqi regime had survived eight years of a disastrous war with Iran and the humiliation of the first Persian Gulf war and then survived and even thrived under the United Nations sanctions regime throughout the 1990s. The declaration of these decrees could not undo a woven network of connections and privileges in Iraqi civil-military relations, and Paul Bremer should have known that. The hard core of the loyal Republican Guards had prepared to disband itself on the eve of the war but only to engage in a prolonged guerrilla fight later. The tactics and skills used by the insurgents in Iraq today are testimony to the Guards' central involvement in the insurgency.

The chaos that fell on Baghdad after the fall of the regime exposed how ill-prepared the US forces were for dealing with the post-conflict situation. The looting of Baghdad began almost immediately after coalition troops arrived in Baghdad. While the Baghdad national museum was being looted, US troops were busy protecting the oil ministry. The poorly protected munitions depots were looted, and nearly all government services came to a halt. The absence of police protection and the prolonged disruptions in electric, water, sewage, and other basic services contributed to the transformation of the initial low-intensity conflict into a much deadlier form of insurgency. On July 16, 2003, General John Abizaid called the increasing attacks on coalition troops a "guerrilla-type campaign," speculating that troops might need to be deployed for up to one year. The August 19, 2003, bombing of the UN's Baghdad office, killing UN representative Sergio Vieira de Mello and twenty-one others, and the August 29 bombing in Najaf that killed eighty-three people, including the leader of the Supreme Council for the Islamic Revolution in Iraq (SCIRI), Mohammad Baqir al-Hakim, were devastating blows to the United States and other coalition members as the new protectors of the Iraqi people. By then, the number of US combat deaths had reached 117, and more had died since the declared end of combat operations than had died during the initial combat.

In the first eight months after the invasion, the Bremer administration tried to recover international support for the coalition occupation of Iraq and to further legitimate the coalition troop presence. The creation of the twenty-five-member Iraqi Governing Council on July 13, 2003, and its August 14 UN Security Council approval were intended to mend earlier splits in the UN Security Council that positioned the United States and Great Britain on one side and France (and Germany) and, to a lesser degree, China and the Russian Federation on the other. Later, on November 15, Bremer's Coalition Provisional Authority (CPA) and the Iraqi Governing Council (IGC) signed an agreement to draft an interim constitution by February 28, 2004, and to transfer power by July 1, 2004. In the meantime, Bremer and the US military were caught by surprise as insurgents stepped up their deadly attacks and the Shi'a religious leadership began to flex its muscle. The number of US soldiers killed in Iraq reached five hundred on January 17, 2004, and soon thereafter the Grand Ayatollah Ali al-Sistani rejected the US proposal for indirect, caucus-style elections. Iraq's Shi'a leadership was not a part of the "grand coalition" of Iraqi exiles who were slated to govern a post-invasion Iraq.

The insurgency was also fueled by ordinary Iraqis who joined the cause because of their loss of livelihood or because of humiliation suffered at the hands of the Americans. The injection of non-Iraqi foreign fighters and al-Qa'ida Jihadists into the Iraqi theater has only served to strengthen the existing resistance, since the war with the coalition forces was already expected to be a long-term conflict. Ba'thists and Jihadists have different visions and agendas for the future of Iraq and are using different strategies in targeting the occupation forces, Iraqi civilians, and the US-supported Shi'a-led government in Iraq. Nonetheless, there is little evidence of in-fighting between these two groups based on their ideological differences or military tactics, which have generally caused more deaths among Iraqi civilians than among the coalition forces. This is not a surprise, however. As long as the US occupation of Iraq persists, it unifies the opposition to the US "design" for the future of Iraqi oil and a long-term military presence, and the presence of US troops in Iraq has been a magnet for foreign fighters and Jihadists. The secular, nationalist Ba'thists may or may not share the radical Jihadists' view of the Shiites as apostates, and the Jihadists may disdain the Ba'thist secularism. Ba'thists hope for a return to the secular, Sunni-dominated era, while the Jihadists yearn for an Islamic caliphate free of all apostates, including all those Muslims who have abandoned the "true" path of Allah. Despite their significantly different goals, they have collaborated in targeting the Shiite-dominated government and the foreign occupiers. For now, political chaos and even civil war serve the interests of both Ba'thists and Jihadists, even if innocent Iraqis are victimized.

Underestimating the Shi'a Factor

Although Ahmad Chalabi and the mainly secular members of the Iraq National Congress (INC) had the attention and support of neoconservatives in Washington, a larger and more popular group of Iraqi oppositionists had spent years organizing in Iran, building the foundation of a future Islamic Iraq. The SCIRI and Hizb al-Da'wah had long-established political and theological links between the seminaries in Qom in Iran and al-Najaf in Iraq, with a clear vision that Iraq would one day become an Islamic republic. Given the traditional ties between the Shi'a leadership in Iran and the Shi'a leadership in Iraq, the Ayatollah Ali al-Sistani's stature in both the Shi'a and Sunni communities, and the suffering of Iraqi people under the secular Ba'thist regime, the clerics in Iraq were inevitably going to rise to the center stage of Iraqi politics. However, the United States made no serious contacts with the Shi'a leadership in Iraq prior to, or in the initial phase of, the invasion, and Jay Garner and Paul Bremer seemed to be unaware or ignorant of the gathering Shi'a power. Clearly, the Shi'a leadership would have not agreed then, nor would it agree in the future, to submit to secular politics and an extended US military presence in Iraq. Nevertheless, the exclusion of prominent indigenous and exiled Shi'a clerics from plans for the future of Iraq certainly added to the mistrust of US intentions.

The clash between US forces and the militia loyal to the fiery and popular Shi'a leader Moqtada al-Sadr on April 4, 2004, was testimony not so much to the divisions within the Shi'a clerical leadership but to their preferred strategies. Despite the CPA issuing an arrest warrant for al-Sadr, his al-Mahdi Army fought US forces for seven weeks until the truce agreement on May 27. The truce was really the product of al-Sistani's call for al-Sadr to stop fighting in order to prevent a premature popular Shi'a rebellion, at a time when the mainly Sunni and Jihadi resistance to the coalition forces meant accepting, for the present, the US "meddling" in the Iraqi affairs. Ayatollah al-Sistani may adhere to the "quietist" school of Shi'a Islam—which calls for clerics to avoid a direct involvement in politics—but his vision for the future of Iraq parallels his Shi'a counterparts in Iraq and Iran who oppose secular political governance and social relations. The Shi'a clerical leadership understands that in light of Sunni Arab and Kurdish opposition to a Shi'a-dominated state, it must enlist the cooperation of non-Shi'a sectors of the Iraqi population. Thus, the key to its political success is the utilization of both cooperation (al-Sistani) and resistance (al-Sadr) to maintain its leverage. However, the Bush administration has been thoroughly oblivious to the networking power of the religious *hawzehs*—religious seminaries—in Iraq and Iran. There are millions of dedicated supporters among Shi'a and Sunni Islamic movements who, having rejected Ba'thism and despising foreign military occupation, continue to strive for an Islamic Iraq.

The United States, from the beginning, had decided to support secular forces in Iraq in both the exiled and the indigenous communities. The Shi'a clerical power, including open clashes with the al-Mahdi Army in Kufa, Karbala, Najaf, al-Kut, and Sadr City, was considered to be a direct challenge to US plans in Iraq. The creation of Iraq's interim administration under Ghazi al-Yawar as president and Ayad Allawi as prime minister was to promote a functional secular government to deal with Iraqis' daily problems. The success of the Allawi administration was therefore dependent upon the position of secular forces in Iraq. However, the revelation of physical and sexual abuse of Iraqi prisoners in Abu Ghraib on April 23, the persistent inflicting of pain on Iraqis and coalition forces by the insurgency, including the beheading of Nick Berg, shown on a video on the Internet on May 11, and the deterioration of living conditions in Iraq continued to undermine the leadership of the US-supported interim administration. It should have come as no surprise when Ayad Allawi's Iraqi National List captured only a small percentage of the vote in the December 12, 2005, parliamentary election. The US administration's ignorance concerning the power of the Shi'a clerics and the unpopularity of the US-backed Iraqi politicians is reflected in a recent report. The co-directors of Conflicts Forum, a London-based group dedicated to providing an opening to political Islam, Alastair Crooke and Mark Perry, observed that "seventy-two hours before the Iraqi people voted on a new parliament, on December 12, 2005, we were told by a senior US administration official that 'detailed data received by the White House' pointed to a 'decisive win' for Ayad Allawi's Iraqi National List." Allawi's victory would turn the tables on the insurgents, this official said gleefully. "Sectarianism will be the big loser." Allawi's prospective triumph was trumpeted repeatedly over the next two days by US news networks quoting administration officials. Weeks later, after the results of the election became known, it was clear that the White House had overestimated Allawi's popularity: His party received just over 5 percent of the vote.[25]

Larry Diamond, a leading US expert on democracy, agreed in 2004, despite his initial opposition to the invasion, to help the Iraq transitional authority with the draft of Iraq's interim constitution, known as the Transitional Administrative Law (TAL). Diamond was pressed by administrators and policymakers to quickly draft the TAL, while addressing the competing concerns of Shiite ambition, Kurdish separatism, and Sunni alienation that followed the invasion. In the end, Diamond's recommendation for a proportional representation scheme for Iraq's general election fell on deaf ears, supposedly because of time and logistical constraints. His critique of the Iraqi operation focuses on several key mistakes. The first US civilian administration arrived in Baghdad with virtually no capacity to function in Arabic; it purged the Ba'th Party and disbanded the army; the United States invaded Iraq with an inadequate level of forces to maintain security; and the administration failed to plan for peace and allowed the Pentagon to set the strategy for postwar Iraq. For Diamond, the administration's worst sin was not going to war but going to war unprepared.[26] Diamond also observed that Ayatollah Ali al-Sistani—the most revered Shiite religious leader—repeatedly proposed more pro-democratic positions than the United States itself and that the Bush administration ignored numerous warnings from its own officials in Iraq that the Shiite heartland was going to erupt (which it did in April 2004).

Diamond seems to think that if the war and occupation had been conducted differently—for example, more troops on the ground, better planning for the occupation, better administration in dealing with the remnants of the former regime—the operation would have ended with the successful achievement of its goals. The problem with such analyses is that they overlook the fact that from the very beginning the Iraqi Shi'a leadership was intent on resisting any plan for a US-supported secular democratic government. The plan for the future of postwar Iraq was inherently based an illusory notion to build a secular, pro-American democracy, promoted by Iraqi secular exiles who were fixated primarily on getting rid of Saddam and not on building a future democratic Iraq. Meanwhile, the Iraqi Islamist exiles were being nurtured in Iran. The Iraqi Shi'a leadership, including members of the al-Hakim family, the former prime minister Ibrahim al-Ja'fari, and other members of both Shi'a opposition groups, al-Da'wah and the SCIRI, were well prepared to fill the vacuum created by the fallen Ba'thist regime.

The Shi'a leadership in both Iraq and Iran were certain from the start that the US long-term goal was to establish its military and economic presence in Iraq, and the Iraqi people remained suspicious of US intentions. Moreover, the economic and political chaos that followed the invasion made the religious leadership of both the Shi'a and Sunni communities a more attractive alternative for restoring dignity to the Iraqi people as well as Iraq's sovereignty. Diamond, writing for *Foreign Affairs* in late 2004, described the nature of the problem, as perceived by the Iraqis:

The coalition never grasped, for example, the fact that, although most Iraqis were grateful for having been liberated from a brutal tyranny, their gratitude was mixed with deep suspicion of the United States' real motives (not to mention those of the United Kingdom, a former colonial ruler of Iraq); humiliation that the Iraqis themselves had proved unable to overthrow Saddam; and unrealistic expectations of the postwar administration, which Iraqis expected to quickly deliver them from their problems. Too many Iraqis viewed the invasion not as international effort but as an occupation by Western, Christian, essentially Anglo-American powers, and this evoked powerful memories of previous subjugation and of the nationalist struggles against Iraq's former overlords.[27]

What has emerged as a powerful alliance of Shi'a groups, the United Iraqi Alliance, is the natural outcome of the changed political environment in Iraq in the aftermath of the collapse of the Ba'thist regime. Despite their differences in leadership and organization, the leading Shi'a parties in the alliance, SCIRI and al-Da'wah, share aspirations for a religiously oriented Iraq, in close cooperation with their counterparts in Iran. It is no secret that leading Shi'a clerics and networks in Iraq and Iran (as well as in Lebanon) have overlapping and complementary personal and religious ties and experiences. There are prominent Shi'a clerics with their feet in both countries' main religious seminaries in al-Najaf and Qom. Ayatollah Ali al-Sistani, for example, was born in Iran but is the leading religious figure in Iraq. The late Grand Ayatollah Abul-Qassim Khoei was born in Iran in 1899 but moved to Iraq at age thirteen and took residence in the holy city of Najaf. The famous al-Sadr family has had a long history of prominent Shi'a clerical leadership in Iraq and Lebanon. The late Grand Ayatollah Sayyid Muhammad Baqir al-Sadr, who was born in al-Kadhimya, Iraq, and worked with Sayed Mohammed Baqir al-Hakim in forming the Islamic movement in Iraq, is the father-in-law of Moqtada al-Sadr and the cousin of both Mohammad Sadeq al-Sadr and Lebanon's Imam Musa al-Sadr. Ayatollah Sayed Mohammed Baqir al-Hakim, cofounder of SCIRI, fled to Iran in 1980 and, along with Iranian Ayatollah Modarresi, cofounded SCIRI. There are currently sixteen grand ayatollahs and twenty-two ayatollahs who are directly or indirectly active in the Qom religious seminaries, many with personal and religious ties with al-Najaf in Iraq.[28] The Bush administration's wishful thinking that the future of Iraq would be a secular democracy was an act of self-deception.

In the ongoing debacle in Iraq and Afghanistan, the leadership in Tehran sees both an opportunity and a threat. Tehran is nervous about the American (and NATO) military presence in Iraq and Afghanistan and the ensuing instability in both of these countries, including drastic increases in drug trafficking and ethnic tension, which have spilled over into Iran. Added to this concern is the well-established US infantry, naval, and aerial presence in the Persian Gulf and in the Caucasus and Central Asia. The socioeconomic and political challenges from within the country, where two-thirds of the population is under thirty years old and national development has tangibly been hurt because of American economic, political, and diplomatic pressure, also have had security implications for Iran. That is, the Iranian leadership strongly believes that the United States is intent on regime change in Iran, especially given the presence of powerful neoconservatives in the Bush administration. Iran's controversial nuclear program has further intensified American political pressure on the government of Iran. Iraq has in the meantime become a playing card in the high-stakes poker game between Tehran and Washington, especially with the escalating financial and human cost of the war in Iraq and Afghanistan and the declining popularity of President Bush. In the end, the crisis in Iraq cannot be resolved without the cooperation of Iran, but the government in Tehran is trying to tie its leverage in Iraq to its ambitions for a civilian, and perhaps military, nuclear program.[29]

Iran is frequently cited as the biggest beneficiary of America's war on terrorism due to the removal of the Taliban in Afghanistan and Saddam in Iraq. But observers of the region hold differing opinions on how the situation in Iraq will impact Iranian policy. Some have argued that there is no unitary Iranian approach when it comes to Iraq. Michael Eisenstadt argues that "there are debates in Tehran that fall in along ideological as well as pragmatic fault lines." In this scenario, Iran would seek a US withdrawal from Iraq in the long run, but a "manageable" state of conflict would be in their short-term geostrategic interests, since this would keep the United States tied down in Iraq. The US military preoccupation in Iraq would work to Iran's advantage, given the controversy over Iran's nuclear program and the threat of UN sanctions or even military action by the United States, Israel, or both. F. Gregory Gause has a different perspective, contending that "a government [in Iraq] that is seen as a viable democratic model might be a source of embarrassment for Iran." Geoff Porter goes even further and argues that "if Iraq were to evolve into an Islamist democracy, this would be a bad example for Iran, which would be forced to entertain alternative forms of an Islamist state that differ from the current iteration."[30]

Although some Sunni Arabs have accused Iraqi leaders of allowing Shi'a Badr members to infiltrate Iraq's security forces and carry out sectarian violence, this does not indicate an Iranian conspiracy to destabilize Iraq for the sake of keeping American troops preoccupied and thus away from Iran.[31] It is true that SCIRI's military wing, the 12,000-strong Badr Brigades, continues to receive financial and training support from Iran's Revolutionary Guard, and Iran also supports Sadr's Mahdi Army, which on occasion has clashed with the Badr Brigades. But the Shi'a religious leadership in Iraq are the natural allies of Iran, no matter the differences in their tactics in dealing with the occupation. Furthermore, the Sunni religious leadership in Iraq does not necessarily see the Shi'a establishment as a primary enemy. The religious doctrinal differences between the two communities are somewhat significant, but both share in common the Quran, the *shari'a* (Islamic law), the Five Pillars of Islam, and the cultural foundations of the faith. Followers of the both sects of Islam have lived together for centuries without a history of communal clashes.[32] The Sunni-Shi'a divide in Iraq is mainly the result of political jockeying among major contenders of power in Iraq and has been exacerbated by American military and political presence, creating the perception that the Shi'a-dominated government is merely an American puppet government that is also being exploited by the Iranians. Shi'as in Iraq, Lebanon, the Persian Gulf states, and elsewhere see an opportunity to break away from their sociopolitical and economic deprivation through Islamic revivalism. Thus the challenge to the United States is to prevent the establishment of an *anti-American* Shi'a-dominated or an *anti-American* Arab Sunni/Shi'a-dominated religious state. This is, however, exactly what is occurring. It is in the long-term American national interest to embrace a democratically, albeit religious, elected Iraqi (and Iranian) government, since the *ulama* (Islamic religious scholars) and Islamists are not inherently anti-American.

Given the historical religious ties and the majority Shi'a population, it is certain that Islam will play a central, if not dominating, role in the future of any Iraqi government. The configuration of an Islamic-oriented government in Iraq is yet to be determined, but the best outcome for Iran is a clerically dominated Iraqi state that is parallel to Iran's but adjusted for the mixed Sunni-Shi'a population and religious leadership, while downplaying ethnic divisions. Moreover, Iran's interests in Iraq are not limited to politics. Tehran also has a commercial stake in Iraq's future. In addition to building a $25 million airport in Basra, Iranian businessmen are buying up property in southern Iraq. Furthermore, a large number of Iranians make religious pilgrimages to Iraqi holy places, and the Iranian government has an interest in ensuring their security.

Conclusion

Contrary to political rhetoric by Bush administration statesmen, the United States is not seriously committed to establishing democracy in the Middle East. The United States has cast a blind eye to human rights abuses in Algeria, Egypt, Saudi Arabia, Jordan, Kuwait, Turkey, Afghanistan, Pakistan, Indonesia, and elsewhere in the Muslim world. President George W. Bush's initial reluctance to invest political capital and actively engage in the "peace process" also has proven damaging to the Palestinian Authority and the Arab states in their dealings with Israel. Removing Saddam from power had little to do with the liberation of the Iraqi people. The connection between the two was mentioned, of course, usually with great enthusiasm, but as Lawrence Freedman stated: "Emancipation was not the reason why the Bush administration went to war or invoked international law to justify it. For Cheney and Rumsfeld, the war was about solving the Saddam problem rather than the Iraq problem, about bringing security rather than justice, about toppling the regime rather than building one. After all, the Bush administration had profoundly said that it was not in the business of nation building and would happily leave it to others."[33]

Freedman further asserted:

To the Bush administration's cavalier assumption that Iraq could be transformed without any extraordinary U.S. efforts, other offenses can be added: the divisive diplomacy that accompanied Washington's rush to war, which tarnished the invasion's legitimacy and then limited international support for an extended occupation; the Pentagon's refusal to commit more troops for postwar reconstruction when so few had won the war; inadequate training, to help U.S. soldiers transition from combat to peacekeeping; disregard for the prospects (and the consequences) of the looting and disarray that followed the fall of Saddam's regime; the decision to disband the defeated Iraqi military; the failure to fully appreciate the implications of excluding former members of the ruling Ba'th party from key administrative posts; the inability to foresee the public relations disaster and the ethical morass that would inevitably result from treating Iraqi prisoners in ways reminiscent of Saddam's methods. The list is not exhaustive.[34]

The US strategy to create a post-invasion secular and democratic Iraq was unrealistic from the start, given Iraq's large Shi'a population, the Shi'a clerical power over their adherents, and their strong connections with religious and political establishments in neighboring Iran. Not only are the numerous strategic and tactical mistakes made in Iraq the result of bad judgment, but they also reflect a lack of fundamental understanding of the nature of Iraq's cultural, religious, and sociopolitical settings. The military and administrative mismanagement of Iraq has also played into the hands of Iraqi opposition to the American military presence. Ironically, these mistakes provide further justification for the decisionmakers to prolong indefinitely the US military presence in Iraq. The competition between the United States and Iraqi Islamists over the future of Iraq is likely to continue for years to come and will not be resolved during the current Bush administration.

The bankruptcy of the neoconservative ideology is perhaps best exemplified by Francis Fukuyama, a leading neoconservative ideologue who has recently distanced himself from the movement:

> Neoconservatism, whatever its complex roots, has become indelibly associated with concepts like coercive regime change, unilateralism and "benevolent" American hegemony. What is needed now are new ideas, neither neoconservative nor realist, for how America is to relate to the rest of the world—ideas that retain the neoconservative belief in the universality of human rights, but without its illusions about the efficacy of American power and hegemony's behavior to bring these ends about.[35]

Fukuyama further observed that "a Wilsonian policy that pays attention to how rulers treat their citizens is therefore right, but it needs to be informed by a certain realism that was missing from the thinking of the Bush administration in its first term and of its neoconservative allies."[36] Finally, pointing out one of the basic flaws in the neoconservative view of Iraq in the aftermath of the fall of Saddam Hussein, Fukuyama asserted that "the war's supporters seemed to think that democracy was a kind of default condition to which societies reverted once the heavy lifting of coercive regime change occurred, rather than a long-term process of institution-building and reform."[37]

The reasons behind what went wrong in Iraq are deeper than only strategic or tactical mistakes committed by the White House, the Pentagon, or the US-appointed administrators in Iraq. In his book, George Packer, a liberal hawk who supported the invasion in the hope of bringing an end to tyranny in Iraq, still insists that the "Iraq war was always winnable; it still is, [and] for this very reason, the recklessness of its authors is all the harder to forgive." Packer recalls in his book the exchange in a meeting between the war hawks and Jay Garner, the head of the Office of Reconstruction and Humanitarian Assistance (ORHA), who had just been replaced by L. Paul Bremer. Packers notes, "None of those present in the meeting, including President George W. Bush, Vice President Dick Cheney, Secretary of Defense Donald Rumsfeld, and National Security Adviser Condoleezza Rice, asked Garner about the realities of the situation in Iraq." The president even jokingly asked Garner, "You want to do Iran for the next one?" to which Garner replied, "No, sir, me and the boys are holding out for Cuba."[38] The cavalier attitude of the central players in the invasion of a sovereign country of 25 million people is just stunning.

Writing in February 2005, James Dobbins, Director of the International Security and Defense Policy Center at the RAND Corporation wrote this assessment of the war:

> The beginning of wisdom is to recognize that the ongoing war in Iraq is not one that the United States can win. As a result of its initial miscalculations, misdirected planning, and inadequate preparation, Washington has lost the Iraqi people's confidence and consent, and it is unlikely to win them back. Every day that Americans shell Iraqi cities they lose further ground on the central front of Iraqi opinion—the war can still be won—but only by moderate Iraqis and only if they concentrate their efforts on gaining the cooperation of neighboring states, securing the support of the broader international community, and quickly reducing their dependence on the United States. Achieving such wide consensus will require turning the US-led occupation into an Iraqi-led, regionally backed, and internationally supported endeavor to attain peace and stability based on the principles of sovereignty and territorial integrity.[39]

Some still seek a military solution to the current US debacle in Iraq. Andrew F. Krepinevich Jr, Executive Director of the Center for Strategic and Budgetary Assessment, believes that the United States needs a strategy revolving around the principles of counterinsurgency warfare. Rather than focusing on killing insurgents, the United States "should concentrate on providing security and opportunity to the Iraqi people, thereby denying insurgents the popular support they need."[40]

However, the failure of the Bush administration in Iraq is more deeply rooted in its lack of understanding of the failure of Iraq's secular politics to deliver socioeconomic and political gains and in its underestimation of the hold of religion on the Iraqi people. The disastrous years of Ba'thist rule were bound to boost the religious *ulama*'s hold on society and politics in Iraq, especially with the Iranians next door. It became clear within a year after the US invasion that "by blowing the top off one of the region's most efficient dictatorships, the United States [had] created a free-for-all for fighters of every hue—Islamist and nationalist, from the homeland and the Diaspora—sparking a contest that [would] influence the course of political Islam for years to come."[41] The invasion and military occupation of Iraq has injected new life into the Jihadists who will not hesitate to sacrifice Iraqi sovereignty and its people in the name of its fight against the Western crusaders. The United States must realize that its fight in Iraq has become part of its war on terrorism *because* of the invasion.

To win the war on terrorism, the United States needs the cooperation of not only moderate Muslims but also Muslim states, some of whom have national goals diametrically opposed to those of the United States. The militant Jihadists are as much, if not more, of a threat to Muslim governments in the region as they are to the United States. The US-Iranian differences over policy goals and objectives could be reconciled if the United States recognized that the Iranian Islamic political system is still evolving toward a more open political system. The Iranian government in the long run has no alternative but to allow the expansion of popular will and civil society. A US-Iranian rapprochement over such common areas of interest as Persian Gulf security, the fight against militant Islamic terrorism, drug trafficking, and investment in energy, industrial, and financial markets is quite possible.

As to the debate over an exit strategy, there are no shortages of opinions. There are suggestions for a "total, speedy, and generous withdrawal,"[42] and ones for a slower, gradual withdrawal after enough Iraqi forces are trained and ready, which has been proposed by the Bush administration and some Democrats, including Senators Joe Biden, Hillary Clinton, and Joseph Lieberman. Others prefer a series of time-tabled withdrawals, a proposal put forth by former CIA Director John Deutch, Senators Carl Levin, John Kerry, Russell Feingold, and Representative John P. Murtha as well as Zbigniew Brzezinski, the Carter administration's national security advisor.[43] Barry Posen, an MIT professor, is among the latest proposing a timetabled withdrawal, suggesting that a low-grade civil war and stalemate are inevitable and that a de facto partition of territory into Sunni, Shiite, and Kurdish areas under a loose federal coalition will occur.[44]

Such exit strategies presume that the initial intent of the US invasion was based mainly on altruistic motives designed to help Iraqi people through the removal of Saddam's brutal regime and the establishment of democratic rule. However, whether the future of Iraq is democratic or not, the US strategy for Iraq demands a long-term military presence in the country. Given US concerns about the security of Israel, the ever-growing importance of Central Asia in countering a rising China in the global geostrategic competition,[45] and the Pentagon's release of the Quadrennial Defense Review (QDR) on February 5, 2006, any sizable withdrawal of US troops from Iraq remains unlikely. The QDR basically reaffirms the 1992 Defense Planning Guidance (DPG) that set the US permanent-dominance doctrine for fiscal years 1994–1999. A likely scenario is that the United States might agree to an "Arab army" presence in Iraq under US command to help with stabilizing Iraq and thwarting the Shi'a influence, which has also made some Sunni-dominated Arab states nervous. Egypt and other members of the Arab League have not been very receptive to the new Shi'a-dominated Iraqi government. Given that the United States is building four new military bases and that the future of the Iraqi territorial and political map is quite uncertain, a long-term US military presence is likely. The United States has for now the option of using its military presence in Kuwait, Qatar, Bahrain, the United Arab Emirates, and Diego Garcia to supplement its military capabilities in Iraq.

The final resolution to the conflict in Iraq rests in a compromise over the division of political power and socioeconomic resources among the contending religious and ethnic rivals. Iran plays a central role in the power play among contenders in Iraq, and the United States must realize that Islam and the *ulama* will continue playing a central role in Iraqi politics and society as both a divisive and a unifying force in the future. It is not unreasonable to assume that any long-term US military presence in Iraq will undercut the legitimacy of Iraqi governments and will be challenged by the Iranian and Syrian governments. The solution to this dilemma can be reached through political rapprochement with these governments to provide for a long-term Persian Gulf security arrangement and to improve chances for a final resolution to the Israeli-Palestinian and Syrian-Lebanese conflicts.

Notes

1. I would like to thank my colleague Stephen Hill for his very helpful comments and editorial suggestions on earlier drafts of this chapter. My thanks also go to the Office of Research and Sponsored Programs at the University of Wisconsin, Eau Claire, for its continued support of my research.

2. BBC, "Report concludes no WMD in Iraq," October 7, 2004.

3. Central Intelligence Agency, *World Factbook,* at http://www.cia.gov/cia/publications/factbook/geos/iz.html.

4. For a better understanding of Islam and state-society relations in the Middle East and Islamic world, see Ali R. Abootalebi, *Islam and Democracy: State-Society Relations In Developing Countries, 1980–1994* (New York: Garland, 2000); Oliver Roy, *Globalized Islam: The Search for a New Ummah* (New York: Columbia University Press, 2004); Gilles Kepel, *The War for Muslim Minds: Islam and the West* (Cambridge, MA: Belknap, 2004).

5. Bremer admits he knew next to nothing about Iraq before he was asked to take over operations there. See L. Paul Bremer III, with Malcolm McConnell, *My Year in Iraq: The Struggle to Build a Future of Hope* (New York: Simon & Schuster, 2006).

6. Martin Indyk, "The Clinton Administration's Approach to the Middle East," address to the Washington Institute for Near East Policy, Washington, DC, May 18, 1993, p. 2, cited in Phebe Marr, "The United States, Europe, and the Middle East: An Uneasy Triangle," *Middle East Journal* 48 (Spring 1994):2.

7. John Waterbury, "Hate Your Policies, Love Your Institutions," *Foreign Affairs* 82, 1 (January/February 2003):58–68, at 58.

8. Keith Garvin, "The One Certainty About Iraq: Spiraling Costs for Americans," ABC News, April 20, 2006.

9. John Mueller, "The Iraq Syndrome," *Foreign Affairs* 84, 6 (November/December 2005):44–54, at 44, 53.

10. Jim Lobe, "Most Iraqis Doubt US Will Ever Leave," Inter Press Service, January 31, 2006. The survey was conducted by the Program on International Policy Attitudes (PIPA) at the University of Maryland for WorldPublicOpinion.org and conducted through face-to-face interviews of 1,150 randomly selected Iraqi adults in all 18 Iraqi provinces in early January, three weeks after the December elections.

11. Peter Bergen and Alec Reynolds, "Blowback Revisited: Today's Insurgents in Iraq Are Tomorrow's Terrorists," *Foreign Affairs* 84, 6 (November/December 2005): 2–6, at 2.

12. See a more recent study by Daniel Benjamin and Steven Simon, *The Next Attack: The Failure of the War on Terror and a Strategy for Getting It Right* (New York: Times Books/Henry Holt, 2005).

13. "Iraq War Illegal, Says Annan," BBC, September 16, 2004. The United Nations Security Council resolution 1441 that was passed unanimously on November 8, 2002, offered Iraq "a final opportunity to comply with its disarmament obligations" that had been set out in several previous resolutions. Resolution 1441 threatened "serious consequences" if Iraq did not meet the UN demands, including "immediate, unconditional, and unrestricted access" to all suspected sites. The resolution, however, did not authorize an automatic military action against Iraq should Iraq fail to abide by its demands.

14. Mark Memmott, "'Downing Street Memo' Gets Fresh Attention," *USA Today*, June 8, 2005. The memo refers to a meeting in Downing Street on July 23, 2002, attended by Blair, Attorney General Lord Goldsmith, Foreign Secretary Jack Straw, ex-defense secretary Geoff Hoon, Sir Richard, former head of the UK armed forces Admiral Lord Boyce and head of the Joint Intelligence Committee John Scarlett.

15. Refer to Downing Street memo at http://afterdowningstreet.org.

16. The casualty figures for coalition forces are readily available. See, among others, "Iraq Body Count," available online at http://www.iraqbodycount.org/.

17. See Thomas R. Mattair, "Exiting Iraq: Competing Strategies," *Middle East Policy Council* 13, 1 (Spring 2006). Mattair examines plans for a US military exit from Iraq offered by Helena Cobban, Lawrence Korb and Brian Katulis, Barry R. Posen, and others in 2005.

18. Jonathan Weisman and Shailagh Murray, "Congress Approves $82 Billion for Wars," *Washington Post*, May 11, 2005.

19. Ibid.

20. Pascal Riche, "The Cost of the War," *TPM Café*, January 5, 2006. The study included costs such as lifetime disability and health care for the over 16,000 injured, one-fifth of whom have serious brain or spinal injuries. It also analyzes the costs to the economy, including the economic value of lives lost and the impact of factors such as higher oil prices that can be partly attributed to the conflict in Iraq. The author's paper also calculated the impact on the economy if a proportion of the money spent on the Iraq war were spent in other ways, including investments in the United States.

21. Michael R. Gordon, "The Strategy to Secure Iraq Did Not Foresee a 2nd War," *New York Times*, October 19, 2004.

22. Michael R. Gordon and Bernard E. Trainor, *Cobra II: The Inside Story of the Invasion and Occupation of Iraq* (New York: Pantheon, 2006).

23. Gordon, "The Strategy to Secure Iraq Did Not Foresee a 2nd War."

24. Ibid.

25. Mark Perry and Alastair Crooke, "How to Lose the War on Terror: Talking with the 'Terrorists,'" *Asia Times,* March 31, 2006. Crooke is the former Middle East adviser to European Union High Representative Javier Solana and served as a staff member of the Mitchell Commission investigating the causes of the second intifada. Perry is a Washington, DC-based

political consultant, author of six books on US history, and a former personal adviser to Yasser Arafat.

26. Larry Diamond, *Squandered Victory: The American Occupation and the Bungled Effort to Bring Democracy to Iraq* (New York: Henry Holt, 2005).

27. Larry Diamond, "What Went Wrong in Iraq," *Foreign Affairs* 83, 5 (September/October 2004):34–56, at 43.

28. The extensive ties that bind the Shi'a *'ulama* in Iran, Iraq, Lebanon, and elsewhere is well known to observers of the Middle East. Basic information is available online at http://en.wikipedia.org/wiki/Qom.

29. For insight into Iran's nuclear program, see Ray Takeyh, "A Nuclear Iran: Challenges and Responses," *Council on Foreign Relations*, March 2, 2006.

30. On the role of Iran in Iraq, see Lionel Beehner, "Iran's Goals in Iraq," *Council on Foreign Relations*, February 23, 2006.

31. Ibid.

32. On the Sunni/Shi'a divide, see Vali R. Naser, "Sunni vs. Shi'a: Religious Rivalry in Iraq and Beyond," *Council on Foreign Relations,* November 3, 2005.

33. Lawrence D. Freedman, "Review Essay, Writing of Wrongs: Was the War in Iraq Doomed from the Start?" *Foreign Affairs* 85, 1 (January/February 2006):129–134, at 130.

34. Ibid.

35. Francis Fukuyama, "After Neoconservatism," *New York Times*, February 19, 2006.

36. Ibid.

37. Ibid.

38. George Packer, *The Assassin's Gate: America in Iraq* (Farrar, Straus and Giroux, 2005).

39. James Dobbins, "Iraq: Winning the Unwinnable War," *Foreign Affairs* 84, 1 (January/February 2005):16–25, at 16–17.

40. Andrew F. Krepinevich Jr, "How to Win in Iraq," *Foreign Affairs* 84, 1 (September/October 2005):87–104, at 88.

41. Mahmood Mamdani, "Review Essay, Whither Political Islam: Understanding the Modern Jihad," *Foreign Affairs* 84, 1 (January/February 2005): at 155.

42. Helena Cobban, "Next Step in Helping Iraqis: Set a Withdrawal Date," *Christian Science Monitor,* July 21, 2005.

43. For a more recent discussion of exit strategies, see Thomas R. Mattair, "Exiting Iraq: Competing Strategies," *Middle East Policy* 13, 1 (Spring 2006):69–83.

44. Barry R. Posen, "Exit Strategy: How to Disengage from Iraq in 18 Months," *Boston Review,* January/February 2006.

45. Zbigniew Brzezinski, *The Grand Chessboard: American Primacy and Geostrategic Imperatives* (New York: Basic Books, 1997).

Part Four

Retrospective and Reassessment

22

The Soviet Perception of the US Threat

Georgiy Mirsky

Throughout history, the official Soviet mentality was chronically one of a besieged fortress. "Capitalistic encirclement" was the key word, the implacable struggle of the two world systems was an axiom, the famous expression *kto kovo* (who will beat whom) both motto and leitmotif. And the imperialist monsters biding their time to attack and destroy the first country of the victorious proletariat changed names: First it was Britain and France, then Nazi Germany and Japan, then the United States. But the essence of the external imperialist threat remained the same, the mortal danger was always there, and the options facing the beleaguered Soviet people never varied: Tough it out or perish.

Soviet citizens always felt they were unique, in more than one way. Even those who knew that life in the West was incomparably better and that the party propaganda praising the advantages of socialism was a huge fraud still believed that, given half a chance, the United States and its allies would attempt to crush the Soviet Union. Why? Because everybody was convinced that the Soviet Union—our country—was the biggest pain in the neck for world capitalism, the source of constant anger, fear, and irritation. By and large people did not question the necessity to maintain our armaments on the same level as the United States or to have allies and military footholds in diverse areas to counteract the US encirclement policy. This was why Moscow's activist policy in the Middle East never met with disapproval, inasmuch as it was regarded as a counterbalance to dangerous US expansion in that sensitive region. Discontent and irritation emerged later when one Arab-Israeli war after another demonstrated the incapacity of Soviet clients to effectively use the weaponry they had received from the USSR.

At this point, a question may be asked: Was it really so important for Kremlin rulers to take into account public opinion, considering the totalitarian nature of the regime? Certainly, political actions used to be taken without anybody in the Kremlin even thinking about the possible reaction of the people. Anything was certain to be approved. However, a protracted pattern of political activity, as distinct from a single action, in a specific area had better be popular and easy to swallow by the masses. The point is that, unlike during Stalin's rule, successor Kremlin regimes were based not so much on the *feuhrerprinzip* (principle of a single leader) as on the principle of collective leadership. It was an oligarchy ruling by consensus that was not confined solely to the Politburo but had to exist in lower party echelons as well. Signals that the "apparatchik aristocracy," the party, and management bosses were constantly sending to the very top might be vague, but still they could give a clue as to the prevailing opinion on specific issues inside the dominant class as a whole. And this opinion largely reflected views and beliefs of much broader sections of the population, even of the masses, it may be said. For, contrary to the concepts of some Sovietologists, the Soviet state, inhuman and antihuman as it was, could still be called the "people's state" in the sense that there was a close affinity between ideas, views, and cultural and social tastes of the rulers and the ruled. Soviet propagandists were not far from the truth when they claimed that they were representatives of the people who were in charge in the Soviet Union. Sure, they were exploiting and hu miliating the people, depriving them of human rights and liberties, condemning them to a miserable and beastly life. However, all of this was being done not on be- half of some closed and privileged strata, as had been the case in prerevolutionary Russia, but on behalf of those sons of peasants and workers who had made it to the top. Thus, the Soviet elite was never socially and culturally alienated or even differ- entiated from the bulk of the population. The big shots and the masses basically shared the same mentality.

This helps to explain why it was important for any long-term political strategy to meet with the approval, if not the actual backing, of the people. Popular tastes, tra- ditions, and prejudices, in their turn, could be used by policymakers for the ration- alization of their line. The Middle East was a perfect example of convergence of popular beliefs—crude and false but mostly genuine—and the Kremlin's realpolitik. A widespread apprehension of US aggressive designs coupled with anti-Semitism (since the US ally, partner, and "vanguard striking force" in the Middle East hap- pened to be a Jewish state, distasteful almost by definition to quite a few Russians, Ukrainians, and others) helped to ensure solid popular backing for an activist and militant anti-American line of Soviet policy in the Middle East. In practice, of course, it was translated into a strategic alliance with left-wing Arab regimes against the US-Israel axis.

What were the motives of the Soviet leadership in the confrontation with the United States in the Middle East? Here, too, we must take as a starting point the overall Soviet concept of the global struggle between socialism and capitalism.

Some Western authors seemed to have overestimated the degree of the ideologi- cal component of Soviet foreign policy. They believed that ideology was paramount in determining the Kremlin's actions. Others, on the contrary, tended to focus al- most exclusively on geopolitics. In fact it was a combination of both. There is no doubt that such people as Nikita Khrushchev, Leonid Brezhnev, Andrei Gromyko, Mikhail Suslov, and the rest sincerely believed in the inherent superiority of social- ism and its ultimate victory over capitalism on the global scale; but at the same time they could not but realize that it was highly improbable for them to actually see the great triumph of Marxism-Leninism in their lifetimes. It was necessary for them to create conditions for this triumph, that is, to strengthen by all means the forces of world socialism and to weaken the imperialist enemy. To achieve this, it was imperative for the Kremlin leaders to change the global balance of forces, foremost in the political and military spheres, since they already lost faith in socialism's ability to achieve greater productivity of labor (in accordance with Lenin's concept). It was, of course, Lenin who predicted that it would be precisely in the sphere of productivity that socialism would eventually prove superior to capitalism. As early as the 1960s it was already impossible to seriously believe in such an eventuality given the obvious and growing gap between the economies of the two world systems. Thus, stress had to be placed on the undermining and sapping of the imperialist forces in the noneconomic sphere since the economy increasingly looked like the Achilles' heel of socialism. The adversary had to be defeated on a different battlefield, and it was clear that it was first in the sphere of military power and second in the ability to appeal to anticolonial, anti-Western sentiments of Third World nations that socialism could really have an edge over capitalism.

As to the first factor—military power—the Kremlin had to be very cautious about using it, especially after the Cuban missile crisis demonstrated the limits of brinkmanship. A world war was tacitly acknowledged to be suicidal, although the top military brass was reluctant to admit it. The awesome military might of the Soviet Union was to be used in three dimensions: First, as a reminder to Western Europe that tens of thousands of Soviet tanks were ready to roll in should the imperialists try to stage a counterrevolution in the socialist camp; second, as a counterbalance to US sea power (this was why so much emphasis was laid on the expansion of the Soviet Navy); third, as a means of arming Soviet allies in the Third World.

The second factor—spreading Soviet influence in the Third World—was more promising, and the prospects seemed bright indeed of transforming the national liberation movement into a strategic ally against the West. Broadly speaking, this was the picture: To strike a military blow at the citadel of world capitalism was too dangerous due to the inevitable nuclear disaster it would entail; internal contradictions of capitalism were growing but the results were too slow in coming; the situation in Europe was frozen, forces on both sides engaged in trench warfare with no prospect of a breakthrough in either direction; the developing countries seething with discontent and driven by the dynamics of anticolonial inertia presented an excellent opportunity of undermining the imperialist system from within rather than engaging it in a frontal clash.

Finally, it must be said that if this kind of global thinking existed in the minds of the top leaders, this was not the case with the people down the road, with those who were planning and implementing the actual policy. For them, it was a given: The cold war was on, the United States was the enemy, everything had to be done to weaken it. It was a zero-sum game not necessarily motivated by ideological hatred and intransigence. The Communist commitment of the diplomats and the scholars in think tanks was actually skin-deep, as evidenced by the subsequent transformation of many of those people in the post–Mikhail Gorbachev era: They have quietly forgotten their Marxism and perfectly adapted to the new situation.

The Soviet Union and the Middle East
in the Eras of Khrushchev and Brezhnev

If, during the Khrushchev and Brezhnev eras (1953 to 1982), you asked any young Soviet diplomat just out of the Institute of International Relations (MGIMO) about the significance of the Middle East for the USSR, he would answer matter-of-factly: Too vital to yield even an inch to the Americans. If you had pressed him for specifications, he would have mentioned the geostrategic dimension first, oil second, and the necessity to back our allies, the Arab anti-imperialist forces, third.

Upon a closer look, however, all three dimensions would prove to be not so terribly vital to the interests of the Soviet Union. From the geopolitical and strategic point of view, nobody in his right mind could imagine US tanks rolling across the Arab deserts to the Caucasus in a new world war. In the "ICBM era" the value of any piece of territory was greatly reduced anyway. As to oil, the USSR had plenty of it to begin with; any attempt to deprive the US allies of Middle East oil would have been extremely dangerous since it was clear that the West would not hesitate to protect its access to that commodity with military force. The only thing left, therefore, was the USSR's strategic alliance with the left-wing Arab regimes.

This alliance was born under Nikita Khrushchev, who, in 1955, struck the famous arms deal with Egyptian President Gamal 'Abd al-Nasser. At the time, Khrushchev overruled the objections of the Soviet ambassador to Egypt, who was dismayed by the very idea of dealing with such a patently non-Communist and politically doubtful character as Nasser. Khrushchev was not inhibited by Marxist dogmatic puritanism. He regarded Nasser and his like as valuable partners in the anti-imperialist struggle. It was a bold and imaginative pattern; fabulous opportunities seemed to be in the offing.

From then on, the new alliance rapidly gained momentum. It expanded to involve Syria, Iraq, and Algeria, and, later, the Palestine Liberation Organization (PLO) and South Yemen. For a brief moment it seemed that Sudan, too, joined the "progressive camp"; Libya always was an embarrassing partner, but Mu'ammar al-Qaddafi's anti-imperialism appeared on balance to be more important than his bizarre theories, which were clearly incompatible not only with Marxism but also with the "revolutionary-democratic ideology" shared by Nasserists and Ba'thists. Typical of our attitude toward Qaddafi was a curious fact: Sometime in the 1970s, after one of his particularly vicious anti-Communist outbursts, it was decided to publish a reply to Qaddafi—not in *Pravda*, of course, but in the *Literary Gazette*, and a high-ranking official in the Central Committee's International Department was entrusted with this job. At the last moment, however, the article, which sounded very lucid and convincing to me, was taken out of the newspaper; apparently somebody higher up in the hierarchy decided that it was not worthwhile annoying the erratic colonel.

Pertaining to ideology, two observations might not be out of place. First, Khrushchev's new course of aligning Moscow with Nasser-type leadership was, of course, a purely pragmatic matter devoid of any ideological overtones. But in a socialist state it had to be rationalized and explained in terms of Marxist theory. This is when academic scholars, myself included, were called upon to work out a plausible theory aimed at proving in a convincing manner exactly why it was not only possible but necessary and highly helpful for the Great Cause to establish an alliance with such people as Nasser. The concept we elaborated was that of "Revolutionary Democracy," a non-Marxist, nonproletarian set of ideas and politics founded first on anticolonialism and second on the alleged impossibility of resolving the urgent problems of the developing countries on the basis of capitalism. The idea was that, although anti-imperialist nationalists were not ready to acknowledge and adopt Marxism's eternal truth, the logic of life would sooner or later teach them that only by following the socialist path could they hope to overcome their countries' backwardness and dependence on imperialism. Thus, the anticolonial, anti-imperialist revolution would inevitably grow into a social one, directed against both foreign and domestic oppressors. The national liberation movement would be transformed into a national-democratic revolution with a clear anticapitalist content and, later, into a popular-democratic revolution of a distinct socialist orientation.

The key terms in this concept were "noncapitalist development" and "socialist orientation." It was assumed that someday Nasser and his ilk would realize the futility of their hopes to modernize their countries and to build an industrial society within the framework of the world capitalist system with the help of the domestic bourgeoisie. Then, socialism would come naturally to them as the only way out of the horrible mess left behind by the imperialist exploiters.

Moreover, these theoretical constructions had very little to do with a genuine desire to build a happy socialist society in the dirt-poor and miserably backward Third World countries. I am not referring now to beliefs and motivations of the scholars who were busy writing memos, papers, and monographs on the issues. To the contrary, actual policymakers were indifferent to the results of "noncapitalist development" in Asia and Africa. What mattered, for them, was the involvement of the states ruled by the "revolutionary democrats" into a worldwide anti-Western coalition. Ideology for them was secondary; it was just instrumental in bringing about decisive change in the correlation of world forces. The Third World leaders who proclaimed their allegiance to socialism, even if only of a homemade and not Marxist variety, were ipso facto committed to the Soviet Union and the socialist community in the international arena. Just how successful they were in regard to the socialist transformation of their states was largely irrelevant. The main thing was to get into the "soft underbelly" of the capitalist system—Asia, Africa, and Latin America—so as to eventually besiege imperialism in its citadel. The more Third World countries proclaimed socialism as their goal, and thus became hostage to Soviet political support, arms deliveries, and so on, the better. Each of these countries could, from that moment on, be regarded as a loss to the United States and its allies: It was a zero-sum game. The propaganda aspect was important, too.

Certainly what mattered for Brezhnev was being able to say in his report at the next party congress: "Comrades, the period under review has demonstrated once more that ideas of socialism are on the march throughout the globe; more countries now stand under the banner of socialism."

In regard to practical politics in the Middle East, the Kremlin's strategy aimed at ensuring a position of strength for the Arab allies in their confrontation with Israel, which was viewed as America's stooge. Disappointment and bitterness set in each time the Arab forces were defeated by Israel; over and over again, an escalation in arms deliveries followed. The more the USSR became committed to the protection of its Arab allies, the more it had to up the ante or else prepare to lose face.

At the same time, there is no evidence that Moscow ever wanted to escalate the Arab-Israeli confrontation to the point of large-scale war. First, Soviet leaders feared that Arab armies would be soundly beaten; second, they were apprehensive about the war spilling over into a US-Soviet armed conflict signaling the outbreak of a nuclear world war. I happened to witness twice the worry and upset of high-ranking Soviet officials as Israeli forces seemed on the verge of closing in on Cairo and Damascus in 1967 and 1973. The PLO, too, was to be supported only inasmuch as it represented a nuisance in harassing Israel, but it was never regarded as a liberation army built up to recapture Palestine or even a part of it.

The official Soviet position, of course, was in accordance with UN Resolution 242. In the International Department of the Soviet Communist Party Central Committee, which was the place where policy guidelines were usually outlined (this also occurred in various academic institutions), debates took place from time to time over goals in the Middle East. The main issue was whether it would serve our interests if Resolution 242 was implemented and a Palestinian entity created. Opinions differed sharply, some people feeling that the Arabs would no longer need our military backing and that Moscow would lose its leverage.

Gorbachev, Perestroika, and New Political Thinking

At first, Gorbachev's foreign policy course was quite traditional, which is not surprising given his background as a career Soviet apparatchik. Even when he embarked on a course of far-reaching domestic reforms, the habitually tough anti-imperialist line showed no signs of slackening. The perestroika leaders, breaking new ground at home, were anxious to cover their flank in the forum of foreign policy. They felt they could not advance on two fronts simultaneously and they were afraid of being perceived as soft on imperialism. So Gorbachev and Shevardnadze preferred to be seen as strong and tough vis-à-vis the West; accordingly, Soviet Middle East policy remained for a time basically unchanged.[1]

Things began to move with the advent of the "new political thinking," particularly when "de-ideologization" of foreign policy was announced. This entailed a decline of ideological priorities and "socialist" commitments abroad. I remember speaking at a conference convened by Shevardnadze in 1987, with all of the Soviet ambassadors abroad participating. When I professed my disillusionment with the practical results of the "socialist orientation" in the Third World, it was a shock to many. However, a group of our ambassadors in the African states approached me after my talk and hastened to thank me for my outspokenness. "At last, somebody has told the truth," they said. "We knew all along that this socialist orientation was a fraud and a failure but, of course, in our official reports things just had to look quite different."

Inevitably, reappraisal of our long-standing line in the Middle East was due to come. More and more, scholars and journalists began questioning the very foundations of our policy in the Arab-Israeli conflict. Doubts were expressed as to the wisdom of our 1967 decision to break off diplomatic relations with Israel. A new approach was shaping up with regard to the Camp David accords.

It is well known that opposition to Camp David and bitter denunciation of Egyptian President Anwar Sadat's political line were the cornerstones of Soviet policy in the Middle East in the 1980s.[2] Much later, in the days of perestroika, I ventured an opinion that it was high time Egypt was readmitted into the family of Arab states. Immediately, a prominent party official with an Arabist background retorted: "Well, and how about the slogan, 'Bury Camp David?'" In spite of the utter absurdity of this position, the official stand on Camp David remained steadfast during the first perestroika years. But this, too, began to change as glasnost gained strength.

Some authors, Western as well as Russian, seemed to underestimate the role of the ideological factor and, correspondingly, of glasnost in the demise of Communist rule. As the ideological barriers were crumbling, suddenly it became possible to question the Soviet past as a whole. When Gorbachev finally, albeit reluctantly, gave the green light to de-Stalinization, little did he think that very soon it would turn into de-Leninization and de-bolshevization. Then, an end to the cold war and to the confrontation era was announced. Almost overnight, the United States ceased to be an enemy; the very word "imperialism" disappeared from the newspapers. The party apparatus suddenly realized that the bottom line was not there any more, the cornerstone fell out, the raison d'être of the system having vanished. This partly explains why the resistance to the overthrow of the Communist regime in the aftermath of the August coup was so feeble: The heart was no longer there; the ideological commitment was gone.

Even before the final collapse, there was a sea change in foreign policy. Anti-imperialism as a guideline disappeared; promoting socialism worldwide became a futile task. Diplomatic relations with Israel had to be restored. De-ideologization meant that our relations with the Arab world were no longer dictated by the commitment to leftist Arab regimes and the need to deny the United States the dominant role in the area. Since the United States was not an enemy any more, why bother about Israel as an enemy foothold?

When the Gulf crisis erupted with the Iraqi invasion of Kuwait, the Soviet Union for the first time sided with the United States in a confrontation with a Third World country—and a socialist-oriented country at that. Some took it very hard. When I spoke at the Academy of the Warsaw Treaty Organization in Moscow at the height of the crisis, I bluntly told my audience that, in my opinion, Saddam

Hussein was a gangster and a butcher. There was an uproar, angry exclamations, and some colonels even walked out. These were the kind of people who had arrived by the hundreds to attend the recent reception at the Iraqi Embassy in Moscow to celebrate the 1958 Iraqi revolution. For them, Saddam is a hero, an anti-American, anti-Jewish, anti-democratic, tough, no-nonsense leader. In short, he is their kind of man.

Faced by strong opposition to his allegedly pro-US policy, Gorbachev tried, for the last time, to play a relatively autonomous role. Middle East adviser Yevgeny Primakov was sent to Baghdad to lobby for a compromise solution. Had he succeeded, it would have been a serious boost to Gorbachev's prestige. First it would have placated the Russian "patriots" unhappy with what they perceived as Gorbachev's subservience to Bush. Second, it could have assuaged the Arabs, who by that time were mad at Gorbachev over the issue of Jewish immigration to Israel. Soviet ambassadors in Arab capitals were reporting to the Kremlin that Soviet prestige in the Arab world was at an all-time low. Arabs felt that Gorbachev (much loved by Bush) could, if he wished, have persuaded the US president to channel the bulk of the Soviet Jews to the United States rather than to Israel. If Gorbachev was not even trying to do this, it could only mean that he did not care about Arabs at all.

Gorbachev, of course, knew that he could not do any such thing. The only way to restore, if only partially, Soviet prestige in the Arab world was to save Iraq from imminent disaster. But Primakov's mission was doomed from the beginning. Later Primakov told me that, given three more days, he would have persuaded Tariq 'Aziz and thus Saddam Hussein to make concessions that would have prevented the US ground offensive. The question arises: Just who did Primakov think he was that the US president would give him three days when everything was already decided and D-Day had already been fixed?

At the subsequent Madrid conference the Soviet Union tried to posture as an independent actor, but nobody took it seriously; the USSR was no longer a superpower. Paradoxically, it was Bush who tried to place the Soviet Union on a superpower basis for the last time. In fact, his "new world order" envisaged a situation in which both superpowers were to continue playing a dominant role in world affairs, but in cooperation and not in confrontation. Gorbachev would undoubtedly have gone along with that, but it was too late. The hands on the clock were nearing midnight.

Post-Communist Russia and the Middle East

Currently Moscow has little foreign policy to speak of. The main trend is to maintain good relations with the West, although the rising tide of Russian nationalism can already be seen as threatening the seemingly well-established pattern. Anti-Western and anti-American backlash in particular is evident in Russian public opinion.

In the foreseeable future, only the Middle East offers Russia the chance to play a role in world affairs. Europe is lost to Russian influence, cut off as it is by Poland and Ukraine both geographically and politically. Even if it were not so, the united Germany effectively prevents Russia from playing any major role in European affairs. The Balkans are a powder keg. In the Far East and Southeast Asia more powerful players are flexing their muscles: Japan, China, the United States. Tropical Africa and Latin America are largely irrelevant to Moscow at this point. The only region left is the Middle East.

In that region Russia has commitments, political and military investments, allies, and leverage of sorts. As a successor state to the Soviet Union, Russia is cochair, along with the United States, of the Geneva Conference. Like the United States, Russia can now wield some influence, although to a far lesser degree, in both the Arab world and in Israel. Russian diplomats can sit at international conferences on the Middle East, pretending to be on equal footing with the United States. Thus, Russia can be perceived (by the Russians themselves, of course, and in Russian public opinion) as not having been pushed out of the picture altogether in world affairs.

Perception is what matters, not substance. As former US Speaker of the House Tip O'Neill once said, all politics is local. For any government in Moscow, it is vital to be seen by the people as not neglecting Russian national interests abroad, as pursuing an independent foreign policy worthy of a great power. The Russians like to think of their country as a great power, no longer as a superpower. An honorable role in the Middle East will be good for their self-esteem. And it is in the Middle East alone that Russia has a tradition of diplomatic success. The Middle East is where its foreign policy future lies.

Notes

1. Information for this point was obtained in conversations the author conducted with Alexander Yakovlev, a top adviser for Gorbachev.

2. Probably the best scholarly expression of Soviet anger and frustration is Yevgeny Primakov's book on Sadat, entitled *Story of Betrayal.*

23

The Push and Pull of Strategic Cooperation

The US Relationship with Turkey in the Middle East

Henri J. Barkey

Not long before the 1974 Cyprus crisis, the US administration decided to move Turkey, along with Greece and Cyprus, from the Near East to Europe. This, of course, was just an organizational change within the State Department, but it would underlie much of Washington's approach to Turkey in the ensuing decades. The importance of Turkey, which was a major US ally during the cold war, was measured largely by its contribution to NATO in its struggle against the Soviet Union. Its strategic location, close to both the Soviet Union and the Middle East (one of the premier theaters for superpower rivalry) and control of the straits are what made Turkey so vital to the United States. With the collapse of the Soviet Union in 1991, Washington continued to insist that Turkey was a European country and, in fact, worked hard to make sure that Ankara remained firmly ensconced in Western institutions by championing its candidacy for European Union (EU) membership.

The new geopolitics of the post-Soviet space opened new arenas of economic and political opportunities for Turkey, despite the fact that it lacked a border with Russia. Turkey could demonstrate that it had a role to play in Central Asia and the Caucasus, hitherto ruled by Moscow, and, with the collapse of Yugoslavia and the subsequent conflicts in Bosnia and Kosovo, in the Balkans as well.

The 1990s witnessed an evolution in the Turkish-American relationship, which came to embrace a great many more subjects and common areas of concern. In addition to traditional issues such as Greece and Cyprus, these included Iraq, Armenia and Azerbaijan, the post–September 11 war on terrorism, oil pipelines from the Caucasus and Central Asia, the Turkish-Israeli rapprochement, and the future evolution of a European security infrastructure. Most important, US commitment to Turkey's candidacy to the EU has remained solid. Despite the confluence of issues,

Ankara's view is somewhat jaundiced by the fact that it has not achieved a sense of parity in its relations with the United States. Criticism of its human rights practices in the 1990s by Washington was a constant irritant for Turkish authorities, who also harbored deep suspicions of US intentions in northern Iraq. Still, Turkey's devastating economic crisis in 2001 was a reminder of how dependent the country is on Washington.

Since the end of the cold war, Ankara's greatest preoccupation has been the Middle East. And it has been in the Middle East that the United States has found Ankara to be most relevant to its own policies and ambitions. During the 1990s, Saddam Hussein emerged as the single most important factor in US-Turkish relations, and Ankara played a critical role in the US policy toward Iraq. With the beginning of the Iraq war in 2003, Turkish-American relations suffered a setback, primarily because Turkey refused to allow a second front against Baghdad through its territory. A further concern is that the war has brought the Iraqi Kurds much closer to independence, which has serious implications for its own Kurdish population.

Finally, in the 2002 elections, the moderate Islam-oriented Justice and Development Party, AKP, came to power, winning an overwhelming majority of seats in parliament. The advent of this party's control of Turkish government brought new risks and opportunities to the relationship. On the one hand, the party's roots were in the anti-Western and anti-American Islamist parties of yesteryear, and the risk of a domestic political confrontation between it and the secular civilian and military establishment would hang over domestic stability. On the other hand, the advent through the ballot box of a moderate Islamist party, committed to European integration, validated the US discourse on democracy.

This chapter focuses on the post–cold war Turkish-American relationship within the context of the Middle East, and for simplicity's sake I define the region to include the Caucasus and Central Asia as well. Despite a contextual focus on the Middle East, I consider other important US-Turkish issues as well.

Recent Origins

The Turkish-American relationship in the post–World War II era dates to Soviet leader Stalin's threats to both Greece and Turkey and the promulgation of the Truman Doctrine in March 1947. The Truman Doctrine would not only mark the beginning of the cold war and the containment policy but would also redefine Turkey's position in the world from a reluctant late participant in the war effort against the Axis powers to a front-line state in the fight against communism. Turkey, together with Greece, joined the NATO alliance in 1952. The change in external alliances was accompanied by an equally dramatic turn of events within Turkey: The one-party state established by Turkey's founder, Mustafa Kemal Ataturk, gave way—albeit slowly and reluctantly—to a multiparty political system, and the new leaders of Turkey made an effort to remain closely attached to the United States.

The Democrat Party that took over the reins of power in Turkey in 1950 was ostensibly more pro United States and, more important perhaps, more market oriented. Once in power, the Democrat administration of 'Adnan Menderes took the lead in the creation of the 1955 Baghdad Pact, a bloc of countries who joined together to thwart Soviet advances into the Arab Middle East.[1] The Baghdad Pact, comprising Turkey, Iraq, Iran, and Pakistan, was short-lived because Iraq pulled out following the 1958 overthrow of the regime in Baghdad. The pact reinvented itself as the Central Treaty Organization (CENTO) although it proved to be of limited use.

The deterioration of US-Turkish relations occurred not because of the Middle East–related problems but rather because of the rivalry with Greece, another NATO ally. The island of Cyprus, home to Greeks and Turks, gained its independence from Great Britain in 1960. The intercommunal conflicts between majority Greeks and minority Turks on Cyprus often brought Turkey to the brink of invading the island in defense of the Turks. In 1964, a last-minute letter from US President Lyndon Johnson threatening Ankara with serious repercussions should it invade the island is credited with stopping the Turkish government from pursuing this course. In 1974, however, following a coup in Cyprus inspired by the ruling military junta in Athens, which had overthrown the constitutional order, Turkish troops intervened. Even though the initial July 1974 Turkish invasion—conducted under the auspices of the London agreement that had formally recognized Turkey, Greece, and Britain as guarantor powers for the island's communities—received mixed international reviews, the Turks followed it up by a second one in August. The latter resulted in the current status quo. The reaction to the second military action was quite drastic: The US Congress, in opposition to the administration's wishes, imposed an arms embargo on Turkey, which would last from 1975 to 1978, further embittering Turkish attitudes toward the United States. In reaction to the embargo, the Turkish Prime Minister, Suleyman Demirel, announced the closure of all US bases in Turkey except for those that had a specific NATO mission, as well as the intention of his government to pursue a policy of rapprochement with Arab and Eastern Bloc countries.

Tensions with the United States coincided with a period of domestic turbulence in Turkey. Starting in the late 1960s, anti-Americanism, largely a mirror image of student movements in Europe and elsewhere around the globe, had permeated all levels of society.[2] In the 1970s, economic difficulties, coupled with the rise of militant left- and right-wing groups, seriously undermined the stability of the Turkish regime. The system seemed to come under siege from every corner of the country and every political tendency; in addition to the left- and right-wing groups, Islamist and Kurdish organizations also began to agitate for a piece of the pie. In turn, the instability of Turkey began to worry Washington as well as key European countries.

The frayed Turkish-American relations began to mend with the lifting of the arms embargo in 1978 and more importantly with the rapid transformation of Turkey's immediate neighborhood. The Iranian revolution created a new revisionist anti-American power in a sensitive region and caused the United States to lose an intelligence perch for eavesdropping on the Soviet Union. That same year, the Soviets invaded Afghanistan, and although Turkey would not figure prominently in the proxy war that Washington would initiate, the cold war was back on, emphasizing once again Turkey's strategic location. Washington, attuned to Turkey's geostrategic importance, was muted in its criticism when Turkish generals took power in September 1980 amid rising political violence and parliamentary deadlock.

The 1980s would usher in a new era in Turkish politics. The centerpiece of this decade was the economic reforms initiated by Turgut Özal. He first unleashed them in January 1980 for Demirel's government; he continued them as minister in charge of the economy during the military interregnum, and he accelerated them following his 1983 victory in the first elections since the coup. In effect, he single-handedly managed to transform Turkey's economy from an inward-looking one to an export-oriented one. Özal's success in the economic sphere brought a degree of self-confidence to Turkey, as the Turkish private sector started to export furiously, especially to Europe. In the years that followed, the economic reforms would be crucial in enhancing Turkey's attractiveness to the EU. Although Özal's approach found favor in Washington, there remained some nagging issues. Among them was the role of ethnic lobbies in Washington, primarily Greek and Armenian, in undermining the Turkish cause. The Greek lobby was seen as responsible for imposing the arms embargo in 1975, and Armenian groups succeeded in bringing up the massacres of Armenians during World War I. Attempts in Congress to pass resolutions commemorating the World War I events brought about strong Turkish reactions, often interfering with the day-to-day business of diplomacy. Ankara's troubles in Congress spurred it to seek its own allies in the United States. In addition to the relatively small Turkish-American lobby, no match for these other well-organized lobbies, Ankara turned to the Jewish-American groups, heralding a future rapprochement with Israel that would eventually come to fruition during the Madrid peace conference in 1991.

US-Turkish Relations Under Iraq's Shadow: Phase I

Iraq's August 1990 invasion of Kuwait represented the first challenge of the post–cold war era. From then on, directly or indirectly, Iraq would cast its long shadow over US-Turkish relations. The Iraq issue is best analyzed in two phases: first is the period from the Gulf war to September 11, 2001; the second phase revolves around the US invasion of Iraq and the ensuing insurgency. Turkey's proximity to Iraq and the basing of US aircraft at the Incirlik air base to maintain a no-fly zone over northern Iraq after the conclusion of the Gulf war would make Turkey a linchpin in Washington's containment strategy of Baghdad. As long as Saddam Hussein ruled Iraq, US policy, as it evolved through the 1990s, could not be implemented without Ankara's help. The Gulf crisis also exacerbated the insurrection by Turkish Kurds in the country's southeastern regions. The often brutal methods employed by the Turkish state to combat this rebellion increasingly put it at odds with its US ally.

At the onset of the Kuwait crisis, President Özal—despite his limited powers as president and facing a great deal of opposition at home—managed to orient Turkish policy behind the United States and its allies in what he was sure would be the winning side. At his instigation, his government closed down Iraq's main export pipelines to the Mediterranean in anticipation of UN sanctions resolutions. Özal struck a cordial relationship with President George H. W. Bush during the crisis[3] and proved quite willing to push his country even further along the path of cooperation with the allies. The opposition to his policies became so fierce that for the first time in Turkish history a chief of staff of the armed forces resigned in protest rather than cooperate with his president.[4]

When the defeated Iraqi regime turned on its own unruly populations in 1991, the Kurds in the north, who had taken advantage of the Gulf war to rebel, began to flee in large numbers to the Iranian and Turkish borders, resulting in a massive refugee crisis. For Turkey, which was confronting a Kurdish insurgency of its own, the inflow of more Kurds into its territory was an unacceptable burden. As a result, the United States, with its allies, put together a force composed of aircraft and ground troops called Operation Provide Comfort (OPC) to successfully force Iraqi troops out of northern Iraq and allow Kurdish refugees to return home. OPC, based in Turkey, required periodic approval by the Turkish parliament, and because of the acrimonious debates it generated, it became a source of tension between Washington and Ankara. These bitter debates were often marked by the quiet, last-minute intervention of the powerful Turkish military in favor of renewing the OPC's mandate. The process, however, did not serve either country well.

Turkish insecurities regarding OPC were directly related to the domestic Kurdish insurgency led by the Kurdistan Workers' Party (PKK) and its leader Abdullah Öcalan, which peaked around 1992. The government felt seriously threatened by the PKK taking advantage of Kurdish-controlled northern Iraq and the sympathetic populace in southeast Turkey. As casualties mounted in the southeast, Turks feared the influence of the Iraqi Kurdish example. Iraqi Kurds, thanks to OPC, were no longer living as subjects of the Iraqi regime and had established their own government structures and had even organized their own elections. Ankara, moreover, was alarmed at the prospect of eventual Iraqi Kurdish independence and its demonstration effect on its own Kurds. As a result, Turkish policy in the 1990s was focused on discouraging Iraqi Kurds from breaking away and on encouraging Saddam's regime to peacefully reintegrate the north. As such, Turkish and American policy diverged significantly over Iraq. A principal proponent of this strategy in Turkey was none other than Bulent Ecevit, who in opposition became the most vociferous critic (together with the Islamist leader Necmettin Erbakan) of US policy and OPC in particular. Ecevit blamed the United States for the failure of the Kurds to reach agreement with Saddam Hussein at the end of the Gulf war and during the Kurdish insurrection in Iraq. In fact, he argued that Washington was planning to create a putative Kurdish state in northern Iraq.[5]

Over time, OPC was restructured, its land component removed, and its renewals routinized; it was renamed Operation Northern Watch (ONW). ONW and its southern counterpart represented a first line of defense for the United States against Saddam, and by reminding Baghdad daily that it did not control its own territory it was a source of psychological pressure on the regime. It would not be an exaggeration to argue that without ONW, Washington's Iraq policy could have collapsed. As the popularity of UN-imposed economic sanctions on Iraq waned in the late 1990s, ONW's importance grew.

However, this was not a one-way street, as both OPC and later ONW provided numerous benefits to Turkey. They represented an important source of Turkish leverage in Washington, which always had to take account of Turkish sensitivities in Iraq and elsewhere for fear of jeopardizing these operations. They also provided a cover for Turkish military incursions into northern Iraq in pursuit of PKK insurgents. More importantly, they helped wed the United States to Turkey's position on the PKK as a terrorist organization and gained Washington's collaboration in Öcalan's apprehension in February 1999 after his eviction from Syria.[6] Öcalan's capture caused the collapse of the insurgency because the PKK decided that in order to prevent the Turkish authorities from executing its leader, it would put a halt to its military operations and would move its fighters from Turkish soil to northern Iraq.

Iraq remained a source of tension in Turkish-American relations throughout the Clinton administration despite the increasing collaboration between Washington and Ankara. Turks were suspicious of US intentions in the region. They were convinced that a significant portion of their own Kurdish problem and the PKK insurgency could be attributed to the absence of "legitimate authority" in northern Iraq (which was controlled by two Kurdish factions at loggerheads with each other), the collapse of their trade relations with Baghdad following the Gulf war, and the imposition of economic sanctions on Iraq. They made it clear that their preference was the reunification of Iraqi territory under the control of the central government in Baghdad. This Turkish position ran counter to US preferences, but the internecine divisions within the Kurdish community between the Patriotic Union of Kurdistan (PUK) and the Kurdish Democratic Party (KDP)—led by Jalal Talabani and Masoud Barzani, respectively—would continue to undermine Washington's position.

Washington invested heavily in trying to resolve these differences. Nevertheless, missteps by the United States helped undercut its Iraq policy. In 1996, the KDP requested Saddam's assistance against the PUK forces. In the ensuing fighting, the Iraqi military took the opportunity to suppress the main US-supported Iraqi opposition group, the Iraqi National Congress (INC), dismantle its infrastructure, and execute many of its agents stationed in northern Iraq. The US response was minimal: It limited itself to lobbing a number of cruise missiles mostly away from the conflict zone. With the demise of the INC, Washington's Iraq policy was transformed from one that aspired to contain the regime's hegemonic ambitions and slowly sow the seeds of regime change into simple containment. When in September 1998 the two Kurdish leaders were brought to Washington to sign off on an agreement that had been negotiated with the help of the Turks, Ankara was incensed that the final document, while paying due respect to the principle of Iraq's territorial integrity, mentioned the prospect of a future federated state in Iraq.

The unresolved status of Iraq, particularly northern Iraq, and the prospect of Kurdish autonomy compelled Turkey to become an active player in northern Iraqi politics. In its determination to eradicate the PKK and prevent the deepening of Kurdish autonomy in the north, Ankara alternated its support among the different

Kurdish factions. It sporadically engaged in large military incursions into the north, based troops there, and with time created the Iraqi Turkmen Front (ITF), composed of members of the Turkish-speaking minority in Iraq, as a counterweight to the Kurds and their aspirations. Trade between Iraq and Turkey flourished, especially after the oil-for-food UN resolution, which stipulated that Iraqi oil exports could be used to import food and medicines. Although this trade did not match pre-war levels, it nonetheless provided Turkey with access to oil, including smuggled oil, and some leverage over the Iraqi Kurds, in particular, the KDP. In order to support Ankara, which had complained bitterly about the losses it had incurred as a result of the Kuwait war, the United States insisted that a majority of the oil to be exported out of Iraq be transported through Turkish pipelines.

The Context Beyond Iraq

Although Iraq was a dominating concern in the 1990s, other issues influenced and enriched the complex US-Turkish relations. Throughout the 1990s, the United States, concerned about Turkish domestic political stability, tried to fortify Ankara by endorsing its quest for European Union membership and by supporting it economically and pushed it to reform its archaic approach to human rights and ethnic relations. The latter effort often produced sharp differences between the two countries, yet Turkish-American relations were on the mend by the end of the decade. When the Clinton administration had actively criticized the undemocratic practices of successive Turkish governments and state institutions and the repression of Kurdish rights and Islamic parties, Ankara, not surprisingly, had taken a dim view of US interference in its domestic politics. Although the Clinton administration was critical of Turkey's human rights practices, it nonetheless simultaneously pursued a number of initiatives designed to improve Turkey's regional standing and strengthen its integration with the world economy, while actively campaigning in Europe at Ankara's behest.[7] These included the push for the construction of an oil pipeline from Baku to the Mediterranean port city of Ceyhan, which would make Turkey a major transit route for Caspian oil; the inclusion of Turkey on the list of the ten Big Emerging Markets, requiring special US attention; and the push for the successful conclusion of negotiations for a customs union with the EU. Later on, when the EU snubbed Ankara at the 1997 Luxembourg summit, Washington undertook a relentless campaign to convince the Europeans that Turkey deserved consideration for membership.

Perhaps the most emblematic moment of this relationship occurred during President Clinton's visit to Turkey in autumn 1999. Spending a record five days in this country (including attendance at the OSCE [Organization for Security and Cooperation in Europe] summit), the president visited with the 1999 earthquake victims and gave a well-received speech at the Turkish Grand National Assembly.

One of the more fundamental changes in Turkish foreign policy after the demise of the Soviet Union and the Gulf war had been its burgeoning relationship with Israel. The dramatic proof of this transformation came about during the tenure of

Prime Minister Necmettin Erbakan, perhaps the single most anti-Israeli and even anti-Semitic Turkish politician, who, under pressure from his armed forces, had to sign an agreement of military cooperation with Israel. The nature of Turkish-Israeli relations was the subject of controversy: For some, it was a "strategic" relationship designed to radically change the balance of power in the Middle East, whereas others have seen it as a development that came about—albeit in an accelerated fashion—following years of deliberate neglect.[8] There were a number of reasons why Turkey decided to embark on cooperation with Israel. The Oslo agreements between Israel and the PLO in 1993 enabled Ankara to relax its approach to Israel. For the Turkish military fighting the PKK insurgency, an opening to Israel served to punish Syria, which had been harboring the PKK chief Öcalan. The close cooperation of Syria's northern and southern neighbors, the two most formidable regional military powers, was received with great alarm in the Arab world.

But among the most important reasons for the rapprochement was the perception in Turkey that improving relations with Israel would help Turkey in Washington. Absent an effective lobby of its own, Ankara had already begun to use its own Jewish citizens to lobby the United States. Still, this was not enough to counter what Ankara had come to believe was the influence of "evil lobbies" or "foreign elements,"[9] meaning the Greek-American and Armenian-American lobbies, with the US Congress. In addition to these, human rights nongovernmental organizations had stepped up their criticisms of Turkey on Capitol Hill, especially with the intensification of the conflict in southeast Turkey. Close cooperation with Israel would help Turkey's image in the generally Israel-friendly US Congress and mobilize some of the Jewish-American groups to lobby in Ankara's favor. From this perspective, the strategy worked; not only did the pro-Israel groups begin to help Turkey, but the courtship has survived the ups and downs of the Israel-Palestinian conflict. Prominent Jewish groups have become a necessary stop for any and all Turkish politicians visiting Washington, including members of the Islamist opposition.

A second reason for the Turkish decision to seek a closer relationship with Israel also had to do with Washington, but not for the reasons suggested above. Turkish officials in the 1990s, with no immediate end in sight to the Kurdish insurrection, became increasingly concerned that arms deliveries from Washington would be subject to human rights scrutiny. Early during the Clinton administration, a helicopter sale got bogged down in the halls of Congress, and Ankara had to withdraw the order rather than face the prospect of a humiliating rejection. Similarly, other contracts with the United States, where applicable, were continuously subjected to these criteria. Israel represented an alternative source of weapons, and given Israel's desire to develop markets for its relatively small arms industry and to improve relations with Turkey, it was unlikely that human rights or any other consideration would undermine such sales.

In addition to the reasons suggested above, Israel had its own motivation for encouraging this burgeoning relationship. One of the more important advantages it derived from the military aspect of the relationship was the ability to train its air force pilots in Turkey, away from the very limited land space offered by Israel itself.

The military dimension of the relationship was shrouded in secrecy and, therefore, attracted far more attention than it perhaps deserved. This is not to say that the military relationship was unimportant to either side—after all, Israeli aircraft routinely train in Turkey, and Israel has managed to participate in and win contracts to sell Turkey a variety of weaponry—but rather that its strategic importance may have been overrated.

During the 1998 crisis with Syria over Öcalan, Damascus and the rest of the Arab world clearly perceived Turkey's greater self-confidence to be a direct result of its new relationship with Israel. Israeli leaders, by contrast, tried to signal Syria that they were not party to this escalation in tensions. The rest of the Middle East, especially Iran, viewed this relationship with alarm, as suggestions were made in the Turkish press that Israel would take advantage of its flight training to destroy Tehran's weapons of mass destruction capabilities. But there was another aspect to this Turkish-Israeli relationship that escaped scrutiny: the economic dimension. Economic ties, unlike military ones, take much longer to bear fruit. While still lagging the close military ties, the Turkish-Israeli economic relationship blossomed with time, benefiting from the fact that Israel enjoyed a free trade agreement with the United States, which provided Turkish exporters with an additional means of reaching the lucrative American market.

As far as Washington was concerned, the Turkish-Israeli relationship was long overdue. The United States provided some incentives, but by and large it took the position that these two countries could decide on their own the limits to their relationship. Joint exercises involving the US Navy with its respective counterparts from Turkey and Israel have been held at yearly intervals. These exercises were mostly symbolic because they restricted themselves to joint search and rescue operations in international waters. When the first of these exercises was conducted, it gave rise to an outcry in the Arab world, whereas the second time it was barely noted. In 2002, however, the three countries announced that they would hold "three comprehensive air maneuvers this year in an effort to improve combat readiness."[10]

Burgeoning ties between the two strong regional allies were welcomed by the United States and especially their extension—albeit before the collapse of the Oslo process—to another US ally, Jordan. This three-way relationship is an example of the "rise of new 'security geometries' or alliances in critical regions" in which the United States, by virtue of its dominant role in these countries' international relations, has the ability to influence the wider region in which they coexist.[11] This did not mean that the United States and Turkey saw eye to eye on all Middle Eastern issues. As much as Washington would have liked to enlist Ankara in its efforts to contain Iran, the fact of the matter was that Turkish-Iranian relations were complex and marked by both cooperation and competition befitting the remnants of two imperial powers. Whereas Turkey welcomed US support for the construction of the Baku-Ceyhan pipeline, Turks also went ahead with a gas pipeline originating in Iran, despite US efforts to isolate Iran. On the other hand, Turks, having complained of Iranian interference in their domestic affairs ranging from support for the PKK to Islamist terrorist groups or other Islamic organizations, have been keenly aware that their neighbor is in the process of developing weapons of mass destruction capabilities, which potentially can be aimed at them. Hence, US attempts at reducing Iran's WMD capabilities have also been welcomed in Ankara.

US-Turkish Relations Under Iraq's Shadow: Phase II

The George W. Bush administration taking the helm in January 2001 included many top officials who had advocated taking a much harder line against Saddam Hussein. The September 11 attacks and the anthrax episode that shut down Capitol Hill simply provided the rationale for the administration's decision to topple the Iraqi leader. As a result, Iraq began to loom larger in US-Turkish relations.

The initial change in the Bush administration's priorities, its intention to pursue terrorists to the ends of the earth, suited Ankara well. First and foremost, for Turkey, which had been fighting its own battle against terrorists, the al-Qa'ida threat was a vindication of its own discourse on terrorism. Ankara, therefore, was confident it would receive greater support against the PKK. Moreover, the obscurantist character of both the Taliban and al-Qa'ida enhanced the ruling secular Turkish civilian and military elites' view that making concessions to Islamists, whether in Turkey or in the Middle East, was the beginning of a slippery slope. Turkey was one of the initial countries to offer Washington its support for the war on terrorism, and by announcing that Turkish troops would be the first to replace the British peacekeeping forces in Kabul, Afghanistan, Ankara further enhanced its image. Turkey tendered not only materiel assistance but also its credentials as a Muslim ally of the United States at a time when many in the Islamic world began to perceive the war on terrorism as a war on Islam. The Ankara government offered its backing despite the fact that large majorities of the Turkish public, according to opinion polls, opposed not only the dispatch of troops to Afghanistan but also the conduct of the US war.[12]

The war in Afghanistan was seen as a new opportunity to solidify Turkey's role and importance in Central Asia. For Ankara, reversing the gains made by a fundamentalist regime that also harbored groups seeking to undermine friendly Central Asian governments was a gain in and of itself, but more important, by taking part in the military operations and helping to stabilize the region, Turkey could further enhance its reputation in the world.[13] In effect, Turkey was getting a second chance—the first being immediately after the demise of the USSR—to spread its influence in Central Asia, and this time it had the added benefit of being nominally part of a winning coalition.

To the great consternation of Turkey the other shoe would soon drop. The Bush administration was not going to be satisfied with just Afghanistan. Iraq was next, and this would create a new set of complications in the relationship. The importance of Turkey to Washington was tested early in the Bush administration when Ankara suffered from a disastrous economic crisis unleashed by a February 2001 fight between President Necdet Sezer and Ecevit. The rapid devaluation of the Turkish lira, the collapse of the banking sector under questionable loans, and the massive layoffs suffered by all sectors of the economy rendered Ecevit's coalition government weak and unpopular. The war on terrorism and Washington's reliance on Turkey for the conduct of its Iraq policy once again highlighted Turkey's strategic importance and convinced the Bush administration—despite internal critics such as Treasury Secretary Paul O'Neill—that it deserved to be rescued through a massive bailout, whereas Argentina, undergoing an equally debilitating economic crisis, did not.

By the time Prime Minister Ecevit visited Washington in January 2002, Iraq had clearly moved to the top of the Bush agenda. Soon after his return from Washington, Ecevit started to publicly distance himself from Saddam Hussein and even warned Baghdad's ruler that unless he complied with UN resolutions, President Bush would act against him.[14] This turnabout in Ecevit's traditional stance regarding Iraq is noteworthy: He claimed to have made it clear to President Bush that should the United States decide to act against Iraq, Ankara expected to be consulted in advance. He also insisted on other conditions, including ensuring the safety of the Turkmen in Iraq, the inadmissibility of an independent Kurdish state in the north of Iraq, and the minimization of Turkish economic losses.

It would not be Ecevit's fate to lead Turkey at the time of the 2003 Iraq war. The Justice and Development Party, AKP, led by former Istanbul mayor Recep Tayyip Erdogan, swept into power in November 2002 by winning 34 percent of the national vote but almost two-thirds of the parliamentary seats. War in Iraq would be an ironic conundrum to face for a leader who in the 1990s had been a devoted follower of the Islamist Erbakan but had now moderated his discourse. Erdogan, due to the political ban on him, had to temporarily relinquish the job of prime minister to his colleague Abdullah Gul, but he found himself immediately courted by President Bush. The US administration, in full war mode, was hoping to get Turkey's permission to station American troops on Turkish soil in preparation for opening a second front against Baghdad. After long and protracted negotiations, the moderate Islamist government decided to support the United States.

The Turkish government drove a hard bargain. It negotiated a large financial package to protect it from the potential negative economic side effects that the war would have entailed. More importantly, it received Washington's approval to enter northern Iraq in the wake of the US 4th Infantry Division to prevent another refugee crisis reminiscent of 1991. In reality, the Turks were anxious for their presence to be felt in northern Iraq as a deterrent to Iraqi Kurdish aspirations for independence.

Events did not turn out as expected. To everyone's surprise, when the government resolution endorsing the US request came for a vote in the Turkish parliament on March 1, 2003, it failed. Although more people voted in favor than against, there were enough members of parliament who abstained while remaining in the chamber that, under Turkish parliamentary procedures, were counted as no votes. The failure of the parliamentary resolution had more to do with the AKP's mismanagement of the vote. In a straw poll conducted on that same morning, the party whips had determined that they had at least a 50-vote margin for success. There was also some confusion regarding the attitude of the military. Although the generals supported the deal, it was clear that both the AKP government and the Turkish General Staff, in view of the public opposition to a deployment of US troops, were anxious to deflect responsibility on the other's shoulder. In an interview with Fikret Bila, a *Milliyet* columnist, three days before the vote, military officials expressed doubts about supporting the American operation and the parliamentary vote.[15] The vote, but especially the perception that the military was unenthusiastic about it, elicited a sharp rebuke from Deputy Defense Secretary Paul Wolfowitz. Still, as the United States continued its preparations for war, American special forces crossed Turkish territory into Iraq to liaise with Kurds and other oppositionists.

Turkish-American relations over Iraq would only deteriorate further after the March 1 vote. On July 4, 2003, US forces in control of northern Iraq arrested a number of Turkish special forces members in the Kurdish town of Sulaymaniyah on suspicion of colluding with ITF members to assassinate the governor of Kirkuk. The Turkish soldiers who were in northern Iraq with American acquiescence received the "al-Qaʻida" treatment: They were hooded and sent to Baghdad for further interrogation.[16] News of the incident shocked the Turkish public and officials, and the arrests became emblematic of the mistrust in Turkish-American relations. Turks began suspecting that the United States was not just intent on punishing Ankara for the March 1 vote. Given Washington's reliance on the Iraqi Kurdish factions, especially after the intensification of the insurgency, it appeared that the United States wanted to sideline Ankara in Iraq in favor of the Kurds. These suspicions were confirmed—though incorrectly American officials would argue—when the American administrator for Iraq, Ambassador Paul Bremer, sided with the Iraqi Kurds to block the deployment of Turkish troops in central Iraq, even though the Turks were responding to a Bush administration request.

The continued war in Iraq further deepened Turkish anxieties about American aims, interests, and capabilities. Ankara expected that among US priorities as the occupying power would be the elimination of the PKK from their hideouts in northern Iraq, but the intensified insurgency prevented the US Central Command from engaging an organization that refrained from attacking American troops. After the PKK abandoned its unilateral cease-fire in 2005, the reluctance of the United States to take on the PKK became a continuous source of frustration in Turkey. The differences over the PKK represented only the tip of the iceberg. Turkey, which hitherto objected to the idea of a federal Iraqi state, had to acknowledge after the constitutional developments in Iraq that the new state was going to be federal in structure. Instead Ankara articulated what it called "red lines" that it wanted respected. These consisted of denying the Iraqi Kurds independence and the oil-rich city of Kirkuk. Ankara claimed that Kirkuk was a Turkmen city and any attempt at changing its ethnic composition would be unacceptable. By contrast, Iraqi Kurdish leaders insisted on the Kurdish character of the city and sought to return Kurdish refugees displaced by Saddam Hussein's ethnic cleansing in the 1980s and 1990s. Both the Transitional Administrative Law and the new Iraqi constitution called for a referendum to determine whether Kirkuk would join the Kurdish provinces in a future federal Iraqi republic. If Kirkuk were to become part of the Kurdish federal entity, Turks fear that the city's oil riches would ultimately lay the foundation of a future independent Kurdistan.[17]

Turkish leaders have continuously voiced concern over the conduct of US military operations. American action in the northern Iraqi town of Tel Afer, where the majority of the population is of Shi'a Turkmen origin, and in Falluja was severely criticized by AKP leaders and parliamentarians. The AKP and its core constituencies view the war in Iraq (and in Afghanistan) as unjustly targeting Muslim populations. Correspondingly, anti-Americanism in Turkey has reached levels never seen before. The government's problem extends beyond its constituency and public sentiment to Turkey's Kurdish problem and its relationship with the military. Having pushed the envelope successfully on critical issues such as the European Union and Cyprus—often in opposition to hard-line domestic interests—the AKP government is vulnerable to accusations of inaction on the PKK's bases in northern Iraq and Iraqi Kurdish aspirations. Should the PKK ramp up its violent activities, domestic pressure in Ankara will correspondingly build up for a military intervention. Such an action could lead to serious disagreements with the US military and the Kurdish forces in Iraq.

The end of the war in Iraq is not yet in sight. Future developments will undoubtedly have additional ramifications. Turkey, for instance, has asked US and Iraqi authorities to delay the scheduled referendum in Kirkuk because it fears a Kurdish victory under current circumstances. Iraqis are unlikely to go along with this request. The Iraq war has soured Turkish-American relations and has encouraged Turkey to opt for what on the outside appears to be a more "stand-alone" foreign policy. On two other Middle Eastern questions closely watched by the US, Syria and Hamas, Ankara broke not just with the United States but also with the Western consensus. Although the West was split on the war in Iraq, the Europeans and Washington had been working in tandem on the decision to isolate both Syria—for its occupation of Lebanon and responsibility in former Prime Minister Hariri's assassination—and Hamas—for its radical pronouncements. Turkey, in contrast, decided to engage Damascus, and when it was criticized, Erdogan claimed that it was he who convinced the Syrian leader Asad to withdraw from Lebanon, an assertion that angered Washington. On Hamas, the Turkish government invited the Syrian-based and most radical elements of Hamas to Ankara immediately after that group's electoral victory in the Palestinian elections. Again, Turkey claimed to be engaging Hamas, an organization on everyone's primary terrorist list, at a time when the West was looking to force it to moderate its discourse and policies. Ankara's action was damaging to its credibility, given that it had lobbied so hard for the Europeans and Americans to denounce and ban the PKK as a terrorist organization.

In general, the AKP government has tried to distance itself from the United States. Although the outcome of the March 1 vote was unintended, and had it passed the circumstances in Iraq could be very different, the fact is that the AKP's actions are consistent with the ideas of the Turkish Islamist camp that date back to the Erbakan years. The AKP government has also distanced itself from Israel, as relations between the two have cooled since the late 1990s. Under the AKP, the new foreign policy is not so much an attempt to oppose Washington as it is to demonstrate that Turkey is an important power. In the minds of AKP leaders, Turkey's geographical location, its much improved economic conditions, its military capabilities, and its historical connections to the Middle East and the Asian continent render Turkey a far more important power than it has aspired to be or been given credit for in the past. The repeated attempts at offering its good offices for mediation in a variety of conflicts, principally in the Middle East, are part and parcel of the AKP's efforts at making Turkey more visible and relevant. In the end, however, the international respect and prestige that the AKP wants to earn for Turkey cannot come at the expense of its relations with the United States precisely because Ankara's close and historical relationship with Washington is one of its most important assets.

Conclusion

Perhaps Turkey's greatest contribution to the United States, as Ian Lesser aptly argued, is a degree of freedom of action or power projection in adjacent areas.[18] Prior to 9/11, despite the vagaries of Turkish domestic politics as widely disparate political parties assumed power in Ankara, both countries had experienced a marked increase in common concerns and interests. This does not hold true any longer. The war in Iraq and the ascendancy of the AKP in Turkey have created some distance between them. This does not mean that the United States will no longer continue to support broad Turkish goals or come to its assistance, as in the crippling economic crisis of 2001. As long as the quagmire continues in Iraq, there is likely to be much more reticence on both sides to engage in the future. This said, the conflict in Iraq also provides unprecedented opportunities for Ankara and Washington to work together to fashion a grand compromise over northern Iraq.[19] However, the current atmosphere of tension has made such discussions very difficult to contemplate at the present time.

It is also important to note that this relationship will continue to be influenced by events outside the Middle East. Among the two most important are Turkey's progression along the European Union membership path and developments in Cyprus. In both of these, the AKP government has taken risks and modified what previously were immutable preconditions. The interplay of these two international issues with domestic politics is likely to create a backlash in Turkey should the Europeans be perceived as turning their backs on Turks. Thus, the possibility exists that particular events could unleash powerful domestic nationalist forces that would severely test Turkey's relations with the West. Turkish-American relations have often surprised even the most seasoned observers. On the eve of the Iraq war, a leading Turkish columnist, Mehmet Ali Birand, observed that Turkish leaders who had long championed a strengthened strategic relationship with the United States were in the horns of a dilemma because of America's war preparations. In essence, he argued, the tables had been reversed: The United States would be asking Turkey to demonstrate its much-touted strategic commitment by supporting its actions in Iraq, and Ankara would have no choice but to comply.[20] Turkey, as the March 1 vote demonstrated, did not follow Birand's prescription. Nevertheless, the United States did not punish Ankara, as some had demanded, but instead sought to stabilize relations and offered a reduced economic package to help Turkey weather the crisis. The current chill in relations will continue as long as the conflict in Iraq remains unresolved, but the setback will not prove to be terribly damaging in the long term.[21]

Notes

1. For an analysis of the period, see George S. Harris, *Troubled Alliance: Turkish-American Problems in Historical Perspective, 1945–1971* (Washington, DC, and Stanford, Calif.: American Enterprise Institute and Hoover Institution, 1972); and Bruce R. Kuniholm, *The Origins of the Cold War in the Near East* (Princeton: Princeton University Press, 1980). Also, see Elie Podeh's chapter in this volume on the Baghdad Pact.

2. Cengiz Çandar, "Some Turkish Perspectives on the United States and American Policy Toward Turkey," in *Turkey's Transformation and American Policy,* ed. Morton Abramowitz (New York: Century Foundation Press, 2001), pp. 128–131.

3. Morton Abramowitz, who was the US ambassador to Turkey at the time of the Gulf war, recounts his experience in obtaining Özal's permission to overfly Turkish territory and access to bases for the war in "The Complexities of American Policy Making on Turkey," in *Turkey's Transformation and American Policy,* pp. 153–156. Özal, in effect, was challenging the traditional cautious modus operandi of Turkish foreign policy; see Malik Mufti, "Daring and Caution in Turkish Foreign Policy," *Middle East Journal* 52, 1 (Winter 1998):48–49.

4. In his memoirs, the resigning chief of the general staff Necip Torumtay tells of Özal's preoccupation with northern Iraq and its possible benefits for Turkey; see his *Orgeneral Torumtay'in Anilari* (Istanbul: Milliyet Yayinlari, 1993), pp. 115–116. Whether Özal, if the opportunity arose, intended to occupy parts of Iraq such as Mosul or Kirkuk has never been clear. In a recent interview, the then-commander of land forces, Dogan Güres, reflected on how Özal would complain about the injustice the British had done at the end of World War I by including those Turkish territories in Iraq. Although General Güres claims to have prepared plans for all possible eventualities, he was never told by Özal that this was his intention; *Yeni Safak* (Istanbul) December 31, 2001.

5. Baskin Oran, *Kalkik Horoz: Çekiç Güç ve Kürt Devleti* (Ankara: Bilgi Yayinevi, 1996).

6. Ecevit even publicly thanked the United States for its help in capturing Öcalan; Kemal Kirisci, "US-Turkish Relations: New Uncertainties in a Renewed Partnership," in *Turkey in World Politics: An Emerging Multiregional Power,* ed. Barry Rubin and Kemal Kirisci (Boulder: Lynne Rienner, 2001), p. 134.

7. For more on US-Turkish relations during the Clinton years, see Henri J. Barkey, "The Endless Pursuit: Improving US-Turkish Relations," in *Friends in Need: Turkey and the United States After September 11,* ed. Morton Abramowitz (New York: Century Foundation, 2003).

8. A representative sample of writings on this topic include Alan Makovsky, "Israeli-Turkish Relations: A Turkish Periphery Strategy?" in Barkey, *Reluctant Neighbor,* pp. 147–170; Ofra Bengio, *The Turkish-Israeli Relationship: Changing Ties of Middle Eastern Outsiders* (New York: Palgrave, 2004); Meliha Benli Altunisik, "Turkish Policy Toward Israel," in *Turkey's New World,* ed. Alan Makovsky and Sabri Sayari (Washington, DC: Washington Institute for Near East Policy, 2000), pp. 59–73; Amikam Nachmani, "The Remarkable Turkish-Israeli Tie," *Middle East Policy* (June 1998):19–29; Anat Lewin, "Turkey and Israel: Reciprocal and Mutual Imagery in the Media, 1994–1999," *Journal of International Affairs* 54, 1 (Fall 2000):239–261.

9. Yasemin Çongar, "The State of Turkish-American Dialogue, *Private View* (Spring 1999).

10. Metehan Demir, "Israel, Turkey, US to Hold Joint Air Maneuvers," *Jerusalem Post,* February 11, 2002.

11. Ian O. Lesser, "Western Interests in a Changing Turkey," in *The Future of Turkish-Western Relations,* ed. Zalmay Khalilzad, Ian O. Lesser, and F. Stephen Larrabee (Santa Monica, Calif.: RAND, 2000), pp. 56–57.

12. Some argued that the Turkish government did not really have a choice in the matter precisely because the United States had come to Turkey's rescue in a number of critical junctures, ranging from the 2001 economic crisis to Öcalan's capture and the push to convince the EU to make Turkey a candidate country. For a forceful exposition of this point of view, see Mehmet Ali Birand, "Türkiye'nin ABD'ye eli mahkum . . . " *Posta,* October 11, 2001.

13. Sedat Ergin, "Türkiye'nin Afganistan sinavi," *Hürriyet,* November 16, 2001.

14. See Cengiz Çandar, "Bagdat'tan Washington'a U dönus?" *Yeni Safak,* January 23, 2002; and *Hürriyet* (Istanbul), January 24, 2002.

15. Fikret Bila, "Ucaksavarlar kime?" *Milliyet,* February 26, 2003. The column got front-page billing with a headline that read, "Askerler Rahatsiz," or "The Soldiers Are Apprehensive." It was later revealed that Bila had talked to the Land Forces commander Aytac Yalman.

16. This appeared to be a rogue operation conducted by some in the special forces command without the knowledge of the higher-ups in the Turkish General Staff. See Henri J. Barkey, "Turkey and Iraq: The Perils (and Prospects) of Proximity," US Institute of Peace Special Report #141, July 2005, p. 10.

17. Ibid.

18. Lesser, "Western Interests in a Changing Turkey," p. 71.

19. Cüneyd Ülsever, "Hükümetin ne Kürt ne de Ortadogu Politikasi Var, II," *Hürriyet,* August 25, 2005.

20. Mehmet Ali Birand, "Türkiye, ABD'ye 'hayir' diyemez," *Posta,* February 12, 2002.

21. Among those who argue that tensions between Turkey and the United States are being exaggerated is Ömer Taspinar. See Ömer Taspinar, "Gerginlik Abartiliyor," *Radikal,* March 21, 2005.

24

The United States and Afghanistan
From Marginality to Global Concern

Marvin G. Weinbaum

The consuming interest for the United States in Afghanistan during most of last half-century was the cold war. Yet until the 1980s, US policy toward Afghanistan formed one of the least confrontational arenas of cold war politics. The United States was satisfied with a low-keyed, limited involvement with the country. Afghanistan was largely conceded as a zone of influence to its Soviet neighbor, although remaining formally nonaligned. A modest US development program, only credible enough to keep Kabul governments from falling entirely under the sway of the Soviet state, complemented Moscow's far larger aid effort. Desperately poor Afghanistan enjoyed a version of neutrality both profitable and nonthreatening. However, in one pivotal sector, aid to the Afghan military, US acquiescence to a dominant Soviet role proved anything but benign.

The decade of the 1980s, preceded by the Soviet military's invasion of December 1979, changed everything for US involvement in Afghanistan. It was a period when US policy was dedicated, above all, toward forcing a Soviet withdrawal and featured a generous, covert program to assist an Islamic-inspired insurgency. Afghanistan, now at the very forefront of a geostrategic competition, suffered devastation to its state and society, even as the conflict contributed in large measure to ending the cold war.

With the departure of the last Soviet troops in early 1989, the United States felt no overriding national interest in Afghanistan, certainly none to match competing US global concerns. Nor did policymakers sense that the United States could contribute materially toward resolving a civil war that began with efforts to defeat a surviving Afghan communist regime and continued with fighting among the victorious parties. It was the appearance and success after 1994 of the Taliban, initially a movement of Islamic students, which redirected Washington's attention to Afghanistan. Exportable terrorism and Islamic radicalism, drug trafficking, and human rights abuses, although already emergent in the country's anarchic setting, became synony-

462

mous with the Taliban and their guest-benefactor Osama bin Laden, alleged mastermind of anti-American activities. The terrorist attacks on New York and Washington in September 2001 quickly transformed a heightened interest into an American engagement in Afghanistan, the dimensions of which few could have previously imagined. The long arm of the US military was directed toward rooting out international terrorism emanating from Afghanistan as the announced first step in an extended global war. It also promised to devolve upon the United States a large share of the international responsibility for helping to rehabilitate and reconstruct the Afghan state and society. More immediately, the fallout of events in Afghanistan deeply impacted US foreign relations across the Islamic world.

The King's Afghanistan

Modern US-Afghan relations might have gone very differently had Washington not rejected requests as early as 1946 for modest military ties, mainly for purchasing arms, from the Afghan governments under Shah Mahmud and Sardar Daoud, both close relatives of King Muhammad Zahir Shah, whose long reign began in 1933. Kabul was rebuffed, however, by US administrations unwilling to forfeit opportunities to cultivate a relationship with the new, prospectively anti-communist state of Pakistan created in 1947. Given the antipathy over their common border between Afghanistan and Pakistan, the United States felt it more rewarding to choose against the smaller, landlocked country. This left Afghanistan scrambling for protection against Pakistan and for the means to fend off an actively imperialist postwar Soviet state. Even though a trade agreement had been signed with the Soviet Union in 1950, until Stalin's death in 1953, Moscow seemed dedicated mainly to increasing the number of communist satellite regimes. Afghanistan, like other nonaligned countries, was by 1955 eligible for military and economic aid, and Prime Minister Daoud welcomed Chairman Khrushchev's offer of $100 million in assistance for various development projects. The same year, Daoud won approval from a specially convened council of traditional leaders for a security treaty with Moscow. In 1956, the first in a series of agreements for arms with the Soviet Union and Eastern bloc countries worth $32 million was signed. As with the development credits, this aid was to be repaid with bartered, although typically undervalued, Afghan commodities.[1] Pakistan had meanwhile signed on in 1954 to the Mutual Security Agreement, making it a military ally of the United States.

Although the Soviet Union was ceded the preeminent role in Afghanistan's economic development, the Afghan royal family and most government officials remained Western oriented, especially after the inauguration of a democratically elected government in 1965. Yet under Prime Minister Daoud, the Soviets were allowed to upgrade the army and air force, including officer training, thus opening the way for domestic communists to infiltrate and subvert the Afghan military and critical sectors of the bureaucracy. The Soviet state also made itself indispensable as it offered, as an alternative to Pakistan's port of Karachi, a northern trade route. Aside from becoming Afghanistan's major trading partner, Moscow also gave backing for a

Daoud-initiated irredentist campaign to carve an ethnic state, to be called Pashtunistan, from most of northwest Pakistan.

Agreements between Kabul and Moscow had the effect of encouraging the United States to offer the Afghan government enough economic assistance to keep Afghanistan from falling effectively within Moscow's orbit. The decision did not come without an internal debate in Washington that went on for several years, beginning in 1954. It pitted those in the State Department who argued for liquidating US involvement in Afghanistan and others who, although not anxious for competition on a project-by-project basis, contended that aid was necessary to keep the Afghans from losing all chance to remain independent and neutral.[2] The Kabul government recognized the advantages accruing to Afghanistan from having the cold war adversaries bid against one another and welcomed aid as well from other donors, including China, West Germany, and Great Britain.

US assistance had actually begun in 1952 with loans for an ambitious water and agricultural development project in the country's southwest Helmand Valley region. By 1956, expanded US aid programs, supported by $15 million in grants, focused on teacher training and other educational programs and various other areas of technical assistance. Together with private American assistance groups, the agricultural, health, and communications sectors were assisted, and food aid was drawn from US surplus stocks. A Peace Corps program was initiated in 1962. Several major infrastructural projects received grants, including construction of a highway from Kabul to the Pakistan border and from Herat to the Iran frontier—in response to a far more ambitious Soviet national road program—and the construction of an international airport in the country's second largest city, Kandahar. By 1974, the United States had given as much as $500 million in assistance in loans, grants, and commodities.

American diplomacy was also active. Afghanistan's long-standing quarrel with the shah of Iran's government over Afghan diversion of the waters of the Helmand River and a tributary had become more acute with US loans for new dams. Quiet US mediation finally brought the two sides together in a treaty signed in March 1973 that regulated and divided the waters.[3] Washington also encouraged mediation by several friendly Islamic countries after Afghanistan's strong advocacy of Pashtunistan resulted in a Pakistan-imposed trade blockade that nearly brought the two countries to war during 1955. In both cases, US strategic interests dictated that it work to lessen tensions between Afghanistan and US-allied countries, lest Moscow be able to exploit further these territorial issues.

Still, the United States never received the political dividends that went to the Soviets. Moscow's projects gained more visibility and were seen as more directly impacting the lives of ordinary Afghans. Washington's development assistance also became less visible after 1956, when the largest projects were completed and funding dropped off considerably. Ironically, behind Washington's largely consistent thinking on Afghanistan from the 1950s through the 1970s lay a concern that were US involvement to deepen, especially were the US to offer military assistance, it could provoke the Soviets to act more aggressively toward Afghanistan.[4]

Although foreign aid brought a measure of prosperity to some sectors of Afghan society, the country remained one of the world's poorest. The assistance also created a large financial debt to Moscow.[5] More consequential still was that it released new social forces that politicized a country unprepared to absorb them institutionally. A new constitution, enacted in 1964 after King Zahir Shah's ouster of the autocratic Daoud in 1963, was supposed to usher in a more open, inclusive system of government. But the king blocked the formation of political parties after they were legislated by the elected parliament. Forcing political activity into more clandestine channels, especially in a country penetrated by foreign influences through aid dependency, would eventually pose a threat to Afghanistan's national integrity.

Post-Monarchy in the 1970s

Taking advantage of cold war rivalries, Afghanistan had managed to escape forfeiting its nonalignment. The communist-led coup of July 1973 that removed Zahir Shah seemed finally to have ended Afghanistan's historic buffer state role. It brought back as president of a soon-to-be-formed Afghan republic the former Prime Minister Daoud. Although Washington accorded recognition to the regime, it grew increasingly wary of Daoud's rule as he embarked on a domestic program with heavy socialist markings. Accompanying this was an expanded Soviet assistance program and the placement of the Afghan army under direct Soviet supervision.[6] In contrast, US economic assistance programs to Afghanistan had already been feeling the pressure of Washington's heavy commitments in Southeast Asia.

Initially, Daoud appeared as only a front man for the dedicated Marxists who returned him to power. But the Afghan president's determination to marginalize his Afghan communist allies soon became evident. Although continuing to welcome Moscow's aid, Daoud was also uneasy about the heightened Soviet presence in the country and was aware of dissatisfaction among Afghans with his attempts at radical transformations of the society and economy. By 1977, Daoud was looking hard for economic and political alternatives that could lessen Moscow's influence. He found them in the region's Islamic states. Pro-Western Iran had, between 1973 and 1975, already given $50 million in assistance and, together with Saudi Arabia, was anxious to upgrade relations with the Kabul regime, promising aid at a level that could eventually dwarf assistance from the Soviet Union.[7]

The Carter administration's plans for Iran as a regional hegemon counted on more cordial relations being forged among Iran's neighbors. Iran as well as Saudi Arabia, Kuwait, and Japan were encouraged to provide economic assistance to Afghanistan.[8] While US Ambassador in Kabul Theodore Eliot encouraged the idea of greater "true" nonalignment by the Daoud government, no plan existed to effect a break by Kabul from Moscow, much less for the United States to replace the Soviet Union. Daoud was nonetheless under criticism from the Afghan political left, for what were perceived to be gradually expanding ties to the United States. Daoud's change of direction was more apparent as he backed away from the Pashtunistan cause in reaching out for a better understanding with Pakistan's Prime

Minister Zulfiqar Ali Bhutto. When Bhutto was deposed in July 1977, his successor, General Zia ul-Haq, indicated that deliberations would continue, and Daoud accepted an invitation to visit Pakistan in March 1978.[9]

The Afghan leader's diplomatic maneuvering came to an abrupt end with a second coup in April 1978, soon to be called the Saur revolution. Although Moscow had misgivings about the growing independence of Daoud's foreign policy, the Soviets had apparently not engineered the overthrow, and Daoud had tried to respect the sensitive lines not to be crossed with his benefactors. Soviet advisers in the capital no doubt knew of the coup plans, and Moscow had worked hard leading up to the coup to bring together the two bitterly divided factions of the communist Peoples' Democratic Party. But the coup was essentially homegrown, an act of revenge by local communists who had been shunted aside by the man they had brought back to power from political oblivion. As before, it required critical backing from units in the Afghan army. Daoud and members of his family, along with high-ranking officials in his regime, were summarily executed.

Further US aid cutbacks took place after the communist takeover. Against the background of a running debate between National Security Adviser Zbigniew Brzezinski and the State Department over how tough to get with the Soviet Union, it was decided to maintain a US presence in Afghanistan and, to the extent possible, to try to influence a communist leadership under President Nur Muhammad Taraki and Prime Minister Hafizullah Amin. US Ambassador Adolph "Spike" Dubs, using his considerable diplomatic skills, appeared to have succeeded during 1978 in establishing working relations with the doctrinaire Marxist yet at times also nationalistic leadership.[10] But Soviet involvement in the country, including the arrival of many more military and civilian advisers, increased in the months following the coup, occasioning several private protests from Washington. When Dubs was kidnapped in February 1979, allegedly by religious fanatics, and then murdered during a suspiciously bungled rescue operation by Afghan government security forces and their Soviet advisers, Washington withdrew its aid program almost entirely and reduced its diplomatic presence in Afghanistan.

More than a year earlier a rural Islamic insurrection had begun against the communist government. Moscow blamed the opposition's success on Amin's insensitive and repressive policies, which it feared could lead eventually to a popular uprising. But when the Soviets in the summer 1979 sought to eliminate Amin, leaving Taraki in full authority, the Moscow-hatched plot backfired, and Amin instead had Taraki killed. Desperate, and fully aware that the Soviets did not trust him and would seek revenge, Amin quietly opened channels to the United States and other countries, hoping to strike a deal to ward off Moscow. Washington, wanting no part of the unpopular, unsavory Amin, ignored his overtures. In late December, the Soviets invaded and killed Amin and his close associates and installed Babrak Karmal, leader of the more Moscow-pliant wing of the Communist Party. Moscow's decision to unleash the Red Army was probably motivated more by fear of rising discontent within the Afghan military than concern about a potent Islamic insurgency. The invasion also carried wider strategic importance, allowing Moscow to take full advantage of opportunities offered by the rapidly declining influence of the United States in the region, most notably in post-revolutionary Iran, which had been Washington's regional police only a short time earlier. From an intelligence standpoint, the invasion was an embarrassment. Despite mounting evidence of a troop buildup, the Carter White House was alerted too late for it to give the Brezhnev government a credible warning not to launch Soviet forces.[11]

Jihad Against the Soviets

For the United States, the Afghan conflict was to become the last great battle of the US-Soviet ideological and military rivalry, and like their previous encounters, it was fought largely through surrogates. If US government policy could be faulted for failing to undertake the public and private diplomacy that might have deterred Moscow from invading Afghanistan, President Carter afterward, feeling personally deceived, reacted angrily. Through public statements as well as economic boycotts and international diplomacy, Moscow faced strong condemnation. More generally, the United States believed it was responding to Brezhnev's increasingly aggressive policies across the Third World. Washington undertook measures to beef up military facilities around the globe, along with efforts to improve relations with China and other countries considered well situated to thwart the Soviets. Taking on Pakistan as an ally in the fight was especially important because the United States had entered into newly combative relations with revolutionary Iran. Indeed, Pakistan could be conceived as strategic compensation for the loss of the shah's Iran. If nothing else, Pakistan itself was to be kept from falling into the Soviet sphere.

It was the view of many US analysts that the Soviets sought with their invasion of Afghanistan to realize a long-held dream of access to a warm-water port. With Pakistan seen as the next target of an expansionist Soviet Union, the Carter administration offered Pakistan's General Zia ul-Haq direct US military assistance. Rejecting the program as inadequate, Zia claimed that Pakistan needed more than Carter's "peanuts" if it were to become the first line of defense against the Soviets, given the potential risks. Only when the incoming Reagan administration promised a far more generous long-term $3.2 billion package of economic assistance and military sales credits did Pakistan agree to become a "frontline state," nurturing the insurgency against the Soviet army and Afghan communist forces.

In his partnership with the United States, Zia ul-Haq hoped that his regime would be able to shed the taint of illegitimacy and international ostracism that it had acquired with the military's 1977 coup against an elected, although faltering, Bhutto government. Direct military assistance from Washington would, most importantly, help Pakistan's military to upgrade defenses against India, a country with close ties to the Soviet Union. The possibility of handing Moscow a defeat in Afghanistan suited Zia's vision of creating friendly Muslim states in the region in order to give Pakistan "strategic depth" in the long struggle with India. At home, the Afghan war helped Zia to sustain his domestic control and delay restoration of meaningful democratic institutions.

Over the course of what became known as a *jihad,* or holy struggle, against the Soviets and their Afghan communist allies, the CIA carried the burden of the US involvement. Eventually, Washington was engaged in the most extensive and expensive covert warfare operation since Vietnam. The assistance to Afghanistan began modestly enough with $30 million going to the resistance forces in 1980, with Saudi Arabia generally matching US funding and the Chinese contributing weapons. Not until the end of 1984, when an allocation of $280 million was announced, was the decision reached by the Reagan administration to escalate the conflict sufficiently to aim for an outright Soviet military defeat. Support increased the following year to $470 million, and in 1987 to $630. In all, during the 1980s, the Afghan Mujahideen received more than $2 billion from the United States, enough to train at least 80,000 fighters.[12]

Large sums of money were funneled to Pakistan's security organizations, notably to a newly empowered Inter-Services Intelligence Directorate (ISID). Purchased weapons were distributed by the ISID among the several Peshawar-based Mujahideen parties expected to carry the brunt of the fighting in Afghanistan. The ISID forced some coordination among these parties, although it showed favoritism toward the most radical and, ironically, most anti-American of the Islamic groups. More secular Afghan nationalists, many with close ties to the United States, were almost entirely excluded from the Pakistani-supervised insurgency.

CIA officials on the scene were not entirely bystanders. Detailed and extensive satellite intelligence was passed on to the resistance, as was training in more sophisticated weaponry and communications equipment.[13] But, for the most part, Washington willingly delegated to the ISID orchestration of the war and rationalized the decision as giving discretion to those in a better position to assess the strategic picture and to know how funds could be used most effectively. In fact, allocations were made by Pakistan only secondarily on the basis of fighting prowess. Most handsomely awarded with arms were those parties that Pakistan felt it could more easily trust and control.

The United States mostly looked the other way as Afghan resistance party leaders living in the border city of Peshawar, Pakistan, enriched themselves through stealing and selling hundreds of millions of dollars of arms.[14] It was also well known by CIA officials who were monitoring the insurgency that the Pakistan army and refugee administrators were siphoning off arms and relief supplies. The partial appropriation of CIA shipments was condoned as a sort of commission to the Pakistan government for the burdens and risks it had assumed in backing the Afghan insurgency, even if a third of supplies never reached their intended recipients.

The Geneva Accords

As early as June 1982, proximity talks had begun in Geneva that allowed Islamabad to avoid direct negotiations with the Marxist regime in Kabul, which it had refused to recognize. The stated objectives of the talks, held under UN auspices in successive rounds over six years, were to end foreign interference and intervention, to realize self-determination and a sovereign Afghanistan, and to repatriate refugees. Plainly, any agreements had to suit the superpowers' cold war strategies. The Soviet Union was deeply engaged in decisions at every stage. The United States, although seemingly more detached from the negotiations, monitored them closely and was present at the final session in Geneva in 1988. Throughout the talks, the United States carried on a dialogue with Moscow over Afghanistan, usually preceded by contacts with Islamabad. Pakistani negotiators, risking forfeiture of US military and economic aid, looked for cues from Washington. However, Pakistan's separate interests, motivated by concern over domestic instability and its own strategic logic, also weighed heavily.[15]

Differences prevailed in Washington over the Geneva negotiations, some linked to issues that touched only peripherally on the Afghan conflict. Cold war conservatives, doubting Moscow's sincerity at Geneva, saw no reason to let the Soviet military off the hook in Afghanistan, or at least only under the most humiliating terms. Their suspicions of the Soviets' intentions at Geneva were shared by pro-Mujahideen lobbies, including many Afghan émigré groups that resented the exclusion of the Afghan parties from the deliberations. Ideological hard-liners and advocates of the *jihad* were also anxious that an agreement leading to a Soviet withdrawal not end arms shipments to the Mujahideen. The Geneva talks were also influenced by US nonproliferation policies. Throughout the 1980s, lobbies on Capitol Hill pressed for Pakistan's compliance with US law and for the relinquishing of its clandestine nuclear weapons program. They demanded that Washington not continue to ignore Pakistani activity and insisted that the White House implement a legislatively imposed aid cutoff—with its obvious implications for the insurgency. These voices were countered by others who stressed Pakistan's contribution not only to the Afghan cause but also as part of a strategy backing Islamic alternatives to communism wherever they could be found.

Some critics of US policy on the left contended that the Soviets were prepared for a military pullout as early as 1983 and that the Reagan administration's desire to perpetuate a conflict bleeding the Soviet state delayed serious negotiations. Although Moscow may, in fact, have been ready to withdraw its armed forces earlier, it would have done so only with international recognition of its Afghan client and a reasonable certainty of the Kabul regime's survival. It was not until 1986, a year after Mikhail Gorbachev assumed power, that the Soviets decided against committing more troops and grew serious about recalling their forces, even if that meant leaving the Kabul government at some risk.

By this time, Moscow had begun to face up to the full economic and political costs of fighting the Mujahideen. The Soviet leadership's decision was influenced by losses it sustained from the introduction of US shoulder-fired, ground-to-air Stinger missiles and the rising tide of domestic opposition to the war in the Soviet Union. Perhaps most of all, Afghanistan posed a prime obstacle to Gorbachev's plans for domestic economic and political reforms.

At the same time, the Reagan administration had begun to take more seriously the UN peace process and appeared ready to accept a nonaligned government in

Kabul. Discussions between Washington and Moscow, suspended since 1982, resumed in mid-1985. With the Soviets signaling their readiness for a settlement, the hard-line opposition in Washington began to melt. Standing in the way of an accord in Geneva, however, was a lack of agreement on a timetable for the Red Army's withdrawal. Other issues, including verification of the pullout and a political formula for governing the country, also had to be resolved with Pakistan.[16]

Soviet willingness by early 1988 to accept a shorter time frame for withdrawal was not matched by agreements on foreign interference and a political settlement. But the United States, seeing no early possibility for an interim government, was anxious not to pass up the opportunity for a Soviet troop withdrawal. On the issue of intervention, both sides settled, in effect, for symmetry in allowing continued military assistance to their respective clients. However, President Zia wanted to hold out until an agreement was reached on a political arrangement that replaced the ruling Marxist regime. Moscow refused to accede to abandoning Afghanistan's communists by excluding them in a future government. Only the direct personal intervention by President Reagan in a phone call to Zia induced the Pakistani president to sign the April 1988 Geneva accords.

Post-Soviet Withdrawal

It was widely predicted that the Marxist government in Kabul would collapse in a matter of months after the last Soviet troops departed in February 1989. Plans were made in Washington to reopen an embassy in Kabul, and assistance was promised to help with postwar reconstruction. Meanwhile, US policy remained aimed at bringing down the Kabul regime through a military victory and replacing it with the Peshawar-based Afghan Interim Government, a collection of Mujahideen parties. But Kabul's communist regime, well stocked with equipment needed to defend itself and continuing to draw economic support from Moscow, refused to surrender and was able to ward off military defeat for three more years. By 1990, Washington was anxious to halt the ongoing bloodshed and began to entertain the possibility that the Peshawar-based parties might have to accept a political reconciliation that involved a broad coalition, including perhaps communist elements.[17] An alternative strategy that might have tried to construct over several years a new political reality, bypassing both the communist and Mujahideen leaders, found little support in either Washington or Islamabad. For its part, Pakistan, particularly its military establishment, was determined to install a government in Kabul over which it would be assured a strong influence. The Pakistani leaders felt that they could control the *jihad* parties in Kabul much as they had in Peshawar.

Without a Soviet presence in Afghanistan, Washington's military aid to the Mujahideen declined; the authorization for arms in 1990 was cut to $50 million from $300 million the previous year. Moreover, supplies of weapons were more closely linked with proven fighting effectiveness, and deliveries slowed with increased evidence that some resistance groups were hoarding their war supplies. The Bush administration also began to question its continued assistance to strongly doctrinaire

Islamic Mujahideen groups, which now appeared to be obstacles to peace and resembled all too closely emerging radical forces across the Muslim world. Understandably, many in Pakistan viewed the US weakening commitment as premature, taken before Pakistan's interests in the region had been secured. Had the communist regime in Kabul not fallen in April 1992, a full US arms cutoff was probably inevitable.

The demise of the government of President Muhammad Najibullah, in power more than five years, followed closely on the heels of the breakup of the Soviet state. Then, despite a Pakistan-brokered accord among the victorious parties, they fought among themselves in a full-fledged civil war more devastating to Afghanistan's capital than was the previous phase of the conflict. Over most of the country, a warlord system instituted a criminalized economy based increasingly on smuggling, extortion, and increased opportunities for income from opium poppy cultivation. The circumstances also allowed for the continued presence of Islamic radicals from Arab and other Muslim countries receiving training and indoctrination much as they had during the anti-communist *jihad.* Large numbers of those in the camps were Pakistanis, some of whom would fight under the patronage of Pakistan's army in the Kashmir insurgency against Indian security forces.

With power ceded to the Mujahideen parties, economic assistance replaced military aid. International assistance was slated for the resettlement of refugees, and the first steps were to be taken in rebuilding the battered economy. However, very quickly it became apparent that serious programs of rehabilitation and reconstruction would have to wait until some force prevailed militarily and could begin to consolidate its authority over the country. Whatever sense of obligation was felt initially by the United States and others to join in rebuilding the country gradually dissipated. Between 1992 and the following year, US funding for Afghanistan dropped 60 percent, to $20 million.

US detachment carried the most immediate implications for Pakistan. With the Soviets gone from Afghanistan, the basis of a US partnership with Islamabad became outmoded, even dispensable. By 1990, Pakistan's nuclear program—which disqualified it for US assistance—was rediscovered. Presidential waivers that allowed for economic and military aid were no longer forthcoming, thus ending nearly a decade of assistance to Pakistan. As a result, the United States lost much of the leverage it had over Islamabad, including any chance that it could steer Pakistani policy on Afghanistan during the next decade.

The ubiquitous conspiracy theorists in Pakistan saw it differently, claiming that the US disengagement in the region had been cooked up with the Russians. The plot was designed, it was alleged, to deny the Mujahideen the full fruits of a victory that would threaten Moscow's control over its Central Asian republics and US influence in the Middle East. It would also thwart Pakistan's emerging contribution to a more powerful post–cold war Islamic world.[18] The reality was far simpler, however. Washington concluded that it had little to offer in finding a political solution and, unlike Pakistan, not a great deal at stake in which factions eventually ruled Afghanistan. The consequences of what might emerge with a weak, factious state were not fully assessed. Although the rising drug trade from Afghanistan was a matter of concern, there was little sense at the time that the trafficking, going mainly to Europe, could be stopped or that production, even if curtailed, would not shift to neighboring states. The threat posed under a system of warlords giving sanctuary to foreign extremists was not fully appreciated.

The period of Mujahideen civil conflict was a low point for Pakistan. Having failed to install its preferred Mujahideen Afghan leader, Gulbuddin Hekmatyar, in power in Kabul, Islamabad displayed its willingness to back any faction able to consolidate power and to provide a reasonably stable government. Above all, Pakistan sought a regime capable of freeing the roads from banditry and other impediments to opening trade routes with Central Asia. Islamabad not only failed in its effort to find a leader or faction that could deliver but instead concluded that those occupying the formal seats of power in Kabul were moving toward closer ties with New Delhi.

The Taliban Era

The answer to Pakistan's search for surrogates in Afghanistan appeared to lie with the Taliban. Mostly students in Islamic schools, frustrated by the predatory militias controlling Kandahar and connecting roads, Taliban fighters surprisingly easily overcame the local authority and set up a self-defined Islamic rule. Pakistan's Minister of Interior Naserullah Barbar moved quickly to adopt this new force, as did the region's powerful trucking cartels. Above all, the Taliban's popular appeal was based on their ability to inject greater law and order, their seeming incorruptibility, and the hope of many ordinary Afghans that these idealistic young men would finally bring peace to the country. Over subsequent months, the Taliban encountered surprisingly little armed resistance as they carried their cause elsewhere in the country. By August 1995, the movement had routed the defenders of Herat, the largest city in the country's west. Only when, that autumn, the Taliban approached the capital, Kabul, and confronted for the first time a disciplined fighting force under veteran commander Ahmed Shah Massoud did they falter. It was also the first serious face-off for the mostly ethnic Pashtun Taliban against fighters from the second largest ethnic minority, the Tajiks.

Taliban success in taking Kabul the second time around in September 1996 ushered in one of the more interesting interludes in US-Afghan relations. By this time, US interests in the country were beginning to revive. Increasingly, the country had become a source of heroin for the international market. Its chaotic political climate also became a gathering place for the military and ideological training of Islamic terrorists preparing to fan out globally with an antiestablishment Muslim and anti-American agenda. The Taliban offered another attraction. With the Taliban seemingly on the verge of victory across the country, the United States decided to establish contacts with the new regime. Some US officials believed that befriending the movement could provide some early dividends. The Taliban seemed to have no particular political agenda and thus stood in contrast to some Mujahideen parties, notably Hekmatyar's, noted for their open hostility toward the United States. Privately, the movement's leaders assured Washington that terrorism and drugs would have no place in their pious rule. The Taliban promised to end poppy growing and indicated a willingness to close down training camps for militants, expelling resident Arabs. The antipathy in Taliban beliefs for Shi'a Islam also recommended the Taliban for a role in the US hoped-for containment of Iran. By contrast, increasing contacts with Tehran by a Kabul regime headed by President Burhanuddin Rabbani, an ethnic Tajik, had sounded alarm bells in Washington. No doubt a factor in US policy through the mid-1990s were plans by an American-Saudi coalition of Union Oil of California (Unocal) and Delta oil companies to build gas and oil pipelines from Central Asia through Afghanistan to Pakistan and then to other Asian markets. But for these pipelines to be constructed, it was necessary that Afghanistan be largely pacified, and the Taliban emerged as the force most likely to secure the risky but potentially highly lucrative investment. The project appealed to Washington because, if it succeeded, it would cut off investment for an Iranian route, thereby denying the Islamic republic the economic benefits of hosting the pipelines. Unocal expected to be able to do business with the Taliban with its attractive promise of future revenue and jobs in an economic recovery. The company's intense lobbying in Washington succeeded in at least giving the strong impression that the commercial venture carried official US sanction.[19]

Although not yet prepared for formal recognition, Washington took tentative steps toward reestablishing an official American presence in Kabul. A series of trips by US officials in autumn 1994 explored reconstruction assistance as well as refugee repatriation, issues of drug trafficking, and the disposition of radical groups. But progress toward de jure recognition slowed abruptly in the weeks following the Taliban's occupation of Kabul. Evidence that the movement was not, in fact, about to sweep to a total military victory no doubt influenced policy. More important, narrow religious doctrines and repressive social policies that the Taliban had previously brought to bear elsewhere in the country were now applied with little modification to the capital city's more secular urban society. Human rights advocates in the United States, especially feminist groups, condemned the Taliban's governing, most notably their elimination of girls' schools and the near impossibility of women's employment. Banning of television and most forms of entertainment marked the Taliban as narrow-minded zealots. So too did their imposition of harsh punishments for criminal offenses, beginning with the murder and public display of the body of former Afghan president Najibullah upon capturing Kabul.

Public and private criticisms against the Taliban increased during 1997, summed up by Secretary of State Madeleine Albright's description of the Taliban as "despicable" during a November visit to Pakistan. Feelings by American policymakers became embittered when the 1998 bombings of US embassies in East Africa were traced to Afghanistan, most specifically to the Saudi Arabian dissident Osama bin Laden, who had taken refuge in Afghanistan. For harboring the alleged perpetrator of these attacks and hosting training facilities for believed terrorists, the Taliban became the United States' number one culprit and target. This was forcefully demonstrated by the cruise missile strike on these camps in August 1998. In hopes of forcing the Taliban to yield up bin Laden to justice and dismantle his al-Qaʻida organization, the United States imposed sanctions on the Taliban early in 1999. Washington also orchestrated the UN Security Council's approval of further sanctions in November 1999. To these were added still another set of sanctions in January 2001. Several of the bans and boycotts were aimed at making it inconvenient for the Taliban leaders to travel and at cutting off their access to funds. Most effective would have been a halt in arms shipments to the Taliban, but it could not be accomplished without the cooperation of neighboring countries, most of all a reluctant Pakistan. The sanctions brought little change in the Taliban's capacity to fight or to enact their policies.

Consumed with feelings of self-righteousness about Islam, the Taliban saw the international demands as a test of their leadership and faith. Increased isolation brought a strengthening of hard-liners among the Taliban's senior officials. Worsening economic conditions made the leadership more reliant on the fund-raising activities of bin Laden and more amenable to his influence. With almost no contacts beyond his immediate entourage, Mullah Omar Akhund was encouraged in the belief that he had emerged as a transnational Islamic leader. Mullah Omar's March 2001 decision ordering the destruction of all the country's pre-Islamic statues—notably the colossal Bamian Buddhas—defied international opinion and ignored Islamic authorities he deemed less enlightened.

Only slowly did the United States and the international community come to appreciate that the Taliban operated with a different, frequently incomprehensible worldview. Many of the strategies that diplomats would ordinarily have expected to sway the Taliban's behavior had little or no effect. Once having decided that an Islamic dictum applied, the leadership cared little for whether Taliban policies damaged the regime politically and economically. Their unwillingness to relinquish bin Laden, although expressed in terms of principle, also reflected a reluctance to break faith with fighters and financial contributors loyal to the Saudi dissident.

The Taliban represented an essentially transient phenomenon, able to pick up the pieces of a failed Afghan state and society. In the absence of viable alternatives, they could remain in power despite their growing unpopularity. Because the Taliban provided a modicum of law and order, and their adversaries had previously demonstrated an incapacity to govern, the Taliban were able to hold the allegiances of key commanders. Close associates of Mullah Omar never challenged him, despite often sharp differences. Perhaps the greatest fear among Taliban insiders was not their defeat by an Afghan opposition but the concern that in their inability to contribute to the country's rebuilding, they could not withstand a force better equipped to meet the basic needs of the people.

The Taliban might, nonetheless, have remained ascendant for some time. The September 9, 2001, assassination of the Northern Alliance's skilled and charismatic commander Ahmed Shah Massoud left the Taliban well positioned to mount a campaign to wrest the remaining 10 percent of the country into their control. Material assistance given to the opposition by Iran and Russia would probably have been insufficient to stave off a Taliban victory. But the balance of forces changed entirely with the US-led coalition's military attack on the Taliban beginning in October. The country was fated to move into a post-Taliban era where, unless a successor political structure was quickly erected and authority asserted countrywide, the return to a warlord system seemed inevitable. Uncertainty also prevailed over whether the international community would limit its involvement to rooting out supporters of terrorism or commit to bringing broad-based government and programs of rehabilitation and reconstruction.

A Karzai Government

Afghanistan in the wake of the Taliban's departure became the first major application of the then prevailing Bush doctrine, which defined US policy as one that would refrain from nation building. American interests might dictate the projection of military power globally, unilaterally if necessary, but the task of rebuilding states and societies would be avoided, left to a country's own people, assisted by an international community that could include the United States. Consistent with this viewpoint, Washington made only a minimal commitment of ground forces. Planned as just the first step in the broader war against international terrorism, US troops were to be deployed only long enough to hunt down the remnants of al-Qa'ida, especially bin Laden and the Taliban's top leadership. This "light footprint," as it was called, also meant that political authority would be handed off to the Afghans as quickly as possible. Just weeks after the ousting of the Taliban, the UN convened a conference in Bonn, Germany, that brought together leaders of the disparate groups that had opposed the Taliban. Hard negotiations, requiring interventions by the UN's special representative and observers from the United States and other countries, resulted in compromise agreements on a political framework and a timetable for forming representative, democratic government in Afghanistan.

Washington's approach largely profited state building while shortchanging security and development. Its policies called for Afghans to take from the outset formal responsibility for the vital political decisions affecting their future. Although foreigners, especially American and UN advisors, would continue to play active behind-the-scene roles, the Afghans would determine their leaders and write and approve their constitution. Hamid Karzai was the American preference as transitional head of government at Bonn, but his credentials as a Pashtun tribal moderate also made him the most viable choice among Afghans. A *Loya Jirgah* (Great Assembly), a traditional gathering of local and national figures, confirmed Karzai as an interim president in June 2002, and a national election in October 2004 gave him a clear popular mandate. In September 2005, Afghans—with international supervision and financing—were able to freely elect a parliament that largely reflected the country's political and social diversity. The early transfer of power also gave ample room for an Afghan government to conduct an independent foreign policy. Above all, a mostly low profile succeeded in allaying the impression that the outsiders, above all the Americans, were there as occupiers, intending to impose a new order on Afghanistan.

A limited American engagement has also had some less fortunate consequences. In the weeks following the Taliban's defeat, the minimalist policy resulted in too few troops being deployed for effective operations along the border with Pakistan. Contracting out much of the task of closing escape routes to the area's unreliable Pashtun tribal militias may have allowed Osama bin Laden and his associates to flee. Nor was there much attention given to providing security for the rest of the country. A UN-sanctioned 5,000-member multinational force (International Security Assistance Force or ISAF) was at the request of the US military restricted in its peacekeeping activities to the Kabul area, presumably out of concern that American support of their activities might be a distraction from US anti-terrorist operations. The political and security vacuum countrywide was quickly filled by private armies headed by regional and local commanders, many of them returning from exile. Absent a central government with a national writ, they carved out a large measure of local autonomy and, in the guise of defending local populations, proceeded to prey upon them.

A light footprint policy that focused almost entirely on American anti-insurgency objectives had another adverse effect. For the first two years there was little evidence that reconstruction had made an impact on the lives of most Afghans. International pledges of aid for Afghanistan, where the United States was a leading donor, had either gone to humanitarian relief programs or was mostly unspent. Security concerns were usually cited as the reason for holding back on projects that had been expected to begin to rebuild roads and other features of the physical infrastructure and rehabilitate the economy, especially its agricultural sector. Nongovernment groups and international agencies, charged with delivering most of the development assistance, found it unsafe to operate in several areas of the country.

By mid-2003 there were indications of changes in American thinking about recovery efforts and security. The reassessment was driven by a growing insurgency from a revived Taliban and its allies and continuing defiance of the central government by regional warlords. An illicit economy, built mainly around opium poppy cultivation, was rapidly expanding. There was increasing appreciation among officials that security could not be separated from reconstruction and that without progress in one there could be few successes in the other. This called for a rededication to getting projects underway along with new commitments of funds from all the donors. It also entailed a fresh look at ways to employ Afghan resources and gain wider involvement of international forces in security and development strategies. An evolving American policy would also require overcoming problems of bureaucratic coordination and establishing a more consistent set of goals.

Over the first eighteen months there had existed a gap between decisions reached in Washington and an ability and willingness of US officials in Kabul to implement them. Weak coordination among agencies reflected differing institutional perspectives and interests. The contrasting priorities of American civilian officials with those of the US military needed to be better reconciled. To address these problems, responsibilities were centralized in the hands of a new American ambassador, the Afghanistan-born Zalmay Khalilzad. His professional background allowed better communication with the Pentagon and access to the White House. Khalilzad brought more coherence to policies by creating a Kabul-based reconstruction group that reported directly to him, while the Washington-based interagency coordinating group was reorganized. During Khalilzad's two-year tenure, he was often criticized for upstaging the Afghan president. However, their strong personal relationship was one of consultation and not dictation.

Several course corrections occurred, though most of them would take considerable time to implement. From the outset, the Afghan National Army (ANA) and national police had been identified as the cornerstones of a security policy. They were expected to gradually assume responsibility for dealing with the country's rampant criminality and at some future date to take over from foreign forces the job of protecting the regime against its enemies. At Bonn, the major security and reconstruction sectors had been divided among several countries. The United States took charge of rebuilding an army slated to eventually number 70,000 troops. But after nearly two years, army recruitment was lagging, and many had deserted. To improve the security situation, Washington increased funding for both the army and police. A new start was intended to improve and accelerate training, raise the low salaries, and pay the recruits more regularly. In early 2006 there were nearly 30,000 ANA troops, present in most provinces. Internal security is provided by the country's 60,000-member police force. While Germany has focused on senior officers, a partnering United States has picked up the pace of training for the large body of police widely viewed as incompetent and dishonest.

A UN-sponsored program to remove weapons from the larger militias has made some headway, but disarmament and demobilization programs have barely touched the hundreds of smaller illegally armed groups that are active in villages and towns. The Japanese government leads efforts to address this problem and funds the reintegration of militia members into society through alternative employment. This program's success has been limited, however, by the lack of job opportunities. Despite the urgency, little progress has occurred in Italian-led efforts to rebuild and reform the judicial system. The United States has stepped in with assistance aimed at training hundreds of judges, prosecutors, court administrators, and corrections officials.

In the most explicit attempt to marry security with reconstruction, the United States began early in 2003 to experiment with Provincial Reconstruction Teams (PRTs). Groups consisting of between 50 and 100 US troops, civilian personnel with political and development skills drawn from several US departments and agencies, and personnel from the Afghan Ministry of Interior were positioned in provincial capitals. Their presence was designed to improve local security, including support for the work of private voluntary organizations and international agencies, but the PRTs also undertake their own small development projects. Many relief and development workers objected to the PRTs' reconstruction activities, as their objectives and those of the military seemed to overlap. Although PRTs have also been frequently criticized for their failure to integrate their activities with local authorities, their number has steadily expanded. In addition, Washington has sought to correct its earlier error in restricting the scope of ISAF's engagement by encouraging other

ISAF-contributing countries (thirty-six in all) to form their own teams. By mid-2006, non-American teams of various sizes were responsible for more than half of the PRTs, which are located in twenty-five of Afghanistan's thirty-four provinces.

Pursuing both security and reconstruction objectives, Washington funded the poppy eradication program in fiscal year 2004 at $220 million and raised it in 2005 to more than $500 million.[20] Although the British remained the lead nation in this sector, the United States has financed the training of special Afghan anti-narcotics squads and sponsored programs providing alternative crops and livelihoods for farmers. President Karzai is committed to drug eradication but has resisted pressures from Washington for a more aggressive approach. Afghan poppy cultivation con-tributes to at least half of the country's gross domestic product and provides a far better income to around 2 million farmers than they would have growing tradi-tional crops. The Kabul government fears that heavy-handed operations that affect mostly small farmers could prove politically destabilizing. The Taliban and their al-lies, who take a cut from the drug trade, have already been able to capitalize on rural resentments. No enforcement stands much chance unless it is also prepared to target the wider community of interests that profit from the drug trade. In addition to the drug dealers, these include local militias and government officials at every level.

Evolving American policies were also evident in a more determined effort to get delayed projects started. By December 2003, the all-important highway from Kabul to Afghanistan's second largest city, Kandahar, had been repaved, and there was promise of accelerated work on other critical roads, as well as restructured education and health projects. Total appropriated US aid spending, both military and nonmil-itary, increased from $737 million in FY 2003 to $1.7 billion in FY 2004, to nearly $4 billion in FY 2005. At a London conference of donor countries and international agencies in early 2006, Washington confirmed its intention to sustain its support of the development portion of its assistance by pledging $1.1 billion for FY 2007.

Despite the apparent resolve and policy adjustments, reconstruction has not met its targets, and the Afghan government's administrative capacity remains crippled by weak skills and pervasive corruption. The insurgency seems destined to continue for some time. Regrouped Taliban militants are increasingly well organized and equipped. With sanctuaries in Pakistan's tribal areas, they have been able to mount guerrilla-style attacks not unlike those seen during the anti-communist *jihad* of the 1980s. American and Pakistani forces cooperate on both sides of the border, sharing intelligence and raiding suspected Taliban safe areas, but a combination of intimida-tion, sympathy toward the insurgency, and healthy bribes to local leaders has limited their ability to check infiltration or capture militants. American policy tries to bal-ance praise for Pakistan's cooperation against terrorism with pressure for a more vig-orous effort to apprehend militants and rein in supportive *jihad* groups inside Pak-istan. Washington mutes its public criticism, however, for fear of politically undermining Pakistan's President Musharraf.

Two agreements reached by the United States in 2005 could have long-term strategic implications for its relations with Afghanistan. Interestingly, these agree-ments sent contrasting messages about the American long-term commitment to the country. In a radical departure, Washington announced its intention to turn over military operations countrywide to a NATO command during 2006. The new arrangements would allow a reduction of 2,500 of the 18,000 American troops in Afghanistan. Several NATO countries within NATO/ISAF agreed to increase their troop commitments and to assume PRT locations previously held by the Americans in the country's more dangerous south. Although the distinction between anti-insurgency and peacekeeping would effectively end, US forces were slated to retain responsibility for military missions along the eastern border areas with Pakistan. But many Afghans who doubt the staying power of the United States in Afghanistan and the region suspect that Washington is signaling with its troop reductions an early American exit. They are convinced that if the al-Qa'ida leadership is captured, American interest in Afghanistan will rapidly fade.

The second agreement, termed a "strategic partnership" between the United States and Afghanistan, was intended to convey a long-term relationship that provides for cooperation in a wide array of economic and social sectors. But the expectation that the agreement allows the United States permanent military basing in the country has aroused controversy in a nation sensitive to the suggestion of foreign occupation. Now that Afghanistan has an elected parliament, Karzai is no longer free to decree laws and reach international agreements as he chooses. The September 2005 contests resulted in a fractious, undisciplined body prepared to assert its independence of the president in many areas of domestic and foreign policy. The parliament may impose new conditions on the relationship with those foreign forces and organizations on which Afghanistan has been so dependent since 2001.

Afghans continue nevertheless to believe overwhelmingly that international assistance, with the United States in a central role, is indispensable to the country's recovery. For all of their concerns about outside meddling and exploitation, Afghan citizens realize that the country lacks the human and material resources to progress very far by itself. Despite the disappointments during the Karzai era, few Afghans would welcome a return of the Taliban. Its rule demonstrated that it has no agenda for addressing the country's basic needs. The insurgency does not seek an early challenge to the Kabul regime. Its strategy is to create enough disruption and intimidation in the countryside, particularly in the Pashtun south and east, for people to lose faith in the central authority's ability to protect them and improve their lives. The Taliban and their allies also bank on sustaining their pressure long enough for the United States and the international community to eventually tire of Afghanistan.

Conclusion

Afghanistan barely figured on the US foreign policy map until late in 1979. Even the Saur revolution in 1978 bringing Afghan communists to power was tolerable. Washington's policy reflected a willingness to recognize, more or less, the Soviet's greater interest in Afghanistan and the American inability to do much about it. Only when the Soviet Union directly intervened militarily and was perceived to have wider strategic ambitions did that view change. But once the Soviet Union was gone, the United States then quickly turned elsewhere, despite a still unresolved conflict. Taliban rule prompted a refocusing, mainly around the issue of terrorism. But the expectation that the country would again fall off Washington's radar screen once the specific threats emanating from within Afghanistan had receded was dashed with the events of September 2001.

What had been inconstancies in US policies and an inclination to downplay Afghanistan's significance calls for further explanation. A good place to start is the steadfast perception of Afghanistan's remoteness, psychologically as well as geographically. The country's location probably helped to motivate Washington's conclusion during the cold war that, with Afghanistan in the Soviet Union's backyard, the United States could not take responsibility for Afghanistan's security along with that of Pakistan's, and the country's chances of independence were actually best served by a slim US presence. Following the Soviet occupation, the problems likely to beset the Afghan state, however regrettable, initially appeared to be sufficiently parochial and distant enough not to impinge on vital American interests.

This failure to recognize fully the regional and global implications of an Afghan nation left turbulent and unreconstructed comes as a consequence of viewing Afghanistan as essentially unique and exotic. It is a picture that portrays the country as hopelessly primitive, rent by unresolved primordial conflicts. Tribal mores and religious fanaticism are thought to make the country largely ungovernable. The image held is of a country where, aside from delivering humanitarian aid, the normal prescriptions for building a viable modern economy and stable, democratic polity are probably not applicable. No doubt the Taliban's often erratic and unacceptable behavior contributed to this view. Even so, it is unfair to Afghan history and underestimates the potential for development and internal cooperation with the right kind of international assistance. Much of what currently seems congenitally an obstacle to Afghanistan's development economically and politically is in fact the consequence of more than a generation of war.

The United States had over time probably undervalued its capacity to contribute to positive changes in Afghanistan. In spite of Washington's penchant for disengagement, throughout the country's civil war most Afghans continued to look for the United States, above all other countries, to help them secure a political settlement.[21] Even some in the Taliban leadership saw little hope of forging a national recovery without the United States. Afghans have always found it difficult to imagine that, after having been so supportive in the 1980s, American leaders could ignore their needs, especially in light of the Afghan *jihad*'s part in bringing down the Soviet state.

Even before the events of September 11, 2001, US policymakers came to realize the errors of the 1990s. By allowing Afghanistan first to descend into virtual anarchy and then succumb to an erratic, despotic theocracy, Washington had left the country vulnerable to exploitation by transnational extremists dedicated to work against American interests. Efforts to target these elements were fruitless until the United States embarked militarily on regime change. In dislodging the Taliban regime along with al-Qaʿida, Washington found itself, despite its predilections, saddled with responsibilities of helping to rebuild an Afghan state and economy.

A broad, sustained international commitment is also required for Afghanistan to have a promising future. The success in the post-Taliban era in evading a potential humanitarian crisis and in realizing the significant political and constitutional milestones has come only with UN-sanctioned, multinational involvement. The challenges confronting the country are many. Deep social and economic deficits leave Afghanistan among the world's most underdeveloped countries. Fledgling judicial and political institutions struggle to establish legitimacy and effective governance. The central government has yet to bring to heel influential regional power brokers. Banditry and corruption are uncontained, while drug production and trafficking distort the economy. Ethnic-linked contention for positions of power and resources threatens national unity. And still unresolved are constitutional issues that divide progressive reformers and religious conservatives.

The United States and the international community are with their presence essentially purchasing time for Afghanistan. In providing resources and helping the country to fend off its enemies, they offer the Afghan state an opportunity to acquire the capacity to address the basic needs of its citizens and provide them physical security. How and when to transfer to Afghan institutions greater responsibilities for development are critical concerns, and both Afghans and their international benefactors will need to manage their expectations. At no time in the foreseeable future is the country likely to witness strong central authority or shed its heavy reliance on outside benefactors. Nor is it likely to measure up to international legal and ethical standards without a more competent and legitimate legal system. At best, Afghanistan may have to settle for becoming a normal less-developed country, albeit one that is sufficiently stable that it will not again become fertile soil for radical forces intent on mounting a regional or global threat. Instrumental to this outcome is the nonintervention of neighboring states and the confidence among Afghans that the United States and international community will not again desert them.

Notes

1. Richard S. Newell, *The Politics of Afghanistan* (Ithaca: Cornell University Press, 1972), p. 128.

2. Leon B. Poullada and Leila D. Poullada, *The Kingdom of Afghanistan and the United States: 1828–1973* (Lincoln, Neb.: Dageforde, 1995), pp. 178–179.

3. Ibid., p. 183.

4. Thomas T. Hammond, *Red Flag over Afghanistan* (Boulder: Westview, 1984), pp. 26–27.

5. By 1979, the Afghans had received from the Soviet Union $2.5 billion in economic and military aid. Bhabani Sen Gupta, *Afghanistan: Politics, Economics, and Society* (Boulder: Lynne Rienner, 1986), p. 12.

6. Lawrence Ziring, *Iran, Turkey, and Afghanistan: A Political Chronology* (New York: Praeger, 1981), p. 97.

7. Ralph H. Magnus and Eden Naby, *Afghanistan: Mullah, Marx, and Mujahid* (Boulder: Westview, 1998), p. 62.

8. Hammond, *Red Flag over Afghanistan,* p. 38.

9. Ziring, *Iran, Turkey, and Afghanistan,* p. 97.

10. Ibid., p. 106.

11. Hammond, *Red Flag over Afghanistan,* pp. 105–106.

12. See Barnett Rubin, *The Fragmentation of Afghanistan* (New Haven: Yale University Press, 1995), pp. 196–201. The full cost for the United States during the course of the anti-communist *jihad* is elsewhere put at $3.3 billion. Marvin G. Weinbaum, *Pakistan and Afghanistan: Resistance and Reconstruction* (Boulder: Westview, 1994), p. 172.

13. Mohammed Yousef and Mark Atkins, *The Bear Trap: Afghanistan's Untold Story* (London: Leo Cooper, 1992), pp. 93–94, 189–194.

14. Tim Weiner, *Blank Check. The Pentagon's Black Budget* (New York: Warner Books, 1991), p. 150. For a description of the CIA's covert assistance to the Mujahideen during the 1980s, see Larry P. Goodson, *Afghanistan's Endless War* (Seattle: University of Washington Press, 2001), pp. 142–143.

15. See Riaz M. Khan, *Untying the Afghan Knot: Negotiating Soviet Withdrawal* (Durham, N.C.: Duke University Press, 1991), p. 170.

16. Rasul Bakash Rais, *War Without Winners* (Oxford: Oxford University Press, 1994), pp. 123–124.

17. Ibid., p. 135.

18. Weinbaum, *Pakistan and Afghanistan,* pp. 92–93.

19. Ahmed Rashid, in *Taliban: Militant Islam, Oil, and Fundamentalism in Central Asia* (New Haven, Conn.: Yale University Press, 2000), pp. 166–169, is among those who contend that US officials vigorously intervened on behalf of the Unocal bid. For a fuller discussion, also see Richard MacKenzie, "The United States and the Taliban," in *Fundamentalism Reborn? Afghanistan and the Taliban,* ed. William Maley (New York: New York University Press, 1998), pp. 96–100.

20. "Afghanistan: Post-War Governance, Security, and US Policy," Congressional Research Service, Report to Congress, March 17, 2006, pp. 44–45.

21. Goodson, *Afghanistan's Endless War,* p. 181.

25

Is It Time for the United States to Give Up on Arab Liberals?

Jon B. Alterman

In the months and years since September 11, the idea that the United States should be more active in promoting democracy in the Arab world has become common-place. President Bush has spoken at length on the topic more than a dozen times, most explicitly during a November 6, 2003, speech at the National Endowment for Democracy. The president's embrace of the idea followed many months of pro-nouncements by senior US government officials that addressed the need for political change in the Arab world—for American interests as well as those of the people in the region—and the need for the US government to play an active role in promot-ing such change.

Although democratization and reform in the Arab world are undisputably desir-able, the US government is going about it in completely the wrong way. The US strategy, as it has been executed, is based on building out from a core of like-minded liberal reformers in the Arab world. In many ways, it is an obvious way to start. As a group, such reformers are intelligent, congenial, well educated, and flu-ent in English. Americans are comfortable with them, and they are comfortable with Americans.

But if we are honest with ourselves, we need to recognize that, as a group, such liberals are aging, becoming increasingly isolated, and diminishing in number. These liberals are losing a battle for the hearts and minds of their countries, and populations are now driven toward younger and more disaffected personalities.

America's problems do not stop there, however. The United States faces three paradoxes. The first is that liberal reformers in much of the Arab world are already seen as clients of foreign powers and as collaborators in a Western effort to weaken and dominate the Arab world. Focusing attention and resources on these reformers runs the risk of isolating them still further, driving a deeper wedge between them and the societies we (and they) seek to affect. In such an event, US efforts are not only in-effectual; they are counterproductive. The second is that conservatives' intimidation of liberals has led many of them to swing their support to existing authoritarian systems. Third, the most vocal proponents of democracy in the Middle East are now Islamists—precisely the groups that most US policymakers are most interested in isolating.

US efforts to promote political openness and change in the Arab world would be far more effective if they stopped trying to coax the disparate sparks of comfortable liberal thought into a flame that sweeps through political systems. Instead, they should concentrate on affecting two targets: regional governments and mass publics. The United States also needs to be willing to work multilaterally to promote reform in a way it has been unwilling to do up to now. If the stakes were lower, the United States could afford the luxury of taking an easier and less effective approach to political change in the Arab world. In today's environment, it isn't nearly sufficient.

In current talk about efforts to reform political life in the Middle East, the Eastern European example looms large. Not only did Eastern European communism crumble after decades of Western effort, but the end of the Soviet Union spelled the diminution, if not the end, of what had been the primary strategic threat facing the United States for a half century.

At its core, the Eastern European experience is thought of this way: Communist tyranny spread, while Western nations kept alive a flickering hope of freedom through overt radio broadcasting, covert support for oppositionists and "prisoners of conscience," and constant government-to-government pressure on human rights and political freedom. A robust policy of public diplomacy and cultural exchanges revealed the obvious: Communist lies about poverty in the West were just that, and the communist world was falling farther and farther behind a rapidly industrializing West.

On the governmental level, the Soviet quagmire in Afghanistan combined with the Reagan administration's stepped up military spending to provoke an internal crisis. On the public level, a series of initiatives to support civil society groups hastened the collapse of corroded and crumbling governments in country after country.

Veteran "cold warriors" view their victory as the product of determination and vision. Unwilling to accommodate authoritarianism, they insisted on a policy of tireless confrontation with the Soviet Union and its clients. Unwilling to accept the inevitability of autocracy, they imagined a future for Eastern Europe that would be capitalist and free. The names of many of the most dedicated of these warriors are familiar today, and they have been prominent figures in the administration of George W. Bush: Richard Perle, Paul Wolfowitz, and Elliott Abrams.

But what of the Middle East? After September 11, 2001, strategic thinkers proclaimed millennial Islamist terrorism to be the preeminent strategic threat facing the United States. But whereas the cold war represented a confrontation *between* governments, this new battle was one brought on by the *failure of* governments. As President Bush explained in London in November 2003, "In democratic and successful societies, men and women do not swear their allegiance to malcontents and murderers, they turn their hearts and labor to building better lives." He continued, "By advancing freedom in the greater Middle East, we help end a cycle of dictatorship and radicalism that brings millions of people to misery and brings danger to our own people."[1] The tools imagined are much the same as those used in the cold war: pressure on governments and fanning the flames of freedom, liberalism, and democracy throughout the Middle East.

While it is obvious to say that the Middle East is not Eastern Europe, it is unsettling to consider just how different the two environments are and how little these differences are acknowledged.

It is useful to start by thinking about the roles of elites vis-à-vis governments. Elites play many roles, but one of the most important for the purposes of the present discussion is the role of mediation. Elites often serve as a lubricant between foreign and domestic systems, using commonalities in travel, education, and language to bridge national divisions. The period of Western imperialism in the Middle East spanned most of the first half of the twentieth century, and in many countries it followed four centuries of Ottoman imperial rule. Throughout, elites played an important collaborative function. "Collaboration" here is not meant pejoratively, but rather in the way suggested by that great historian of British imperialism, Ronald Robinson, who writes of "two interconnecting sets of linkages . . . one consisting of arrangements between the agents of industrial society and the indigenous elites drawn into cooperation with them; and the other connecting these elites to the rigidities of local interests and institutions."[2]

Early twentieth-century Levantine elites were a worldly bunch, often multilingual and tolerant, if a bit corrupt. Under their guidance, parliaments arose throughout the region, often unifying on the need to end European colonial rule. But as we know, many of the stories of the elites in the Middle East ended badly. Tales of self-indulgence and profligate spending on their part only sharpened dismay at the Arab world's continued subjugation to European powers. Collaboration took on a negative coloration, as the elites were seen as too feckless to win true independence. The sin of the elites, in the eyes of many, was exemplified by the creation of the state of Israel, widely seen to be a solution to a European problem on the back of a weak and divided Arab nation.

When nationalist revolutions swept the Arab world in the 1950s, those revolutions were a repudiation of that weakness. Elites were tossed out as foreign fops, and new indigenous elites—Manfred Halpern's much-vaunted "new middle class"—set about defining a new and "truly authentic" form of Arabism.

In truth, traditional Arab elites have never recovered the high ground. Widely perceived to be agents of foreign interests—however one construes foreign in an Arab context—the old families have clawed their way back to influence but have largely done so on the terms of their tormentors. Liberalism remains suspect, part of a Western plot to weaken and subjugate rather than strengthen and liberate. Elite messengers and their messages remain besmirched.

Compare this to Eastern Europe, where it was the communists' utilitarian socialist universalism that was a foreign import. While one cannot quite point to a golden democratic past in Europe, there was not a sense, as there was in the Arab world, that the patrimony of liberal thinking was weakness and foreign domination—quite the opposite.

In addition, the role that elites play in any society is changing, driven by communications technology and a surge in popular culture. One need not accept the idea of a single global village to appreciate the familiarity—or at least, perceived familiarity—many people feel with societies half a world away. Whereas the old elites transcended the local through their travel and knowledge of foreign languages, newly emergent elites participate in a global, or at least regional, culture that may have little to do with dominant European-derived paradigms. The collaborative role that traditional elites have played is less mysterious, and the interests of foreign powers are more obvious to local audiences.

The rise of an increasingly independent popular culture has an important effect on our discussion. Elites have lost much of the agenda-setting role they had enjoyed in years past. What matters most in attracting an audience now is having a message, not merely having an outlet. Stolid state-run broadcasters have seen their audiences desert them, and they have had to change their message. Audiences now control what they pay attention to, not information bureaucrats. The broadcaster with his finger on the pulse of the public mood, not the one with the ear of the minister of information, plays the primary agenda-setting role in modern Arab societies. Such communication is increasingly unmediated, as television brings arguments and rebuttals straight into the living rooms of its viewers.

In an environment overflowing with clashing ideas that easily cross borders, it has long seemed that much of Arab discourse is centered around an idea of defining what is "authentically Arab." For years, part of such an identity involved support for the Palestinian cause. But in recent years, the explosion of communication from the grass roots has created competing notions of everything from music and style to religious practice, all of which affects people's daily lives. The Arab world is no more likely to arrive at a single conclusion of what it is to be an Arab than Americans are to arrive at a conclusion of what it is to be an American. However, this process is nonetheless defining what is "un-American" and, by extension, what is "un-Arab." Because of the legacy suggested above, old liberal elite views of a just Arab society are falling outside the bounds of Arabs' imagined common future.

Washington has many heirs to the liberal elite tradition in the Arab world. They often fill posts in the World Bank and other international institutions, work for the US government, or labor in academia. They talk of the misdirection of the Arab world and the need for change. We notice their accents when they speak English, and we hail them as authentic voices for change in the Middle East. But what Washington doesn't hear is that many of these people have accents when they speak Arabic as well. Their speech marks them as Arabs who have left, who have fundamentally compromised, or been compromised. One colleague used the evocative phrase "native aliens" to describe them; their most valuable commodity is that they have Western ideas but non-Western passports.[3]

In academic circles in the early 1990s, it was hard not to hear of Nawal al-Saadawi, the prominent Egyptian feminist, novelist, and physician who fled her own country under death threats. But I will never forget the words of one of my Egyptian professors, a prominent female professional in her own right, who practically spit in disgust saying (in Arabic), "She doesn't belong to us, she belongs to you."

In the past several years, the Egyptian government has appeared to be conducting a prosecutorial witch-hunt against Egyptian-American sociologist Saad Eddin Ibrahim. While the government officially accused him of misappropriating money from the European Union, the sponsor had no complaints about the use of funds. It was widely whispered that Ibrahim's misfortune had nothing to do with the funding and everything to do with his flamboyant criticism of so-called Arab republics that had hereditary rule—Syria in practice, and Egypt in theory, if presidential son Gamal Mubarak rose to the presidency. Ibrahim's case aroused little interest in Egypt, and his valedictory lap occurred in the United States rather than there. But when Senator Patrick Leahy speculated about earmarking $2 million for his NGO, the Ibn Khaldun Center, four prominent members of the board resigned in protest. All the while, not a single cent changed hands.

Three additional points are in order. The first is to make clear that all Arab liberals do not come from elite backgrounds. A good number—although probably a minority—come from modest backgrounds. But the fact remains that support for liberal ideals as they are promoted and articulated in the West remains almost entirely an elite province, whether that of those born into an elite rank or those who have come up into such ranks. What we often refer to as "like-minded individuals" form a distinctive group, and a decidedly elitist one.

The second point is that as old elites are pushed aside, new elites are emerging. Such elites come from religious backgrounds, the media, the military, or some combination. What is important to note here is that the new elites tend to come from sectors of their societies that are often illiberal, while old liberal elites are increasingly marginalized.

Conservative groups conduct an active, creative, and impressive array of activities and services that affect people's daily lives: providing care to the sick, food to the hungry, and spouses to the unmarried. They seek leadership positions in professional organizations and civic groups. All too often, Arab liberals' activities end when they deliver copy to their editor.

What is happening in the Arab world today smacks a bit of what the sociologist William Julius Wilson described happening in black neighborhoods in Chicago in the 1960s and 1970s. Whereas segregation had created all-black communities that had both rich and poor, desegregation created black communities that were uniformly poor and had far higher incidents of violence and crime than had obtained during segregation. In the Arab world, liberal elites cluster ever more closely around Western embassies in capital cities and work in international institutions, while the bulk of the Arab world grows more angry, more desperate, and more estranged from those liberal elites with whom Western governments deal most often.

All putative liberals in the Middle East do not fall into this category. In religious and secular circles alike, new thinkers are emerging who seek to create new syntheses of "authentic" Arabness (or Islam) and modernity. As a group, they come to the idea of liberalization through different paths—some through socialism, and others through Islamism—and they have seen the failure of their previous ideologies. But such thinkers often go beyond the bounds of what Americans are comfortable with. Many reject the idea of secular government, and they embrace the idea of armed resistance, be it against Israel or the United States. They are committed to neither women's rights nor laissez faire economics. To some in the West, their ideas seem like watered-down liberalism; to others, their ideas are an example of what Senator Daniel Patrick Moynihan used to refer to as "defining deviancy down." They are deeply wary of the United States government, and the United States government is deeply wary of them.

Instead, the US government has sought to work with traditional partners, seeking to engage them through a program called the Middle East Partnership Initiative (MEPI), established by the Bush administration in 2002. MEPI has identified economic cooperation as an initial step toward respect for rule of law, transparency, and an end to cronyism, but many of the partnership's first efforts consisted of conferences and training. Urgency in getting the partnership up and running has meant grasping for low-hanging fruit, and an overwhelming push for women's empowerment has helped ensure participation is mostly limited to capital city elites. One of the programs is, perhaps, typical. The Business Internship for Young Arab Women seeks forty women between the ages of twenty-two and thirty with high proficiency in English to live in the United States for three to six months. However desirable this may look from a US standpoint, the number of women with such English skills is quite limited, yet not nearly as limited as the number whose families—both mothers and fathers—would consider it appropriate for their daughters to live independently overseas at such a tender point in their lives. While the intent is noble, anyone with even a passing knowledge of the Middle East must recognize what a small segment of Arab society would benefit from such a program. And there is a chilling statistic: Of thirty-four civil society organizations listed as "partners" on the MEPI Web site, there is but a single Arab organization among them.

MEPI is, of course, an overlay on existing aid programs in the Middle East, run either by the US Agency for International Development (USAID), US embassies, or both. In case after case, such programs are directed toward the activities of what can only seem to be a client class of Western-educated elites whose governments permit such activities so long as they remain politically inert. In Jordan, the embassy supports a panoply of semi-royal charities like the Noor Al Hussein Foundation, the Royal Society for the Preservation of Nature, and similar organizations. Indeed, Jordan's so-called nongovernmental organizations are so tightly tied into the government that they gave rise to the acronym "GONGO," meaning "government-organized nongovernmental organization." In the words of one friend in the White House, the typical aid recipient in the Middle East is the son of an ambassador, with a German mother, who happens to run an NGO.

US efforts to promote democracy have also run aground on the hard shoals of reality. Throughout the region, concerted efforts at democratization have yielded results that are mixed at best. For example, many in the Bush administration expected

Iraq to be the jewel of US efforts to promote political change in the Middle East, sweeping aside a brutal socialist dictatorship and installing a democratic, capitalist system that would be an inspiration throughout the Middle East. Hundreds of billions of American dollars later, Iraqi national politics are marked by sectarian strife, political dysfunction, and a growing Islamicization of public life. Ahmed Chalabi, the expatriate darling of many administration figures and the clear leader of the Iraqi opposition in exile before the fall of Saddam, polled only about 30,000 votes nationwide (out of approximately 12 million) in the December 2005 elections. Well-meaning efforts to train would-be Iraqi politicians and jump-start a political process have collapsed under assassinations, intimidation, and infighting. Iraq inspires far more fear than respect in the Middle East and stands as an example to many of how alternatives to an unsatisfactory status quo may be even worse.

The Palestinian Authority seemed poised for progress after the death of Yasser Arafat in November 2004, especially after then Prime Minister Mahmoud Abbas swept a multiparty election with more than 60 percent of the vote three months later. Early optimism gave way to pessimism, however, as Abbas was unable either to assert effective control over his own Fatah Party and the Palestinian Authority or to make diplomatic progress with Israel and the United States. Worsening economic conditions, persistent corruption, and a complete breakdown in party discipline all contributed to Hamas's victory in parliamentary elections in January 2006. Western denunciations of the party and its platform, combined with widespread hopes—even in the Arab world—for its failure, have left many wondering how the US government will square the circle between supporting democratic elections and sanctioning the victors of those elections.

The most interesting example may be Egypt, which for several months was a critical test case of the Bush administration's democratization policy. Egypt is not only a key ally of the United States (on military cooperation, Arab-Israeli peace issues, and counterterrorism) but also a massive aid recipient, receiving more than $2 billion annually in military and financial assistance. President Hosni Mubarak appeared to be among the first Arab leaders to blink in the face of the US democratization strategy, announcing suddenly in February 2005 that he would open the presidential elections in September of that year to multiple candidates, instead of conducting it as a referendum on his presidency as in the past. Some observers saw this as a chink in the armor of authoritarian rule, and anticipation grew for both the presidential elections and the parliamentary elections that followed two months later. In the State Department, and in the White House, attention shifted toward Egypt.

The results were sobering. President Mubarak hardly broke a sweat in his campaign, handily defeating his rivals. The next closest finisher won less than 10 percent of the vote, and most challengers fared significantly worse. Egyptians hardly felt they had a viable choice. When parliamentary elections rolled around two months later, candidates from the Muslim Brotherhood (running as independents) did surprisingly well, and candidates from traditional opposition parties did surprisingly poorly. Egypt had broken up its elections into three rounds to ensure that a judge could monitor each polling station. Brotherhood gains in the relatively open first round were a shock to many in the ruling party; over the next two rounds, reports documented the return of old tactics such as voter intimidation and violence, ferrying government employees to boost votes for the ruling party, and the shutting down of polling stations. When the dust settled, the ruling party had maintained its grip on power, but the Muslim Brotherhood was by far the largest opposition group, winning 88 of the 454 seats. The rest of the opposition parties, including old leftist and socialist parties, won only a dozen seats in all. Perhaps most chillingly, President Mubarak's most prominent challenger, Ayman Nour, lost his seat in the parliament; a month later, the courts convicted him of fraud and sent him to prison, a symbol to many of what happens when one openly challenges the status quo. Nour had met several times with Secretary of State Condoleezza Rice, and as a secular opposition figure with a taste for populism, he was clearly operating in a political space that US government officials wanted to expand. It was also a space that the Egyptian government sought to regulate closely.

The US government should not continue to pursue a policy of democratization that concentrates on support for liberal voices in illiberal societies. Doing so is likely to exacerbate US problems rather than solve them, driving deeper wedges between those with whom the United States seeks to work and those whose attitudes it seeks to influence. Liberal elites are not proving to be successful opinion leaders in their own communities, and closer ties to the West often serve to estrange them from, rather than embed them in, such communities. Think about it as a plant: If all of the sun and all of the nutrients come from one direction, it will not grow tall and strong—it will be weak and bent, and no amount of food or sunlight will make it right as long as it all comes from a single direction.

Greater tolerance, transparency, and openness in the Middle East would indeed serve US interests, and it would serve the interests of the people of the Middle East as well. But to be effective, efforts must be concentrated in three areas. The first is on the government-to-government level. As countless US government officials have recognized, the US government cannot go on doing what it has been doing, relegating these issues to the bottom of a long list of agenda items for bilateral discussions. However, in order to implement such a program effectively, we need to be alert to two dangers. The first is that it will fall into the trap of excusing repression as a necessary part of the war on terrorism. Foreign governments know how vulnerable the United States is on this issue, and they will attempt to use it to excuse a range of abuses. The US government should not take the bait.

The second is that the US government needs to consistently and aggressively push for greater freedom of association in the Middle East, even for those whose views it finds despicable. It is understandable that foreign governments are sensitive about US intervention in their domestic politics, but the veto that some exercise over any nongovernmental group taking money from overseas is unacceptable.

The second area of work is with the broader publics in the Middle East. The US government needs to have far more modest goals with far broader segments of the population in the Arab world. The depth and breadth of animus against the United

States poisons the environment for any values it espouses, and merely neutralizing some of this opposition would represent a significant advance.

In order to pursue such a strategy, the United States would need to work with an array of nontraditional partners. Some may say things the US government doesn't agree with on issues relating to women, Israel, or any of a number of issues. The US government needs to abandon the idea that cooperation with an individual or group means embracing their every belief. It need not and should not. In addition, the United States will have to move away from accounting rules that pose an intimidating, if not impenetrable, barrier to many groups. Fiduciary responsibility is necessary, but it must be a tool to promote accountability rather than a barrier to action.

Another area to think about in this regard is stepping up activities of American organizations that have nothing to do with the US embassy in a particular country. Corporations, foundations, NGOs and a range of other groups could carry out activities successfully without the imprimatur—or encumbrances—of official US government endorsement. The US government should vigorously pursue such strategies on their own merits, as well as get around some of the problems mentioned above.

A third area of activity is greater coordination with other countries and groups of countries, particularly the European Union. Europeans share a quite similar analysis of trends in the Arab world, yet they are far more aware because they see large expatriate populations in their own countries threatening domestic security. Despite the deep commonality of goals between the Middle East Partnership Initiative and the Barcelona Process, neither side understands much about the other. There are at least two advantages to cooperation with the EU. The first is that the EU doesn't carry the stigma in the Middle East that the United States does, making it a less threatening actor on the domestic stages of the region. Equally important, however, coordinated pressure and incentives stand a far better chance of working than competing ones, diminishing the possibility that targeted countries would seek to play the United States against the EU and increasing the likely efficacy of outside efforts.

How should one approach Arab liberals in all of this? None of this is to argue that the US government should abandon them or cast them off. They continue to play valuable roles in our society and in their countries of origin. But Americans need to recognize that such liberals are unlikely to be effective catalysts for the change that all agree is necessary. Stepping up US support for these elites runs the risk of drawing them even further out from the societies we seek to influence, isolating them and pulling their societies even farther away from the direction in which we want them to go.

If the United States is to be successful in these efforts to promote political openness and change, it must keep in mind two things. The first is a healthy understanding of the limits of US abilities. The second is to remember that when others rely on us to create change, it diminishes the likelihood of that change actually occurring by de-legitimizing its authenticity and by breeding complacency or passivity among those whose action is most needed.

There is another challenge facing the United States as well, and that is remembering that what is important is not how things sound and feel in Washington but how they sound and feel in the Middle East. In their classic book *Africa and the Victorians,* Robinson and Gallagher observed, "In the end it was the idea and the analysis of African situations in Whitehall, and not the realities in Africa as such which moved Victorian statesmen to act or not to act."[4] With so much high-level interest in the Middle East, the United States runs the risk of being guided by conventional wisdom rather than true knowledge. In that event, the outcomes would almost certainly be worse than those that many in Washington agree they need to be.

Notes

1. http://www.whitehouse.gov/news/releases/2003/11/20031119–1.html.

2. Ronald Robinson, "Non-European Foundations of European Imperialism," in *Studies in the Theory of Imperialism,* ed. Roger Owen and Bob Sutcliffe (London: Longman, 1972), p. 121.

3. I am grateful to Hakan Yavuz at the University of Utah for this phrase, although I absolve him of any responsibility for the other ideas expressed here.

4. Ronald Robinson, John Gallagher, and Alice Denny, *Africa and the Victorians: The Official Mind of Imperialism,* 2nd ed. (London: Macmillan, 1981), p. 21.

26

New US Policies for a New Middle East?

William B. Quandt

September 11, 2001, is one of those dates that Americans will remember and reflect on for a very long time. Did this unprecedented terrorist attack on the United States show the bankruptcy of years of US involvement in the Middle East? Many Americans seemed puzzled. "Why do they hate us so much?" became a common question. After all, don't we support peace and stability in the Middle East? Don't we promote economic development and democracy?

Paradoxically, the answer to why September 11 happened can be found not just in some of the obvious flaws in US policy in the Middle East—its support for repressive regimes, its failure to resolve the Israeli-Palestinian conflict, its sanctions against Iraq—but also must be understood, in part, as a result of the remarkable success of US policy over the preceding fifty years. Because the United States was the most powerful player in the Middle East, because so many regimes were beholden to it, Washington became the target of the grievances of all those who were unhappy with the existing order in the region. If a Saudi or an Egyptian wanted to overthrow the regimes in Riyadh or Cairo, he might try direct action against those targets. But such efforts have been thwarted quite successfully in recent years, in part because of support given to those regimes by the United States. Ironically, striking at the United States became the least dangerous means, or so it must have seemed to Osama bin Laden and his followers, to bring down the hated regimes that had done so much to weaken and corrupt Islamic political movements in the previous decade. Had all gone as planned, the United States would have reacted harshly and indiscriminately to the September 11 attacks, outraging Arab public opinion, delegitimizing pro-American regimes, and setting the stage for the eventual overthrow of the existing order.

But it seems unlikely to turn out that way. Just as Saddam Hussein in 1990 had calculated that Arab public opinion might shield him from the power of US retaliation, so must have Osama bin Laden counted on widespread support from angry

Muslims throughout the region. And there was a great deal of anti-American sentiment around, both in 1990 and in 2001. But US power was not deterred, nor was it indiscriminate, and a surprisingly large number of Middle Eastern and Central Asian states ended up cooperating in the initial phase of the "war on terror."

President George W. Bush had come to office just nine months before the attacks of September 11, 2001, without a fully developed plan for the Middle East. But he did come to office with a team of policy advisers who had sharply defined views on the region. Some, like Vice President Dick Cheney and Secretary of State Colin Powell, were veterans of the George H. W. Bush administration, while others, like Secretary of Defense Donald Rumsfeld, had served in various capacities with presidents Ford and Reagan. In addition, a flock of so-called neoconservatives occupied secondary positions at the Department of Defense and in the White House. Many of them were identified with views calling for the transformation of the Middle East—overthrowing Saddam Hussein, fully backing Israel, and promoting the spread of democracy.

It took some time after 9/11 for President Bush to embark on an entirely new approach to dealing with the Middle East. His initial inclination seemed to be to strike back at al-Qa'ida and to topple the Taliban regime in Afghanistan where Osama bin Laden had found refuge. That was accomplished fairly quickly and without great loss of life. But some in the Bush administration argued for a more ambitious policy of remaking the Middle East, starting with the removal of Saddam's regime. Sometime during 2002, President Bush made the fateful decision to embark on this strategy, arguing in public that Iraq possessed weapons of mass destruction and had ties to al-Qa'ida. Powell managed to slow down the rush to war, but only for a few months. In March 2003, the US-led invasion of Iraq began, and with it a new era for American policy in the Middle East. To appreciate how great a departure this policy was from traditional approaches, we need to look back a bit, and then to reflect on the likely consequences of this radical approach to remaking the Middle East.

Despite 9/11, one could argue that US policy in the Middle East since World War II had been remarkably successful *in terms of the standard definition of US national interests.* Although this is a contested view, I think it is reasonably accurate within the framework of stated US objectives in the Middle East.

The normal definition of US interests in the Middle East throughout the cold war era had consisted of essentially three points. One was to ensure that the Soviet Union, our global rival and adversary, did not succeed in extending hegemony into the Middle East. Given what we now know, that may never have been a likely prospect, but after World War II, with US-Soviet competition for influence in Iran and Turkey and the establishment of the Kremlin's domination in Eastern Europe, there was a real concern that Soviet power would extend quickly into the Middle East and perhaps be very difficult to contain. For the entire post–World War II period up to 1990, the problem of how to deal with the Soviet Union was number one on the list of Middle East policymakers in Washington.

The second issue was oil. There were times when access to oil was taken for granted, but everyone understood that the Persian Gulf region was the single largest source of oil in the world; indeed it comprises two-thirds of the globe's proven oil reserves. We simply could not ignore the strategic significance of that fact.

Third was the special relationship between the United States and Israel. The relationship has not always been a comfortable one, but every president since Harry S Truman has felt a special commitment to Israel's security and well-being that has not been matched by a comparable commitment to any other single state in the region.

If one takes these three points as the definition of Washington's major interests in the region—containing the Soviet Union, oil, and Israel's security—we can then determine how successful US policy had been up until 9/11. Compared to our policy in Southeast Asia, for example, US policy in the Middle East had been a relative success, certainly in terms of costs, both human and economic. Calculating the human costs to the United States of pursuing our policies, with all the mistakes made over this entire fifty-five-year period, it is estimated that at most some 500 Americans had lost their lives in Middle East–related violence up to 2001 (plus almost 3,000 more in the September 11 attacks). In Southeast Asia, the comparable number exceeded 50,000. This is not meant to minimize the importance of those losses in the Middle East, only to put them in perspective.

In economic terms, the cost of pursuing US policies in the Middle East is not so easy to calculate. For implementing Middle East policy between 1945 and 2000, Congress authorized, just in terms of budget outlays, expenditures of about $200–250 billion (in current dollars), which, of course, seems like a huge amount of money. This works out to somewhat more than $4 billion per year over this entire period. These numbers are inexact at best, but compared to the costs of supporting the North Atlantic Treaty Organization (NATO) or financing the war in Vietnam, the expense for US policy in the Middle East had been quite low until the Bush administration decided to intervene in Iraq.

With respect to the US interest in Middle East oil, it is probably no exaggeration to say that if the United States and its allies had not had access to that resource at low prices in the 1950s and early 1960s, the rebuilding of Europe and Japan along democratic lines as a bulwark against Soviet expansion would have been exponentially more costly. In a way, then, the Middle East did fit into the grand strategy of the United States during this era.

To appreciate how much changed with the invasion of Iraq, consider the costs to America of the first three years of the war, from spring 2003 to spring 2006. In human terms, more than 2,300 Americans were killed and more than 15,000 wounded, many very seriously. The cost of the war was staggering when compared with costs up to that time, probably equaling all the expenditures for Middle East policy in the previous fifty years—well over $300 billion in direct costs. And the price of a barrel of oil, which had been relatively level in the mid-twenty dollar range before the Iraq war, was up to seventy dollars per barrel by mid-2006.

Prior to 9/11 and the Iraq adventure, the United States had relied on a series of policy instruments to pursue its goals in the Middle East: economic and military assistance, arms sales, covert interventions, military presence, diplomacy—particularly in the Arab-Israeli peace process beginning in 1967—but only rarely the direct use of US military forces, as in Lebanon in 1958 and 1982 and the war against Iraq in 1990–1991. During the cold war era, the US public seemed willing to support these policies, by and large. There were occasional debates and protests but never anything like the massive alienation from official policy that occurred as the costs of our involvement in Southeast Asia grew in the 1960s and 1970s. For the most part, Democrats and Republicans, year after year, were prepared to support the main thrust of US policy in pursuit of widely supported American national interests. Both President George W. H. Bush and President George W. Bush, the first in 1990–1991 and the second in 2001–2002, were able to count on extremely high levels of public support for their military responses to what seemed to be direct threats to US interests in the Middle East. It was only as the costs of the Iraq war—both economic and human—continued to grow in 2005 and the perception set in that American objectives could not be easily achieved that public opinion began to turn decisively against the war.

The Gulf crisis and war of 1990–1991 looks very much like the end of one phase in US foreign policy—a kind of watershed between the cold war and the post–cold war eras. It occurred just as the Soviet Union was disintegrating, but when the United States was still fully mobilized following the intense military buildup under the Ronald Reagan administration in the 1980s. Oil was seen to be at risk. Washington's military strategy promised success with relatively few US casualties. The United States had Arab allies on its side to fight against another Arab regime, and it had other countries willing to help foot the bill. That is what made it possible to mobilize the 500,000 US troops to fight the war efficiently and successfully, and to sustain public support. But note, this was not the beginning of a new burst of enthusiasm for redrawing the map of the Middle East. Pax Americana was not on the minds of official Washington after settling accounts with Saddam Hussein in Kuwait. Instead, Saddam Hussein was allowed to remain in power, and the United States relied on sanctions, containment, and deterrence—tried and true policies from the cold war arsenal—to deal with the remaining threat from Iraq.

The apparent inertia in US Middle East policy after the cold war came to an end on September 11, 2001. The initial reaction of striking at al-Qa'ida and the Taliban regime in Afghanistan was a standard "realist" response to a direct attack on the United States. It was only after the fall of the Taliban in late 2001 that the real debate got underway in the Bush administration about whether and how to refashion American policy in the Middle East. As it turned out, this supposedly conservative president opted for a remarkably ambitious policy consisting of several main themes: first, the war on terror would be pursued aggressively; second, the Saddam Hussein regime in Iraq would be overthrown and disarmed; third, pressure would be exerted on Iran and Syria to change their hostile foreign policies; fourth, the Israeli-Palestinian conflict would be placed on the back burner, and Israeli prime minister Ariel Sharon would be supported as he developed his own new approach to dealing with the Palestinians. In all of these initiatives, the United States would act according to its own definition of its interests. If others chose to participate in these initiatives, they would be welcome. But Bush would not waste much time or energy on multilateral diplomacy.

As time went on and the ostensible reason for invading Iraq became questionable—there were no weapons of mass destruction, and ties to al-Qaʻida were flimsy at best—the Bush administration developed a new rationale for its Middle East policy. Arguing that terrorism had its roots in the undemocratic nature of Middle East regimes—an intriguing and controversial proposition—the Bush administration declared that its goal was to fight terror by bringing democracy to the Middle East, starting with Afghanistan and Iraq. No longer would friendly dictators be coddled—or so the rhetoric implied. To say the least, this was a dramatic departure from anything that had come before. Could the United States really deliver on this ambitious new program for the Middle East? Let us look at the issues one by one, though they are all interconnected.

Iraq

When George W. Bush was running for president in 2000, he could not possibly have imagined that Iraq would become the defining issue of his presidency—if he were, indeed, to win. Well, he did win—sort of—and Iraq did become the defining issue, at least in the eyes of most commentators in early 2006. How did this happen?

The decision to invade Iraq stemmed from the reaction to 9/11, the transformational views on the Middle East of the neoconservatives, and Rumsfeld's desire to disprove the Powell Doctrine, which held that the United States should use force only when it had a massive military advantage and a clear exit strategy. The decision to go to war in Iraq in March 2003 with about 150,000 US troops was also anchored in a remarkably optimistic view of what would likely occur. The military correctly understood that Iraq's army would not put up much of a fight, but the planners of the war also had a naïve notion that they would be met by grateful Iraqis who would quickly transition to a pro-American democracy. Within months, in this view, most American troops would be on their way home. All that needed to be done was to remove Saddam and his top henchmen, install a government of pro-US Iraqi exiles (Ahmed Chalabi, Ayad al-Alawi), and Iraq could then rely on its oil wealth to develop its economy and to buttress its democratic leanings.

The war planning was faultless, as far as it went—which was to Baghdad and the fall of the regime. But it made little provision for what would happen after the war, and the political planning was even more incompetent. From the outset of the post-Saddam era, there were too few American troops to guarantee security, a problem compounded by the decision to disband the Iraqi army and to purge the government of most Baʻth party cadres. Instead of a functioning Iraqi state without Saddam, the Americans all of a sudden confronted chaos. Over the ensuing months, as a robust insurgency began to take hold in the Sunni areas of Iraq, Iraqi politics began to polarize along sectarian lines.

By mid-2004, Americans realized that they needed to put more of an Iraqi face on the day-to-day governing of Iraq. A provisional authority was created and elections were called for January 2005. Those elections resulted in large-scale participation on the part of Kurds and Shi'as—the two groups that had suffered most under Saddam—but an almost total boycott by the Sunni Arab minority. The next months were spent fighting the insurgency, including a small but virulent element of foreign fighters aligned with al-Qa'ida who seemed intent on fomenting sectarian violence. In addition, work began on a constitution, which was ratified in the fall of 2005, again with Shi'a and Kurdish support but Sunni opposition (especially to its federal provisions, which could leave the Sunni areas without access to a fair share of central government oil revenues). With considerable effort, Sunnis were persuaded not to boycott the elections held in December 2005, elections that were supposed to set in place the first "permanent" democratic government of the country.

By the time these elections were held, American opinion was turning against the war, and many were losing faith that a US-imposed democracy could be established there. Instead, the new Iraq was beginning to look ungovernable, fragmented, sectarian, not very democratic, filled with religious zealots, and tilting ominously toward Iran. This was not exactly what the Americans had had in mind when they sent troops into battle three years earlier.

Into 2006, it is difficult to see success in Iraq. If, by chance, a loosely federated Iraq, semi-democratic in nature, relatively peaceful, and intent on rebuilding its shattered economy were to emerge in coming years, many Americans might still conclude that the whole costly enterprise was worth the lives and money. A few might still believe in a more robust democratic, pro-American outcome, and if that were to happen it would vindicate the Bush policy. But it seemed just as likely that Iraq would remain a deeply fractured society and troubled polity, riven by sectarian and ethnic disputes, prone to violence, and allying on many regional issues with neighboring Iran. This would be a clear setback for the Bush administration and for US policy in the Middle East.

Regardless of which of these scenarios comes to pass, the Bush team seemed to have concluded as of early 2006 that the time had come to lower expectations, to signal that troops would be withdrawn, and to prepare public opinion for a realistic definition of "victory"—Saddam was gone from power, Iraqis had a chance to create their own state, the prospect that Iraq would build weapons of mass destruction was remote, and the germ of democracy may have been planted in the heart of the Middle East, even if it would take years to come to fruition.

Iran and Syria

Toward the end of the Clinton administration, both Syria and Iran were countries with whom the United States seemed to be trying to improve relations. Syria's legendary leader, Hafiz al-Asad, had died in May 2000, and many expected that his son and heir, Bashar, would prove to be something of a reformer. Iran, which had been at odds with the United States ever since the 1979 revolution, had received a number of signals from the Clinton administration that better relations might soon be a possibility. The fact that the elected president of Iran, Muhammad Khatami, was an outspoken reformer also seemed to indicate that a thaw between Tehran and Washington might be imminent. But in neither case was that to happen.

As early as January 2002, President Bush had gone on record labeling Iran as a charter member of the "axis of evil," along with Iraq and North Korea. The main complaints were that Iran supported terrorism, was hostile to Israel, and was pursuing a nuclear program that might have the potential to produce highly enriched uranium.

Among neoconservatives, there were some who felt that Iran was even more of a threat than Saddam's Iraq. But Bush's decision in early 2003 to invade Iraq put the Iran issue on hold, at least for the time being. No one in Washington wanted to face two simultaneous military confrontations in the Middle East, especially since Iran was a very large country, and there was no obvious *casus belli*.

The irony of the Iraq operation was that it managed to accomplish in a few weeks what Iran had been unable to do in eight years of war—namely, to overthrow Saddam Hussein. In addition, if Iraq was to be a democracy, as the Americans insisted, it seemed likely that the Shi'as would eventually come to power, and Iran had close ties with the two major Iraqi Shi'a groups. From Iran's perspective, the changes in Iraq were a big strategic plus, provided that American troops eventually withdrew.

One lesson from the crisis of 2003 was that the United States was much less likely to challenge militarily a country that had nuclear weapons, such as North Korea, than one that simply had a nuclear research program, like Iraq. Iran seemed to act on this lesson by accelerating its moves in the direction of an actual weapons capability, while constantly denying any such intent.

The American response was harsh, but short of direct threats to use force. Indeed, apart from maintaining unilateral—and not very effective—sanctions on Iran, the United States reluctantly agreed to let a number of European states explore the possibility of working out a compromise with Iran that would allow Tehran to pursue its nuclear research without developing its own ability to enrich uranium. The talks dragged on throughout 2005 and into 2006 without reaching a conclusion. Meanwhile, Iran elected a new hard-line president, Mahmoud Ahmadinejad, making any near-term reconciliation between the United States and Iran quite unlikely.

The one place where there were hints of a change was in Iraq itself. There, the American envoy, Zalmay Khalilzad, was authorized to make contact with Iranian officials to discuss the security situation in Iraq. Those talks began in April 2006, but they were conducted against the backdrop of warnings from conservative circles in Washington that military force might be the only remaining option for dealing with Iran's nuclear program.

Syria was a different matter altogether. The United States had maintained diplomatic relations with Damascus since the 1970s and frequently held high-level talks, primarily about the Arab-Israeli peace process. Clinton had come close to reaching an agreement between Israel and Syria in early 2000. However, in the new atmosphere that prevailed after 9/11, Syria's support for radical Palestinian and Lebanese groups, its alignment with Iran, and its generally thuggish behavior in Lebanon were all problematic for the Bush team. During 2004, in a rare moment of cooperation with France, the United States supported UN Security Council Resolution 1559, which called for Syrian withdrawal from Lebanon and the disarming of the Hizbollah militia, Syria's firmest ally in the country.

In February 2005, an immense bomb blast in Beirut killed former Lebanese Prime Minister Rafiq Hariri, and most observers suspected that Syria was behind this act of terrorism. Pressure mounted on Syria to comply with Resolution 1559, and by summer 2005 Syrian troops did finally withdraw, ending a thirty-year presence in Lebanon. This did little to ease the tensions between Damascus and Washington, however, and by early 2006 there was no sign that US-Syrian relations would improve any time soon. At the same time, with the war in Iraq still demanding a major US military commitment, there was little chance of direct US military action against Syria.

Israel-Palestine

One might have thought that 9/11 would have convinced Americans to make an all-out effort to resolve the Israeli-Palestinian conflict. After all, one of the major sources of anti-Americanism in the region was the ongoing violence in Israel-Palestine and the perception in much of the Arab and Muslim world that the United States was unreservedly supporting Israel. But the Bush team was worried that pressure on Israel would be seen as bending to the demands of terrorists, and this was ruled out from the beginning. In addition, Bush seemed to have a good opinion of Israeli Prime Minister Sharon and a very dim one of PLO leader Yasser Arafat. Thus, in early 2002, when Arafat was believed to have lied to Bush about an apparent arms smuggling operation, Bush essentially ordered that official contact with Arafat be ended. During the summer, the president gave an important speech in which he called for creation of a Palestinian state, existing side by side with Israel, but the call was coupled with a demand that Palestinians carry out far-reaching political reforms. In short, as long as Arafat was in charge, the United States would do little on the peace front.

In response to pressure from British Prime Minister Tony Blair, Bush did agree, shortly after the invasion of Iraq in spring 2003, to put forward a so-called Road Map for Israeli-Palestinian peace negotiations. Part of the goal was to hold out some hope to Arabs that the United States would use its influence to moderate Sharon's harsh policies at a time when Arab opinion was being agitated by the war in Iraq. The Road Map demanded that the Palestinians end their use of violence against Israel, called on Israel to stop building settlements, and laid out a series of steps that might result in a Palestinian state with provisional borders within a matter of years. Since there was no agreed mechanism for making any of the provisions of the Road Map actually occur, it quickly bogged down, with Palestinians saying they could not improve the security situation until Israel stopped erecting settlements and pulled back troops, and Israelis arguing that they would do no such thing until the attacks ceased.

Meanwhile, Arafat was becoming increasingly isolated—physically and politically. Sharon would have no dealings with him, and soon the Americans joined in shunning him. In fall 2004, Arafat's health took a sudden turn for the worse, and on November 11 he died in a Paris hospital. His successor, much to the satisfaction of American officials, was the relatively moderate Mahmoud Abbas (Abu Mazen), who was elected president in a relatively free election in January 2005.

Meanwhile, Sharon had begun to develop a strategy that would effectively bypass the Road Map. He proposed not negotiations but unilateral Israeli steps that would change realities on the ground. One part of the plan was the construction of a barrier/wall between Israelis and Palestinians. The barrier would follow the 1967 lines in some areas, while in others it would intrude into the West Bank in very disruptive ways for Palestinians. Many thought they could see the outline of Israel's de facto future borders in the route of the barrier/wall. The second part of the strategy was to evacuate Israeli settlers—about 8,000 of them—from Gaza, leaving this area entirely in Palestinian hands but tightly surrounded by Israel. Optimists thought that Sharon's initiative, carried out successfully in mid-2005, might be followed by further unilateral moves that would bring about a reduction in the violence and a period of de facto peaceful coexistence between Israelis and Palestinians. Pessimists were more inclined to see the Gaza disengagement as a way of gaining time for consolidating Israel's position in crucial parts of the West Bank, while completing the construction of the barrier.

Bush's attitude toward all of this was a typical mixture of disengagement, support for Sharon, and occasional pronouncements about what the future shape of a peace agreement would look like. At his most expansive, Bush put forward a view that called for two states, Israel and Palestine, living side by side. Israel would not be expected to withdraw all the way to the 1967 lines, but those lines should serve as the main point of reference when final borders would be drawn up. In addition, Bush said explicitly that a Palestinian state should be democratic, contiguous, and economically viable. In a nod to Israeli sensitivities, he said that Palestinian refuges could not expect to return to homes in Israel proper. For some reason, he did not go on to say that they should receive generous compensation for their losses, although that would certainly be part of any full statement of the American position. Only on Jerusalem and its future was Bush notably silent. But even more important, beyond his words he seemed to have no strategy to make any of this happen. Indeed, up until the moment in early 2006 when Ariel Sharon suffered a massive stroke, Bush seemed to believe that the best stance for the United States was to hold back and let the parties work their way through their respective elections, scheduled for early in 2006, and then assess the new political realities that would face him. Such a restrained approach was called into question with the departure of Sharon from the political stage and the subsequent victory by Hamas in Palestinian parliamentary elections in late January 2006. In short, Bush began 2006 without a credible strategy for Israeli-Palestinian peace, just as events on the ground were casting a dark cloud over the future.

Israeli elections were held in March 2006. The party formed by Sharon before his stroke, Kadima, won, but with only 29 of the 120 seats in the Knesset. The new prime minister, Ehud Olmert, would preside over a multiparty coalition of the center. In theory, this gave him room to engage in negotiations, but the harsh reality was that the Hamas victory and dominance of the Palestinian side made such negotiations unlikely. Instead, Olmert spoke of unilateral steps that would set Israel's border over the next four years. While this was unlikely to bring peace, it might be the best that could be hoped for, given the president's other preoccupations in the region and his flagging support on the home front.

Democracy

The last of the major themes of the Bush administration's Middle East policy was democratization. The policy has not been fully elaborated by any means, but the main idea is that the time has come for the United States to place more emphasis on political and economic reform in the region. There is an audience for such views. Middle Easterners do want to see economic change, they do want to see more responsible and accountable governments, and they are fed up with the corruption of their own leaders. But there is always the dilemma for the United States of trying to impose its own views, which may ultimately produce a negative nationalistic backlash. The issue of how best to support reformist regimes may not be so easy to avoid in the future.

Many of the leaders with whom the United States has had cordial relations—the Saudi royal family, Egypt's Hosni Mubarak—are getting on in years, and succession will soon take place to a new generation of leaders, as it has already in Jordan, Syria, Morocco, and several of the small Gulf states. This will be the moment when we will see if the United States is inclined to go beyond rhetoric and provide actual support and encouragement for democratization. It is simply not a viable stance to argue that the Middle East is an exception to the trend toward democracy because of some alleged incompatibility of Islam and democracy, and the Bush administration has now stated that forcefully. Indonesia, the largest Muslim state, has shown that opposition to a dictator who had clung to power too long can take the form of demands for more democracy. The same may be expected in many parts of the Middle East in the years ahead. In Indonesia, the United States finally encouraged Suharto to step down. Similar moments will doubtless confront future American presidents in the Middle East. Clinging to the old order while professing a belief in democracy will not serve American interests.

At the same time, if democracy is simplistically equated to the holding of elections, and if those elections are held in conditions of turmoil, occupation, or economic distress, then the results may be quite unfortunate for those who hope for liberal, tolerant, pluralistic outcomes from elections. Indeed, elections in 2005–2006 in Egypt, Iraq, and Palestine showed the strength of Islamic parties in mobilizing voters against incumbents. Even in Iran, hardly a showcase for democracy, contested presidential elections in 2005 brought a hard-line figure to the fore to replace the relatively moderate Khatami. In short, the results of recent elections may temper the enthusiasm of some in the Bush administration for rapid democratization as the panacea for the region's ills. Other goals, such as creating conditions of security, spurring economic growth, ending foreign occupations, establishing competent political institutions, fostering a free press, and bolstering civil society may all be recognized as essential components in a serious strategy for encouraging democracy.

Conclusion

Although the United States has protected its basic interests during the past fifty-plus years, it has often done so by dealing with illegitimate regimes, a situation that still exists today and that is increasingly worrisome. As of 2006, the United States actually has quite good relations with many governments in the region, with the exception of Iran, Syria, and Sudan. But at the more popular level—among both Islamists and nationalists—there is a deep antipathy for US policies. In the future, threats to US influence will be difficult to deal with because they will be less clear-cut, as the al-Qa'ida phenomenon demonstrates. The fragility of the regimes in the region is a reality over which the United States has very little influence. It is tremendously difficult to resuscitate a regime that has lost its fundamental legitimacy. The United States, for example, probably could not have done a great deal to prevent the Iranian revolution by the time it reached a critical mass.

In the future, the United States, despite the perception that it is the only remaining global power, cannot hope to impose a design of its own on the Middle East. There is a certain inevitability that Middle Easterners will view the United States with suspicion simply because it is the most powerful country in the world—quite apart from its policies. No country that feels weak and vulnerable will feel comfortable dealing with a much more powerful country, so there is now built into the structure of diplomacy one strike against the United States. On the one hand, everyone is awed by US power, but on the other, they distrust it. This suggests that the Middle East will remain a troubled area and that the United States will face many obstacles in its efforts to pursue its multiple goals in the region and to combat terrorism, challenges made more serious by the erosion of serious interest in foreign policy in many circles in the United States.

27

Islamist Perceptions of
US Policy in the Middle East

Yvonne Yazbeck Haddad

For more than five decades, the umbrella ideology of Islamism has cast an increasingly large shadow as Islamist groups strive to create a unified ethos in order to enhance their own sense of empowerment in facing repressive regimes and what they view as Western and Zionist hegemonic policies in the Muslim world. Designed as an alternative to liberal humanism and socialism, as well as to fundamentalist secularism and Marxism, Islamism has left itself vulnerable to attacks from various quarters, including the regimes of some Arab countries, secularists, Zionists, humanists, socialists, feminists,[1] and most recently the government of the United States that has since 9/11 dubbed Islamists as evil. During the past twenty years, the US press and some people in the US academy and government have created a consummate stereotype, commonly identified as "Islamic fundamentalism" or "Islamic extremism."[2] In October 2006, President Bush identified the enemy but distinguished it from the religion of Islam: "Some call this evil Islamic radicalism, others militant jihadism, still others Islamo-fascism. Whatever it is called, this ideology is very different from Islam."[3] Individuals and groups who fall into this category tend more and more to be demonized by those who oppose or fear them, rendering them unworthy of being taken seriously in their criticism of US policies.[4] Thus, Islamism as an "-ism" increasingly provides a handy means of objectification for those who seek to undermine its legitimacy.

Currently, a profound sense of victimization on the part of Islamists has led to the development of a parallel stereotype: the alliance between Israel and the United States, which is generally depicted as "the crusader-Zionist conspiracy," the Western demon bent on the eradication of Islam.[5] This perception has its roots in the worldview of the Muslim Brotherhood, "the mother of all Islamist movements" in Egypt. Hasan al-Banna, who founded the Muslim Brotherhood in 1928, identified a comprehensive venue of operations for his organization in order to realize his futuristic vision of a vibrant Muslim nation (the *'umma*). The focus was to be on the development of a new Muslim human being brought about through moral and spiritual rearmament, a new society actualized through economic development and social justice, and a new vibrant nation free of foreign domination. He perceived the Muslim nation to be in mortal danger as a consequence of the abolition of the office of the caliphate (the generally acknowledged leader of the Islamist community dating to the initial successor of the Prophet Muhammad) in 1924 by Mustafa Kemal Ataturk in Turkey. The caliph had provided a sense of Islamic unity maintained by commitment to Islamic values in societies governed by Islamic law. From his vantage point, foreign interests, at the time mainly British, appeared to work diligently to divide the Muslim world into nation-states to facilitate their subjugation and to insist on implementing the Balfour Declaration of 1917, which had promised a national homeland for European Jews in Palestine. For al-Banna, the Balfour Declaration was not only a means of maintaining colonial interests in the area but was a continuation of European crusader designs on the holy lands.

Many different views and perspectives are represented under the rubric of Islamism. It is currently popular in Western scholarship to distinguish between the mainline Muslim Brotherhood on one side and al-Jama'at al-Islamiyya, Islamic groups such as al-Takfir wa al-Hijra, al-Jihad, and al-Qutbiyyun in Egypt, Hamas of Palestine, and Hizbollah of Lebanon on the other. The Islamic groups are generally referred to as militants, extremists, or terrorists, whereas the Muslim Brotherhood and its affiliates in other Arab countries, such as the Islamic Action Front of Jordan and Jam'iyyat al-Islah of Kuwait, are perceived as more moderate and willing to participate in the democratic process.

Ahmad Kamal Abu al-Magd, a former cabinet member in the regime of Anwar Sadat in Egypt, distinguishes between five groups seeking Islamization. The first call themselves the *Salafiyyun* and are noted for their inflexible adherence to the classical teachings of Islam, leaving little room for modern reinterpretation.[6] The second group is the Sufis, who emphasize the spiritual dimension of Islam and focus their efforts exclusively on seeking a spiritual revival. The third group carries the banner of Islam but is in total rebellion against the prevailing Muslim condition. Attempting to move beyond Islam, they are nonetheless eager to hang on to Islamic slogans. The fourth group consists of several movements adamant in their demand for the reinstitution of Islamic law *(shari'a)* as the constitution of the state. For them, the control of political power is the most effective way to work for Islam. The fifth group that al-Magd identifies is composed of the moderate majority who believe in the use of reason in applying the teachings of Islam as a guide for life.[7]

Although all Islamists appear to agree on an agenda of bringing about the kinds of changes that provide empowerment and well-being for Muslim society, they differ on the means of actualizing change and on issues of political and religious pluralism in an Islamic state. Meanwhile, there is general agreement among Islamists and secularists that US foreign policy in the Middle East has been skewed in favor of Israel since the 1967 Arab-Israeli war (also known as the Six Day War, or June War). This perception has left an indelible mark on Islamist identity and its worldview. This chapter analyzes these perceptions and the Islamist response. It is based on

Islamist literature, which is polemical on the Palestinian self-rule question and generally hostile toward Israel and US foreign policy. Illustrations used in this chapter are taken mainly from Islamist journals, newspapers, and other publications and are supplemented with interviews I conducted with Islamists in Jordan, Egypt, Kuwait, Tunisia, and the United States.

Islamism: A Reaction to Disempowerment

Islamism is not a reactionary movement; it does not want to replicate the Islamic community of the Prophet Muhammad in the seventh century. Rather, it seeks control of the present and future of Muslim destiny.[8] From its inception it has been reactive, responding to direct and imagined challenges posed by internal conditions as well as its violent encounter, during the past two centuries, with a dominant West, which has insisted that the only universal values worth adhering to are those developed in the West during the Renaissance and the scientific revolution and embodied in rational, liberal, or Marxist thought. Its ideologues operate with a heightened awareness of the importance of monitoring events in the world, particularly those that affect their lives, and responding to them. They see themselves as manning a defensive operation, the responsibility of which is to safeguard society from total disintegration.[9]

Islamism was initially a reaction to the internal sense of decay in Muslim society. A central theme in most Islamist literature is a response to the deep awareness of the backwardness of Muslims, a critical assessment of what went wrong historically, and an effort to rectify the situation in order to bring about a vibrant future. Revival is seen by its advocates as a crucial means of infusing life into a community that is bogged down in centuries-old ideas and traditions that have led to the ossification of Islamic society, restricting its ability to adapt to the fast-changing reality of the modern world. The revivalists produced a literature that portrayed Islam as a forward-looking, creative, and open ideology receptive to movement and change. They sought to remove the shackles of Islamic society, freeing it from the constraints of the values and interpretations of the past. Their goal was to initiate involvement in the unfolding history of the world, taking control of the lives of their constituency and participating in shaping the future. Unity of the community was seen as an essential component of this venture.

The challenge of modernity to the prevailing Islamic system arrived already formulated and fully developed, in an alien environment where a different set of issues was being addressed. Westernizers, both indigenous and foreign, perceived European models as prefabricated systems that were transferable and ready for borrowing and implementation because they had worked in the West; hence they advocated liberalism, secularism, and socialism. Since the 1967 Arab-Israeli war there has been a growing perception that imported, Western, ready-made models of development and modernization, touted as instant solutions for domestic and foreign problems, have failed to bring about the results hoped for by advocates. More important, they are perceived to have failed even in the West itself.

Islamism is a reaction to the denial of the right of self-determination. The lack of democratic institutions and the absence of governments that operate under the law and for the well-being of the people in the region are increasingly identified as major causes of backwardness. Islamist leader Tawfiq Muhammad al-Shawi of Egypt, for example, identifies such specifics as the following: the lack of freedom of determination (the right to choose the ruler) on the part of the polity and the lack of accountability on the part of the ruler; the fact that the *shari'a* has been replaced in most countries by laws legislated by governments; the separation of the law from government, that is, the replacing of an independent jurisprudence by a European model in which "law is the will of the state"; and the loss of a comprehensive unity, a by-product of Western efforts to divide and conquer.[10]

Islamism is a reaction against disempowerment and what is seen as the irrelevance of the nation-states created in the region as a result of the Sykes-Picot Agreement constructed during World War I, through which the British and the French artificially divided much of the Middle East into spheres of influence that were later sanctioned through postwar agreements into the mandate system consisting of state units that had hitherto not existed. There is general consensus in Islamist literature that the dominant world order that has prevailed since the nation-states in the area were carved out has not allowed for the inclusion of Arabs as full citizens of the world. Arab nations and peoples have continued to be subservient to foreign domination, which Islamists describe as a continuing predatory relationship.[11] Their diagnosis is based on the belief that the core problem is the failure of these nation-states to adhere to the sources of strength in Islam itself that brought about the great and powerful Islamic civilization of the medieval world. In many cases, the analysis goes on to show that the ideology that is supposed to bring about the revival of Muslim society and its potency in the world, although cast in Islamic idiom, continues to rely on Western standards and values as necessary for that revival.

Islamism is also a reaction to a profound feeling on the part of Muslims that they have been victimized over the centuries at the hands of Western Christians. The litany of perceived outrages includes European treatment of Muslims during the crusades. They cite the fact that Eastern Christians, Jews, and Muslims in Jerusalem were massacred by the Western invaders during the First Crusade whereas Salah al-Din (Saladin) treated the crusaders magnanimously by giving them assurance of safe passage after he led the Muslim recapture of the city eighty-eight years later in 1187. It includes the *reconquista* in Spain during which a ruthless de-Islamization policy gave Muslims the options of conversion, expulsion, or execution. It includes the colonialist movements of the nineteenth and twentieth centuries, along with the activities of Christian missionaries. It also includes the reality that in the Soviet Union, Muslims living under Communist hegemony were not allowed to practice their faith or study the tenets of their religion. And it includes the perception that for a century, Zionism has been one more element of the long and continuous effort supported by Christians to eradicate Islam and Muslims from the holy places. Bosnia and Kosovo are seen as further manifestations of European efforts to eradicate the indigenous European Muslim population.[12]

Along these lines, Islamists perceive Christian missionary activity as having been designed to separate Muslims from Islam. These efforts are believed to have been inspired by the long history of Christian fanaticism against Islam, culminating in the commissioning of missionaries to march under the banner of Christ into Muslim countries in order to convert them. The legacy of missionary sermons and speeches (now translated into Arabic) provides a rich illustration of the accuracy of this perception. For example, it has been noted that although there had been concern over the Jewish danger, the Bolshevik menace, and the yellow peril, Islam posed the greater danger since it alone is capable of expanding and forming a wall against imperialist interests.[13]

Islamism is a reaction to the demonization of Islam. Muslims are offended and angered at the way in which Islam has been defamed in inflammatory political statements, such as former US Vice President Dan Quayle's comparison of Islamic fundamentalism to Nazism and communism,[14] and statements supporting Zionist interests in popular novels, such as Leon Uris's *The Hajj*.[15] Islamists are very aware that since the late 1970s there has been a dramatic increase in the number of articles in the US press dedicated to Muslim-bashing. These tend to depict Muslims as irrational and vengeful and motivated by religious zeal and fanaticism that arise out of an innate hatred of the West, its Judeo-Christian heritage, and its secularist values. For Muslims, among the most infuriating statements was the 1990 Jefferson Lecture on "Islamic fundamentalism" by prominent Arab historian Bernard Lewis,[16] which generated a heated response from many sources. Islamists observe that Lewis identified historical and cultural differences as the causes of Muslim anger, completely ignoring the specific policies and actions of Western nations that foster the perception among Muslims that, as long as the lives of Westerners are not at stake, fairness does not matter. One Muslim author wrote: "His twenty-six-page address was remarkable for the absence of the word 'Israel.' Nor was any mention made of the United States support of the Zionist state, which inflames Muslim passions worldwide. Any US diplomat who has served in a Muslim country or taken even a cursory glance at Muslim media can verify this feeling."[17] Since 9/11, American officials as well as evangelical Christian leaders have felt free to demonize Islam. Lt. Gen. William G Boyken, Deputy Undersecretary of Defense for Intelligence and War Fighting recalled his service in Somalia and boasted: "I knew that my God was bigger than his. I knew that my God was a real God, and his was an idol." Former Attorney General John Ashcroft stated, "Islam is a religion in which God requires you to send your son to die for him . . . while Christianity is a faith in which God sent his Son to die for you." Televangelist Benny Hinn preached: "This is not a war between Arabs and Jews. It is a war between God and the devil." Franklin Graham, in an interview on Belief.net said: "I believe the Qur'an teaches violence. It does not teach peace, it teaches violence." Other religious leaders focused their diatribe on the Prophet Muhammad, inflaming Muslim sentiments worldwide. Rev. Jerry Vines, former president of the Southern Baptist Convention said, "Muhammad was a demon-possessed pedophile." Pat Robertson on the CNBC program, *Hannity & Colmes,* in September 2002 commented: "This man Muhammad was an absolute wild-eyed fanatic. He was a robber and brigand." Jerry Falwell, on *60 Minutes* on October 6, 2002, stated, "I think Muhammad was a terrorist."

Such distorted presentations of Islam are seen by Muslims as conscious efforts at revisionist history, inspired by contempt for Islam or motivated by political considerations in an attempt to maintain unwavering US support for the state of Israel. They tend to validate for Islamists their perceptions that the West has a double standard by which it measures events in the area.

Islamism is increasingly a reaction to what is perceived as Western and Zionist fears of Islam. Although the theme of the "threat of Islam" may have been manufactured for Western political reasons,[18] it provides a useful tool in recruiting young Muslims into the fold. The "mighty" West and Israel, which have humiliated and subjugated Muslim nations, claim that they fear nothing but Islam. If the oppressors know what is the source of strength, they ask, when will the Muslims awake?[19]

Islamism is a reaction to Zionism. Israel's 1967 preemptive strike, which resulted in a devastating defeat of Jordan, Egypt, and Syria, is generally referred to as *'udwan*, or aggression. Its policies are perceived as Judaizing and aimed at disempowering, dispossessing, and displacing the Palestinians in an effort to destroy their identity. What is perceived as its persistent rejection of United Nations (UN) resolutions and violation of the Geneva Convention have fostered, nursed, and inflamed the Islamic response. It is enhanced by what is seen to be US intervention at the United Nations in support of these policies, which has made the international community ineffective in implementing resolutions that would uphold justice.[20] Israeli justifications for the confiscation of property as its divine right and Western silence regarding these activities elicited a response from Abdullah Kannun, a noted North African author and a member of the Higher Council of Islamic Research of al-Azhar, that is typical among Islamists. Advocating the Islamization of the conflict, he affirmed that although the Arabs are the protectors of Palestine, the land belongs to all Muslims. Muslims must therefore be aware of the connection between Zionism and the kind of Christian religious zealotry that was experienced earlier by the Muslims during the crusades: "The Palestinian issue is an Islamic, not only an Arab issue. Zionism is the stepdaughter of imperialism *(rabibat al-isti'mar)*. Imperialism is the hidden image of the Crusades undertaken by Western Christians against the Muslims of the East."[21]

On another level Islamism can be said to be a kind of mirror image of Zionism. It may be seen as an attempt to emulate what is perceived as a winning Israeli formula in which religious zeal, divine justification, scriptural proof-texting, and victimization are employed to mobilize Jewish as well as Euro-American Christian support for the state. For some Muslim observers, the essence of the issue is that the state of Israel is a Jewish state. "Zionism is therefore the means of the Jewish religion to realize itself, a means of the Jewish people to create their unity in confrontation with all others in the region," says Kamil al-Baqir, a leading Islamist.[22] The question thus remains: Why is it acceptable for Jews to have a Jewish state and not for Muslims to form an Islamic state? Islamist leader Abdullah Kannun notes that the "educated civilized West is not ashamed to boast of its Christianity, to explain Zionism

in its religious context, and to support it by quotations from the Bible, but the ignorant, underdeveloped East is ashamed to call for an Islamic revenge."[23]

Islamism and the "Double Standard"

Islamism is a reaction to what is perceived as the double standard *(al-izdiwajiyya)*
that is used by the West in its foreign policy in the Middle East. For example, in de-
monizing the Islamists, Westerners claim that there is no room for religion in the
modern nation-state.[24] Islamists consider this not only to be hypocritical in light of
Western support for Israel and enduring and prominent symbols of religiosity in the
West but, in a very profound way, to be the proof of the double standard. Hence
they believe that the West is not against religion per se but against Islam. "Pakistan
and Israel," says one writer, "are two countries created solely on the basis of religion
and faith. But you may read in the Western press that Pakistan is backward and reactionary because it has emerged in the name of religion. Nothing whatsoever of
this nature is said about Israel."[25]

There is a growing perception among Islamists that Jews and Christians, driven
by religious fanaticism, triumphalism, and imperialism, have been engaged in a
"thousand-year war" with Muslims, which the latter are losing because they are not
driven "by a parallel religious sentiment in order to repel this fanatic aggression."[26]
Major events in the area have contributed to this perception, such as the civil war in
Lebanon, which has cast an aura of suspicion on the allegiance of Arab Christians
and the efficacy of Arab nationalism, the success of the Iranian revolution, which
validated for the faithful the Qur'anic teaching that God will give victory to those
who believe, and Operations Desert Shield and Desert Storm, which were widely
perceived as a vindication of the projected Islamist worldview that blamed "the
problem of Israel" on Western bigotry and religious fanaticism and were seen as a
continuation of the crusader-Zionist efforts to destroy Islam.[27]

Muslims have been intrigued by the fact that Israel and its supporters boast that
it is the only democracy in the area. They note that it functions as a democracy "for
Jews" while denying religious minorities—both Christian and Muslim—equal access to resources such as water,[28] housing,[29] health, education,[30] jobs, and the ability
to purchase land. Some go so far as to argue that Israel's actions have been devoid of
any compassion or human values.[31] The former executive secretary of Islamic Jihad
in Palestine, Dr. Fathi Shikaki, said in an interview, "I would ask them how they
could talk about justice, democracy, and human rights while a methodical process of
genocide has been taking place for decades against the Palestinian people."[32]

Muslims are very aware of the double standard that comes into play when the US
press, members of the academy, and some government officials label Muslims as extremists. They see that the charge of extremism is arbitrary depending on the interest of the accuser. According to Islamist leader 'Abd al-Baqi Khalifa, for example:

> Extremism is ascribed to violent events according to the interests of those who are
> making the judgement. For example, the war in Afghanistan prior to the Mujahideen

was presented by the Soviet media as a war of evil people against the Russians who had come to Afghanistan to develop it and restore security to the area and prevent American domination over it. In the American and Western media it was depicted as a war of liberation undertaken by the Afghan people against an invading army.[33]

Khalifa further notes that the international press is under the influence of the decisionmakers and acts as their mouthpiece providing epithets for those they seek to criticize. Thus, "the warriors of Abkhazia are separatists, the southerners in Sudan are [liberationists], the demonstrators in Moscow are criminals and in Peking are freedom lovers, the Kurds in Iraq are victims, in Turkey, they are professional criminals. These are the contradictory depictions that have made the word 'extremist' predominantly a kind of political curse word rather than a name for anyone in particular."[34]

Islamists perceive that there is a pronounced discrepancy between professed US values and US actions; that justice, self-determination, and human rights appear to be victims of national interest; that in the last analysis "might makes right"; and that Muslims are rendered weak *(mustadh'afun)* by the empowerment of Israel. Aware of the enormity of the Holocaust and of European-Christian guilt for the sins of Nazism and anti-Semitism, they still question why Western society found a way to expiate those sins at the cost of Palestinian-Christian and Muslim lives. They note that the Ecumenical Council convened by the pope asked Christians to stop cursing Jews in the Catholic Church and that the World Council of Churches absolved the Jews from the historical events that led to the crucifixion of Jesus Christ. Yet, they ask, why is this the fault of the Muslims? Why, they ask, should the Arabs of Palestine pay the price for this error by the church with their homeland, their dignity, their present, and their future?[35] "When various churches compete to please Israel and flatter the Jews, does this point to anything but that the religious leaders have sold their conscience to Satan . . . ? The Arabs [of Palestine] are threatened by general extinction, their homes are blown up, their villages eradicated from existence, and still [their efforts at] self defense are considered a crime and an insurrection. . . . This dreadful tribulation is bound to awaken sleeping Islam."[36]

Islamists and the Gulf War

To Islamists, Western hypocrisy and duplicity were manifest in the Gulf war. The real motive was never to defend international law, enforcement of which varies from case to case and depends on whether the aggressor is a Western country or a Third World country. The objective of that campaign was to "control the oil resources, protect Israel, and achieve US hegemony over the West [Europe] itself."[37]

Operations Desert Shield and Desert Storm tapped into a reservoir of Islamist distrust of Western policies in the Middle East that have long been depicted as hypocritical, duplicitous, and racist. Even as the US administration in 1991 insisted that there was no linkage between Kuwait and Palestine, Muslims throughout the world saw indisputable parallels between the two that fostered the already strong perception of the double standard of Western dealings in which the United States violated the very values it professed. These parallels include issues relating to boundaries, the use of weapons, and rewards for aggression. Desert Storm/Desert Shield was perceived by Islamists as a link in the chain of Christian oppression of Muslims. Islamists initially condemned the Iraqi aggression against Kuwait. However, when the United States assumed the leadership in redressing the aggression and did not allow for a negotiated settlement, the majority saw US intervention as a continuation of colonial policies designed to rob Arabs and Muslims of their wealth, to foster the dismemberment of the Muslim peoples by maintaining their divisions into nation-states, and to destroy Arab power in order to maintain Israel's supremacy in the area.

Islamists ask why Iraq's aggression was immediately redressed while that of Israel has been relegated to diplomacy and negotiations that have been protracted over thirty-five years. They heard the George H. W. Bush administration affirm there could be no room for negotiation or delay in regard to the Iraqi invasion of Kuwait. They ask why Saddam Hussein had to implement the UN resolutions immediately and completely, given that Israel has been allowed to circumvent all UN resolutions except the one recognizing it as a state, with which it has only partially complied, since the resolution also stipulates the existence of a Palestinian state and the repatriation or compensation of the refugees. The following statement typifies the Arab feeling toward what is perceived to be a double standard:

> Everybody in Congress stated accurately that Iraq stood in violation of the United Nations Charter and United Nations resolutions. But no one congressman or congresswoman mentioned the potential relevance of the fact that in the 23 years before Iraq started violating the United Nations Charter, Israel had been violating it every month and every week and every day. No one mentioned the 42 United Nations Resolutions on the subject. So while they were invoking the legitimacy of the United Nations, none in Congress had enough honor, enough self respect, enough integrity even to acknowledge that there was another country besides Iraq in the Middle East which at that moment stood in violation of the United Nations Charter.[38]

Islamists heard President Bush and Secretary of State James Baker affirm repeatedly that aggression should not be rewarded—yet they recall that when Israel invaded Lebanon in 1982, the United States gave it the green light. They remember that 20,000 Lebanese and Palestinians were killed and over 30,000 wounded during the invasion and that Israel also used US chemical weapons of mass destruction (napalm, phosphorus, and fragmentation bombs) against civilian targets. When the United Nations passed a resolution to apply sanctions on Israel, the United States vetoed the measure. Soon after, the US Congress voted $1.5 billion as a gift to Israel to compensate for the cost of the war. Islamists also remember that in October 1990, during Operation Desert Shield, Israeli troops "massacred" seventeen Muslims at the Aqsa mosque. The fact that Congress soon afterward authorized a $700 million grant to Israel is seen by Islamists as a reward for the taking of Muslim life.

The Bush administration accused Saddam Hussein of not respecting the international boundaries set by Britain. Islamists have questioned why, after more than a half century, the United States has not restricted Israel to the boundaries delineated for it by the United Nations and why it has been allowed to continue occupying territories designated for Palestinian residence as well as parts of Syria and Lebanon.

The Bush administration justified the military operation against Iraq by depicting Iraq's invasion of Kuwait as a violation of Kuwait's right to self-determination. Islamists ask why the United States acquiesces in Israeli occupation and annexation of Palestinian territory and refuses to recognize the Palestinian right to self-determination. In denying that Iraq occupied Kuwait to liberate Palestine, Secretary Baker said, "No one should enslave a people in order to liberate another." Islamists agree but fail to understand why US policymakers permit Israel to "enslave" the Christians and Muslims of Palestine in order to liberate the Jews.

Another example for Muslims of the US double standard was the tragic situation in Bosnia. The hesitation by the American administration to intervene was seen by Islamists as living proof of the contradiction in Western conduct. Noting that the Western conscience in general had been sympathetic to the plight of Bosnian Muslims, they found it strange that "Western policymakers have not bothered to translate the sympathy of their nations into action, and all they do is maneuver so as to contain the trends in Western public opinion. . . . Instead of acting to save Bosnian Muslims from Serbian concentration camps, the West [was] content with guaranteeing the passage of food and humanitarian aid as if to feed the Muslims before being slaughtered."[39] Muslims see a discrepancy in the way that Americans respond to human tragedies, which seems to be determined by the religious affiliation of the victims as Jewish or as Muslim. "Both the Holocaust and the slaughter of Bosnian Muslims are emotional issues; yet what makes questioning the extent of the Holocaust off limits and criticism of Bosnian Muslims, who are undergoing a similar campaign of extermination by the Serbs, acceptable? Muslims are no less sensitive to the mass executions of their European brethren than are Jews in America of their European counterparts."[40]

For many, the initial double standard in the policy toward Bosnia provided yet more proof of Western perfidy, one more example of Western outrages committed against Muslims and people of the Third World.

> The West's collusion and connivance, which has so far enabled the Serbs to seize more than 70 percent of Bosnia before occupying it completely, serves to obliterate five centuries of Islamic civilizational presence in Europe. It will only bring back to the minds of Muslims the repetitive image of the Westerners and their conduct when they occupy other people's countries: physical liquidation, usurpation of land, obliteration of cultural and civilizational remains, and enslavement of those who remain alive, stripping

them of their cultural identity. The tragedy in Bosnia is that of Andalusia, that of Palestine, that of the Red Indians in America, and that of the black peoples in Africa.[41]

And when the forces of NATO and the United States went in to end the Serbian ethnic cleansing aimed at de-Islamizing Bosnia and Kosovo, Islamists saw the intervention as one inspired by European self-interest, as they did not want Muslim refugees and asylum seekers to emigrate to Western Europe, while US officials portrayed it in a way that demonstrated they care for international order and Muslim life—and from the Muslim perspective, as long as it is not in Palestine.

Islamists and the "New World Order"

In 1992, Munir Shafiq, a Christian with Marxist sympathies who had converted to Islamism in the seventies, wrote an Islamist analysis of US policy in the Middle East as it appeared to be unfolding as a consequence of the declared "new world order." His assessment is typical of the genre of Islamist literature on the subject. Shafiq warned about several important changes in US policy that became possible after the success of Operation Desert Storm, noting that these changes were reminiscent of earlier colonial intervention in the region. Desert Storm left parts of the Arab world under "American military occupation," he said, a hearkening to the post–World War I period, when Muslims fought each other for the spoils promised by the British only to find themselves sectored and chopped up. Shafiq called the US-Soviet-Zionist decision to open Soviet Jewish immigration to Palestine the establishment of "Israel II," since the number of immigrants could reach 3 million, doubling the Jewish population of Israel. He warned:

> Thus while there was jubilation at the end of the Cold War, a [new] war has been declared on the Arabs and the Muslims through this frightening emigration which can be seen as Balfour Declaration II, or Israel II. No one, no matter what good intentions he may harbor towards the United States of America, can but see this immigration of millions except as an aggressive act against Palestine, the Arabs and the Muslims similar to that of the Balfour Declaration.[42]

Shafiq noted that the US policy of disarmament, disempowerment, and dismemberment of Iraq and the ensuing policy of economic strangulation following the 1991 Gulf war, left that nation in a position worse than that which was obtained during the colonial hegemony after World War I: "Anyone who connects these sanctions to what happened in Kuwait makes a grave error." He insisted that the sanctions imposed on Iraq after the war supported the primary US goal of maintaining the strategic military superiority of Israel over all Arab countries combined. The Arabs are to be restricted to arms that can maintain their regimes and suppress their own people, but not any "arms with teeth." The purpose is to maintain an Iraq that is paralyzed internally with no central authority and no possibility of extending its authority within its borders for some time to come.

Shafiq termed the establishment by the West of the no-fly zones in Iraq to protect the Kurdish north and the Shiite Arab south as Sykes-Picot II, a reincarnation of Sykes-Picot I, the operation that is seen as originally carving up and dismembering the Islamic body. These inequitable divisions are seen as maintaining Western interests through the maldistribution of wealth and resources in the region. Regardless of the success of its divide-and-conquer policy, he said, the West has not been satisfied with the developments in the area during the past four decades. Nasserism, Palestinian resistance, and the rise of Iraq threatened Western interests, hence the new policies affirming the Zionist plan for hegemonic dominance of the area. Shafiq argued that in order to achieve the Israeli strategic vision of the Balkanization of the Arab world, the policy has been to "seek to divide the region according to religious affiliation, ethnic origin, nationalist identity, regional and sectarian interests, in essence, the recasting of the area as a mosaic of minorities."[43] It will also seek to impede any scientific or technological progress in Arab and Muslim nations.

He went on to say that US interest in promoting an Arab-Israeli peace is an effort to recast the configuration of the area. It seeks to sacralize Israel as part of the Middle East regardless of Arab and Islamic interests, Arab and Islamic security, or dreams of an Arab and Islamic common market or economic integration. In order to achieve this, the United States has resorted to nineteenth-century colonial policies of utilizing military force under the guise of international legitimacy.[44] The new strategic role for Israel in the region, Shafiq said, is different in some aspects from that which was obtained during the cold war. Its overwhelming superiority in arms will be maintained as a reserve and combat-ready force to be called upon in time of need. If peace with the Arabs is achieved, there will be no need to keep its forces deployed at the borders in constant readiness. Its new role calls for a greater political, diplomatic, and economic participation throughout the Arab world, which is to be dismembered in order for Israel to partake of water resources, the marketplace, and development projects.[45]

Islamists and the Zionist Lobby

The Islamist literature depicts the West as dominated by the Zionist lobby. This image has had several mutations as Zionist influence is perceived to have gained control of the inner circles of policymakers who determine the destiny of the region. Interviews I conducted with Islamists in Egypt in 1985 made clear that they resented the double standard with which they were treated. One leader talked about the "evenhanded" policy, which was then the buzzword used by the administration to describe the habit of the West "to stroke Israel with the palm of their hand and whack us with the back." That same year, the joke in Jordan was, Why doesn't Israel want to become the fifty-first state of the United States? The answer: It would then have to be satisfied with being represented by two senators whereas now it has 100.

In interviews I conducted in 1989, the image of Zionist control of the US government became even more dominant. One Islamist depicted the United States as a colony of Israel (a view that is shared by Arab secularists). He compared the state of affairs in the United States with the former British rule over Egypt, noting that there were three specific areas in which British power manifested itself. First, Egyptians were not allowed to have an independent foreign policy but had to defer to Britain for direction. Second, there were foreign British residents in Cairo who made sure that Egyptian policy was in accord with the interests of Britain. Third, Egyptian tax revenues were sent to Britain to sustain its power. He drew the parallels by concluding, "What you have in the United States is a government that is unable to formulate an independent foreign policy without first asking how will Israel react. Secondly, the Congress is accountable to the Israeli lobby, which functions as a foreign agent placing the welfare of Israel above that of the United States. In the third place, the lobby assures the flow of billions of US tax dollars to Israel."

Unwavering support for the state of Israel in the US Congress is taken for granted by Islamists. Members of Congress were seen as fearful of losing their jobs if they questioned unqualified support for Israel. By being thus silenced, Congress was seen by Islamists as sanctioning acts of violence by Israel as well as supporting Israeli policies, through routine funding, of "dehumanizing" the Palestinian people. This did great damage to US credibility. One Egyptian Islamist referred to the "Hostages on the Hill" in reference to the US Congress. The image has not improved. The influence of the Zionist lobby is perceived as being unprecedented in US history. With the ascendancy in the Bill Clinton administration of Martin Indyk, a former Zionist lobbyist who is perceived as supporting Likud policies, to the National Security Council in charge of US policy in the region, some Islamists referred to the "Israeli-occupied White House."[46] The election of George W. Bush did not bring about the hoped for rectification in American foreign policy; rather it ushered in the power of the neoconservatives, who are decidedly pro-Israeli.

US Foreign Policy and the Clinton Administration

For Islamists, the Clinton administration assumed authority at a critical time in history. Due to the collapse of the Soviet empire, the US administration was not only able to implement its policies unimpeded by considerations of balance of power, but it also chose to shed its cooperative arrangements with old "allies," such as Pakistan and the Afghan Resistance Movement, and to rearrange its priorities. Clinton began what was perceived as a tilt toward India at the expense of Pakistan, the latter an ally during the cold war who had for years supported the policies of the United States and had allowed operations against the Soviet Union to be launched through its territory into Afghanistan. The dumping of Pakistan and the abandonment of Afghanistan were perceived as part of US duplicity and a sign of its increasing control by Zionist interests. The United States would feign friendship only when it needed to use nations for its own interests.

The Arab and Islamic worlds found themselves weak and divided in the wake of Desert Storm. Not only was there apprehension on the part of Islamists concerning the new world order as it was being shaped, but they also felt victimized by increasing demonization that targeted them as the potential enemy. The Clinton administration did not initiate anything that would allay these fears. The prevailing perception is that the Arabs continue to provide the convenient target for proving US virility, hence the unleashing of "Tomahawk diplomacy" against Baghdad (a reference to US Tomahawk cruise missiles). Although many among the Islamists would have welcomed the killing of Saddam Hussein, the targeting of an industrial complex confirmed for the Islamists their suspicion that the United States sought to maintain Israeli scientific and technological superiority while denying the Arabs any such opportunity.

Furthermore, it increasingly looked as though Iraq had become the proving ground for US manhood. Not only had President George H. W. Bush declared that the victory in Desert Storm had wiped away the defeat of Vietnam, but it was perceived that President Clinton began his administration by bombing Iraq in order to prove that he was not afraid of war and that he was not a draft dodger. When Madeleine Albright assumed office as secretary of state, she had to prove her "manhood" by bombing Iraq. Albright, while ambassador to the United Nations, had already demonstrated on two occasions to the Islamists that she placed little value on Arab life. To her the children of Lebanon and Iraq were disposable in the larger scope of maintaining US interests in the Middle East. When Boutros Boutros-Ghali, secretary general of the United Nations, refused to suppress UN reports and a video that proved that the Israeli army during Operation Grapes of Wrath in South Lebanon had on April 18, 1996, deliberately targeted the UN headquarters at Qana (which resulted in the massacre of more than 100 women and children who had taken refuge there), Albright was incensed and made sure that he was not reelected to the post again.[47] On May 12, 1995, appearing on *60 Minutes,* she was asked by Leslie Stahl, "We have heard that half a million children have died [in Iraq]. I mean that's more children than died in Hiroshima. And—and you know, is the price worth it?" Albright replied, "I think this is a very hard choice, but the price—we think the price is worth it."[48]

Despite their struggle for empowerment during the twentieth century, Islamists feel, it has been determined that Arabs should be maintained in weakness, mediocrity, and subservience. For many in the Islamist movement, the actions of the Clinton administration and its pronouncements confirmed the perception of many Muslims that it is Tel Aviv that dictates policy in the area. The fact that over two dozen former employees of the Israeli lobby were directing US administration policy in the Middle East led Muhammad Husayn Fadlallah of Lebanon to write: "The current American administration has become almost completely Jewish, if not in origin then in its clear and infamous political affiliation."[49] Clinton's statements in response to terrorist activities made it clear that the United States condemned violent radicalism and extremism in any form, yet he praised Islam as a religion and emphasized that there was no inevitable "clash of civilizations" between the West and the Islamic world. These comments were welcomed in the Islamic world, but most Muslims remained unconvinced and essentially responded by saying that actions speak louder than words.

An address by Martin Indyk (former assistant secretary of state for the Near East and North Africa) on May 18, 1993, raised further concern about the future of the region. Indyk outlined a Manichaean vision, one where the world was portrayed as a potential nightmare should the nationalists or Islamists realize their dream and form a united front. The alternative vision that he promoted was one of harmony and bliss in which Israel would attain its "normalization" in the region. He stated:

> In other words, the "vision thing" was very clear to this president before he came into office. He understands that the Middle East is finely balanced between two alternative futures: one in which extremists, cloaked in religious or nationalist garb, would hold sway across the region, wielding weapons of mass destruction loaded into ballistic missiles; and the other future in which Israel, its Arab neighbors and the Palestinians would achieve an historic reconciliation that would pave the way for peaceful coexistence, regional economic development, arms control agreements, and growing democratization throughout the Middle East.[50]

In his address, Indyk dismissed the Islamists as a set of "troublemakers." He declared them to be the by-product of "decades of neglect and dashed hopes for political participation and social justice that have nurtured some violent movements cloaked in religious garb that have begun to challenge governments across the Arab world with the potential of destabilizing the region."[51] His remedy was to create a market economy and provide some vision of democracy. Unfortunately, his emphasis on the "vision" rather than the reality, coupled with the US record of support for autocratic regimes and silent approval of the subversion of democratic elections in the Occupied Territories, in Algeria, and in Egypt had most Islamists apprehensive at the prospect.

Indyk stated that the United States is not an impartial arbiter of the peace process; rather he affirmed that "the President and the Secretary of State made it clear that our approach in the negotiations will involve working with Israel, not against it. We are committed to deepening our strategic partnership with Israel in the pursuit of peace and security."[52] This affirmation did not bode well for permanent peace in the area and in fact probably assured further growth of the Islamist movement. Furthermore, it served to undermine the very regimes (Egypt and the Gulf nations) the United States wishes to support. Those regimes were put in the position of seeming to collude in the empowerment of Israel at the expense of the Arab population.

In his speech to the Jordanian parliament in 1994, President Clinton appeared to be reiterating Indyk's vision of a Manichaean worldview. He portrayed the Middle East as "an arena of struggle between the forces of tyranny and freedom, terror and security, bigotry and tolerance, isolation and openness." In the process, he spelled out for Islamists the choices between good and evil in the area, with the good being assured when they associated with Israel. Meanwhile, administration policy appeared to depict Islam in a similar fashion: At one end of the spectrum is Islam, represented by the faith that is confined to personal belief and ritual practices, and on the other are extremist groups that insist on the political dimension of Islam and therefore are dubbed violent and terrorist. Although this policy affirms a respect for the religion of Islam, it is a disemboweled Islam that has no input into human, social, economic, or political values, which some Islamists have dubbed "American Islam." Meanwhile, the Clinton administration made several unprecedented gestures to the American Muslim community to demonstrate their inclusion in the American mosaic. The president sent greetings to Muslim leaders in the United States on the occasion of the Islamic holiday. He also included Islam in his directive that employees can display religious objects of their particular faith at their workstations. The First Lady invited Muslim representatives to the White House for *iftar* (breaking the Ramadan fast) dinners, to the consternation of some in the Zionist lobby who accused her of hobnobbing with terrorists with blood on their hands.

Such symbolic gestures, however, did not change the Islamist perception that the Clinton administration associated international terrorism with Muslims. The Clinton administration's promoting and signing of the Anti-Terrorism Act of 1996 after the Oklahoma City bombing, which sanctioned the profiling of Arabs and Muslims (not in the image of Timothy McVeigh) at airports as potential terrorists, is seen as proof of such perceptions:

> The West attempts to tie international terrorism with Islam, while the historical record is studded with the crimes of the West which confirm that all forms of extremism and terror were invented in the West which spreads them in the world through the Mafia, Nazism, Neo-Nazism, racial discrimination, abduction of heads of state and ambassadors, stalking the leaders of national liberation movements, assassination of innocent civilians, attacking peaceful cities with nuclear bombs, using internationally banned weapons, poisoning water sources and food supplies, blockading civilian populations and denying them their right to life.[53]

Several generations of Arabs have been socialized to believe that Palestine is an Arab Issue. Each generation has been provided with "proof" of the injustice perpetrated against the Palestinian people so as to cement this perception. "The question of Palestine was not the only Arab issue; rather, it was their central issue." The Arabs have also had the burden of dealing with the issues of division and unity, of economic retardation and development, of resources and dependency, and of their perception of their civilization.[54] Since 1967, the issue of Palestine has been adopted increasingly as part of the Islamic agenda. It seems all too clear that an unjust peace that thwarts all hopes will only intensify the anger at what is seen as long-standing injustice and will fuel the flames of Islamist reaction.

After the 1967 Arab-Israeli war, one American administration after another invited the Arabs to trust American evenhandedness and come to the peace table and reap the benefits. And they have come. Over fifteen Arab nations for a time established some sort of relationship with Israel after the signing of the Oslo agreement and the Madrid peace conference of 1991. The consequences were perceived to be the increased arrogance on the part of the Israeli government. Many in the area feel that the Islamists were vindicated, that Israel does not want peace but pacification and the legalization of its acquisition of the rest of the land of the Palestinians with the indigenous population relegated to isolated Bantustans, while the presidents of the Palestinian Authority are to become the enforcers for Israeli security interests. As one Islamist put it, "the peace process turned out to be the process by which Israel acquires Palestinian land piece by piece by piece."

Increasingly, people in the area believe that the peace process is based on the flawed idea that the United States is an impartial mediator. Speeches by President Clinton and Vice President Gore on the occasion of the fiftieth anniversary of the declaration of the state of Israel make evident that the United States is not impartial "but act[s] in support of Israel and its act of aggression to confiscate land, deport its occupants and eradicate what is left of the Muslim population of Palestine."[55] Or as a June 1988 statement signed by twenty-six Kuwaiti organizations put it, "Fifty years have passed and Israel's record of aggression grows larger, and with it grows the condemnation of the international organizations which are incapacitated by the American veto which stands at the ready to support the oppressor against the oppressed."[56]

The peace process engaged in by the Clinton administration was suspect from the beginning because the diplomats charged with shepherding it through were from the Israeli lobby and were working in support of Israel's interest. Not one had an Arab background; hence there was an underestimation of what the Palestinians, Arabs, and Muslims would find acceptable. At issue was the fact that the Arabs believed that they had given up all they could at Madrid. They had accepted Israel within its 1967 borders, relinquishing 78 percent of original Palestine for the Jewish state. But Israel wanted more land. It wanted to maintain settlements established on confiscated land in the West Bank and Jerusalem, a policy that is in violation of international law as set by the Geneva Convention and reiterated by a variety of UN resolutions. This was justified as necessary because of its security needs, that it was the dream of generations of Jews who had suffered during the Holocaust, and that Israel had won the war. To the Islamists, such demands were seen not only as excessive greed but in a very profound way as an unjust solution to the problem.

Arabs argue that it is unjust to expect the Palestinian Christians and Muslims to relinquish their rights to their lands and homes in order to satisfy Israel's expansionist security needs. That would reward Israel for what the Arabs call its War of Aggression (of 1967). If the argument is that Israel had won it by war, that in the final analysis might makes right, then, they say, the Arabs should wait until a new generation is able to rise and become strong enough to take it back. If Israel's acquisition of land is based on religious justification that 16 million Jews consider Jerusalem as the religious center of their life, they question why the sentiments of 1.3 billion Muslims about Jerusalem are not being taken into consideration. They question why Judaism is being privileged. If the argument is that God had promised the land in the Hebrew scriptures, they question why the Qur'an, the final revelation of God, which sees that the Jews will be dispersed throughout the world, is not taken into consideration.

The final product of the peace process undertaken by the Clinton administration was seen not as Prime Minister Barak's "generous offer," as depicted by President Clinton; rather it is seen as the affirmation of the Israeli dream of legitimizing its acquisition of more land while keeping the Palestinians out. President Clinton's spin on the offer was dismissed as duplicitous. The protracted negotiations of the peace process provided the cover for Israel to more than double the illegal settlements. Clinton had used the power and prestige of the United States to empower Israel rather than to provide a just and equitable solution that could finally bring peace to the area. He had worried more about having Barak reelected and having his wife elected as a senator from New York than about the fate of millions of Palestinians who had suffered under the longest occupation in history.[57]

US Foreign Policy and the George W. Bush Administration

Muslims expected a more equitable policy from the George W. Bush administration. During the presidential debates, he had questioned the use of racial profiling legislated by the Clinton administration, which had targeted Arab Americans. Furthermore, in the estimation of Arab and Muslim Americans, a change in administration would remove the Israeli lobby from the center of policymaking. They had noted that the lobby was instrumental in defeating the reelection bid of George W. Bush's father (because it did not forgive his policy of demanding a halt to the construction and expansion of settlements on the West Bank). Consequently, George W. received the endorsement of the major Muslim and Arab organizations, and a large number of Arabs and Muslims in the United States registered and voted for the first time, accounting for 2 percent of the votes received by the Bush-Cheney ticket. Muslims believe that their votes were the decisive margin in Florida. They had not paid attention to the promises he had made to the Zionist lobby. He was later to boast that he had borrowed twenty policy wonks from the American Enterprise Institute, noted as the home of neoconservatives and unconditional supporters of Israel.[58] In essence, while the Clinton administration relied on Zionists with connections to the Labor Party in Israel, the Bush administration utilized those who had a long-standing relationship with Benjamin Netanyahu of Likud.

The initial policy of the George W. Bush administration was to keep Arab and Muslim Americans at arm's length. Symbolic gestures of inclusion initiated by the Clinton administration were discontinued. Muslim and Arab Americans seeking an audience with policymakers were at first ignored. Later, a scheduled meeting with Vice President Dick Cheney was canceled, and at another meeting, one of the participants was removed by security despite the fact that he had a special security clearance because he was an intern in a senator's office. And true to form, one of President Bush's first ventures into foreign policy was to send the air force to bomb Iraq. It was a very loud signal not only to prove to the US electorate that he was a true patriot and had not avoided the fighting in Vietnam but also to put the Arabs on notice that the containment of Iraq would continue.

From the beginning, President Bush wanted to keep his hands off the Arab-Israeli conflict. In the process, he allowed the Israeli authorities to continue to grind down the Palestinian resistance to the occupation. His public and highly publicized refusal to meet with Yasser Arafat, while repeatedly welcoming Prime Minister Sharon to the White House, sent an important message to Islamists that he was in total support of Israel and its policies. Whenever the Palestinians reacted to Israeli aggression, Bush blamed Arafat and the Palestinians. Such open support of Sharon infuriated Muslims and Arabs overseas; Sharon was particularly reviled because he was implicated in four massacres perpetrated against the Palestinians. They were particularly aggrieved when Bush met with Sharon after the Israeli shelling and demolition in Ramallah around the headquarters of Yasser Arafat. Bush had earlier expressed his frustration by saying, "Enough is enough," which led some to believe that he was finally disgusted enough to restrain what was perceived to be Israeli aggression. But upon meeting with Sharon, Bush declared him a "Man of Peace." This led the moderate top Palestinian negotiator, Saeb Erekat to say, "When I hear the president saying that Sharon is a man of peace after he has destroyed our way of life, and after the Jenin refugee camp, I don't know if this is not a reward for Israeli terrorism against the Palestinian people."

Another policy adopted early in the Bush administration that aggravated Islamists was its refusal to engage in a discussion of what was perceived to be Israeli racial policies. Their anger was demonstrated in Muslim publications all over the world when the United States and Israel walked out of the UN World Conference Against Racism, Racial Discrimination, Xenophobia, and Related Intolerance held in Durban, accusing participants that the conference had been "hijacked" by Israel's enemies. For Islamists that fact demonstrated once again America's lack of concern for Palestinians under what is perceived to be an oppressive Israeli occupation that openly discusses means of containing Palestinians within fences, transferring them to other countries, or getting rid of them because they do not fit into its definition of a Jewish state. One Islamist asked, "If this is not racism, what is?"

And then there was the 9/11 attack on the World Trade Center in New York and the Pentagon in Virginia, and Americans asked, "Why do they hate us?" Osama bin Laden's statement provided an answer that few US policymakers wanted to hear. He identified US foreign policy vis-à-vis the Arab-Israeli conflict, US containment of Iraq, which had degraded the lives of the Iraqi people and led to their suffering, and US troops stationed in the Gulf, who maintained American hegemony in the area and supported autocratic regimes. His message was blunted by a parade of former US policymakers, diplomats, and army brass who appeared on American television stations around the clock to assure the American public that they hate us because of our "democracy," our "culture," and our "values." And as Raghida Dergham of the Lebanese daily *al-Hayat* has said, not one dared to tell the American people that "it is the policy, stupid." The Arabs who perpetrated the horrible terrorist acts in the United States were suspected of being the same group that had hit American installations of command and control elsewhere: two embassies in Africa, the USS *Cole* in Yemen, and the Khobar Tower in Saudi Arabia where American troops lived. They had not attacked any of America's cultural monuments—not one Pizza Hut, Mc-Donald's, or cathedral had been bombed. For those who continue to question whether there was any connection between the destruction of 9/11 and our foreign policy, Robert Fisk of the British *Independent* pointed to the fact that the last will of Muhammad Atta, who led the suicide bombers on 9/11, was written on April 18, 1996, the day of the Qana massacre.

After the attacks of 9/11, the Bush administration declared a "global war on terrorism." The attack on American soil was so momentous that it was deemed to have "changed America forever." To his credit, President Bush reached out to the Arab and Muslim American communities and assured them that the United States was waging war not against Islam but against terrorism. He called on the American people not to take out their anger and frustration on American Muslims. At the same time, his administration incarcerated more than 5,000 Arabs and Muslims using the hastily legislated Patriot Act. Racial profiling of Arabs and Muslims continues to be a common practice. Meanwhile, there was very little movement in adjusting US foreign policy to demonstrate more evenhandedness and justice. The Bush administration was caught in a double bind: If it altered its policies, it could be perceived as caving in to the terrorists; at the same time, the constant blaming of Palestinians for the bloodshed in Israel/Palestine and the daily saber-rattling for regime change in Iraq raised questions about US sincerity. The majority of Muslims overseas believed that the United States had declared war on Islam. The administration's policy, implemented by the American diplomatic corps, of trying to root out fundamentalist Islam from textbooks and *madrasas* in Muslim countries has infuriated Islamists. They have questioned what right "Mufti Bush" has to decide what true Islam is. The fact that the administration bombed the Taliban, which had not perpetrated 9/11, and the large number of Afghan civilian casualties raised suspicions that the motive was retribution. No one doubted US might and ability to destroy Islamists, but they reserved the right to think for themselves and to hold their own interpretations of the Qur'an. Many continue to question whether current policies are raising a new generation of Islamists who will seek to avenge what they perceive to be a war on Islam, despite the assurances by the Bush administration to the contrary, and they await justice for the Palestinians.

Western commentators point to the fact that various Arab governments appear to have wearied of the Palestinian leadership and the Palestinian cause. The Gulf war precipitated an exodus of Palestinians from yet another Arab country, Kuwait, while Operation Iraqi Freedom emptied them out of Iraq. That, however, does not translate into Muslim abandonment of the issue of Palestine and Jerusalem. For Islamists, the danger facing the Muslims is not "the Palestine problem" as much as the "problem of Israel." For Muslims, Palestine is a cause. It represents the demand for the right of a people to self-determination, democracy, and freedom. It is also the demand that the West recognize that an Arab person is equal to a European person or, as some Palestinians put it, that a European Jew is not better than a Palestinian Christian or Muslim and has no superior right to rob, destroy, expel, kidnap, or kill without consequences. Palestine is a demand for the end of the colonial era, an end to the era of "Christian arrogance"[59] and "Jewish insolence,"[60] a demand that the superior international Islamic law prevail, which would guarantee justice and freedom to Muslims and to religious minorities who dwell among them.

Islamists believe that American foreign policy has targeted them as worthy victims for annihilation. They hope that one day the West will wake up to the tragedy it has perpetrated. Those in the West may yet apologize for the destruction of Palestine; they may even offer restitution, but will they ever be able to correct the wrong that they have done? As Rashid Qabbani, the mufti of Lebanon put it:

> The West has been brilliant in the crime of ridding itself of the Jewish problem and dumping it into the heart of the Arab world by supporting the Zionist entity and [establishing] Israel in Palestine in 1948. After WWII Western nations began seeking forgiveness from Israel for what Nazism had done to the Jews. Will the Western conscious[ness] awake one day to seek forgiveness for the crime which they committed by establishing Israel in Palestine and by evicting the Palestinian people from their homes and land? Will the West seek forgiveness for the suppression, terrorizing, and humiliation that Israel has been meting out for fifty years to the oppressed Palestinian people and for the loss of their land at the hand of the West? Should it occur, of what value will Western apology be? For it is the West that daily provides Israel with the weapons of mass destruction, prepared for the annihilation of the Palestinians and the Arabs.[61]

Operation Iraqi Freedom and Its Consequences

One of the transformations that took place post–9/11 was in President George W. Bush himself, who now refers to himself as the "war president."[62] After September 11, 2001, the president proceeded to plan for the invasion of Iraq, a plan promoted by the neoconservative advisors in his administration.[63] In seeking the support of the American people for the global war on terrorism, the Bush administration utilized a variety of themes, including creating a climate of fear about the alleged imminent danger from a nuclear attack by Saddam Hussein. When these assertions were questioned, then National Security Adviser Condoleezza Rice, on September 8, 2003, retorted: "The problem here is that there will always be some uncertainty about how quickly he can acquire nuclear weapons. But we don't want the smoking gun to be a mushroom cloud." Furthermore, despite the fact that Saddam was a secularist, he was initially depicted as an accomplice of al-Qa'ida. Later, he was condemned as a monster who had gassed his own people (even though the biological and chemical weapons are suspected to have been provided by the United States). He could not be trusted with possessing weapons of mass destruction that he would surely aim at the United States. At the same time, the propaganda for war provided the public with a moral justification for attacking Afghanistan and Iraq, bathing the war in the virtues of, among other things, liberating the oppressed women of Islam from fanatical oppressive Islamists. The goal became the modernization and democratization of Islamic society. Washington eventually promised the refashioning of Iraq as a beacon of democracy that would serve as a model for the entire Middle East.[64]

Muslims took note of the fact that Operation Iraqi Freedom was a preemptive war. From their perspective, there was no virtue in the attack. Although they despised Saddam Hussein, they perceived the goal of the US-led invasion in more sinister terms, as one that was driven by the motive of weakening the Arabs and Muslims and empowering Israel. They accused the Bush administration of dealing with the consequences of terrorism while turning a blind eye toward its causes. Arabs and Muslims are aware that terrorism is a response to American policies that empower autocratic regimes and implement Israeli and Zionist policies that are harmful to Arabs and Muslims and therefore breed hatred. They noted that the US government could not acknowledge this truth since it would indict itself, and therefore it projects the blame on others. Hence the Bush administration declared a global war on terrorism, in which it assumed a total monopoly in deciding the nature of the war, its timing, its targets, the means to be utilized, and the manner in which it would be conducted.[65]

Islamists saw the war in Iraq as a two-pronged attack that utilized military power and media deception. While various spokesmen of the Bush administration boasted about "Shock and Awe" to neutralize the Iraqi army and pacify the population, Islamists saw the attack as proof of American brutality and addiction to state terrorism in order to gain control of the oil fields of Iraq. On Arab television American military tactics looked indistinguishable from those that Israel utilized in the Occupied Territories. The two occupations appeared to blend into a coordinated attack against Muslims, especially after US rhetoric conflated terrorism against the United States with resistance to Israeli occupation in Palestine and Lebanon. "Shock and Awe" did not cow Arabs and Muslims; rather, it inflamed their passions against the West and its supporters, a sentiment that spawned a large number of volunteers for the insurgency. The American media was perceived by Muslims as assuming the role of the self-censoring and embedded servant of hegemonic imperialist goals "which have no association with freedom or democracy."[66]

While a great deal of ink has been spilled discussing the war, its motives, goals, and conduct, two foci of Islamist literature are worth noting: the growing rejection of violence as a tactic to achieve the goals of the Islamic movement and the continued rejection of perceived US schemes to bring the Muslim world under its cultural hegemony and to empower Israel over the Arabs and Muslims.

Several Islamist leaders have published *shari'a*-based interpretations that denounce terrorist bombings targeting civilians. They have also expressed their opinion that these bombings are based on a misinterpretation of Islamic teaching and have been counterproductive and therefore against the interests of Islam. The renunciation of violence by these Islamic groups was not a consequence of the demonstration of American resolve and power, whether in Afghanistan or in Iraq. For example, the Jama'ah Islamiyya, which was responsible for the first attack on the World Trade Center in 1993, renounced violence on July 5, 1997. They called for the cessation of armed operations and the shedding of blood as a means of achieving the goal of Islamizing society. This declaration was signed by its leadership and approved by Sheikh Omar 'Abd al Rahman from his prison cell in the United States.

The group split, and those who refused to subscribe to peaceful resistance perpetrated the terrorist activities in the late 1990s in Luxor, Upper Egypt,[67] while others joined al-Qaʻida.

This literature notes that violence has been counterproductive and has not achieved its goals. Hijacking airplanes has not put a stop to air travel in the world. Nor has targeting a bank eliminated the banking industry or kept people from dealing with banks. Likewise, bombings are not going to force the United States to alter its policies. Rather, violence has brought great injury to the cause and goals of the Islamic movement since it has led to the identification of *jihad* with terrorism, an interpretation promoted by many Israelis and the Americans as a way to de-legitimate resistance movements in Palestine and Lebanon as well as in Chechnya and Iraq. Israeli and American rhetoric depicts all resistance as terrorism and asserts that "all Muslims are terrorists, the word Islam means terror, all are engaged in killing civilian women and children."[68] Thus, some Islamist leaders have concluded that "*jihad* for the sake of *jihad,* fighting for the sake of fighting is the wrong model of *jihad.* It is an erroneous interpretation of this great Islamic duty."[69] This view contends that America's aggression should not legitimate what is against the Islamic *shariʻa,* the killing of innocent people. America's crimes against Arabs and Muslims are evident and cause a great deal of grieving; however, they should not be used as an excuse to weaken the *ʻumma* or provide the United States with an excuse to interfere in the internal affairs of Arabs and Muslims.[70]

The literature admits that the perpetrators are right that the US treatment of Muslims is laced with arrogance and contempt, evident in the legislation passed by Congress as the "Sudan Peace Act,"[71] the "Iraq Liberation Act,"[72] and the "Syria Accountability Act,"[73] while four hundred congressmen voted in support of a resolution to not put pressure on Israel to implement the Road Map, which would bring about the creation of a Palestinian state—this despite the fact that the Road Map, from its inception to its final formulation, was an Israeli project.[74] It is also evident in the treatment of prisoners of war in Afghanistan, detainees at the prison at Guantánamo Bay in Cuba, and those held at the Abu Ghraib prison in Iraq. This treatment is seen in the Arab and Muslim worlds as an example of America's disdain for human rights as well as international conventions.[75] Islamists continue to see President Bush as a hypocrite and a liar not only because of the deception about the reasons for the invasion of Iraq but also because of the spin about the noble goals of the invasion. They note for example that in a November 6, 2003, speech at the National Endowment for Democracy, he focused on the theme of democracy in the Muslim world. He commended the leaders of autocratic countries—Bahrain, Jordan, Kuwait, Morocco, Oman, Qatar, Saudi Arabia, and Yemen—but condemned the "Palestinian leaders who block and undermine democratic reform."[76] But when the Palestinians elected representatives he did not approve of, specifically the Hamas parliamentary victory in January 2006, Bush sanctioned the blockade of the freely elected Palestinian government, which was intended to starve it into submission.

Another peeve is the promotion by the Bush administration of the Greater Middle East Partnership project that was perceived to be an American political strategy to abrogate the Arab identity by adding far-flung Muslim nations under a new geographic umbrella.[77] The term Middle East was designed by colonial powers. Its geographic reach has always been elastic and flexible, determined by Western interests. In earlier times it had included Iran, Turkey, and Cyprus, but the Greater Middle East had an even larger reach. To Islamists, its goal appears to be the eradication of the Arab identity. They would become Middle Easterners instead of Arabs. Some perceive it as a reincarnation of an old project to refashion the Arab nations according to Western dictates and Israeli design. The idea had first been floated by Shimon Peres, former prime minister of Israel, by which he depicted the Middle East at peace, with Israel managing the area's resources and controlling its trade.[78]

Islamists continue to be suspicious of the Bush administration's goals in Iraq. They maintain that under the rubric of pluralism and democracy, the American government appears to be in the process of dividing the country according to ethnic and sectarian identities. They note that the record of the US occupation does not inspire hope. It is accused of insisting on giving US companies the right to develop the oil industry, robbing the Iraqis of their wealth. It is also accused of initially placing shady characters in charge of the Iraqi government, of allowing the theft of archeological treasures, and of subverting the intellectual and religious culture of Iraq by replacing the school curricula with materials conceived and written in the United States.[79]

Suspicion of America's motives is pervasive in the Muslim world, and the US desire to unilaterally dictate norms and culture is a serious concern in the Middle East. The fear is that the globalization promoted by the United States will result in the Americanization of Arab and Muslim culture. This Americanization can be imposed through "Shock and Awe" if necessary, with total disregard for any freedom of choice or democratic input by Muslims.[80] The hope in the Arab and Muslim worlds is that Americans will recognize that the international order that was unilaterally abrogated by the United States must be restored. The hope is that the American people will initiate that change.[81]

Notes

1. For example: "The black intellectual trend has lately been able to make Islam a synonym to terrorism and darkness through the media which is controlled by the 'Muslim' states. He who prays five times a day is an iniquitous terrorist . . . she who wears a hijab is an iniquitous terrorist; he who reads the Qur'an is an iniquitous terrorist, and he who refuses usury, drinking, Eastern dancing, social dancing and mixing of men and women is an iniquitous terrorist; he who advocates the study of Islamic history and Islamic religion is an iniquitous terrorist; he who calls for an Islamic economic, cultural, political unity is an iniquitous terrorist. . . . Anyone who belongs to Islam is bloody and reactionary who must be destroyed. What would satisfy them is for the Muslims to abandon Islam and follow others in religion, thought, way of life and conduct . . . only then would it be proper to call them enlightened."

Hilmi Muhammad al-Qa'ud, "Al-Fikr al-Aswad . . . wa al-Fitan al-Thaqafiyya," *al-Mujtama'* 24(1081) (December 28, 1993), p. 56.

2. In an interview, Dr. Fathi Shikaki, secretary-general of the Islamic Jihad Movement in Palestine, protested the designation of terrorist. See Omar Maxwell, "No Peace Until Palestine Is Free," *Inquiry* 1(6) (January 1993), p. 21: "I do not know how the Palestinian is described as a terrorist when his scream is a response to his pain and suffering while defending his land against Jewish Russian soldiers, who had never (and neither their fore-fathers) set foot in any inch of Palestine. The West's attempt to homogenize our countries is the source of all terrorism and chaos. We are calling for peace based on justice, rights and dignity. We must be dealt with as equals and as carriers of a great civilization. Only then will peace prevail in our region and the whole world."

3. "President Bush Delivers Remarks at the National Endowment for Democracy," October 6, 2006, http://www.whitehouse.gov/news/releases/2005/10/print/20051006-2.html. "President Bush Delivers Remarks to the Joint Armed Forces Officers' Wives' Luncheon," Bolling Air Force Base, October 25, 2006, http://www.findarticles.com/p/articles/mi_m0NTQ/is_2005_Oct_25/ai_n15950433

4. An example: "In recent days, the West has started to triumphantly declare that in today's world, Arabs do not matter. For them Muslims also do not matter and they would like to keep it that way. The media and Western political and propaganda machines are assiduously asserting that Islam is incompatible with civilization. Their main points are that Islam lacks democracy, is devoid of compassion and has no rights for women. In doing so they have splendid examples, or in fact props; Saudi Arabia is rendering the best service. It is allegedly run according to the Quran, so there is no democracy and no rights." Abdurrahman Abdullah, "The Final Battle for the Soul of Afghanistan," *Inquiry* 1(3) (June 1992), p. 19.

5. See, for example, Muhammad 'Amara, "al-Ta'addudiyya: al-Ru'ya al-Islamiyya . . . wa al-Tahaddiyat al-Gharbiyya" [Proceedings of the Conference on Political, Sectarian and Ethnic Pluralism in the Arab World] (Herndon, Va.: IIIT, 1993), pp. 1–34.

6. For a sampling of Salafi literature, see 'Abd al-Rahman 'Abd al-Khaliq, *al-'Usul al-'Ilmiyya li al-Da'wa al-Salafiyya* (Kuwait, 1402H); 'Umar Sulayman al-Ashqar, *Ma'alim al-Shakhsiyya al-Islamiyya* (Kuwait, 1984). For a criticism of Salafi thought, see Muhammad Fathi 'Uthman, *al-Salafiyya fi al-Mujtama'at al-Mu'asira* (Cairo, 1982).

7. Ahmad Kamal Abu al-Magd, *Kitab al-Quwmiyya al-'Arabiyya wa al-Islam* (Beirut, 1980), pp. 32–33. For a different categorization, see Khurshid Ahmad, "Islam and the New World Order," *Middle East Affairs* 1(3) (Spring/Summer 1993), pp. 10–11.

8. See Yvonne Yazbeck Haddad, "The Authority of the Past: Current Paradigms for an Islamic Future," in *The Authority of the Past*, ed. Toby Siebers (Ann Arbor: University of Michigan Institute for the Humanities, 1993). For Islamist discussions on the future, see Ahmad Kamal Abu al-Magd, "Al-Muslimun Da'wa li-Iqtiham al-Mustaqbal," *al-'Arabi* 292 (March 1983); Fu'ad Muhammad Fakhr al-Din, *Mustaqbal al-Muslimin* (Cairo, 1976); 'Abd al-'Aziz Kamil, *al-Islam wa al-Mustaqbal* (Cairo, 1976); 'Abd al-Halim 'Uways, *al-Muslimun fi Ma'rakat al-Baqa'* (Cairo, 1979); Sayyid Qutb, *Islam: The Religion of the Future* (Chicago: Kazi Publications, 1977).

9. Muhammad al-Ghazali, *Ma'rakat al-Mushaf fi al-'Alam al-Islami* (Cairo, 1964); Muhammad al-Hasani, *al-Islam al-Mumtahan* (Cairo, n.d.); Muhammad Farag, *Al-Islam fi Mu'tarak al-Sira' al-Fikri al-Hadith* (Cairo, 1962); Muhammad al-Ghazali, *Kifah Din* (Cairo, n.d.); Muhammad Jalal Kishk, *al-Ghazu al-Fikri* (Cairo, 1975); 'Abd al-Sattar Fathallah Sa'id, *al-Ghazu al-Fikri wa al-Tayyarat al-Mu'adiya li al-Islam* (Cairo, 1977).

10. Tawfiq Mahmud al-Shawi, "Istratijiyya 'Ilmiyya li al-Tayyar al-Islami," *al-Mujtama'* 24(1081) (December 28, 1993), p. 22.

11. Abdullah, "The Final Battle," p. 19.

12. One author described the minarets of Yugoslavia in the following words: "This remains a living testimony to the glorious and often forgotten Islamic heritage of the last remnants of Europe's indigenous Muslim population, a people, a society, a civilization possibly on the verge of extinction. This is not a fate different from the fate experienced by the indigenous Muslims of Sicily, Italy, Spain, Portugal, Hungary, Malta, etc. many centuries earlier." Saffet Catovic, "Europe's Islamic Heritage in Jeopardy," *Inquiry* 1(6) (January 1993), p. 28.

13. See Ziyad Muhammad 'Ali, *'Ida al-Yahud li al-Haraka al-Islamiyya* (Amman, 1982), p. 21.

14. Graduation speech at the US Naval Academy, Annapolis, Maryland, May 30, 1990.

15. "We Muslims are very distressed at the growing number of attacks of the Western Jewish American media against Islam. . . . We are prone to think that the Jewish and Zionist groups with all their great influence in the West and America have determined to turn the West against Islam and to push Christianity and Islam into a violent confrontation that will destroy both and keep the Zionists as winners." Ghannushi, in an interview appearing in *al-Majalla* 24(1081) (December 28, 1993), p. 28.

16. See Bernard Lewis, "The Roots of Muslim Rage," *Atlantic Monthly* 226(3) (September 20, 1990). An editorial by Charles Krauthammer appearing in the *National Review* reiterates the same ideas, as does "The New Crescent of Crisis: The Global Intifada," *Washington Post,* February 16, 1990. Cf. Daniel Pipes, "The Muslims Are Coming, the Muslims Are Coming," *National Review,* November 19, 1990, pp. 28–31.

17. Mowahid H. Shah, "A New Cold War Within Islam?" *Christian Science Monitor,* July 30, 1990, p. 19.

18. In an interview with the first secretary of the US embassy in Qatar, Yusuf al-Qaradawi is reported to have said: "It is not in America's interest to be an enemy of Islam, the Islamic forces and the Islamic movements that are balanced and moderate. However, there are individuals and powers who have an interest in maintaining that Islam is something to fear and revile. They envision for American policy makers and to those in power that Islam is a frightening demon which represents what they call the green threat which they must be cautious of after the passing away of the red Communist threat. This in reality is a myth. For Islam, especially that represented by the moderate groups which we advocate, is not a danger to anyone." *al-Mujtama'* 24(1081) (December 28, 1993), p. 31.

19. David Ben-Gurion, the first prime minister of Israel, is reported to have said, "We fear nothing but Islam"; Yitzhak Rabin reportedly declared, "The religion of Islam is our only enemy"; and Shimon Peres warned, "We will not feel secure until Islam puts away its sword." 'Ali, *'Ida,* pp. 45–46.

20. 'Abd al-Hamid al-Sayeh, *Madha Ba'd Ihraq al-Masjid al-Aqsa?* (Cairo, 1970), pp. 23, 178ff.

21. Abdullah Kannun, "Al-Muslimun wa Mushkilat Filastin" in *Kitab al-Mu'tamar al-Rabi' li-Majma' al-Buhuth al-Islamiyya,* pp. 36, 38.

22. Kamel al-Baqir, "Jawhar al-Qadiyya al-Filastiniyya" [The Essence of the Palestinian Issue], in *Kitab al-Mu'tamar al-Rabi'* [Book of the Fourth Conference], p. 136.

23. Abdullah Kannun, "Makanat Bayt al-Maqdis fi al-Islam," in *Kitab al-Mu'tamar al-Rabi' li-Majma' al-Buhuth al-Islamiyya,* vol. 2, p. 39.

24. "And it was the West, champion of the separation of Church and State, cradle of secularism, that helped in the creation of this state founded on the idea of the return to the Promised Land. The intrusion of religion into politics didn't bother European socialists, nor American technocrats. Neither did it bother the atheists of Moscow who were the first to recognize the State of Israel." Habib Boulares, *Islam: The Fear and the Hope,* p. 25, as quoted in *Inquiry* 1(3) (June 1992), p. 42.

25. Muhammad M. al-Fahham, "The Restoration of Jerusalem," in *The Fifth Conference of the Academy of Islamic Research* (Cairo: Government Printing Office, 1971), p. 53.

26. Muhammad al-Ghazali, *Qadhaif al-Haqq* (Kuwait, 1984), p. 109.

27. Yvonne Yazbeck Haddad, "Operation Desert Shield/Desert Storm: The Islamist Perspective," in *Beyond the Storm,* ed. Phyllis Bennis and Michel Moushabeck (New York: Olive Branch Press, 1991), pp. 248–260.

28. See Konstantin Obradovik, ed., *The Inalienable Rights of the Palestinian People* (London: Outline Books, 1985), pp. 292–301.

29. Ibid., pp. 245–291.

30. Munir Farah, "Impact on Education," in *Occupation: Israel Over Palestine,* ed. Naseer A. Aruri (Belmont, Mass.: AAUG, 1983), pp. 295–318; and Naseer Aruri, "Universities Under Occupation," in the same volume, pp. 319–336.

31. See, for example, Hasan Khalid, "Kalimat al-Wufud" [Statement of the Delegates], *Kitab al-Mu'tamar al-Rabi': al-Muslimun wa al-'Udwan al-Israili,* vol. 2 (Cairo, 1968), p. 29.

32. Maxwell, "No Peace Until Palestine Is Free," p. 22.

33. 'Abd al-Baqi Khalifa, "al-Tatarruf: Mafahimuh . . . Asbabuh . . . Nata'ijuh . . . 'Ilajuh," *al-Mujtama'* 24(1076) (November 23, 1993).

34. Ibid.

35. al-Ghazali, *Qadhaif,* p. 223.

36. Ibid., p. 225.

37. Rachid Ghannouchi, "Islam and the West: Realities and Prospects," *Inquiry* 2(7) (March/April 1993), p. 45.

38. "The Great Betrayal," *Al-Mashriq* (January-February 1991), p. 9.

39. Ghannouchi, "Islam and the West," p. 46.

40. Ahmad Abul Jobain, *Islam Under Siege: Radical Islamic Terrorism or Political Islam?* Occasional Papers Series No. 1 (Annondale, Va.: United Association for Studies and Research, June 1993).

41. Ghannouchi, "Islam and the West," p. 46.

42. Munir Shafiq, "al-Istratijiyya al-Amerikiyya wa-Athar al-Nizam al-'Alami al-Jadid 'Ala al-'Alam al-'Arabi," *Qira'at Siyasiyya* 2(1) (Winter 1992), p. 10.

43. Ibid., p. 22.

44. Ibid., p. 19.

45. Ibid., p. 23.

46. "This is a surrender to the Jews who have assumed the power in the United States, so that the White House and those in it have become an instrument in the hand of the Jews." Unsigned editorial, "al-Wilayat al-Muttahida Taraf Munhaz Yad'am Isra'il wa-Atma'aha," *al-Majalla* 29(1299) (December 5, 1998), p. 9.

47. Boutros Boutros-Ghali, *Unvanquished: A U.S.-U.N. Saga* (New York: Random House, 1999), pp. 250–257; for press reports about the Qana massacre, see: http://almashriq. hiof.no/lebanon/300/350/355/april-war/index.html.

48. http://home.att.net/~drew.hamre/docAlb.htm.

49. Muhammad Husayn Fadlallah, *Ru'a wa Mawaqif*, vol. 3 (Beirut: al-Markaz al-Islami al-Thaqafi, 1997), p. 10.

50. Martin Indyk, "Address to the Soref Symposium, Washington Institute, May 18, 1993," p. 3.

51. Ibid., p. 8.

52. Ibid., p. 17.

53. Zaghlul al-Najjar, "Kayf Yara al-Muslimun al-Ghaarb? . . . wa-madha Yakshha al-Gharb min al-Islam? Surat al-Gharb Tarikhiyan wa-Nafsiyan 'Ind al-Muslimin," *al-Mujtama'* 29(1302) (February 6, 1998), p. 52.

54. Salim al-Hoss, "Qadiyyat al-'Arab Ba'd al-Salam," *al-Majalla* 727 (January 16–21, 1994), p. 38.

55. Unsigned editorial, "al-Wilayat al-Muttahida Taraf Munhaz Yad'am Isra'il wa-Atma'aha," *al-Majalla* 29(1299) (May 12, 1998), p. 9.

56. "Bayan Min Jam'iyyat al-Naf al-'Am bi-Munasabat Murur Khamsin 'Aman 'Ala Ightisab Filastin," *al-Mujtama'* 29(1302) (February 6, 1998), p. 14.

57. For details of the Camp David meeting, see Clayton Swisher, *The Truth About Camp David: The Untold Story About the Collapse of the Middle East Peace Process* (New York: Nation Books, 2004).

58. "President Discusses the Future of Iraq," Office of the Press Secretary, White House, February 26, 2003.

59. See, for example, the repeated references to crusader arrogance in Fathi Bakhkhush, "Daqqat Sa'at al-Jihad: al-Umma fi Khatar" [The Hour of Jihad Has Struck: The Nation Is in Danger] *Risalat al-Jihad* 9(93) (November 1990). He condemns the US-led coalition of Desert Storm: "The Crusaders have come this time with a military campaign under the leadership of oppressive America, arrogant with its devastating power" (p. 58). He also writes that the Islamic nationalist rejection of US policies in the region has enraged "oppressive American Crusaderism" because it perceives it as a "threat to its contending power and its [ability] to impose its arrogance on the world" (p. 59). He also calls the forces gathered for Desert Storm "the greatest terrorist Crusader force in history," which can only be resisted by a religious response. "If one of the characteristics of this age is that American arrogance has reached the highest peak, a parallel characteristic is the ability of armed believing nations to mire this arrogance in the dust (p. 61).

60. Yitzhak Shamir is quoted as having boasted in a radio broadcast that "he is proud of the terrorist record of the Stern Gang including the assassination of Swedish Count Bernadotte on a United Nations Peace Mission in 1948, the assassination of Lord Moyen, the British Minister of State for Middle East Affairs, and the massacre of Deir Yasin." See "Kalla al-Sihuniyya Haraka 'Unsuriyya" [No, Zionism Is a Racist Movement] *Risalat al-Jihad* 10(103) (October 1991), p. 6. Cf.: "The Israeli enemy backed by the forces of imperialism, never ceases to disclose his real designs which are no less than wresting more Arab territories, and thereby impudently paying no heed to the legitimate rights of the Palestinian people." Abdul-Aziz Kamel, "The Opening Address," *Sixth Conference of the Academy of Islamic Research* (Cairo: al-Azhar, 1971), p. 17. Abba Eban, former Israeli ambassador to the United Nations, was reported to have said, "If the General Assembly were to vote by 121 votes to 1 in favor of Israel returning to the Armistice lines . . . Israel would refuse to comply with that decision." *New York Times,* June 19, 1967.

Several examples are cited by Fahmi al-Huwaidi, the popular Egyptian journalist, including the following: "The most recent example of 'good intent' comes from Morocco during the middle of January when the Moroccan government handed Israel the remains of Jews who drowned when their boat overturned while attempting to flee to Israel in the fifties. Israel's response to this gesture was insolent and in bad taste. It marked the event by placing a cornerstone for the erection of a monument to commemorate the victims in Maaleh Edumim, the large settlement established between Jerusalem and Jericho in the West Bank and which the Palestinians seek to have removed." Fahmi al-Huwaidi, "Bayn Bolard wa al-Shaykh Ahmad Yasin: Jawasisuhum Lahum Thaman wa-Munadiluna bila Thaman!" *al-Majalla* 729 (January 30–February 5, 1994), p. 34.

61. Rashid Qabbani, "al-Gharb Yamuddu Isra'il bi-kul Aslihat al-Damar al Shamil," *al-Mujtama'* 29(1299) (May 12–18, 1998), p. 25.

62. In his February 7 (broadcast on February 8), 2004, hour-long Oval Office interview with Tim Russert on NBC's *Meet the Press* (http://www.americanprogress.org/site/pp.asp?c=biJRJ8OVF&b=28200&printmode=1), President Bush declared himself to be a "war president." Bush: "I'm a war president. I make decisions here in the Oval Office in foreign-policy matters with war on my mind. Again, I wish it wasn't true, but it is true. And the American people need to know they got a president who sees the world the way it is. And I see dangers that exist, and it's important for us to deal with them."

63. Grant F. Smith, *Deadly Dogma: How Neoconservatives Broke the Law to Deceive America* (Washington, DC: Middle East Policy, 2006).

64. Al-Rifa'i and Qubaisi, *Amerka*, p. 256. See also Muhammad Hasanain Haykal, *Al-Imbaratoriyya al-Amerikiyya wa Ighara ala al-Iraq* (Cairo: Dar al-Shuruq, 2003), pp. 239, 255.

65. Isam Na'man, *Al-Arab Ala Muftaraq Istishraf Tahadiyyat ma Ba'd September 11, 2001* (Cairo: Sharikat al-Matbu'at li al-Tawzi' wa al-Nashr, 2002), pp. 23–24.

66. Al-Rifa'i and Qubaisi, *Amerka*, pp. 238.

67. Osama Ibrahim Hafiz and Asim Abd al-Majid Muhammad, *Mubadarat Waqf al-Unf: Ru'ya Waqi'iyya wa Nazra Shar'iyya* (Cairo: Islamic Turath Bookshop, 2002). For publications against violence after 9/11 by the same press, see Hamdi Abd al-Rahman al-Azim, Najih Ibrahim Abdullah and Ali Muhammad Ali al-Sharif, *Taslit al-Adwa Ala ma Waqa' fi al-Jihad min Akhta*, 2002; Najih Ibrahim Abdullah and Ali Muhammad Ali al-Sharif, *Hurmat al-Ghulu fi al-Din wa-Takfir al-Muslimin*, 2002; Ali Muhammad Ali al-Sharif and Osama Ibrahim Hafiz, *al-Nusuh wa al-Tabyin fi Tashih Mafahim al-Muhtasibin*, 2002; Karam Muhammad Zuhdi, Najih Ibrahim Abdullah, Ali Muhammad Ali Sharif, Osama Ibrahim Hafiz, Hamdi Abd al-Rahman Abd al-Azim, Fuad Muhammad al-Dualibi, Asim Abd al-Majid Muhammad, and Muhammad Isam al-Din Dirbala, *Tafjirat al-Riyad: al-Ahkam wa al-Athar*, 2003; Karam Muhammad Zuhdi, Najih Ibrahim Abdullah, Ali Muhammad Ali Sharif, Osama Ibrahim Hafiz, Hamdi Abd al-Rahman Abd al-Azim, Fuad Muhammad al-Dualibi, Asim Abd al-Majid Muhammad, and Muhammad Isam al-Din Dirbala, *Istratijiyyat Tafjirat al-Qa'ida: Al-Akhta wa al-Akhtar*, 2004. For a detailed memoir detailing the activities of al-Jama'at al-Islamiyya, see Muntasir al-Zayyat, *al-Jama'at al-Islamiyya: Riwaya min al-Dakhil* (Cairo: Dar Misr al-Mahrusa, 2005).

68. Karam Muhammad Zuhdi, Najih Ibrahim Abdullah, Ali Muhammad Ali Sharif, Osama Ibrahim Hafiz, Hamdi Abd al-Rahman Abd al-Azim, Fuad Muhammad al-Dualibi, Asim Abd al-Majid Muhammad, and Muhammad Isam al-Din Dirbala, *Tafjirat al-Riyad: al-Ahkam wa al-Athar* (Cairo: Maktabat al-Turath al-Islami, 2003), p. 52.

69. Zuhdi et al., *Tafjirat al-Riyad*, p. 40.

70. Ibid., p. 116.

71. Public Law 107–245, October 21, 2002.

72. Public Law 105–338, October 31, 1998.

73. Public Law 108–175, December 12, 2003.

74. Zuhdi et al., *Tafjirat al-Riyad,* p. 12.

75. Al-Rifa'i and Qubaisi, *Amerka,* pp. 299–300.

76. "Remarks by the President at the 20th Anniversary of the National Endowment for Democracy, US Chamber of Commerce," White House, November 6, 2003.

77. For an extensive discussion of the topic, see Al-Rifa'i and Qubaisi, *Amerka.*

78. Shimon Peres and Arye Naor, *The New Middle East* (New York: Henry Holt, 1993).

79. Al-Rifa'i and Qubaisi, *Amerka,* p. 256. See also Muhammad Hasanain Haykal, *Al-Imbaratoriyya al-Amerikiyya wa Ighara ala al-Iraq* (Cairo: Dar al-Shuruq, 2003), p. 290.

80. Al-Rifa'i and Qubaisi, *Amerka,* pp. 36, 152.

81. Ibid., p. 238.

Postscript

Americans and the Muslim World— First Encounters

Robert J. Allison

Before the geographic area we now call the Middle East was called the Middle East, before the British colonies on the North American mainland became the United States, and before petroleum powered the world's economy, Americans and Muslims had a strange and profound encounter. This encounter was part of the long afterglow of the Crusades, as when English mercenary John Smith, fighting for the Austrians against the Ottoman Turks, was captured in Transylvania. Smith killed his Muslim captor and escaped, returning by way of Russia to England, which he left again, this time to sail west and found the colony of Jamestown. In 1645, as novelist and naval historian James Fenimore Cooper tells us, a ship built in Cambridge, Massachusetts, fought an Algerian ship in the Atlantic, in what Cooper called the first American naval battle. In the 1680s, New Yorkers raised money to redeem sailors captured in North Africa, and in 1700, an American sailor returned to Boston from captivity in Algiers. The Puritan clergy used his story of captivity and resistance to Islam to bolster the faith of their flocks.

Eighteenth-century American and European literature made the Muslim world a counterpoint to the idea of individual autonomy, the central feature of the emerging American ideology. Political writers, such as John Trenchard and Thomas Gordon in England, the authors of *Cato's Letters,* and Charles Secondat Montesquieu in France, author of the *Persian Letters* and *Spirit of the Laws,* used Muslim states such as Morocco, Turkey, and Algiers as examples of how not to construct political societies. The American colonists who rebelled against England in 1776 and then set to forming their own political society had not only read these books, but they had incorporated them into their way of thinking. In the Barbary states of North Africa, and in the Ottoman Empire, at least as it was presented to them by European writers, Americans saw an example of the kind of political society they did not want to create.

Travelers and other observers saw signs of decay in Muslim societies, and Americans were determined to avoid the causes and thus prevent the symptoms. The most influential book on the subject was the Abbé Volney's *The Ruins, or a Survey of the Revolution of Empires* (1792), a meditative reflection drawn from his travels in Egypt and Syria. *The Ruins* speculated on how the great Mesopotamian civilization came to collapse, and Volney found the answer in political intolerance fed by religious fanaticism. President Thomas Jefferson found Volney's *Ruins* so important that he undertook to translate it, enlisting the help of American diplomat and poet Joel Barlow.

This ideological picture of the Muslim world was colored by the experiences of American sailors held captive in Algiers, Tripoli, and Morocco. Between 1785 and 1815, a dozen American ships were captured by the North African states, who held the sailors hostage. This captivity forced American leaders to grapple with a variety of problems: What was the responsibility of the US government to its citizens? Should the United States pay ransom for citizens held captive? Should the United States pay tribute to foreign powers in order to protect its citizens? Different American leaders had different responses to these questions. John Adams calculated that paying tribute to Algiers would be less expensive than fighting a war, that Americans were the most reluctant people on earth to pay the kind of taxes that would be required to build a navy, and since Britain and France paid tribute to Algiers, there was no harm in the Americans emulating their example. Thomas Jefferson, on the other hand, believed it would be essential to American liberty to fight Algiers and Tripoli, not only to protect American citizens but to demonstrate to England and France that the Americans were a different sort of people, who would not engage in the kind of corrupt diplomacy of Europe. Jefferson's assertion of America's "difference" won the day, and one of his administration's first acts in 1801 was to send an American fleet to the Mediterranean to blockade Tripoli. The pope praised the American navy for subduing Tripoli, accomplishing what the Christian nations of Europe had been unable, or unwilling, to do.

The captivity of American sailors in Algiers raised another issue, directly related to the idea that Americans were less corrupt and more noble than Europeans and that the Americans had created a political society whose virtue would endure forever. The Americans who wrote about their captivity in Algiers called the experience slavery. The irony of Americans being held as "slaves" in Africa was lost on very few. Benjamin Franklin's last published work was a parody of a Georgia congressman's defense of African slavery in America, putting the Georgian's words in the mouth of a Muslim official justifying the enslavement of Christians in Algiers. Royall Tyler, author of the first American play, wrote a novel entitled *The Algerine Captive,* connecting American captivity in Algiers to American complicity in the African slave trade.[1]

American misunderstanding of the Muslim world rested on a profound ignorance of the Islamic religion, Muslim society, and the wild misinterpretations of the prophet Muhammad, who was known to eighteenth-century European and American writers as "Mahomet." Puritan minister Cotton Mather contrasted the liberty with which Europeans and Americans could reason with the tyranny of Muslim society. Heaven shone on *"our Parts of the Earth"* in allowing "Improvements of our *modern Philosophy,*" while no follower of the "thick-skull'd Prophet" was permitted to question the scientific truths revealed to Muhammad.[2]

We do not know where Mather learned about Muhammad, but the only English-language biography of Muhammad had been written in 1697 by Anglican clergyman Humphrey Prideaux. Prideaux's interest in Muhammad was only coincidental to his real purpose, which was to expose the folly of religious indifference. Prideaux had planned to write a major work on Constantinople's fall to the Muslims in 1453. But his growing alarm at the state of English society, the "giddy humour" with which too many young people embraced "fashion and vogue" rather than religion, and the ease with which men and women criticized the church, alarmed Prideaux, and he wrote his book on Muhammad as a sober warning. Mecca had been a prosperous trading town, the people had been more attentive to their commercial interests than to their spiritual needs, they had allowed the faith of their fathers to degenerate, and Muhammad had exploited their religious laxity to impose his own religious and political agenda. The Muhammad emerging from Prideaux's work, and from the other English-language tracts on Islam, was an ambitious man. His ambition found a religious outlet, and the Meccan merchants' religious indifference allowed him to secure his religious tyranny.[3]

Prideaux's "Mahomet" was a warning sign in the young American republic of the 1790s. Many Americans welcomed the French revolution that enshrined liberty and reason in the place of monarchy and tradition. But others worried about the consequences, and in France's revolution they saw an anarchy that would ultimately be replaced by a tyrant. Vice President John Adams reached back into French history, writing a series of essays warning about the consequences of anarchy and disorder. In England, Edmund Burke warned in *Reflections on the Revolution in France* that liberty would be the victim of equality. Thomas Paine responded to Burke with his *Vindication of the Rights of Man,* which seemed, on its arrival in America, to be as much an answer to Adams as to Burke. Secretary of State Thomas Jefferson had an advance copy of Paine's pamphlet and sent it to the printer with a note praising Paine's attack on "the political heresies" that had lately sprung up, confident that "our citizens would rally again round the standard of common sense." Paine's book was printed in America with Jefferson's endorsement on the cover. American readers took Jefferson's jab at "political heresies" as a reference to Vice President Adams. In response to this perceived attack on Adams, his son, John Quincy, writing under the name Publicola, compared Jefferson to "the Arabian prophet" who called on "all true believers in the Islam of democracy to draw their swords," and paraphrasing the Muslim creed "There is no God but Allah, and Muhammad is his Prophet," the younger Adams had Jefferson and his zealous supporters shouting, "There is but one Goddess of Liberty, and Common Sense is her prophet."[4]

The situation seemed similar to that of seventh-century Mecca. Jefferson was a well-born, respectable man like Prideaux's Muhammad, but by countenancing the free thought of Thomas Paine and others, he would ultimately destroy the liberty he pretended to defend. In 1795, a Philadelphia publisher specializing in religious works published the first American edition of Prideaux's *Life of Mahomet,* and Prideaux's preface, warning of the dangers of infidelity and religious indifference, seemed especially pertinent in the new nation.

But this was not the only possible reading of Prideaux's *Mahomet.* The Adams administration, which took office in 1797, tried to quell the political storm by imposing a sedition act, making it a crime to criticize or bring ridicule upon the president. One of the fifteen victims of the act was Vermont Congressman Mathew Lyon, who was sent to federal prison for suggesting that President Adams appointed men to office for their political loyalty rather than their accomplishments and that the president was fond of pomp and parade. (Lyon was reelected to Congress while in prison.) Having seen how far criticizing the president directly would take him, Lyon's son James, a printer, launched an indirect criticism. While his father was in jail, James Lyon published the second American edition of Prideaux's *Life of Mahomet,* this one without the preface warning of infidelity. Without this preface, the book takes on a different cast, and the Mahomet is a religious zealot who will tolerate no opposition and forbids "all manner of disputing about his religion," just as Adams and the Federalists had forbidden political disputes. Prideaux's conclusion could not have been more eloquently phrased for Lyon's purpose: "And certainly there could not be a wiser way devised for upholding of so absurd an imposture than by thus silencing, under so severe a penalty, all manner of opposition and disputes concerning it."[5] If Lyon had said this, his prison term would have been extended.

A second biography of Muhammad appeared in America in 1802, with the descriptive title *The Life of Mahomet; or, the History of that Imposture which was begun, carried on, and finally established by him in Arabia: and which has Subjugated a Larger Portion of the Globe, than the Religion of Jesus has yet set at Liberty.* The anonymous author found Islam to be "deeply affecting to a Philanthropic heart," as it degraded men and women "to the rank of brutes by the consummate artifice and wickedness" that had been created by one man, the prophet Muhammad. Islam had so depraved its adherents that this author thought they could be saved only by Christian conquest to free them from "that system of blasphemy and iniquity by which they are at present enslaved." Missionaries and teachers would be helpless against the rulers who used "carnal weapons" on their subjects and respected no argument but force.[6]

Muslim societies were more than distant symbols. In 1785 and 1793, Algiers captured a dozen American ships and held over one hundred American sailors captive. In this crisis, Susanna Rowson, an English actress living in America, wrote a play, *Slaves in Algiers, or, a Struggle for Freedom.* Loosely basing it on Cervantes's *Il Cautivo,* Mrs. Rowson added a tangled family dynamic to make her story current with an American audience. Although the Western characters Constant, Augustus, Olivia, and Rebecca are essential to the plot, the story centers on Fetnah, who has been sold into the dey's harem by her father, the merchant Ben Hassan, who began his career as a London rag merchant and had betrayed everything in his quest for wealth—he had left England for Algiers, had converted from Judaism to Islam, and finally had sold his daughter to the dey because he and Fetnah's mother "loved gold better than they did their child."[7]

Ben Hassan will do anything for money; Fetnah, though the Dey's "chosen favorite," laments her imprisonment in the splendid palace. "I like them very well," she says of the luxury surrounding her, "but I don't like to be confined." She asks, is "the poor bird that is confined in a cage [because it is a favorite with its enslaver] consoled for the loss of freedom? No! tho' its prison is of golden wire, its food delicious, and it is overwhelmed with caresses, its little heart still pants for liberty: gladly would it seek the fields of air, and even perched upon a naked bough, exulting, carrol forth its song, nor once regret the splendid house of bondage."

Fortunately for Fetnah, at this moment Rebecca arrives in Algiers "from that land where virtue in either sex is the only mark of superiority. . . . She was an American." Rebecca, also consigned to the dey's seraglio, assures Fetnah that "woman was never formed to be the abject slave of man" and stirs Fetnah's natural love of liberty. Fetnah declares, "I feel that I was born free, and while I have life, I will struggle to remain so." Fetnah accepts the struggle, and the virtuous Americans even convince the dey to accept it, telling him to "sink the name of subject in the endearing epithet of fellow-citizen," and he agrees to "reject all power but such as my united friends shall think me incapable of abusing." The Americans tell the dey to prove by his conduct "how much you value the welfare of your fellow creatures," as they return to the land "where liberty has established her court," hoping for the day when "Freedom" will "spread her benign influence" through every nation.[8]

The Americans in Susanna Rowson's play are great teachers, teaching the dey how to be a better ruler and teaching the people of Algiers to be good citizens. The American war against Tripoli (1801–1805) gave the Americans more opportunities to teach the lesson of American prowess and virtue. From the first naval engagement in August 1801 until the peace treaty was signed in June 1805, Americans regarded the war as a constant lesson in their own distinctive national character. President Jefferson was determined to cut the American military budget, to chastise Tripoli, and to do both as a lesson to European nations on proper modes of international conduct. Jefferson's decision to blockade Tripoli rather than launch a direct attack and to blockade using the smallest possible force led to disaster, as the *Philadelphia,* the second-largest ship in the American fleet, ran aground off Tripoli in October 1803. But the navy turned this disaster into a triumph, as Lieutenant Stephen Decatur and a small crew disguised themselves and a captured Tripolitan vessel and sailed into Tripoli harbor in February 1804, destroying the *Philadelphia* without losing a man. Americans saw Decatur's deed as evidence of their own prowess and courage. The naval bombardment of Tripoli in August 1804 gave further proof of American courage, and when Tripoli and the United States signed the treaty on board the USS *Constitution* (the first time a Barbary state signed a treaty on an enemy warship), it confirmed for Americans their new place in the world.[9]

Barely a year after the war began, a play conveying this message was performed on the New York stage. No copies survive of *The Tripolitan Prize, or, American Tars on an English Shore*. We know it only from a caustic review by Washington Irving. The American tars reach the English shore after being chased by a Tripolitan ship—it seems a violent storm in the Mediterranean sent both ships to the English channel, where they fight it out. Improbable as this may have been, it allowed the Americans to win their battle against Tripoli within sight of England, and on the stage, crowds of Englishmen and women watched the American victory. Irving noted with sarcastic disgust that the American audience, particularly those in the galleries, spent the entire play "hallooing and huzzaing" the American captain and his crew on stage. The captain bellowed at one point, "What! an American Tar desert his duty!" and the American audience responded "Impossible! American Tars forever! True blue will never stain!!" The battle, Irving wrote, was "conducted with proper decency and decorum," after which "the Tripolitan very politely gave in—as it would be indecent to conquer in the face of an American audience."10

We do not have such rich records of the audience response to other literature written in response to the Tripolitan war. But these cultural effusions—plays, poetry, novels, and paintings—all convey the same themes the audience celebrated in *The Tripolitan Prize* and *Slaves in Algiers*. Joseph Hanson's 1806 poem, *The Musselmen Humbled, or a Heroic Poem in Celebration of the Bravery Displayed by the American Tars, in the Contest with Tripoli*, said that the Americans had won the war against Tripoli as they were armed with "the formidable powers of justice and freedom," which gave them "that invincible courage, which terrified and overcame the plundering vassals of the tyrannical bashaw." Hanson asked, "[W]hat can be effected by the slaves of tyrants? who fight for plunder and despotic masters: who defend no laws, but such as are oppressive; and protect no pow'r, but that which disrespects 'em."11

An 1812 play by Bostonian James Ellison, *The American Captive, or Siege of Tripoli,* saw this same reason for the American victory. In the play, Abdel Mahadi had seized power in Tripoli from his older brother, Ali ben Mahadi, whom he said was too weak to rule. Ali was "too mild to reign," he had "courted peace, and peace attain'd created heavy taxes!" Instead of peace, Ali should have "courted the crimson hand of war." Abdel, on the other hand, will use "*plunder*" to preserve his power and save his subjects from "that damn'd abyss, to which my brother's mild and milky reign had doom'd them." Plunder alone "can prop our sinking realm" and save it from the "misery and want" brought by peace. Ali's daughter, Immorina, and her fiancé lament this triumph of "*ambition*" over "*virtue*," taking solace that while "*crime* may for a season triumph," only "*virtue*" can secure "a monarch's bliss, his count[r]y's welfare, and his subjects' love."12

As in Rowson's *Slaves in Algiers,* this debate on internal affairs is enriched by the arrival of American captives. In this play, one of Abdel's cruisers has captured an American ship. The arrival of Americans causes great excitement in Tripoli, as one Tripolitan woman asks Immorina, "Do you know what *Americans* are?" Immorina answers, "*Men*, are they not, like other men?" "Pshaw," the old woman says, the Americans are "*Indians!* Yes indeed, *Indians!*" They would scalp any man or woman they caught, "and I'm sure this proves them not to be *men*." Immorina corrects her.

The Indians, she says, are the natives of America but only "inhabit the western regions of that vast country, and are savage, and barbarous, like our wild Arabs." On the other hand, "those whom we denominate Americans" are like the Europeans in "customs and manners," are civilized, polished, enterprizing, brave, and hospitable.[13]

The civilized, polished, enterprising, brave, and hospitable Americans are represented in this play by Captain Anderson, the captured master of the ship. Anderson and Abdel form a striking contrast of American and Tripolitan power. In their first meeting, Abdel is decked out in a "sumptuous Turkish habit," his turban decorated with a large diamond crescent, his jeweled sash barely hiding the dagger on his hip. Abdel asks Anderson if his father is a noble. Anderson replies, "If to be the son of him who served his country, in the time of peril, be that which you call noble, I am of the most noble extraction, but if, from pamper'd lords and vicious princes, alone descend the gift, then I am not." Anderson's father bore "the proudest title man can have"—he was "An honest man."[14]

Anderson contrasts not only with the corrupt and gaudy Abdel but also with other American characters in the play. Jack Binnacle, one of Anderson's crew, wonders why the United States does not simply "blow Algiers, Tunis, and Tripoli up, and put an end to these nests of pirates?" Anderson applauds Binnacle's spirit and pledges to "fight till my heart-strings snap" rather than "be tributary to any nation," but he wants a permanent solution. Simply destroying the coastal cities would allow marauders like Abdel to move into the interior. Anderson wants to reform Tripoli so tyrants like Abdel cannot flourish. Anderson's plan, carried out with the help of Princess Immorina and the Jew Ishmael, is to escape from Tripoli, secure support from the navy for the deposed Ali, who will return to power and end the depraved power of Abdel once and for all.[15]

To the tune of "Washington's March," Anderson and Ali return to Tripoli, and Anderson prays "to be granted that heroic courage, that energy of soul, which so distinguish'd the father of my country, the matchless hero of the western world." Anderson kills the despotic Abdel, declaring that "*A slave* has power to strike a *tyrant* dead." Although Immorina tells Anderson that he now ranks "among the Prophets," the American is more interested in being placed alongside Washington.[16]

As in Susanna Rowson's *Slaves in Algiers,* and *The Tripolitan Prize,* Anderson in *The American Captive* teaches the Muslim tyrant a lesson. A contemporary American songwriter promised that if any despot dared insult the American flag, "We'll send them Decatur to teach them 'Good Manners.'"[17]

And yet some American writers questioned the ability of their country to teach moral lessons to others. In the spring of 1787, while her father, the American minister to France, toured the southern part of that country, sixteen-year-old Martha Jefferson wrote to keep him informed of events in the world. Germany, Russia, and Venice, she reported, were at war against Turkey, and the plague had struck in Spain. She only briefly mentioned these world events, but then she found a story that captured her interest. "A virginia ship comming to spain," she wrote, "met with a [Algerian] corser of the same strength. They fought and the battle lasted an hour and a quarter. The Americans gained and boarded the corser where they found chains that had been prepared for them. They took them and made use of them for the algerians themselves." Martha saw the irony in this turn of events. But instead of relishing the American victory, she saw only compounded tragedy. "They returned to virginia from whence they are to go back to algers to change the prisoners to which if the algerians will not consent the poor creatures will be sold as slaves." The Algerians had wanted to enslave the Americans, a fact that might have justified their own enslavement. But not to Martha Jefferson, who asked her father, "Good god have we not enough? I wish with all my soul that the poor negroes were all freed. It greives my heart when I think that these our fellow creatures should be treated so terribly as they are by many of our countrymen."[18]

The capture of American sailors, who were put to work in Algiers or Tripoli, touched Americans' consciences. The plight of these "slaves" in Algiers and Tripoli stirred Americans to raise money for their redemption. The Americans could boast that they had created a society different from the tyrannies of the Old World, but the captivity of Americans in North Africa reminded them that this was not the case. In Ellison's *The American Captive,* Jack Binnacle, a captive sailor, tells Hassan the overseer about America. "It's a charming place, Mr. Overseer; no *slavery* there! All freeborn sons!" Hassan answers, "No Slavery, hey? Go where the Senegal winds its course, and ask the wretched mothers for their husbands and their sons! What will be their answer? *Doom'd to slavery, and in thy boasted country, too!*"[19]

A New England newspaper ran an item in 1794 headed "Profession versus Practice," a satire on fugitive slave ads, and an attack on "ranting southern demagogues," like Thomas Jefferson, who preached "*universal equality*" while practicing "*piratical barbarity.*" The ad promised a reward for the return of an "American slave" to his master, "Ibrahim Ali Bey" of Algiers. It described the slave as an "ungrateful Villain" and "incorrigible infidel," who refused to renounce "his Christian errors" and had escaped with a "borrowed" manumission certificate. Freed slaves, the ad warned, were lending their freedom papers to other slaves, who used this "new invented species of *robbery*" to escape. How odd, the ad concluded, that these Christians would think this sharing was "*meritorious.* What strange, absurd ideas the Christians must have of *merit.*"[20]

The true story of a free black man helping an enslaved African escape appeared in several New England papers in 1795 and was paired with the story of an American captive redeemed from Algiers. Cato Mungo, reportedly an African prince, was returned by benevolent friends to Ouidah, in West Africa, and George Burnham, an American captain from New York, was ransomed by friends in 1794. Cato Mungo and George Burnham's stories were paired under the heading "Curses of Slavery," and the pairing made Burnham's suffering seem slight. Cato Mungo gave a "long and melancholy account of the treatment of the poor Africans in that land of cruelty" and suggested that Africans take "some measures" to redeem "such of our brethren as it would be in our power to restore to their families and connections." He repeated in horror that "several of the Royal family of this kingdom" were now "doing drudgery in the kitchens of the *United States!!!*"[21]

Cato Mungo had been helped to escape by Mawyaw, a free black man living in Connecticut, where slavery was still legal. Although slaves in Connecticut were treated more decently than were slaves in other states, they were still slaves. Mawyaw had helped Cato Mungo escape to Massachusetts, where slavery had been abolished in 1783. Connecticut's legislature had recently rejected an emancipation plan, Mawyaw reported, allowing "self-interest" to check its benevolence. Although the state was giving away millions of dollars' worth of public lands, "their souls were not large enough" to free African slaves. The legislators "did not think themselves justifiable in taking away the property of individuals," Mawyaw reported. He was not surprised: He noted that Americans "could not find in themselves generosity enough" to redeem their countrymen "now in slavery in the kingdom of Algiers." Americans were in no position to assert their moral superiority to the Algerians.

Benjamin Franklin's last published essay carried this same theme. Franklin, as president of Pennsylvania's antislavery society, had signed a petition to Congress in 1790 calling for an end to the slave trade. Franklin may have expected this to be his last public act. But a Georgia congressman, James Jackson, took to the floor of the House to denounce Franklin for suggesting that slavery was morally wrong. Jackson blasted Franklin and the Quakers, who had also submitted an antislavery petition, for being overzealous moral meddlers whose ignorant and misguided efforts at reform would undermine both the American economy and the well-being of the slaves. Slavery, Jackson said, was justified by religion, economics, politics, and history. The Georgians who enslaved Africans lifted their slaves out of barbarism and taught them the Christian virtues. If the slaves were freed, Jackson said, it would ruin Georgia's economy, since no one would work in the rice fields and these blacks would not work unless they were forced to do so. And what would happen to the freed people? They would not stay and work, and if they moved to the frontier, the Indians would kill them. Georgia's keeping of slaves was the benevolent option, as it taught slaves Christianity and allowed them to cultivate Georgia's rice.

Franklin read Jackson's speech in the *Federal Gazette* in March 1790. Franklin knew he had to reply. No American political leader had ever publicly said that slavery was a good thing: all had been committed to its extinction. Jackson's speech marked a change. Franklin knew he had to respond. Franklin had written his first newspaper essay more than seventy years earlier, had later tangled with Cotton Mather and the British ministry in print, and knew how to devastate an adversary. He wrote his response to Jackson under the name "Historicus" and said he liked Jackson's speech very much. It reminded him of something he had read many years before, a speech given by the dey of Algiers.

Sidi Mehemet Ibrahim, the dey of Algiers, had given a speech similar to Jackson's in 1687. Franklin said he had read it in a book called *Martin's Account of his Consulship.*[22] The dey was provoked by a group of religious zealots, the Erika, or "Purists," who had petitioned Sidi Mehemet to abolish Christian slavery and piracy, which the Erika said were unjust and against the teachings of the Qur'an. Franklin then quoted Sidi Mehemet's speech, which turned out to be James Jackson's speech, with Erika substituted for Quakers and Christian slaves substituted for Africans. James

Jackson's argument justifying the slavery of Africans in America also justified the enslavement of Americans in Africa.

Algiers should not give up enslaving Christians, Sidi Mehemet warned, as it would ruin the nation's economy merely to gratify "the whims of a whimsical sect." He asked, "If we forbear to make slaves" of Christians, "who in this hot climate are to cultivate our lands? Must we not then be our own slaves?" As for the freed slaves, Sidi Mehemet and Jackson both feared they would not easily make the transformation to freedom. If the Christians stayed, they could not be considered the equals of Muslims. They would not "embrace our holy religion; they will not adopt our manners; our people will not pollute themselves by intermarrying with them."

They would become "beggars in our streets" and would pillage Algerian property. They would not work unless they were forced to do so, and if sent to the frontiers, they were too ignorant to establish a "good government" and would be massacred by wild Arabs. They were not to blame for their ignorance or weakness—these were traits they brought with them from their backward homelands, where most peasants, Spanish, Portuguese, French, and Italian, were treated as slaves. The Algerians had improved their lives by allowing them to work "where the sun of Islamism gives forth its light." Sending the freed people home would be denying them this benefit; it would send them "out of light into darkness."

After listening to Sidi Mehemet's arguments, the leaders of Algiers decided, according to Historicus, that to go on record as saying that slavery violated moral law was "at best *problematical.*" Algiers would hold on to slavery, and so, in 1790, would the United States. Franklin had made up the Erika, Sidi Mehemet, and *Martin's Account of his Consulship.* But unfortunately, he had not made up James Jackson. The similarities between Jackson's real speech and Sidi Mehemet's fictional one showed that "men's interests and intellects operate and are operated on with surprising similarity in all countries and climates, whenever they are under similar circumstances."

Franklin knew this better than most of his countrymen. They thought they had seen in the Muslim world all that they hoped to avoid in the new world: political and religious tyranny, subjugation of women, and craven self-interest. They also believed that they had created a political system that would prevent these evils, or at least hold them in check. Americans had developed an image of themselves and their society by looking at the Muslim world, holding an image of people and places that helped them, they thought, construct their own nation and identity. But Franklin told them their image of themselves was wrong, only partly because they carried in their heads a hopelessly distorted picture of Muslim history and society.

Notes

1. For more on these themes, see Robert J. Allison, *The Crescent Obscured: The United States and the Muslim World, 1776–1820* (New York: Oxford University Press, 1995); Ray Watkins Irwin, *The Diplomatic Relations of the United States with the Barbary Powers, 1776–1816* (Chapel Hill: University of North Carolina Press, 1931); and James Field, *America and the Mediterranean World, 1776–1882* (Princeton: Princeton University Press, 1969).

On the general perceptions of Islam in the West, see Norman Daniel, *Islam and the West: The Making of an Image* (Oxford: Oneworld, 1993).

2. Cotton Mather, "The Christian Philosopher" [1721] reprinted in *Cotton Mather* (n.p.).

3. Humphrey Prideaux, *The History of the Life of the Great Imposter Mahomet* (Philadelphia: Stewart and Cochran, 1796), 2–3.

4. Merrill D. Peterson, *Thomas Jefferson and the New Nation: A Biography* (New York: Oxford University Press, 1970), 438, 440.

5. Humphrey Prideaux, *The True Nature of Imposture, Fully Displayed in the Life of Mahomet* (Fairhaven, Vt.: James Lyon, 1798), 76–77.

6. *The Life of Mahomet; or, the History of that Imposture which was Begun Carried on, and Finally Established by Him in Arabia; and Which has Subjugated a Larger Potion of the Globe, than the Religion of Jesus has Yet Set at Liberty. To Which is Added, an Account of Egypt* (Worcester, Mass.: n.p., 1802), 83–84, 85.

7. Susanna Haswell Rowson, *Slaves in Algiers, or a Struggle for Freedom* (Philadelphia: n.p., 1794), 5.

8. Ibid., 9 10, 65 68, 71, 72.

9. For a striking example of this, see the song written by Francis Scott Key honoring the heroes of Tripoli, which in verse and cadence became the foundation of the "Star-Spangled Banner," which he wrote a few years later during the War of 1812 against England. Allison, 204–206.

10. Irving's review from the *New York Morning Chronicle,* quoted in William Dunlap, *History of the American Theatre* (New York: J. and J. Harper, 1832), 301–302.

11. Joseph Hanson, *The Musselmen Humbled; or a Heroic Poem in Celebration of the Bravery Displayed by the American Tars, in the Contest with Tripoli* (New York: n.p., 1806), 3, 7–9.

12. James Ellison, *The American Captive, or Siege of Tripoli* (Boston: n.p., 1812), 9, 12, 35.

13. Ibid., 24–25.

14. Ibid., 20–21.

15. Ibid., 18–19, 37–38.

16. Ibid., 34, 51.

17. *New York Evening Post,* 15 March 1806.

18. Martha Jefferson to Thomas Jefferson, Paris, 3 May 1787. *Papers of Thomas Jefferson,* Julian Boyd et al., eds. (Princeton University Press, 1950), 11:334.

19. Ellison, *American Captive,* 37–38.

20. "Profession vs. Practice," Boston *Federal Orrery,* 24 November 1794; Boston *Mercury,* 25 November 1794; Newburyport *Morning Star,* 26 November 1794.

21. "Curses of Slavery," *Rural Magazine, or Vermont Repository* (March 1795), 118–124. Cato Mungo's story was reprinted in Salem *Gazette,* 13 January 1795; Boston *Federal Orrery,* 29 January 1795; Portsmouth *Oracle of the Day,* 31 January 1795. For African Muslims enslaved in America, see Allan D. Austin, *African Muslims in Ante-Bellum America* (New York: Routledge, 1996).

22. Benjamin Franklin, "On the Slave Trade," *The Works of Benjamin Franklin,* Jared Sparks, ed. (London: Benjamin Franklin Stevens, 1882), 2:517–521.

About the Editor and Contributors

Ali R. Abootalebi is associate professor of Middle Eastern and international studies at the University of Wisconsin-Eau Claire. He is author of *Islam and Democracy: State-Society Relations in Developing Countries, 1980–1994* (2000).

Erika Alin is associate professor of political science at Hamline College in St. Paul, Minnesota. Her publications include *The United States and the 1958 Lebanon Crisis: American Intervention in the Middle East* (1995).

Robert J. Allison chairs the History Department at Suffolk University in Boston. He is the author of *The Crescent Obscured: The United States and the Muslim World, 1776–1815* (2000) and *Stephen Decatur: American Naval Hero 1779–1820* (2005).

Jon B. Alterman is director of the Middle East program at the Center for Strategic and International Studies in Washington.

Amatzia Baram is an associate professor in the Department of Middle Eastern History and director of the Jewish-Arab and Middle East Research Centers at the University of Haifa. Among his publications are *Culture, History, and Ideology in the Formation of Ba'thist Iraq, 1968–1989* (1991) and *Building Toward Crisis: Sadam Husayn's Strategy for Survival* (1998).

Henri J. Barkey is the Bernard and Bertha Cohen Professor of International Relations at Lehigh University. Most recently he served on the US State Department's Policy Planning Staff (1998–2000), working on issues related to the Eastern Mediterranean and the Middle East. His numerous works include *Turkey's Kurdish Question* (with Graham Fuller, 1998), and *Turkey and Iraq: The Perils (and Prospects) of Proximity* (2005).

JoAnn A. DiGeorgio-Lutz is an associate professor of political science at Texas A&M University-Commerce. A specialist on the PLO, she has published articles in *Mediterranean Quarterly* and *International Studies Quarterly*.

Sir Sam Falle is a retired British diplomat. He served in Iran from 1949 to 1952, in Lebanon from 1952 to 1955, on the Middle East oil desk in London from 1955 to 1957, and in Iraq from 1957 to 1961. He was ambassador to Kuwait from 1969 to 1970, and he has also been ambassador to Sweden and high commissioner to Singapore and Nigeria. His remarkable autobiography is titled *My Lucky Life, in War, Revolution, Peace and Diplomacy* (1996).

Robert O. Freedman is the Peggy Meyerhoff Pearlstone Professor of Political Science at Baltimore Hebrew University and visiting professor of political science at The Johns Hopkins University. Among his publications are: *Moscow and the Middle East* (1991), *Israel Under Rabin* (1995), and *The Middle East Enters the 21st Century* (2002).

Mark Gasiorowski is professor of political science and director of the international studies program at Louisiana State University. His books include *Mohammad Mossadeq and the 1953 Coup in Iran* (coeditor, 2004); *U.S. Foreign Policy and the Shah: Building a Client State in Iran* (1991); and *Neither East nor West* (coeditor, 1990).

F. Gregory Gause III is associate professor of political science at the University of Vermont. Among his publications are *Oil Monarchies: Domestic and Security Challenges in the Arab Gulf States* (1994) and *Saudi-Yemeni Relations: Domestic Structures and Foreign Influence* (1990).

James Gelvin is professor of history at the University of California–Los Angeles. He is the author of *Divided Loyalties: Nationalism and Mass Politics in Syria at the Close of Empire* (1998), *The Modern Middle East: A History* (2004), and *The Israel-Palestine Conflict: One Hundred Years of War* (2005).

Fawaz A. Gerges is visiting fellow at the Center of International Studies at the Woodrow Wilson School of Public and International Affairs at Princeton University and is a faculty member at Sarah Lawrence College. His publications include *The Superpowers and the Middle East: Regional and International Politics, 1955–1967* (1994).

Shafeeq N. Ghabra is professor of political science. He served as the first and founding president of the American University of Kuwait (2003–2006) and a former director of the Kuwait Information Office in Washington, D.C. (1998–2002). He has published four books, including *Palestinians in Kuwait: The Family and the Politics of Survival* (1987).

Yvonne Yazbeck Haddad is professor of history at Georgetown University. She has published numerous books and articles on Islam, including *Contemporary Islam and the Challenge of History* (1982) and *The Islamic Impact* (1984).

Peter Hahn is professor of history at Ohio State University and Executive Director of the Society for Historians of American Foreign Relations. He is the author of *Crisis and Crossfire: The United States and the Middle East Since 1945* (2005); *Caught in the Middle East: U. S. Policy Toward the Arab-Israeli Conflict, 1945–1961* (2004); and *The United States, Great Britain, and Egypt, 1945–1956: Strategy and Diplomacy in the Early Cold War* (1991).

Paul W. T. Kingston is associate professor of political science at the University of Toronto, Scarborough College. A specialist on Middle East development policy during the immediate post–World War II period, he is author of *Debating Development: Britain and the Politics of Modernization in the Middle East, 1945–1958* (1996).

David W. Lesch is professor of Middle East history at Trinity University in San Antonio, Texas. Among his books are the following: *Syria and the United States: Eisenhower's*

Cold War in the Middle East (1992); *1979: The Year That Shaped the Modern Middle East* (2001); and *The New Lion of Damascus: Bashar al-Asad and Modern Syria* (2005).

Georgiy Mirsky is a distinguished scholar at the Institute of World Economy and International Relations in Moscow. He is the author of numerous books and articles in Russian and English, and he has been an adviser to Soviet and Russian leaders.

Malik Mufti is associate professor of political science at Tufts University. He is author of *Sovereign Creations: Pan-Arabism and Political Order in Syria and Iraq* (1996), as well as articles on Turkey and Jordan in the *Middle East Journal* and *Comparative Political Studies*.

Elie Podeh is associate professor and head of the department of Islam and Middle Eastern Studies at the Hebrew University of Jerusalem. Among his publications are *The Decline of Arab Unity: The Rise and Fall of the United Arab Republic* (1999); *The Arab-Israeli Conflict in Israeli History Textbooks, 1948–2000* (2002); and *Jewish-Arab Relations: From Conflict to Resolution?* (co-editor, 2005).

Jeremy Pressman is assistant professor of political science at the University of Connecticut and research fellow at the Crown Center for Middle East Studies at Brandeis University. He is co-author of *Point of No Return: The Deadly Struggle for Middle East Peace* (1997).

William B. Quandt is the Edward R. Stettinius Professor of Politics at the University of Virginia. He served as a staff member on the National Security Council from 1972 to 1974 and from 1977 to 1979 and was actively involved in the negotiations that led to the Camp David accords and the Egyptian-Israeli peace treaty. Among his many books are: *Peace Process: American Diplomacy and the Arab-Israeli Conflict Since 1967* (third edition, 2005) and *Camp David: Peacemaking and Politics* (1986).

Bernard Reich is professor of political science and international affairs at George Washington University. His books include *The United States and Israel: Influence in the Special Relationship* (1984), *Securing the Covenant: United States–Israel Relations After the Cold War* (1995), and *Political Dictionary of Israel* (2000).

Gary Sick is the executive director of the Gulf/2000 project at Columbia University, a research and documentation program. He was the principal White House aide for Iran on the National Security Council staff at the time of the Iranian revolution and hostage crisis and is the author of two books on US Persian Gulf policy.

Janice Gross Stein is Belzberg Professor of Conflict Management and the Director of the Munk Center for International Studies at the University of Toronto. She has published a number of articles and books on Middle East affairs and international relations, including *We All Lost the Cold War* (1984) and *Peace-Making in the Middle East: Problems and Prospects* (1985).

Marvin G. Weinbaum is professor emeritus of political science at the University of Illinois at Urbana-Champaign. From 1999 to 2003 he served as senior analyst on Pakistan and Afghanistan in the Bureau of Intelligence and Research at the US State Department. He is currently a scholar-in-residence at the Middle East Institute. Among his numerous publications are the following books: *Afghanistan and Pakistan: Resistance and Reconstruction* (1994) and *South Asia Approaches the Millennium: Reexamining National Security* (coeditor, 1995).

Steve A. Yetiv is a professor of political science at Old Dominion University. He is the author of *The Persian Gulf Crisis* (1998); *Expanding Foreign Policy* (2004); and *Crude Awakenings* (2005).

Index

LaVergne, TN USA
08 September 2009
157141LV00023B/113/P